DICTIONARY OF CONTRASTING PAIRS

Also by Adrian Room

Dictionary of Cryptic Crossword Clues
Dictionary of Trade Name Origins
Naming Names: A Book of Pseudonyms and Name Changes with a 'Who's Who'
Room's Classical Dictionary
Room's Dictionary of Confusibles
Room's Dictionary of Distinguishables
Place-Name Changes Since 1900: A World Gazetteer
Dictionary of Confusing Words and Meanings
Dictionary of Translated Names and Titles
A Dictionary of True Etymologies
Dictionary of Changes in Meaning
Dictionary of Coin Names

A DICTIONARY OF CONTRASTING PAIRS

Adrian Room

ROUTLEDGE
London and New York

First published in 1988 by
Routledge
11 New Fetter Lane, London EC4P 4EE

Published in the USA by
Routledge
in association with Routledge, Chapman & Hall, Inc.
29 West 35th Street, New York, NY 10001

Set in Linotron Baskerville
by Input Typesetting Ltd, London SW19 8DR
and printed in Great Britain
by Richard Clay Ltd, Bungay, Suffolk

Library of Congress Cataloging in Publication Data

Room, Adrian.
Dictionary of contrasting pairs.

Bibliography: p.
1. English language—Synonyms and antonyms—
Dictionaries. I. Title.
PE1591.R746 1988 432'.1 87–20509

British Library CIP Data also available
ISBN 0–415–00217–6

CONTENTS

The other night, from cares exempt,
I slept – and what d'you think I dreamt?
I dreamt that somehow I had come
To dwell in Topsy-Turveydom! –
Where vice is virtue – virtue, vice:
Where nice is nasty – nasty, nice:
Where right is wrong and wrong is right –
Where white is black and black is white.

(W. S. Gilbert, *Bab Ballads, My Dream*)

INTRODUCTION

A typical polite after-meal or workbreak conversation often goes something like this:

'Tea or coffee?'
'Coffee, please.'
'Black or white?'
'White, please.'
'With sugar or without?'
'With sugar, please.'
'One or two?'
'Just one, please.'

Every day of our lives we are faced with contrasting choices like this, and indeed a standard working day is itself a kind of mirror image of itself, so that we perform opposite or contrasting actions. We wake up, get up, wash and dress, have something to eat, and go to work. At work, the day is usually divided into two halves, morning and evening, with a midday meal in between and very likely with a break ('elevenses') in the morning and another ('tea break') in the afternoon. We then return home, have something to eat, and finally undress and wash, get into bed, and go to sleep. True, the two halves are not exactly parallel, and there is a longer spell at home in the evening than there is in the morning. Men, too, do not (fortunately) have to 'unshave' themselves in the evening. But otherwise we are really reversing in the evening what we have done in the morning, and the words and verbs involved are standard opposites for what happens: wake up/go to sleep, get up/go to bed, dress/undress, go out to work/return home from work, and so on. Meanwhile 'morning' is in one sense the opposite of 'evening', but in another way it is also contrasted with 'afternoon'. Even the acts of dressing and undressing involve opposing actions, such pairs of verbs as put on/take off, do/undo, tie/untie, button up/unbutton, tighten/loosen.

Such daily routines and standard conversations may seem unimportant or trivial. They reflect a wider and more universal state of affairs, however, in which contrasts and opposites are seen to play a regular part. Existence on earth is not merely a matter of mornings and evenings, but of day and night, sun and moon, summer and winter, and at its most basic, birth and death. As members of the human race, we are male or female, as are most of our 'lesser brethren' the animals, and we can be young or old, fat or thin, tall or short, clever or stupid, hungry or thirsty, rich or poor, nice or nasty, loved or hated. Indeed, almost every regular or familiar word has an associated or contrasted opposite, with one implying 'not the other'. A 'stupid' person is thus by implication not intelligent, and an 'old' man is by definition no longer young. To go 'down' the stairs is the exact opposite of going 'up' them, and to 'sleep' is not to 'wake'.

Such associated contrasts can extend to terms and verbs that on the face of it appear to have no obvious opposite. A dog is often thought of as a domestic pet contrasted with a cat, a table is associated with a chair, red is the 'opposite' of blue, and a colour photo is mentally compared with a black and white one. If I write you a letter, you then read it, and that is the associated action; if I watch TV, I also listen to it, and the two senses are regarded as complementary; if a schoolchild is playing, he is not working, and that is the difference; and so on.

Such contrasting associations cut across language and nationality, and are certainly not specifically English. In 1977, for example, a Russian work with the forbidding title of *Dictionary of Associated Norms in the Russian Language* was published by Moscow University. The book contains the results of an oral survey made a few years earlier in which between 500 and 700 intelligent young or middle-aged individuals were asked to say which word first sprang to mind when a given word was spoken to them, with 500 such 'word stimulants' in all. The frequency of the responses was then recorded. For many words, the most common association was a contrasting or opposite one, and they included the following, which not only proves the universal 'rule of association by opposites' but gives something of an insight, and a genuine one at that, into the Russian character.

Stimulus	*Response*	*Stimulus*	*Response*
grandfather	grandmother	new	old
big	little	answer	ask
war	peace	father	mother
newspaper	magazine	daddy	mummy
give	take	bad	good
girl	boy	arm	leg
day	night	sit	stand
village	town	hear	see
daughter	son	ask	answer
uncle	aunt	magazine	newspaper
life	death	old	young
look for	find	table	chair
cinema	theatre	stand	sit
finish	begin	Saturday	Sunday
love	hate	heavy	light
people	animals	depart	arrive
mother	father	fall	get up
place	time	morning	evening
young	old	surname	forename
find	look for	good	bad
beginning	end	clean	dirty

True, not all responses were as universal, and the most common reaction to 'dark', for example, was 'forest', with 'light' only in second place. But for all the others, it was the opposite that came first, even when presented either way (i.e. 'good' produced 'bad', and 'bad' suggested 'good', and other examples of this type can be seen in the table). And even allowing for the difference of language, in which contrasting words perhaps rhyme or alliterate, the responses are much as those made in similar surveys conducted in other countries, such as Britain and the United States. (One such alliteration which possibly prompted the contrast is in the pair that produced English 'table' and 'chair', since the Russian words for these are respectively *stol* and *stul*. We shall be returning to the matter of rhyme and alliteration later.)

Contrasting words constantly occur in our everyday language, not least in the many everyday sayings and proverbs that spring to mind. 'Red sky at night, shepherd's delight', we say, observing an evening glow, and continue, 'red sky in the morning, shepherd's warning'. There are really two pairs of contrasts here: not only 'night' and 'morning', but 'delight' (something good to come) and 'warning' (something bad to come). Even 'rain before seven, fine before eleven' has its meteorological contrast, as has the more long-term 'oak before ash, expect a splash; ash before oak, expect a soak'. More general and succinct sayings have similar contrasts, such as 'more haste, less speed', 'east, west, home's best', 'like father, like son', and the humorous 'heads I win, tails you lose' (which contains *three* pairs of opposites, but has a first half meaning the same as the second!).

Some proverbs, although not themselves containing a contrasting comparison, can often be matched with a contradictory saying, so that 'Too many cooks spoil the broth' can be countered with 'Maybe, but many hands make light work'.

It seems to have been Hippocrates who originated the classical saying, 'Art is long, but life is short' (in Greek, *ho bios brachys, hē de technē makrē*, and in Latin *ars longa, vita brevis*), and there are many literary quotations besides proverbs that embody contrasting concepts as food for thought. One need look no further than the opening chapters of the Book of Genesis in the Bible to find some familiar ones: 'And the evening and the morning were the first day', 'The greater light to rule the day, and the lesser light to rule the night', 'Male and female created he them', 'As gods, knowing good and evil', 'It shall bruise thy head, and thou shalt bruise his heel', and so on. This is to say nothing of equally well known New Testament contrasting quotations, such as 'Many are called, but few are chosen', or 'Alpha and Omega, the beginning and the ending', or 'Many that are first shall be last, and the last shall be first'. The Prayer Book has such contrasts, too, as in those of the Marriage Service: 'For better for worse, for richer for poorer, in sickness and in health'.

When contrasting words are combined ('good and evil', 'for better for worse') as distinct from being opposed ('Many are called but few are chosen', 'More haste, less speed'), the result is a totality of concept, a comprehensiveness, so that 'male and female' implies *all* humans, regardless of sex, but 'male or female' points to the difference between the two sexes. Even so, the words themselves remain as contrasts in their own right, and 'evening' is still the opposite of 'morning' even though the biblical quotation above combines the two to denote a complete day, a perfect unit of time.

Readers of more modern literature than the Bible or Prayer Book cannot fail to notice similar contrasting ideas and expressions in the works of several authors, to say nothing of the titles of world famous classics such as *War and Peace*, *Crime and Punishment*, *Le Rouge et le Noir*, and so on. In the poetical works of Tennyson, for instance, contrasts abound, whether to indicate totality or opposition. Among some of the most memorable, and most frequently quoted (whatever their actual merit in poetical terms) are: 'Now sleeps the crimson petal, now the white', 'Man is the hunter; woman is his game', 'Every moment dies a man, Every moment one is born', 'Without one pleasure and without one pain', 'Weeping, weeping late and early, Walking up and pacing down', 'As the husband is, the wife is', 'Ring out the old, ring in the new', 'Cannon to right of them, Cannon to left of them', and probably the best known of all, 'For men may come and men may go, But I go on for ever'. This last (from 'The Brook') compares two concepts, birth and death ('coming' and 'going') and transience ('Men may come and men may go') and permanence ('But I go on for ever'). Such compound contrasts are satisfying, and add to the richness and profundity of the written text. (See the pair **true/false** in the Dictionary for one of Tennyson's most interesting compound contrasts.)

Nor are such contrasts confined to language in literature. It can also occur in the particular action or situation that develops, often for deliberately comic or intriguing effect. Lewis Carroll used contrast and opposition to evoke a fantasy 'topsy-turvy' world in *Alice in Wonderland* and *Through the Looking-Glass*. In the former book Alice dwindles to such a small size that she fears she may disappear altogether – then she suddenly grows outlandishly large. When she encounters the puppy, she is tiny, but it is enormous (playing with the puppy is to Alice 'very like having a game of play with a cart-horse'). Then although Alice keeps her normal size in *Through the Looking-Glass*, many of the other characters are the reverse of what one expects, so that what appear at first to be bees buzzing round the flowers are in fact tiny elephants, and the Gnat with whom Alice converses is huge ('"about the size of a chicken," Alice thought'). It is an upside-down or inverted world in both books – more specifically, a reflected one in the second – and literal 'ups' and 'downs' constantly reoccur in them, as well as many inverted spoken puns and riddles, making nonsense of logic. Alice regrets her claim in the Mad Hatter's Tea Party that 'meaning what she says' is the same as 'saying what she means', and in the Trial Scene ('Who Stole the Tarts?') the King of Hearts cannot decide whether 'important' or 'unimportant' is the right word to describe the fact that Alice knows 'nothing whatever' about the affair. (See **Tweedledum/Tweedledee** in the Dictionary, for another Carrollian contrast.)

Such inversion of logic and the grotesque emphasis on contrast and opposition is the source of much humour and entertainment generally, so that we enjoy being unexpectedly presented with 'black' when we were expecting 'white', and in hearing a shout when we would have expected a whisper. We think that the conjurer has nothing in that box, but he has something; we are sure that the knife-thrower will hit the young lady tied to the wall, but he misses; we are convinced that those two lines in the optical illusion are divergent, but they are actually parallel; we expect the comedian called Lofty to be a tall man, but he is a dwarf. Indeed, many comedians themselves work best as contrasting pairs: one tall man and one short, or one fat man and one thin; one 'straight' man and one 'wit', or one clever man and one 'thick'. One need only mention such famous pairs as Laurel and Hardy, Abbott and Costello, Morecambe and Wise and Little and Large to see this contrasting principle in action. (The very names of the last pair serve to emphasize this contrast.)

In a sense, we are also 'role actors' in our daily lives, and similarly feature in a sort of contrasting capacity when we speak to someone. To the doctor we are a patient, to the shop assistant a customer, to the bus conductor or ticket collector or air hostess a passenger, to the waiter a diner, to the hotel porter a guest, to the teacher a pupil, to the theatre actor a member of his audience. We are constantly thus in a contrasting 'him and me' or 'her and me' association, an individual 'interface' in which our roles are regarded as complementary. A doctor is not a doctor if he has no patient to treat, and a shop assistant cannot perform her job if she has no customer to serve.

Like writers and actors, too, artists employ contrast and opposition in their paintings, not simply in a balance of light and shade (the Italian word that relates to this, 'chiaroscuro', is itself a contrasting combination of *chiaro*, 'light' and *oscuro*, 'dark') but in the actual subjects. Many 'old masters' depicted contrasting characters or subjects, especially biblical, mythological or allegorical, such as *Adam and Eve*, *St George and the Dragon* (which is really 'Good and Evil') and *Age and Youth*. Rubens painted *The Union of Earth and Water*, and Pieter de Hoogh *Mistress and Servant*. The many versions of the *Adoration of the Magi* (or *Adoration of the Shepherds*), too, contrast the human and the divine, the adult and the child, the wealthy and the humble, the worldly and the eternal. Appreciating such contrasts in a painting is just as satisfying and rewarding for the viewer as it must have been for the painter himself. Joseph Wright of Derby's painting *The Forge*, for example, contrasts a sleeping countryside with active, working people, a cold, natural moonlight with a hot, manmade fire in the forge, a rich client watching with a country blacksmith working.

Also watching the blacksmith in Wright of Derby's picture are a woman and a man, and the difference between the sexes, and the mutual attraction between them, is one of the most pervasive contrasts in our lives. Despite talk of 'equal opportunities', and 'equality of the sexes', which is right and laudable as far as many occupations and situations are concerned, the fact remains that the biological difference between male and female is one of the most influential in our thought and language. Feminists seek to denounce those, especially (and usually) men, who contrast the sexes, but contrast there is, whatever is said, and the human race, or indeed the animal world, would not survive if it were not for the complementary biological roles performed by either sex. As they say, 'it takes two', and not two of a kind, either. Without going into traditional attitudes (the 'strong' or 'macho' male as against the 'sweet' or 'sexy' female), one need merely consider the many ways in which language distinguishes between the sexes, not simply by gender ('man' and 'woman') but by relationship ('husband' and 'wife', 'son' and 'daughter') and occupation ('waiter' and 'waitress') as well as social or other rank ('king' and 'queen', 'master' and 'mistress', 'Mr' and 'Mrs'). We certainly think of animals and birds in this way, and there is all the difference in the world between a 'cow' and a 'bull', or a 'cock' and a 'hen'. Where else do we get our milk and our eggs, even if either can provide our meat?

So gender differences will form a significant factor in the selection of contrasting pairs that are included in the Dictionary, and I have devoted Appendix II (p. 291) to an examination of the more precise linguistic features involved.

It is now time to say something about the actual entries, and to explain *how* they were selected. Clearly, there are hundreds if not thousands of ways in which contrasts and opposites can be expressed, and a finite choice had to be made. On the whole, I have selected those pairs of words that are the most familiar, even absurdly so, such as 'black' and 'white', 'up' and 'down', 'in' and 'out'. In each entry, I have tried to illustrate the most important ways in which the respective words or concepts occur in the language, for example in set phrases or semi-technical usages, and where appropriate I have added an etymology or two, or drawn a parallel in another language. Some contrasting words, too, I have quoted in short extracts from literary or other sources, so that the reader can see them at work, as it were. On the other hand, in an increasingly complex and 'professional' world, it would have been wrong to omit some more specialized contrasts that we frequently encounter or use in our day-to-day lives. So the reader will also find such contrasts as 'analogue' and 'digital', 'atrium' and 'ventricle', 'bid price' and 'offer price', 'centrifugal' and 'centripetal', even 'zygodactyl' and 'heterodactyl'. This last may seem incomprehensible or unimportant to most of us, but to ornithologists it is significant, even essential. And, with a little knowledge of basic Greek roots, it is not so incomprehensible after all.

Basic Greek roots are largely but not exclusively the subject of Appendix I (p. 281), where a selection of common contrasting prefixes and suffixes is provided, together with examples and comments. There the reader will not only find the opposite of 'eu-', as in 'euphoria' (it is 'dys-'), but can also see how prefixes, and to a lesser degree suffixes, sometimes have different 'opposites' to designate a contrasting term. Thus 'mega-' can be paired with 'micro-', and 'micro-' in turn with 'macro-', while 'mono-' can have 'di-' (or 'bi-') or 'poly-' to serve as its contrast. Many quite common and familiar scientific terms contain Greek or Latin prefixes or suffixes, and the Appendix is a convenient way of selecting some of the more common ones that are found in 'opposites'.

It is sometimes a toss-up with a contrasting pair of words which one occurs to one first. We tend to think of 'black and white', for example, not 'white and black', and to talk of 'sacred and profane' rather than 'profane and sacred'. If a quantity or 'progression' of some kind is involved, it will normally be the lower or 'earlier' one first, as in 'sunrise and sunset', 'prefix and suffix', 'single and double'. With the gender differentiation, too, *pace* the feminists, it is traditionally (but not always) the male who precedes the female in such pairings, so that one has 'man and woman', 'dog and bitch', 'lad and lass'. But whatever the pairing, the reader will always find the second of the two words listed separately alphabetically to refer to the first, so that if 'outer' comes to mind before 'inner', it will be found in its alphabetical place to cross-refer to 'inner/outer', and similarly

'Iraq' will cross-refer to 'Iran'.

There seems little doubt that some contrasting pairs remain firmly in our minds in a particular order because they either rhyme or alliterate (begin with the same letter). This factor lies behind such pairs as 'but and ben', 'Cancer and Capricorn', 'dot and dash', 'fair and foul', 'flotsam and jetsam', 'hare and hounds', 'latitude and longitude', 'little and large', 'make and break', 'purl and plain', 'saint and sinner' (the 'goodies' usually come first) and 'town and gown'. And the very fact of the rhyme or alliteration, which we always enjoy in language, helps to promote and strengthen the regular usage in speech or writing of the contrast it actually expresses. 'Trick or treat?' 'Yin or yang?'

Finally, I hope that the somewhat 'encyclopedic' nature of some of the entries may not put the reader off, but on the contrary interest and where necessary inform him. Such entries are the necessary consequence of the complex technical world in which we live.

But, in there among all the technicalities, let us not forget that it is the small and unremarkable brown nightingale that has the sweetest song, and the large and showy peacock the harshest and most strident call.

Acknowledgments

My overall acknowledgments are really due to the authors, writers and compilers of the dictionaries and many other books that I consulted during work on this Dictionary, since without their professional information and linguistic researches I could not have begun to make my own compilation of contrasting entries. For more precise details regarding such sources, the reader should see the last section of the Dictionary, 'By way of a bibliography' (p. 294).

For his particular personal permission to reprint his poem 'Short Thoughts' in the **reader/writer** entry (p. 203) I am indebted to D. J. Enright. The poem is taken from *Instant Chronicles*, published by Oxford University Press in 1985.

For information concerning the socio-economic structure of Scotland, I am similarly personally indebted to Angela Moar, a native of that lovely but sometimes misunderstood land.

Finally, and importantly, I am greatly indebted to Norman Franklin for his editorial support and professional advice, especially in scientific fields, thus preserving me from what might otherwise have been a rash of 'bloopers'.

Adrian Room
Petersfield, Hampshire

Aa

A[1]/B
In many designations, 'A' indicates something that is bigger or better than its 'B' counterpart, such as an 'A'-road (a main one) as distinct from a 'B'-road (a smaller, minor road, often linking two 'A'-roads across country), and in some schools, a class lettered 'A' (such as '4A') may denote one that is academically brighter than its 'B' equivalent ('4B'). In some continental schools, however, where a shift system is worked, 'A' designates the morning or early shift, and 'B' the later, or afternoon one. For some time after the Second World War, a 'B'-film was a shorter, 'supporting' film shown as well as the main one. The latter, however, was not known as the 'A'-film, but simply as the 'main feature'. In more recent times, the 'B' side of a pop record has become the term for a performer's piece or song that is regarded as less original or popular than that on the main, 'A' side. (Although in some cases the so called 'B' side has proved as much of a commercial hit as the 'A', and there have also been records with two equally good songs, promoted as a 'double A side'.) In enumerating or evaluating, as in listing points in an argument, or marking a piece of schoolwork, 'B' is always seen as inferior to 'A', or less important than it. In the expression 'from A to B', the contrast is not one of quality, however, but simply of location, with the reference to two different places or points between which one needs to travel. (Compare 'from A to Z' in the next entry.)

A[2]/Z
The first and last letters of the English alphabet, of course, and therefore implying a marked degree of quality or disparity, or a completeness or thoroughness (as in knowing a subject 'from A to Z'). The reference, too, can be a literal alphabetical one, as in the series of London street plans called *A to Z* or simply *A–Z*, where the streets are listed alphabetically in an index (usually from Abberton Walk to Zoffany Street). Compare **alpha/omega**.

A4/A5
The two most common sizes of typing or writing paper, with 'A4' the larger (297 × 210 millimetres, or about $11\frac{3}{4} \times 8\frac{1}{4}$ inches), with 'A5' half this in length when folded (i.e. 148 × 210 millimetres, or about $5\frac{7}{8} \times 8\frac{1}{4}$ inches). The latter size can be used for correspondence with the writing or typing running across the wider or narrower area, i.e. with the 210 millimetres measuring along the top or down the side.

A5 see **A4**

abduction/adduction
The two words are anatomical terms, describing opposite movements of limbs. 'Abduction' (literally, 'leading away') is the act of moving an arm or leg away from the body, sideways (i.e. raising it), while 'adduction' ('leading to') is bringing a limb back down to the body from the side. These movements take place technically in the coronal plane (see **sagittal/coronal**). The corresponding verbs are 'abduct' and 'adduct'.

Abel see **Cain**

abroad see **home**[1]

absent see **present**[1]

absentee see **truant**

absolute ceiling see **service ceiling**

absolute monarchy/constitutional monarchy
'Absolute monarchy' is the ruling of a country by a monarch without any limit on his powers, and in particular without any constitution that could limit them. A 'constitutional monarchy', as in the majority of countries today that have a monarchy (including Britain), is one in which the power of the monarch is restricted by a constitution, so that he or she 'reigns but does not rule'. 'Absolute monarchies' are thus effectively things of the past, such as the rules of Louis XIV in France or Queen Elizabeth I in England, while modern states with 'constitutional monarchies', apart from Britain, include Belgium, Denmark, Japan, Jordan, Kuweit, Luxembourg, Malaysia, Morocco, Nepal, the Netherlands, Norway, Spain, Swaziland, Sweden and Thailand. The only country in the world today that can be properly called an 'absolute monarchy' is Saudi Arabia (which is also virtually the only country to be partly named after its first monarch, Ibn Saud). See also **monarchy/republic**.

absolute music see **programme music**

absolutism/relativism
In philosophy and religion, 'absolutism' is the doctrine that there is one absolute being (God) who predetermines or ordains the actions of men. 'Relativism' holds that laws do not come from God or a supreme being, but that knowledge and moral values depend on (i.e. are relative to) a person's nature or his situation at a given moment. 'Relativists' would thus have listened to Oliver Cromwell's plea to the Church of Scotland in 1650 to abandon the Stuart cause: 'I beseech you, in the bowels of Christ, think it possible you may be mistaken.' The corresponding adjectives, 'absolute' and 'relative', are frequently found in scientific usage, so that a temperature of 'absolute' zero, for example, is the one that is the lowest obtainable in theory (−273.15°C or −459.67°F), while the 'relative' density of a substance is the ratio of this density to that of a standard substance under specified conditions. (For gases, the standard used is often air or hydrogen at the same temperature and pressure as the substance.)

absorb/adsorb
As with the **abduction/adduction** pair above, it is the prefixes that give the contrasting meanings here, especially in chemistry. Thus, if calcium chloride 'absorbs' water, the latter is dissolved into the acid, and when palladium metal 'adsorbs' hydrogen, the gas accumulates on it in the form of a thin film. The corresponding nouns are 'absorption' and 'adsorption'.

abstract/concrete
As applied to nouns, something that is 'real' and that actually exists, as perceived by the senses, is 'concrete', while something that is merely an action, or a quality, or a state, is 'abstract'. For example, 'love' is 'abstract', while a 'poem' (that you can see or hear) is 'concrete'. However, 'concrete' poetry is poetry in which the way the words are displayed and printed is designed to have a special visual effect.

AC/DC
These two common abbreviations, referring to types of electric current, apply to 'alternating current' and 'direct current'. With 'AC', the voltage alternates so that the current reaches a maximum in one direction before decreasing and reversing to reach a maximum in the opposite direction. The process is repeated continuously several times a second, and 'AC' is the kind of electricity transmitted by electricity companies. With 'DC', as in batteries and fuel cells, the current flows in one direction only. The big disadvantage of 'DC' is that it cannot be transmitted at high voltages over long distances. In colloquial use, the phrase 'AC/DC' is sometimes used to mean 'bisexual', implying that such a person is

like an electrical appliance that functions on both types of current.

accent see **dialect**

Access/VISA
These are the two most popular types of bank credit card in Britain (see **charge card/credit card**), with the latter still sometimes known as a 'Barclaycard', after Barclays Bank, who first issued it. There is little difference in the way the two cards operate, although cash advances can be cheaper with a 'VISA', since (in 1988) it is possible to use it to obtain money for up to eight weeks at a fee of only 1½%, while 'Access' charges ½% per week as interest on an advance. The main difference between the two is in the issuer: 'Access' cards are issued by the three main banks apart from Barclays (i.e. Lloyds, Midland and National Westminster), as well as the Royal Bank of Scotland, while 'VISA' cards are issued by Barclays, the Bank of Scotland, the Trustee Savings Bank, and a number of building societies. However, it is not necessary for a cardholder to bank at a particular bank in order to obtain one or other of the cards, and many people hold both. (Figures issued in late 1985 showed that there were almost equal numbers of cardholders for both: 8.2 million.)

acclivity see **declivity**

acid/alkali
In chemistry, an 'acid' is a compound that produces hydrogen ions in water, while an 'alkali' absorbs them. When this happens mutually, the two combine to form a salt. An 'acid' thus neutralizes an 'alkali', and is popularly known as the compound that turns litmus paper red, while an 'alkali' (today usually referred to in chemistry as a 'base') will turn such litmus paper back to blue again. An example of a common 'acid' is sulphuric 'acid' (H_2SO_4), used in many industrial processes and formerly known as 'oil of vitriol', while a common 'alkali', also important in industry, is sodium hydroxide ($NaOH$), also still known as 'caustic soda'.

across/down
The two main types of clues or 'lights' (as professionals call them) in crosswords, with the 'across' words filled in from left to right, as in normal writing, and the 'down' answers from top to bottom. In many European crosswords, the two kinds are known as the equivalent of 'horizontal' and 'vertical', which is just as accurate, although rather more formal. (The actual word 'crossword' does not refer so much to the 'across' clues as to the fact that the words cross or intersect.)

active[1]/dormant
The two main types of volcano, with an 'active' one erupting regularly, while a 'dormant' one can lie inactive for some time before erupting. When a volcano ceases to erupt altogether, it is called 'extinct', in which case it is really no longer properly a volcano, if by this word is meant 'mountain or hill that erupts regularly or periodically'. Among well known 'active' volcanoes are Etna, Vesuvius, Stromboli and Cotopaxi, while 'dormant' volcanoes include Popocateptl in Mexico, Tongariro in New Zealand, and Soufrière, in the West Indies. (The famous Chimborazo and Kilimanjaro are believed to be extinct.)

active[2]/passive
In a general sense, 'active' implies 'doing', while 'passive' means 'being done to', 'being on the receiving end'. In grammar, an 'active' verb is one that indicates the action performed by the subject of the sentence, as in 'The boy *kicked* the ball', so that a 'passive' verb indicates the action done to the recipient, as in 'The ball was *kicked* by the boy'. An electronic device is 'active' if it uses electrical power to amplify or control an electrical signal (as transistors and valves do), while it is 'passive' if it does not use electrical power (as capacitors and resistors do not). In medicine, 'active' immunity is the kind that is long-lasting and produced by antibodies within a living organism, but 'passive' immunity is produced by the transfer of antibodies to a living organism, usually by injection into the bloodstream.

acute[1]/chronic
The two terms are used of contrasting types of illness or disease, with one that is 'acute' being usually 'short and sharp', such as appendicitis, and one that is 'chronic' being recurring and usually long in duration, such as 'chronic' bronchitis. (The latter word derives ultimately from Greek *chronos*, 'time'.) The distinction is sometimes blurred by the fact that 'chronic' can be used colloquially of any ache or pain, to mean simply 'bad', 'severe', so that a 'chronic' headache could medically be really an 'acute' one.

acute[2]/grave
The two words are used for the two common types of accent in French (and also some other languages), where the 'acute' (marked as *é*) often denotes a so-called 'closed' or 'tight' vowel sound (as in *fiancé*), while a 'grave' indicates an 'open' or 'long' vowel sound (as in *père*). In ancient Greek, an 'acute' accent was used to indicate a spoken or sung pitch that was higher than that of neighbouring syllables or vowels, whereas a 'grave' denoted a lower or falling pitch. Both words are themselves of French origin, with something like the French pronunciation still preserved for 'grave' (rhyming with 'suave'), although in other general senses, when 'grave' means 'serious', for example, it rhymes with 'save'.

acute[3]/obtuse
In mathematics, an 'acute' angle is one less than a right angle (i.e. less than 90°), whereas an 'obtuse' angle is one greater than this. In transferred use, an 'acute' person is a perceptive or shrewd one, while an 'obtuse' person is a dull-witted or insensitive one.

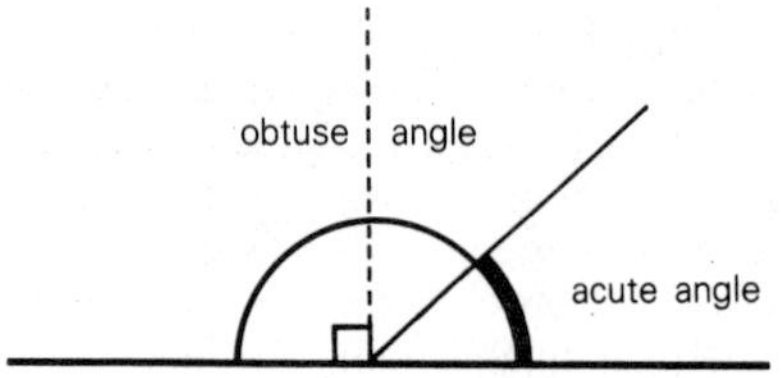

AD see **BC**

Adam/Eve
The two names are used in a number of contexts, from metaphorical to commercial, to mean 'basic man' and 'basic woman'. They familiarly occur as the first man and first woman to be named in the Bible, where 'Adam' is simply called 'the man' down to Genesis 2:19, and where the name of 'Eve' (given her by 'Adam' 'because she was the mother of all living') first occurs in Genesis 3:20. In the biblical story, however, it is undoubtedly 'Eve' who is the heroine and the enterprising one, and it was she who 'saw that the tree was good for food' and who 'took of the fruit thereof, and did eat, and gave also unto her husband with her'. See also **Cain/Abel**, **man/woman**.

add/subtract
Two of the basic but opposite arithmetical processes, whereby figures are respectively totalled or reduced by being either combined or by the lesser being taken away from the greater. The two words are themselves of Latin origin, with 'add' from *addere*, 'to put to', and 'subtract' from *subtrahere*, 'to draw away'. See also **plus/minus**.

adduction see **abduction**

adsorb see **absorb**

adult/infant
In the legal definition, an 'adult' is a mature (or 'major' person) over 18, while an 'infant' is someone under this age, a 'minor' (see **major/minor**). The usual contrast is not this legal one, however, but that of **child/adult** (which see). 'Infant' literally means 'unable to speak', from the Latin.

adult see **child**

advance[1]/retard
The contrast here is between a verb meaning 'speed up' and one meaning 'slow down', as applied to something mechanical, for example. Hence the letters 'A' and

'R' found on the regulators of some clocks and watches formerly, although properly these stand for the French equivalents of *avancer* and *retarder*. (Modern clocks often have a plus or minus sign for this function.) In a more general sense, to 'advance' something is to bring it forward in time, as when one 'advances' the date of a meeting, but here the opposite verb is not so much 'retard' as 'delay' or simply 'put back'.

advance[2]/retire
The two verbs are often used in a military context, so that an army will 'advance' when it goes ahead to attack the enemy or occupy territory, and will 'retire' when it is itself attacked. The latter manoeuvre is sometimes diplomatically known as 'withdrawing', as if the army were moving back not in order to retreat under pressure, but as a deliberate tactical ploy, made to gain a subtle advantage.

aerodynamics/aerostatics
'Aerodynamics' is the study of gases, especially with regard to the various forces such as 'lift' and 'thrust' and 'drag' that operate on an object as it moves through the air (typically, an aeroplane). 'Aerostatics' is the study of gases in equilibrium and of solid bodies immersed in them (typically a balloon in the air, which progresses not under its own motive power but by means of the various air currents, 'thermals' and so on). Compare **dynamic/static, thrust/drag**.

aerolite/siderite
These are the two main types of meteorite, with an 'aerolite' a stony meteorite, consisting of silicate minerals, and a 'siderite' an iron one, usually consisting of about 94% iron and about 6% nickel. A very few meteorites contain a mixture of stone and iron, and these are known as 'siderolites'. The root Greek words behind the names are *aer*, 'air', *lithos*, 'stone' and *sideros*, 'iron'.

aerostatics see **aerodynamics**

aestivate see **hibernate**

affirmative/negative
In general terms, 'affirmative' means 'agreed' (or 'yes'), and 'negative' means 'not agreed' (or 'no'). More narrowly, in logic, an 'affirmative' proposition asserts the truth of the predicate (the statement that says what a thing is or does), for example in the sentence 'All dogs have four legs'. A 'negative' proposition, on the other hand, denies the truth of the predicate, as in the sentence 'No man is immortal'. Compare **positive/negative**.

African elephant/Indian elephant
The difference between the two kinds of animal is greater than their respective countries. The 'African elephant' (*Loxodonta*) has larger ears and a flatter forehead, and is also darker grey in colour and inclined to be fiercer, which means that the 'Indian elephant' (or Asian elephant) (*Elephas*) has smaller ears, a more pronounced forehead, and is lighter grey in colour and often gentler. Additionally, the 'African elephant' has two sensitive 'finger-tips' at the end of its trunk, whereas its Indian cousin has only one. The famous Jumbo, formerly of the London Zoo, who gave his name to large objects generally (such as 'jumbo packs' and 'jumbo jets') was an 'African elephant'.

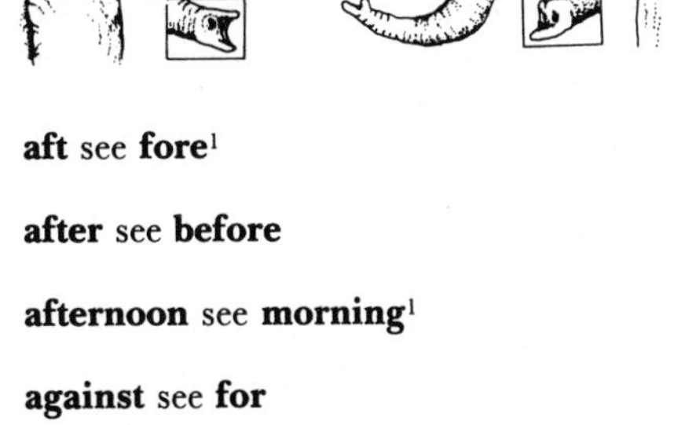

aft see **fore[1]**

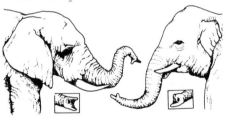

after see **before**

afternoon see **morning[1]**

against see **for**

agnate see **cognate**

agnostic/gnostic
The Greek prefix *a-* on 'agnostic' shows it to be literally the opposite or negative of 'gnostic'. The word as a whole was invented in 1869 by the English biologist T. H. Huxley as an actual contrary to 'gnostic', with the intention, therefore, that it should mean 'unknown' as applied to the existence of God. (He himself denied, however, taking the biblical phrase 'to the Unknown God' in Acts 17:23 as the basis for the word.) So in the original sense, 'gnostic' meant 'holding that spiritual truths can be known about phenomena beyond the material', and 'agnostic' meant 'holding that nothing can be known beyond material phenomena', with the whole dispute being decidedly metaphysical. Later, however, 'agnostic' began to mean loosely 'doubting in the existence of God', and came to be contrasted more with 'atheist' (who denies the existence of God) or with 'Christian' (who believes in the existence of God).

agoraphobia see **claustrophobia**

ahead/astern
The two are the opposite directions or positions with regard to a boat or ship, respectively 'forward' or 'in front' of it, or 'backward' or 'behind' it. A ship's 'head' is its front part or bows. Compare **stem/stern**.

air see **earth**

airmail/surface mail
These are the two contrasting ways of sending mail abroad from Britain and most other countries, with 'airmail' being quicker but more expensive (and with weight and other restrictions), and 'surface mail' being slower but cheaper. As the terms indicate, mail sent by 'airmail' is flown by aircraft, while the 'surface' referred to in the alternative method is that of land or sea (compare **land/sea**). The two types of communication became established as alternatives only in the twentieth century, when mail began to be regularly sent abroad by air. In Britain, 'airmail' is particularly thought of as applying to mail sent to countries outside Europe, for which a special blue 'airmail' sticker is used, although in fact most mail to Europe also goes by air (without being specifically designated as 'airmail').

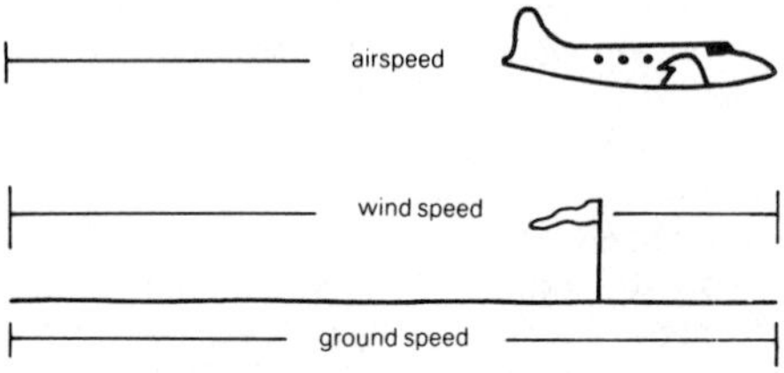

airspeed/groundspeed
Of a flying aircraft, its 'airspeed' is its speed relative to the air through which it travels, while its 'groundspeed' is the speed with which it travels over the ground. These will obviously differ, and it is thus the job of a navigator on an aircraft to calculate a so-called 'triangle of velocities', whose three sides are heading and 'airspeed', track and 'groundspeed', and wind direction and speed.

à la carte/table d'hôte
These two French terms mean literally 'by the card' (i.e. 'as on the menu') and 'host's table', and denote the two basic types of meal served in a restaurant or hotel. An 'à la carte' meal has dishes that can be selected individually at individual prices from the menu, while a 'table d'hôte' lunch or dinner is one at a fixed price for the whole meal, with the main dishes selected by the manager (or the chef). Eating 'table d'hôte' is therefore not so expensive as 'à la carte', but one has a much more limited choice of courses. 'Carte' as a word for a menu or 'bill of fare' was in use in English in the nineteenth century ('The carte was examined on the wall, and Fanny was asked to choose her favourite dish', Thackeray, *Pendennis*, 1850), and 'à la carte' came into fashion at about the same time.

ale see **beer**

alive/dead
The two basic states of a being that has been born, either living or no longer having life. The nearest the two terms come to be equated, although they are clearly diametric opposites, is when jointly applied to a 'wanted' person or criminal (or animal), who must be captured 'dead or alive'. (If 'alive', he will at least be captured and rendered harmless; if 'dead', he is harmless anyway.) A more general metaphorical description 'dead-and-alive' can be used of a person or place or activity to mean that he or it is dull and of no interest. The phrase implies 'alive but as good as dead'. Compare **live/dead**, **life/death**.

alkali see **acid**

allegro/lento
The contrast is not so much a musical one (which would more accurately be 'presto', or 'fast', as against 'lento', or 'slow'), but a linguistic one. In modern philology, an 'allegro' form of a word or phrase is one in which the sounds are run together, as in everyday speech. For example, the 'allegro' form of 'library' is 'libry', and of 'how do you do' is 'howd'yedo'. (Compare the former domestic servant's 'yes'm', for 'yes, madam'.) The 'lento' form is thus the opposite of this, with the word or phrase spoken out in full, and more slowly than usual.

allopathic/homoeopathic
The terms relate to medical treatment. Conventional medicine uses 'allopathic' treatment, in which substances are given or administered that produce effects opposite to the cause of the disease. 'Homoeopathic' medicine, on the other hand, treats disease by giving very small doses of a remedy that in a healthy person would produce the same symptoms as those of the disease. (This follows the old Latin tag of *Similia similibus curantur*, or 'Let like be cured by like'.) 'Homoeopathic' medicine was introduced in Germany in the early nineteenth century, and today has a small but significant number of adherents in many countries. Greek 'allo-' means 'other', and 'homoeo-' means 'like', while '-pathic' means 'suffering'.

alpha omega

A α Ω ω

alpha/omega
The first and last letters of the Greek alphabet (which word is itself based on 'alpha' and the second Greek letter, 'beta'). In a general but rather literary way, the phrase 'alpha and omega' can be used to mean 'essential thing', 'that which is most important' (compare **A/Z**). In the Bible, the phrase is used in Revelation 1:8 to signify the eternity of God: 'I am Alpha and Omega, the beginning and the end, saith the Lord'. Popularly, both 'alpha' and 'omega' can equally indicate an extreme or 'ultimate', without 'omega' having the connotation that 'Z' has when compared with 'A'. For this reason, both words are as popular as each other for use as commercial names.

altruistic/egotistic
An 'altruistic' person is one who puts others (Latin *alter*) before himself, and an 'egotistic' person is one who put himself first (Latin *ego*, 'I'). Thus 'altruism' implies unselfishness, even if of rather a self-righteous kind, and 'egotism' means self-centredness.

AM/FM
The two abbreviations relate to radio transmissions, and respectively stand for 'amplitude modulation' and 'frequency modulation'. 'AM', in the sending of a carrier wave, thus means that although its frequency stays unchanged, its amplitude varies ('modulates') in accordance with the amplitude of the input signal. With 'FM', on the other hand, the frequency modulates while the amplitude of the carrier wave remains unchanged, and this is the standard system used for radio broadcasts on VHF ('very high frequency'), hence the abbreviation 'VHF/

FM' used by the BBC for many of its radio programmes, as distinct from ones that are transmitted on longer waves.

a.m./p.m.
The two abbreviations, despite their learned Latin origin, have long been used in Britain to denote a time in the morning or one in the afternoon or evening (such as '9.0 a.m.' or '6.0 p.m.', with an insular reluctance to adopt the 24-hour clock). The abbreviations stand for *ante meridiem* (not 'ante meridian', as sometimes heard or seen), meaning 'before noon' and *post meridiem*, 'after noon', and both have been in regular use since the eighteenth century.

amateur/professional
These terms denote contrasting sporting statuses, so that technically an 'amateur' is a sportsman or woman who has never competed for money, whereas a 'professional' receives payment. As a result of the distinction, a concept of 'pro-am' has developed, applied to a contest (often, a golfing tournament) in which 'amateurs' compete against 'professionals'.

amelioration/pejoration
The terms basically mean respectively 'improving' (or 'making better') and 'deteriorating' (or 'making worse'). They are used technically in the study of language to indicate a word or meaning that has improved over the years or worsened. For example, the present word 'nice' originally meant 'foolish' or 'silly', so has undergone 'amelioration'. On the other hand, modern 'silly' originally meant 'holy' or 'happy', so has been subject to 'pejoration'. The terms themselves are based on Latin *melior*, 'better' and *peior*, 'worse'.

amis loyaux see **faux amis**

anabatic/katabatic
Geographically, an 'anabatic' wind is one that blows up a hill or mountain slope, especially during the day, while a 'katabatic' one blows downhill, especially at night, when the air cools and becomes denser. In his *Anabasis*, the Greek historian Xenophon describes the expedition, under his own leadership, of the mercenaries of Cyrus the Younger from Sardis to Cunaxa in Babylonia (their *anabasis*, literally 'going up'), followed by their retreat to the Black Sea after the death of Cyrus (their *katabasis*, or 'going down').

anachronism/parachronism
Strictly speaking, an 'anachronism' is the mention, usually in a literary work, of something that is properly too early for it, whereas a 'parachronism' is the reference to someone or something that is really too late for the particular work. However, 'anachronism' (literally 'back in time') is commonly used for a wrong timing generally, whether too early or too late, as is recognized by the *Oxford English Dictionary* in its entry for the word: 'Said *etymologically* (like *prochronism*) of a date which is too early, but also used of too late a date, which has been distinguished as *parachronism*.' The latter (the late mention) is by far the most common, and occurs either deliberately or out of carelessness several times in Shakespeare, for example, where the play *Julius Caesar* has a reference to clocks striking and where, in *Antony and Cleopatra*, Cleopatra plays billiards. Similarly, in 1856 the actor Charles Keane complained of Shakespeare's *The Winter's Tale* that 'chronological contradictions abound, inasmuch as reference is made to the Delphic Oracle, Christian burial, an Emperor of Russia, and an Italian painter of the sixteenth century'. Compare **prochronism/metachronism**.

anadromous see **catadromous**

analogous/homologous
These terms are used in opposite senses in biology to refer to organs and parts of a creature. If they are 'analogous', they have the same function but have evolved differently, such as a whale's paddle and a fish's fin. If they are 'homologous', they have evolved the same way but now have different functions, such as a whale's paddle and a bat's wing. The words derive from Greek *analogos*, 'proportionate', and *homologos*, 'agreeing'.

analogue/digital
In their most familiar senses, an 'analogue' clock or watch is one that indicates the hours, minutes and seconds by means of hands on a dial, the age-old method. A 'digital' clock, by contrast, shows the times by means of figures or digits, typically as '14:28' for 2.28 p.m. An 'analogue' (more usually, 'analog') computer is one that performs arithmetical operations by using some physical quantity, such as mechanical movement, while a 'digital' computer (always an electronic one) is one using an input of combinations of numbers, letters and other characters by means of a particular programming language, with this represented inside it in a binary notation. In another specialized application, 'analogue' is used of conventional discs (records) and tapes, while 'digital' is used of compact discs (CDs) which have their sound quantified as a number or numbers. See also **record/cassette**.

analysis/synthesis
In its most general sense, 'analysis' means the division of something into its different parts so that their relationship to each other or their value can be examined. 'Synthesis' is the opposite of this, the combining of a number of parts into a complex whole. In Kantian philosophy, 'analysis' involves the separating of a particular concept from another that contains it, while 'synthesis' is the unifying of a particular concept with another that is *not* contained in it. In philology, an 'analytic' language is one such as Chinese, and to a lesser extent English, that uses different functions of words and a particular order of words to express meaning, whereas a 'synthetic' language is not an artificial one but one such as Latin, Greek or Russian, in which meaning is usually expressed by the addition of various prefixes and suffixes ('endings') to a root term. (See **declension/conjugation** here.) This means that in a 'synthetic' language, one word can be much more meaningful than in an 'analytic' one, since it contains a 'synthesis' of elements. For example, compare the 'synthetic' Latin *regebantur*, as a single word, with its 'analytic' English equivalent in four words, 'they were being ruled'.

anapaest/dactyl
In classical verse, an 'anapaest' is a so-called 'foot' that consists of two short syllables and one long one, as in the following English line:

Wĭth ă hēy/ănd ă hō/ănd ă hēy/nŏnnȳ nō.

A 'dactyl' is the opposite of this, consisting of one long syllable followed by two short ones, as in the line:

Wīt wĭth hĭs/wāntŏnnĕss/lāstĕth deăth's/
bĭttĕrnĕss.

'Anapaest' literally means 'striking back' in Greek, i.e. 'reversed', since it is a reversed 'dactyl'. 'Dactyl' itself means literally 'finger', with the three syllables compared to the three joints of the finger, one long and two short.

ancient/modern
In historical terms, 'ancient' indicates the earliest known period of civilization, down to at latest the fifth century AD, and thus embracing 'Ancient' Greece and 'Ancient' Rome. 'Modern' history thus runs from about the end of the Middle Ages (the fifteenth century) to the present time. In combined form, the two words are familiar as the title of *Hymns Ancient and Modern* (colloquially known as 'A and M'), a collection of Christian hymns for church use first published in 1861 and still quite popular. Several of the hymns were translations from the Latin, so can with some justification be called 'Ancient'.

and/or
As an entire phrase, the expression is fairly common to denote a possible addition or alternative, as 'soldiers and/or sailors', meaning either one or the other or both. When first current in the nineteenth century, the phrase had 'and' printed over the word 'or', and could be found mainly in mercantile documents. See also **either/or**.

angel/devil
The respective 'goodie' and 'baddie' of heaven or Christian mythology. In the Bible, 'angels' feature chiefly as intermediaries between God and man, as their name suggests, since it originates from Greek *angelos*, 'messenger'. 'Devils', on the other hand, and notably their leader, *the* 'Devil', are fallen 'angels', who lapsed from grace either because of their envy (of men) or through pride. In Christian lore, two of the main 'angels' (archangels) were Michael and Gabriel while the chief 'devil', the ruler of hell, was Satan or Lucifer. Pictorially, the two types of being are associated respectively with wings and haloes and with horns and hooves (and a forked tail, in the case of the 'Devil'). Loosely and popularly, 'angel' means simply a 'good' or attractive person, and 'devil' a bad or 'awkward' one ('She's a real angel'; 'He's a little devil').

angiosperm/gymnosperm
In botany, an 'angiosperm' (literally 'vessel seed') is a seed plant such as the buttercup or rose that has its seeds in a closed ovary; otherwise, it is simply a flowering plant. A 'gymnosperm' ('naked seed'), by contrast, is a woody seed-bearing plant such as a conifer or yew that produces naked seeds, which are not closed in an ovary. See also **monocotyledon/dicotelydon**.

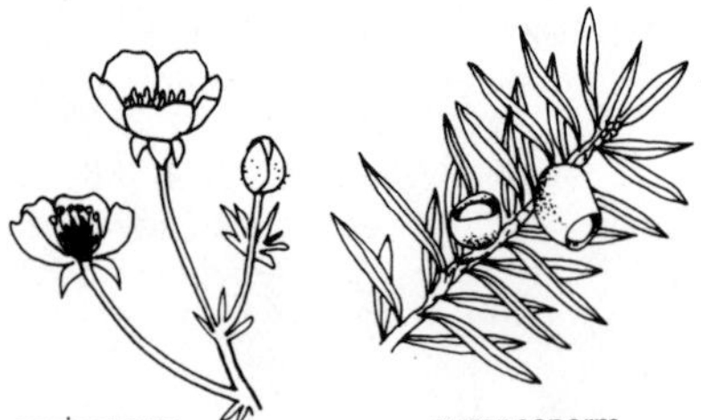

anhedral see **dihedral**

animal/vegetable
Despite the popular parlour game of 'Animal, vegetable or mineral', the dichotomy is really between 'animal' and 'vegetable', because the distinction is between living creatures that can move voluntarily and respond to stimuli, on the one hand, and plants, that can do neither, on the other. There is thus an 'animal' kingdom and a plant kingdom to embrace these two main types of living organism, and if a further contrast is needed, they can be matched together against the members of the 'mineral' kingdom, which comprises all non-living organisms, such as minerals and rocks. Compare also **fauna/flora**.

animate/inanimate
As adjectives, the two words mean literally 'living' and 'not living'. They have a special use in the field of language, to describe classes of nouns referring respectively to living persons or animals, and non-living ('dead') objects. In Russian, for example, the form of the accusative case of masculine nouns varies depending whether the reference is to an 'animate' being or not. (Perversely, the actual word for 'animal' in Russian is neuter, so is grammatically 'inanimate'!)

anode see **cathode**

anorexia/bulimia
These are the medical terms for the contrasting conditions sometimes also known as 'compulsive fasting' and 'compulsive stuffing'. 'Anorexia' (or 'anorexia nervosa') is more common among young people than older, afflicting girls rather than boys, and consists of an abnormal aversion to food as a result of an emotional or psychological disturbance. 'Bulimia', whose subject range is less narrowly defined, involves a pathologically insatiable hunger, usually as the result of a brain lesion rather than an emotional disturbance. The literal sense of 'anorexia' is 'without appetite' (Greek *a*-, 'not' and *orexis*, 'appetite'), which is a hideous misnomer, since a person so afflicted can have a raging hunger that she strives desperately to suppress. 'Bulimia' means literally 'ox hunger' (Greek *bos*, 'ox' and *limos*, 'hunger').

answer see **question**

antagonist[1]/protagonist
Properly, in drama or fiction, an 'antagonist' is the character who is opposed to ('anti') the hero, who is the 'protagonist', with the words thus meaning respectively 'one who struggles against' and 'one who struggles first' (Greek *protos*). So in Shakespeare's *Othello*, for example, Iago is the 'antagonist' to the hero Othello, the Moor 'protagonist'. Popularly, however, 'protagonist' has come to be understood as 'one who supports a cause', with the first part of the word wrongly taken as *pro-*, 'for', and this has distorted the true opposition between the terms. See also the next entry.

antagonist[2]/synergist
These two medical terms are used to apply respectively to a drug that counteracts the action of another drug or substance in the body (such as one that transmits nerve impulses), and a drug that increases or enhances the action of another. Morphine and atropine are thus familiar 'antagonists', and a stimulant drug such as caffeine is a 'synergist'.

Antarctic see **Arctic**

antepost see **starting price**

anterior/posterior
In a number of technical senses, the terms are used to mean 'front' (at or towards it) and 'rear' (likewise), literally 'more before' and 'more after', from Latin. In anatomy, for instance, 'anterior' can be used as a synonym for 'ventral', and 'posterior' for 'dorsal' (see **dorsal/ventral**), and in botany the 'anterior' part of a flower or leaf is the one farthest away from the main stem, while a 'posterior' part is situated nearest to the stem.

anti see **pro[1]**

anticline see **syncline**

anticlockwise see **clockwise**

anticyclone see **cyclone**

antidote see **poison**

antipope see **pope**

antistrophe see **strophe**

antithesis see **thesis[1]**

antonym see **synonym**

apart see **together**

aperitif/digestif
The two French words are commonly somewhat pretentiously used to denote respectively an alcoholic drink drunk before a meal to whet the appetite, and one drunk after as an aid to digestion. Typically, both are spirits or at least fortified wine, such as a cocktail for the 'aperitif' and a liqueur as a 'digestif'. The idea of the 'aperitif' is to serve as an 'opener' (but not an aperient!). Both are really an excuse to drink and enjoy alcohol apart from the wine that actually accompanies the meal.

aphelion see **perihelion**

apodosis/protasis
In grammar, 'apodosis' is used to refer to the main clause of a conditional sentence (the part that does not begin with 'if'), as the italicized words in: 'If you were to ask me, *I would come at once*'. 'Protasis' is thus the counterpart of this, the subordinate clause (beginning with 'if'): '*If you were to ask me*, I would come at once'. The two terms have the respective meaning 'giving back', 'returning' (i.e. answering) and 'putting forward', 'extending' (i.e. proposing).

apogee/perigee
In astronomy and astronautics, the 'apogee' of a natural or artificial satellite or spacecraft is its furthest point in orbit from the Earth, while the opposite is its 'perigee', its closest point to the Earth in its orbit. Thus the 'apogee' of the Moon from the Earth is 406,800 kilometres, and

its 'perigee' 356,400. Greek *apo-* means 'away', *peri-* means 'round', and *ge* means 'Earth'.

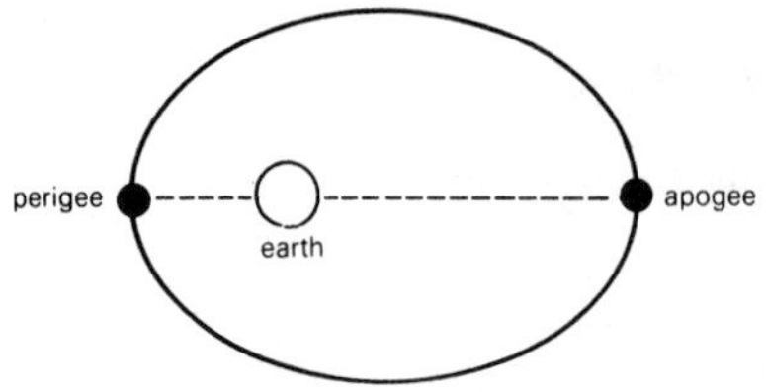

Apollonian/Dionysian
The two terms derive respectively from the names of the Greek gods Apollo and Dionysus. Apollo was the messenger of the gods, and himself the god of light, poetry, music, healing and prophecy. Dionysus, by contrast, was the god of wine, fruitfulness and vegetation and of general 'permissiveness'. So Apollo represents 'sweetness and light' and Dionysus 'wine, women and song' (among other things), with the result that the corresponding adjectives have come to denote opposing strains or tendencies in drama and literature from Greek tragedy onwards. In modern times, D. H. Lawrence might thus be said to be a 'Dionysian', while Gide and Stendhal could be regarded as 'Apollonians'. It was the German philosopher Nietzsche who introduced the terms in his *The Birth of Tragedy out of the Spirit of Music* (1872).

a posteriori see **a priori**

appearance/reality
To take the terms philosophically, 'appearance' is the outward or phenomenal manifestation of things, or the world as revealed by the senses (as it appears to be), while 'reality' denotes what actually exists, independent of human awareness (i.e. as it 'really' is). For most of us, however, who are not philosophers, the 'appearance' of a thing is its 'reality', and the tree that grows outside my house is in 'reality' a tree because it has the precise 'appearance' of one.

applause/slow handclap
Two rather interesting ways in which an audience expresses its approval or disapproval of a performance, with spontaneous clapping meaning 'well done!' (the faster the clapping, the greater the approval), and a deliberate 'slow handclap' meaning 'rotten!' or 'get on with it!' Clapping (spontaneous or unsynchronized applause) is virtually universal in signifying approval, but the 'slow handclap' is more a British phenomenon. When Russians give a 'slow handclap', for example, it indicates approval, as if the audience are 'in accord' in their verdict.

applied see **pure**

a priori/a posteriori
In logic, an 'a priori' argument is one made from obvious or self-evident propositions, already made, proceeding from cause to effect, or a general law to a particular instance. For example: 'It grows dark early every winter, therefore, as today is 6 February, it will grow dark early this evening'. An 'a posteriori' argument reasons from particular facts to a general law, or makes a conclusion about a cause from observing the effects. Not all 'a priori' or 'a posteriori' arguments are necessarily correct, of course, and in some cases there can be ambiguity. In his *Modern English Usage*, H. W. Fowler cites the classic example of the statement: 'God's in his heaven – all's right with the world'. This will be 'a priori' if it means 'Since we know God is in heaven, therefore all is right with the world', but 'a posteriori' if it means 'The world is obviously good, therefore there must be a God in heaven'. The two terms are Latin, meaning literally 'from the previous' and 'from the latter'.

Arabian camel/Bactrian camel
The 'Arabian camel' or dromedary (*Camelus dromedarius*) has one hump on its back, while the 'Bactrian camel' (*Camelus bactrianus*) has two, and that is the main and obvious difference. Additionally, the 'Arabian camel' cannot withstand the cold as well as the 'Bactrian camel', since the latter has a thicker coat and shorter legs.

It is a swifter runner, however – hence its alternative name of 'dromedary' (Greek *dromas*, 'running'), as it was used in races. There is a difference of habitat, too, as the names indicate, with the 'Arabian camel' found in India, the Middle East and North Africa, and the 'Bactrian camel' in Central Asia ('Bactria' was an ancient country of south-west Asia more or less corresponding to modern north Afghanistan). To most Europeans, the 'Arabian camel' with its single hump is probably the 'proper' one.

Arabic numerals/Roman numerals

These are the two main kind of number used in European languages today, with 'Arabic numerals' the familiar 1,2,3,4,5,6,7,8,9,10, and 'Roman numerals', corresponding to these, I,II,III,IV,V,VI,VII,VIII,IX,X. 'Arabic numerals' are really of Indian origin, but are so called since western Europeans learned about them through Arab writers. The present system of 'Roman numerals', in which '1988', for example, is written 'MCMLXXXVIII', was fairly recent to develop, and in classical times there were different systems for expressing multiple figures. In everyday usage, 'Arabic numerals' normally serve for main enumeration, and 'Roman numerals', often in small letters, for secondary enumeration, especially where letters of the alphabet are not used, and in many books 'Roman numerals' are used for introductory pages and 'Arabic numerals' for the main text. 'Roman numerals' did originate with the Romans, however, as can be seen by the fact that 'C' stands for Latin *centum*, 'hundred', and 'M' for *mille*, 'thousand'.

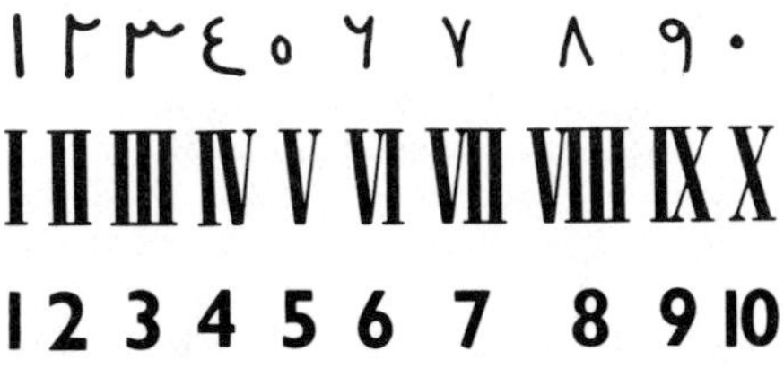

arable/ley

'Arable' land is land that can be or actually is tilled for growing crops, while 'ley' land (or just 'ley') is today simply grassland or pastureland (although formerly regarded as 'arable' land put down specially to grass).

archaism/neologism

An 'archaism' is a word or phrase that is old or obsolete, sometimes used in literature for special effect, especially in poetry down to the nineteenth century. One example is this verse from Thomas Parnell's *A Fairy Tale*, where the words in italics were all 'archaisms' when it was written (in about 1700):

With that Sir Topaz, hapless youth!
In accents faultering, ay for *ruth*
  Intreats them pity *graunt*;
For *als* he been a mister *wight*,
Betray'd by wandering in the night
To tread the circles haunt.

A 'neologism' is the opposite, a word that has been newly coined for a special reason, such as to give a name to a new scientific process, or market a new type of garment. Examples of 'neologism' are 'astronaut', 'cybernetics', 'catsuit' and 'yucky'. 'Neologisms' can thus be created from existing words or elements, or devised as an entirely original word. Certainly many current 'archaisms' were once 'neologisms'.

Arctic/Antarctic

The two names for the opposite polar regions of the world, with the 'Arctic' round the North Pole, and the 'Antarctic' round the South. The name of the latter indicates its geographical location 'anti' or opposite the 'Arctic', which in turn takes its name from Greek *arktos*, 'bear', since it lies beneath the constellation of the Great Bear (Ursa Major), one of whose stars is the Pole Star.

Arhat/Bodhisattva

'Arhat' is the term in Buddhism for a monk who at death passes to Nirvana, where he is in a state of absolute bliss and release from the cycle of reincarnation.

'Bodhisattva' is the word for a Buddhist who although he has attained perfect bliss and enlightenment, refrains from entering Nirvana in order to save others, and so is worshipped as a deity. The two terms derive direct from Sanskrit, and mean respectively 'worthy of respect' and 'one whose essence is enlightenment' (literally 'enlightenment being').

arithmetic progression/geometric progression
'Arithmetic progression' is a mathematical progression in which numbers increase by a constant amount, e.g. 3, 6, 9, 12, 15, etc. In 'geometric progression', the increase is one of constant ratio, e.g., 1, 2, 4, 8, 16, 32, etc. (where each number is doubled).

arrière-garde see **avant-garde**

arrival/departure
The two words are chiefly associated with the times at which various types of public transport arrive or depart, such as trains and aircraft, with each traditionally abbreviated in timetables as 'arr' and 'dep'. Mainline stations and airports thus have 'arrival' and 'departure' boards or displays for the benefit of travellers or those meeting them. The two words have different endings ('-al' and '-ure') because of their particular development from Old French, and although some nineteenth-century writers attempted to introduce a form 'departal', it never caught on.

arsis see **thesis**[2]

artery see **vein**

artificial see **genuine**

artiodactyl/perissodactyl
Two impressive words that to a zoologist describe an important difference in various types of hoofed mammals (ungulates). Ones that are 'artiodactyl', like the pig, hippopotamus, camel, deer and cow, have hooves with an even number of toes, while those that are 'perissodactyl', such as the horse, rhinoceros and tapir, have hooves with an odd number of toes. The terms, based on Greek, mean literally 'even-numbered toes' and 'uneven-numbered toes'. See also **odd/even**, and for a similar sort of digital distinction (but of direction, not number), compare **zygodactyl/heterodactyl**, the last entry in this main text.

art music see **folk music**

arts/sciences
We have all come across such phrases or titles as 'The art or science of fly fishing' (or whatever), and have probably wondered, 'which is it?' Which subjects, disciplines or pursuits are 'arts', and which 'sciences'? The question has exercised the minds of several writers over the ages. When specifically contrasted, the difference has been expressed in different ways. In his *Logick* (1725), Isaac Watts, better known as the hymn-writer, wrote: 'This is the most remarkable distinction between an art and a science, viz. the one refers chiefly to practice, the other to speculation'. Subsequently, William Jevons in his *Elementary Lessons in Logic* (1870) was to write: 'A science teaches us to know and an art to do', and this may well be the best and simplest definition still. However, when it comes to the academic side, we need to be more precise, and it really boils down to the fact that what is not a 'science' is an 'art', i.e. is concerned traditionally with literature, languages, philosophy or what might be thought of as a 'cultural' subject. (This would embrace the 'aesthetic' subjects such as music, painting and the fine 'arts' generally.) 'Science', therefore, deals with systemized knowledge, as the name implies (Latin *scire* means 'to know'), and in turn embraces the so-called natural 'sciences' such as physics, chemistry and biology. However, there is a distinct overlap, since one can make a systematic study of a language, and this subject itself has spawned many 'sciences' (e.g. sociolinguistics and semiotics). So perhaps the 'knowing' and 'doing' division is the most satisfactory as a general guide, with the 'doing' aspect of 'art' seen in related words such as 'artefact' and 'artifice'. The full title of the Royal Society of 'Arts', too, is

the Royal Society of 'Arts', Manufacturers and Commerce, embracing both 'art' and 'science'.

ASA/DIN
'ASA' (or more fully, 'ASA/BS') stands for 'American Standards Association/British Standard', and 'DIN' stands for German '*Deutsche Industrie Norm*' (or 'German industry standard'), and the two are different ways of expressing the speed of a photographic film. 'ASA' gives the formula as $0.8/E$, where E is the exposure of a point that is 0.1 density units above the so-called fog level on the characteristic curve of a particular sensitized material. (This is somewhat technical: 'fog level' is the term for the density of a developed photographic material that has not been exposed to light, and 'characteristic curve' is a graph of the density of such a material.) 'DIN' uses a logarithmic formula to express the speed, in which although E ('exposure') is still 0.1 units above the fog level, the formula itself is $-10\log_{10}E$. Of the two systems, 'ASA' is the more widely used, and is the simpler, since it is not logarithmic (a film of 200 'ASA' is thus twice as fast, and requires half as much exposure, as one of 100 'ASA'). For a 'DIN' film, every increase by three doubles the speed, so that a 50 'ASA' film equals 18 'DIN', 100 'ASA' equals 21 'DIN', and so on.

ascend/descend
To 'ascend' is to go up, of course, and to 'descend' to go down. From these two basic verbs, terms such as 'ascender' and 'descender' have developed, and also 'ascendant' and 'descendant'. In printing, an 'ascender' is that part of a lower case letter (see **upper/lower**) that extends above the body of the letter, such as in 'b' or 'h'. A 'descender' is the opposite: that part of a letter that descends below the main body of a letter such as 'x' or 'n', for example 'j', 'p' and 'y'. Compositors may need to take these into account in certain cases, for example when a letter with an 'ascender' comes directly below one with a 'descender' in a text with minimal spacing between the lines. In astrology (not astronomy!), the 'ascendant' is that part of the zodiac that rises above the eastern horizon at a given moment (in particular, a person's birth), while the 'descendant' is the point exactly opposite to this (on the so-called ecliptic or 'great circle' of the sky).

Ashkenazi/Sephardi
The names belong to the two main divisions of Jewish people. The 'Ashkenazi' are of German or East European descent and spoke Yiddish. The 'Sephardi' are non-Yiddish-speaking and are the western branch of European Jews that settled in Spain and Portugal. The names relate respectively to Ashkenaz, the son of Gomer (Genesis 10:1 and I Chronicles 1:6), and to Sepharad, a region mentioned in Obadiah 1:20 and thought to have been Spain. The 'Sephardi' spoke Judaeo-Spanish, or Ladino, and are far fewer in number today than the 'Ashkenazi'. However, the chief rabbinate of Israel has both an 'Ashkenazi' and a 'Sephardi' chief rabbi.

Asia see **Europe**

assets/liabilities
The 'assets' of a business are its property and the amount of money owing to it, as entered on the credit side of its balance sheet (see **credit/debit**). 'Assets' can be technically fixed, current (see **current assets/fixed assets**), liquid (i.e. as actual money, or easily convertible into money), or intangible (i.e. able to be sold but having no intrinsic value). Its 'liabilities' are basically its debts or obligations, which will be entered as claims on the debit side of the balance sheet.

assonance/dissonance
'Assonance', as typically found in poetry, is the use of the same vowel sound with different consonants, or of the same consonant with different vowels, so as to produce a special effect of euphony. For example, 'holy Moses' (same vowel, different consonants) or 'creaking and croaking' (same consonants, different vowel). (The latter variant is also known

as 'consonance'.) 'Dissonance' is the opposite of this, with the use of cacophonous or 'jarring' consonants and vowels. Browning has 'dissonance' in these lines from *Childe Roland to the Dark Tower Came*:

What made those holes and rents
In the dock's harsh swarth leaves, bruised as to baulk
All hope of greenness? 'tis a brute must walk
Pashing their life out, with a brute's intents.

For something like the equivalent in music, see **consonance/dissonance**.

astern see **ahead**

astrology see **astronomy**

astronomy/astrology
'Astronomy' is the science that deals with the study of the stars and of celestial bodies in general. 'Astrology' is the pseudo-science that purports to interpret the occult influences of the stars and planets on the lives of humans. Originally, however, 'astrology' was a proper science, and embraced what is now 'astronomy', and was divided into so-called natural 'astrology', which calculated the movements of the heavens (or the supposed movements), and judicial 'astrology', which studied the supposed influence of the stars on human destiny, as modern 'astrology' does. It is perhaps rather surprising that it was not the '-ology' form to be adopted for the modern science, since this ending is much more common than '-onomy' for the names of sciences today (e.g. biology, geology, psychology, philology, zoology, etc). The '-nomy' actually means 'arrangement', 'management', as in 'economy' and 'autonomy'.

Atlantic/Pacific
Apart from the Indian Ocean, the 'Atlantic' and 'Pacific' are the two main oceans of the world, regarded respectively as dividing the Old World (Europe) from the New (North America) and as separating America and Asia. Seen differently, the 'Atlantic' is the great ocean of the western world, and the 'Pacific' that of the East, with corresponding implications of 'civilization' and the exotic. It is perhaps significant in this respect that 'transatlantic' is a much more common term than 'transpacific'. If the two areas had been smaller, there is a chance that they could have come to be called the 'Western' and the 'Eastern' oceans. (In fact, the sixteenth-century Spanish explorer Vasco Balboa did call the 'Pacific' the 'Southern Sea' by contrast to the 'Northern Sea', i.e. the 'Atlantic', since he approached it when travelling southwards.) As it is, the 'Atlantic' has a name based on that of the Atlas Mountains, beyond which it lies, with the name in turn related to that of the mythical 'Atlantis', while 'Pacific' means 'peaceful', as Magellan encountered no storms when crossing it from South America to the Philippines a few years after Balboa's discovery.

atlas see **caryatid**

atrium/ventricle
In anatomy, the 'atrium' is the upper chamber of the heart that receives blood from the veins (see **vein/artery**) and forces it downwards into the 'ventricle', from which it is pumped into the arteries. The words themselves are rather unusual in origin. Latin *atrium* was the term for a courtyard open to the sky in a Roman house, while 'ventricle' is a diminutive of *venter*, 'belly'. An older name for 'atrium' was 'auricle', as a diminutive of *auris*, 'ear'.

attack[1]/counterattack
A 'counterattack' is not simply the repelling of an 'attack', as it is made, but in effect another, answering 'attack' made some time after the initial 'attack'. This is therefore in contrast to certain other words with 'counter-', where the opposing action is simultaneous (e.g. counterattraction, counterbalance, counterclaim, counterculture, counterpart, counterpoint).

attack[2]/defend
The opposing verbs are familiar from both warfare and sport, with one side or the other aiming to advance and win ('attack')

and the other trying to prevent such an advance and to protect its 'base' ('defend'). In both activities, one side can divide its participants into those who 'attack' (such as the forwards in football) and those who 'defend' (such as the backs), and even in cricket, the bowlers are sometimes seen as the side that 'attacks', while the batsmen 'defend'. To 'defend' thus acquires a meaning which is not only 'prevent an attack' but 'be prepared for an attack', with the two actions effective simultaneously.

Attic/Doric
In literature, 'Attic' is sometimes used to denote writing that is urbane and sophisticated, while 'Doric' is rustic and unsophisticated. The reference is to the Greek regions of Attica (capital, Athens) and Doris, south of Thessaly. Hence the term 'Attic wit', meaning refined or delicate wit, and the significance of the word 'Doric' in these lines from Milton's *Lycidas* (referring to an 'uncouth swain'):

He touch'd the tender stops of various quills,
With eager thought warbling his Doric lay.

attract/repel
The verbs respectively indicate 'drawing to' and 'pushing from', whether of scientific substances or human characteristics. In their adjectival forms, the words can mean generally 'pleasant', 'nice', or 'unpleasant', 'nasty', as 'He has an attractive smile' and 'It was a repellent sight' (or a 'repulsive' one, since the two words are related in the original Latin).

aubade see **serenade**

auction/Dutch auction
The difference is that in an 'auction', the bids go up, with the sale made to the highest bidder, while in a 'Dutch auction' the price starts high but is gradually lowered for the item until it is acceptable to a bidder. The adjective 'Dutch' is used in a number of opprobrious ways to refer sarcastically to something that is the opposite of the genuine thing, with the 'Dutch auction' just one of them. (Others are a 'Dutch uncle' who is a severe critic, a 'Dutch treat' in which each person pays for himself, and 'Dutch courage', which is induced by alcohol.) The origin of this derisive usage probably stems from the rivalry between the English and the Dutch in the seventeenth century.

auction bridge see **contract bridge**

audio/video
The 'split' here is virtually the one that exists in the pairs **radio/TV** and **sight/sound**, so that the connotation of the terms is the same: anything that is 'audio' is less immediately striking but capable of great emotive force, with anything 'video' having a direct and sometimes powerful (if superficially) visual appeal. 'Audio' thus relates basically to any equipment, such as a recorder or a tape or disc, that is concerned with the transmission or reproduction of sound, while 'video' equipment (recorders, tapes, discs, etc.) involves the transmission of a visual medium (more exactly, one with vision and sound), such as a televised programme, recorded film, or 'homemade' production. From the 1980s, the two media were essentially part of the world of pop music and discotheques, and it is curious that the three words *audio, video, disco* just happen to have (in stuffy Latin) the meaning 'I listen, I see, I learn'. There must be a moral in this somewhere.

augment/diminish
In general terms, to 'augment' is to increase, and to 'diminish' to decrease. The verbs have one or two special uses, however, such as in music, where to 'augment' an interval is to increase by a semitone (e.g. C to G 'augmented' is C to G sharp), and to 'diminish' an interval is to reduce it by a semitone (e.g. so that C to E when 'diminished' becomes C to E flat). Strictly, only a major or perfect interval can be 'augmented', and a minor or perfect one be 'diminished'. See also **major/minor**, **sharp^2/flat**, **perfect/imperfect**.

augmentative see **diminutive**

aunt see **uncle**

aural see **oral**[1]

aurora australis see **aurora borealis**

aurora borealis/aurora australis
The Latin names mean respectively 'northern aurora' and 'southern aurora', and refer to the natural phenomena known also in English as 'northern lights' and 'southern lights'. The better known is the former, seen in high northern latitudes in the form of streamers or arches of light in the sky, and believed to be caused by solar particles entering the Earth's upper atmosphere. See also **north/south**, and compare the next entry.

austral/septentrional
The two terms are specialized or rarish equivalents of 'south' and 'north' when used adjectivally, so that an 'austral' wind is a south one, and a 'septentrional' state is a northern country. The origins of the words lie in mythological or astronomical Latin, with *auster* actually meaning 'south wind' and 'septentrional' deriving from *septentriones*, literally 'the seven ploughing oxen' (*septem*, 'seven' and *triones*, 'ploughing oxen'), otherwise the constellation of the Great Bear (Ursa Major), which lies over the North Pole (see **Arctic/Antarctic**). The 'southern' sense of 'austral' lies behind the name of Australia, which was marked on maps in classical times, when its existence was only conjectured, as *Terra incognita australis*, 'the unknown southern land'.

automatic see **manual**

autumn see **spring**

autumnal see **vernal**

avant-garde/arrière-garde
The French phrases mean literally 'vanguard' and 'rearguard', and have come to be used in English in the field of fine arts to apply respectively to experimental or 'advanced' artistic techniques, and to conventional ones, i.e. to those artists or intellectuals who follow the 'avant-garde'. The former phrase became current from the early 1900s; the latter only from the 1960s (too late to be recorded in the *Supplement* to the *Oxford English Dictionary*). See also **vanguard/rearguard**.

ave/vale
The two Latin words mean respectively 'hail' and 'farewell', and have been traditionally combined in the tag *Ave atque vale*, 'Hail and farewell', originating as the words of Catullus before his brother's tomb, quoted from these lines in his *Carmina*:

> Nunc tamen interea haec prisco quae more parentum
> Tradita sunt tristi munere ad inferias,
> Accipe fraterno multum manantia fletu,
> Atque in perpetuum, frater, ave atque vale.

These have been translated by Sir William Marris as follows:

> Yet take these gifts, brought as our fathers bade
> For sorrow's tributes to the passing shade;
> A brother's tears have wet them o'er and o'er;
> And so, my brother, hail, and farewell evermore!

In fact, in Roman use 'ave' could itself mean both 'hail' (at a meeting) and 'farewell' (at a parting).

away see **home**[2]

Axminster see **Wilton**

aye/no
'The ayes have it!' The two terms are still used in some formal situations when a vote is made, with 'aye' meaning 'yes' (or 'for') and 'no' what it says (or 'against'). The best-known usage is in the House of Commons on the occasion of a vote or

'division', when Members of Parliament either vote orally 'aye' or 'no' or proceed into separate lobbies for the purpose, the 'ayes' voting in a lobby to the right of the Speaker, and the 'noes' to his left. It is still uncertain whether 'aye' originated in the 'aye aye, Sir', of sailors, or as an alternative to 'yea', or as a representation of 'I', expressing agreement.

Bb

B see (1) **A**[1] (2) **H**

bachelor/spinster
'Bachelor' (regularly misspelt 'batchelor' in a wide range of printed and handwritten texts) has the basic meaning 'unmarried man', while 'spinster' means 'unmarried woman'. The ideal marriage match is thus between one and the other. Today the terms are normally used, however, only in legal documents and in the Church of England 'Banns of Marriage' duly published orally during a church service (describing the two parties on the lines of 'John Edward Bloggs, bachelor, of the parish of Little Downland' and 'Emily Jane Biggs, spinster, of this parish'). In its sense 'university graduate', 'bachelor' is sexless and can be used of men and women. The words themselves have no reference at all to the unmarried status. 'Bachelor' derives, through Old French, from the Latin word for 'farmworker', and 'spinster' means 'woman who spins'. French does rather better with *célibataire* for either, this deriving directly from the Latin word for 'unmarried' (like a 'celibate' priest in English).

back see (1) **forward**[1] (2) **front**

backbencher/frontbencher
In the British House of Commons, a 'backbencher' (who sits on benches or seats at the back of the chamber, furthest from the centre) is a Member of Parliament who holds no office in either the Government of the day or the Opposition (see **Government/Opposition**). By contrast, a 'frontbencher' (who sits on the seats nearest to the centre of the chamber, on either side of the house) is a leading member of the Government, such as a minister, or his equivalent in the Opposition. There are also 'crossbenchers', who are neutral or independent members (peers) in the House of Lords, where they sit on benches set at right angles to those occupied by members of the Government and the Opposition. See also **front/back**, **Lords/Commons**.

background see **foreground**

backhand see **forehand**

backsight see **foresight**[1]

backspin see **topspin**

backwardation see **contango**

backwards see **forward**[1]

backwash/swash
The first of these words is probably better known than the second. 'Backwash' is the splash or dashing movement of water as caused by retreating waves (on a river bank, for example, after a boat has passed at speed). A word is therefore needed for the dashing of water caused by an advancing wave, such as one falling on the beach by the sea, and this is 'swash'. The basic word is probably imitative in origin, but does also suggest 'wash'.

Bactrian camel see **Arabian camel**

bad see **good**[1]

baddies see **goodies**

bank see **bond**

banker/pocket
These are stationers' or office-workers' terms for the two basic types of envelope. A 'banker' envelope has a long flap down one side; a 'pocket' envelope has its flap

at one end. The words are hard to find in standard dictionaries. For the connection with 'bank', see **bond/bank**.

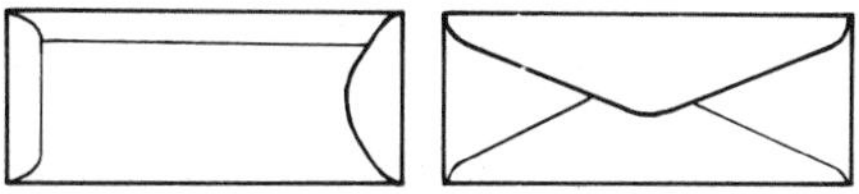

pocket banker

bas relief/high relief
The two French terms (semi-French in the latter case) are used in sculpture or design-work generally to denote a style in which the forms project respectively slightly or considerably from the background, without being separate from it. The proper French words are *bas relief* ('low raised work') and *haut relief* ('high raised work'), and also sometimes occur in their Italian forms of 'basso relievo' and 'alto relievo'.

bas relief

high relief

bass see **treble**

bat/bowl
The two main contrasting activities in the game of cricket, in which one player of a side hits the ball ('bats'), both protecting his wicket and at the same time endeavouring to score runs (points), while another player of the opposing side throws him a ball ('bowls') in an attempt to hit his wicket or dismiss him from the game in some other way (or at least to prevent him from scoring). In principle, the batting side are the defenders in the contest, and the bowling side the attackers (see **attack/defend**). Rather surprisingly, the words 'bowl' and 'ball' are not related, although they are closely associated in the game.

battery/mains
The two main sources of electricity for various instruments and tools, from radios to electric razors. Many instruments, such as radios, can be 'battery' or 'mains' powered, with the latter type of supply generally regarded as cheaper and 'steadier'. However, instruments powered by 'battery' are obviously more versatile, since they can be taken almost anywhere, and in making the choice between the two, a would-be purchaser is usually obliged to solve the equation of 'constant cheap power' versus 'versatility'. On the whole, the larger the electrical device, and the greater its complexity, the more likely it will be to have 'mains' power (as a refrigerator or television set), while a simple, portable implement, such as an electric torch, which *has* to be versatile, will almost always be powered by 'battery'. Finally, some 'mains' powered devices have 'battery' back-ups that come into operation if there is a power failure, especially when they operate constantly, like an electric clock. See also **AC/DC**.

battery see **free-range**

BBC/ITV
The two main organizations transmitting television in Britain, with the 'BBC' (British Broadcasting Corporation) government-controlled but enjoying a large degree of independence, and 'ITV' (Independent Television), as the familiar name for the television side of the IBA (Independent Broadcasting Authority), not government-sponsored. This means that the 'BBC' derives its income mainly

from the sale of television licences, but also partly through a government grant, while 'ITV' derives its whole income through advertising (hence its alternative name of 'commercial television'). The difference between the TV programmes produced by the two organizations is less discernible now than it was when 'ITV' first transmitted in the late 1950s. For many years, the 'BBC' had a reputation for 'safe and stuffy' programmes, while the 'ITV' broadcasts were seen as generally brighter and aimed at the 'mass' viewer. The distinction was thus something like that discussed in the entry **quality paper/popular paper**. Today, however, the difference is more sharply defined. Many viewers consider that 'ITV' news programmes, for example, are better than those on the 'BBC', but in the mid-1980s drama on 'BBC' was as good as anything on 'ITV'. A comparison between the two has also polarized round the inclusion of advertisements. The 'BBC' has no advertising, whereas 'ITV' programmes are constantly interrupted by 'commercials'. Many people feel that if the 'BBC' accepted commercial advertising, its present high standards would not suffer. Moreover, viewers would no longer have to pay the licence fee, which they now do whether they watch either the 'BBC' or 'ITV'!

BC/AD

In many but not all countries in the western world, these are the two Christian eras, 'Before Christ' and 'Anno Domini' ('the year of the Lord'), with the abbreviated versions varying from one language to another (e.g. French *av. J.-C.* or *avant Jesus-Christ* and *après J.-C.* to correspond, German *v.Chr.*, in full *vor Christi Geburt*, or 'before the birth of Christ', and *n.Chr.*, otherwise *nach Christi Geburt*, 'after the birth of Christ', and so on). The system of reckoning eras like this was introduced by Dionysius Exiguus in the sixth century 'AD' to designate the years in a table he had drawn up for fixing the date of Easter. The unofficial Jewish equivalents of 'BC' and 'AD' are 'BCE' ('Before the Common Era') and 'ACE' ('After the Common Era'). Muslims date their years 'AH', i.e. 'Anno Hegyrae', or from the year of the Hegira (AD 622), that of the flight of Muhammad from Mecca to Medina.

bear/bull

These are the two opposite types of speculators on the Stock Exchange, with the terms also applied to the stocks and shares themselves. A 'bear' speculates on a falling market, so sells his shares in the hope of buying them in again later and so making a profit. A 'bull' gambles on a rising market, so buys shares while he thinks the price is reasonably low, hoping to sell them later at a higher price for a profit. The first term seems to originate in the proverb about 'selling the bear before you have his skin', with 'bull' coming to be associated with the other animal (perhaps as both are powerful and have associations with sport and risk-taking).

beast see **bird**

beau/belle

The two French words denote respectively a handsome man or 'fop' and a beautiful woman or 'fine lady'. The latter word has been fairly widely used in certain stock phrases such as 'bathing belle' (with almost half a pun on the former 'diving bell') and 'belle of the ball', and has also been appropriated for some named railway trains, such as the former Brighton 'Belle' and Bournemouth 'Belle' (both seaside trains having associations with bathing 'belles'). 'Beau' has much more of a historical and romantic ring, such as the various dandies called by the nickname ('Beau' Brummel, 'Beau' Nash, and so on). 'Belle' has not been used as a woman's nickname in this way, despite the fact that 'beau' and 'belle' are exact gender equivalents.

beaux-arts/belles-lettres

The French terms mean literally 'fine arts' and 'fine letters'. 'Beaux-arts' is really exactly the same as 'fine arts' itself, so means painting, sculpture and music, where what is important is the aesthetic appeal. The phrase relates in particular to the classical decorative style of the École des Beaux-Arts in Paris. The literary equivalent of 'beaux-arts' is thus 'belles-lettres', originally conceived (in France) as embracing grammar, rhetoric and poetry. Today, when used at all, it means either 'fine writing' or perhaps, more academically, 'the humanities'. It somehow has an amateurish ring about it, implying almost an affectation of literary style, which 'beaux-arts' does not have.

bedder see **gyp**

bee/wasp
As insects, 'bees' differ from 'wasps' in that their mouthparts form a proboscis, enabling them to lap nectar from flowers, and that they have hairs on their bodies enabling them to pick up pollen from the flowers. 'Bees' also differ from 'wasps' by storing the honey and pollen in their nests. There is also another distinction. The 'bee' has a sting that is barbed, and when it stings, it stays in the wound. A 'bee' sting will thus need to be removed. A 'wasp' sting is not barbed, however, so merely the site of the sting will need to be treated. Incidentally, it is only the worker 'bee' that stings (see **drones/workers**).

beefcake/cheesecake
These apparent comestibles actually relate to pictures or poses of the human figure, especially those of the husky male and the attractive female that are designed to emphasize their sexual appeal. It was the 'cheesecake' that came first, originating in the 1930s in the United States, where the term came to apply to a 'pin-up', or picture used for publicity purposes, especially one that concentrated on 'leg art'. The slang term itself seems to have arisen as an embodiment of a pretty woman who was 'good enough to eat', so that the word links up with other slang designations such as 'sweetie pie', 'peach', 'cookie' and even perhaps 'tart' and 'crumpet'. 'Beefcake' then followed in the 1940s, with the rise of handsome he-men filmstars such as Alan Ladd, and the word here was a humorous copying of the feminine equivalent. And although there is a real edible 'cheesecake' (made with cream cheese, cream and sugar), there is no 'beefcake' to accompany it as a matching meat dish.

beer/ale
Although 'beer' and 'ale' are popularly equated as the familiar staple pub drink, today 'ale' is commonly used for the 'real' brew, otherwise genuine draught 'beer' as distinct from canned and bottled 'beer'. Originally, too, 'ale' differed from 'beer' in that it was unflavoured by hops. Today, too, 'ale' (especially the real thing) is more bitter, stronger and heavier than 'beer'.

before/after
The two words are familiar in pictorial advertisement for various remedies and treatments (e.g. slimming products), where a person is shown 'before' and 'after' treatment. Many advertisers are fond of comparisons and contrasts ('More comfort, less cost', and so on), and the 'before' and 'after' appeal is one of the standard ones.

beginning/end
Unlike the pair **start/finish** (which see), 'beginning' and 'end' often denote the first and last stages of something, not the first and last moments. So 'in the beginning' means 'at first', 'in the early days', and 'at the end' means 'at last', 'in the final stages'. The two words are often

contrasted in a single sentence, such as 'from beginning to end', and both have been preserved in some memorable quotations. Among these are T. S. Eliot's 'In my beginning is my end' and Churchill's almost equally philosophical words during the Second World War: 'This is not the end. It is not even the beginning of the end. But it is, perhaps, the end of the beginning' (Speech made on 10 November 1942, of the Battle of Egypt).

behind see **in front**

being/nothingness
There could hardly be a contrast more extreme than this, implying existence on the one hand, and non-existence on the other, with all that each individually entails. The words are familiar as the title of the long philosophical treatise by Sartre (in the original French, *L'Être et le Néant*), in which he attempted to present his main arguments for his theory of existentialism.

belle see **beau**

belles-lettres see **beaux-arts**

ben see **but**

benevolent/malevolent
The two words derive from Latin, and mean respectively 'wishing well' and 'wishing evil' (see **good/evil**). A 'benevolent' old man is thus kindly, but a 'malevolent' one is wicked and harmful. Shakespeare had two characters Benvolio and Malvolio, respectively in *Romeo and Juliet* and *Twelfth Night*, and they are good-willed and ill-willed in keeping with their names. In considering this pair of opposites, it should be noticed that 'benefactor' and 'malefactor' are not true opposites, since although a 'malefactor' does evil, a 'benefactor' is specifically a person who aids another financially, a patron.

benign/malignant
In medicine, a 'benign' growth or tumour is one that does not cause grave structural damage in the body, whereas a 'malignant' growth does, and spreads. The Latin *bene* and *male* roots, 'good' and 'ill', are at the base of the terms, as they are behind the words in the entries above and below.

benison/malison
A 'benison' is a blessing, and a 'malison' a curse, especially a spoken one. In this sense, they can thus be fairly well equated with 'benediction' and 'malediction'. Both words, however, are now decidedly poetic, if not archaic. For the acts they embody, see **bless/curse**.

bent see **straight**[1]

bequest/devise
In law, a 'bequest' is a gift of personal property left to someone in a will. A 'devise', by contrast, is a gift of real property (i.e. immovable property such as land and tenements). The two verbal forms are often combined in a 'blanket' formula in many wills, on the lines of, 'To my son John, I bequeath and devise . . .'.

Beta/VHS
These are the commercial names of the two leading video cassette recorders and video cameras, with 'Beta' (or 'Betamax') first introduced by Sony in 1975 and 'VHS' (standing for 'video home system') introduced by the firm of JVC at almost the same time. The difference in quality between the two types of videotape is small – the tapes pass over the heads in a slightly different way and at different speeds – but the purchaser or renter of one or the other (recorder or camera) needs to know that, maddeningly, the two systems are not compatible. On the whole, 'Beta' recorders came to be regarded as having a slightly superior picture quality, but by the mid-1980s had lost out to 'VHS', which dominated the market.

better/worse
'For better for worse' is one of the best known phrases from the 'Solemnization of Matrimony' or wedding service in the Prayer Book. As grammatical comparatives (respectively of 'good' and 'bad'), the two words are remarkable for their quite

different forms, with no expected 'gooder' and 'badder'. (The same sort of thing, however, happens in other languages, such as French *meilleur* and *pire* for the comparative degrees of *bon* and *mauvais*.) The reason why this happened is unclear. (Dr Robert Burchfield, Editor of the Oxford English Dictionaries, doubts that *any* reason can be found for the irregularity, since 'comparatives and superlatives have never fitted into a single pattern' [private letter, 6 March 1986].)

bevel see **chamfer**

biannual/biennial
Two trickishly similar opposites. 'Biannual' means 'twice a year'; 'biennial' means 'every two years'. The latter word is used for a plant that completes its life cycle in two years, as distinct from the 'annual', for which one year is enough, and the 'perennial', that grows for at least three years. The former word is mostly used for periodic publications, for which an alternative such as 'twice yearly' or 'six-monthly' could be an unambiguous alternative description.

bid price/offer price
On the Stock Exchange, the 'bid price' is the price at which the marketmaker is prepared to buy a particular security, and the 'offer price' is the one at which he is prepared to sell. The difference between the two prices that he quotes is called the 'spread'.

biennial see **biannual**

big/little
What is the difference between the members of the couplets **great/small** and **little/large**? There is a considerable overlap. But on the whole 'large' often has a suggestion of volume or space (compare 'a big room' and 'a large room'), while 'little' often has an overtone of affection or even pettiness that 'small' does not have (compare 'poor little feet' with merely 'small feet', and 'silly little mistake' with 'small mistake'). For a consideration of 'great', see **great/small**.

big bang theory/steady state theory
These alliterative terms have gained currency to express the two main theories on the origin of the universe. The 'big bang theory' posits that about 10,000 million years ago, all the matter in the universe was hurled in all directions by a cataclysmic explosion so that all the components are still flying apart. As a more peaceful alternative to this, the 'steady state theory' postulates that the universe has always existed and has always been expanding, with matter thus being created continuously. The Sun, and therefore indirectly the planets (and therefore our own Earth), would therefore very likely have been a cosmic spin-off from one or other of these processes.

big end/little end
In some of the earlier days of motoring, and even not so early, one of the major disasters that could befall a driver would be for his 'big end' to go. This meant that the larger end of the rod connecting the piston to the crankshaft in the engine had become detached from its main body, or had fractured. The opposite end of the rod was therefore the 'little end'.

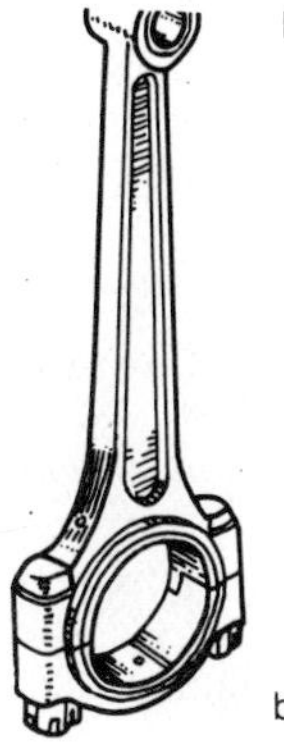

Big-endians/Little-endians
These characters are nothing to do with the connecting rod of the entry above! They are the rival factions, or two of them, in *Gulliver's Travels*, who keenly disputed whether a boiled egg should be broken at

the big end or the little end. The work was largely a satire, of course, and the 'Big-endians' and the 'Little-endians' represented the Catholics and Protestants, or rather the heated disputes between them. The terms subsequently came to stand for any petty dispute, especially one involving doctrine. (Swift's book also had rival wearers of high heels and low heels.) See also **Catholic/Protestant**, **Lilliput/Brobdingnag**.

bilateral see **unilateral**

bilateral symmetry see **radial symmetry**

billy goat/nanny goat
The colloquial or even standard terms for, respectively, a male and a female goat. The words are based on Christian names: 'billy goat' on Billy (William), and 'nanny goat' on Nanny (Anne). The nicknames seem to have become current no earlier than the late eighteenth century, and it is just possible that the American outlaw known as 'Billy the Kid' may have come to be so called under their influence, although his real name was actually William Bonney, and 'kid' was already established to mean 'rogue' in his time (1859–81).

biplane see **monoplane**

bird/beast
The phrase 'birds and beasts' is sometimes used to refer to the two main groups of living creatures ('animals') who inhabit nature or even constitute it. The genesis of the comparison is perhaps in medieval text, as echoed in the children's hymn by Sabine Baring-Gould 'Now the day is over', which has the lines:

> Birds and beasts and flowers
> Soon will be asleep.

birth/death
The two words that denote the beginning and end of life, also used in a transferred sense to mean 'origin' and 'cessation' of something, such as 'birth of a new era' and 'death of colonialism'. The pair of opposites contains near rhyming words, which doubtless helps their mutual association, as well as their link in their sense of 'extremes'. Hence the appeal of both to poets, as in T. S. Eliot's coupling of them in *Journey of the Magi*. If anything, however, the comparison is even more vivid in the couplet **life/death**, which see.

bitter/sweet
Here the two words describe tastes that are respectively unattractive and attractive, harsh and repellent (such as coffee dregs) or pleasant and 'moreish' (as sugar). The words are even combined as 'bitter-sweet' to denote something that is both pleasant yet sad, such as a last farewell or childhood memories. Literally the description could apply to an apple. The combined term is an old one, and can be found in Chaucer. Compare **sweet/sour**.

bitch see **dog**[1]

black/white
Of all colours, 'black' and 'white' are the supreme contrasts, since 'black' implies complete absence of light and 'white' is the result of full light. (Strictly speaking, neither are true colours, as they have no hue of themselves.) Both words have strong overtones, too, of evil and goodness, malignity and sanctity, with much of this derived from things that are themselves 'black' or 'white' such as night (which is dark and 'shady') and snow ('pure as the driven snow'). And doubtless milk would not be the same nourishing and healthy drink if it were any colour but 'white'! On the whole, there are more 'sinister' phrases with 'black' than 'pure' ones with 'white' (blackguard, blackleg, blackmail, blacklist are merely a few), but there are also a few contrasting opposites. Among them are 'black' magic, which is evil, and 'white' magic, which is harmless, 'black' bread, which is dark and coarse, and 'white' bread, which is light-coloured and relatively fine in texture (see also **brown/white** in this connection). Sometimes the 'bad' and 'good' distinction is not present, and the reference to colour pure and

simple. In the Orthodox Church, for example, the 'black' clergy are the monks, who wear black robes, and the 'white' clergy are the parish priests, who wear (or wore) white, while other dress differences distinguish the pair **black tie/white tie** (which see). In more recent times, a 'whiteout' has developed by contrast to a 'blackout', when the concealing or masking agent is snow or fog, not darkness. For another modern couple, see **black hole/white hole** below. 'In black and white' is now a familiar phrase to mean 'in writing', 'as officially printed', referring to the 'black' text on 'white' paper, and an additional contrast has developed for **colour/black and white** (which also see). For the human race, there is an obvious visible difference between those people with 'black' skins and those with so-called 'white'. Most of the former now prefer to think of themselves as simply 'blacks', whereas formerly they were widely known as 'negroes', a word that has now become an offensive term. Again, for tea and coffee drinkers, the choice is often between 'white' (with milk) and 'black' (without), in particular for the latter drink, where 'white' may also mean 'with cream' as well as 'with milk'. Taste and habit obviously comes into the choice of one or the other, although it is the 'black' variant here that is socially often regarded as the superior one. See also **tea/coffee** and compare **ebony/ivory**.

black and white see **colour**

blackcock/greyhen
These are the names of, respectively, the male and female black grouse. The different sexes are named after their prevailing colours, with the female lighter than the male, as in a number of other birds. (The male blackbird is black, but the female brown, for example.)

black hole/white hole
Two quite recent astronomical designations for hypothetical bodies. A 'black hole' is a region of space that has probably resulted from a collapsed star. It has a very high density and a gravitational field from which no radiation (in particular, light) can escape. A 'white hole', however, does emit radiation and is believed to be the converse of a 'black hole'.

black tie/white tie
The reference is to one or other of a specific type of formal evening dress worn by men: 'black tie' means a dinner jacket, black waistcoat and black bow tie; 'white tie' means a tailcoat, white waistcoat and white bow tie. The former is much more common than the latter, and the words 'black tie' are enough in themselves on an invitation to designate the required type of evening dress.

blank verse/rhyme
'Blank verse' is unrhymed verse, common in English literature, and especially drama, from the sixteenth century. Without the discipline and potential artificiality of 'rhyme', it can thus be quite close to ordinary speech, even though remaining indisputably poetry. Milton used it in *Paradise Lose*, for example, as in the following lines (in pentameters, as was much 'blank verse'):

> Now came still evening on, and twilight gray
> Had in her sober livery all things clad;
> Silence accompanied, for beast and bird,
> They to their grassy couch, these to their nests,
> Were slunk, all but the wakeful nightingale.

See also **hexameter/pentameter**.

bless/curse
The contrast between the two, with their implied wish for another's good or evil, has long attracted writers of all ages and tongues, as for example in the Bible: 'And I will bless them that bless thee, and curse him that curseth thee' (Genesis 12:3). Literature, too, has long favoured the formula 'Blessed be . . .' and 'Cursed be . . .', with the former found also in the Bible (in the Beatitudes, where one would expect it) and the latter in various writers,

such as the author of the ballad *Helen of Kirkconnell*:

Curst be the heart that thought the
thought,
And curst the hand that fired the shot.

A well-known combination of both wishes comes in the two lines of Shakespeare's Epitaph:

Blest be the man that spares these
stones,
And curst be he that moves my bones.

Two comprehensive 'curses' in literature can be found in R. H. Barham's poem *The Jackdaw of Rheims* and in Laurence Sterne's *Tristram Shandy* (Book III).

blonde/brunette
From French, these are the two terms that have come to be adopted in English for 'fair-haired woman' and 'dark-haired woman'. Grammatically, 'blonde' is feminine, but despite this can also be used of a fair-haired male, especially the traditional 'blonde beast' or Nordic type. 'Brunette', in turn, has a diminutive suffix that is used when the word designates a younger person. Use of the words in France itself may not relate to hair colour at all, however, and if a waiter enquires in a *bistrot* or café, 'Monsieur veut une blonde?', it could simply be that he wishes to know whether the customer requires a light beer or a dark (*une brune*).

blood see **body**[1]

blow see **suck**

blue see **red**[2]

blue-collar worker see **white-collar worker**

Blues[1]**/Greens**
The 'Blues' and the 'Greens' were the names of rival companies in Byzantium who competed in chariot races, with the colour of each displayed on the chariot. (There were originally four colours, red, white, blue and green, but the last two came to absorb the others.) The rivalry dates from the revolt of AD 532, when there were riots in the circus at Constantinople in the reign of Justinian.

Blues[2]**/Lifeguards**
The 'Blues' (otherwise the Blues and Royals) and the 'Lifeguards' are the two regiments of the British Army that form the Household Cavalry (as part of the sovereign's personal guard, appearing on public occasions). They differ in the complementary colours of their uniforms: the 'Blues', obviously enough, wear blue uniforms, while the 'Lifeguards' wear scarlet jackets and helmets with white plumes. Between them, the two regiments thus comprise the three 'red, white and blue' colours of the Union Jack, the British national flag.

blunt see **sharp**[1]

board/lodging
As applied to accommodation, especially when provided for an employee, 'board' means 'food', 'meals' (the 'board' is the dining table), while 'lodging' means 'bed'. A variation on this is the 'bed and breakfast' ('B & B') offered to a tourist by a 'boarding' house or a private home, especially one licensed to provide such accommodation.

boarding school see **day school**

Bodhisattva see **Arhat**

body[1]**/blood**
In Christian doctrine, the human 'body' and 'blood' of Christ, which were changed but not abandoned at the Resurrection, and which are represented by the two consecrated elements of the Eucharist, the bread and the wine (see **bread/wine**). In the Roman Catholic Church, the Miracle of the Mass turns the bread and the wine into the 'Body' and 'Blood' of Christ, and the two together are known as a 'sacrament'. For Anglicans, the bread and wine of the Communion Service are usually more symbolic in this respect. See also **Catholic/Protestant**.

body²/soul
The two contrasting components of a human being, his physical 'body' and his intangible 'soul', the latter being his spiritual or immaterial part, regarded by many as surviving the 'body' after death (see **life/death**). The words are used in combined form to express some idiomatic senses, so that 'to keep body and soul together' means to survive, and basically 'body and soul' means the entire human self or being. The contrast between the two is often brought out in religious and philosophical writings, so that the Prayer Book speaks of 'those things which are requisite and necessary, as well for the body as the soul', and the separation of the two at death, as referred to, is a favourite subject for poets. In his *Tamerlaine*, Nicholas Rowe, the eighteenth-century writer, thus talks of death being 'the last sad adieu 'twixt soul and body', and more familiarly, Charles Sprague Hall was to remind us a century later that although 'John Brown's body lies a mould'ring in the grave', 'his soul is marching on!' In modern medical terminology, both words combine in 'psychosomatic', referring to a physical state or disorder caused by emotional or mental factors. The origin of the term lies in Greek *psyche*, 'soul' and *soma*, 'body'.

Bokmål/Nynorsk
These terms are used for the differing official forms of written Norwegian. 'Bokmål', formerly known as 'Riksmål', developed through the gradual adaptation of written Danish, and was adopted during the union of Norway and Denmark in force from the late fourteenth century to the early nineteenth. 'Nynorsk', formerly known as 'Landsmål', was created by the language scholar Ivar Aasen in the mid-nineteenth century to continue the tradition of Old Norse, by means of adapting dialects of the western part of the country. 'Bokmål' is today in much wider use than 'Nynorsk', and although there have been plans to fuse the two languages in a common tongue, to be called 'Samnorsk', nothing has so far come of this, and the transition has been strongly resisted. 'Bokmål' means literally 'book language' (and 'Riksmål', 'national language'), while 'Nynorsk' means 'New Norwegian' (and 'Landsmål', 'nationwide language'). 'Samnorsk' means 'same Norwegian'.

boldface see **lightface**

Bolsheviks/Mensheviks
Although commonly understood to mean simply 'Russian communists', the 'Bolsheviks' were historically those radical members of the Russian Social Democratic Party that seized power in Russia in the 1917 Revolution (see **February Revolution/October Revolution**). Subsequently, the name was adopted as an alternative for the Communist Party in that country, but was officially dropped as a designation in 1952. The 'Mensheviks' (the 'baddies' from the Soviet point of view) were the members of the less radical wing of the Russian Social Democratic Party who believed in the gradual achievement of socialism by constitutional methods, unlike the 'Bolsheviks', who favoured revolution. They were mainly active before and during the 1917 Revolution. The two names respectively mean 'those in the majority' and 'those in the minority', since the 'Bolsheviks' were the larger faction. (Russian *bol'she* means 'more', and *men'she*, 'less'.)

bolt see **nut**

bond/bank
These are the terms for the two main types of writing and typing paper. 'Bond' paper is the superior, strong white kind of paper, formerly popular for 'top copies', while 'bank' is the thinner paper, mostly used for 'carbon copies'. 'Bond' paper is so called since it was originally used for bonds and other important documents. (It was also adopted for the commercial names of some types of writing paper, such as 'Basildon Bond'.) 'Bank' paper, also known as 'flimsy', was formerly used by banks for foreign letters to save on postage.

boo see **hurray**

boom/slump
Economic opposites, with 'boom' a rising period of economic growth, with increasing wages and profits (and prices), and full or near-full employment, and 'slump' a sharp decline in the economy, with a steep fall in prices and much unemployment. A prolonged 'slump' is usually known as a 'depression'. Both terms originated in these senses in the United States in the nineteenth century.

borrow see **lend**

boson/fermion
In nuclear physics, a 'boson' is an elementary particle (a minute particle of matter) that obeys relations stated by Einstein and the Indian physicist Satyendranath Bose, and that has a spin (ability to apparently rotate round its own axis) which is either zero or integral (equal to a whole number). A 'fermion' is a similar particle that obeys relations stated by the Italian physicist Enrico Fermi and his English colleague Paul Dirac, and that has a half-integral spin. Put another way, the 'boson' occurs in nature only in symmetrical states, and the 'fermion' only in antisymmetrical states. Both terms were proposed by Dirac in 1947, in his *Principles of Quantum Mechanics*. Electrons, protons and neutrons are all 'fermions' (see **proton/electron**), while typical 'bosons' are photons and pions (pi-mesons).

bottle see **jug**

bottom see **top**[1]

bound/free
Although conjuring up basic images of slavery and freedom, the two terms are used as technical opposites in certain fields and sciences. For example, in linguistics, a morpheme (meaningful part of a word) is 'bound' when it cannot exist separately from a word, so that it is always 'bound' to it. Examples are 'un-' in 'unlikely' and '-er' in 'reader'. A 'free' morpheme can thus exist independently, such as 'book' (which can be used on its own or in a combination such as 'bookmaker').

bourn/burn
A 'bourn' (or 'bourne') is the word for a small stream, sometimes an intermittent one, in the south of England, such as at Bournemouth or one of the Wiltshire or Dorset villages called Winterbourne (where the stream dries up in summer). A 'burn' is a small stream in Scotland, such as at the various villages called Burnside and in the names of many streams themselves, known as 'Burn of . . .' (e.g. Burn of Boyne, Burn of Davidston). The latter word is fairly familiar from the writing of Scottish poets, such as Stevenson's 'abune the burn' and Burns' 'adown some trotting burn's meander'. The two words are related.

bowl see **bat**

box pleat/inverted pleat
A 'box pleat', in dressmaking, is a flat double pleat made by folding under the fabric on either side of it, so that one folded edge faces right and the other left. An 'inverted pleat' is a reversed 'box pleat', with the fullness of the material turned inwards. In this way the two folded edges will face each other on the same side of the fabric.

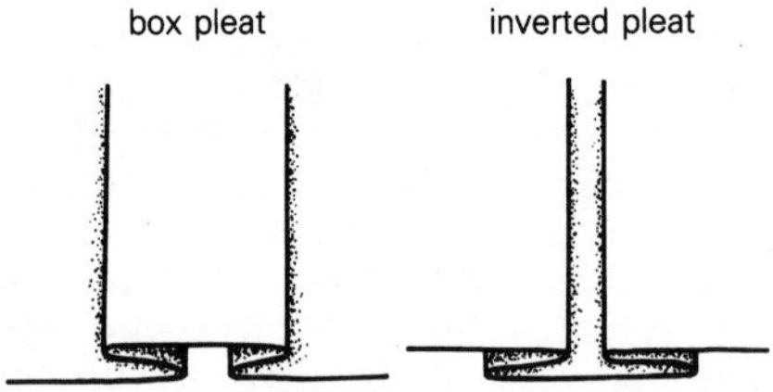

boy/girl
The words for the male and female child, respectively, with each until recently often associated with education or the general upbringing of children. (Most junior state schools, especially the old 'elementary' schools, even had separate entrances for the two sexes, designated 'BOYS' and

'GIRLS'.) 'Boy', too, has long had an almost aggressively 'male' association in various stock phrases, such as 'one of the boys', 'jobs for the boys', when used of men, and even simply 'old boy' as used of a former member of a school, particularly a public school. 'Girl', as the feminists have not been slow to point out, has mostly lacked such positive overtones, and indeed has taken on negative or 'weak' ones, especially in its derivative and diminutive forms such as 'girlish' and 'girlie'. In similar vein, 'boys will be boys' implies that one must make allowances for youthful exuberance, but 'all girls together', as used of a group of women, suggests an almost playful or desperate rallying of forces in time of crisis or celebration. Even 'old girl' can sound patronizing or disrespectful by comparison with the 'chummy' use of 'old boy' ('Try this, old boy', and 'Come on, old girl').

bradycardia see **tachycardia**

brain/brawn
The dichotomy here is between intellect and sheer brute strength, and application of 'mind' or 'matter', as appropriate. A little thought ('brain') will often succeed, however, where physical force ('brawn') will not, and despite the 'impact' that certain he-men and 'muscle-men' may have, at least visually, it is usually the 'brain' that will bring the more rewarding prize. The two types are traditionally represented by the intellectual or 'swot' and the 'tough guy' or strong man, the latter displaying his powers as 'beefcake' (which *Chambers Twentieth Century Dictionary* actually defines as 'brawn as distinct from brain'; see **beefcake/cheesecake** for more). The 'brawn' in this contrasting pair is exactly the same word that, in British usage, means 'jellied meat loaf', and as such is related to an Old English word meaning 'flesh'.

brake horsepower/indicated horsepower
'Brake horsepower' is the horsepower of an engine measured by the resistance of an applied brake. An engine's 'indicated horsepower' is its power output calculated from the mean effective pressure in the cylinder (as derived from an indicator diagram, representing the cyclic variations of pressure and volume here, and the speed of the engine in revolutions per minute). The 'indicated horsepower' exceeds the 'brake horsepower' (also sometimes called the 'useful' horsepower) by the power lost in friction and pumping.

branch see **root**

brandy/whisky
Connoisseurs of these strong drinks claim that 'brandy' livens one up, but 'whisky' calms one down! One should therefore prefer 'whisky' for an alcoholic nightcap. In origin, 'brandy' is a spirit distilled from grape wine, but 'whisky' is distilled from fermented cereals. See also **whisky/whiskey**.

brass see **woodwind**

brawn see **brain**

bread/wine
In the Christian church, these are the two main elements of the Eucharist, the 'bread' representing the Body of Christ, and the 'wine' his Blood (see **body/blood**). In themselves, 'bread' and 'wine' are basic food and drink (although not as basic as 'bread' and water). Literary references to 'bread' and 'wine' are frequently religious in tone, therefore, although not quite so much in Edward Fitzgerald's translation of *The Rubáiyát* of Omar Khayyám, where there is an augmented combination of

> A Jug of Wine, a Loaf of Bread – and
> Thou.

break see **make**

break-up see **freeze-up**

breve/macron
A 'breve' is a curved mark or accent (˘) placed over a vowel to show that it is short; a 'macron' is a straight mark (¯)

similarly placed to show that the vowel is long. The two signs are used in the *Oxford* and some other dictionaries for this purpose, when indicating pronunciation. For example, 'hăt' with its short vowel, and 'hāte' with its long one. 'Breve' is the Latin word for 'short' (hence English 'brief'), and 'macron' the Greek word for 'long' (hence English 'macrobiotic', literally 'long-lived').

brick/rendered
These are the two main types of external wall finishes, as seen in many houses, with 'brick' meaning what it says, and 'rendered' meaning that the 'brick' has been covered with plaster. If a firm is to install double glazing in a house, one of the first things they will need to know is whether the walls round the windows are 'brick' or 'rendered'. The latter will need special care.

bride/groom
The respective designations of a woman who is about to be married, or who has just been married, and her husband-to-be, or her newly wed husband. 'Groom' is really short for 'bridegroom', where the second half of the word was originally *guma*, 'man' in Old English, but became 'groom' under the influence of the identical word that also happened to mean 'man' (as well as 'servant'). The 'bridegroom' was thus the 'bride's man'. The full form was not regularly shortened to 'groom' until the seventeenth century, and is first found in this usage in Shakespeare. In the Prayer Book, the terms are not used for the couple, who are referred to before, during and after the ceremony as 'the Man' and 'the Woman'. The word 'bride' has twice as many glamorous associations as 'groom', and in many senses the man is (for once) eclipsed by his female partner. (It is 'Here comes the bride', not 'Here come the bride and groom', and there is no equivalent of any kind for 'blushing bride' as far as the grovelling groom is concerned.)

bridge/tunnel
There are two main ways of crossing a river or channel, either over it, with a 'bridge', or under it, with a 'tunnel'. Similarly, where a main road or trackway needs to keep level as much as possible, as on a railway, 'dips' such as rivers and some valleys can be crossed with a 'bridge' (even when it is called a 'viaduct'), and 'rises' such as hills can be traversed through a 'tunnel'. Where a fairly extensive stretch of water needs to be crossed, either a 'bridge' or a 'tunnel' can serve the purpose, with advantages (and disadvantages) for each. Specialized developments of a 'bridge' and a 'tunnel', in particular for road traffic, are respectively a 'flyover' and an 'underpass'. Pedestrians will be more familiar with a 'footbridge' and a 'subway'. (The latter word does not mean 'underground railway' in Britain, as it does in the United States.)

bright/dim
The two adjectives denote the degree of intensity of light or intelligence, with some electric lights having special 'bright/dim' switches (as in railway sleeping cars). For some time from the 1920s or so, cars had 'dimmers' in the United States ('dippers' in Britain) to enable the headlights to be directed downwards or 'dipped'. Somehow the two words manage to suggest their own qualities, so that 'bright' fortuitously rhymes with 'light' and 'right', and 'dim' suggests 'damp' and 'doom'.

bring/fetch
Two opposites that sometimes cause problems to learners of English. 'Bring' means 'carry or take from that place to this' ('Bring me that book, would you?') whereas 'fetch' means 'go to that place and carry or take back' ('Fetch me a cloth, could you?').

broad/narrow
'Broad' implies a great width, as a 'broad' river or a 'broad' staircase, while 'narrow' is the opposite, implying a short, restricted distance across, such as a 'narrow' lane or a 'narrow' belt. In some instances, 'wide' can serve as well as 'broad' for a distance across, especially where a measurement is concerned (one thus has a 'wide' belt, not

really a 'broad' one), but 'broad' and 'narrow' are traditional contrasts where thoroughfares are concerned, as they were for Molly Malone, who 'wheeled her wheelbarrow through streets broad and narrow'. See also the related **standard gauge/narrow gauge**.

broadsheet/tabloid
These are the two terms for the two main sizes of newspaper, with 'broadsheet' the large size and 'tabloid' the small. The terms also still have something of a split indicated in the pair **quality paper/popular paper** (which see), since quality papers, especially daily ones, are still mainly 'broadsheet', while the popular papers are largely 'tabloid'. In the printing trade, 'broadsheet' is the standard term for a sheet of paper that has not been folded, hence the use of the word for a newspaper that is printed on this type of sheet. 'Tabloid', however is less obvious. It originated as a trade name for a type of medicinal tablet, but later came to be used of newspapers with smaller pages that reported the news in 'condensed' form.

Brobdingnag see **Lilliput**

brother/sister
Apart from the obvious designations as males and females, respectively, who have the same parents, the two words are also used in various types of community, from religious orders (with the words used in effect as titles) to fellow trade-unionists or other 'campaigners for a cause'. Feminists, in particular, have extensively adopted 'sister' as a term or symbol of affiliation. (Latin *filius*, 'son', on which this last word is based, is also related to English 'feminine', so seems in order here.) The use of 'brother' as a slang exclamation ('Brother, look at that!') seems more likely to have originated among the 'underworld' than in a religious community.

brown/white
The main contrast here is between 'brown' bread, which is made of dark flour, such as wheatmeal or wholemeal, and 'white' bread, which is made from 'white' flour. The distinction has acquired a connotation of something that is specially nutritious or wholesome for whatever is 'brown', with the 'white' equivalent being merely standard. This applies not only to bread but also to such foods as eggs, rice and even sugar, to the extent that 'brown' sugar is now seen as 'the best' and 'white' as purely basic, fit mainly for cooking and routine 'cuppas'. In actual fact, 'brown' sugar is unrefined, or at most partially refined, while 'white' sugar is the proper thing, and is fully refined in its purest form! (See also **wholefood/junk food**, **yin/yang**.)

brownie see **cub**

brunette see **blonde**

Brythonic/Goidelic
These are the respective terms for the two main groups of Celtic languages, with 'Brythonic' the southern group, including Welsh and Cornish in Britain and Breton in France, and 'Goidelic' the northern group, incorporating Irish Gaelic ('Erse'), Scottish Gaelic, and Manx. Many similarities can be detected in all Celtic languages, but the similarities are most marked in the two groups as named, with the 'Goidelic' languages even closer to one another than the 'Brythonic' ones. The word 'Brythonic' is related to 'Breton', and 'Goidelic' to 'Gaelic', and even the terms themselves still have alternative forms, which can complicate things. ('Brythonic' is also known as 'Brittonic', for example, and 'Goidelic' as 'Gadhelic'.) See also **P-Celtic/Q-Celtic**.

BST see **GMT**

buck/doe
The word 'buck' is used for the male of a number of animals, in particular the hare, kangaroo, rabbit and reindeer, while 'doe' is used as the female of these. 'Buck' has acquired a number of additional senses, all deriving from the male animal (including 'fine fellow', 'jump in the air' and even 'dollar', this last from 'buckskin'), but 'doe' is still almost exclusively used in its

original meaning (unlike, say, 'bitch', 'filly' or 'cow').

built-in see **free-standing**

bulimia see **anorexia**

bull see (1) **bear** (2) **cow** (3) **ox**

bullock see **heifer**

Bundesrat/Bundestag
The 'Bundesrat' is the title of the upper house of the parliament of Federal Germany (West Germany), and the 'Bundestag' is that of its lower house. The German words mean literally 'federation council' and 'federation diet'.

Bundestag see **Bundesrat**

burn see **bourn**

but/ben
The two little words are usually taken together ('but and ben') to designate a tiny Scottish house, where strictly speaking the 'but' is the outer room of a two-roomed cottage (in practice, usually the kitchen), and 'ben' is the inner room. The words derive respectively from Old English *butan*, 'outside' and *binnan*, 'inside'. The joint association is a homely one, as in a poem by Robert Burns of 1786:

> Some kind, connubial dear,
> Your but-and-ben adorns.

butter/margarine
'Butter', familiarly spread on bread and used for cooking, is made from cream by churning. 'Margarine' is a substitute for it, similar in appearance and consistency, but prepared from vegetable and animal fats by emulsifying them with water and adding small quantities of milk, salt, vitamins (by law), colouring matter and the like. However, both 'butter' and 'margarine' contain at least 80% fat, as stipulated by government regulations, and many types of both products have a similar content of saturate and polyunsaturate fatty acids. Even so, 'margarines' that are 'high in polyunsaturates', although having the same fat content as other kinds of 'butter' and 'margarine', have a higher proportion of polyunsaturate fatty acids, for example as in such vegetable oils and sunflower oil and corn oil, and these are believed to reduce the level of cholesterol in the blood. For this reason, 'margarine' is often regarded as 'healthier' than 'butter'. On the other hand, 'butter' is undoubtedly more 'natural', so also has a healthy image. In recent years, manufacturers of each product have taken to slanging their opposite number, so that the consumer has become both confused and exasperated by the whole advertising campaign, and has simply chosen whichever suits his or her needs or pocket best.

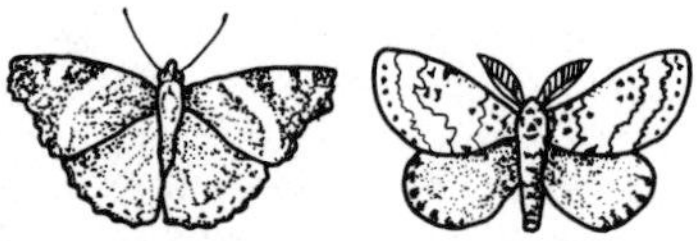

butterfly/moth
The main difference between the two large-winged flying insects is this: the 'butterfly' flies mainly by day, is brightly coloured with knobbed or club-shaped antennae, and holds its wings vertically when at rest; the 'moth' mostly flies at night, is dull-coloured, with spindle-shaped, threadlike or comblike antennae, and holds its wings flat when at rest. The 'moth', too, often has a connecting hook for fastening its wings together, which the 'butterfly' does not have.

buy/sell
Two of the most basic of human economic activities, where the ideal situation is 'buying' at a low price and 'selling' at a high, thereby making a profit or a saving (or both). Some people engage in professional 'buying' and 'selling' as their main occupation, and these include so-called 'marketmakers' (dealers on the Stock Exchange, formerly known as

'jobbers' and 'brokers') and members of import-export concerns. See also the next entry.

buyer's market/seller's market
In the world of finance and economics, a 'buyer's market' is a market in which supply exceeds demand, enabling buyers to influence prices. A 'seller's market' is the opposite, a market in which demand exceeds supply and in which the sellers can thus influence the prices. Both situations involve the professional business of buying and selling (see the entry above) and demand considerable financial expertise. See also **supply/demand**.

Cc

cabinet see **shadow cabinet**

cache-sexe see **jockstrap**

cacography see **orthography**

cacophony see **euphony**

Cain/Abel
The well known biblical brothers are respectively murderer and murdered, and their names are sometimes used for a fratricide or other especially 'vengeful' killing. In the story itself, 'Cain' was the eldest son of Adam and Eve (see **Adam/Eve**) who killed his brother 'Abel' out of jealousy when the latter's sacrifice of the firstlings of his flock proved more acceptable to God than his own sacrifice of the fruits of the ground. The tale may refer to the everlasting quarrel between nomads and farmers, as the crops of the latter are damaged by the herds of the former. The elder brother's name is preserved in the phrase 'to raise Cain', meaning 'make a great fuss', 'cause a scandal', with the reference similar to that in 'raise the Devil', that is, cause the person mentioned to appear. (The phrase has also prompted the corny old riddle: 'Why were Adam and Eve rowdies? Because they raised Cain'.)

call/put
On the Stock Exchange, a 'call' or 'call option' is an option to buy a fixed amount of shares at a fixed price within a specified period, usually three months. A 'put' or a 'put option' is the exact opposite of this, an option to sell a fixed amount of shares under similar conditions. Option dealing is not for the faint-hearted since the shares may not rise in value in the way that the speculator had predicted they would, and they may indeed fall, in which case he would have been better taking out a 'put' option. See also **buy/sell**, **buyer's market/seller's market**, and the next entry below.

call loan/time loan
A 'call loan' is a loan that is repayable on demand, which could well be at an embarrassing moment for the borrower. Its counterpart is a 'time loan', which must be repaid on or before a specified date. Despite the disadvantage mentioned, a 'call loan' is the preferable type, since with luck the lender may forget to 'call', or may at least waive his right to do so. Moreover, there is no restriction on time.

calyx/corolla
Botanically, a 'calyx' is the sepals of a flower regarded collectively, forming an outer envelope that protects the flower bud inside. A 'corolla' is the petals collectively, forming an inner envelope. Botany is full of Latin (or neo-Latin) words, and these two mean respectively 'shell' and 'little crown'.

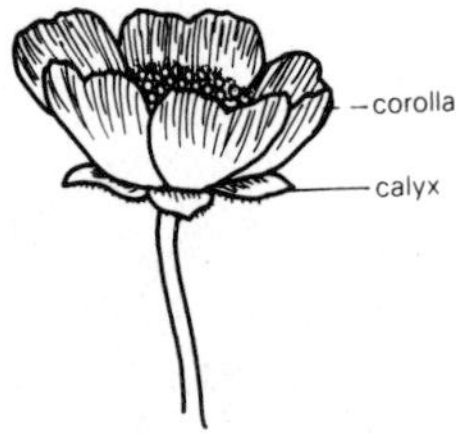

Cam see **Isis**

Cambridge see **Oxford**

cameo/intaglio
A 'cameo' is a gemstone or medallion with an engraving of two or more coloured layers, arranged in such a way that the background is of a different colour to the raised design. An 'intaglio' is a similar

gem or ornament, but one with a sunken or incised design, as opposed to the relief design of the 'cameo'. Both words come from Italian, and although the original meaning of 'cameo' is uncertain, 'intaglio' means 'engraved', literally 'cut in', with the second part of the word related to English 'tailor' (who is really a 'cutter').

Cancer/Capricorn
These are the respective names of the two tropics, with 'Cancer' in the northern hemisphere (as a line of latitude at $23\frac{1}{2}^\circ$ north), and 'Capricorn' parallel to it in the southern hemisphere (at a latitude of $23\frac{1}{2}^\circ$ south). The names refer to the corresponding signs of the zodiac at this latitude on the celestial sphere (the 'dome' of the sky). 'Tropic' literally means 'turning' (from the Greek), and refers to the ancient belief that the Sun turned back at the solstices (see **equinox/solstice**). The tropic of 'Cancer' is the northernmost latitude reached by the overhead Sun, and the tropic of 'Capricorn' the southernmost. For more astronomy, see the next entry.

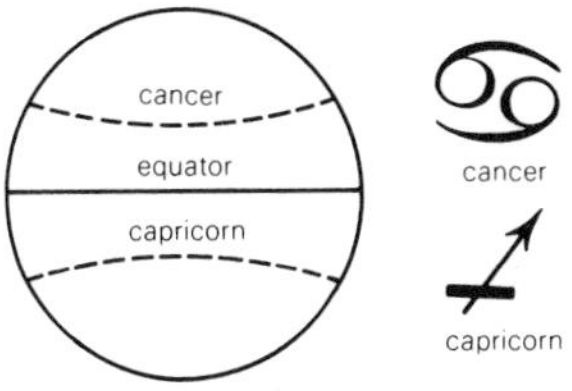

Canis Major/Canis Minor
'Canis Major' (the 'greater dog') is a constellation in the southern hemisphere close to Orion, with its main star as Sirius, the 'Dog Star', the brightest in the sky. 'Canis Minor' (the 'lesser dog') is also close to Orion, but is in the northern hemisphere, and its main star is Procyon. (This last name means literally 'before the dog', and refers to the fact that it rises before Sirius.)

Canis Minor see **Canis Major**

Canterbury/York
The two cathedral cities, respectively in the south and north of England, represent the two provinces or archdioceses of the Church of England, with the Archbishop of 'Canterbury' the spiritual head of the Church, officially titled 'Primate of All England', and the Archbishop of 'York' known as the 'Primate of England'. The Archbishop of 'Canterbury' was originally the papal legate, and thus today has many powers which the Archbishop of 'York' does not. For another rivalry involving the latter city, see also **York/Lancaster**.

canticum/diverbium
In the drama of Ancient Rome, the 'canticum' was the part of a play that was declaimed or sung, as distinct from the 'diverbium', which was the term for the spoken dialogue. There are several 'cantica' in the plays of Plautus, but very few in Terence. The Latin words mean respectively 'something sung' and 'dialogue'. (A rare word 'diverb' exists in English for a type of proverb with two contrasting parts, for example: 'England is a paradise for women, and a hell for horses; Italy is a paradise for horses, but hell for women'. There is really a double contrast here, with the two opposing halves themselves containing a contrast.)

Cantonese see **Mandarin**

cantoris see **decani**

capital-intensive/labour-intensive
In commerce and economics, 'capital-intensive' means that a fair amount of capital (such as buildings and machinery) will be needed in the production of something, as compared to other costs involved. In this way, when labour costs rise, the process of production may become more 'capital-intensive'. A business or industry that is 'labour-intensive', on the other hand, uses more labour than capital or land. In a sense, therefore, 'intensive' almost equates to 'expensive', depending whether more money is needed to purchase and run the machines or to pay the men and women who operate them.

capitalism see **communism**

capital letter/small letter
The two types of written or printed letter, of course, with much argument at times about whether a word should or should not begin with a 'capital letter' or a 'small letter'. The general tendency is for the 'small letter' to take over, as any glance at eighteenth-century English will show, when many nouns were written with a 'capital letter'. Here is a typical example: 'There is two sorts of Indian Silk called Culgees, the one is Satten, the other is Taffety. They are much used for Handkerchiefs, and for Lining of Beds, and Gowns for both Men and Women' (*The Merchant's Warehouse Laid Open*). Today, the only words with a 'capital letter' here would be 'Indian' and those of the title. Some business texts and advertisements still use 'capital letters', however, as if this makes particular words more important, or somehow makes the text as a whole more authoritative. (An example, taken to extremes: 'From The Longest Established Window Company In The Area Comes The Very Latest In Window Technology' [*The Messenger*, 12 February 1986, a free local advertising paper].) This sort of usage has been playfully seized on by some humorous or children's writers in fictional works, e.g. 'I am a Bear of Very Little Brain, and long words Bother me', in A. A. Milne's *Winnie-the-Pooh*. See also the reference to 'upper case' and 'lower case' in **upper/lower**.

capon/poulard
En route from the farmyard to the kitchen, a 'capon' is a castrated male chicken, especially fattened for eating, and a 'poulard' is a hen that has been spayed and similarly treated. The words are from French, with the former probably ultimately deriving from Greek *kotein* 'to cut', and the latter related to English 'pullet' (which is a young hen, as yet unspayed). See also **castrate/spay** if doubt remains about these operations.

Capricorn see **Cancer**

Capulets see **Montagues**

cardinal number/ordinal number
The 'cardinal numbers' are the ordinary enumerating ones, otherwise one, two, three, four, five, etc. The 'ordinal numbers' are those used for giving the order, such as first, second, third, fourth, fifth, etc. 'Cardinal' really means 'principal' here, and ultimately derives from Latin *cardo*, genitive *cardinis*, 'hinge', since it is the type of number on which the others 'turn' or depend.

carrot see **stick**[1]

carvel-built see **clinker-built**

caryatid/atlas
In sculpture, a 'caryatid' is a supporting column (as for a portico) that represents a draped female figure. The male equivalent of this is an 'atlas' (or a 'telamon'), with the male much less draped than the female (so that his muscles and rippling torso can be admired). Both types of architectural art date from classical times, and one of the best examples of 'caryatids' is the porch of the Erechtheum, at the Acropolis in Athens, which still has its original six figures, now over two thousand years old. Some modern 'atlantes' are the seventeenth-century ones supporting the balcony of the town hall at Toulon, France, and the even more recent nineteenth-century ones at the entrance to the New Hermitage Museum in Leningrad. 'Atlas' obviously derives from the name of the classical giant. 'Caryatid' comes from Greek *Karuatides*, the title of the priestesses at Caryae in Laconia, while 'telamon' has its origin in Greek *tlenai*, 'to bear'. See also **Atlantic/Pacific**.

cassette see (1) **record** (2) **reel-to-reel**

castrate/spay
The two verbs denote the process of removing, respectively, the testicles of a male (animal or human) and the ovaries of a female (animal only), thus preventing either from breeding. This can be done for a number of reasons, of which the chief

two are (as applied to an animal) to render it sterile or to make it more docile, especially when it is being prepared for food. Some 'castrated' and 'spayed' animals have special names, such as 'gelding' (of a horse) or 'poulard' (of a hen; see **capon/poulard**), but a 'castrated' male human is known as a 'castrato' (especially when this was done, as formerly, to preserve a fine high singing voice) or 'eunuch' (when appointed as the guard in a harem). The verb 'castrate' is ultimately related to 'caste', denoting a special type of class of person, and 'spay' relates to the kind of fencing sword known as an 'épée'. See also **ox/bull**.

cat see **dog**[2]

catadromous/anadromous
Two specialized words that simply mean, of fishes, 'breeding down-river' and 'breeding up-river'. The former word, for instance, applies to eels that migrate down rivers to the sea to breed, and 'anadromous' is used of such fishes as the salmon, which migrates up rivers from the sea to breed. The words, based on Greek roots, mean literally 'down-running' and 'back-running'. For a related subject, see **coarse fish/game fish**.

catalyst/inhibitor
In chemistry, a 'catalyst' is a substance that increases the rate of a reaction without itself undergoing any chemical change. A substance that does the opposite, and slows down a reaction, is an 'inhibitor' (also sometimes known as an 'anticatalyst'). Iodine is a 'catalyst', for example, when it accelerates the decomposition of acetaldehyde, and any antioxidant, that retards deterioration by oxidation (as with petroleum products or rubber, for example) will be an 'inhibitor'. Most phenols are antioxidants and so 'inhibitors'. 'Catalyst', from the Greek, literally means 'dissolver'.

catamaran/trimaran
The distinction between the two types of sailing craft is that a 'catamaran' is twin-hulled and a 'trimaran', as its name suggests, has three hulls (two flanking the main hull). The latter word has been based on the former, as if the 'cata-' had some sort of numerical sense. It does not, however, and is not even the same element as found in such terms as 'catapult' or 'cataract', where it means 'down'. 'Catamaran' is thus not of Greek origin at all, but is a Tamil word, *kattumaram*, meaning literally 'tied timber'. The 'trimaran' made its appearance as a word only in the 1950s.

catarrhine/platyrrhine
If an animal or a person is 'catarrhine', it means that it or he or she has nostrils set close together and opening downwards (like baboons). If on the other hand the face is 'platyrrhine', it has widely separated nostrils that open to the side (like American monkeys). (As used of humans, who are normally 'catarrhine', the term 'platyrrhine' means that the nose is unusually short and wide.) The two words mean literally 'downward nose' and 'flat nose'.

categorical imperative/hypothetical imperative
Two opposing philosophical terms from Kantian ethics, which makes them sound formidable. However, they are quite easily understood: the 'categorical imperative' is the moral principle stating that one's behaviour should be motivated by duty, not the prospect of reward, but the 'hypothetical imperative' means that one's conduct is governed by necessity, not by morality. The terms themselves thus relate to an 'imperative' or command that is 'categorical' or absolute, not involving any conditions, and one that is 'hypothetical', since the command is conditional, effective only on the assumption that something is so, i.e. that there actually is a necessity.

cathode/anode
A 'cathode', in physics, is an electrode (wire conducting an electric current) by which electrons leave an external circuit and enter an electrical device (usually via a conducting liquid). An 'anode' is an electrode by which electrons leave a device and enter an external circuit. Put another

way, a 'cathode' is the positive terminal of a battery delivering a current, while an 'anode' is the negative terminal. See also **positive/negative**. The words literally mean 'way down' and 'way up', with the second half of the word representing Greek *hodos*, 'way'.

Catholic/Protestant
Two of the chief divisions (alas) in the Christian world, denoting respectively the Roman 'Catholic' Church, whose head is the Pope (the Bishop of Rome), and those Christians who at the time of the Reformation (in the sixteenth century) separated from the Roman Church and who do not acknowledge the Pope as their head. (The 'protest' that gave the 'Protestants' their name was not one actually against the Pope, but by a group of German 'reforming' churchmen who opposed the decision of the 'Catholic' majority in the so-called Diet of Spires, which passed legislation to end all toleration of Lutherans in 'Catholic' districts.) 'Catholics' attach supreme importance to the eucharist or 'Mass', in which they hold that the consecrated bread and wine become the Body and Blood of Christ (see **body/blood**, **bread/wine**), while they also oppose the remarriage of divorced people and some forms of birth control, and attach great emphasis to the religious life (as for monks and nuns). They also hold a high place in their worship for the saints and in particular for the Virgin Mary, as the 'Mother of God', and their doctrine includes a belief in purgatory (an intermediate state for souls before they pass to heaven or hell). Until relatively recently, too, most 'Catholic' church services were in Latin. For 'Protestants', almost all this, where even believed or practised, is noticeably 'played down', although there are some members of the Church of England (the so-called 'High Church') who approach 'Catholic' belief and doctrine (and certainly ritual) in their Christian way of life. The trouble about the word 'Catholic' is that it has more than one meaning. As commonly used (as here), it means 'Roman Catholic', but with a small 'c' it means 'universal', even in religious contexts. There is thus no anomaly in members of the Church of England (which is strictly speaking a 'Protestant' church) asserting their belief, as they do publicly in reciting the Apostles' Creed in church, in the 'holy Catholick Church' (to use the spelling of the Prayer Book). See also **high/low**, **Republicans/Loyalists**.

caudal see **cephalic**

cause/effect
The coupling here is a common one to explain a particular occurrence or incident or attitude: if there is no 'cause', a thing cannot happen, but if there is a 'cause', there will be an 'effect'. The terms really belong to philosophy, and Aristotle, for example, held that there were four types of 'cause' that could bring about an 'effect', including even a thing's nature (its 'formal cause') or its purpose ('final cause'). Some very important 'effects' can be produced by quite small or slight 'causes', like the missing horseshoe nail that caused the loss of a battle and the downfall of an entire nation.

Cavalier see **Roundhead**

calvalry/infantry
Originally, and properly, the 'cavalry' were the mounted troops of an army, on horseback, although today the term denotes an armoured motorized unit (with the exception of mounted troops used for ceremonial occasions, such as the Household 'Cavalry'). The 'infantry', by contrast, were and still are those army units that go on foot, with certain regiments still including the word in their name, such as the Durham Light 'Infantry'. Both words derive directly from Italian, respectively from *cavaliere*, 'horseman' (compare English 'cavalier') and *infante*, 'boy', 'footsoldier' (compare English 'infant'). The 'infantry' were thus historically the young men who went on foot and attended the knights, who were the 'cavalry' in medieval times. The emphasis on going on foot as the role for the 'infantry' is seen in the very term 'foot', used in the British army to apply specifi-

cally to them. This, too, is found in regimental names, such as the 67th (South Hampshire) Regiment of Foot, who distinguished themselves in the Indian campaigns of the early nineteenth century. For a similar sort of distinction, see **footpad/highwayman**.

Ceefax/Oracle
These are the respective names of the teletext services provided by the BBC and the IBA (see **BBC/ITV**), as received on specially adapted television sets. Both services have news summaries, sports results, weather reports, travel information and the like, but 'Oracle', since it is broadcast by the IBA, also includes advertisements ('commercials'). (Teletext is not the same as Prestel, which is viewdata: see **teletext/viewdata**.) The two names derive from 'see facts' and apparently the ordinary word 'oracle', i.e. with reference to the priest or priestess in classical times who prophesied the future and whose authority was respected (and doubtless also with an indirect reference to the phrase 'consult the oracle', meaning 'ask someone in authority for information'). Inevitably, there were those who felt that 'Oracle' should be an acronym, so one was duly invented: 'Optional Reception of Announcements by Coded Line Electronics'.

ceiling see **floor**

celestial/terrestrial
'Celestial' means 'relating to the skies' (the 'heavens') and 'terrestrial' 'relating to the earth'. Both terms are used in astronomy, more commonly the former, as one might expect, in such expressions as 'celestial equator', as distinct from the one on Earth, and 'celestial globe' for a model of the skies, as against a 'terrestrial' globe, or model of the Earth in the form of a sphere. A 'terrestrial' telescope, however, which is used for sighting objects on Earth, has as its opposite number an 'astronomical' telescope, not a 'celestial' one. The terms derive respectively from Latin *caelum*, 'heaven' and *terra*, 'earth'. The pairing works better in some languages other than English, where the word for 'heaven' is the same as the word for 'sky' (e.g. French *ciel*, German *Himmel*, Russian *nebo*). In 1960 Stravinsky composed an opera for television called 'The Flood', based on the biblical story of Noah's Ark, in which the main characters are the 'Celestials' (God and Lucifer), who sing their parts, and the 'Terrestrials' (a narrator, the caller, Noah) who talk.

Celsius see **Fahrenheit**

Celtic/Rangers
The two famous rival Scottish football teams, both based in Glasgow. The encounters between the two have been accompanied by numerous scenes of violence. Nor is the rivalry merely a sporting one, since 'Celtic' has traditionally drawn its supporters from immigrant Irish Catholics, while 'Rangers' has been represented by native Scottish Protestants. Thus what in other circumstances should have been a friendly (but professional) football match, played to a sporting code, has many times turned into a virtual religious and even racial battle. ('Celtic' here is always pronounced 'Seltic'.) A number of relevant cross-references can be made here, so see, as desired, one or more of the following: **amateur/professional**, **Brythonic/Goidelic**, **Catholic/Protestant**, **emigrant/immigrant**, **P-Celtic/Q-Celtic**. (By some curious literal fluke, 'Celtic' contains five letters of 'Catholic', and 'Rangers' incorporates five letters of 'Protestant'.)

centralization/decentralization
These typical terms from managerial jargon denote respective policies of bringing some organization, such as a government body, under central control (typically, in London), and of reorganizing it into several, usually autonomous units (so dispersed round the country). Either policy has its supporters and detractors.

centrifugal/centripetal
The terms are to do with mechanics or engineering, and mean respectively (and literally) 'flying from the centre' and 'seeking the centre'. A 'centrifugal' pump

thus works by means of 'centrifugal' force, which acts outwards on a rotating body, making the medium involved move away from the axis. (This can be visually observed in a spin drier.) A 'centripetal' force, not so commonly found in practical use, acts inwards, sending the medium to the centre. One example of 'centripetal' force in action is found in a train rounding a bend: it does not leave the track (because of 'centrifugal' force) since the flanges of the outer wheels on the outer rail force it inwards. In practice, therefore, a 'centripetal' force is used to keep an object moving in a circle, instead of flying outwards. Although the 'petal' of 'centripetal' is not the same as the 'petal' of a flower, the word is in fact used in botany to apply to certain inflorescences (arrangements of the flowers on the stalk) that develop from the outside towards the centre, while a 'centrifugal' inflorescence develops outwards.

centripetal see **centrifugal**

centum see **satem**

cephalic/caudal
In anatomy, 'cephalic' and 'caudal' are used as alternatives to the pair of adjectives **superior/inferior** (which see) when describing position. The terms derive respectively from Greek *kephalē*, 'head' and Latin *cauda*, 'tail'. See also in this respect **head/tail**.

chair see **table**

chalk/cheese
'They're as different as chalk and cheese', we say, of two people with contrasting natures or characters, or of two related people, such two brothers or sisters, who look quite unlike each other. The expression is basically an old one, and occurs for instance in John Gower's *Confessio Amantis* of the late fourteenth century: 'Lo, how thei feignen chalk for cheese'. The point is that at first glance, 'chalk' and 'cheese' are similar: both white, both crumbly, and both fairly solid. Yet one is edible and the other quite inedible, and this basic difference lies under their outward appearance. The phrase is also used of someone who is unable to distinguish one thing basically from another, or who is generally ignorant: 'He doesn't know chalk from cheese'.

chamfer/bevel
In engineering drawing or architecture, a 'chamfer' is an angle, usually of 45°, that has been cut on the corner or edge of a solid in such a way that the sharp edge (the 'arris') is removed and replaced by a narrow strip. A 'bevel' is similar, except that the angle as a whole is other than a right angle (i.e., neither of the two oblique angles is 45°). However, 'bevel' can be used of the flat narrow strip even when it occurs in a 'chamfer', so care needs to be used with the two words. 'Chamfer' derives from Old French and literally means 'edge break' (*chamfrein*), whereas 'bevel', also from Old French, means 'yawning', 'gaping'.

chancellor/vice-chancellor
At most universities, the 'chancellor', although obviously senior to the 'vice-chancellor', is purely a nominal or honorary head, while the actual head and chief executive or administrator is the 'vice-chancellor'. The 'chancellor' therefore is most in evidence only on ceremonial occasions. This is the illogical British system. In the United States, the arrangement is effectively reversed and more logical, with the 'chancellor' the chief administrative officer and the 'vice-chancellor' his or her deputy.

chapel see **church**[1]

characteristic/mantissa
In mathematics, the 'characteristic' is that part of a common logarithm that is before the decimal point (as a whole number), so that the 'mantissa' is what follows the decimal point. For example, the common logarithm (to base 10) of 20 is 1.3010, and of this the 'characteristic' is 1, and the 'mantissa' .3010. The latter term derives from Latin, and is ultimately an Etruscan

word meaning 'something added', 'makeweight'.

charge card see **credit card**

Charybdis see **Scylla**

cheese see **chalk**

cheesecake see **beefcake**

cherubim/seraphim
Milton wrote of the 'helmed Cherubim' and 'sworded Seraphim' who are 'seen in glittering ranks with wings display'd'. What is the difference? The 'cherubim' (plural of 'cherub') are the second of nine orders of angelic beings in the celestial hierarchy (the traditional ranking of angels). As such they are immediately inferior to the 'seraphim' (plural of 'seraph'), who are the highest order. Popularly, 'cherubic' means 'chubby-faced and innocent-looking', like a young child, while 'seraphic' is used to mean 'blissful', as in a 'seraphic smile'. The words are directly Hebrew in origin.

child/adult
The split here is between 'young person' and 'mature person', with the words themselves sometimes used to denote exclusion or (which is not quite the same thing) exclusiveness. For example, certain theatrical performances may be designated as 'unsuitable for children', and certain erotic or even plainly pornographic literature is marked as 'for adults only'. It is difficult to be dogmatic about the point at which a 'child' becomes an 'adult', since this can depend on so many factors. (For a legal angle, see **adult/infant**.) In older literature, the contrast is frequently between 'child' and 'man', as in the biblical 'When I became a man, I put away childish things', and Wordsworth's famous 'The child is father of the man', meaning that as a person is as a 'child', so will he or she be when an 'adult'.

chinaman see **googly**

Christian name/surname
Most people in the western world today have two distinct names, a 'Christian name' (or forename, or first name, or given name, since not all bearers are even nominally Christians), and a 'surname' (or family name). The former, although coincidentally borne by many other people, depending on its general popularity and allowing for variations in language, is very much a 'personal' name, with some degree of informality allowed for a stranger to use it. The latter, the 'surname', is normally the same as the other members of the person's family, in particular his or her parents, and is usually regarded as a more formal and 'official' name, often given or signed merely for identification purposes. The difference between the two names is thus respectively in effect that of 'private' or 'personal' and 'public' or 'official'. The 'surname' emerged in many European countries only in the twelfth and thirteenth centuries, mainly to serve as an identifying name when there were many bearers of the original name. (Hence the actual word 'surname', meaning one that has been added on top of the existing name.)

Christmas/Easter
The two greatest festivals of the Christian church, celebrating respectively the earthly birth of Christ and his heavenly 'rebirth' or Resurrection (after his Crucifixion on Good Friday). The degree of popular celebration attached to each depends, broadly speaking, on the division of the church involved: the Western Church (including the Roman Catholic and Anglican) regards 'Christmas' as the more 'festive' of the two, while the Eastern Church (the Orthodox) celebrates 'Easter' with the greater ritual and devotion (and, it must be said, religiosity). For this reason, at least in Catholic and Protestant countries, 'Christmas' has now been popularized to a highly secular degree, and has become a season of material merrymaking. This means that 'Easter', although also having its popular secular side (mainly in the form of Easter eggs and springlike associations), is largely uncelebrated as a

festival in its own right. The two occasions, too, have virtually polarized into 'indoor' (i.e. winter) and 'outdoor' (i.e. spring), and 'Easter' is the key day for the tourist and holiday season to start in Britain and many other European countries. One final distinction: 'Christmas' falls on a fixed date (25 December) but a varying day of the week; 'Easter' falls on a movable date (anything between 21 March and 25 April), but a fixed day of the week (Sunday).

chromatic/diatonic
In music, a 'chromatic' scale is one ascending or descending in semitones, and consisting of twelve notes (for example from middle C on the piano up or down to the higher or lower C through all the notes). A 'diatonic' scale is the standard one of eight notes in Western music, for example from middle C up or down an octave on only the white keys. A 'diatonic' key can be major or minor (see **major/minor**). The two terms mean literally 'coloured' and 'extended'.

chronic see **acute**[1]

church[1]/chapel
In Britain, and especially in England, the division is between the established 'Church' of England and the 'chapels' of the Protestant or Nonconformist 'churches' (the so called 'Free Churches'), with the latter sometimes popularly regarded as a kind of 'us' by contrast to the much larger and longer existing 'them', where 'them' is part of the 'Establishment' in the authoritative or socially superior sense. The contrast is thus something on the lines of **Catholic/Protestant**, at least historically, but there is also a strong 'social' split, as expressed typically about an engaged couple that 'His people are "Church", but hers are "Chapel"'. This division was long seen in Wales, with 'Church' equating with the rich landowners, the Tories and the English-speakers, and 'chapel' represented by the farmers and industrial workers who were Welsh-speaking. The very words for the 'chapel' worship indicate their difference: 'Nonconformist' and 'Free' (i.e. not conforming to the established 'church' and free from this establishment). See also the next entry.

church[2]/state
The two bodies are usually regarded in Britain as the two leading representatives of the 'Establishment', i.e. of the institutions that govern and influence public life, with the 'church' (the 'Church' of England, in this case) being the religious institution, and the 'state' (the government) the secular one. Mutually, the 'Church' and the 'state' are interrelated, since the former is granted certain privileges by the latter and in return must fulfil certain obligations. The 'bridge' between the two exists in the form of the sovereign, who is not only head of 'state' but also (since it is the established 'church'), head of the 'Church' of England. The nature of the difference between the two institutions would alter significantly if ever the 'Church' becomes disestablished from the 'state'.

cif/fob
The two commercial abbreviations stand for 'cost, insurance, freight' and 'free on board', and relate respectively to the way in which the trade figures are calculated for imports and exports. 'Cif' indicates that the exporter pays not only the cost of transportation of the goods but also the insurance on their passage, as well, of course, as paying for the goods themselves. (If only the price of the imported goods is reckoned, the total cost is clearly understated.) 'Fob', on the other hand, does not take transportation or insurance costs into account for exports, since these will be paid by the country that is purchasing the goods. The goods themselves are thus 'free on board' the ship that exports them.

circumcised/uncircumcised
The difference is more than a surgical one, and frequently denotes a sharp religious division, even a social one. In the Bible, for example, 'circumcised' equates to 'Jew', and 'uncircumcised' to 'Gentile' (see **Jew/Gentile**). Hence St Paul's

teaching in the New Testament that 'in Jesus Christ neither circumcision availeth any thing, nor uncircumcision'. Because of this association, 'uncircumcised' came to mean 'impure', 'irreligious' in the writings of travellers, for example, down to the twentieth century, and referred to the peoples of the non-Christian world, by contrast with the spiritually 'purified' Christians. In the modern world, the distinction can also be a racial one, as well as a religious, since Hindus are 'uncircumcised' while Muslims are 'circumcised'. The word itself means basically 'cut round' (i.e. the foreskin of the penis), and has its equivalent in other languages (e.g. German *beschneiden*, Russian *obrezat'*).

cisalpine/ultramontane
The two contrasting terms, with their opposite prefixes, mean respectively 'this side of the Alps' and 'that side of the Alps' (more precisely, 'beyond the mountains'), referring to regions lying either south of or north of the Alps (i.e. as viewed from Rome). In the history of the Roman Catholic Church, 'cisalpine' relates to a movement that sought to minimize the authority of the pope and to lay stress on the independence of the various branches of the Church. 'Ultramontane' implied the reverse: a stress on the influence of the pope and a central authority, as distinct from local independence. A French satellite state called the 'Cisalpine Republic' was set up in northern Italy by Napoleon in 1796 and existed until 1802.

civilian/military
Government (state) employees in Britain are broadly divided between those who are in the armed services (the 'military') and those who are not, and so are 'civilian' staff. There is no anomaly in the fact that many 'civilian' employees actually work closely with the 'military' in one capacity or another (e.g. as instructors, clerks, catering staff), nor is there in the fact that each branch of the armed forces is headed by a minister who is himself a 'civilian'. Indeed, the Civil Service is so called to denote that it is a government body distinct from the 'military' (as well as incidentally the legislative and judiciary branches). Where 'civilian' and 'military' employees work together, there can sometimes arise an implicit division of opinion as to which of the two lives and works in the 'real' world.

classical[1]/pop
The two main divisions of music, as experienced by the everyday listener and enjoyer of it. The division is very loosely 'age' versus 'youth', or possibly 'highbrow' as against 'lowbrow', since much 'classical' music is mentally demanding and intricate, while by its very definition, much 'pop' (i.e. popular) music is 'easy listening'. There is also a split between 'serious' and 'trivial', since concert-going (to 'classical' music) is a cultural affair, while much 'pop' music is used simply as undemanding background music, or for pure entertainment. However, things are not really as simple as this, and there can be 'light' 'classical' music (e.g. Strauss waltzes) just as there can be 'heavy' or complex 'pop' (when it is usually called something else, such as 'heavy metal', or in a general way, as 'rock'). See also the next entry.

classical[2]/romantic
If Bach and Mozart are 'classical' composers, and Brahms and Schumann are 'romantic' ones, where does one draw the line? Roughly, 'classical' music is that of the sixteenth century to the end of the eighteenth, which is really 'pure in proportion and beauty', that is, a virtual work of art in itself, with due form, balance, contrast and the like. This means that 'romantic' music is generally later, and mainly consists of music that expresses the emotions, or develops a literary or pictorial idea. Put another way, 'classical' music is 'head', and 'romantic' music is 'heart'. However, Mozart, especially in his last works, sometimes borders on the 'romantic', and Beethoven, although indubitably a 'classical' composer, at times edges even further across the divide. See also **programme music/absolute music**.

claustrophobia/agoraphobia
The literal meaning of the two psychological afflictions are 'fear of locked-in places' and 'fear of public gathering places', otherwise a morbid dread of being confined in an enclosed space or exposed and vulnerable in an open one. In a sense, the terms can overlap, since a person who tends to 'come over all funny' in church, for example, is really more prone to 'agoraphobia', as it is not the confinement that bothers him but the presence of the other people, and in a church on his own he might be quite unaffected.

clean/dirty
Apart from the obvious contrast, the two words are used in some special senses to mean 'uncontaminated' and 'contaminated'. For example, in nuclear warfare, a 'clean' weapon is one that produces little or no radioactive fallout, while a 'dirty' one would cause widespread contamination. In a less specialized field, a 'clean' joke is one without any innuendoes, while a 'dirty' joke is a smutty or indecent one. A 'clean' wound, too, is an uninfected one, while a 'dirty' wound is the opposite, and is potentially more serious.

clear/pearl
Of electric light bulbs, a 'clear' bulb is one with transparent glass, through which the filament can be seen, while a 'pearl' bulb has frosted glass, so that one cannot see the filament. 'Clear' bulbs can be glaring, and cast hard shadows, but they can make glass light shades sparkle. 'Pearl' bulbs give a more diffuse light, but are aesthetically better to look at in cases where a light bulb has to be exposed. (A 'pearl' bulb should not be confused with an 'opal' one, which has translucent white glass.)

clear see **thick**[1]

clerical/lay
These are the two standard adjectives to apply to a member of a church who is a priest or who is not. ('Clerical' relates to 'clergy' and also 'clerk'; 'lay' derives ultimately from Greek *laos*, 'people'.) Paradoxically, at least in the Church of England, many 'lay' members are even more 'churchy' than the clergy, and make their opinions felt in media ranging from parish councils to the press ('Letters to the Editor').

clingstone/freestone
A 'clingstone' is a fruit, usually a peach, in which the flesh clings to the stone. A 'freestone' is one in which it does not. All nice and clearcut!

clinker-built/carvel-built
The terms relate to shipbuilding, or more exactly boatbuilding. If a boat is 'clinker-built' it has the lower edge of each external plank or plate overlapping the upper edge of the one below it. If it is 'carvel-built', it has planks that meet flush at the seams. The words themselves derive from 'clinch' and (probably) 'caravel', the latter being a former kind of sailing ship.

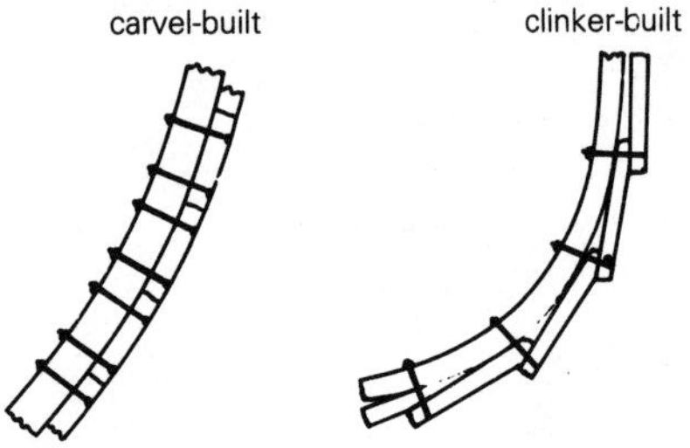

clockwise/anticlockwise
The two expressions are a fairly handy way of saying 'rotating to the right' and 'rotating to the left', i.e. in the same direction as the hands of a clock when viewed from the front. But people and objects must have been making such circular movements long before the introduction of clocks with hands, if only in mystic ceremonies. So what words were used then? (Incredibly, the *Oxford English Dictionary* gives a first recording of 'clockwise' only as late as 1888, and of 'anticlockwise' only in 1898, when it began to supersede the somewhat earlier 'counterclockwise', also first noted in 1888.) The answer lies in **withershins/deasil**, which see.

closed see **open**[1]

coarse/refined
The pair of opposites here can be used of such abstract things as taste and manners ('coarse manners', 'refined taste'), and can also sometimes serve for other distinctions. One of these is a 'coarse' metal, which by definition is one that has not been 'refined', although in many cases the more common opposites for concrete objects are 'coarse' and 'fine', as in 'coarse cloth', 'fine cloth'. 'Coarse' was originally spelt 'course' and meant simply 'ordinary', 'such as is found in the course of things'. For another 'coarse' comparison, see the next entry.

coarse fish/game fish
The division here is basically 'salmon' and 'not salmon'. A 'coarse fish' is a freshwater fish that is not a member of the salmon family (*Salmonidae*), whereas a 'game fish' does belong to this family. In the world of angling, to which the terms belong, 'coarse fishing' (so called because of the coarse texture of the skin of such fish) is much more popular than 'game fishing' (so named since catching the fish is the 'sport' of the angler).

cock/hen
In their most general sense, 'cock' is the male of a bird and 'hen' its corresponding female. Popularly, however, the two names relate to the farmyard birds, whose respective younger versions are known as the 'cockerel' and the 'chicken'. The **male/female** duality can be seen in the names of several birds, such as 'peacock' and 'peahen', 'moorcock' and 'moorhen' (as the red grouse), but in the case of the 'woodcock' the name applies to both sexes, and the 'hen harrier' is not so called because it is female, but because it is a hawk that harries 'hens'! D. H. Lawrence punned on both words when he wrote: 'There are the women who are cocksure, and the women who are hensure' (*Assorted Articles*, 1930). See also **stag party/hen party**.

code see **plaintext**

coffee see **tea**

cognate/agnate
In genealogy or genetics, 'cognate' is the term used to mean that a person is related by blood to another, or shares a common maternal ancestor. The opposite is thus 'agnate', meaning that the person's kinship can be traced back only through the male line. The terms have some legal usage, and derive from Latin words meaning respectively 'born together' and 'born additionally'.

cold see **hot**

cold-blooded see **warm-blooded**

cold front/warm front
Recorded here separately from the main **hot/cold** entry, for ease of distinction, these two meteorological terms describe the main types of advancing air mass: a 'cold front' is the boundary line between a warm air mass and the cold air that is pushing from beneath it and behind it as it moves; a 'warm front' is the boundary between a mass of warm air and the cold air above it, which is rising at a less steep angle than at a 'cold front'. An 'occluded front' is a line where the 'cold front' has overtaken the 'warm front', raising it from ground level. On a weather chart, a 'cold front' is conventionally indicated as a line with triangles, while a 'warm front' is shown as a line with semicircles. An 'occluded front' has these symbols alternately.

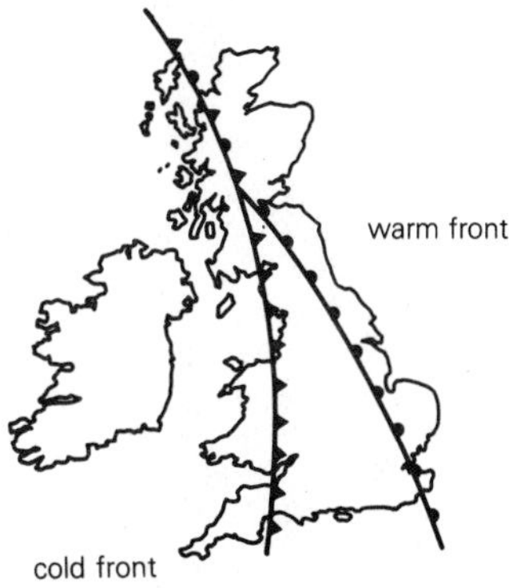

collection see **delivery**

Collegers see **Oppidans**

colour/black and white
The big contrast here is in photography, the cinema, and television, where a 'black and white' picture was originally the norm until 'colour' photography and film techniques were developed. Although 'colour' photographs of a kind were made in the nineteenth century, their commercial development only really took off with the introduction of Kodachrome roll films in the 1930s and Kodacolour films in the 1940s. 'Colour' films gained prominence at about the same time, but 'colour' television followed on a regular basis only in the late 1960s. There are still those who say that 'black and white' photography and films have a quality that 'colour' lacks, and who claim that 'black and white' films have an air of documentary authenticity that 'colour' films often lack. The mainly 'black and white' photography in newspapers reinforces this concept. In Britain, there were still two and a half million owners of 'black and white' television sets in 1988, as against over sixteen million 'colour'. However, this is hardly surprising in view of the big difference in the licence fee, with 'black and white' ('monochrome') only £21 at this time compared to the hefty £62.50 for 'colour'.

coloured/white
The terms here, often also spelt with a capital letter, relate specifically to skin colour, so that technically a 'coloured' person is anyone who is not a 'white'. In practice, however, 'coloured' often means 'black' in this sense, although in South Africa, for instance, 'coloured' means specifically 'of mixed race', and although the South African parliament now contains a 'white' House of Assembly and a 'coloured' House of Representatives (as well as an Asian House of Delegates), it still has no black members. See also **black/white**.

colt/filly
These are the two words for, respectively, a young male horse and a young female, in particular one aged under four who takes part in a race. Although the names have also entered the human domain, with 'colts', for example, used for the male players of a junior sports team, and 'filly' gaining the slang sense 'girl', the latter word is not related to French *fille* but comes from Old Norse *fylja*, and is actually related to English 'foal'.

combination/permutation
In mathematics, a 'combination' is an arrangement of the numbers or terms of a set into particular groups, without any set order within the group. For example, the 'combinations' of a, b and c, taken two at a time, are ab, bc, ac. If the arrangement is ordered, these are 'permutations', and will thus be given for the same instance as ab, ba, ac, ca, bc, cb. The two words are sometimes used together as a general sort of phrase to mean merely 'different varieties', 'various ways', such as the reply of a waiter in a restaurant when asked what dish he recommends: 'Well, Sir, there are all sorts of permutations and combinations you can try.'

come/go
Apart from the two basic senses of the common verbs ('proceed or move in this direction', 'proceed or move in that direction'), 'come' and 'go' are quite frequently combined to denote a constant movement, often a restless one, as when hospital patients are disturbed by the ceaseless 'coming and going' of medical and surgical staff, visitors, cleaners and so on. Rather curiously, the two words are also used for particular bodily emissions, with 'coming' denoting an act of orgasm and 'going' denoting an act of urination or defecation. This is because the former is regarded as 'arriving', i.e. is awaited as a sort of 'product', while the latter has words such as 'to the toilet' understood. At a more academic level, see **go up/come down**.

come down see **go up**

comedy/tragedy
At their most basic, a 'comedy' is an

amusing or humorous play, and a 'tragedy' a serious or sad one, with the combination of both types called a 'tragi-comedy'. The two types of drama date from classical times, however, and have been interestingly defined since then. The twelfth-century dramatist Johannes Januensis, for example, said that 'comedy' differed from 'tragedy' because it concerned the doing of ordinary people, whereas 'tragedy' had to do with kings and persons of importance. Similar definitions have stated that 'comedy' has a humble style of writing, while 'tragedy' is lofty, or that 'comedy' begins with misfortune and ends in joy, while 'tragedy' is the opposite. The words themselves mean respectively 'sung village festival' and, more surprisingly, 'goat song', with the latter apparently relating to some kind of ritual in which goats were sacrificed (Greek *tragos* is 'goat'). The second half of each word is from the Greek verb 'to sing', giving English 'ode'.

commoner/scholar
The academic distinction here is something like that of the pair **Oppidans/Collegers** (which see), but at university level, where a 'commoner' is an ordinary student or undergraduate who is not on a scholarship, when he or she is obviously known as a 'scholar'. At Oxford a 'scholar' is regarded as being 'on the foundation', meaning that he is entitled to financial support from the funds of a particular college, as endowed by a particular individual or trust.

Commons see **Lords**

communism/capitalism
These two contrasting 'isms' are those of the **East/West** split, and in particular designate the political and social philosophies of the superpowers, respectively Soviet Russia and the United States. However, not all Russians are by any means 'communists', any more than all Americans or other westerners are 'capitalists'. To a certain degree, each term is viewed by its opposite proponents as a 'dirty word', since a belief in 'communism' implies a strong opposition to 'capitalism', which has private enterprise as its own economic basis. The very terms define their key concepts of 'community' ('all for one, and one for all') and 'capital' (material wealth). In its modern sense of 'Marxism-Leninism', 'communism' as a word first arose in the writings of Marx and Engels. 'Capitalism' is an almost contemporary term, arising in the mid-nineteenth century. See also the next entry.

Communist China/Nationalist China
'Communist China' is a name quite frequently used for the Chinese People's Republic, i.e. mainland China, while 'Nationalist China' is an unofficial name for Taiwan (properly called the Republic of China), the island state off the south-east coast of 'Communist China' that was formerly known as Formosa and that became the last territory of the Chinese Nationalist government in 1950 when Chiang Kai-shek withdrew there.

complex see **simple**[1]

composer see **librettist**

composite number see **prime number**

compound see (1) **element** (2) **simple**[2]

compressor see **expander**

compulsory/optional
The two terms are frequently used in a fairly formal context when a choice cannot or can be made, for example in an examination paper, which will have 'compulsory' questions (that must be answered) and 'optional' ones (that may be or need not be). In some cases, however, there is no 'optional' equivalent, for example for 'compulsory purchase', meaning the purchase of a house by a local or other authority whether the owner wishes to sell or not, and in other instances the better contrast to 'compulsory' is expressed by 'voluntary', such as the difference between 'compulsory military service' and 'voluntary military service' (not 'optional').

con/senza
In music, the two Italian words, meaning respectively 'with' and 'without', are used for certain directions to players, e.g. 'con sordini' means 'with mutes' (for example, to trumpet players), and 'senza sordini' would then be the direction to remove them. (To a pianist, however, 'con sordini' means 'dampen the strings by depressing the left pedal', and 'senza sordini' means 'depress the right pedal so that the strings vibrate unhindered'.) See also **with/without**.

con see **pro**[2]

concave see **convex**

concentric see **eccentric**

concord/discord
Musically speaking, a 'concord' is an interval or chord that (for want of a better word) sounds 'satisfying', while a 'discord' is the opposite, a chord that is 'unresolved' and seems to be leading on to something more acceptable. For example, in the opening bars of the Bach chorale illustrated here, the thirds of the chords in the first five beats are all 'concords', and give a feeling of satisfaction. The chord of the seventh in beat 6, however (the 'seventh' is C added to D with its third and fifth of F# and A), is a 'discord', and we are unhappy until it is resolved in the next chord.

concrete see **abstract**

confirm/deny
The two verbs are sometimes used in non-committal statements made to the media, such as 'The company would not confirm or deny that the product had been sold' (usually taken to mean a tacit confirmation: they did not say 'no', therefore they could well mean 'yes').

congruent/similar
The two adjectives are used in mathematics (more precisely, geometry) to describe contrasting types of triangles. One that is 'congruent' is equal in size and shape to another, while a 'similar' triangle is one that has the same angles as another, but sides that are of a different length. 'Congruent' literally means 'meeting together'.

conjugation see **declension**

conjunction/opposition
In astronomy, 'conjunction' is the term used to refer to the position of a planet or the Moon when it is in line with the Sun as seen from the Earth. The planets are in inferior 'conjunction' when they are between the Earth and the Sun (this can only happen to Mercury, Venus or Mars), and in superior 'conjunction' when the Sun lies between the Earth and the planet (likewise). 'Opposition' refers to the position of one of the other planets (Jupiter, Saturn, Uranus, Neptune, Pluto) or the Moon when it lies directly opposite the Sun as seen from the Earth. When in 'conjunction', the planet thus has the appearance of minimum (nil) separation from the Sun; when in 'opposition' it is as far away from it (exactly opposite) as it could be. See also **superior/inferior**.

connotation see **denotation**

Conservative/Labour
The names of the two chief opposing political parties in Britain since the First World War, with the third party of significance the Liberals (more recently the Liberal-Social Democratic Alliance). The 'Labour' Party is that of the left wing, as its name implies (it claims to represent the interests of labour, i.e. the working classes), so that the 'Conservative' Party is that of the right, standing for the preservation (or as its name suggests, 'conser-

vation') of established institutions and advocating private enterprise. The division is thus between 'state-owned' and 'private', or, put another way, 'nationalization' and 'denationalization' (where nationalization already exists). The 'Conservative' Party developed in the 1830s out of the former Tory Party (see **Whig/Tory**), and its members are still known as 'Tories' as an alternative name. The 'Labour' Party evolved in the early years of the twentieth century, and its members are also known as 'Socialists'. Since the Second World War, there have been exactly equal numbers of 'Conservative' and 'Labour' governments – six each to date. Traditionally, most 'Labour' support comes from the big cities and the north of England, while 'Conservative' supporters mostly live and work in rural England or the south. See also **left/right**, **north/south**.

consonance/dissonance
In music, 'consonance' and 'dissonance' are really the respective effects produced by a 'concord' and a 'discord' (see **concord/discord**). However, acoustically speaking, there is no distinction to be made between the two, and many chords or musical intervals have only a relative degree of 'consonance' or 'dissonance', depending on the historical period of the composition in which they occur and the subjective ear or psychological reaction of the listener. Compare **assonance/dissonance** for something similar but more clearcut in literature.

consonant see **vowel**

constitutional monarchy see **absolute monarchy**

constructive/destructive
The two contrasting or opposite adjectives are sometimes applied, either individually or jointly, to criticism, which can thus be helpful or well intended ('constructive') or adverse and truly critical ('destructive').

consubstantiation see **transubstantiation**

consumer/producer
The two agents who keep the economy going, with the 'consumer' needing or using the product supplied or manufactured by the 'producer'. We are all of us 'consumers', and as such are liable to be at the mercy of the marketing practices of the 'producers', who have the power to fix prices, quality, availability, and so on of their products.

contagious/infectious
A 'contagious' disease is one passed on by direct contact with the individual who has it, or at least with his or her clothing. An 'infectious' disease is one transmitted without actual contact, but by micro-organisms such as bacteria. Examples of 'contagious' diseases are chicken pox, venereal disease and leprosy, while 'infectious' diseases include influenza, tuberculosis and poliomyelitis. In the 1980s, the 'contagious' disease AIDS ('*a*cquired *i*mmune *d*eficiency *s*yndrome'), at first popularly associated with homosexual men, was constantly in the headlines, and in 1986 became the object of a government-sponsored (and explicitly worded) campaign. (In fact, AIDS is in a sense both 'contagious' and 'infectious', since it is the contact between the body fluids of the two persons that causes the transmission of the virus that then infects the body. However, the infection cannot occur without the initial contact.)

contango/backwardation
In the jargon of the Stock Exchange, 'contango' is a premium paid by a buyer of shares to a seller so as to postpone delivery until a future day of settlement, as officially fixed. 'Backwardation' is the opposite: a premium paid by a seller to a buyer to postpone delivery similarly, with such postponement usually being speculative. The terms can relate to the charges themselves or to the actual postponement. 'Backwardation' therefore refers to the 'keeping back' of the delivery. The origin of 'contango' is more obscure, and the word appears to be a sort of alteration of 'continue', as the postponement of delivery of the stock involves a 'continuation' of

the deal until a future date. Both terms emerged in regular use only in the mid-nineteenth century.

content/not content
The obvious opposites, the second negating the first, are officially used in the House of Lords (see **Lords/Commons**) as expressions of agreement or disagreement with a motion, respectively, and thus correspond to the 'aye' and 'no' of the House of Commons (see **aye/no**). The result of a vote would therefore be recorded in something like the form: 'Content 84, Not Content 23'.

contract see **expand**

contract bridge/auction bridge
'Contract bridge' is the more common version of the card game, in which tricks won in excess of a particular number ('overtricks') do not count towards winning the game although they do add points to the final score. 'Auction bridge' differs from this in that the overtricks *do* count towards winning the game. 'Auction bridge' was the earlier form of the game to develop, with 'auction' referring to the bidding. 'Contract bridge' is so called since the object of bidding is to secure the final contract. See also **grand slam/little slam**.

Contras see **Sandinistas**

convergent see **divergent**

convex/concave
An object that is 'convex', such as a lens or a mirror, is one that bulges outwards, and one that is 'concave' curves inwards. The words derive from Latin and literally mean 'vaulted' and 'arched', with *cavus* meaning 'hollow'. One way to remember the difference is to associate 'concave' with 'caving in' (helpful semantically, but incorrect etymologically!).

cooked see **raw**

cooking apple/eating apple
'Cooking apples' (or 'cookers') are the larger, usually greener varieties that are best eaten cooked (although some kinds can be eaten raw if one is not too particular about taste or texture). 'Eating apples' ('eaters') are therefore the more common sorts (also more expensive than 'cookers') that are designed to be eaten uncooked. One common variety of 'cooking apple' is Bramley's seedling, while there are many kinds of tasty 'eating apple', from Worcester Pearmain to Cox's Orange Pippin. 'Cooking' sherry or wine is a cheap variety used to flavour a dish.

cool/warm
The two words are opposites to mean 'rather cold' and 'rather hot', as applied to weather or the temperature of water, for example. There are even abstract applications, such as a 'cool reception' and a 'warm welcome'. However, 'cool' can have favourable or unfavourable associations ('cool' drink, 'cool' wind), and in colloquial use 'real cool' can mean 'excellent', 'marvellous'.

Copernican system see **Ptolemaic system**

cops/robbers
The two groups are opposing sides of 'goodies' and 'baddies' in police chases (often comic filmed ones) and children's games. Both types of activity originated in the United States, apparently in the early twentieth century. See also **cowboys/Indians**, **goodies/baddies**.

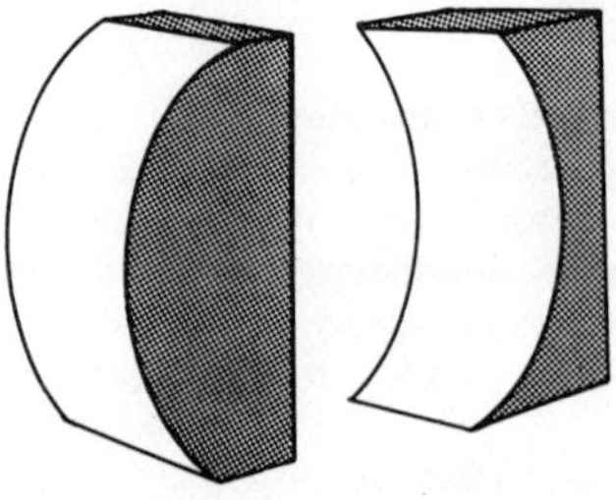

corolla see **calyx**

coronal see **sagittal**

coulisse see **parquet**

counterattack see **attack**[1]

count noun/mass noun
Grammatically speaking, a 'count noun' is a noun that refers to something that can exist in the plural without any change in meaning, for example 'book', 'tree' or 'attack' ('books', 'the trees', 'two attacks'). A 'mass noun' exists only in the singular in its regular sense, and usually refers to a substance or concept, such as 'water' or 'justice'. 'Mass nouns', too, are not used with the indefinite article ('a' or 'an'), whereas 'count nouns' are. 'Count nouns' are sometimes also known as 'unit nouns'.

country see **town**[1]

course/wale
The two terms relate specifically to knitting. The 'course' is the horizontal rows of stitches, and the 'wale' the vertical row. (The latter word is related to 'weal'.) For another knitting link-up, see **purl/plain**.

court see **quadrangle**

cow/bull
The two familiar words for, respectively, the mature female and the mature male of any species of cattle, with the terms also applied to other animals such as elephants, whales and seals (e.g. 'bull elephant', 'cow seal'). See also **ox/bull** and compare **heifer/bullock**.

cowboys/Indians
Like 'cops and robbers' (see **cops/robbers** above), this is a children's game of North American origin, with the two sides representing the battles between the 'cowboys', the tough American ranch hands and horsemen, and the native American 'Indians', especially in the nineteenth century.

cradle/grave
The first and the last resting places of a human being, as occurring in the expression 'from the cradle to the grave', meaning 'for the whole of a person's life'. The phrase appears to date back to at least the seventeenth century, and now has an alternative equivalent in the rhyming 'from womb to tomb'.

creationism/traducianism
The two terms denote theological contrasts. 'Creationism' is the belief that God creates the souls of humans at either their conception or their birth. 'Traducianism' is the theory that the soul is transmitted to a child by its parents in the basic act of generation. Some theologians have used the latter theory to explain the doctrine of original sin (i.e. that sin has been innate in man since Adam's first sin of disobedience in the Garden of Eden).

credit/debit
In banking and accounting, 'credit' is the amount of money or balance in a person's favour, while 'debit' is the opposite – the balance that he owes. It has long been traditional practice in bookkeeping for 'credits' to be entered in the right-hand column of a balance sheet, and 'debits' to be entered on the left. This arrangement is still observed in a bank's balance sheet ('statement of account') with the balance itself (the running total after 'credits' have been added and 'debits' deducted) shown in a third column. Related opposites here are 'creditor' and 'debtor', with the former the word for a person who is owed money by the latter. See **red/black**, **assets/liabilities**.

credit card/charge card
A 'credit card' is one issued by a bank (for examples, see **Access/VISA**) which enables the holder to obtain goods, services and even cash on credit, so that he settles up wholly or partly later, usually monthly. A 'credit card', too, has a fixed credit limit as determined by the holder's requirements and resources. A 'charge card' is not issued by a bank but by a

commercial organization such as a club or store (well known examples are the American Express and Diners Club cards, and those issued by such chain stores as Marks and Spencer and Boots). Some but not all of these, especially the more expensive, charge an annual fee and also one for joining, and require the holder to pay off his monthly statement in full, without any credit or 'minimum payment' in this sense. However, such types of 'charge card' have no upper credit limit, and may charge no interest (although the chain store cards do), since payment is made in full.

creole/pidgin
Both terms are used for a type of 'mixed' language. The 'pidgin' really comes first, since it is a speech system evolved to provide a means of communication between people who have no common language. In other words, it is a sort of 'bastard' language, based initially on English and Chinese in the nineteenth century, that came to be used for trading and business contacts only. ('Pidgin' is itself a corruption of the word 'business'.) When a 'pidgin' (based on whatever languages, for example French, Portuguese or English) becomes the regular language of a community, it evolves into a 'creole'. This has notably happened in the West Indies, so that Barbados has an English-based (Caribbean) 'creole'. The word 'creole' itself goes back through Portuguese *crioulo*, as a term for a white person born in the colonies, to Latin *creare*, 'to create'.

crescendo/diminuendo
The musical terms, taken directly from Italian, mean respectively 'increasing' (i.e. louder) and 'diminishing' (i.e. softer), and occur as directions in a score or part to players or singers. They are traditionally abbreviated as 'cr' and 'dim', and have occurred in this form in some hymnbooks as a direction to the choir or congregation to sing gradually more loudly or more softly. However, in some cases they have been wrongly taken to serve as 'expression' guides, and to stand for 'cry' and 'dim' by some hymn singers. This is understandable when they appear against such lines as:

And we believe Thy Word,
dim Though dim our faith may be;
cr Whate'er for Thine we do, O Lord, We do it unto Thee.

See also **piano/forte**.

Croatian see **Serbian**

crooked see **straight**[2]

crosses see **noughts**

cross-ply see **radial**

cross-saddle see **side-saddle**

cry see **laugh**

cryptogam/phanerogam
In botany, a 'cryptogam' is a plant that does not produce seeds, for example mosses and ferns. The opposite is a 'phanerogam', that does produce seeds, with this category embracing the majority of plants. 'Phanerogams' are now technically known as 'spermatophytes' (see **angiosperm/gymnosperm**). The two contrasting terms mean literally 'hidden marriage' and 'visible marriage', while 'spermatophyte' means, more accurately, 'seed plant'. 'Cryptogams' reproduce by means of spores.

cub/brownie
The names are those of the junior members (boys and girls) of, respectively, the Scout Association and the Girl Guides Association. 'Cubs' (formerly, 'Wolf Cubs', and today officially 'Cub Scouts') are aged from eight to ten, and 'brownies' (in full, 'Brownie Guides') are in a similar age group, although a girl can join any time after her seventh birthday. The two groupings thus correspond at a junior level to the **scouts/guides** sector (which see), with however 'brownies' outnumbering 'cubs'. Historically, 'cubs' arose after scouts, and 'brownies' after 'cubs' (but also after guides: see their senior counterparts for the details). 'Cubs' are so called

with reference to the wolf cubs with whom the native baby Mowgli was brought up by Mother Wolf in Kipling's *Jungle Books*, while 'brownies' are so named for their brown uniform (but also, no doubt, with some reference to the good-natured goblins called 'brownies' who carried out helpful household services in popular stories).

cum dividend see **ex dividend**

cumulus/stratus
There are different terms for the various cloud formations, but these two are basic opposites, since a 'cumulus' cloud is one that develops vertically and produces rain and hail storms, while a 'stratus' cloud spreads horizontally and produces steady rain (but not storms). The names denote their form, as Latin *cumulus* means 'mass', while *stratus* means 'layer'.

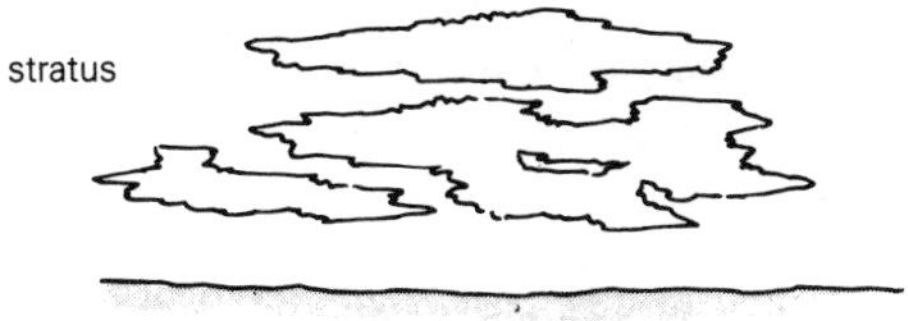

cunnilingus see **fellatio**

current account/deposit account
At a bank, a 'current account' is the standard one that carries no interest and against which cheques can be drawn at any time. A 'deposit account', on the other hand, earns interest and usually requires notice for a withdrawal to be made from it. A customer can have both types of account, but they normally operate separately, and if one becomes overdrawn, the bank will not automatically 'top it up' from the other. In the United States, a 'current account' is known as a 'checking account', while 'deposit accounts' are called 'savings accounts'.

current assets/fixed assets
The 'current assets' of a firm or business are its stocks, shares and money owed that can be readily converted into cash. Its 'fixed assets', by contrast, are its more or less permanent assets, such as machinery and fixtures, that cannot be quickly converted. 'Fixed assets' also includes the intangible asset of 'goodwill', that is, the firm's reputation and general standing among its customers.

curse see **bless**

curved see **straight**[3]

cyclone/anticyclone
In meteorology, a 'cyclone' is a 'depression' or 'low', otherwise a mass of air moving at below the normal atmospheric pressure and often bringing rain. An 'anticyclone' (or 'high') is thus the opposite: a mass of moving air of a higher pressure than the surrounding air, and usually bringing fine or settled weather. In the northern hemisphere, winds in an 'anticyclone' blow clockwise around the centre, but in the southern hemisphere they blow anticlockwise. (In winter, too, there are two types of 'anticyclone' in Britain, one with overcast skies and the other with clear skies and frosty nights. See the final sentence of **summer/winter**.)

cylinder see (1) **rotary** (2) **upright**

Dd

dactyl see **anapaest**

dah see **dit**

dam see **sire**

dame see **principal boy**

dan see **kyu**

dark/fair
The two opposites that describe hair colour or complexion, and that for hair correspond to the pair (here reversed) **blonde/brunette**, which see. What is interesting is that 'dark' has retained its single meaning since Old English usage, whereas 'fair' developed only in the sixteenth century from the word that meant (and still means) 'beautiful', 'pleasing'. This suggests that 'fair' hair is more attractive than 'dark'. If so, this could be because we all have an innate tendency to be attracted to anything that is light or bright (such as the sun or the seaside), and not to favour anything 'dark' (such as the night or an object that is obscured in some way). In theory, therefore, a person with 'fair' hair or a 'fair' complexion is one with a 'sunny' nature, and instantly likable, whereas a person with 'dark' hair or a 'dark' complexion may be more indrawn, or at least mysterious. For a further consideration of this contrast, see **fair young man/'Dark Lady'**. See also the next entry and likewise **light/dark**.

dark see **light**[1]

Dark Ages see **Middle Ages**

'Dark Lady' see **fair young man**

darkness/light
The best way to describe the former word is to say that it is the absence of the latter. In our subconscious, 'darkness' is mostly associated with a blank or void or 'nothingness', while 'light' stands for a fullness and completeness. 'Darkness' is thus dead of night, with all its sinister overtones, while 'light' is the noonday brightness and life. Not for nothing did primitive man seek to have fire in his dark cave, and whatever its theological or symbolic interpretation it is certainly significant that the whole Bible opens with 'darkness' and that God's first command was 'Let there be light' (Genesis 1:3). For the more practical implications of the two states, see **light/dark**, and compare also the entry above. (See even **night/day**, too.)

dash see **dot**

daughter see **son**

dawn/dusk
The two terms stand for the coming of light at the beginning of the day and the fading of light at the end. Or to invert this: 'dawn' marks the end of the night, and 'dusk' its onset. For reasons that have been touched on in the entry above, 'dawn' thus symbolizes hope and optimism, while 'dusk' can denote the fading of hope and a sense of impending gloom. However, in practical terms, 'from dawn to dusk' simply means 'the whole day long'. Even so, 'dawn' has a greater emotive content than 'dusk', if only because of the 'dawn chorus', or early singing of birds to herald a new day. (There is sometimes a 'dusk chorus', although not so called, for example when starlings gather, but it

tends to be merely an unromantic disturbance rather than something to stop and listen to.)

day see **night**

day school/boarding school
As popularly understood, a 'day school' is a non-resident one, where the pupils attend each day for lessons and activities, often for only five days a week, while a 'boarding school' is one where the pupils reside during term-time, with their timetable thus catering for weekend lessons and activities. In Britain, most 'boarding schools' are in the private sector, typically as public or preparatory schools. However, many 'boarding schools' do also take non-resident pupils, who are known as 'dayboys' or 'daygirls' respectively, or generally (and rather confusingly) as 'day boarders'. Pupils sleeping at the school are then known as 'boarders'. See also **public/private**, **state/private**.

DC see **AC**

de see **men**

dead see (1) **alive** (2) **live**[1]

deaf/dumb
A contrast is often implied between a 'deaf' person, who cannot hear, and a 'dumb' person, who cannot speak, with the former condition often resulting in the latter, at least to an effective degree. For this reason, special 'deaf and dumb' alphabets and signs have been devised so that those afflicted can communicate visually.

deasil see **withershins**

death/resurrection
In the Christian religion (and also in some pre-Christian religions), 'resurrection' is the process by which a person comes back to life after 'death', as exemplified by the 'Resurrection' of Christ from the tomb three days after his 'death'. This is not quite the same as the contrast between 'life' and 'death', since many Christians hold that their 'resurrection' after their 'death' will occur only at the 'Second Coming' of Christ. Theologians are still in some dispute, however, as to what kind of 'body' a resurrected person will have when this happens. The word itself literally means 'rising again'. See also **life/death**.

death see (1) **birth** (2) **life**

debit see **credit**

decani/cantoris
The pair of rather rarefied words belongs to church ritual and services, so that in a church choir, that has singers on both sides, 'decani' is the same side as the dean (Latin *decanus*), otherwise the south side (with the altar at the east end), so that 'cantoris' is on the north side, the same as that of the precentor (Latin *cantor*), who directs the choral services in a cathedral or certain churches. Where a choir sings alternately, first one side, then the other, their music parts are often marked with these terms (usually abbreviated as 'dec.' and 'can.'). The words are actually Latin genitives ('of the dean', 'of the precentor'), with 'side' understood.

decathlon see **pentathlon**

decentralization see **centralization**

deciduous/evergreen
The two terms, one technical-looking, the other easily understood, are used respectively of trees that do or do not shed their leaves in winter. Among 'deciduous' trees are the familar oak and elm, while 'evergreen' trees include the pine and holly. 'Deciduous' literally means 'falling down', from Latin *decidere*. It seems strange that no Latin-based word has developed botanically for 'evergreen'.

decimal/duodecimal
The mathematical terms relate respectively to counting and reckoning systems based on ten or twelve. Most countries of the world today have a 'decimal' monetary system, for example, often with one major

unit subdivided into a hundred others (such as the British pound and pence, or American dollar and cents). The 'duodecimal' system was long in use in Britain, however, with twelve pence to the shilling (and 240 to the pound) until as recently as 1971. Today, too, the British still use inches and feet (twelve inches to the foot) to express many common measurements, in particular that of a person's height, while many shops still sell everyday goods in 'duodecimal' lengths or widths as well as 'decimal' ones. (This often results in clumsy dual measurement details, as e.g. 'address labels 4″ × 2″ (102 × 49mm)', and mail order catalogues may well use one system or the other or both, depending which they feel the customer will or should know.) See also **metric/imperial**.

declension/conjugation
The rather impressive (and outwardly not very meaningful) terms are grammatical ones relating respectively to the different case endings of a noun (or adjective) or personal endings of a verb, that is, in a so-called 'inflected' language (notoriously Latin) that has such endings. Thus, Latin (since we are talking about it) has five noun 'declensions', with the first including the familiar *mensa*, *mensa*, *mensam*, *mensae*, *mensae*, *mensa* for the six cases of the word for 'table' (singular only here). It has four 'conjugations' of verbs, too, with again the best recalled perhaps being the first, which includes (in the present indicative) *amo*, *amas*, *amat*, *amamus*, *amatis*, *amant*, for 'to love'. The designations, themselves sometimes confused by learners of the language in question, mean literally 'bending aside' (since the endings of the cases deviate from the norm, or nominative) and 'joining together' (since the different forms of the verb are all mutually related). The jargon of grammar is quite horrendous, and had to be understood and memorized by the wretched classics student until quite recent times. However, at least *The Public School Latin Primer* made itself clear when it said 'Nouns are DECLINED. Verbs are CONJUGATED' (Parts of Speech, paragraph 11, section 2).

declination see **right ascension**

declivity/acclivity
A 'declivity', in geography or generally, is a downward slope, while an 'acclivity' is an upward one. The *clivus* seen in each is the Latin for 'slope'. (English 'cliff' is not related to this, however, but derives from another source.) Compare **syncline/anticline**.

decrease see **increase**

decree absolute see **decree nisi**

decree nisi/decree absolute
Both terms feature in divorce proceedings, with a 'decree nisi' a provisional decree or legal order for the two parties to separate, and a 'decree absolute' an order making the divorce final. The former normally leads to the latter, unless cause to the contrary is shown. Hence the Latin *nisi* ('unless') of the first decree. In English, the 'nisi' is pronounced 'nigh-sigh' (which obviously can lead to poetic puns, some of them not very funny).

deduction/induction
The terms relate to the process of reasoning. In logic, a 'deduction' is the drawing of a particular conclusion from general premisses, while an 'induction' is the contrary: the drawing of a general conclusion from particular premisses. The two processes are known respectively as 'deductive' and 'inductive' reasoning. Here is an example of a 'deduction': All war is wicked; the battle between Ruritania and Urbitania is a war; therefore the battle between Ruritania and Urbitania is wicked. And here is an 'induction': My dog likes chasing cats; my neighbour's dog likes chasing cats; therefore it is likely that most dogs like chasing cats.

deep/shallow
The opposing terms are mostly used of water or some other liquid, with 'deep' meaning 'of great depth' and 'shallow' meaning 'of little depth'. ('Shallow brooks murmur most, deep silent slide away', Sir Philip Sidney, *The Arcadia*.) By extension,

both words can apply to non-material things, such as 'deep' love or 'shallow' remarks (ones lacking any serious thought or perception). English is lucky having 'shallow' as the opposite to 'deep', since some languages simply have to say the equivalent of 'not deep' (e.g. French *profond*, 'deep' and *peu profond*, 'shallow', Italian similarly *profondo* and *poco profondo*). The word itself is probably related to 'shoal'.

deep structure/surface structure
In so-called 'generative grammar', as formulated by the American linguist Noam Chomsky, 'deep structure' is the 'real' underlying structure or meaning of a sentence, as against its 'surface structure', which is its grammatical arrangement when written out on paper. For example, the 'surface structures' of these two sentences are identical: 'Jim expected Joy to read his letter' and 'Jim persuaded Joy to read his letter'. Here the 'surface structure' is noun + verb + noun + infinitive + possessive adjective + noun. The 'deep structure' of the two sentences is different, however, since although the first can be transformed as follows: 'Jim expected that Joy would read his letter', the second cannot (you can't say: 'Jim persuaded that Joy would read his letter'). So what appears on the surface may mask a hidden grammatical snag or conceal a hidden meaning.

de facto/de jure
In law, something that is 'de facto' is known to exist, whether legally or not, such as a country's 'de facto' political regime. 'Du jure', however, means 'by right', 'legally', such as the recognition that is extended 'de jure' to the new regime. The Latin phrases literally mean 'from the fact' and 'from the law'.

defecate see **urinate**

defence see **prosecution**

defend see **attack**[2]

defendant see **plaintiff**

definiendum see **definiens**

definiens/definiendum
These two terms belong to the art of lexicography, so have a rightful place in this dictionary. They look imposing, but they are quite straightforward: the 'definiens' is the word or words used to define or explain the meaning of another word, while the 'definiendum' is the word or phrase that needs to be defined. Thus in this (simplified) dictionary entry, 'young goat' is the 'definiens' and 'kid' the 'definiendum': '**kid** *n.* young goat'. (And in this sentence you have just read, there are actually two 'definientia' to define two 'definienda'.) The Latin words means respectively 'defining' and 'thing to be defined'.

definite article/indefinite article
In languages that have them, these are the respective grammatical terms for the words corresponding to 'the' (such as French *le*, *la*, *les*) and to 'a' or 'an' (French *un*, *une*). 'Definite' since 'the' is used to denote a particular noun, and 'indefinite' since 'a' does not specify which is meant. 'Article' since this is the literal translation of Latin *articulus* which was itself, in classical times, a translation of Greek *arthros*, literally 'joint' (and the term used for the Greek 'definite article').

deflation see **inflation**

deictic/elenctic
'Deictic' means literally 'showing' in Greek, and is the term used in logic to denote something proved by direct argument. 'Elenctic', on the other hand, means literally 'refuting', and denotes the refuting of an argument by proving the opposite (usually by means of deductive reasoning: see **deduction/induction**).

deist/theist
A 'deist' is someone who, although acknowledging the existence of God, holds that religion is based on reason rather than divine revelation. A 'theist', by contrast, is someone whose belief in God is based on both reason *and* divine revelation. The

two theological terms were synonymous until the eighteenth century, when they were differentiated in such a way that the 'deist' was regarded as a kind of 'negative' believer, and a 'theist' as a 'positive' one. (See also **agnostic/gnostic**.)

de jure see **de facto**

dele/stet
These two opposite terms belong to printing and proof-correcting, so that a 'dele' is a sign (in the form of a letter 'd' written with a flourish) denoting that what is marked should be deleted, while 'stet' (marked with a dotted line under the relevant text) means that what has been previously deleted should now be left as it was, and should be printed. The words are straight from Latin and mean respectively 'obliterate' and 'let it stand'. 'Dele' (which is pronounced 'deely') was earlier known as 'deleatur' ('let it be obliterated'), and may have partly developed as an abbreviation of this.

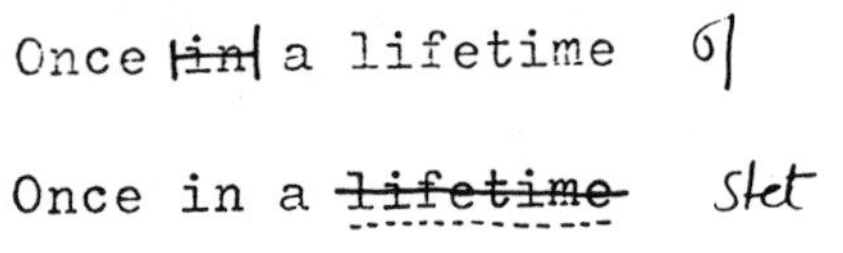

delivery/collection
The two words are familiar from postboxes and Post Office literature (especially in the sign that appears in a post office window), indicating respectively the times when mail is 'delivered' to addresses and when it is 'collected' (for sorting and despatch) from the postbox. English uses 'collection' in this sense where many other languages use a word based on a verb such as 'empty' 'lift up', describing the basic action of the postman who clears the box. Thus 'collection' in French is *levée*, in Italian is *levata*, in German *Leerung* ('emptying') and in Russian *vyemka* ('taking out'). English sees the postman as gathering all the letters from different postboxes (and originally from houses as well).

demand see **supply**

demand deposit/time deposit
In the world of banking, a 'demand deposit' is one from which withdrawals can be made without notice. A 'time deposit', however, requires advance notice, or a particular date to be specified. (Sometimes 'time deposit' can also mean that a deposit has to be made for a particular length of time.) Both types operate in a deposit account (see **current account/deposit account**).

Democrat/Republican
Although not distinctly 'left' and 'right' in the same way as the two main British political parties (see **Conservative/Labour**), the American 'Republican' party is really more right of centre than the 'Democratic' party, and is more the party of 'big business', whereas many 'Democrats' are 'small' men. The 'Democratic' party, too, has much of its support among working people and Black voters, whereas many 'Republicans' are found among farmers and in the capitalist world of the big cities. 'Democrats' thus favour social reform and cooperation between nations, while 'Republicans' support a discernible government role in the country's economic and social life. In short, to some extent each party lives up to its name in a modified sense, with the 'Democrats' putting the emphasis on the people (Greek *demos*) and the 'Republicans' more concerned with the role of the state (Latin *res publica*).

demotic/hieratic
These two terms relate to different types of hieroglyphics. When 'demotic', the hieroglyphics were simplified, and were used in Ancient Egypt by the ordinary literate person who was not a member of the priesthood. The term thus literally means 'of the people' (compare the entry above). 'Hieratic' hieroglyphics were more complex, and were a cursive form of writing used by the priests. The name here comes from Greek *hieros*, 'holy', 'sacred', from which 'hieroglyphics' itself comes (as literally 'holy carving'). For another use of 'demotic', see the next entry.

Demotic/Katharevusa
Here the terms relate to the Modern Greek language. 'Demotic' is the spoken form of Modern Greek, now increasingly used in standard literature. By contrast, 'Katharevusa' is a now much less frequent form of Modern Greek, formerly used for literature (not the spoken language). It derived from the Attic dialect of Ancient Greek, and included many archaic features. 'Demotic' means literally 'of the people' (see the entry above), and 'Katharevusa' derives from Greek *katharos*, 'pure'.

denominator see **numerator**

denotation/connotation
The difference here is in the verbs 'denote' and 'connote'. To 'denote' something is to mean it directly or explicitly; to 'connote' it is to give its meaning indirectly or allusively. To put it rather formally: the 'denotation' of the word 'dog' is the group of animals that belong to this family, while the 'connotation' of 'home' is a combination of security and comfort.

deny see **confirm**

departure see **arrival**

deposit account see **current account**

depression see **elevation**

descend see **ascend**

descriptive see **prescriptive**

destructive see **constructive**

devil see **angel**

devise see **bequest**

dexter see **sinister**

dextrorse see **sinistrorse**

diachronic see **synchronic**

dialect/accent
A 'dialect' is the form of a standard language spoken in a particular geographical area or by members of a particular social or occupational group. As such, it will have its distinctive vocabulary, grammar and pronunciation, differing from the norm. A distinctive example of a 'dialect' in Britain is the Scottish form of English, as seen, for instance, in the writings of Robert Burns, e.g.

> Fair fa' your honest sonsie face,
> Great chieftain o' the puddin'-race!
> Aboon them a' ye tak your place,
> Painch, tripe, or thairm.
> (*To a Haggis*)

An 'accent' is the pronunciation of a language, whether the standard ('accepted') form or a 'dialect'. One can thus have an 'accent' that is neutral, Cockney, Scottish, Oxford, foreign, or the like. We all thus speak with some sort of 'accent', but we do not all speak a 'dialect'. The term itself literally means 'conversation' (compare 'dialogue').

dial telephone/press-button telephone
The 'dial telephone' is the old familiar sort, with a dial numbered anticlockwise from 0 to 9, and with the number obtained by rotating this clockwise with the finger ('dialling'). In the mid-1980s, such telephones began to be rapidly replaced by the 'press-button telephone', where the figures are arranged in a 'bank' (usually, in four rows of three, from top to bottom), and with the number obtained by pressing the successive buttons that correspond to the figures. (Moreover, such telephones are found as 'one-piece', with earpiece and mouthpiece combined in a single instrument, or 'two-piece', where the receiver rests vertically on a cradle.) What is interesting is that people still talk of 'dialling' a number on a 'press-button telephone', even though it has no dial (by definition, a 'dial' must be circular), and even in telephone directories ('phone books') telephone users are given information about 'dialling' certain numbers. Many users still have 'dial telephones', of course, but soon there will be few left and a new verb will be needed to refer to the buttons.

(Perhaps 'press' is the obvious choice, although 'key in' or just 'key' is increasingly heard.)

diastolic/systolic
These are medical terms, and relate to the function of the heart and to blood pressure. The peak pressure of blood in the arteries occurs when the heart contracts, and is known as 'systolic' pressure (Greek *systellein*, 'to contract'). The lowest pressure is the 'diastolic' pressure (Greek *diastellein*, 'to expand'), and this occurs when the heart relaxes. (Doctors express blood pressure as a double reading in such a form as '130/80', where '130' represents 'systolic' pressure, and '80' represents 'diastolic' pressure. The figures represent the height of a column of mercury in millimetres: hence the thermometer-like device on the instrument with which the doctor measures a person's blood pressure, the impressively named sphygmomanometer.) See also **vein/artery**, **atrium/ventricle**, and if necessary **expand/contract**.

diatonic see **chromatic**

dicotyledon see **monocotyledon**

dictionary/encyclopaedia
At their most basic, a 'dictionary' gives the spelling, definition and (often) origin of a word or phrase, while an 'encyclopaedia' gives information. However, both are normally arranged alphabetically, and a 'dictionary' can certainly include a good deal of information, especially if it includes proper names. There are also 'encyclopaedic dictionaries' which are a combination of both. So what is the difference? The answer is roughly as follows: 'encyclopaedias' usually give much more extensive information than 'dictionaries' do; 'dictionaries' deal primarily with definitions, while 'encyclopaedias' contain articles dealing with topics; although 'encyclopaedias' may give the literal meaning and origin of a word, they usually do not, and instead they write about the topic or subject that the word denotes. Or to simplify, 'dictionaries' are about words; 'encyclopaedias' are about things. But there are many exceptions. (How about this present 'dictionary'? Perhaps it is more of an 'encyclopaedia', given its range of subjects and its way of writing about them? Yet surely it is hardly what we think of as an 'encyclopaedia'.) Finally, perhaps an actual example of the treatment of a word in a 'dictionary' and an 'encyclopaedia' may help, for the sake of comparison:

> **oxlip**/|oks |lip/*n* a Eurasian primula (*Primula elatior*) similar to the cowslip, but unscented and having larger flowers [(assumed) ME *oxeslippe*, fr OE *oxanslyppe*, lit., ox dung, fr *oxa* ox + *slypa*, *slyppe* paste – more at SLIP (cf COWSLIP)] (*Longman Dictionary of the English Language*, 1984)

> **Oxlip**, *Primula elatior*, a handsome plant with a very limited distribution in woodlands in the eastern part of England, mainly near Saffron Walden. It is intermediate in character between the primrose and the cowslip, but may be distinguished from the rather common hybrid between these two plants by the absence of folds in the throat of the tubular flower. (*Everyman's Encyclopaedia*, 1978)

different see **same**

differential calculus/integral calculus

'Differential calculus' is an algebraic procedure to find the curve of a line from the area or the slope from a line. 'Integral calculus' is the converse, and is used to find the area under a curve or the line from the slope. Both methods use special types of graphs.

digestif see **aperitif**

digital see **analogue**

dihedral/anhedral
The two terms relate to aerodynamics and aircraft design. On an aeroplane, the 'dihedral' is the angle formed between an upward- or downward-sloping wing and

the horizontal, whereas the 'anhedral' is the angle between a downward-sloping wing (only) and the horizontal. The angle at which an aircraft's wings slope is important for ensuring its stability, and has to be calculated accordingly in its design.

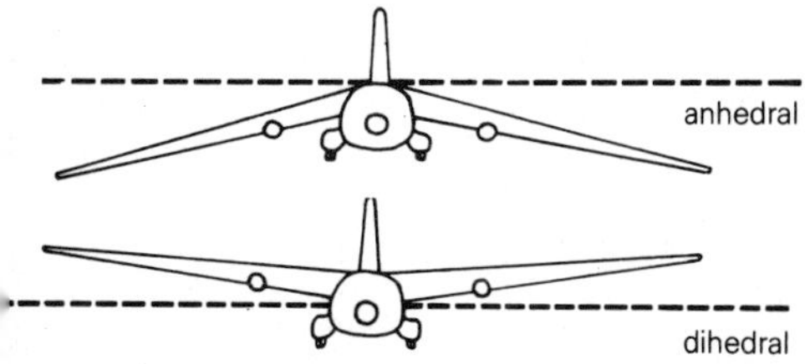

dim see **bright**

diminish see **augment**

diminuendo see **crescendo**

diminutive/augmentative
In language, a 'diminutive' is the form of a word that indicates the object's small size and often implies affection or triviality. It can either occur by a suffix on the word (as 'statuette'), or by an actual shortened form, as commonly with names (as 'Mike' for 'Michael', or even 'peke' for 'Pekinese'). The suffix '-y' or '-ie' is also commonly used to make the 'diminutive' of a name (such as 'Johnny' for 'John', and 'Annie' for 'Anne'). An 'augmentative' is the opposite, indicating a large size and often implying an awkwardness or ugliness. They are not so common in English, although some words ending in '-ard' have adopted this 'augmentative' suffix from the French, as in 'bastard', 'coward' and 'wizard', and similarly in words ending in '-oon' deriving from the Italian 'augmentative' suffix '*-one*', so that 'balloon' is a large 'ball' and 'bassoon' is a large 'bass' instrument.

DIN see **ASA**

dinner see **lunch**

Dionysian see **Apollonian**

direct[1]/indirect
Apart from the everyday senses (a 'direct' route, an 'indirect' route), the terms have one or two more specialized uses. In grammar, for example, 'direct' speech denotes the exact words a person says ('I'll come tomorrow'), while 'indirect' speech reports the spoken words with due grammatical changes ('He said that he would come the following day'). Then in football, a 'direct' free kick is one awarded (as a penalty) so that a direct shot at the goal can be made, while an 'indirect' free kick requires the ball to be passed to another player before a shot at goal can be made. (Neither of these is a so called 'penalty kick', which is a free kick awarded for an offence in the penalty area.) Again, in the financial world, 'direct' tax is tax that is levied directly from the person or organization that pays it, while 'indirect' tax is levied on goods and services and is paid indirectly by the person or organization buying the goods or using the services. However, not every 'direct' usage has an 'indirect' counterpart, and the 'direct' method of teaching a language, for example (with minimal use of the learner's mother tongue), has no 'indirect' method to oppose it, nor formerly were there any 'indirect' grant schools to contrast with 'direct' grant schools (receiving grants direct from the Department of Education and Science, not from the local education authority). Sometimes, too, the opposite of 'direct' is another term altogether. Compare, for instance, **AC/DC**, and see the next two entries below.

direct[2]/retrograde
In astronomy, 'direct' is used of a heavenly body that moves from west to east on the celestial sphere, as planets generally do. 'Retrograde', therefore, is used of a body, such as a satellite, that moves in a direction opposite to that of a larger neighbouring body. Phoebe, for example, the satellite of Saturn, has a motion that is 'retrograde' to that of its parent planet, whose motion round the Sun is 'direct'. ('Retrograde' literally means 'going backwards'.)

direct access/sequential access
In the language of computers, 'direct access' (also known as 'random access') is a method of reading data from a file without reading through the whole file from the beginning. This is made possible by a 'direct access' memory, also often known simply as a 'RAM' ('random access memory'). 'Sequential access' requires the data to be read (in sequence) from the beginning of the file.

director see **producer**

dirty see **clean**

disc/tape
See **record/cassette**.

disc brake/drum brake
Most brakes on motor vehicles are so-called 'friction' brakes, and these are divided into 'disc brakes' and 'drum brakes'. When a 'disc brake' is applied, two calliper-operated pads rub against a flat disc attached to the hub of the wheel. By contrast, a 'drum brake' is one that presses brake shoes against the inside walls of the brake drum when it is applied, with the brake drum itself being a cast-iron drum attached to the hub of the wheel. 'Disc brakes' came to be installed in standard cars much later than 'drum brakes', and were first exploited in racing cars, where in turn they had been adapted from the 'disc brakes' used on large aircraft when landing.

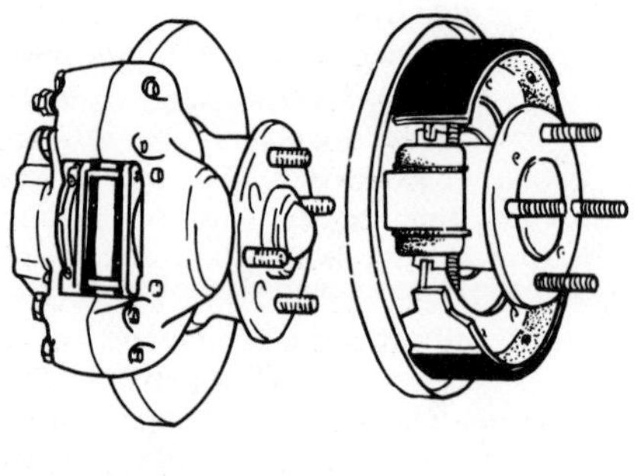

discord see **concord**

discount/premium
On the Stock Exchange, 'discount' is used for a deduction made in the market price of a security for some reason, e.g. when investors price shares at a 'discount' to their theoretical net value. The opposite of this is 'premium', used for a sum paid in addition to the market value of an asset (by comparison with another).

disc wheel/wire wheel
These are two contrasting types of wheel on motor vehicles. A 'disc wheel' has a round pressed disc in place of spokes, while a 'wire wheel' has the rim of the wheel held to the hub by wire spokes. 'Wire wheels' are (or were) mainly found on sports cars.

dissonance see (1) **assonance** (2) **consonance**

distaff side see **spear side**

distal/proximal
The two terms are used in anatomy to describe the position of a muscle, bone, limb or the like. 'Distal' means 'farthest from the centre' (or point of attachment or origin), while 'proximal' means 'nearest to the centre', or closest to the point of attachment. For example, talking of the arm, the fingers are 'distal' to the body or trunk, while the shoulder is 'proximal' to it. The two words are now also used by dentists to describe the relative positions of teeth, and themselves are nineteenth-century creations, with 'distal' based on 'distant'.

dit/dah
The two little words are sometimes used as verbal equivalents for the 'dot' and 'dash' symbols of Morse code, so that letter 'C', for example (- · - ·), is read out as 'dah dit dah dit', and 'SOS' comes out as 'dit dit dit, dah dah dah, dit dit dit'. See also **dot/dash** itself.

diurnal/nocturnal
The adjectives mean respectively 'of the day' and 'of the night', and have mostly technical or scientific applications, so that

'diurnal' animals are ones that are active in the day (like man), while 'nocturnal' ones are active at night (such as hedgehogs). The words can also have a rather stilted or poetic general sense, however, such as Wordsworth's 'earth's diurnal course' and Thomas Hardy's 'some nocturnal blackness' (though even that he linked up with hedgehogs). The origins of the words lie in Latin *dies*, 'day' and *nox*, genitive *noctis*, 'night', with the second half of each term as in 'journal'.

diverbium see **canticum**

divergent/convergent
The two terms here belong to psychology. 'Divergent' thinking is thinking in a way in which several different ideas or solutions are produced from a single idea of problem, otherwise (loosely) a 'fertile imagination' or 'flow of ideas' (the answer to an author's prayer). 'Convergent' thinking is therefore the opposite, and is a type of thinking in which an overall or common concept is obtained from several divergent sources (perhaps the answer to an inventor's prayer). If you are good at IQ tests, you are probably a 'convergent' thinker, while the creative person uses 'divergent' thinking. In ophthalmology, a 'divergent' squint is one in which the eyes turn outwards ('walleye') and indicates long sight; a 'convergent' squint has the eyes turning inwards ('crosseye') and is a sign of shortsightedness. In mathematics, a 'divergent' series has no limit (e.g. 2, 4, 6, 8), while a 'convergent' series tends towards a limit (e.g. 1, ½, ¼, ⅛).

divide see **multiply**

dock leaf see **stinging nettle**

doe see **buck**

doff see **don**

dog[1]/bitch
Although 'dog' can be used of a male or female animal, 'bitch' is used exclusively of the female, and in this context (say, a discussion on breeding) 'dog' will mean the male. The words are sometimes used of other animals, so that a 'dog' fox is a male one (although the female is not a 'bitch' but a vixen). Both terms, too, are used as contemptuous jargon for a man or a woman ('dirty dog', 'stupid bitch'). 'Bitch' is a pure Old English word, perhaps related to 'back' (although not to French *biche*, 'doe'). For a further consideration of 'dog', see the next entry.

dog[2]/cat
The two animals are the two most popular domestic pets in Britain and many countries. (In Britain in 1986, for example, there were believed to be about six million 'dogs' as pets and more than five million 'cats'.) Yet although virtually equating in popularity as pets, there are distinct contrasts between the two, which may perhaps sometimes reflect the character or nature of their respective owners. A 'dog' is essentially a 'public' animal, enjoying activity and 'conversation' in company. A 'cat', on the other hand, is a private creature, well able to tolerate (and even prefer) its own company. A 'dog', too, is by nature a dependent animal, often with its whole life and every action subordinate to the wishes of its master or mistress. A 'cat', however, although often glad of the patronage and attention provided by its owner (especially at mealtimes), is almost entirely independent of him, doing what it wants when it wants. (A 'dog' waits for the outer door to open so that it can go for a walk with its owner; a 'cat' simply wants to be released to its outside territory on its own.) 'Dogs', again, are in a sense very much male creatures, while 'cats' are feminine. Compare, for instance, the bluff, business-like way in which a 'dog' covers its excreta with vigorous kicks of the hind legs, while the 'cat' does likewise fastidiously and carefully with its front paws. Without being sexist, it is thus possible to see a 'dog' as similar to a boy (it likes action, sport, noise, excitement, hearty meals, and much that is physical). A 'cat', by contrast, is more girl-like (it is particular and delicate in its habits, enjoys self-grooming, dislikes loud or harsh noises, is relatively 'low profile' and even

self-effacing). Finally, to mention the fairly obvious, a 'dog' is a daytime animal, quite content to sleep while its owner sleeps at night. The 'cat', though, is (or can be) a creature of the night, often sleeping by day. Small wonder that the two are often openly antagonistic to each other, with the hostile initiative often taken, typically enough, by the 'dog'. And when it is raining 'cats and dogs', it is really pouring. The saying may echo a medieval belief that 'dogs' were linked with winds, and 'cats' with storms, so that the 'cat' symbolizes the rain and the 'dog' its violence as it lashes down. But domestic 'dog' and 'cat' *can* live in harmony!

don/doff
The two verbs are now somewhat dated equivalents for 'put on' and 'take off', so that one can 'don' a coat or 'doff' one's hat. The words originate in the phrases 'do on' and 'do off', and in Shakespeare's time were even written 'd'on' and 'd'off'.

don'ts see **do's**

Doric see **Attic**

dormant see **active**[1]

dorsal/ventral
In anatomy, the two terms are sometimes used as alternatives to 'anterior' and 'posterior', since they literally mean 'back' and 'abdomen'. 'Dorsal', thus, relates to the back or spinal part of the body, and 'ventral' to the front, or belly. In zoology, too, a 'dorsal' fin is one on a fish's back, while a 'ventral' fin is underneath it. The contrasting terms have almost exclusive scientific usage, and are hardly ever found in general writing.

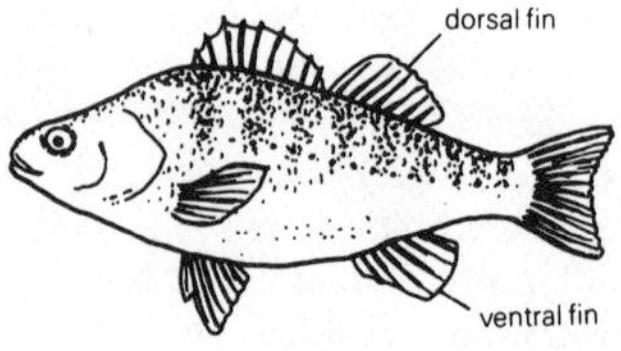

do's/don'ts
Taken as a phrase, the 'do's and don'ts' of a thing or situation are a summary of what one should or should not do, often at a fairly informal but none the less meaningful level. There are usually four or five of each, with the 'don'ts' frequently given first. This is because doing something wrong can cause more serious consequences and damage than doing it the right way. They are often found in instruction manuals for mechanical appliances or in directions for the use of some piece of specialized equipment, with 'do' or 'don't' printed in bold type, e.g. '**Don't** store the cassette in a warm place; **Don't** attempt to disassemble the plastic case; **Do** protect the cassette against dust; **Do** store it in its protective packet'. The expression itself seems to have originated early in the twentieth century, and a little book was published in 1902 called 'Golf do's and don'ts'.

dot/dash
'Dots' and 'dashes' are the two alternating symbols used in the Morse code, with the 'dot' a written or printed point (or a short 'blip' of sound or light) and the 'dash' a line (or longer emission of sound or light). The idea of using the two symbols was the brilliantly simple one selected by the inventor of the code that bears his name, the American artist Samuel Morse, who died in 1872. His own surname in Morse is an elegant combination of the six 'dots' and six 'dashes' that comprise it: —— ——— ·—· ··· ·

double see **single**[1]

double scull see **pair-oar**

doves/hawks
'Doves' are peaceful birds, and 'hawks' aggressive attackers. Hence the adoption of their names for the two possible sides in a dispute, with the 'doves' advocating a conciliatory settlement (and no war), while the 'hawks' take a belligerent attitude and demand vigorous action. The respective terms originated quite recently, at the time of the Cuban missile crisis of

1962. As the *Saturday Evening Post* for 8 December reported that year: 'The hawks favored an air strike to eliminate the Cuban missile bases', while 'The doves opposed the air strikes and favored a blockade'. (In the event, the 'doves' won and Khrushchev was obliged to back down.) Notice the close comparison here between the 'hawks' and the diving aircraft, while the 'doves' are not airborne at all but are on the surface of the water (echoes of Noah's ark, perhaps).

down see (1) **across** (2) **up**

downbeat see **upbeat**

downer see **upper**[1]

downstage see **upstage**

downstairs see **upstairs**

downstream see **upstream**

downwind see **upwind**

drag see **thrust**

drake see **duck**

drawbridge see **swingbridge**

drink see **food**

drive/putt
In golf, a 'drive' is a long shot, especially one played from the tee with a 'driver' (a club specially effective for such shots). A 'putt', by contrast, is a short, gentle stroke, designed to send the ball into the hole (or towards it) on a 'putting' green. A 'drive' is thus a stroke made at the start of a game or 'hole', and a 'putt' one made at the end of it. 'Drive' here implies 'forceful move', while the term 'putt' is simply an alteration of 'put' (fittingly originating in Scotland, the home of golf).

drones/workers
The two main types of bees in a hive. The 'drones' are male. They have no sting and gather no honey and have the sole function of mating with the queen. (They gave their name to the human 'drones' who are parasites and live off the work of others.) The 'workers' are female, and are the bees who, as their name implies, do all the work, including the gathering of honey and the carrying out of protective duties (hence their sting). 'Drones' are not so called because they 'drone', but the other way round – the buzzing or humming sound known as 'droning' is derived from the bees. See also **bee/wasp**.

drop see **hoist**[1]

drug see **placebo**

drum/tub
The two words describe the two types of top-loading washing machine. 'Drum' machines are rather like front loaders (see **front loader/top loader**) but have an opening for the washing to be put in and taken out in the side of the drum. 'Tub' machines are closest to the original washing tub (hence their name), and their chief advantage is that clothes can be added during the washing process. They are expensive to run, however, as they use a lot of hot water.

drum brake see **disc brake**

drunk/sober
Put basically, being 'drunk' is being intoxicated (i.e. poisoned) by alcohol, usually to such an extent that one's faculties are impaired. But the many colourful comparisons show that it is a state of supreme happiness and irresponsibility to some who become thus: 'drunk' as a lord (as a fiddler, as a fish, as a boiled owl). Being 'sober' (as a judge, but not much else) means being in solemn and serious command of one's faculties, not having touched any alcohol. Relatively, however, 'sober' suggests 'dull', 'unimaginative', or implies the absence of what can make being 'drunk' an attraction.

dry see (1) **sweet**[1] (2) **wet**

dry iron/steam iron
These are the two main types of domestic electric iron. The 'dry iron' is the basic sort, and is both lighter and cheaper than a 'steam iron' and also less bulky. The 'steam iron', using its spray or 'bursts' of hot steam, is more versatile, however, especially as it can act as a 'dry iron' as well. Apart from this, it is simpler to use, since the ironer has no need to worry about the right degree of dampness. Likewise it gives a better finish to what it irons, especially seams. However, it has one disadvantage: if it uses hard water, scale can build up inside, impairing its proper functioning and effectiveness. So the basic difference is really that of **wet/dry**, as one iron uses water and the other does not.

DSK see **QWERTY**

dualism/monism
'Dualism', in philosophy, is the theory that considers reality to consist of two independent and fundamental principles, typically, mind and matter (see **mind/matter**). 'Monism', by contrast, is the doctrine that reality consists of only one substance, that is, either mind or matter. In a general sense, 'dualism' is what this dictionary is about.

duchess see **duke**

duck/drake
'Duck' is the word for the bird in general, with 'drake' used exclusively for the male. (The two words are not related.) The pleasant pastime of 'ducks and drakes', or the skimming of flat stones over a still surface of water, derives its name from the fact that the birds (of either sex) are similarly associated with movement over water.

duke/duchess
A 'duchess' is rather more than simply the wife of a 'duke', although she obviously can be this, since some 'duchesses' are in effect 'dukes' in their own right (although called by the feminine equivalent of the title). However, all British 'duchesses' at present are the wives or widows of a 'duke'. The feminine form derives from French (as do similar ranks of nobility such as 'countess' and 'viscountess'). 'Duchess' is also a slang word for 'wife' ('I'll have a word with the duchess'), hence the Cockney term 'dutch' for a wife, as a short form of this. (Albert Chevalier popularized the word with his song *My Old Dutch.*) 'Duke' does not have a similar usage, except as a nickname for a smart or showy man, or a 'champion' in some way (such as the American jazz composer and pianist, Duke Ellington, whose real forenames were Edward Kennedy).

dumb see **deaf**

duodecimal see **decimal**

duplex see **simplex**

durable goods/perishables
'Durable goods' (or 'durables') are ones that are fairly longlasting and need to be replaced only infrequently, such as cars, refrigerators and cookers. 'Perishables', on the other hand, have a short life and will decay or 'go off' soon. Most foodstuffs (such as fruit, vegetables, butter and eggs) are therefore 'perishables'. The two terms need to be used when such things are marketed, stored or transported. Economists, too, are interested in the way consumer spending varies for each type of goods.

dusk see **dawn**

Dutch auction see **auction**

dwarf see **giant**

dynamic/static
The application of both terms is largely technical and scientific, so that 'dynamics', for example, is the branch of mechanics that deals with the forces that cause bodies to move, while 'statics' studies forces that produce a state of equilibrium among solid bodies (as for a pendulum or a rope and pulley). In computer jargon, a 'dynamic' memory is one that needs to have its contents

updated or refreshed from time to time, while a 'static' memory does not need this, and has devices that will ensure the indefinite retention of stored information. At their most basic, the two terms relate respectively to things that are moving (Greek *dynamis*, 'power') and things that are standing still (Greek *statikos*, 'causing to stand'). Compare **mobile/stabile**.

dysphemism see **euphemism**

Ee

eared seal/earless seal
The descriptive distinctions are self-explanatory. The 'eared seal' belongs to the family *Otariidae*, and apart from its visible earflaps has fairly well developed hind limbs with which it can progress over land. The 'earless seal' belongs to the family *Phocidae*, and has no external earflaps and only rudimentary hind limbs, as well as a body covering of hair. The latter is the 'true' seal and the one seen around the coast of Britain, for example.

earless seal see **eared seal**

early/late
The interesting thing about these opposite words is that they often apply to a subjective state, so that one man's 'early' can be another man's 'late'. ('I don't like to go to bed too late' really doesn't say very much, except that I like to have proper sleep, or that I enjoy relaxing in bed before sleeping.) There is always, however, an implied comparison, so that if a train arrives 'late' it arrives after its scheduled time, and if I arrive 'early' at the bank, I have to stand and wait for it to open. 'Early' often has a suggestion of correctness or enterprise, while 'late' can imply laziness or apathy. It is the 'early' bird that catches the worm, after all, and 'early' to bed and 'early' to rise are said (without much justification) to result in good health, wealth, and wisdom. (Although compare the simple nuisance of 'too early' with the awful finality of 'too late'!)

earned income/unearned income
'Earned income' is what we are paid for our regular work or job. 'Unearned income' sounds like some sort of handsome gift, but it is actually taxman's talk for income from savings and investment, otherwise income from capital. Some people object to the term, saying that this kind of income is not 'unearned' at all, since they have worked hard to build up their savings. But until a better term is invented, we will have to live with it.

earth/air
In ancient and medieval cosmology, 'earth' and 'air' were two of the opposing elements that, together with the two elements **fire/water**, constituted the universe. In a later contrast, 'earth' was the name of the world (of land and sea, see **land/sea**) as distinct from the (material) heaven or sky. See also **heaven/hell**.

east/west
'East is East, and West is West, and never the twain shall meet', wrote Kipling, and sometimes it certainly seems like it, especially when 'East' means the communist world and 'West' the capitalist (see **communism/capitalism**). The contrast between the two points of the compass is usually quite sharp. The sun rises in the 'east', for example, but sets in the 'west'. The 'east' thus symbolizes the dawn, and the 'west' the dusk. In Britain, a city's 'East' End is often its poor district, unlike its rich 'West' End. This was long true in London. In other cities, a different distinction has developed: 'East' Beirut is Christian, while 'West' Beirut is Muslim. It is perhaps unfortunate that in English the words are so alike, since a carelessly written 'east' can be taken for a 'west'. A similar distinction exists between the various derivatives, such as eastern/western, eastwards/westwards, easterly/westerly, and so on. (But see also the next entry for a different contrast.)

Easter see **Christmas**

easting/northing
In map reading, an 'easting' is the distance eastward in longitude from a given reference point, and is expressed by the first half of a map grid reference. The 'northing' is thus the similar distance north in latitude from this point, and appears as the second half of the grid reference. Such references can be accurate to 100 metres on a standard Ordnance Survey map with a scale of two centimetres to one kilometre (1:50 000). The necessary figures for the 'eastings' and 'northings' appear in the margins of the maps, and so enable the particular site to be given as a six-figure reference that is unique to it. For example, the reference for Horseshoe Hole Farm in north-west Norfolk, near King's Lynn, is 557 241. Here '557' is the 'easting' and '241' the 'northing', with the 'easting' read off from the western margin of the map, and the 'northing' worked out from the southern edge. The terms themselves originated on mariners' charts in the seventeenth century. See also **latitude/longitude**.

easy/tight
Apart from the everyday senses of the words (shoes with an 'easy' fit or a 'tight' fit), the terms are used in economics. Here an 'easy' market is one with a low demand in which prices tend to fall. A 'tight' market is the opposite: one with excess demand and with prices tending to rise. In general, 'easy' money is readily obtainable, too, and when money is 'tight' it is hard to come by.

eating apple see **cooking apple**

ebb[1]/flood
An 'ebb' tide is one that is receding, or is at its lowest point; a 'flood' tide is one that is rising, or is at its highest point. Low water, is thus an 'ebb' tide at its lowest point, and high water is the peak of a 'flood' tide. The word 'ebb' is related to 'of' and so to 'off', since both are of the same origin. The idea is of a tide that is 'running off'.

ebb[2]/flow
In general, water that is 'ebbing' is receding, or getting shallower, while water that is 'flowing' is advancing or becoming deeper. Both words can be used metaphorically, although 'ebb' is more commonly used than 'flow' in this way. A person's strength can thus 'ebb' or become weaker, but not 'flow'. Together, 'ebb and flow' is sometimes used to denote an unstable or vacillating state, or a ceaselessly changing one, such as the 'ebb and flow' of traffic in a city, or the 'ebb and flow' of one's daily life. 'Flow' and 'flood' are related words. See the previous entry.

ebony/ivory
There is a frequent implied and certainly visual contrast between the two words and the substances themselves, with 'ebony' a hard black wood, and 'ivory' the hard white substance found in the tusks of elephants. Both, too, are seen in piano keys, and both substances are used for contrasting effect in furniture design and ornamentation. In its issue for 30 November 1922, for example, *The Times* reported that the newly discovered Tutankhamun's tomb in Egypt contained 'a stool of ebony inlaid with ivory'. In the Bible, too, one can read how merchants brought (among other riches) 'horns of ivory and ebony' to the city of Tyrus (Ezekiel 27:15). It may even be possible that the present spelling of the word 'ebony' was modelled on that of 'ivory'. In modern transferred usage, as a further contrast, 'ebony' has come to mean 'black-skinned', and the magazine *Ebony* is the largest magazine for blacks in the world. Somewhat confusingly, a term 'black ivory' arose in the nineteenth century to denote African slaves regarded as objects of commerce, and the expression appeared in the title of the novel by the writer of stories for boys, R. M. Ballantyne, *Black Ivory: Adventures Among Slavers* (1873). Finally, the continuing contrast between the two was popularized in 1982 when the pop song 'Ebony and Ivory', sung by the black singer Stevie Wonder and the white singer Paul McCartney, became the number one hit. (The visual element was

doubly emphasized here, since apart from the skin colour of the singers, the song was sung by Wonder at the black and white piano keyboard.) See also **black/white**.

eccentric/concentric
'Eccentric' circles are ones that may overlap but that do not have the same centre. 'Concentric' circles, on the other hand, although not necessarily the same size, will have exactly the same centre.

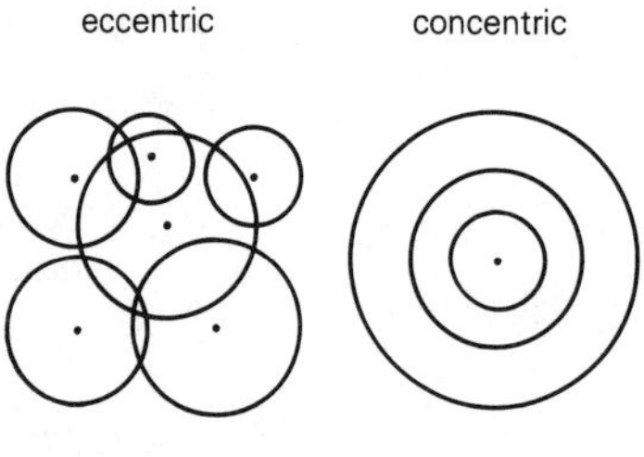

ectoplasm see **endoplasm**

edh see **thorn**

effect see **cause**

e.g./i.e.
The two common abbreviations have contrasting uses. 'E.g.' (from Latin *exempli gratia*, 'for sake of an example') refers to the words that follow, while 'i.e.' (Latin *id est*, 'that is') refers to the words that have just been mentioned. 'E.g.' thus introduces examples, while 'i.e.' gives an explanation. Here they are in action, so that the difference can be seen:
Jim is keen on martial arts, 'e.g.' judo, karate and kendo.
Jim is keen on martial arts, 'i.e.' the combative sports or methods of self-defence that came to us from the East.

ego/id
The two Latin terms ('I' and 'it') derive from the teaching of Freud, which held that a person's 'ego' is his conscious mind, the part of him that is aware of the environment, while his 'id' is his unconscious mind, full of primitive urges and instincts. Freud taught that a person's 'ego' tries to mediate between the world and his 'id', to make the world meet the 'id's' desires. He also contrasted the 'ego' and the 'id' with the 'superego', which he held to be that part of the unconscious mind that acted as a conscience for the 'id'. In popular parlance, however, 'ego' simply means 'morale', 'self-image', and there is no implied contrast with 'id', which therefore has no popular usage.

egotistic see **altruistic**

egress see **ingress**

Eights Week see **May Week**

either/or
Taken individually, both words indicate a choice, with 'either' preceding the first choice and 'or' following it (and any subsequent choice). In this way, there is no difference in meaning ('take either a cup or a mug' means the same as 'take a cup or a mug'). But as a joint expression, 'either/or' implies a compulsory choice between only two things: 'It was an either/or situation: either we attacked them or they attacked us.' It is possible the phrase may owe something to the Danish equivalent *enten-eller*, which was the title of a book by the Danish philosopher Kierkegaard. Either way, the choice is a binding one. Compare **neither/nor**.

Electra complex see **Oedipus complex**

electric see **electronic**

electricity see **gas**

electron/positron
An 'electron' is an elementary particle of matter that carries a single negative charge. It is a constituent of an atom, orbiting round the nucleus, and is the cause of an electric current. A 'positron' carries a single positive charge, and is of the same weight as a proton. It is of transient existence, produced by certain nuclear disintegrations. When a 'positron'

collides with an 'electron', they mutually disintegrate, because the electrical charges cancel out and produce a burst of energy. The name of the 'positron' is actually based on that of the 'electron'. See also **proton/electron**.

electron see **proton**

electronic/electric
In general, a machine or instrument that is 'electronic' is popularly understood as being more complex and sophisticated (and modern) than one that is 'electric'. The distinction is that an 'electronic' instrument, such as a computer or television set, is controlled by transistors or microchips that are themselves powered or activated by an 'electric' current. An 'electric' appliance, on the other hand, does not have such components and operates directly from an electricity supply, such as a vacuum cleaner or a cooker. A good example of the contrast can be seen in an 'electric' and an 'electronic' typewriter. An 'electric' typewriter has a quantity of 'works' that operate it through a motor powered by the electricity supply. An 'electronic' typewriter, however, has virtually no bulky 'works' inside it at all except a small unit that is in effect a microcomputer. 'Electronic' instruments have many advantages over 'electric' ones, and are becoming increasingly common in everyday use.

element/compound
In chemistry, an 'element' is a basic substance (105 are known) that consists of atoms of one kind only. Examples are carbon (C), copper (Cu), hydrogen (H) and oxygen (O). A 'compound' is thus a substance consisting of two or more 'elements' combined. Examples are hydrogen sulphide (H_2S), combining hydrogen and sulphur, and sulphuric acid (H_2SO_4), combining hydrogen, sulphur and oxygen. All the 'elements' appear in Mendeleev's periodic table (see **period/group**).

elenctic see **deictic**

elevation/depression
These are terms used in surveying. The 'elevation' is the angle between a line from the observer to an object above him and a horizontal line. The 'depression' is the angle between the line from an observer to an object below him and a horizontal line. An 'elevation' would thus produce a figure for a house on a hill, and a 'depression' for a building below one in a valley.

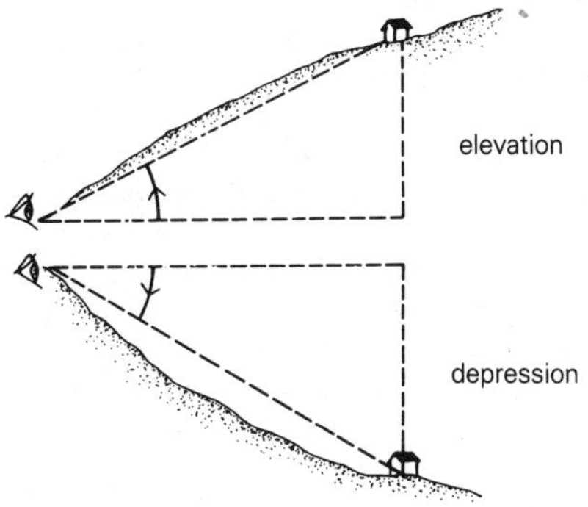

elevation see **plan**

elite see **pica**

em/en
The two small words denote units of measure in printed material, especially as used in spacing. An 'em' was formerly the area of a 12-point capital letter 'M', and an 'en' half this. The actual spacing (between words) is made by a piece of type-metal called a 'quadrat' (or simply 'quad'), and in ascending order of width can be 'en' (–), 'em' (—), 'two-em' (——) or even 'three-em' (———).

embolus/thrombus
Medically speaking, an 'embolus' is a blood clot, air bubble or other particle that is transported by the bloodstream until it is lodged in a blood vessel and obstructs it, so impeding the circulation. A 'thrombus' is also a blood clot, but one that remains attached to its point of origin, without being transported in the blood. The Greek origins of the terms mean

respectively 'stopper' and 'clot', so do not denote the essential mobile/static difference between them.

emigrant/immigrant
Both are forms of 'migrant', and denote a person going or coming to live in another country. An 'immigrant' is someone who has arrived (from abroad); an 'emigrant' is someone who has left (from his native land). Depending from which end he is considered, a single person can thus be both an 'immigrant' and an 'emigrant'. ('E-' = 'ex-' or out, and 'im-' = 'in-'.) Compare **migrant/resident**.

emperor/empress
An 'empress' is the wife or widow of an 'emperor', or else a woman who holds this rank in her own right. Both words came into English from French (where, however, their modern equivalents are more obviously distinguished as *empereur* and *impératrice*, leaving English with the awkward spellings).

empress see **emperor**

empty see **full**

en see **em**

enclitic/proclitic
In language, an 'enclitic' is a word or particle that is joined on to another word without any accent of its own, for example the 'que' of Latin *Arma virumque cano* ('I sing of arms and the man') or the 'not' of English 'cannot'. A 'proclitic' also has no independent accent, but is joined to the *front* of the word, like the 't' (meaning 'it') of ''tis true'. (Compare **prefix/suffix**.) The words mean literally 'leaning on' and 'leaning forward'.

encyclopaedia see **dictionary**

end see **beginning**

endogamy/exogamy
These two terms belong to the field of anthropology. 'Endogamy' is marriage within one's own tribe or family unit, in other words, intermarriage. 'Exogamy' is marriage outside such a unit, so that a person's spouse comes from another tribe or village (as decreed by some tribal laws). The second part of each word means 'marriage', while the two prefixes mean respectively 'inside' and 'outside'. Compare the next entry.

endonym/exonym
The first term here does not exist in any dictionary, so I have invented it to serve as a useful opposite to the second word, which does exist. To take the second word first: in the field of name studies (onomastics), an 'exonym' is the name of a place abroad that is different from its native form in one's own language. For example, the French 'exonym' of 'London' is 'Londres', and the Italian 'exonym' is Londra. Since there are a fair number of such names (English 'Moscow' for native 'Moskva' is another, as is 'Rome' for 'Roma'), it is useful to have a term that denotes the native name of a (native) place. The 'endonym' of 'Rome' is thus 'Roma', and of 'Moscow' it is 'Moskva'. The second part of each term means 'name' (as in 'pseudonym'), and the first parts are the same Greek prefixes as in the previous entry. Compare also the next entry.

endoplasm/ectoplasm
The opposing terms here relate to cytology (the study of cells). The 'endoplasm' is the inner, relatively liquid part of the cytoplasm (the jellylike material round the nucleus), while the 'ectoplasm' is the outer, relatively rigid part of the cytoplasm. On the two words, 'ectoplasm' became popular in the 1920s for the substance that was supposed to emanate from the body of a medium in a spiritualist seance and to turn into a human shape or face. (Some fine fake photographs of 'ectoplasm' were devised to amaze the gullible public.) The two Greek prefixes here mean obviously enough 'inner' and 'outer', with 'ecto-' an alternative for the 'exo-' of the two entries above.

end-rhyme see **head-rhyme**

engaged see **vacant**

engaged tone see **ringing tone**

enlarge/reduce
To 'enlarge' something is to make it larger, and to 'reduce' is to make it smaller. The best known use of the opposite terms is probably for photography, where an 'enlargement' is a print that is larger than the negative from which it is made. (As such, it is also quite often known commercially as an 'enprint', which is usually one 5 × 3½ inches in size.) 'Reductions' are the opposite, although here the 'reducing' is done (for example, by means of a photocopier) for reasons of size or economy, not for display purposes. (When 'enlarging' or 'reducing' are done by copier like this, the opposing terms are frequently 'magnification' and 'reduction', not 'enlargement'.)

entrance/exit
The 'entrance' is of course the way in, and the 'exit' the way out. The words are quite interesting in themselves. 'Entrance' derives fairly obviously from French, where the verb corresponds to English 'enter'. 'Exit', however, is pure Latin, meaning 'he goes out'. The English word seems to have derived partly from this, as a stage direction to an actor, and partly from Latin *exitus*, 'departure'. Today both words are becoming more formal by comparison with the more homely 'way in' and 'way out'. But see also **ingress/egress**.

environmentalism/hereditarianism
The two lengthy terms are part of the jargon of psychology (typically, some may say). They are easy to understand, however. 'Environmentalism' is the theory that a person's behaviour is chiefly influenced by his environment. On the other hand, 'hereditarianism' is the school of thought that lays stress on the importance of a person's heredity in determining his behaviour. The dispute between the 'environmentalists' and the 'hereditarians' has been going on for decades now, and is still unresolved.

EP see **LP**

epigenesis see **preformation**

epilogue see **prologue**

epistle/gospel
The two words are used for the two Bible readings that are given in the Holy Communion service in the Church of England and several other Christian churches. The 'epistle', which comes first, is taken from one of the 'Epistles' of the New Testament, that is, one of the apostolic letters of the saints Paul, Peter, James, Jude or John. The congregation sits while the 'epistle' is read. There then follows the 'gospel' (often after a hymn), for which the congregation stands. This is taken from one of the four 'Gospels' of the New Testament, i.e. the books of Matthew, Mark, Luke or John. The 'epistle' (in the Church of England) may well be read by a layman, but the 'gospel' is usually read by the officiating clergyman (or at least an ordained minister). By their very nature, the 'epistle' is mostly didactic, while the 'gospel' usually recounts part of the narrative of the life of Jesus. Irregular worshippers seeking uplift at a Communion service on Easter Day may have some problems with the 'epistle' prescribed for the day in the Prayer Book, which deals with 'fornication, uncleanness, inordinate affection, evil concupiscence, and covetousness'. Not so much uplift as downfall.

equinox/solstice
The words are sometimes confused. They are also virtual opposites! The 'equinox' (Latin 'equal night') occurs on two occasions in the year (see **vernal/autumnal**) when day and night are of equal length. This happens on about 21 March and 23 September, when the Sun crosses the Equator. The 'solstice' (Latin 'sun standing still') occurs also on two occasions in the year (summer and winter) when we have respectively the longest day and the shortest. The two 'equinoxes' are thus marked by a balance, and the two

'solstices' by extremes. Compare **Cancer/ Capricorn**.

ermine/vair
In heraldry, 'ermine' is a 'fur' conventionally represented by black 'ermine' tails on a white field (background). 'Vair' is the other 'fur', represented by alternate rows of blue and white bells or shields. On a coat of arms, the 'ermine' certainly looks much more like a real fur. 'Vair' (related to English 'variegated') is said to represent the fur of a squirrel, while 'ermine' actually names the animal (the stoat).

Eros/Thanatos
In psychology, 'Eros' (or 'eros') is the term for those life instincts, especially the sexual ones, that aim for self-preservation and the uninhibited enjoyment of things. 'Thanatos' (or 'thanatos'), by contrast, is the other primal instinct that seeks death. Both are strictly Freudian concepts, and both take their names from Greek gods: 'Eros' was the god of sexual love, and 'Thanatos' the personification of death. (Their names actually mean 'love' and 'death' in Greek.)

erythrocytes see **leucocytes**

esoteric/exoteric
'Esoteric', which is by far the commoner word, means 'intended for the enlightened minority', such as an 'esoteric' cult or an 'esoteric' style of writing. 'Exoteric' therefore means the opposite, and denotes something that is (or is intended to be) intelligible to more than the select few. One could thus have an 'exoteric' account of a philosophical viewpoint, or an 'exoteric' explanation of an complex scientific process. This present dictionary aims to be more 'exoteric' than 'esoteric'. The words derive from Greek and basically mean 'internal' and 'external'.

essentialism see **progressivism**

ethical see **proprietary**

euphemism/dysphemism
A 'euphemism', which is better known than its opposite, is an inoffensive or milder word substituted for a coarse or indecent one, especially in matters of sex, death, excretion, religion and other frequently 'taboo' areas. For example, a 'euphemism' for 'die' is 'pass on', and one for 'urinate' is 'spend a penny'. Interestingly, some words or phrases that were originally 'euphemisms' have now acquired a much more 'basic' sense, and often need a new 'euphemism' to express them. On example is 'intercourse', which after all means literally only 'business', 'dealing'. A 'dysphemism' is thus the use of an offensive or 'blunt' word in place of an innocuous one, such as the Australian 'Pommy bastard' for 'British immigrant' and 'kicked the bucket' for 'die'. The words literally mean 'good speech' and 'bad speech', with 'dysphemism' based on 'euphemism'.

euphony/cacophony
The words literally mean 'good sound' and 'bad sound', and can be used in a fairly general sense, especially in adjectival form. One can thus speak of a person's 'euphonious' voice, or talk of a 'cacophonous' argument. In literature, and particularly poetry, some writers deliberately employ 'euphony' or 'cacophony' for special effect. Many of Keats's poems have lines of 'euphony', as for example the following, with its soft 'm's' and 's's', from his *Ode to a Nightingale*:

> Perhaps the self-same song that found a path
> Through the sad heart of Ruth, when sick for home,
> She stood in tears amid the alien corn.

And in these lines from Tennyson's *Morte D'Arthur*, the first three lines of strident 'cacophony' are followed by two of smooth and soothing 'euphony':

> The bare black cliff clanged round him, as he based
> His feet on juts of slippery crag that rang
> Sharp-smitten with the dint of armed heels –
> And on a sudden, lo! the level lake,
> And the long glories of the winter moon.

See also **assonance/dissonance**, **concord/discord**.

Europe/Asia
Together, 'Europe' and 'Asia' form (as 'Eurasia') one of the great land masses of the world, while individually representing the **east/west** (or **oriental/occidental**) divide. 'Asia', too, represents the old culture, the ancient religions, while 'Europe' stands for the new civilization and modern religion, especially that of Christianity, itself now also split into east and west, or in the **Catholic/Protestant** division. There is similarly a political split between the capitalist west ('Europe') and the communist east ('Asia'), all the more since the latter continent contains two of the world's leading communist powers, Soviet Russia and China. There is, again, a contrast between the relatively small states of 'Europe' and the large countries of 'Asia'. Finally, the east/west division is even seen in the names of the continents themselves, since (if this theory is correct) the name of 'Europe' derives from an Assyrian word meaning 'west', 'sunset', while 'Asia' is said to mean the opposite, 'east', 'sunrise'.

eurytropic see **stenotropic**

Eve see **Adam**

even see **odd**

evening see **morning**2

evensong see **matins**

evergreen see **deciduous**

evil see **good**2

ewe see **ram**

exception see **rule**

exclamation mark see **question mark**

exclude see **include**

ex-directory/in the book
The two phrases are used, respectively, for a telephone subscriber whose number is not or is in the directory. 'Ex-' here means 'out of', as distinct from 'in', and the phrase as a whole seems to have arisen some time in the 1930s, when subscribers began to realize the advantages of being excluded from the directory (the chief one being that one's number and address remain private, and are not public knowledge). The phrase 'in the book' arose at about the same time, or indeed a little earlier, as it occurs in a story by Agatha Christie of 1925 ('You might ring up a number for me now. Look it up in the book', *The Secret of Chimneys*). The fact that the public invariably referred to the telephone directory as 'the book' led British Telecom (who are responsible for the telephone system in Britain) to rename its regional directories in the mid-1980s as simply 'The Phone Book'.

ex dividend/cum dividend
'Ex dividend' means 'without dividend', and applies to the purchase of shares bought either during their normal payment period or during a specified period before this. The purchaser of such 'XD' shares is thus not entitled to the current or imminent payment. 'Cum dividend' means simply 'with dividend', and applies to the purchase of shares that will qualify for the next dividend payment. In some cases, shares can have both an 'ex dividend' price and a higher 'cum dividend' price.

exhale see **inhale**

exit see **entrance**

exogamy see **endogamy**

exonym see **endonym**

exoteric see **esoteric**

expand/contract
To 'expand' is to grow larger in size or volume, and to 'contract' is to grow smaller in this way. Many substances

'expand' when they are heated and 'contract' when they cool. Metals do this, hence the use of mercury in thermometers. The words have certain technical uses, but often without the other opposite sense. For example, although muscles 'contract', they don't 'expand' but simply 'relax', and although one can 'expand' a mathematical expression (as the sum of several terms of a series), one does not often 'contract' one. Such usages apply when the 'growing larger' or 'growing smaller' is the chief function of the thing involved, and when it does not equally do either. Compare also the next entry.

expander/compressor
In electronics, an 'expander' increases the variations in signal amplitude in a transmission system, while a 'compressor' reduces them. This is one instance where the opposite of 'expand' is not 'contract'. Compare the previous entry.

expenditure see **income**

explicit see **implicit**

explode/implode
Apart from the popular 'explode' meaning 'blow up', 'go off', the word has the opposite 'implode' for one or two technical uses. One of them is in phonetics, when to 'explode' a consonant is to pronounce one (such as 'p' or 't') with a sudden release of air. To 'implode' is to do the opposite, so as to pronounce a consonant with a sucking in of air. We don't have these in English, but they can be heard in the so called 'clicks' of some African languages, when the tongue is pressed against the teeth or the roof of the mouth and then suddenly pulled away. (The nearest we get to this is in the sound written 'tut tut' or 'tsk tsk' to represent a sign of disapproval or reproach.) However, when a light bulb or a vacuum flasks bursts in, it can be said to 'implode'. So to 'explode' is to burst as the result of internal pressure, but to 'implode' is to collapse as the result of external pressure.

export see **import**

expressionists see **impressionists**

extension see **flexion**

extensive/intensive
Here the two terms apply to the world (or field) of agriculture. 'Extensive' farming (not so frequently encountered) means farming with a minimum use of capital or labour. 'Intensive' farming, on the other hand, is farming with increased capital and labour. In this way, productivity can be increased without the need to farm more land or use more raw materials, and the farmer will concentrate on such things as tilling the ground more thoroughly, using more fertilizers, and so on.

exterior see **interior**

external see **internal**

extramarital see **premarital**

extrapolate see **intrapolate**

extravert see **introvert**

extrinsic see **intrinsic**

extrusive/intrusive
The two terms here relate to geology, and in particular to igneous rocks, that is, those produced by volcanoes. 'Extrusive' rocks are those formed by cooling lava when it has poured out of a volcano and solidified. 'Intrusive' rocks are formed by lava forcing its way in between layers of existing rocks, and there cooling and solidifying. The terms literally mean 'thrusting out' and 'thrusting in'.

Ff

fact/fiction
'Fact' is what is real; 'fiction' is what is imaginary and unreal. Yet 'fact' is said to be stranger than 'fiction'! Perhaps it is, since although 'fiction' depends on the imagination, which can devise anything, however bizarre or unlikely, it is also known to be unreal. 'Fact', therefore, is expected to conform to observed and experienced patterns, and when it doesn't, it is remarkable for its departure from the norm. Sometimes, an inventive author's 'fiction' can become 'fact', as with the scientific devices and machines of Jules Verne. Many titles of his novels are no longer 'fiction', but simply 'fact', such as *Twenty Thousand Leagues Under the Sea* and *From the Earth to the Moon* (although not yet *Journey to the Centre of the Earth*). See also **fiction/non-fiction**.

facultative/obligate
The two terms belong to biology. If a living creature is 'facultative', it can exist under more than one type of environment when it has to. The classic example is a 'facultative' parasite that can exist either as a parasite proper, by living off a 'host', or as a so-called saprophyte, when it lives off dead decaying matter. An 'obligate' parasite, on the other hand, is obliged to live off its host, and cannot exist in any other way.

Fahrenheit/Celsius
The two names are familiar as methods of recording temperature, with 'Celsius' formerly known better as 'Centigrade'. 'Fahrenheit' is the scale that registers the freezing point of water (or melting point of ice) at 32°, and the boiling point of water at 212°. For the simpler 'Celsius', water freezes at 0° and boils at 100°. Although most Britons are now familiar with 'Celsius' temperatures for the weather, some people still prefer to think of a hot day in terms of 'Fahrenheit', since 'in the eighties' sounds much 'higher and hotter' than 'nearly thirty'. Paradoxically,

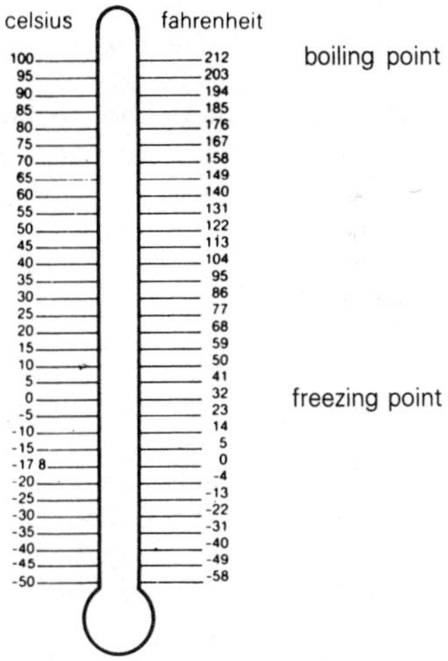

too, a winter temperature of 'under twenty' can sound colder than one of 'minus six'. (Many laymen are suspicious of minus quantities.) Even body temperature is still frequently thought of in degrees Fahrenheit, with 98.6° (formerly 98.4°) being 'normal' and anything over 100° indicating trouble. (In 'Celsius', standard body temperature is 36.9°.) 'Fahrenheit' is the name of the German physicist who invented the mercury thermometer in the eighteenth century and devised the scale as we know it today. He divided the interval between the temperature of a mixture of ice and water and body temperature into 64 equal parts, with freezing point at 32° and body temperature thus (slightly mismeasured) at 96°. 'Celsius' is the name of the Swedish astronomer Anders Celsius, who invented his 100-degree scale at about the same time that Fahrenheit devised his own. 'Centigrade', meaning simply 'hundred degrees', was a term that followed only a hundred years later.

fail see **pass**

fair/foul
'Fair is foul and foul is fair', intone the witches in *Macbeth*. 'Fair' usually means 'good', 'favourable', such as 'fair weather' and 'a fair wind', as well as 'honest' (a 'fair decision'). 'Foul', however, means 'bad', 'unfavourable', 'dishonest', such as 'foul weather' or 'by foul means'. The phrase 'come fair or foul' means 'whether we have good luck or bad', and 'by fair means or foul' implies 'even if we have to break the law'. See also **dark/fair**, and compare the next entry.

fair see **dark**

fair young man/'Dark Lady'
Here we have not just a literary contrast but a poetic mystery. The two characters are those of Shakespeare's *Sonnets*, with the 'fair young man' featuring in the first 126 Sonnets, and the 'Dark Lady' (the 'Dark Lady of the Sonnets', as she is often called) coming in the remainder, which number up to 154 but with the last two of these fairly conventional and serving merely to end the sequence. The 'fair young man' is an unmarried blond youth; the 'Dark Lady' is a raven-haired married woman. Shakespeare seems to have been fond of both of them, and in the Sonnets urges the youth to marry and so reproduce his beauty. He is referred to by such expressions as 'this fair child', 'my lovely boy' and so on, while the lady is a 'black beauty'. Much literary detective work has gone into an attempt to reveal their identities, but so far no theory has been truly convincing and no explanation accepted as conclusive.

falcon/tercel
A 'falcon' can be generally a member of the genus *Falco*, the bird of prey, but narrowly the 'falcon' is the female of this bird, and the 'tercel' is the male, at any rate in the sport of falconry. The latter word has an interesting derivation, with its ultimate origin from Latin *tertius*, 'third'. This referred to the old tradition that only one egg in three hatched a male chick.

fall see **rise**

fallen see **living**

false see **true**

far see **near**[1]

Far East see **Middle East**

farewell see **hail**

fast see (1) **feast** (2) **slow**

fat/thin
Many 'fat' people are really 'thin' inside, as George Orwell noted in *Coming Up For Air* ('Has it ever struck you that there's a thin man inside every fat man?'). Both words can imply an excessive degree of 'bigness' or 'leanness', or at least an unexpected amount (a 'fat' profit is greater than one expected, and a 'thin' disguise a poor one). Sometimes there is rivalry between the opposites, as in the 'Fattypuffs' and 'Thinifers' of the children's stories.

father see **mother**

faun/satyr
In classical mythology, a 'faun' was a rural deity in the form of a man with a goat's ears, horns, tail and feet. A 'satyr' was similar, as a minor woodland god in the form of a goatlike man. However, the 'faun' belonged to Roman mythology, and the 'satyr' to Greek. Moreover, 'fauns' were relatively gentle creatures, associated with pastoral pursuits, while 'satyrs' were actively lascivious, and much given to drinking wine and chasing nymphs. Properly, too, 'satyrs' had no horns. The 'faun' derives its name from the Roman god Faunus, who came to be identified with the Greek pastoral god Pan. The 'satyr'

has a name that can be traced back to the Greek *satyros* but that ultimately is of uncertain origin. See also **fauna/flora**, **nymphomania/satyriasis**.

fauna/flora
The alliterative terms have come to denote, respectively, the animal life of a place and its plant life. One can thus talk of the 'fauna and flora' of Iceland, for example, or of the Solomon Islands, especially when they are subjects of study. The words take their names from classical mythology, with 'fauna' borrowed from Fauna, the sister of the god Faunus (see previous entry), and 'flora' from Flora, the Roman goddess of flowers. The terms were popularized in the titles of books published by the great Swedish botanist Linnaeus: in 1745 he brought out his *Flora Suecica* (Latin, 'Swedish flowering plants') and a year later his *Fauna Suecica* ('Swedish animals'). Compare also **animal/vegetable**.

faux amis/amis loyaux
The two French terms literally mean 'false friends' and 'true friends'. 'Faux amis' is the phrase used in language study to denote a word in one language that becomes falsely associated with a similar or even identical word in another, although the two words have quite distinct meanings. For example, French *impotent* and English 'impotent' are 'faux amis', since the French word actually means 'crippled', and French *courtier* means 'broker', not 'courtier' (which is *courtisan*). By contrast, 'amis loyaux' (although not such a common term) are words that do actually correspond, to the relief of the language learner, such as French *correspondre* and English 'correspond'. Several scientific terms are 'amis loyaux', such as (in French) *solution* and 'solution', *moment d'inertie* and 'moment of inertia'.

feast/fast
This is one of those pairs of opposites represented by words that are disconcertingly alike. (Others are **stem/stern**, **yin/yang** and the prefixes **hyper-/hypo-**, for which see Appendix I.) Not surprisingly, 'feast' and 'fast' have been seized on by several writers who wish to couple them as opposites. For example, in Shakespeare's *Timon of Athens*, Flavius, rebuking Timon for his gluttony and greediness, speaks of 'Feast-won, fast-lost', and there has long been a proverbial phrase 'either a feast or a fast' in English to describe an 'all or nothing' situation ('Dock labour has been graphically described as "either a feast or a fast". Good wages may be earned in a short time. [. . .] On the other hand, work is not always obtainable', *Daily Telegraph*, 26 July 1912). The original contrast was more than 'eating a lot' as against 'eating nothing', since the two words referred to religious occasions: a 'feast' was to be observed with rejoicing and was intended to serve as a contrast to a 'fast', which was to abstain from food as a sign of penitence or in order to exercise self-discipline. Doubtless the similarity of the words helped, however, in their 'association of opposites'. The words are actually of quite different origins: 'feast' derives ultimately from Latin *festus*, 'joyful', while 'fast' is an Old English word (and basically meaning 'hold fast').

feather/square
These two terms belong to rowing. When an oar is 'feathered', it is turned parallel to the water in between strokes, mainly to lower wind resistance. When it is 'squared', it is turned perpendicular to the water at the beginning of a stroke, in order to make maximum impact and give the greatest 'pull' when submerged. The alternating movements can best be seen in the action of a good canoeist.

February Revolution/October Revolution
Both events occurred in Russia in 1917 and marked contrasting stages of the Russian Revolution. The 'February Revolution' took place in March as an uprising in which the tsar abdicated and as a result of which a provisional government was established. The 'October Revolution' was the seizure of power by the Bolsheviks under Lenin in November, when this uprising was transformed into a socialist

revolution. The latter was thus *the* Revolution, and is the one normally meant by 'Russian Revolution'. The names do not correspond to the months in which they occurred since at the time the Russian calendar was still the 'Old Style' Julian one. See **Gregorian calendar/Julian calendar**, **old/new** and even **Bolsheviks/Mensheviks**.

fee simple/fee tail
In property law, a 'fee simple' relates to land that can be inherited by any heirs of the owner and can in fact be transferred by him to anyone he wishes. A 'fee tail' is the opposite, and denotes that the land can be inherited only by a particular line of heirs. 'Fee' here means 'land held or inherited' (in this sense it is still sometimes spelt 'fief'), and the two terms are French ones meaning 'simple fee' and 'cut fee', with 'tail' related to modern French *tailler*, 'to cut'.

fee tail see **fee simple**

fellatio/cunnilingus
The two are technical (or psychosexual) terms for contrasting sexual acts. 'Fellatio' is oral stimulation of the male genital organs, and 'cunnilingus' that of the female. When this is performed simultaneously by both people, the act is sometimes called 'soixante neuf' (French for 'sixty nine', from the position when lying of the two persons). 'Fellatio' derives from Latin *fellare*, 'to suck', while 'cunnilingus' literally means 'vulva licker' (Latin *lingere*, 'to lick', is directly related to *lingua*, 'tongue', and so to 'linguistics' and 'language'). See also **suck/blow**.

female see **male**

feme covert/feme sole
The terms still exist in law as applying to, respectively, a married woman and an unmarried one (the latter embracing spinsters, widows and divorcees). The literal Anglo-French meanings are 'covered woman' and 'woman alone'. 'Covered' implies that the woman is 'covered' or protected by her marriage.

feminine see **masculine**

fermion see **boson**

fetch see **bring**

few see **many**

fiancé see **fiancée**

fiancée/fiancé
Possibly these are the two most nearly corresponding of all contrasting words (for others see **feast/fast**, above). But in the French from which they directly come, the adding of an 'e' to a masculine word to denote its feminine equivalent is a common occurrence, even when the 'e' is silent, as it is here. It seems strange that English has had to borrow the pair to denote, respectively, a woman or a man who is engaged to be married. (The pair **bride/groom** are too close to the actual marriage, and may already have gone through the ceremony.) Even French, which uses the same pair, usually prefixes the words with a clear sex-indicating word, such as *le fiancé* or *ma fiancée*. The words literally mean 'promised one' and are indirectly related to 'faithful'. They came into popular use in English only in the mid-nineteenth century, before which the words used were 'affianced', 'betrothed' or simply 'engaged', as still now.

fibula see **tibia**

fiction/non-fiction
The contrasting terms are currently used by bookshops, libraries and the reading public generally for 'imaginative literature' (in effect, mainly novels and short stories) and factual works (in effect, any literature that is not 'fiction'). It seems a pity that a more positive term could not have been found for the negative-sounding 'non-fiction'. Somewhat confusingly, too, there is now also a 'non-fiction novel', which is one about real situations, with real characters. An example is Truman

Capote's *In Cold Blood* (1966), in which he retells the events of a multiple murder of a Kansas family and follows the lives of the two murderers to the moment of their execution. See also **fact/fiction**.

fiction see **fact**

figurative see **literal**

file see **rank**[1]

filly see **colt**

fils see **père**

final see **initial**

finger/toe
What is interesting here is that for these opposites, English has two distinct words, with no need for any accompanying qualification. In French, for example, while 'finger' is *doigt*, 'toe' is *doigt du pied*, as it were, 'digit of the foot'. Italian is similar, having respectively *dito* and *dito del piede*. Even Russian does the same thing, with 'finger' being *palets* and 'toe' *palets nogi*. The identification of the two with each other goes back to classical times, where similarly Latin *digitus* and Greek *daktylos* also meant either 'finger' or 'toe'. German, however, does have two separate words, each of them similar to the English, respectively *Finger* and *Zehe*. But it is the latter word, with English 'toe', that relates to Latin *digitus*, not 'finger', which thus has another origin, and probably relates to 'five' and 'fist'. Although extremities, 'finger' and 'toe' are not commonly linked (compare **head/tail**, **head/toe**).

finish see **start**

finite/infinite
The two opposites tend to belong to philosophy, with anything that is 'finite' being limited in size, space or time, and anything that is 'infinite' being unlimited. In mathematics, too, a 'finite' number is one that can be counted or measured, and an 'infinite' number has an unlimited quantity of digits, factors, terms or whatever. One example of an 'infinite' figure is one with a so-called 'recurring' decimal, in which a digit or series of digits repeats itself endlessly at some stage after the point. The fraction 'one third' expressed as a decimal is an 'infinite' number of this type, since it runs 0.33333 . . . etc. *ad infinitum*. (In mathematical shorthand, a recurring decimal like this is indicated with a dot over it, thus: $0.\dot{3}$) The concept of anything 'infinite' is a complex one, since everything in our lives is 'finite', including life itself.

Finno-Ugrian see **Indo-European**

fire/water
The two are frequently regarded as basic opposites, since 'fire' is hot and dry and 'water' is cold and liquid. More importantly, 'water' extinguishes 'fire', so is a 'counteracting opposite' like the members of the pairs **acid/alkali**, **stinging nettle/dock leaf**. The phrase 'to go through fire and water' is an old one, occurring in the Bible ('We went through fire and through water', Psalm 66:12), and denotes two of the greatest natural dangers to man, that of being burnt or drowned. Finally, the two are coupled in other sayings, such as 'Fire and water are good servants but bad masters' and 'You can't mix fire and water'. 'Fire' and 'water' are also ancient 'elements': see **earth/air**.

first[1]/last
Contrasting opposites if ever there were, with a whole range of familiar phrases and expressions containing them. Among the best known are the biblical 'Many that are first shall be last; and the last shall be first' (Matthew 19:30), 'First to come and last to go' (found also in Longfellow's *The Musician's Tale*), 'First in, last out' (redundancy principle in some companies and government departments), 'I'm the first, and I shan't be the last' (proverb), 'First up, last down' (ambiguously, of someone who goes to bed early and gets up late, or rises early and goes to bed late), and of course 'from first to last' (from beginning

to end), 'first and last' (all importantly), and in isolation in enumerating or positioning ('You go first, then Jill, then me last'). Many things that are 'first' also have a 'last' equivalent, such as 'first' name and 'last' name (otherwise **Christian name/surname**), 'first' thing and 'last' thing (as the earliest and latest act or time), and, in a military setting, 'first' post and 'last' post (the first and second bugle calls at the time for retiring, with the latter also played separately at a funeral or memorial service). Compare the next entry.

first[2]/second
The contrast here is one of status or priority, with 'first' implying something that is superior to the 'second'. Some examples are: 'first' class and 'second' class (of passenger accommodation or as a postal service), 'first' cousin and 'second' cousin (the former is a child of one's uncle or aunt, the latter is a child of the 'first' cousin of either of one's parents), 'first' base and 'second' base (which must be touched in that order in baseball by a player attempting a run), 'first' lieutenant and 'second' lieutenant' (military ranks of junior officers, especially in the United States, with the 'second' the junior), and, more generally, 'firsthand' and 'secondhand' (of something coming directly or indirectly from its source). In many other cases there is a 'third', but here the enumeration proper begins, and the contrast status begins to be blurred or weakened. Compare the last entry.

fissiped/pinniped
The pair sound like a comic duo or the heroes of a children's comic, but in fact they belong to zoology, and more narrowly to types of animals' toes. Dogs, cats, bears, and other carnivores are 'fissiped', that is, they have toes that are separated from one another. Seals, sea lions, walruses and other aquatic animals are 'pinniped', or have simply a flipper as a leg and no separate feet at all, and certainly no individual toes. (According to this definition, Edward Lear's Pobble must thus have been a 'pinniped'.) The terms literally mean 'split foot' and 'fin foot'.

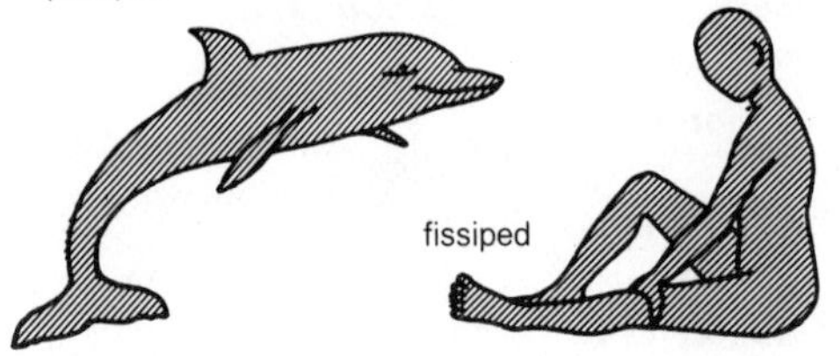

fixed/variable
The overall contrast here is between something that is immovable or unchanging and something that isn't. A 'fixed' cost, for example, does not alter during the production of something, but a 'variable' cost does. (Commercially, 'fixed' costs include those of land, buildings and machinery, but 'variable' costs relate directly to production, since the costs of buying raw materials at different prices is involved. A firm's wages bill can be 'fixed' or 'variable', depending if one is talking about agreed rates or overtime and special rates.) In astronomy, a 'fixed' star is one so far away that it appears to remain still when compared to the others. A 'variable' star, however, is one that varies in brightness, so is not really in proper contrast to it. For the contrast between the 'fixed' wing and the 'variable' wing of an aircraft, see **swing wing/fixed wing**, and for 'fixed' assets, see **current assets/fixed assets**.

fixed assets see **current assets**

fixed wing see **swing wing**

flat see **sharp[2]**

flat race see **steeplechase**

Fleming/Walloon
A 'Fleming' is a native or inhabitant of Flanders, the former principality that now corresponds to south-west Belgium and north-east France, with his native

language being Flemish. A 'Walloon' now also lives in this same region, but is one who speaks French, or a dialect of French. (He is really the 'intruder' since his name means 'foreigner'. In this sense it is related to 'Welsh', who were also originally 'foreigners' in a land dominated by the Anglo-Saxons.) So 'Flemings' and 'Walloons' thus speak entirely different languages, with Flemish being a Germanic language and French a Romance one (see **Romance/Germanic**). They therefore symbolize the language division that really exists throughout the whole of Belgium, as Flemish and French are its two official tongues. (Road signs will thus direct tourists to Kortrijk or Courtrai, Brugge or Bruges, Gent or Gand.)

flexion/extension
The terms here relate to anatomy and to movements of the body. If the body and neck moves forwards (so that it 'nods' or 'bows'), this is termed 'flexion'. The opposite, backward, straightening-up movement is thus called 'extension'. Both movements can also apply to the limbs. If the leg or arm bends at the knee or elbow when it moves in the sagittal plane (see **sagittal/coronal**), this will be flexion, and when it straightens out, this will be 'extension'. The terms mean simply 'bending' and 'straightening out'.

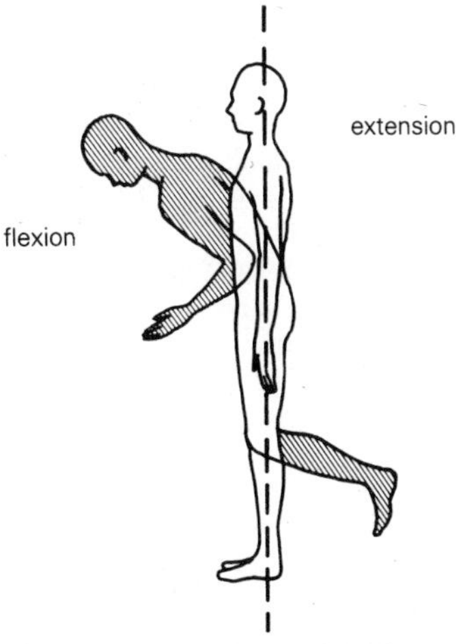

flier/winder
Two rather specialized opposites, but nevertheless straightforward ones. A 'flier' is a rectangular step in a straight flight of stairs, and is so called because it 'flies' up or down (as part of the flight). A 'winder' is a step on a spiral staircase, or one that goes round a corner, as its name suggests. The difference may not seem very important – many people are more concerned about the **upstairs/downstairs** distinction – but it matters to builders of staircases!

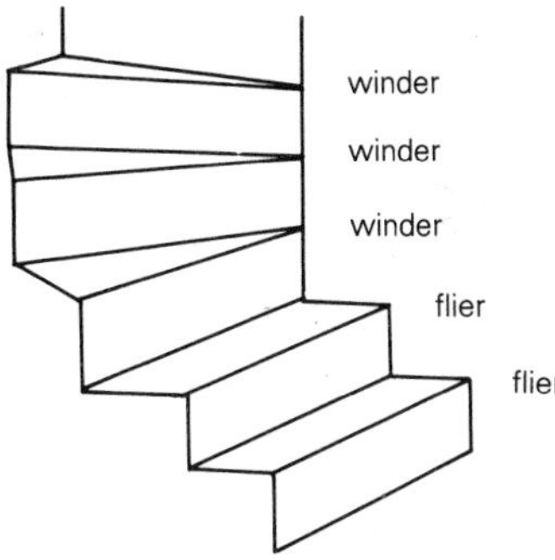

flood see **ebb**[1]

floor/ceiling
If a room has bookshelves 'from floor to ceiling', then it has them all the way up the walls, since the 'floor' is the base of the room and the 'ceiling' covers it overhead. 'Floor' and 'ceiling' can have some transferred senses, such as a 'floor' under wages (their lower limit), and a 'ceiling' on prices (their upper limit). (Compare also **service ceiling/absolute ceiling**.) The word 'floor' is related to Latin *planus*, 'level', and so to English 'plain'. 'Ceiling' is probably related to Latin *caelare*, 'to carve' rather than to Latin *caelum*, 'heaven' (and French *ciel*, therefore). Either way, it is certainly not so called because it 'seals' the room!

flora see **fauna**

flotsam/jetsam
'Flotsam' is really a legal term meaning 'wreckage of a ship found floating', while

'jetsam' means 'goods thrown overboard to lighten a ship in distress'. (The latter word particularly applies to such goods when subsequently washed ashore.) Both 'flotsam' and 'jetsam' become Crown property if the owner does not claim them within a year and a day. Taken together in figurative use, 'flotsam and jetsam' can mean 'vagrants' (the 'flotsam and jetsam of society'), or merely 'odds and ends' (a spare room full of 'flotsam and jetsam'). The words were adopted as the stage names of a pair of comic singers in the 1930s, with 'Flotsam' being the bass singer B. C. Hilliam, and 'Jetsam' the countertenor Malcolm McEachern. They always 'signed off' with the phrase, 'Yours very sincerely, Flotsam and Jetsam'.

flow see **ebb**[2]

fluorescent lamp see **tungsten lamp**

flutter see **wow**

fly see **hoist**

FM see **AM**

fob see **cif**

foe see **friend**

foible/forte
The two words could almost be general opposites in their respective senses of 'weakness' and 'strength' ('Cream cakes are one of her foibles', 'Scuba diving is his real forte'). However, the true contrast here is a technical one, and belongs to the sport of fencing. Of a sword's blade, the 'foible' is the most vulnerable part, from the middle to the tip. The 'forte' is its stronger section, between the hilt and the middle. 'Foible' is an obsolete French word meaning 'feeble', while 'forte' is the modern French (grammatically feminine) word for 'strong'. ('Forte' was originally pronounced 'fort', but seems to have altered its pronunciation under the influence of Italian 'forte', the musical term for 'loud'.) The general senses appear to have developed from the fencing uses in the seventeenth century. See also **strength/weakness**.

folded/rolled
The question invariably asked of a purchaser of gift wrapping paper. Neither method is really satisfactory: if the sheet is 'folded' it has to be creased before it can be used for wrapping; if it is 'rolled' it can become damaged or bent during its journey from the shop to one's home (or the wrapping point). Probably the best type of gift paper is the sort that has been pre-folded, and can be taken flat, just as it is.

folio see (1) **page** (2) **quarto**

folk music/art music
'Folk music', in its 'pure' sense (unalloyed with rock music), is music that has been passed down orally from generation to generation, with its original 'composing' often lost in the mists of time. 'Art music', by contrast, is music that has been consciously composed, and that can be ancient or modern (for example one of the pair **classical/romantic** and even **classical/popular**).

food/drink
The two basic necessities to maintain life, with 'drink' more vital than 'food' if one is to be in short supply. Since 'drink' denotes not only the liquids we consume but the act of swallowing them, one might have expected a word based on 'eat' for the complementary solid nourishment. (This happens in German, for example, where *essen* is the verb 'to eat' and *Essen* the noun 'food'.) However, we have been left with 'food', which is related to 'feed' and 'fodder', so perhaps the word development is logical enough after all.

foot see **hand**

footpad/highwayman
These two highway robbers had a distinction. The 'footpad', as his name indicates, went on foot, while a 'highwayman' was mounted on horseback. (The 'pad' of

'footpad' is related to 'path'). In his *Letters of a Russian Traveller*, published in the 1790s, the Russian writer and traveller Karamzin compared the two types of robber to the infantry and the cavalry, respectively, and the difference is indeed the same. (See **cavalry/infantry**.)

for/against
Two very basic opposites, traditionally associated with a vote or 'show of hands' to express an agreement (or approval) or a disagreement (or rejection) of a motion. Both words have several other uses, with 'for' about twice as versatile as 'against', but their contrasting senses, as here, are among their most frequent. See also **aye/no**.

fore[1]/aft
The contrasting terms used to correspond to 'front' and 'back' of a ship, and themselves related directly to 'before' and 'after' in a spatial sense. 'Fore' is an old word, but 'aft' developed only in the seventeenth century, probably from 'abaft'. For other nautical opposites see **ahead/astern**, **stem/stern**. Compare also the next entry.

fore[2]/hind
Here the contrast is between the front and back legs of a horse or other four-legged animal, with the resulting combination usually written as one word ('foreleg' and 'hindleg'). There are other corresponding contrasts with 'fore' and 'hind': see **foresight/hindsight** below, for example.

foreground/background
These two opposites usually relate to a view or to a picture, where the 'foreground' is the part of the scene nearest the viewer (at the front) and the 'background' is furthest from the viewer (at the back). The words also have transferred senses to mean 'position of prominence' and 'inconspicuous position'. In this meaning 'foreground' is much the same as 'forefront'. However, there is no 'backfront' to serve as its opposite! In its different uses as a non-contrasting word, 'background' is much more common than 'foreground'.

forehand/backhand
The two opposites here belong to sport, and especially to games such as tennis and squash. A 'forehand' stroke is made with the palm of the hand facing the direction of movement of the racket (and ball), while a 'backhand' stroke, which is more difficult and more complex, is made with the back of the hand facing this direction. In certain other specialized senses, a 'backhand' is not necessarily the opposite of a 'forehand'. For example, in riding, the 'forehand' is that part of a horse that is in front of the rider sitting in the saddle. 'Backhand', however, is handwriting that slopes to the left (backwards), instead of being upright or sloping to the right, as normally.

foreign see **native**

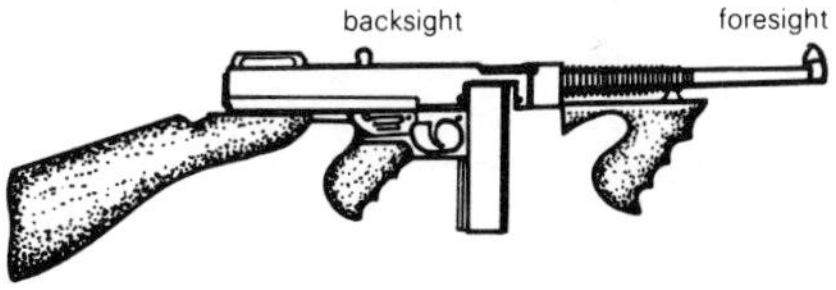

foresight[1]/backsight
This pair of opposites (which should be contrasted with the next entry) has its best-known use in shooting and surveying. On a gun, for example, the 'foresight' is the one nearest the muzzle, while the 'backsight' is the one nearest the eye of the person firing (who lines both up when aiming). In surveying, a 'foresight' is a reading taken to the next point from which one will survey, while a 'backsight' is a reading taken back to the last point from which one surveyed. A surveyor thus makes a series of 'foresights' and 'backsights' while progressing from one station to the next.

foresight[2]/hindsight
Here the opposites usually have a transferred usage, not a literal meaning. 'Foresight' is thus the prudent 'looking forward' to the future, with provision made for it. 'Hindsight' is the embarrassing realization

that one did not do the right thing at the time, or that one did not understand a situation properly. In other words, one is 'wise after the event'. However, 'hindsight' can also be used in a literal sense to mean the same as 'backsight' (see entry above).

fork see **knife**

former/latter
Strictly speaking, 'former' should be the first of two things, and 'latter' the second (only), although many people use 'former' to mean simply 'the first mentioned' and 'latter' as 'the last mentioned'. (For example, it is really incorrect to say 'Tom, Dick and Harry met up at the former's house' as there are three people mentioned.) The words have some uses in special names or titles. For example, the 'Former Prophets', in the Hebrew Bible, are the books of Joshua, Judges, I–II Samuel and I–II Kings, while the 'Latter Prophets' are those books that in Christian tradition are known simply as 'the Prophets' (and which are themselves divided into the Major and Minor Prophets). 'Former' is indirectly related to 'before' and 'latter' to 'late' and 'last'.

forte see (1) **foible** (2) **piano**

forward[1]/back
As contrasting adverbs, 'forward' means 'ahead', 'to the front', 'onwards', while 'back' means 'to the rear', 'reversing one's progress', otherwise 'advancing' and 'retreating'. 'Forward' usually implies progress, and 'back' retrogression, as in Lenin's famous saying 'One step forward, two steps back', as a common experience in the lives of individuals, the history of nations and the development of political parties. To 'look forward' to something is to await it eagerly, but to 'look back' can be simply to reminisce.

forward[2]/reverse
In certain instances, 'forward' and 'reverse' are adjectives of opposite meaning. For example, a 'forward' gear is one that drives a vehicle forward (in the sense of the entry above), while a 'reverse' gear sends it back. In sport, too, a 'forward' dive is one made from a standing position facing the water, when the body is propelled forward, while a 'reverse' dive is one made from the same position but with the body rotating backwards. (A dive like this made when the diver faces away from the water is called a 'back' dive, so really belongs to the **forward/back** pair of the entry above.) Compare, however, **obverse/reverse**.

forwards/backwards
See **forward/back** above.

foul see **fair**

four-stroke engine/two-stroke engine
These are the two main types of internal combustion engine, especially the petrol engine as used in motor vehicles. The 'four-stroke engine' (as found in most cars) has a piston that makes four strokes for each explosion, with these strokes making two revolutions of the crankshaft. The strokes are technically known as 'induction' (when the fuel and air mixture from the carburettor comes in), 'compression', 'expansion' (or 'power') and 'exhaust' (when the burnt gases are expelled). The 'two-stroke engine' (as used in many motorcycles as well as stationary motors such as pumps) is thus one in which the piston makes only two strokes for every explosion, these being 'ignition' (or 'injection') and combined 'compression' and 'expansion' ('power'). Separate 'intake' ('induction') and 'exhaust' strokes, as for the 'four-stroke engine', are not necessary, since exhaust and intake take place at the same time from separate ports near the end of the 'power' stroke. The 'two-stroke engine' tends to be less efficient than the 'four-stroke engine', mainly because of the loss of unburnt fuel in the exhaust.

fox/vixen
As with many animals and birds, the name of the male ('fox') is also used for the animal generally, with 'vixen' here reserved for the female. As applied to humans, 'fox' and 'vixen' have much the same senses that 'dog' and 'bitch' have

when addressed to men and women, so that a 'old fox' is a cunning or sly person, but a 'wretched vixen' is a spiteful or ill-tempered woman. (The word is used much less commonly than 'bitch'.) The two basic words are closely related, as can be clearly seen in their German equivalents: *Fuchs* and *Füchsin*.

free see **bound**

free house/tied house
As applied to pubs, a 'free house' is one that sells the products of a range of breweries, whereas a 'tied house' must sell only the drinks of the brewery that owns or rents it. So 'free' does not mean that the pub provides drinks without payment, alas, but that the owner or licensee is 'free' to buy his drinks from wherever he likes, or even to brew his own.

free-range/battery
The contrasting terms here apply to hens and their eggs. 'Free-range' hens are ones that are kept in natural or 'non-intensive' conditions, while 'battery' hens, as their name implies, are housed in enclosed cages, and are treated as mere egg-producing robots. 'Free-range' eggs may taste better. See **brown/white**.

free-standing/built-in
The alternative here applies to domestic appliances such as cookers, and especially relates to the kitchen, where space is often at a premium. The advantage of a 'free-standing' appliance is that it can be moved and taken with one if leaving the house altogether. However, a 'built-in' appliance is now generally the norm, particularly in a 'fitted' kitchen, where such equipment can be just as efficient as any 'free-standing' unit and as easy to clean. However, when you move house, you can't take it with you. See also **gas/electricity**.

freestone see **clingstone**

freestyle see **Graeco-Roman**

freewheel see **pedal**

freeze/thaw
These two opposites most commonly relate to the formation of ice on water, or the transformation of water to ice, with the 'thaw' reconverting the ice back to water after a 'freeze'. The terms can also be used in a transferred sense to apply to relationships between two people or groups of people, or to describe a person's individual manner or attitude ('He began to thaw after a while, when he saw I meant him no harm'). In some countries, the literal 'freeze' coincides with winter, and the 'thaw' in early spring is eagerly awaited. Compare the next entry.

freeze-up/break-up
The opposites here are literal ones, referring to the annual 'freeze-up' of rivers, lakes and topsoil in autumn or early winter that occurs in such countries as the United States and Canada. When the ice finally melts in early spring, and the waters begin to flow again, that is the 'break-up' (relating specifically to the breaking up of the ice). Compare the entry above.

French vermouth/Italian vermouth
'French vermouth' (or just 'French') is the dry variety, and 'Italian vermouth' (or just 'it') is sweet. Vermouth itself is the alcoholic drink with a white wine base that is flavoured with aromatic herbs and often drunk as an aperitif, or used in some mixed drinks (for example with gin). Compare **aperitif/digestif**, **mixed/straight**, **red/white**, **sweet/dry**.

fresh[1]/salt
'Fresh' water is simply water that is not 'salt', so is basically water that is drinkable, unlike sea water, which is 'salt' and undrinkable (unless processed in some way). 'Fresh' is a versatile adjective, but this use of it in English is not shared by many other languages. In French, for example, *eau fraîche* means simply 'newly drawn water', while 'fresh water' is *eau douce* (literally 'sweet water'). The same applies in German, where 'fresh water' is *süßes Wasser* ('sweet water' again). Compare the next entry.

fresh[2]/stale
In this case the pair of opposites applies to foodstuffs such as bread and beer. 'Fresh' bread is newly baked (and delicious); 'stale' bread is hard, musty and dry from being kept too long. 'Fresh' beer is newly drawn or brewed, and 'stale' beer is flat and tasteless. The two words can also apply to air ('fresh' air is usually outside, and invigorating, while 'stale' air can be found in some enclosed rooms and spaces, where it is stagnant or foul). The opposites can similarly be used of information or news, so that 'fresh' information is recent and new (and probably additional to what there was already), while 'stale' news is already familiar and not new at all (as news should properly be). Compare the entry above for another contrast to 'fresh'.

friar see **monk[1]**

friend/foe
The contrast here is chiefly a specialized military one, used to establish the identity of an unknown person or vehicle. If it is 'friend' it is 'one of ours'; if 'foe', 'one of theirs'. The two words have long been traditionally combined as a challenge (with the question 'Friend or foe?' either implied or even actually asked), and this dates back to at least medieval times. Apart from this phrase, 'foe' is not frequently used in English, and the more common 'enemy' is preferred. Doubtless the alliteration helps to preserve the coupling here, as it certainly does in the German equivalent of 'friend or foe' which is *Freund oder Feind.*

frog/toad
Apart from the 'water/dry land' difference ('toads' are aquatic only when breeding), 'frogs' are smooth-skinned while 'toads' have a rough skin, and 'frogs' progress by leaping, while 'toads' hop. There are therefore three distinct ways in which the creatures can be differentiated. Zoologically, too they belong to different families: 'frogs' are members of the *Ranidae* family, while 'toads' are from the *Bufonidae.*

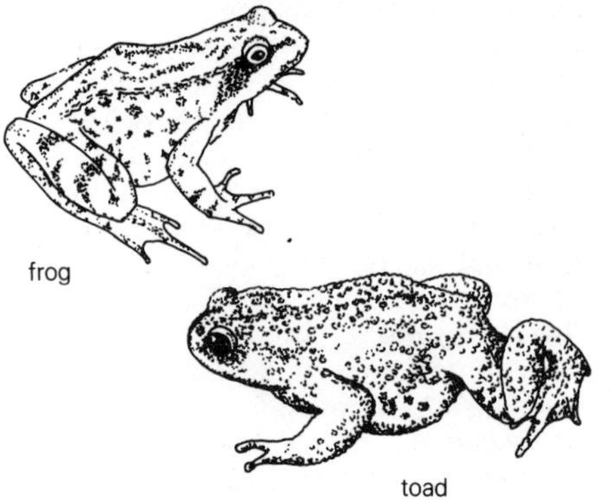

from/to
There are dozens of phrases linking these two prepositions of opposite meaning. Among them are 'from A to B' (see **A/B**), 'from A to Z' (see **A/Z**) and similar expressions that link different opposites or contrasts (e.g. 'from dawn to dusk', 'from start to finish', 'from father to son', 'from cradle to grave'). The two words can also appear on postal packets, with 'to' indicating the address of the recipient, and 'from' that of the sender. Indeed, in human communications they are essential when linking two names or pronouns ('from me to you', 'from Tom to Sue, with love', and so on). It is perhaps rather unusual that English has retained a four-letter word for such a very common sense as 'from', and many languages have much shorter words for the pair, e.g. French *de/à*, German *von/zu*, Italian *da/a*, Russian *ot/do*. But compare the expression 'to and fro', meaning 'This way and that' (where, however, the shorter 'fro' derives from Old Norse, not Old English).

front[1]/back
In many instances, 'front' implies a person or thing that is more important than another, while 'back' can mean the reverse, and indicate something minor or unimportant or at least inconspicuous. For example, the 'front' door of a house is the main one, on to the street, while a 'back' door is a more 'private' one, used for ordinary or 'business' occasions. A 'front'

garden, because of its position, will thus often be a flower garden, while the 'back' garden is where the vegetables are grown and the dog is kept. There may even be a difference in function: a 'front' tooth is not only more prominent but is used for biting, while a 'back' tooth is for chewing or grinding. In many cases, however, the opposite of a 'front' term will not be a 'back' one, and vice versa. There may even be no opposite at all. For example, there are no 'front' equivalents for a 'backbone', a 'backfire', a 'backlash', or a 'backpack'. Compare **in front/behind** and the next entry below.

front[2]/rear
As distinct from the pair **front/back** (above), 'front' has an opposite 'rear' in a mostly more formal context, and frequently as a noun, not an adjective. For example, an army can advance on a broad 'front' while taking care to defend its 'rear', and a builder or estate agent may talk of the 'front' of a house as distinct from its 'rear'. (An estate agent will talk of a 'large garden to rear', not a 'big back garden'.) Compare **in front/behind**.

front loader/top loader
Two different types of washing machine. A 'front loader' (the majority now) has a door at the front through which clothes are placed and from which they are removed after washing. A 'top loader' has its opening at the top. The great advantage of a 'front loader' is that it can be snugly placed under a work surface. On the other hand, there is no danger of water spilling out of the door with a 'top loader', and clothes can also be added during the washing process. 'Top loaders' are themselves distinguished as one of the pair **drum/tub** (which see).

fruit/vegetable
Broadly and popularly speaking, a 'fruit' is sweet, and often eaten uncooked, while a 'vegetable' is usually not regarded as sweet and is normally cooked. Many types of 'fruit', too, grow on trees and in orchards, such as apples, plums and pears, while a number of 'vegetables' grow as plants in the ground or even come from below ground, such as carrots, turnips and other 'root' plants. In a meal, also, 'vegetables' usually accompany the meat or savoury course, while 'fruit' is frequently served up for sweet (or 'pudding'), or eaten as a dessert at the end of the meal. Sometimes, what is actually a 'fruit' is popularly regarded as a 'vegetable', since it goes with the main meat course. The best example of this is the tomato, which is eaten both cooked and as a salad. Properly, though, it is a 'fruit', although is often not noticeably sweet and never served as a 'pudding'. Even more notable is the so called 'vegetable' marrow, which although always eaten as a 'vegetable', is in fact a 'fruit'! The word 'fruit' thus needs to be defined, and it is as follows: 'succulent edible body of a seed plant, especially one having a sweet pulp containing the seed'. Put more simply, if the 'fruit' has 'pips', seeds or stones, it *is* a 'fruit', not a 'vegetable'. It will thus be seen that certain other 'vegetables', such as the cucumber, are really 'fruits'. So perhaps the popular division of the two, as in the first sentence above, is actually the most sensible after all.

full[1]/empty
There can be an intermediate stage, of course, such as 'half full' and 'half empty' (the former being positive, and the latter more negative), but basically 'full' implies being 'topped up' and unable to hold any more, while 'empty' means 'containing nothing'. In a transferred sense, a 'full' life is a busy and satisfying one, while an 'empty' life is a dull and apparently pointless one. The two are frequently contrasted in saying and quotations, such as 'An empty purse causes a full heart' and 'He that is full of himself is very empty'. See also the next entry.

full[2]/half
Although the opposite of 'full' is usually regarded as 'empty', there are some instances where the contrasting word is 'half'. This particularly applies to the status of a thing or person, or its value.

For example, a child can travel 'half' fare, and be admitted to certain public performances at 'half' price. If a young child, he or she may have a 'half' portion of food when eating out with the family, and wear clothes that are in 'half' sizes. Other contrasts of this type (field of activity in brackets) are: 'half back' and 'full back' (football), 'half moon' and 'full moon' (astronomy), 'half nelson' and 'full nelson' (wrestling) 'half time' and 'full time' (sport) and 'half length' and 'full length' (photography or portraiture). In many cases, however, the 'full' equivalent does not have this word actually expressed, such as 'half brother' and 'brother', 'half hour' and 'hour', 'half dollar' and 'dollar'. In other cases, the corresponding word to 'full' is 'part' (see next entry).

full-time/part-time
A person who works 'full-time' or studies 'full-time' does it all the time, working for the whole day or week, or studying for the whole term. If the time for which a person works or studies is restricted, and less than the accepted norm, he will do this 'part-time'. A 'part-time' waitress might thus receive half pay (as distinct from full pay), and a 'part-time' student may have another job to attend to (even if only a 'part-time' one). Compare the entry above.

functional disease/organic disease
A 'functional disease' is one in which there is no observable change in the actual material form or arrangement of any organ or part, but simply a disturbance or reduction in its function. For example, a 'functional' heart disease could involve an irregularity in its action, but no detectable alteration in its actual physical formation and composition. An 'organic disease', on the other hand, does involve a physical change in the structure. An 'organic' heart disease would therefore be detectable in the form of an alteration in shape, size, tissue or the like. Diseases can be categorized in other contrasting ways: see, for example, **acute/chronic**, **benign/malignant**.

fundamental/harmonic
These two terms are virtual opposites in music, as applied to a particular note. The 'fundamental' is the 'proper' or main note, as usually heard, and this sounds together with its 'harmonics', which are always at higher frequencies and that together with the 'fundamental' give the note its characteristic pitch. (The 'harmonics' are sometimes called 'overtones' or, less commonly, 'upper partials'.) The overall effect can best be heard when a bell is struck, with its main or strongest (and usually lowest) note its 'fundamental' and all the higher reverberations its 'harmonics'. A violin player can sometimes produce an effect whereby a note's 'harmonics' are heard without the 'fundamental'. This is done by playing a string while simultaneously touching it at its centre or some other point. This touching prevents the whole string from vibrating and so the 'fundamental' from sounding. See also **treble/bass**.

funny ha-ha see **funny peculiar**

funny peculiar/funny ha-ha
The semi-serious phrases are sometimes used in conversation to distinguish the two most common senses of 'funny', i.e. 'comical' ('The man was wearing a funny hat') and 'strange' ('The man was wearing funny shoes'). The phrases are used after a person has just said something with the word 'funny' and the listener wants to know which sense was meant: 'Funny' as 'peculiar' or 'funny' in a way that makes you laugh ('ha-ha')? For example, one person says: 'I saw a really funny picture yesterday'; the other person then says 'Funny peculiar, or funny ha-ha?' The first person then explains which sense he meant. The phrases themselves are fairly recent in English, and only really became popular in the 1930s. Perhaps they first occurred in the dialogue of a film or comedy act somewhere.

further education/higher education
The terms may seem similar but they represent a clear distinction, even if not quite so obvious as that of **primary/**

secondary. They relate to education after school-leaving age. 'Further education' applies to education received outside universities, and will include training in technical and commercial skills. 'Higher education' is provided by universities and polytechnics, and is thus broadly more academic than 'further education', which has a practical basis.

future/past

Adelaide Ann Proctor, who wrote 'A Lost Chord' ('Seated one day at the organ . . .'), also wrote, with perhaps more practical significance:

> The Past and the Future are nothing,
> In the face of the stern To-day.

She was probably right. Whatever is 'past' is over and done with, and cannot be altered. Whatever is 'future' is still to come, and so is hypothetical. What really matters is what is happening *now*. However, in time (and also in tense, for language-learners), the 'future' and the 'past' are opposites, and represent the alterable forward view, and the unalterable view left behind one.

Gg

gaffer/gammer
The two words can be used as affectionate or rather patronizing names for an old man or an old woman, respectively, especially one who lives in the country. 'Gaffer' is much more common than 'gammer', however, and has acquired other senses. These include the name of the chief lighting technician in a film or TV studio, and a semi-colloquial nickname for a foreman or overseer in an industrial concern or a factory, so that 'the gaffer' is virtually the same as 'the boss'. The words themselves look like shortenings of 'grandfather' and 'grandmother', although some linguists claim that they derive from 'godfather' and 'godmother'. See **godfather/godmother** in this respect.

gain/loss
The words relate to the acquiring of something and the losing of it, whether in a general way or in a specialized usage. To make a 'gain' usually means to make money or a profit, so that to make a 'loss' means to do the reverse, and to be 'out of pocket' (see **profit/loss**). 'Gain' and 'loss' are terms also used of an electrical appliance, relating to the increase or decrease respectively in its power. (In this sense, 'gain' is the same as 'amplification'.) The general contrast between the words can be seen in such sayings as 'One man's gain is another man's loss', and the moral application of the comparison has been used in several religious contexts, especially to warn against the danger of pride (as in the hymn line 'My richest gain I count but loss').

galley proof/page proof
These terms belong to printing and publishing. 'Galley proofs' are proofs of a book submitted to a reader on long 'galleys', or strips of paper about three pages in length. As such, they are much easier to correct or rearrange than the 'page proofs' which are the subsequent stage, and which show the printed matter in the form it will consequently take in the actual book. At 'page proof' stage, therefore, the reader can see if the compositor has made the corrections accurately, and can compile the index. In simpler books, without a large number of illustrations or tables, the first stage of 'galley proofs' is often omitted. The word 'galley' apparently associates the printer's tray of type with a hot baking tray in a kitchen, and this is turn suggests a link with the kitchen or 'galley' on a ship. Today, however, most printing does not involve the use of any actual type at all, but if it is the printed matter is 'cold set', and it is only the ink that is hot, not the type. (When the ink makes contact with the cold paper it quickly solidifies.)

game fish see **coarse fish**

gamekeeper/poacher
In their most familiar senses, a 'gamekeeper' is a person employed on a private estate to 'keep the game', that is, to take charge of the breeding and feeding of the game animals or birds that are being reared so that they can later be hunted for sport and food. (The procedure may seem a strange and contradictory one, but is logically exactly the same as cattle farming, for example, or pig rearing, although the sporting element is absent here.) The 'poacher', on the other hand, is the lawbreaker who hopes to steal the game that the 'gamekeeper' is endeavouring to protect. They are thus sworn enemies, and on different sides of the fence (quite literally, in many cases). The two words have gained some figurative currency recently in the expression

'poacher turned gamekeeper', meaning that a person changes from opposing or attacking a policy to defending it. The phrase is mostly associated with business and industry, and with views supporting or attacking trade union policy, for example. The converse phrase, 'gamekeeper turned poacher', is also used. When Lord Gowrie, formerly Minister for the Arts, was appointed as chairman of Sotheby's, the famous art auctioneering firm in London, he went on record as commenting, 'You've heard of the poacher turned gamekeeper, now you see the gamekeeper turned poacher' (*The Times*, 24 October 1985). He meant that he was now going to promote Britain's artistic heritage for export, instead of trying to prevent its export.

gammer see **gaffer**

garden peas see **processed peas**

gas/electricity
Both forms of power are common in people's homes, with many houses having both 'gas' and 'electricity' supplies, typically using 'gas' for cooking and heating, and 'electricity' for lighting and for running several appliances such as refrigerators and television sets. There is always an implied contrast between the two, however, whether in terms of cost, efficiency, safety or for some other reason. For heating, 'gas' is generally regarded as cheaper than 'electricity', and as easier to control. It does require a special flue to be installed, however. 'Electricity' is on the whole more expensive (although probably not at 'off-peak' times and rates), but is easier to install and does not require a flue. When it comes to cooking, 'gas' is also cheaper; moreover, cookers that use 'electricity' are more expensive to buy. Certainly, a 'gas' grill is cheaper than one heated by 'electricity'. Many people prefer 'gas' for cooking, too, since it provides fast heat and is easy to regulate. But again, 'electric' cookers are available in a wide range of types, with refinements such as solid plates, radiant rings, etc., that 'gas' cookers cannot have. So the overall contrast is a fairly complex one.

gay/straight
The two terms are contrasting words used by homosexuals to mean respectively 'homosexual' and 'not homosexual' (i.e. heterosexual). 'Gay' became widely used in this sense only in the late twentieth century, to the extent that many people consciously avoid using it (an unmarried man is no longer a 'gay bachelor', and it is better to have an enjoyable evening out than a 'gay party'). 'Straight' implies 'regular', 'normal', as compared to a 'deviant' or 'bent' (or even 'kinky') sexual proclivity. See also **homosexual/heterosexual**, **homosexual/lesbian**, **straight/bent**.

gee-up/whoa
These are the two contrasting commands to a draught horse to make it either start or stop. ('Gee-up' can also be used to an already moving horse to make it turn to the right.) The terms also have some colloquial use in ordinary human talk, for example (to a slow child), 'Come on, gee-up!' or (to someone filling one's glass too full), 'Whoa, that's enough!' The child's word 'gee-gee' for a horse derives from 'gee-up', with the command itself apparently a combination of the two exclamations 'gee!' and 'hup!', the latter now wrongly associated with 'up'.

gemeinschaft/gesellschaft
As they stand, the two words are German for 'community' and 'company'. The terms are used in sociology for two contrasting social groups. A 'gemeinschaft' is a group whose individual members are united by common ties such as loyalty to a cause, family ties, shared beliefs, or some similar unifying force. A 'gesellschaft' is a social group in which the binding force is a practical one, with a division of labour and with each individual expressing a self-interest in the activity of the group. In a 'gemeinschaft', thus, the common link is a personal, informal one; in a 'gesellschaft' the link is an impersonal, formal one, often made merely for

convenience. The terms were devised and elaborated by the German sociologist Ferdinand Tönnies in his work *Gemeinschaft und Gesellschaft* (1887), usually translated into English as 'Community and Association'.

general anaesthetic see **local anaesthetic**

generalist see **specialist**

Gentile see **Jew**

gentleman/lady
The contrast here is in the use of the terms in certain ways for a man and a woman. A 'gentleman' is a man regarded as having qualities of refinement, good manners and 'breeding', and as coming from a good family (not necessarily an aristocratic one). A 'lady' is a woman similarly regarded. In their most general uses, the words can apply politely to any man or woman, in such sentences as 'He's a very helpful gentleman' and 'Who's the next lady to see me?' The terms are thus common when referring to strangers in a shop or other public place ('I think this gentleman is before me', 'I think that lady's dropped a glove'). Compare **man/woman**, **lord/lady**, **ladies/gentlemen**.

gentlemen see **ladies**

genuine/artificial
The division here is between 'true' and 'false', or 'real' and 'unreal'. Yet something that is 'artificial' can be just as effective as a thing that is 'genuine', or even more so, since it may not possess some of the latter's disadvantages. In this context, the real contrast is therefore between 'natural' and 'manmade', such as an 'artificial' fly used by anglers in place of a 'genuine' or real one. However, as applied to such things as emotions, feelings, and the like, 'genuine' has the implication of 'good', while 'artificial' implies 'bad'. (For example, 'genuine' affection is real and earnest and heart-felt, but an 'artificial' laugh is a forced or insincere or even mocking one.) When 'artificial' is used of a manmade or synthetic replacement for part of the body, the contrasting word is not 'genuine' but either 'real' or 'natural'. For example, 'artificial' teeth can replace 'natural' teeth, and an 'artificial' limb can be used instead of a real one. 'Artificial' respiration, too, is given when a person's 'natural' respiration has apparently failed. See also **true/false**.

genus/species
In the various categories of biological classification for living things, 'genus' and 'species' are frequently contrasted, not simply because they are major categories, but because in the traditional system of binomial nomenclature, the 'genus' and 'species' are used together for naming purposes. The 'genus' (from Latin meaning 'race') is one of the groups into which a so called 'family' is divided, and which itself contains one or more 'species' (Latin meaning 'kind'). For example, the domestic cat is *Felis domesticus*, where '*Felis*' is its 'genus' (in the family *Felidae*), and '*domesticus*' is its 'species'.

geocentric/heliocentric
The words (based on Greek) literally mean 'earth-centred' and 'sun-centred', so are alternative terms for the theories propounded respectively by Ptolemy (who maintained that the Sun revolved round the Earth) and Copernicus (who believed, as we generally now do, that the Earth goes round the Sun). In this respect see **Ptolemaic system/Copernican system**. In the world of astrology (as distinct from astronomy), 'geocentric' relates to calculations of the positions of the planets as seen by an observer on the Earth, while 'heliocentric' astrology bases its interpretations with reference to the Sun as centre.

geography see **history**

geometric progression see **arithmetic progression**

Germanic see **Romance**

gesellschaft see **gemeinschaft**

get/produce
These two nouns (not verbs) are used in the equestrian world to denote, respectively, the entire offspring of a male horse (a stallion) or a female (a mare). 'Get' relates to the biblical 'begotten' and 'begat' (meaning 'father') while 'produce', more obviously, relates to the act of giving birth or of 'bringing forth' the young animal. The words are also used in their verbal sense and can be found in special stud books and directories (e.g. 'An ideal horse to get hunter foals' or 'This mare has produced four foal winners'). Compare **sire/dam**.

giant/dwarf
In their most familiar sense, the words are obvious contrasts for a person who is larger than average, and one who is smaller, especially when this tallness or shortness is the result of some genetic fault. In a transferred sense, the terms can thus imply great stature (or status) or insignificance, accordingly (a 'giant' in the world of physics, a puny 'dwarf' when it comes to creative ideas). The saying that 'A dwarf on a giant's shoulders sees further of the two' has also been quoted by a number of writers, from medieval times to the present. In astronomy, the words have technical uses, so that a 'giant' star is a very bright one with a great mass, and a 'dwarf' star, rather more precisely, has a brightness that is ordinary or less than normal, and a size that is relatively small, but is of a high density. See also the prefixes **giga-/nano-** (p. 285).

Gilbert/Sullivan
There have been several well-known pairs of librettists and composers, responsible for the words and music of a musical work such as an opera, and 'Gilbert' and 'Sullivan' are among the most familiar, at least in the English-speaking world. The comic operas (or operettas) of the Victorian era were the joint products of Sir William Gilbert (who wrote the words) and Sir Arthur Sullivan (who composed the music), and it is in their contrasting roles here that one chief difference between them lies. The other was in their differing personalities, since 'Gilbert' was gruff and domineering, while 'Sullivan' was gentle and charming. This 'clash' led to a quarrel that lasted for four years. In the end, however, they were reconciled and the music won through. (According to David Eden, in *Gilbert and Sullivan: The Creative Conflict*, published in 1986, 'the life instincts in Sullivan overcame the death instincts in Gilbert'!)

girl see **boy**

Girondins/Montagnards
These were the names of the two rival political parties in France at the time of the Revolution, with the 'Girondins' being the moderates, or even the right-wingers, who were in effect republicans, and the 'Montagnards' the extreme revolutionary left-wingers, who held that complete centralization of government was necessary, and who eventually overthrew the 'Girondins' and took control of the Jacobins, who were also revolutionary radicals and so similarly opposed to the 'Girondins'. The 'Girondins' were so called since many of them came from the department of the Gironde. The 'Montagnards' (literally 'mountain men') were so named because they occupied the highest benches in the assembly. (And the Jacobins derived their name from the convent of St Jacques in Paris where they originally met.) The 'Girondins' are sometimes known in English as 'Girondists', and their main opponents given as the Jacobins, not the 'Montagnards'.

give/take
'Give and take is fair play', 'Give him an inch and he'll take an ell', 'It blesseth him that gives and him that takes', 'Whoever gives, takes liberty'. These are just a few of the many sayings and quotations that combine the two opposing words, and there are just as many with the alternative pairing of 'give' and 'get'. The basic concept is of presenting something that is one's own to someone else ('giving') and acquiring something from someone else that is their own ('taking'), although of course it is quite possible to 'give' without

'taking', and one can 'take' without 'giving' anything in return. Yet 'giving' and 'taking' as reciprocal actions are part of our daily lives, especially in such everyday activities as shopping and travelling and in the very act of conversation, whether 'business' or 'pleasure'. 'Give and take' is itself a phrase that implies mutual concessions being made, benefits being shared, or ideas being exchanged. It seems we prefer to balance the two: 'taking' without 'giving' is unreasonable and unsociable; 'giving' without 'taking' is unnatural and even suspect.

glossy/matt
Of a photograph, 'glossy' means smooth and shiny, with a bright, light-reflecting surface and noticeable contrast of colours (or of shades of black and white). A 'matt' photograph, however, has a relatively dull appearance, with a lacklustre surface that is also slightly roughened. The colour contrasts are similarly more muted. Many people prefer a 'matt' surface since this eliminates glare and undue reflection, and also gives a photograph more of a picture-like quality. 'Matt' here is simply a commercial spelling of 'mat', which in turn comes from French *mat*, itself literally meaning 'dead' (from the Arabic) and occurring in the latter half of the word 'checkmate' in chess (which means 'the king is dead'). Compare the next entry below.

glossy magazine/pulp magazine
The first and obvious contrast here is in the type of paper on which the magazines are printed. 'Glossy magazines' (or simply 'glossies') are printed on glossy paper, as their name implies, with this being of a high quality and suitable for the many colour photographs that a 'glossy' carries. A 'pulp magazine', on the other hand, is printed on low quality, roughish paper, suitable for texts and certain graphical effects, but hardly for clear, sharp photographs. The main differences between the two types apart from this are that 'glossy magazines' are expensive and 'up-market', and often deal with fashion, while 'pulp magazines' are cheap, self-consciously 'down-market', and contain mainly trite or sensational material or stories, some of which, nevertheless, have attracted a cult readership. 'Pulps', too, are mainly a feature of the American market rather than the British. (In the United States, incidentally, 'glossies' are more usually known as 'slicks'.) Examples of 'glossy magazines' are *Harpers & Queen*, *Country Life* and *Playboy*, while two well known American 'pulp magazines' are *Amazing Stories* (a classic of the genre) and the more modern *Eerie Country*. Many of the original American science fiction and fantasy 'pulps' of the 1930s have now generally yielded in popularity to comics, however.

GMT/BST
Here the contrast is one of time or season (or both). 'GMT' ('Greenwich Mean Time') is the standard time for Britain during the winter months and itself serves as a basis for calculating the time in a number of other countries round the world. 'BST' is 'British Summer Time', when the clocks are advanced one hour in the spring (until the autumn) to make optimum use of natural daylight hours. Many other countries have a similar system of summer time. Britain has experimented with other time systems in the past, at one stage even having a 'Double Summer Time' (two hours ahead of 'GMT'), and on another occasion doing without 'BST' at all. However, the present system seems to suit most people, and does give a welcome extra hour of daylight in the evenings. 'GMT' is so called since it is the local time at Greenwich, through which the 0° meridian passes.

gnostic see **agnostic**

go see (1) **come** (2) **stop**[1]

goats see **sheep**

godfather/godmother
These are the male and female godparents or 'sponsors', who in the Christian church accept responsibility for the Christian upbringing of the child from the moment of his or her christening (baptism). In the

Church of England, 'there shall be for every Male-child to be baptized two Godfathers and one Godmother; and for every Female, one Godfather and two Godmothers' (Book of Common Prayer). Today, since membership of the Church of England is often a purely nominal thing ('Religion: C of E'), the godparents themselves are frequently little more than honorary uncles and aunts, taking little or no interest in their godchild's religious upbringing (but duly coming up with an annual birthday and Christmas present until they are grown up). However, 'godfathers' and 'godmothers' have existed since medieval times, and are a long-established arrangement. More recently, 'godfather' (but not 'godmother') has acquired a more sinister sense as a word for the head of a criminal organization, especially the Mafia. (For more on this, see the American films of the 1970s, *The Godfather* and *The Godfather, Part Two*, from the novel by Mario Puzo.)

godmother see **godfather**

Goidelic see **Brythonic**

gold/silver
The two precious metals are frequently contrasted, but always with the implication that 'silver' is inferior to 'gold', even if itself valuable. The difference can be seen not simply in coins (a 'gold' sovereign, a 'silver' crown) but in medals, awards, prizes and scores. A 'gold' medal is the award made to a competitor who comes first in a number of sports contests, for example, notably athletics, with the runner-up gaining a 'silver' (and the one coming third a 'bronze'). A 'gold' disc, likewise, is an award (in the form of a golden gramophone record) made to an artiste whose record has reached a specified sales figure, especially in pop music, with a 'silver' disc going to sales at a lower but still impressive figure. (However, both are topped by a 'platinum', which is awarded for the best sales of all.) There was even both a 'golden' age and a 'silver' age in classical mythology. The 'golden' age was the first and best, when all was prosperity, happiness and innocence (not necessarily in that order). The 'silver' age was in more marked contrast to it, and followed it, with the original prosperity turned to coarse opulence, and the innocence replaced by irreligion. Both actually and symbolically, too, the yellow of 'gold' suggests the bright sun, and the white 'silver' the pale moon. For alchemists, too, 'gold' symbolized man or king, and 'silver' woman or queen. Finally, consider the old proverb, 'Speech is silver, silence is golden'.

good[1]/bad
Hamlet voiced the theory: 'There is nothing either good or bad, but thinking makes it so'. The reasoning is debatable, but at a less philosophical level, for most people, the difference between 'good' and 'bad' is all too apparent. Indeed, the distinction is so basic that it is on a par with 'right' and 'wrong'. So perhaps it is best here to concentrate on the actual usages of the opposites. A 'good' man is virtuous, a 'bad' man is a wrongdoer. Fresh fruit is 'good' for you, but too many rich puddings and sweets are 'bad' for you. 'Good' money is sound and financially reliable; 'bad' money is unsound or worthless. If you have a 'good' night you have slept well and soundly; if you have had a 'bad' night you have slept poorly or fitfully. If a child is 'good' at games, he or she plays well; if a child is 'bad' at mathematics, the subject is found to be difficult (or even poorly taught). Finally (for the purposes of this entry, which must be finite), 'Good riddance to bad rubbish'. (But see the next entry.)

good[2]/evil
Here the 'big divide' is chiefly a theological and philosophical one, with much speculation about the origin of 'evil' in a world that apparently began as 'good' (see the first chapter of Genesis, and also **Adam/Eve**). As for the contrasting pair **good/bad** (above), there are many sayings and quotations that embody some observation about the two opposite states, whether from a moral or some other angle. These can range from the fairly profound

'Bear with evil and expect good' to the more homely 'Many a good cow has an evil calf'. Whatever our view of 'good' and 'evil', at whatever level, the association of 'good' with 'God' and 'evil' with 'Devil' (who personifies it) is a purely chance one, and the words are not linguistically related. In modern usage, too, 'evil' is a much more 'rarefied' word than 'bad', its virtual equivalent, although in medieval times it was much more common, and was in general use as a word denoting any kind of disapproval or disparagement. Hence its common use (in an everyday sense) in the Bible, for example: 'A good tree cannot bring forth evil fruit' (Matthew 7:18), where today we would talk about 'bad' fruit.

goodbye see **hello**

goodies/baddies
Two fairly good-natured opposites denoting characters or persons who take sides as 'good' and 'bad', with the former conventionally winning (at least in many fictional contexts). The words almost certainly arose in the 1930s with reference to the characters in a western movie, with the 'goodies' often being cheered and the 'baddies' booed (see **hurray/boo**). The implication was that the 'goodies' were the 'good men' and the 'baddies' the 'bad men', and doubtless the words actually developed as a shortened form of one or the other. (For some time before this, a real-life criminal, such as a gangster or gunman, was known in American slang as a 'bad man', possibly as an English translation of the Spanish term *malo hombre*.) The general use of the two terms as contrasting designations, however, probably dates from only about the 1950s, by which time 'goodies' and 'baddies' had moved from the cinema screen into the wider world of politics and moral issues. See also **good/bad** and **good/evil**, above.

goods/services
As used in economics, 'goods' are commodities that are tangible and (usually) movable, and that are not consumed at the same time as they are produced. An example might be grain or oil. 'Services', on the other hand, are commodities such as banking that are mainly intangible and are normally consumed at the same time as they are produced.

googly/chinaman
Such delightful names could only belong to the esoteric game of cricket, where they both indicate a ball bowled in such a way that, on bouncing, it turns towards the leg (right) side of a right-handed batsman, although looking as if it might turn to the left. The difference is that a 'googly' is bowled by a right-handed bowler, and a 'chinaman' by one who is left-handed. (However, a 'googly' can also be bowled by a left-handed bowler so long as it turns to the *off* or left side of a right-handed batsman after bouncing.) The origin of 'googly' is unknown, although it is on record that the technique of bowling them was first practised by the cricketer B. J. T. Bosanquet in the 1890s. A 'chinaman' apparently gets its name from the fact that it was first bowled by the Chinese-born West Indian cricketer Ellis Achong in the 1930s (although evidence suggests that such a style was already in existence). The suggestion that the 'googly' is so called because it makes the batsman go 'googly-eyed', since he doesn't know which way the ball is going to turn, is pleasant but cannot be substantiated. However, it is certainly a fact that both senses of the word are recorded as emerging more or less simultaneously, in the early 1900s. See also **leg/off**.

gospel see **epistle**

go up/come down
Apart from the obvious opposites of 'ascend' and 'descend', the two terms are also used in more specialized contexts to denote contrary actions. For example, a university student, especially one at Oxford or Cambridge, 'goes up' when he enters the university, or returns to it after a vacation, and 'comes down' when he leaves it, or at the end of a term. (From

the university end, this latter action will be seen as 'going down'.) The analogy is that of travelling to an important place such as London, since when journeying to the capital one usually 'goes up' to it, and when returning home, one 'comes down' from it. For more of the implications and niceties here, see the pair **up/down**. Metaphorically, too, if a person 'goes up' in the world, he or she moves to a higher social or other position, while to 'come down' in the world is to sink to an unacceptably low level of living, especially when one has been used to better things.

Government/Opposition
The contrasting terms are officially used in Britain for the government in power and for the members of the political party who oppose it in Parliament. (The degree of officiality even extends to the formal name for each side being 'Her Majesty's Government' and 'Her Majesty's Loyal Opposition'.) In practical terms this means that Parliament contains not only a 'Government' but a sort of officially recognized 'Anti-Government', campaigning to oust it and take its place. In actual terms the 'Opposition' is thus to an extent the same as the Shadow Cabinet, at least as far as its senior ministers are concerned. (See **shadow cabinet/cabinet**.) The titles have been in use since the eighteenth century, although the extended formal title (for the 'Opposition') originated as a quip in a speech made to Parliament on 10 April 1826 by John Cam Hobhouse, the future Baron Broughton: 'It was said to be very hard on his majesty's ministers to raise objections to this proposition. For his own part, he thought it was more hard on his majesty's opposition (a laugh) to compel them to take this course'.

gown see **town**[2]

Graeco-Roman/freestyle
The two contrasting terms relate to the sport of wrestling. The 'Graeco-Roman' style imposes restrictions, in that the wrestler may not use his legs to gain a fall and no hold may be applied below the waist. 'Freestyle', on the other hand, imposes no restrictions at all, and the wrestler may use any hold or throw that he chooses. (It is thus 'no holds barred', to use an expression that itself derives from wrestling of this type.) The name 'Graeco-Roman' alludes to the fact that the style is similar to that practised by the ancient Greeks and Romans. 'Freestyle' is self-explanatory.

grand mal/petit mal
Here the two French expressions mean literally 'big illness' and 'little illness' and are used of severe and mild forms of epilepsy, respectively. 'Grand mal' involves loss of consciousness in an epileptic fit for up to five minutes, accompanied by violent convulsions. 'Petit mal' denotes loss of consciousness for only thirty seconds or less, or even no actual loss of consciousness at all, while convulsions, if any, are mild and occur more as muscle spasms and twitching. The terms arose only in the nineteenth century and answer to the much more formal Latin names for the two types of *epilepsia gravior* and *epilepsia mitior*, with the latter words here meaning respectively 'graver' and 'milder'.

grand piano/upright piano
The basic difference here is that in the 'grand piano', the strings are arranged flat or horizontally, while in the 'upright piano' they are arranged (obviously) in an upright position, or vertically. The 'grand

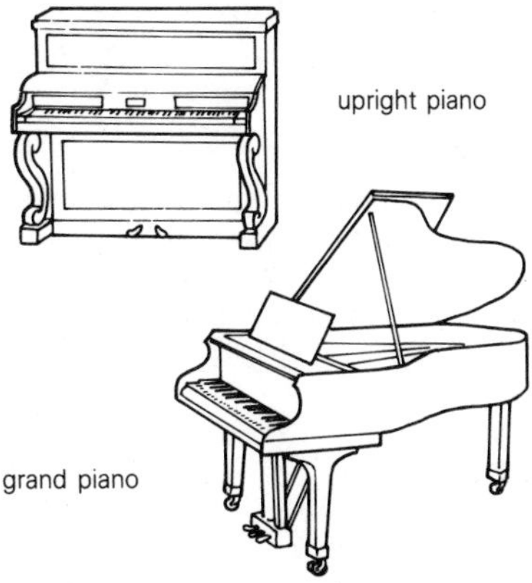

piano' is familiar from its appearance at concerts and recitals, and in the homes of serious musicians (of whatever type of music). The 'upright piano' is the more homely one found in modest homes and dotted around schools, clubs and pubs. The 'grand' is named for both its size and appearance, and has been so designated since the late eighteenth century. (Music is fond of things that are 'grand', such as a 'grand overture', a 'grand chorus', a 'grand finale' and, above all, 'grand opera', whose very title is more than daunting.)

grand slam/little slam
Most people have heard of a 'grand slam' without realizing that there is also a 'little' one. The expressions belong to the game of bridge. A 'grand slam' is the winning of thirteen tricks by one player or side in a single hand. A 'little slam' is the winning of all tricks *except one* (frustratingly enough). A 'grand slam' has come to be extended to other games and sports, where it can denote the winning of all the major tournaments in a year, especially in tennis. The 'slam' here does not seem to derive from the fact that the winning player 'slams' his cards on the table, but probably has some other origin. It is still uncertain what it is.

granny see **reef knot**

graphics see **text**

grass court see **hard court**

grave see (1) **acute**[2] (2) **cradle**

great/small
'All creatures great and small' is somehow much more poetic and memorable than 'All creatures big and little', or even 'large and small'. 'Small', however, is the standard opposite to 'great', which itself is an imposing and rather formal alternative to 'big' or 'large'. It can imply 'big' in a special way, so that a 'great' tree is unduly large and possibly old, and a 'great' crowd is an exceptionally sizeable one. However, although 'small' is the standard contrary to 'great', in animal and bird names the 'great' form usually has no fixed opposite, since the word simply denotes a creature larger than the average or than the most common kind. There is thus a 'great' ape as opposed to a standard one, and a 'great' tit as one bigger than the most familiar sort. With astronomical creatures, though, the opposite is usually 'little', as with the 'Great' Bear and the 'Little' Bear, for the two constellations. In everyday and popular use, therefore, 'great' opposes 'small', which itself has the same sense of 'unduly so' that 'great' has. This can be seen in various proverbs and sayings, such as 'The great fish eat up the small', and 'Great engines turn on small pivots'. Consider, too, the biblical exhortation, 'Be not ignorant of any thing in a great matter or a small' (Ecclesiasticus, 5:15). Compare **big/little**, **large/small**, **major/minor** and the next entry below.

greater/lesser
As they stand, the two words mean 'bigger' and 'smaller'. They are commonly associated, however, with the names of animals and plants, such as the 'greater' black-backed gull and the 'lesser' black-backed gull, the 'greater' celandine and the 'lesser' celandine. (It must have been the latter that Wordsworth meant when he wrote, somewhat cloyingly, of the 'flower that shall be mine', which was 'the little celandine'.) The opposites also occur in some geographical names, especially of island groups, such as the 'Greater' Antilles and the 'Lesser' Antilles in the West Indies. (For more about the latter, see **leeward/windward**.) A curious use of 'greater' without any 'lesser' is in the names of some British cities with their suburbs, such as 'Greater' London and 'Greater' Manchester'. In such cases, 'Great' would really serve just as well. (However, 'Greater' Britain was not simply 'Great' Britain, but was a name used for a while in the nineteenth and twentieth centuries to mean the British Empire, or Britain with her colonies.)

Greeks/Romans
There is usually an implied contrast

between the Ancient Greeks and the Ancient Romans that extends beyond the mere difference in language. The 'Greeks' are usually thought of as more ancient or 'historical' (which they were), more advanced culturally and intellectually (disputably so) and generally more exotic and esoteric. The 'Romans', on the other hand, are mostly seen as more 'down to earth' (with their gladiatorial combats and central heating) and generally more approachable and accessible. The difference in concepts must arise at least partly from the fact that the Roman Empire extended to most of Europe, including Britain. Therefore, although decidedly 'classical', their lifestyle was more worldly and has left its mark to this day in many countries in the form of 'Roman' settlements, castles and roads. The 'Greeks' were geographically more remote, as well as historically, and their current image reflects this. However, at a popular level there is still much real ignorance about both races and nations. (It was Disraeli who said of his wife, 'She is an excellent creature, but she can never remember which came first, the Greeks or the Romans'.) See also **Trojans/Greeks**.

Greeks see **Trojans**

green see **red**[3]

Greens see **Blues**[1]

Gregorian calendar/Julian calendar
The 'Gregorian calendar' is our present one, with its 365 days in most years and a leap year occurring in every year whose number can be divided by four (except those centenary years, such as 1900, that cannot be divided by 400). It was introduced in 1582 by Pope Gregory XIII (hence its name) as a revision of the 'Julian calendar' which had been brought in way back in 46 BC by Julius Caesar (hence *its* name). This earlies calendar was similar to the 'Gregorian', but had a beginning of the year that was not fixed as 1 January and leap years that occurred in centenary years, as well as every fourth year. Gregory XIII introduced his reformed calendar because the 'Julian' one was by then 'out' by as much as eleven days. This was the result of the inaccurate calculations made by Caesar's astronomer Sosigenes, who had over-estimated the length of the year by eleven minutes. Over the years and centuries, this had amounted to a sizeable discrepancy. England switched to the 'Gregorian calendar' in 1752, while the Eastern Orthodox Church has still not changed.

greyhen see **blackcock**

grey squirrel see **red squirrel**

groom see **bride**

gros point/petit point
In needlepoint embroidery, 'gros point' is a large cross-stitch covering two horizontal and two vertical threads. 'Petit point' is a small diagonal stitch across single threads (also known as a 'tent stitch'). The clearly French terms mean 'large point' and 'small point', with the 'point' the stitch made by the needle.

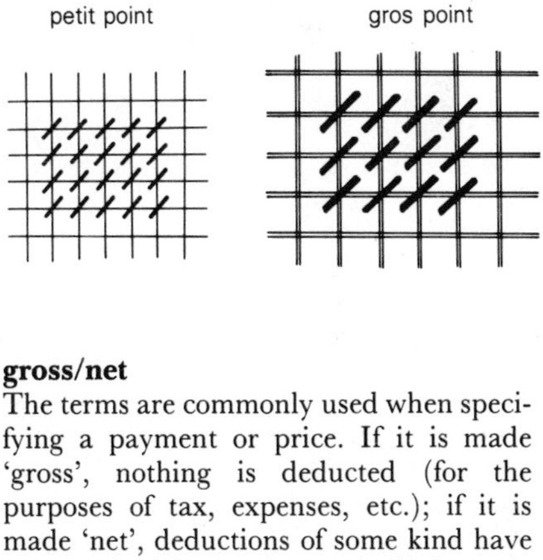

gross/net
The terms are commonly used when specifying a payment or price. If it is made 'gross', nothing is deducted (for the purposes of tax, expenses, etc.); if it is made 'net', deductions of some kind have been made. The words can similarly apply to weight, with the 'gross' weight of something including that of its container, wrapping and the like, and its 'net' weight that of the thing itself, the contents inside the container. (Most foodstuffs have their 'net' weight indicated, even where it is not

specified as such, e.g. 'Chopped Chicken in Jelly 198 g 7 oz', i.e. 'net'.) 'Gross' ultimately derives from Latin *grossus*, 'thick', and 'net' (still sometimes spelt 'nett') from French *net*, 'neat' (i.e. with nothing added).

Gross-schreibung/kleinschreibung
An admittedly rather academic pair of opposites, but quite an interesting one. They are the German for, respectively, 'big writing' and 'little writing', and relate to the German practice of writing nouns with capital letters. (For example, 'A father and his son are going through the wood' is *Ein Vater und sein Sohn gehen durch den Wald.*) Most Germans, and those learning German, accept this situation, but there has been a small but steady campaign to 'decapitalize' and to change from *Gross-schreibung* to *kleinschreibung*. Among the campaigners have been such noted figures as Wagner and the writers Stefan George and Bertolt Brecht. The main advocators, however, were the Grimm brothers, the famous philologists and story writers, who were authors not only of *Grimms' Fairy Tales* but of a *Deutsches Wörterbuch*, or 'German Dictionary', where they actually practised what they preached, and in which all nouns appear with small letters. Somewhat surprisingly, many English dictionaries, when quoting German nouns, follow this practice, and print them with small letters. Even the great *OED* and its *Supplements* do. Until some unified linguistic policy is declared, however, German nouns, like English names, will have to continue to be written with capital letters, since this is the established norm. See also **capital letter/small letter**, and even **upper/lower**.

ground speed see **air speed**

ground wave see **sky wave**

group see **period**

Guernsey see **Jersey**

guest see **host**

guide see **scout**[1]

guilty/not guilty
'Prisoner at the bar: how do you plead, Guilty or Not Guilty?' The legal question is the traditional one posed by the judge in a courtroom to the accused, who can reply as either 'Guilty' or 'Not Guilty', depending whether he admits the offence or denies it. However, it is the jury who must decide whether he is actually 'guilty' or 'not guilty' of the offence. In English law, too, the defendant will be assumed to be 'not guilty' however he pleads, until the jury has given its verdict (which will thus either confirm this, or state that he is 'guilty'). In Scottish law, the equivalent of 'not guilty' is 'not proven', which in many cases may actually correspond more accurately to the real state of things, especially if evidence is slim or confused. Compare **innocent/guilty**.

guilty see **innocent**

gymnosperm see **angiosperm**

gyp/bedder
Although relating to university jargon, these are not the old 'Oxbridge opposites' (see **quadrangle/court**, for example, or **May Week/Eights Week**). A 'gyp' is the term at Cambridge University (and also at Durham) for a male college servant, while a 'bedder' is a female servant (at Cambridge only). As her name implies, one of her main duties is to make beds and clean students' bedrooms. 'Gyp' may derive from 'gypsy', perhaps since originally the work of today's 'gyps' was done (on a casual basis, simply as odd jobs) by 'hangers on' who led an unsettled way of life like that of gypsies. But to complete the picture, see also **scout**[2]**/gyp**.

gyp see **scout**[2]

Hh

H/B
The contrast here is in the two basic types of pencil lead. An 'H' pencil is one with a hard lead, used by artists for precise and detailed work. A 'B' pencil has a soft lead, used generally for gentler and 'fuller' drawing. The letters stand respectively for 'hard' and 'black'. (In the United States, 'F' for 'fine' is used instead of 'H'.) For pencils used for writing, the degree of hardness is normally indicated by a number, from 1 (the softest) to 4 (the hardest). Artists' pencils can range from 8'B', the softest, to simply 'H' (or 'F'), the hardest. For drafting (engineering drawing) pencils, the hardness usually ranges from 'HB', as the softest, to 10'H', the hardest. Some older pencils have degrees of hardness indicated by a repetition of the letter, such as 'HH' or even 'HHH', and for degrees of softness similarly ('BB' and 'BBB').

hail/farewell
The contrasting expressions are now mainly found in historical (or humorous) contexts, with 'hail' used as a form of greeting, and 'farewell' said at a parting. (Compare the corresponding modern pair **hello/goodbye**. See also **ave/vale**.) There are dozens of familiar quotations with each word individually ('Hail, fellow, well met', 'Sweets to the sweet; farewell': respectively Swift and Shakespeare), but not quite so many combining them. (The best known is probably the English translation of Catullus's famous *Atque in perpetuum, frater, ave atque vale*: 'And forever, O my brother, hail and farewell!') 'Hail' basically means 'be healthy', and is related to 'hale', 'whole' and 'healthy' itself. 'Farewell' means what it says: 'fare well', i.e. 'go well', 'may you have a good journey'.

half see **full**

hammer[1]/sickle
The two contrasting devices are familiar as the crossed emblems on the flag of Soviet Russia. The contrast lies in the application of the two implements: the 'hammer' represents industrial workers, and the 'sickle' peasants, or the country labourers. So the split is basically that of **town/country**. Russians actually say the words the other way round: *serp i molot*, 'sickle and hammer'. It will be noted that the two implements, as they appear on the Russian flag (in the top lefthand corner, surmounted by a star), actually resemble a type of cross, with the handles of the 'hammer' and 'sickle' pointing in different directions. In this respect the emblem as a whole corresponds to the actual cross found on other national flags, e.g. Norway, Greece, and of course the United Kingdom with its 'Union Jack'.

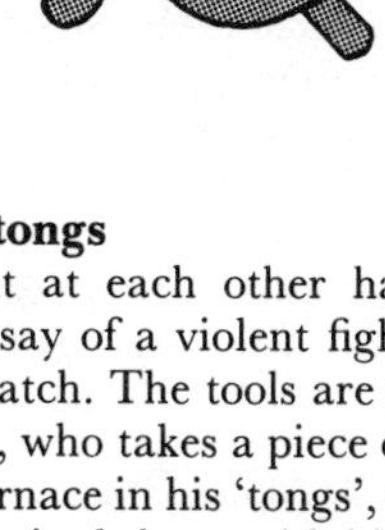

hammer[2]/tongs
'They went at each other hammer and tongs', we say of a violent fight or verbal slanging match. The tools are those of the blacksmith, who takes a piece of hot metal from the furnace in his 'tongs', and beats it into the required shape with his 'hammer', one implement in each hand. The metaphorical contrast is really that of the battling or arguing parties.

hand/foot
Here the two parts of the body correspond as the outer elements of limbs, respectively the arm and the leg, and although anatomically they can to some extent be equated (both have five digits and a similar bone arrangement), they obviously serve different purposes, with the 'hand' generally much more versatile than the 'foot'. However, they are both used for 'doing things' (if only hitting and kicking), so need to be restrained, rightly or wrongly, on occasions. Hence the need to bind a prisoner 'hand and foot' to prevent him from striking or running. In a pleasanter context, if one waits on a person 'hand and foot', one serves him or her more than dutifully, using the 'hands' to bring and take things and the 'feet' to arrive and depart.

hard/soft
As well as the obvious opposites ('hard' ground, 'soft' ground), there are some fairly specific or specialized uses of the two words. A 'hard'-boiled egg is one cooked so that its white and yolk solidify, while a 'soft'-boiled one has a 'runny' yolk. 'Hard' porn (pornography) relates to the explicit portrayal or description of the sexual act, while 'soft' porn is usually not much more than titillating (and in many cases even legal, or tolerated by the law). 'Hard' drugs are addictive or habit-forming ones, such as cocaine and heroin, while 'soft' drugs such as cannabis or its milder form, marijuana, are not addictive. 'Hard' roe is the eggs of the female fish, especially when still enclosed in the membrane of the ovary, while 'soft' roe is the sperm of a male fish, especially when still in the testis. 'Hard' sell is a term for aggressive salesmanship, but 'soft' sell uses gentle if cunning persuasion. Of a computer, 'hardware' means its physical parts and components, whether electric or electronic, while its 'software' is its programs. Your 'hard' palate is the roof of your mouth, and your 'soft' palate is the fold at the back of this, where it more or less separates your mouth and throat. See also below **hardwood/softwood** and the related **hard court/grass court** and **paperback/hardback**.

hardback see **paperback**

hard court/grass court
These are the two contrasting types of tennis court, each requiring a different technique, but broadly with the 'hard court' giving a faster game, and the 'grass court' one that can be more complex, since the ball is harder to control accurately on grass, which itself can present a varying surface depending on the weather and its own condition and 'geography'. (This can also affect the movements and stance of the player, of course.) Chronologically, the 'grass court' came first, but both were in existence already in the late nineteenth century.

hardwood/softwood
'Hardwood' is the wood of a broad-leafed tree, such as the ash, oak and beech, as distinct from 'softwood', which is the wood of a coniferous tree, such as the pine. Put another way, 'hardwood' trees are angiosperms, while 'softwood' ones are gymnosperms (see **angiosperm/gymnosperm**). Most 'hardwoods' really are harder than 'softwoods', as their name implies. However, a few 'hardwoods' are actually softer than most 'softwoods'. (One example is the South American balsa.) On the whole, 'hardwoods' are much more versatile than 'softwoods', but 'softwoods' are more readily available and are cheaper.

hare[1]/hounds
The 'hare' is chased; the 'hounds' do the chasing! That is the contrast of the chase, and more precisely of the sporting diversion otherwise known as a 'paperchase'. The 'hare' is thus a runner who sets off ahead of the others and lays a trail. The 'hounds' then start after him, and by following the trail attempt to catch him. If they succeed, they have won; if they fail, the 'hare' has won. The sport dates from at least the first half of the nineteenth century, and a 'hare and hounds' features

in the famous school story *Tom Brown's Schooldays* by Thomas Hughes ('Please, sir, we've been out Big-side Hare-and-Hounds, and lost our way'). The two types of animal are also paired in the expression 'to run with the hare and hunt with the hounds', said of a person who tries to keep in with both sides in some way, or who actually does so. Compare the next entry, and in a different sort of field, see **rabbit/hare**.

hare²/tortoise
The contrast here is between the 'hare' who runs fast, and the 'tortoise' who moves only slowly – but who wins the race. The allusion is to Aesop's fable, 'The Hare and the Tortoise', in which the 'hare', confident of an easy victory over the slow 'tortoise', decided to have a short nap. While he was asleep, the 'tortoise' walked past him and won. (Moral: Slow but sure wins the race.)

hare see **rabbit**

harmonic see **fundamental**

harmony/melody
The two terms, themselves rather harmonious and melodious, are the two contrasting elements that make music what it is. 'Harmony' is the arrangement or composition of the different notes, instruments, voices or chords. 'Melody' is the 'tune', or the message that they convey. It is naturally possible to have a 'melody' without any 'harmony' in the strict sense of the word, but 'harmony' without 'melody' is virtually impossible, except for isolated snatches of music. The terms also apply to the study of each particular musical art, so that 'harmony' studies the way in which chords combine and are structured, while 'melody' (although not all musicians would accept the definition) is the 'Method of ranging single musical Sounds in a regular Progression, either ascending or descending, according to the established Principles' (Charles Avison, *An Essay on Musical Expression*, 1751). Put another way, 'harmony' is all that is 'vertical' in musical composition, while 'melody' is what is 'horizontal'.

hate see **love**

haurient see **urinant**

have-nots see **haves**

haves/have-nots
The contrasting terms are quite recent ones to denote the rich and the poor, especially as considered in the joint expression 'the haves and the have-nots', with the implication that the 'haves' possess not simply wealth, but also security, while the 'have-nots' are regarded as deprived or oppressed. In most contexts, too, the reference is specifically to the rich nations of the world and the poor. The expression seems to have originated soon after (and perhaps even as a result of) the First World War.

hawks see **doves**

he/she
The male and the female, with 'he' also used to denote people in general: 'He that hath ears to hear, let him hear'. Feminists and some grammarians object to the latter use of 'he', but what is the alternative? One can endlessly say 'he or she', but after a while this seems cumbersome. One can say 'they' or 'those': 'Those who have ears to hear, let them hear'. But this blurs the singular implication of 'he'. One can devise a pronoun that is not gender-specific, such as these proposals by various professors and educators in the United States: 'co', 'et' (with the 'e' of 'he' and 'she' plus the 't' of 'it'), 'hesh', 'hir', 'jhe' (pronounced 'gee'), or simply 'person' ('Person that has ears to hear, let person hear'). The problem remains. It is purely coincidental that 'she' contains the letters of 'he', just as 'female' contains 'male' and 'woman' contains 'man'. In Old English, the two pronouns were even closer, so that 'he' was *hē* and 'she' was *hēo*. This was clearly confusing, and 'she' developed to differentiate the sexes.

head[1]/tail
'From head to tail' is one fairly standard way of expressing the total length of an animal, since its 'head' is usually its foremost part and its 'tail' its hindmost. In a metaphorical sense, we say 'I can't make head or tail of it' when we fail to understand something, or cannot puzzle it out. The reference is as if to a strange kind of animal, i.e. one whose 'head' or 'tail' cannot be reliably located. Apart from these expressions, 'head' serves as the opposite of 'tail' in a number of special uses. Among them are the 'head' and 'tail' of a coin (otherwise its pair of **obverse/reverse**), a 'head' wind (against one) and a 'tail' wind (behind one), and a 'head' lamp (at the front of a vehicle) and 'tail' lamp (at the rear). However, many 'head' phrases will have no corresponding 'tail' ones, simply because humans have no 'tails'! Compare the next entry below.

head[2]/toe
'From head to toe' is an expression corresponding to 'from head to tail' (see above) when indicating the overall height or body length of a person. ('From head to foot' is another way of saying the same thing.) There are no contrasting 'head' and 'toe' phrases in an individual sense simply because the two parts of the anatomy are so different. However, 'head' can be the opposite of 'foot' in such terms as the 'head' and 'foot' of a bed (top and bottom of it), or purely as the top and bottom of other objects (such as the 'head' of this page and the 'foot' of it).

header see **stretcher**

head rhyme/end rhyme
In poetry or verse, 'head rhyme' is the same as alliteration, and is found when the same letter occurs at the beginning of successive words (as trivially in 'Goosey goosey gander, Whither shall I wander?' and as more seriously in Pope's 'bookful blockhead' 'With loads of learned lumber in his head'). 'End rhyme' is therefore the familiar kind, occurring at the ends of words on successive lines as in the majority of 'standard' poetry and verse, including this laconic limerick:

> There was a young lady of Leeds,
> Who planted her garden with seeds,
> The birds came along
> And ate every one,
> So now she has nothing but weeds.

heart/mind
The contrast here is a stock one to denote a person's emotional or moral nature ('heart') as distinct from his or her intellect or 'brains' ('mind'). The words are coupled not merely in everyday speech ('We must turn our hearts and minds to this important matter') but are found in various quotations, such as Matthew Arnold's 'With women the heart argues, not the mind'. A similar comparison also occurs with 'heart' and 'head' ('Tell me, where is fancy bred?'), where the alliteration helps. However, 'mind' is a more accurate counterpart to 'heart' when it denotes the intellect or powers of reasoning.

heaven/hell
There are quotations and sayings galore that contrast the two great religious 'abodes of the dead' (one must suffice: perhaps it should be Milton's 'Better to reign in Hell, than serve in Heaven'), with other contrasts implied, such as 'good' and 'bad', 'blessed' and 'cursed', 'up' and 'down', 'angel' and 'devil', 'saint' and 'sinner', and so on. As with other pairs of opposites, the alliteration helps to bind the words in their 'attraction of opposites'. See also as entries the pairs mentioned (e.g. **good/bad**, **bless/curse**, etc.).

heavy see **light[2]**

heel/toe
The terms for the back and front part of the foot are sometimes used to express contrasting functions or senses, particularly when the analogy with a real 'heel' and 'toe' is fairly close. One notable geographical example is the 'heel' of Italy (its southeast extremity) and the 'toe' of Italy (its southwest end, where it 'boots'

Sicily). In motor racing, drivers use a technique called 'heel and toe' (or 'toe and heel'), in which one foot is on the brake and accelerator simultaneously, so as to change gear quickly (with the 'heel' operating the brake, and the 'toe' the accelerator). In the sport of road walking, too, the 'heel-and-toe' style is used, in which the 'heel' of the front foot touches the ground before the 'toes' of the rear one leave it.

heifer/bullock
A 'heifer' is a young cow, especially one that has not had more than one calf, and a 'bullock' is a young bull, and especially a gelded (castrated) one. The origin of 'bullock' is fairly obvious (it is a diminutive of 'bull'). The origin of 'heifer' is still uncertain. The word may relate to 'high', as if the animal was a 'high stepper' when it walked.

heliocentric see **geocentric**

hell see **heaven**

hello/goodbye
First, the origins. 'Hello' (also spelt 'hallo' and 'hullo') is actually an alteration of 'hollo', the call used to attract attention, with its own derivation uncertain. 'Hello' is not thus related to 'hail' as a form of greeting (see **hail/farewell**). 'Goodbye' is a shortening of 'God be with you', a wish (or a blessing) made for a person at a parting or departure. No doubt 'God' became 'good' because of similar expressions, such as 'good day', and 'good night'. (For a similar commendation to God, compare French *adieu* and Spanish *adios.*) 'Hello' is more versatile in its usage than 'goodbye', since it is not only an everyday greeting, but a standard response when answering the telephone (used also in other languages, such as French *allô*) and an exclamation of surprise (such as the comic policeman's 'hullo-ullo-ullo!'). Hence the former 'hello-girl', who was a telephone operator. (The term dates back to the United States in the nineteenth century.) Some people use the expression 'It's hello and goodbye' to indicate a short meeting or a brief visit, for example, when one is introduced to a person who one will probably never see again.

hemeralopia/nyctolopia
The two technical terms denote defects of eyesight. With 'hemeralopia', the patient has reduced vision in bright light. With 'nyctolopia', there is an inability to see properly in faint light, or when it is dark. The latter condition is commonly known as 'night blindness'. As they stand, the words have Greek origins which mean respectively 'day blind eye' and 'night blind eye'. 'Hemeralopia' is sometimes called 'day blindness'. More confusingly, however, it is sometimes used to denote night blindness. This is because 'night blindness' is taken to mean that the person so afflicted can see better by day, or as if the actual word 'hemerolopia' were derived from the two Greek elements *hemera*, 'day' and *ops*, 'eye' (overlooking the middle *alaos*, 'blind').

hen see **cock**

hen party see **stag party**

here/there
The best thing that can be done here (and there) is to give the most common derivative opposites with their meanings. If 'here' means 'in or to this place' and 'there' means 'in or to that place', then 'hereabouts' means 'somewhere round here', and 'thereabouts' means 'somewhere round there' (or 'approximately', as when one says, 'There were thirty people at the station, or thereabouts'). 'Hereby' is a formal word meaning 'by this means' ('I hereby declare . . .' means 'This declaration that I am making means . . .'), and 'thereby' means 'by that means' (or 'in connection with that', for example in the stock phrase, 'and thereby hangs a tale', i.e. 'there's an explanation or story behind that'). There are other much more formal opposites beloved of legal sticklers (such as 'heretofore' and 'therewith'), but about the only one in regular (and formal) use is 'herewith', used of something enclosed

with a letter ('Please find herewith' means 'I have enclosed'). As a unified phrase, 'here and there' means 'in places' or 'at times' ('His speech was rather boring, here and there'), and 'neither here nor there' means 'irrelevant' ('What he said was neither here nor there'). Related words, with contrasting pairs beginning respectively 'h' and 'th', are 'hither' and 'thither' and 'hence' and 'thence', with a further link-up existing in the pair 'this' and 'that' (see **this/that**).

hereditarianism see **environmentalism**

hero[1]/heroine
The 'great man' and 'great woman' (actually or fictionally) have titles that derive from the Greek, respectively *heros* and its feminine, *heroine*. However, the Greek mythological priestess Hero, who killed herself when her lover Leander drowned, has a name that does not mean 'heroic' (which she was not), but probably 'dedicated to Hera' (the goddess to whom the Roman Juno corresponded). In much more modern times, 'heroin' (the drug) is probably so named because a person taking it feels 'heroic'. 'Hero' can be used of anyone, male or female, in a general sense ('She was a real hero', meaning she was very brave). Compare the next entry, and see also the relevant comments in Appendix II (p. 291).

hero[2]/villain
Here we have the principal 'goodie' and 'baddie' (see **goodies/baddies**) of a stage production, or a work of fiction. In a melodrama, or pantomime, the 'hero' is traditionally greeted with a cheer, while the 'villain' is hissed or otherwise derided (see **hurray/boo**). It was the emergence of the stage 'villain' that gave rise to the expression 'villain of the piece', meaning the person who has caused some kind of trouble (with the 'piece' being the play). For the origin of 'hero', see the entry above. 'Villain' comes from the former French word meaning 'peasant' (so is related to both the historical 'villein', or village peasant, and the Roman 'villa').

heroine see **hero[1]**

hers see **his**

heterodactyl see **zygodactyl**

heterodox see **orthodox**

heterogeneous see **homogeneous**

heterosexual see **homosexual**

hexameter/pentameter
A 'hexameter' is a line of verse consisting of six metrical units ('feet'), while a 'pentameter' has five such units. The two forms were used in classical poetry, where they can be found in so called 'elegiac couplets', first a 'hexameter', then a 'pentameter'. This example was quoted by Coleridge:

> In thĕ hĕx|āmĕtĕr | rīsĕs thĕ |
> foūntāin's | sīlvĕrў | cōlūmn,
> In thĕ pĕn|tāmĕtĕr āye | fāllĭng ĭn |
> mēlŏdў | bāck.

In more conventional English poetry, such contrasting 'hexameters' and 'pentameters' are rare, and the best examples remain in classic verse.

hibernate/aestivate
When an animal 'hibernates' it spends the winter in a dormant condition, and its metabolism slows right down. If it less commonly 'aestivates', however, it spends the summer in such a state. The words derive respectively from Latin *hibernus*, 'of winter' and *aestivus*, 'of summer'. Among well known animals that 'hibernate' are the dormouse, badger, hedgehog and squirrel, as well as some reptiles and insects. Some land snails 'aestivate' in desert regions when it becomes too hot and dry for them to maintain a normal existence. In a sense, man 'hibernates' in cold countries during the winter, reducing activity to minimum, and can up to a point 'aestivate' in hot or tropical climates in the summer, if only by means of a daily siesta (which looks as if it ought to relate to 'aestivate' but does not).

hide see **skin**

hieratic see **demotic**[1]

high/low
The two opposites have engendered a wide family of contrasting expressions, many of them specialized. Here is a selection of the most important. 'Highbrow' means 'being or seeming to be intellectually superior'; 'lowbrow' means 'being or seeming to be intellectually unsophisticated'. 'High' Church, in the Church of England, means 'attaching importance to the role of the priesthood, to rites and rituals (nicknamed 'smells and bells' by some Anglicans), and to the Catholic tradition'; 'Low' Church means that all these things are minimized, and importance is attached to the evangelical tradition (particularly, in some cases, where 'fire and brimstone' preaching is concerned). (Broadly, too, 'High' means male and conservative; 'Low' means family oriented and liberal. It is the 'Low' churchpeople who support the idea of women priests; the 'High' oppose this.) 'High' spirits are exuberant and active ones; 'low' spirits mean depression, dejection, and impassivity. 'High' key, of a painting or photograph, means that tones are mainly light or bright, with little contrast; 'low' key means that the colours are subdued, with few highlights. In linguistics, Old 'High' German (for example) is a form of German that was spoken in southern Germany, where the terrain is higher. (This became the standard modern German.) Old 'Low' German was thus spoken in northern Germany, where the land is lower. (This was the forerunner of modern Dutch.) Finally, back in church again (but this time Roman Catholic, or at any rate 'High' Anglican), 'High' Mass is an elaborate solemn mass (communion service), with music and much ritual; 'Low' Mass is a relatively simple or 'said' mass (without incense, for example). If you wish to attend a 'High' Mass, you may have to search 'high and low', or all over the place, before you find a church where it is held. See also **higher/lower**, **Highlands/Lowlands**, **high jump/long jump**, **upper/downer**, **bas relief/high relief**.

higher/lower
Apart from their obvious literal senses, the words have some special uses of interest. 'Higher' criticism is the use of scientific technique to determine the origin and literary sources of the books of the Bible. 'Lower' criticism is the textual criticism of the Bible, that is, an examination of those texts that exist to establish the original text. In botany (or more exactly, mycology), too, the 'higher' fungi are ones with well-developed hyphae (body filaments), while 'lower' fungi have only rudimentary hyphae, or even none at all. Generally, a more common pairing for 'lower' is 'upper' (see **upper/lower**).

higher education see **further education**

highjump/longjump
Two contrasting types of jump in athletics, with the 'highjump' testing the maximum height a sportsman can reach, and the 'longjump' (in the United States, 'broadjump') seeing how far he or she can jump. Both terms were already in use in the nineteenth century. (However, the modern expression 'to be for the high jump', meaning to be due for punishment, refers to the 'high jump' made by a person when executed by hanging.)

Highlands/Lowlands
The contrasting geographical terms relate to Scotland. The 'Highlands' are the northwest mountainous part; the 'Lowlands' are the flat central area, around the valleys of the Forth and Clyde, where they separate the Southern Uplands from the 'Highlands'. The 'Highlands' (formerly called the 'Highland') are usually thought of as the 'typical' Scotland, since it is there that the Celtic element is strongest, and the region contains some of the wildest and most beautiful scenery in the country. As Robert Burns, Scotland's national poet, wrote:

Farewell to the Highlands, farewell to the North,
The birth-place of valour, the country of worth.

Edinburgh and Glasgow are both in the 'Lowlands', incidentally, which points to yet another difference between the regions: the 'Highlands' are almost exclusively rural, while most of Scotland's important towns and cities are in the 'Lowlands'.

high relief see **bas relief**

highwayman see **footpad**

hill/valley
'Hills' go up, above one; 'valleys' go down, below one! One the whole, this geographical difference is true. It will not apply to all countries, for example, and in a desert land, or one with few or no rivers, there will be no valleys. The local inhabitants will therefore not make this contrast, but instead 'hills' as against 'plains'. For most of Europe, and a number of other countries, the 'hill' and 'valley' divide will be the normal one, though. A not very well known proverb runs: 'He that stays in the valley shall never get over the hill' (in other words, 'Think big!'). The Bible has several references to 'hills' and 'valleys', including the familiar: 'Every valley shall be exalted, and every mountain and hill shall be made low'.

hind see **fore**[2]

hindsight see **foresight**[2]

hinny see **mule**

hiragana/katakana
'Hiragana' is one of the Japanese systems of writing based on Chinese ideograms ('word pictures'), and 'katakana' is the other. 'Hiragana' (literally 'flat kana') is used in newspapers and general literature; 'katakana' ('side kana') is used mostly for scientific work and official documents. ('Kana' is the term for the Japanese syllabary, or the list of signs that roughly equates to the 'alphabet' of other languages.)

his/hers
'Belonging to him', 'belonging to her', especially in commercial or humorous use to denote the possessions of a husband and wife (e.g. as marked on towels, pillows, etc). The pair are also sometimes used to denote things (e.g. lavatories) that are designated exclusively for males or females, respectively. Grammatically, 'his' now serves as both an adjective ('his' coat) and a pronoun (the coat is 'his'), while 'hers' is the pronoun only (the coat is 'hers'), with the corresponding adjective being 'her' ('her' coat). Sometimes a joke rustic form is used, as in: 'This chair is his'n, and that chair is her'n'. This correctly reflects the old grammar, however, for there was a pair in southern English dialect of 'hisn' and 'hern'. (There were also 'ourn', 'yourn' and 'theirn'. The forms probably developed by association with 'thine' and 'mine'.)

historic see **primary**[1]

history/geography
The two contrasting studies or disciplines still have much of a schoolroom patina on them, with 'history' associated with rather dull kings and queens and '1066 and all that', while 'geography' still suffers from its 'soft' image, as a rather nebulous subject dealing with maps and mountains and boring imports and exports. Indeed, the two can be said to have something of an implied 'male' and 'female' image respectively. (As recently as 1985, an advertisement for a new car showed the vehicle in a field accompanied by the wording 'Executive class. Economy class. Geography class.', and a picture of three schoolgirls, one holding a bunch of flowers, under the approving gaze of an undoubtedly spinsterish teacher, making the whole thing like a 'nature ramble'.) In actual fact, both studies are highly specialized and can be quite academic. The difference between them is that the 'historian' researches events in time, while the 'geographer' studies objects and occur-

rences in space. Put another way, 'history' is 'vertical' (or diachronic), working mainly in a temporal medium; 'geography' is 'horizontal' (or synchronic), working mainly in a spatial medium. Of course the two overlap, particularly in such fields as local 'history' and historical 'geography'. But the contrasts are clear enough, even if 'history' has now come to be regarded as the 'brainy' subject, while 'geography' is the 'practical' one. Compare **synchronic/diachronic**.

hit/miss
A 'hit' is 'on target' and a 'miss' is 'off target' (either short of it, or beyond it, or to one side of it). The words can apply to precise sports (from archery to gunnery), or to successes and failures in general ('She was a real hit'; 'A miss is as good as a mile'). If something is 'hit or miss' it is unpredictable or haphazard or 'happy-go-lucky'. The expression dates back to Shakespeare's time.

hog/sag
Technical opposites, to be precise nautical, because they relate to shipbuilding. If a vessel is 'hogged', it droops at the bow and stern because of a structural or design fault; if it 'sags', its keel droops or bulges in the centre. In other words, 'hog' refers to the keel like a hog's back, or bulging inwards, and 'sag' means what it says, since the keel 'sags' outwards. A keel should run straight along the bottom of the vessel as it has to serve as the foundation for the structure of the hull.

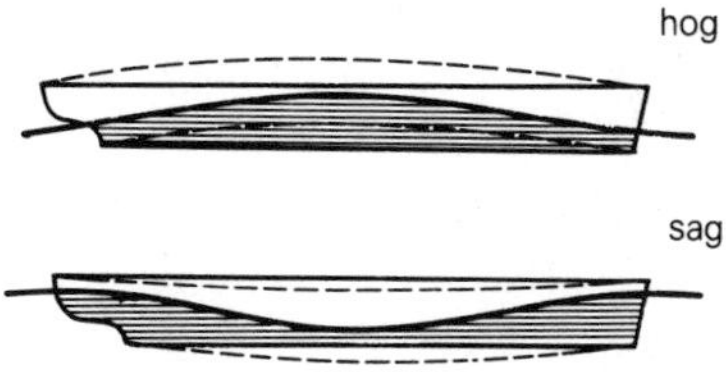

hoist[1]/drop
Another nautical pair (see the previous entry). The 'hoist' of a sail is its height above the deck when it has been hoisted on its own yard ('rope'). The 'drop' of a sail is its height when it is attached to a fixed yard.

hoist[2]/fly
Still nautically, although also on land. The 'hoist' of a flag is its inner edge, nearest the staff or 'pole'. Its 'fly' is thus its outer edge. The rope that hoisted the flag will have been attached to its 'hoist', and the other part is the one that 'flies' free. Hence the terms. See also the entry above.

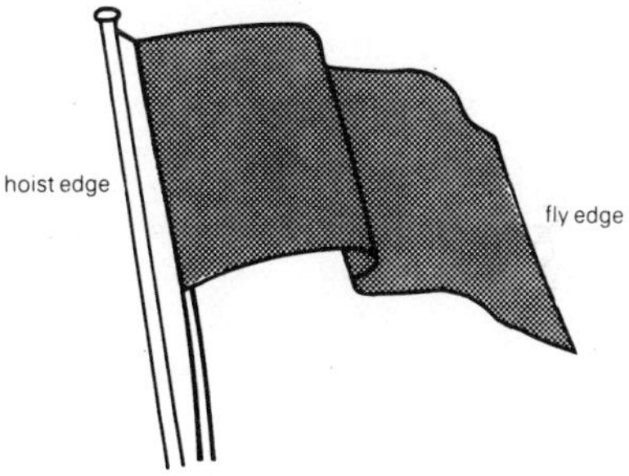

home[1]/abroad
'Home' is in this country, 'abroad' is in that country, overseas. When no motion is involved, one should say 'at home' as an exact opposite to 'abroad', although when travelling, 'home' is correct. ('I returned home a week after I had gone abroad.') In modern use, 'abroad' can be used as a noun to correspond to 'home', as in: 'Abroad is too expensive for me, I much prefer home'.

home[2]/away
The chief contrast usually made here is in a sporting fixture, such as a football match. This can take place as a 'home' game or an 'away' one, depending whether it is played on one's own field or on that of one's opponents. Those who bet good money on the results of football matches know that a 'home' win may be more likely than an 'away' one, since the team will be familiar with their own ground, and will not have become tired through travelling.

homoeopathic see **allopathic**

homogeneous/heterogeneous
'Homogeneous' means 'composed of similar parts', 'having a uniform structure or content'. One can thus have a 'homogeneous' cargo on a ship, where only one type of goods is carried, or live in a 'homogeneous' neighbourhood, where everyone has the same social or other background. 'Heterogeneous' therefore means 'consisting of different parts', 'having a varied content or texture', such as a 'heterogeneous' chemical compound, containing different elements, or a 'heterogeneous' theatre audience, where there was a wide variety of people. Daniel Defoe wrote:

> Thus from a Mixture of all Kinds began,
> That Het'rogeneous Thing, an Englishman.

homoiousian see **homoousian**

homologous see **analogous**

homoousian/homoiousian
Only theologians could have a contrasting pair as nicely differentiated as this in sense and spelling. The terms relate to the Trinity, the exact nature of which has exercised the minds of Christian theologians and scholars wonderfully over the centuries. 'Homoousian' means 'holding that the Son is of the same substance as the Father'. 'Homoiousian', therefore, means 'holding that the Son is of like, but not identical substance with the Father'. The terms arose as two theological 'sides' in Byzantium, and in their original Greek literally meant (respectively) 'of the same substance' and 'of like substance'. 'Like' is of course not the same as 'same'. But we need pursue the theology no further here!

homosexual[1]/heterosexual
This is perhaps one of the most familiar 'homo-' v. 'hetero-' pairings, as applied to people who (the minority) are attracted to their own sex and those (the majority) who are attracted to the opposite sex. The 'homo-' is sometimes wrongly thought of as being the Latin for 'man'. It is, but not in this word, where it is the Greek for 'same' (see page 285). For a further consideration of this aspect, see the next entry below. The terms are relatively recent, and date from only the late nineteenth century, where they first occurred in the work of the German neurologist Krafft-Ebing, who specialized in the study of sexual deviations. Compare **gay/straight**.

homosexual[2]/lesbian
Perhaps partly because of the association with Latin *homo*, 'man' (see entry above), or simply because male 'homosexuals' have generally been more prominent in the public eye, 'homosexual' is often used of male 'gays' and 'lesbian' of women. The latter usage is correct, because 'lesbians' get their name from the homosexuality attributed to the Greek woman poet Sappho, who lived on the island of Lesbos. However, 'homosexual' can quite properly be used of both men and women, since it denotes an attraction to the same sex. 'Lesbian' as a term arose at about the same time that 'homosexual' and 'heterosexual' did (see above). See also **gay/straight**.

honours degree see **pass degree**

horizontal see **vertical**

horse chestnut/sweet chestnut
The contrast is a fairly well-known one: 'horse chestnuts' are inedible, while 'sweet chestnuts' are not only edible but delicious when roasted on a cold winter's day. 'Horse chestnuts' are more familiarly known as 'conkers', and as seen in this annual autumn sport, popular with children. The tree is said to be so named since the fruit (the 'nut') was formerly used in the treatment of respiratory ailments in horses. The two types of chestnuts are not related as species: the 'horse chestnut' is *Aesculus hippocastanum*; the 'sweet chestnut' is *Castanea sativa*.

host/guest
'Mankind is divisible into two great

classes: hosts and guests', wrote Sir Max Beerbohm. And so it has long been socially, with the 'hosts' entertaining and the 'guests' being entertained. However, for a time in the thirteenth and fourteenth centuries 'host' meant both 'host' ('one who entertains') and 'guest' ('one who is entertained'). The duality of meaning was not simply fortuitous, since both words, which are still close in appearance and spelling today, originally had a common source. This was ultimately Latin *hostis*, 'stranger', 'enemy', or in Medieval Latin, 'army', i.e. 'hostile strangers'. It is thus the 'stranger' aspect that unites the two opposite senses, since a proper 'host' is a stranger to his 'guests', and they are 'strangers' to him. Latin *hostis* then developed an alternative form *hospes*, genitive *hospitis*, to give the modern sense of 'host', with the former 'army' sense still detectable in the other sense of 'host', that means 'large number' (a 'host' of flies or of problems). Both Latin words then came to produce a large number ('host'!) of words in English, through French, that are related to looking after or being looked after, such as 'hospital', 'hospice', 'hostel', 'hotel' and even 'ostler' (who was originally a 'hostler', or stableman at an inn). 'Hostage' belongs here, too, as he is a person who is 'looked after' as a pledge. However, before the word came into English from French, it was influenced by another Latin source. This was *obses*, genitive *obsidis*, also meaning 'hostage' but having a literal sense 'one who sits before'. An English derivative of this is the word 'obsession', which originally meant 'siege' in the sixteenth century (i.e. a 'sitting before' a town or fortress). A historic survival of the 'host' who was both 'host' and 'guest' can be seen in the so called 'Hoastmen' of Newcastle-on-Tyne. Today, they are the members of the City Corporation or Guild. Formerly, however, they had the function of receiving 'guests' (called 'hosts') who came to Newcastle to buy coal and other commodities. The Seal of the Corporation still shows a 'Hoastman' in his official robes receiving a stranger with the words 'Welcome my oste'. The familiar 'mine host' as the pub landlord gets his semi-jocular title from Shakespearean times. Words in other languages also reflect the mutual link between the terms, from Ancient Greek *xenos*, 'stranger' to Modern Russian *gost'*, 'guest'. English 'ghost' is not related to either, though, however friendly or unfriendly it is.

hot/cold
Contrasting conditions and states that affect every day (and night) of our lives, with the familiar 'H' and 'C' of the water taps. (Problems can arise abroad for the unwary, since 'hot' taps can be marked 'C', and in Italian *caldo* means 'hot', not 'cold'. For a similar linguistic inconvenience see **ladies/gentlemen**.) 'Cold' can quite often mean 'formerly hot', so that 'cold' meat is meat that was cooked earlier (and was 'hot') but has now cooled down, and 'cold' soup is soup that should be 'hot' (unless a deliberately chilled variety). On the whole, however, 'hot' is used of things that are normally 'hot', so that there are no 'cold' cross buns, 'cold' pots (as a stew) or 'cold' peppers. 'Hot' often has an overtone of 'exciting' or even 'dangerous', such as a 'hot' news story (a recent and possibly sensational one), a 'hot' potato (in the transferred sense of a sensitive matter or situation) and 'hot' stuff (of a person who impresses by sheer 'zing', in a quality such as intellect, ability or sexual attraction). 'Cold' can denote the opposite, such as 'cold' comfort, which is poor consolation, a 'cold' shoulder, which implies rejection or lack of sympathy ('He just gave me the cold shoulder when I asked for help'), and 'cold' water, in its usage to indicate deprecation or indifference ('She simply poured cold water on my suggestion'). To 'blow hot and cold' is to vacillate or display uncertainty (often first favouring then rejecting, like a disloyal lover). The reference is not to a wind blowing but to one of Aesop's Fables, in which a traveller blew alternately on his fingers to warm them and on his soup to cool it.

hounds see **hare**[1]

House of Representatives/Senate
In the United States, the 'House of Representatives' is the lower chamber of Congress, while the 'Senate' is the upper chamber. The 'House of Representatives' has 435 members, elected every second year from all the states, but with the allocation of seats based on their population. The 'Senate' has 100 members, two from each state, serving six years, but with a third of them elected every two years. If both chambers pass a bill, it becomes an Act of Congress if accorded the consent of the President. Compare **Lords/Commons**, **Bundesrat/Bundestag**, **Lagsting/Odelsting**.

Houyhnhnms/Yahoos
The names of the inhabitants of Houyhnhnmland (pronounced probably 'Whinnimland'), the imaginary country of Gulliver's fourth voyage in Swift's *Gulliver's Travels*. The 'Houyhnhnms' are the superiors, a race of horses (whose name was probably based on 'whinny'), who personify everything that is good in mankind and who live an idyllic existence. They hold in subjection the inferior race of 'Yahoos', who are filthy human brutes (with their name probably based on a coarse exclamation such as 'ugh!'). They represent everything that is bad and degrading in the human race (as it mostly is, according to Swift). The 'Yahoos' gave the word 'yahoo' to the English language to mean a coarse or brutish person. The 'Houyhnhnms', understandably, did not popularly catch on, despite their virtues. For more mythical horses, see the next entry. See also **Lilliput/Brobdingnag**.

Hrimfaxi/Skinfaxi
In Scandinavian mythology, 'Hrimfaxi' was the horse of the night, while 'Skinfaxi' was the horse of the day. Every night, drops fell from the bit of 'Hrimfaxi' to form the dew, while the mane of 'Skinfaxi' brought the light of the sun. Their respective names mean 'frost mane' (more closely 'rime mane') and 'shining mane', with '-faxi' preserved in the English names Fairfax and Halifax (with 'fax' formerly a word in English for a person's hair).

hug/kiss
Both can obviously relate to a show of affection, especially when the 'kiss' is on the lips. On the whole, however, a 'hug' is almost exclusively a gesture of affection only, and a much greater, literally 'all-embracing' one than the mere touch of the 'kiss', which when given not on the mouth (e.g. on the cheek or, now somewhat affectedly, on the hand) is simply a conventional mark of respect or reverence. One can thus 'kiss' a stranger, but not 'hug' him or her (unless the circumstances are exceptional, or the practice accepted in the country concerned). In traditional English letter-writing, too, there is even a contrast between the symbols for each: a 'hug' is an 'O' (representing the encircling embrace), while the 'kiss' is an 'X' (standing for the contact of the lips). For what it's worth, too, 'hug' derives from an Old Norse verb meaning 'comfort', 'soothe', while 'kiss' is apparently purely imitative of the sound made (and could perhaps even be related to 'suck'). For another contrasting use of 'O' and 'X', see **noughts/crosses**.

hurray/boo
The two traditional words said (or shouted) to express approval on the one hand or disapproval on the other. Normally, they are voiced in response to something, such as the appearance of the 'hero' in a pantomime, or that of the 'villain' similarly. Often they occur as a reaction to good news or bad news ('Lads, we have won' – 'Hurray!'; 'I'm going to stay as long as I like' – 'Boo!'), with 'hurray' much more common. 'Hurray' (also spelt 'hooray' and 'hurrah') is likewise the formal word used to cheer a person, a losing team in a sports match, and the like, when it is introduced by 'Hip, hip hip' (as the standard 'three cheers', with the whole phrase repeated three times). 'Hurray' has thus long had a link with the greeting of royalty or winning a victory in battle, as well as various military ceremonies generally (but particularly the navy, with its old shanty line 'Hoo-ray and up she rises'). In more jargonistic use, one now has so called 'boo'

words and 'hurray' words, otherwise current words or names that are out of favour or in, usually on a 'fashionable' basis. For example, 'These days, "police" is a boo word', meaning that the police have come in for some criticism, and the word does not have its former connotations of security, helpfulness, friendliness and so on. This use of 'boo' and 'hurray', although quite common in journalism, is not one that has found its way into many (if any) dictionaries.

husband/wife
The sense of 'married man' and 'married woman', each with regard to the spouse, is so well known that no more need really be said about it. However, it is interesting that English is one of the few languages where 'husband' has no reference to the male or man, as such, but simply means 'householder', 'one bound to a house'. Other languages have a word related to Latin *maritus*, 'husband' (as in English 'marital') or to the equivalent of 'man'. So one has:

English	man	husband
French	homme	mari
Italian	uomo	marito
Spanish	hombre	marido
German	Mann	Mann
Russian	muzhchina	muzh
Welsh	gŵr	gŵr
Irish	fear	fear

hybrid see **monolithic**

Hyde see **Jekyll**

hydraulic see **pneumatic**

hydrogen see **oxygen**

hyperbole/litotes
In language study, a 'hyperbole' is a type of exaggeration that obviously cannot be literal ('I was frightened to death'), with a 'litotes' the opposite, a special understatement, often with 'not' or 'no' ('The article was not without interest', meaning that it was interesting). 'Hyperboles' are common in everyday speech and conversation, but on the whole 'litotes' are used for literary effect, except in such stock phrases as 'not half' and most of all 'not bad'. ('What did you think of the play?' 'Not bad, not bad at all.') 'Hyperbole' literally means 'thrown over', and 'litotes' means 'simple'. (It is also sometimes known as 'meiosis', which literally means 'lessening'.)

hypermetropic see **myopic**

hypothetical imperative see **categorical imperative**

Ii

iamb/trochee
The two terms are those of metrical feet (syllable groups) in poetry, with an 'iamb' being an unstressed syllable followed by a stressed one (as in the word 'display' or 'delight'), and a 'trochee' the opposite (as in 'baker' or 'pansy'). The 'iamb' is much more common than the 'trochee' in English verse since it follows the usual speech pattern, as in Robert Louis Stevenson's:

> In winter I get up at night
> And dress by yellow candle-light.
> In summer quite the other way, –
> I have to go to bed by day.

The 'trochee', with its stressed syllable followed by an unstressed, can soon become monotonous, as typically in Longfellow's *Hiawatha*:

> From the waterfall he named her,
> Minnehaha, Laughing Water.

The origin of 'iamb' is obscure, and the meaning of Greek *iambos* is uncertain. 'Trochee', however, literally means 'running' (Greek *trochos* means 'wheel'). Compare **anapaest/dactyl**.

ice skates see **roller skates**

id see **ego**

idealism see **materialism**

i.e. see **e.g.**

ignoble see **noble**

illiterate see **literate**[1]

immigrant see **emigrant**

immortal see **mortal**

imperfect see **perfect**

imperfective/perfective
In grammar (and by comparison with the pair **perfect/imperfect**), 'imperfective' and 'perfective' denote a so-called 'aspect' of the verb in some languages, with an 'imperfective' verb denoting that an action or event was or is still in progress at a particular time (or was or will be so), and a 'perfective' verb showing that the action is completed (or was or will be so). This is a particular feature in Russian, for example, where *ya pisal* means 'I was writing' (but hadn't finished), and so is 'imperfective', while *ya napisal* means 'I wrote' (and finished writing), and so is 'perfective'. Up to a point the terms can also apply to English, where these very verb forms just quoted can also be regarded respectively as 'imperfective' and 'perfective'. (However, 'I wrote' could be either: 'I wrote to her every day' would be 'imperfective', because I never completed the writing, but 'I wrote to her yesterday' would be 'perfective', as I wrote once and finished writing.)

imperforate see **perforate**

imperial see **metric**

implicit/explicit
If I make an 'implicit' remark, I hint or suggest something without saying so directly. For example, 'I have seen better performances' implies that this was a bad one. If I make an 'explicit' remark, I 'spell it out' directly, so might say 'That was a very bad performance'. 'Implicit' can even apply to something not even stated at all, but that can be deduced, such as, 'I'm taking a coat' (meaning 'I think it's going to rain'). In recent years, 'explicit' has come to acquire the sense 'graphically

frank', 'revealing everything', with regard to sexual descriptions, which were formerly mostly 'implicit'. The words themselves, derived from Latin, mean respectively 'folded in' and 'unfolded'.

implode see **explode**

imply/infer
Although the senses of both often blur in popular usage, strictly speaking 'imply' means 'say indirectly', 'mean', and 'infer' means 'deduce', 'conclude'. Thus, I can 'imply' a thing when I say it indirectly, and I can 'infer' a thing when you say it indirectly. For example, 'I am not implying that you made a mistake' means that I do not mean that you are wrong, and 'Are you inferring that I'm a fool?' means that I have concluded that you were probably saying this.

import/export
'Imports' are brought into a country, while 'exports' are what a country sends abroad. When a country 'imports' more than it 'exports', its economy is not so healthy, but when it 'exports' more than it 'imports', things are obviously going well and trade is booming. The 'port' of both words is not the same as the 'port' that means 'town by the sea with a harbour'. The former means 'carry' (i.e. in or out of the country), and the latter comes from Latin *portus* (related to modern English 'ford' and 'fare', so is to do with 'going').

impressionists/expressionists
These names, sometimes spelt with capital letters, are used of two artistic schools or groups. The 'impressionists' sought to re-create in their paintings an 'impression' of the physical world that they saw, particularly through the effects of light. Among well-known 'impressionists' were Monet, Renoir, Pissarro and Sisley. The 'expressionists', on the other hand, who followed them chronologically, sought to give 'expression' to their emotions in what they painted, rather than portray what they saw. Some well-known 'expressionists' were the German Marc, the Norwegian Munch and the naturalized Briton Kokoschka. 'Impressionists' (who were mainly French, and active in the late nineteenth century) were objective, while the 'expressionists' (who were mainly German and Russian, and active in the early twentieth century) were subjective. The 'expressionists' arose as a reaction to the 'impressionists', and chose their name accordingly to indicate this.

in/out
Our everyday life is full of 'ins' and 'outs' (and also of general 'ins and outs', or complexities). Every time we open a door, we go 'in' or 'out', and constantly receive and take things (that come 'in') while sending or transmitting others (that go 'out'). There are some interesting special applications of the words. If a fashion or social trend is 'in' it is acceptable and even copied; if it is 'out' it is regarded as not worthy of recognition or attention. Most offices or secretaries have an 'in' tray for correspondence received, and an 'out' tray for letters to be despatched. At a hospital, an 'in' patient is a resident one, while an 'out' patient is a visiting one, coming on a particular day by appointment. After a cabinet reshuffle, various ministers are 'in' (appointed) or 'out' (dismissed). In tennis, 'van in' (short for 'advantage in') is a winning point to the server, and he needs only one more point to win the game. 'Van out', on the other hand, means the advantage has gone to the receiver, who will now be in the same winning position. Finally (for this particular entry), the 'In' and 'Out' Club is a nickname for the Naval and Military Club in London, so called not for the quick turnover in its membership but simply because the words 'IN' and 'OUT' were originally painted on the pillars at the entrance to its courtyard in Piccadilly.

inanimate see **animate**

inboard/outboard
On a ship or boat, 'inboard' relates to anything in it or on it, especially an 'inboard' motor, which will be within its hull. Anything 'outboard' will therefore be

outside the main hull or structure, so that an 'outboard' motor, as used with many small boats, is one that can be operated at the stern, where it will be mounted externally. On an aircraft, 'inboard' relates to anything close to its main body, or actually inside the fuselage, while something that is 'outboard' will be near the wing tips.

include/exclude
It was Samuel Goldwyn who is said to have commented 'Include me out' on one occasion when a deal was being discussed. One sees what he meant, but more orthodoxly 'include' implies 'in', and 'exclude' 'out'. The corresponding adjectives, 'inclusive' and 'exclusive', are frequently associated with prices or charges, with 'inclusive' indicating that there are no 'extras', and 'exclusive' meaning that additional charges must be made ('£15 exclusive of VAT'). 'Exclusive' also has the sense 'special', 'unique' in a commercial sense ('our exclusive offer'), where there is no contrast with 'inclusive'.

income/expenditure
The terms are traditional opposites for the money that a person earns and the money that he spends, otherwise what comes in and what goes out. ('Expenditure' is sometimes also known, in a rather general way, as 'outgoings', which is really a more accurate opposite linguistically, since to 'go out' is the opposite of to 'come in'.) 'Expenditure' is not the same as 'expenses', because it involves *all* payments made, not merely ones arising as the result of some particular deal or settlement.

increase/decrease
The words mean fairly generally 'grow in size or quantity' and 'lessen in size or quantity', and correspond to similar opposite senses such as **enlarge/reduce**, **expand/contract**, **augment/diminish**, and so on. On the face of it, one might have expected a word 'excrease' as the opposite of 'increase'. However, the '-crease' means 'grow' (Latin *crescere*), and 'ex-' means 'out', and one cannot 'grow out' but only 'grow less', with the 'de-' serving to denote the reverse of the original action (as in the pair **inflation/deflation** below). Even so, there are many pairs of opposites in 'in-' and 'ex-' as can be seen in the selection that follows.

incubus/succubus
Both are types of demon, and belong to the world (or sub-world) of the supernatural. An 'incubus' is a male spirit that in folklore is said to have sexual intercourse with a woman when she is asleep. A 'succubus' is the opposite: a female demon who is believed to visit a sleeping man for a similar purpose. The words are of Latin origin, and mean literally 'lying on' and 'lying under' (with regard to the common position during the act). Rather unexpectedly, 'succubus' is grammatically masculine. The feminine form, 'succuba', certainly existed, but was eventually ousted, doubtless under the influence of 'incubus', with the significance of the masculine ending forgotten.

indefinite article see **definite article**

independent school see **maintained school**

Indian elephant see **African elephant**

Indians see **cowboys**

indicated horsepower see **brake horsepower**

indicative/subjunctive
The terms are those of so called grammatical 'moods'. The 'indicative' mood makes a statement, such as 'it is raining and I am cold'. The 'subjunctive' mood, by contrast, relates to a verb used to express something uncertain, hypothetical or wished for, such as 'If I were you' or 'Far be it from me' (or 'Suffice it to say'). In English, the 'subjunctive' survives only in a few stock forms like these. In foreign languages, however, it continues to flourish generally as an added complexity for the learner of the language concerned whether French, German or classical

Latin, meaning that many verbs will have two sets of tenses, one 'indicative' and one 'subjunctive'. The terms themselves are designed to show that the 'indicative' points out or 'indicates' something objective or factual, while the 'subjunctive' is (or was) often found in 'subjoined' or subordinate clauses. Both words look awkward because they are rather contrived translations of Greek terms, respectively *oristike*, 'defining', and *hypotaktike*, 'subordinating'.

indirect see **direct**[1]

Indo-European/Finno-Ugrian
Most of the languages of Europe, as the family name indicates, are 'Indo-European', that is, they are all to some degree (some quite closely) mutually related, and all developed from a hypothetical (reconstructed) parent language called 'Indo-European'. (The first half of the name denotes that many Asian and Indian languages also belong to this family, with Sanskrit, the language of Hinduism, one of its oldest representatives, and so close to the original 'Indo-European'.) Within the 'Indo-European' family of languages are the two important branches differentiated as **Romance/Germanic**, with others being Slavonic or Celtic languages, and two of the oldest represented by Latin and Greek (see **Greeks/Romans**). 'Indo-European' languages, too, easily outnumber the 'Finno-Ugrian'. As the latter's family name suggests, its two chief representative languages are Finnish and Hungarian, also European languages, to which can be added certain languages spoken in the Soviet Union, such as Estonian, Ostyak and Vogul. The main difference between the actual families is that most 'Indo-European' languages are synthetic (see **analytic/synthetic**), while 'Finno-Ugrian' languages are 'agglutinative', that is, they build up words from component parts, with each having a fixed meaning (this is not quite the same as 'synthetic', where an ending such as Latin *-um* can stand for more than one meaning). For example, Hungarian *Magyarországban* means 'in Hungary', literally 'Magyar-land-in', with *ország*, 'land' and *ban*, 'in' added ('agglutinated', as it were 'glued on') to *Magyar*.

indoor/outdoor
The two contrasting adjectives mostly relate to games and clothes. Thus, 'outdoor' games (mostly the main 'sporting' ones) include cricket, football, golf, tennis and baseball, while some of the better known 'indoor' games are billiards, snooker, dominoes, darts and almost all so-called 'board' and card games. Some games can be played in a covered court or building, even a few traditional 'outdoor' ones such as tennis. But this doesn't really make them 'indoor' games in the popular sense, and such games as basketball and squash are regarded as more 'outdoor' than 'indoor', even though they are almost always played inside a building. 'Indoor' therefore often implies 'in the house', 'at home'. With clothes, most people have an 'indoor' article and an 'outdoor' one corresponding to it, such as 'indoor' shoes (slippers, house shoes) and 'outdoor' shoes (boots, walking shoes), and a general term such as 'coat' can mean an 'indoor' one like a jacket, or an 'outdoor' one, like an overcoat or raincoat. There is also a divide between 'indoor' plants (decorative house plants) and 'outdoor' plants, that grow in the garden. The corresponding adverbs are 'indoors' and 'outdoors' (or 'out of doors').

induction see **deduction**

in esse/in posse
The terms are legal ones, still in their original Latin. 'In esse' means 'actually existing', and 'in posse' means 'potentially'. For example, beneficiaries can be 'in esse' (i.e. alive) at the time a will is made, and a person's funds can total a certain amount 'in posse' (not in reality). The expressions have been also used in theological and other learned contexts, and they are usually written or printed in italics. The poet Thomas Gray, in a letter dated 1756, wrote: 'You are not however to imagine that my illness is *in esse*; no, it is only *in posse*'.

infant see **adult**

infanta/infante
The 'infanta' was formerly the title of the daughter of a king of Spain or Portugal, while the 'infante' was his son (especially one who was not the heir to the throne). The words are respectively the feminine and masculine of the word for 'infant', in either Spanish or Portuguese.

infante see **infanta**

infantry see **cavalry**

infectious see **contagious**

infer see **imply**

inferior see **superior**

infield/outfield
In some sports, especially cricket and baseball, the 'infield' is the central area of the field, respectively near the wickets and enclosed by the bases. The 'outfield' is therefore the area that is outside the pitch (between the wickets) in cricket (where it is also called 'the deep') and beyond the lines connecting the first, second and third bases in baseball. The terms feature largely in sports reports and accounts of matches or games.

infinite see **finite**

infinity see **zero**

inflation/deflation
In economics, 'inflation' is the term for a continuing increase in prices. (Economists differ in their opinions as to what causes it.) 'Deflation' is the reverse, when prices fall. This is often engineered by a government to halt 'inflation'. It can do it by raising taxation or by cutting government spending (or both).

infra see **supra**

infralapsarian/supralapsarian
The rather impressive terms are not botanical designations but theological. An 'infralapsarian' was someone who believed that it was only after the Fall (in the Garden of Eden) that God decreed who was predestined to salvation and who was not. A 'supralapsarian' held that it was before the Fall. The terms derives from the Latin prefixes *infra*, 'below' (i.e. after) and *supra*, 'above' (i.e. before), with the rest of the word based on *lapsus*, 'fall' (as in English 'lapse'). The contrasting doctrines were important in Calvinistic theology in the seventeenth century. See also **supra/infra**.

infra-red/ultra-violet
The terms, meaning literally 'below the red' and 'above the violet', relate to areas of electromagnetic radiation that lie outside opposite ends of the visible spectrum. 'Infra-red' rays have a wavelength between that of red light and microwaves, and are usually perceived in the form of heat, hence their use in heat treatment, as well as in photography. 'Ultra-violet' rays have a wavelength between the violet end of the spectrum and X-rays, and they are popularly used in 'sun lamps' for providing an artificial suntan.

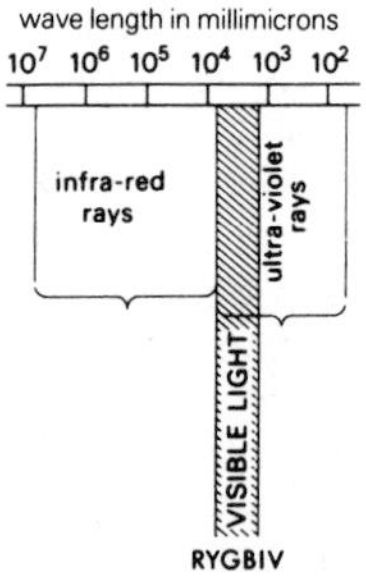

in front/behind
These are opposite adverbs of position or direction. To walk 'in front' is to walk ahead of someone or something; to walk 'behind' is to walk to the rear of a person, following him. Motion is not necessarily involved, and a tree can grow 'in front' of a house, or 'behind' it, for example. The contrast is thus similar to that of **front/rear**, or even **front/back**.

ingress/egress
Two somewhat stilted words corresponding to 'entrance' and 'exit' (or simply 'way in' and 'way out'). The terms have something of a legal ring to them, as in the expression 'right of ingress' or the contrary, giving a person a lawful right to enter somewhere. A story is told of a circus owner who, finding that the public were reluctant to leave the 'big top' after the performance, had a prominent notice placed by the way out with the wording 'To the egress'.

inhale/exhale
To 'inhale' is to breathe in, and to 'exhale' to breathe out. The second part of the word comes from Latin *halare*, 'to breathe'. The opposites have mostly a literal sense, with no transferred usage.

inhibitor see **catalyst**

initial/final
The pair of opposites have mainly a formal use, corresponding to 'first' and 'last', such as for an 'initial' payment in an agreement, or a 'final' warning of some possible penalty. As a noun, 'initial' has come to mean the first (capital) letter of a name, especially when they stand on their own ('Your initials are the same as mine').

inner/outer
The meanings of the opposites can be either 'interior' or simply 'further in' ('exterior' or 'further out'), often depending on the number of things so designated. There are a number of technical or scientific uses. In astronomy, for example, the 'inner' planets are those that have orbits nearest to the Sun (i.e. Mercury, Venus, Earth and Mars), while the 'outer' planets are further out (Jupiter, Saturn, Uranus, Neptune and Pluto). Somewhat similarly, 'inner' space is the environment at or near the surface of the Earth, and in particular under the sea, while 'outer' space is probably more familiar as the space outside the Earth's atmosphere, especially so-called 'interstellar' space. In anatomy, the 'inner' ear (also called the internal ear) is the basic organ itself inside the head, with its auditory nerve, 'labyrinth' and so on, while the 'outer' ear is the visible external part, that gathers sound waves and sends them to the eardrum. On a shooting target, as in archery, the 'inner' is the ring nearest the centre or bull's-eye while the 'outer' is the outside ring, furthest from the centre. Some geographical names have a distinctive 'Inner' and 'Outer', such as the 'Inner' and 'Outer' Hebrides in Scotland, with the former being nearest the mainland, and the latter also known as the Western Isles. Former 'Inner' and 'Outer' Mongolia have now altered their original status as territories: 'Inner' Mongolia is today a region of northeast China, while 'Outer' Mongolia is the Mongolian People's Republic (from 1924), an independent state. In Peking (or Beijing), the 'Inner' City contained the Imperial City (and inside that the Forbidden City), while the 'Outer' City was (and is) the main commercial district. Britain, too, has 'inner' cities, as a fairly recent term for the older, more densely populated and usually more impoverished area of a city. However, there is normally no explicit 'outer' city as the rest of the urban complex. See also the next entry below.

inner-directed/other-directed
In psychology, 'inner-directed' is used of a person to mean that he or she is guided more by conscience and moral values than by external pressures to conform. 'Other-directed' means that the person will therefore be guided or motivated chiefly by external influences. The awkward terms were devised in 1950 by the American sociologist David Riesman for his study entitled *The Lonely Crowd*.

innocent/guilty
The words are mainly used as opposites in a non-specialized sense, such as an 'innocent' remark (one made unaware of its significance) or a 'guilty' look (whether actually so nor not). However, the two can also have legal uses ('I declare this man to be innocent of all charges') except (in England) for a verdict, which uses the terms of the pair **guilty/not guilty**. Often

the opposite of an 'in-' word (when this means 'not', as here) is simply the rest of the word without it, as for the pair **organic/inorganic**. However, although there is a word 'nocent', it is now very rare and seldom used.

inorganic see **organic**

in personam/in rem
As they stand, the two Latin terms literally mean 'against the person' and 'against the matter'. They are used in legal jargon for an action brought either against a specific person or persons or, on the other hand, against property. For example, an action or judgment made 'in personam' could be to impose some kind of obligation on someone, while one made 'in rem' could be in order to recover a piece of property or the use of it.

in posse see **in esse**

input/output
'Input' usually relates to the supplying or adding (or 'putting in') of a quantity of power, information, energy, material or the like somewhere. In computer technology, for example, 'input' is the data fed or keyed in to the computer. 'Output', therefore, is what a person or thing produces, manufactures or 'puts out', such as an author's 'output' (the books that he writes) or a factory's 'output' (the goods that it manufactures). Again, in computers, the 'output' is the information it produces. (There is even a term 'input/output' of computers, relating to the operations that control its specific 'input' and 'output'.)

in rem see **in personam**

insane see **sane**

inside/outside
As well as the obvious, general opposite meanings ('inside' the house, 'outside' the car), the words have certain uses as sporting terms. In football, for example, the 'inside' right and 'inside' left are two players who cover the midfield area and operate mainly as attackers, supported by the 'outside' right and left (wingers) who cover the outer edges of the pitch. In motoring, too (not always such a sport), the 'inside' lane is the part of the road nearest the edge on a dual carriageway, while the 'outside' lane is the one nearest the centre of the road, used for overtaking. In another field of activity (and a kind of sport with different rules), an 'inside' job is a crime committed with the help of someone who has knowledge of the layout and operations of the premises involved, and who probably works there (as in a bank), while an 'outside' job is a crime carried out without such assistance. Finally, an 'insider' is a person who is a recognized member of a group or organization, and party to its secrets, while an 'outsider' is someone who is not so included.

instantaneous exposure see **time exposure**

instant coffee/ground coffee
'Instant coffee' is coffee that can be made from powder or granules almost 'instantly', by having boiling water poured over it. 'Ground coffee' (or 'roast coffee') is 'real' coffee that has to be made by brewing and/or filtering and percolating. The precise terms used are sometimes vague and also misleading, since even 'instant coffee' was (and in a sense still is) 'ground coffee' or 'roast coffee'. Coffee manufacturers and marketers like to choose the words that make the coffee sound as 'real' as possible, even when it is 'instant'. See also **tea/coffee**.

inswinger/outswinger
Cricketers will know all about these. An 'inswinger' is a ball that turns from the off to the leg side when it is bowled, while an 'outswinger' is one that swerves from the leg to the off. See also **leg/off** and compare **googly/chinaman**.

intaglio see **cameo**

integral calculus see **differential calculus**

intensive see **extensive**

interior/exterior
The basic reference here, of course, is to what is 'inside' and what is 'outside'. There are also some specialized uses. In filming, for example, an 'interior' shot is one made inside a building, studio or the like, while an 'exterior' shot is made outside, out of doors. In mathematics, an 'interior' angle is one inside a triangle, square or other figure, between two of the lines, while an 'exterior' angle is one between a line extended from the side of a figure and one of its sides itself. In a government, the minister of the 'interior' will be responsible for the internal affairs of a country (what is known in Britain as the 'Home Secretary'), but there is normally no minister of the 'exterior', but usually a 'foreign' or 'overseas' minister (in Britain, 'Foreign Secretary'). An 'interior' decorator is one who paints and decorates indoors, while one who works on the outside of a house or building is simply a 'painter and decorator'. Compare **internal/external** below.

internal/external
As with the pair **interior/exterior** of the entry above, there are some special uses of the opposites. For example, an 'internal' degree is the normal type of academic degree awarded to someone who has studied at a university. An 'external' degree, however, is one awarded to a person who has not actually attended the university, but who has probably studied by means of a correspondence course. Still on the academic side, an 'internal' examiner is one on the staff of the school or institution where the students are to be examined, but an 'external' examiner comes from outside, and is not connected with the place. Most people have heard of an 'internal' combustion engine, where the combustion that generates the heat (that is converted into the energy) takes place inside the engine itself, usually in a cylinder. But did you know that there is also an 'external' combustion engine? This is one, such as a steam engine, where the fuel is burned outside the combustion chamber.

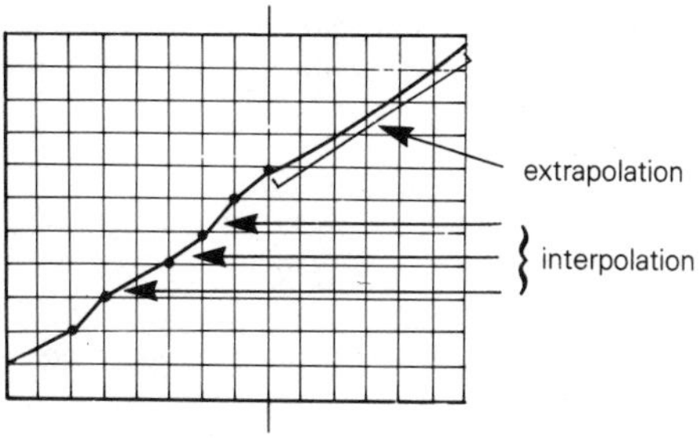

interpolate/extrapolate
In one of its narrowest senses, to 'interpolate' (in mathematics) is to estimate the value of a function between values that are already known, so that to 'extrapolate' is to estimate beyond these values, normally by extending a line or curve on a graph. In a looser sense, the words are not exact opposites, since 'interpolate' usually means 'add to a text' (often in order to falsify or corrupt it), and 'extrapolate' can mean simply 'infer', 'deduce', when predicting something by past experience or known facts. Both really have the idea of altering something, as Latin *interpolāre* means 'refurbish'. In English, 'extrapolate' was devised from 'interpolate'.

interpreter see **translator**

in the book see **ex-directory**

intransitive see **transitive**

intrinsic/extrinsic
In a general sense, 'intrinsic' means 'essential', 'in itself', as when one says that an object has no 'intrinsic' value (but may have a great sentimental value). 'Extrinsic', less commonly used in this way, therefore means 'not in itself', 'extraneous', as questions that are 'extrinsic' to the subject being discussed (i.e. they are not relevant to it). In anatomy, 'intrinsic' muscles (for

example), are ones located inside another organ, as those in the ear or the larynx, while 'extrinsic' muscles are situated outside an organ, and are attached to it, like those of the tongue. The root of the word is ultimately Latin *sequi*, 'to follow', with the prefixes *intra*, 'inside' and *extra*, 'outside'.

introvert/extravert
The contrasting words, although having some general use ('He's a real introvert'), properly belong to psychology, where an 'introvert', as the name suggests, is someone who is 'turned inwards', and whose interests are directed inwards to his or her own thoughts. An 'extravert' (also spelt 'extrovert') is therefore the opposite, an 'outgoing' person whose attention and interests are directed entirely to everything that is external. In zoology, if an organ is 'introverted' it is turned inside out, like the finger of a glove can be. Some molluscs have hollow organs that can do this. However, 'extravert' is not used as an opposite of this process.

intrusive see **extrusive**

invalid see **valid**

inverted pleat see **box pleat**

inverted snob see **snob**

invisible see **visible**

in vitro see **in vivo**

in vivo/in vitro
The opposing terms here relate to biological processes. If a process takes place 'in vivo', it does so inside the body or inside a living organism. If it takes place 'in vitro', it does so under artificial conditions outside the body, usually in a vessel such as a test tube, culture dish, or the like. A so-called 'test tube baby' is one that has been conceived (by artificial insemination) 'in vitro', outside the mother's body. The Latin phrases mean literally 'in a living thing' and 'in glass'.

inwardly/outwardly
The words are quite often used for contrast in a single sentence, for example, 'Inwardly I was very apprehensive, but outwardly I managed to stay calm'. The usage like this often suggests that a deception or hidden danger lies 'inwardly', while 'outwardly' all is not what it appears to be. The concept is thus often something like that of a 'wolf in sheep's clothing', and indeed the biblical source of this saying contains one of the words: 'Beware of false prophets, which come to you in sheep's clothing, but inwardly they are ravening wolves' (Matthew 7:15).

Iran/Iraq
The contrast here is a good deal more than the single letter that distinguishes these two neighbouring Middle East countries, in open conflict with each other since 1980. The differences between the two are part of the general clash of religious and political interests that have long divided and fragmented the Middle East, and the present 'Gulf War', as the conflict is known, has its roots in the early years of the twentieth century, when both countries made opposing territorial claims. (Iran was then known as Persia.) More simply, the two lands were neighbouring 'rivals for supremacy', as often happens (consider any 'colonialist' or expansionist regime), here as the two largest states of the Persian Gulf. (At present, 'Iran' has a population nearly four times as large, however, as that of the 12 million of 'Iraq'.) But the real source of the current war, apparently insoluble, is the religious differences of the two: 'Iran' practises a form of Islam (Shi'ism) that is in conflict with the form of Islam predominant in 'Iraq' (Sunnism). For the further story, see **Shi'ite/Sunnite**.

Iraq see **Iran**

irenics/polemics
In Christian theology, 'irenics' concerns itself with unity between the various sects and denominations, while 'polemics' deals with religious controversies and differences. The terms can also have an appli-

cation outside theology to relate respectively to 'peace' studies and 'war' studies. Greek *eirene* means 'peace' and *polemos*, 'war'.

is/isn't

Perhaps two of the most basic contrasts or opposites one can have, that a thing 'is' so or 'isn't'. Despite the essential philosophical possibilities, however, the pair, in combination, are commonly associated with the response of a pantomime audience or of one child quarrelling with another. Thus, in the pantomime, one of the characters makes a statement that is patently absurd and that is denied by another. This leads to the exchange, 'Oh, yes it is!', 'Oh, no it isn't!', taken up by the audience in support of the one or mockery of the other. With children, the exchange is much briefer and degenerates into a heated and rapid altercation confined to, 'Is!', 'Isn't!', 'Is!', 'Isn't!', *ad nauseam et infinitum.*

Isis/Cam

These are the names of the rivers that flow respectively through Oxford and Cambridge, with the 'Isis' being an alternative name for the Thames at this point. The two are thus sometimes used to stand for one or other of the university pair **Oxford/Cambridge**, particularly in literary or academic use. For example, in one of his *Ecclesiastical Sonnets*, Wordsworth wrote of 'Isis and Cam, to patient science dear!', and in *The Dunciad*, Pope declared,

> May you, my Cam and Isis, preach it long!
> The Right Divine of Kings to govern wrong.

At Cambridge, the 'Cam' is still known by its alternative name of 'Granta' (as exemplified in the nearby village of Grantchester). The name of the 'Isis' arose as a form of the second half of the Latin name of the Thames, *Thamesis.*

isn't see **is**

Italian vermouth see **French vermouth**

italic/roman

These are the names of the two standard sorts of printing type, with 'roman' the more common and usual (and as this is now printed), and 'italic' the 'sloping' version (*like this*), mostly used for special emphasis. The same names, especially 'italic', can apply to handwriting. (For 'italic' writing a special broad-nibbed pen is used, so that the vertical and horizontal strokes are thick and the sloping strokes are thin.) 'Roman' is so named since it refers to the characteristic upright form of lettering in the inscriptions of Ancient Rome. 'Italic' is much more recent in origin, and describes the kind of type used in the early sixteenth century to print an edition of the works of Virgil that was published in Venice by Aldo Manuzio and dedicated by him to Italy.

italic

roman

ITV see **BBC**

ivory see **ebony**

Jj

Jack/Jill
The two names, familiar as the boy and girl of the nursery rhyme ('Jack and Jill went up the hill'), are sometimes used as generic names for a man and woman, or boy and girl, especially in literature. The particular image is usually of two young people, as in the lines from Puck's song in Shakespeare's *A Midsummer Night's Dream*:

> Jack shall have Jill;
> Nought shall go ill.

(Shakespeare did not invent the phrase, which was already well known.) Compare **Adam/Eve**.

jar see **straight glass**

Jeff see **Mutt**

Jekyll/Hyde
The names are those of the two principal characters in Robert Louis Stevenson's novel *The Strange Case of Dr Jekyll and Mr Hyde*. In this, Dr 'Jekyll', aware of the duality of good and evil in himself, discovers a drug enabling him to create a separate personality that would absorb all his evil instincts. This is Mr 'Hyde', whose personality he periodically assumes in order to give expression to his evil instincts. The personality becomes dominant, and 'Hyde' commits a murder. 'Jekyll' now finds himself increasingly unable to revert to his original dual form, and when about to be arrested for the murder, takes his own life. (All this by the author of *A Child's Garden of Verses*, although even *Kidnapped* centres on a murder.) The phrase 'Jekyll-and-Hyde' has thus come to refer to a person's good and bad nature, whether considered overall or as comprising the two opposing sides individually. We all have a 'Hyde' in conflict with our more desirable (and usually more public) 'Jekyll'.

Jersey/Guernsey
The names are those of the two principal islands of the Channel Isles group, popular with British (and French) tourists in the holiday season. With regard to the islands themselves, 'Jersey' is the larger and more populous, and also the more southerly of the two. The islands are also equally well known for their cattle and for the quality and quantity of the resulting milk, with 'Jersey' cows usually fawn-coloured (all over) and 'Guernsey' cows normally a mixture of fawn and white. ('Guernsey' cows, too, are larger than 'Jerseys'.) Topographically, the difference between the two islands can be well observed from the air: 'Jersey' is well wooded and slopes down to the south; 'Guernsey' has far fewer trees (and far more greenhouses), and has its lower region in the north. 'Jersey' thus has the warmer climate, since not only is it further south, and nearer the French coast, but it is sheltered from north winds and Atlantic gales by high land on its northern and western coasts. (Both islands, too, have their own individual parliaments, currencies and postage stamps.) There are also contrasting garments named after the islands. A 'jersey', the better known, is simply a jumper or pullover or sweater in general, but a 'guernsey' is specially a thick type of 'jersey'. (Both were so named because they were traditionally worn by sailors. Significantly, the 'guernsey' is the thicker garment, as needed on the island with the cooler prevailing climate.) However, rather confusingly, 'jersey' is also used as the name of a fine machine-knitted fabric used not for jumpers but for thin shirts and dresses. As such it can be made from a range of fabrics, including

wool, silk and nylon, while the 'jersey' that is a jumper is usually made of wool or some similar manmade yarn.

jet engine see **piston engine**

jetsam see **flotsam**

Jew/Gentile
Basically, if biblically, a 'Jew' is a person whose religion is Judaism and who at least notionally has descended from the ancient Israelites, while a 'Gentile' is anyone who is not a 'Jew', or who was not one in biblical times. Since a 'Gentile' was outside the accepted religion, the word became synonymous with 'pagan' or 'heathen'. At the same time, since most non-'Jews' were Christians, the term 'Gentile' also came to mean 'Christian'. The word arise from Latin *gentes*, 'the nations', itself a translation of the term for 'Gentiles' used in the Hebrew Bible, which was *goyyim* (or, with the definite article, *hagoyyim*, 'the nations'), meaning all the nations of the world who were not 'Jews' and so did not belong to the 'Chosen People'.

Jill see **Jack**

jock strap/cache-sexe
These are the names of the two minimal garments used for covering (and in the case of the male, supporting) the genital organs of the two sexes. The 'jock strap' is worn by male sportsmen and athletes, and the 'cache-sexe' by agile and athletic women when performing in circuses and strip clubs, when it is usually spangled and sometimes artistically or whimsically shaped. Both names are understandably somewhat euphemistic. The 'jock' of the male garment is a nickname for the organ it supports, while the feminine equivalent is French for 'sex-hider'. (In this respect it conforms to other French ornamental devices, such as the 'cache-pot' which holds a flower pot while discreetly masking it, and the 'cache-peigne', literally 'comb-hider', that is an ornament at the back of a woman's hat.) Another minimal garment that can be worn by both men and women is a 'G string'. This is simply a small piece of material covering the genitals that is supported by a thong or other string around the waist. It was originally worn by American Indians (men and boys), but in the twentieth century the name was extended to a similar garment worn by female artistes and strippers. It differs from a 'cache-sexe', however, in being more functional (or mandatory). (The 'G' is unexplained, although the word is also sometimes spelt 'gee-string'. No word beginning with 'G' suggests itself, nor does the garment resemble the shape of this letter, as say a 'Y-Front' does.)

John Doe see **Richard Roe**

John o'Groats see **Land's End**

joint/several
The terms occur in legal documents, where 'joint' refers to a combined ownership or obligation of some kind, and 'several' means each individually, without sharing. The legal phrase 'jointly and severally' thus serves as a 'blanket' term to cover combined and individual references.

jug/bottle
In its immediate past, the phrase 'jug and bottle' was used for the bar of a public house where drinks could be obtained for consumption off the premises, in other words, as the equivalent of the modern off-licence (see **on/off**). Originally, however, the words denoted a distinction: 'jug' referred to beer, while 'bottle' meant wine. As such, the nouns could be used outside the context of the public house to denote these respective drinks, as when the English preacher Robert South, in one of his famous sermons, fulminated against 'the sordid temptations of the jug and the bottle'.

Julian calendar see **Gregorian calendar**

junior see **senior**

junk food see **wholefood**

jus sanguinis/jus soli
The Latin expressions mean literally 'law of blood' and 'law of soil', and are legal terms. 'Jus sanguinis' refers to the principle that the nationality of a person at birth is the same as that of his or her parents, while 'jus soli' maintains that the nationality is determined by the country or territory where the person was born. The terms thus express the way in which a person's nationality can be determined: by his parents or by his motherland or fatherland.

jus soli see **jus sanguinis**

Kk

katabatic see **anabatic**

katakana see **hiragana**

Katharevusa see **Demotic**

Kentishman see **Man of Kent**

kharif/rabi
In India and Pakistan, 'kharif' is the term used for a crop that is harvested at the beginning of winter. It is thus distinct from 'rabi', which is a crop harvested at the end of winter. The words mean respectively 'gathering' and 'spring', and derive from Arabic. For something like an equivalent, see **spring wheat/winter wheat**.

kilometre/mile
The 'kilometre' is the standard unit of road distance in most European and many other countries, while the 'mile' remains as the norm in Britain and other English-speaking countries, notably the United States and Canada. A 'mile' is just over one and a half 'kilometres' in length (more exactly 1.609), while at sea a nautical 'mile' is somewhat longer, and is equal to 1.852 'kilometres'. The popular comparison is much like that of the pair **Fahrenheit/Celsius**, and is actually that of **metric/imperial** (which see).

king/queen
The male and female pair are familiar figures from sovereign states to games of cards and chess, so hardly need an introduction. What is rather unexpected is that as somewhat similar English words, they are not related. 'King' is basically related to 'kin', while 'queen' has the root sense 'woman', 'wife' (and so is related to the first part of the word 'gynaecology'). In many other languages, the word for 'queen' is the feminine form of that for 'king', thus:

French	roi	reine
German	König	Königin
Italian	re	regina
Latin	rex	regina
Russian	korol'	koroleva

kiss see **hug**

kleinschreibung see **Gross-schreibung**

knife/fork
The 'knife' is for cutting and laid to the right of the plate; the 'fork' is for raising the food to the mouth and laid to the left. That is the chief contrast between the two eating implements, although in some countries the 'fork', which is normally manipulated by the left hand, may be transferred to the right when the 'knife' has been used for cutting up the food on the plate. There is a phrase 'to play (or ply) a good knife and fork', meaning to eat heartily, and a 'knife-and-fork' man (or breakfast, or whatever) implies a heavy involvement with food and 'tucking in'.

kolkhoz/sovkhoz
The two Russian words denote different types of farm in the Soviet economy. A 'kolkhoz' is a collective farm in the proper sense of the term (the word is the Russian abbreviation for *kollektivnoye khozyaistvo*), otherwise a type of cooperative undertaking by a number of peasants (often a village or group of villages) who pool their land and other resources and are paid by the state for the amount of work they put in and the quantity (and quality) of their produce. A 'sovkhoz' (short for *sovetskoye khozyaistvo*, literally 'Soviet farm') is also an agricultural enterprise, but differs from a 'kolkhoz' in that it is run on industrial

lines with the workers receiving regular wages. There are fewer 'sovkhozes' than 'kolkhozes', but they cover a much larger area. (In 1985 there were nearly 23,000 'sovkhozes' and 27,000 'kolkhozes'. However, these figures are dramatically different from 1940, when there were more than 230,000 'kolkhozes' but only just over 4000 'sovkhozes'.)

kung fu see **tai chi chuan**

kyu/dan
In judo, a 'kyu' is one of the six grades for less proficient competitors, with the sixth 'kyu' the lowest. By contrast, the 'dan' is one of the ten Black Belt grades for the professionals or experienced, with the tenth the highest (although almost impossible to attain, and the highest a westerner has managed to date is the eighth 'dan'). In karate, there are eight 'kyu' grades (the eighth the lowest), followed by ten 'dan' grades (the first the lowest). In Japanese, 'kyu' means 'class' and 'dan' means 'grade', 'step'.

Ll

Labour see **Conservative**

labour-intensive see **capital-intensive**

lad/lass
'Come lasses and lads, get leave of your dads', runs the old traditional song, urging the young men and women to dance round the maypole. The words still have a 'period' ring to them, although to call a boy 'lad' and a girl 'lass' is still common practice in certain parts of Britain, especially the north, with each having its own diminutive form, respectively 'laddie' and 'lassie'. Although somewhat similar, no link has been proved to exist between the words, and indeed their precise origin is still uncertain. 'Lass', however, is not a shortened form of 'ladess', as some people like to think! The plurals of each are sometimes used flippantly for the designations of a male and female toilet in a public house (see next entry below for the more conventional indication).

ladders see **snakes**

ladies/gentlemen
As the plurals of the 'polite' pair **gentleman/lady**, 'ladies' and 'gentlemen' have two familiar usages. The first is to preface a speech to a public gathering, in order to draw attention to the words that follow ('Ladies and gentlemen, allow me to present . . .'). The second is to announce the location of (or way to) a public lavatory, where the two words must be unique among euphemisms, since the object they designate is not actually mentioned at all. This second usage is quite recent, and appears to have arisen only in the present century (as has that of the abbreviated 'gents' for the men's convenience). With regard to the 'address' usage of 'Ladies and gentlemen', there is some evidence that until about the mid-eighteenth century, the order of the words was the other way round, so that a speaker would begin, 'Gentlemen and ladies'. Most languages are now the same as the modern English order, although (even if the location varies) French has something similar in the *Bonjour, monsieur-dame* ('Good morning, Sir and Madam') with which the shopkeeper traditionally addresses his customers. Public lavatories are now often marked simply 'Men' and 'Women', and loo visitors in European countries can amuse themselves seeing whether the words translate as this or as the equivalent of 'Gents' and 'Ladies'. (A basic knowledge of the language is certainly needed here, and tales have been told of more than one Englishwoman who has hurriedly entered the building marked 'Uomini' in Italy only to retreat from it equally hastily.) See also **Sir/Madam** and even **Sir/Miss**.

lady see (1) **gentleman** (2) **lord**

Lagting/Odelsting
These are the two names of the upper and lower chamber, respectively, of the Norwegian parliament (itself called the Storting). The words actually mean 'law parliament' and 'allodium parliament' ('allodium' being in English legal use the term for an estate held in absolute ownership in feudal times), while 'Storting' means 'great parliament'. (The common '-ting' here is really the same as English 'thing', but the sense of 'parliament', 'assembly' is still active in the name of the 'hustings' of an election, where the basic sense is 'house assembly'.)

laid see **wove**

Lancaster see **York**

land/sea
Until 'air' came along to make a third element for travelling in, 'land' and 'sea' held the sole right as a contrasting pair of elements over which man could make his way, as he still mostly does. The contrast is even more basic since the two represent the alternating surfaces of the earth, one dry, the other wet. (Overall, the earth has a surface that is three parts 'land' to seven parts 'sea' or water, with the proportion two to three in the northern hemisphere, but only one part 'land' to nearly five 'sea' in the southern hemisphere.) The pairing of 'land' and 'sea' is common in literature, from Milton's 'thing of sea or land' in *Samson Agonistes* to Wordsworth's 'thing that never was, on sea or land' (referring to a picture of Peele Castle in a storm). Nor should one overlook, presumably, Kipling's embarrassing:

> When 'Omer smote 'is bloomin' lyre,
> He'd 'eard men sing by land an' sea.

In a more artistic area, the 'seascape' developed as a contrast to the 'landscape' and has so far not in turn engendered an 'airscape'.

landlady see **landlord**

landlord/landlady
The contrast here is both exact and inexact. Exact, in that a 'landlady' can be a female 'landlord', as a woman who owns land or a building for leasing or renting. Inexact, in that a 'landlord' runs a public house, but a 'landlady' is also the female proprietor of a boarding house. In the latter sense, the correspondence is basically there (a boarding house and a public house are both places where guests can stay), but as popularly used the 'landlord' is the man behind the bar and the 'landlady' the sometimes fearsome woman who devises a host of rules and regulations to be observed by her resident guests (especially by the seaside).

Land's End/John o'Groats
The names are those of the extreme south-western and north-eastern points of mainland Britain, respectively, and are traditionally paired in the expression 'from Land's End to John o'Groats', meaning 'from one end of Britain to the other' (for the record, 847 miles by road). No doubt the somewhat similar structure of the names reinforces their mental association (they both have awkward apostrophes and consist of two words). No other country appears to have a similar expression, although the geography needs to be right, as it is in Britain. However, the English phrase 'from Dan to Beersheba' runs it close and has the same basic sense of 'from one end of the kingdom to the other'.

langue/parole
The French words mean respectively 'language' and 'word'. They were chosen by the Swiss linguist Ferdinand Saussure to distinguish the language people use mentally, in their thoughts, and the language they use when they are actually speaking. The use of the terms was somewhat modified later, however, to denote on the one hand a language regarded as a system of elements within a community of speakers, and on the other the linguistic behaviour of an individual when speaking. Noam Chomsky subsequently introduced a similar dichotomy with his terms 'competence' and 'performance'.

langue d'oc/langue d'oïl
Another French couplet. Here the expressions mean respectively 'language of *oc*' and 'language of *oïl*', both being designations of differing types of dialect in Frence in medieval times. 'Langue d'oc' was the group of dialects spoken in the south of France, and is usually regarded as including Provençal. 'Langue d'oïl' was the group spoken in the northern half of France (north of the Loire), and was the basis of modern French. The distinctive *oc* and *oïl* were respective words for 'yes', with *oc* ultimately from Latin *hoc* and *oïl* from Latin *hoc ille* (with *fecit* understood), the latter meaning 'this he did'. (It was *oïl*, however, that gave the present standard French *oui* for 'yes'.) 'Languedoc' became the name of a province in the south of France, and today 'Languedoc' wines from the region are still so called.

langue d'oïl see **langue d'oc**

large/small
Here one is in the rather complex group of 'size opposites' that includes **big/little**, **great/small** and **little/large**, among others. 'Large' is contrasted with 'small' in a limited number of uses and expressions, not nearly as extensive as 'big' versus 'little'. Anatomically, one has the 'large' intestine and the 'small' intestine, with the former being the rear division of the intestine that is shorter and wider than the latter. Mentally, a person can be either 'large'-minded or 'small'-minded. If the former, he will be broad-minded and generally liberal in outlook. If the latter, he will be narrow-minded, petty and intolerant. When it comes to names of types of creatures, one needs to be careful. A 'large' white is a breed of pale-coloured pig with a big, long body, but a 'small' white is a white butterfly (whose 'large' version is normally known as the cabbage white). But perhaps one of the most common uses is in the pair of 'large'-scale and 'small'-scale. A 'large'-scale map covers a geographically 'small' area in some detail; a 'small'-scale map covers a geographically 'large' area with little detail shown. In a general sense, the two mean simply 'extensive' and 'limited' (as a 'small'-scale operation).

large see **little**

lass see **lad**

last/next
These are opposites in time, so that 'last' week was the one before this one, and 'next' week is the one after this one. So similarly one has 'last' month and 'next' month, 'last' year and 'next' year, 'last' time and 'next' time, and so on. 'Last' thus has two main meanings. For the other, see **first/last**.

last see **first**[1]

late see **early**

lateral thinking/vertical thinking
'Lateral thinking' is the method of solving problems by unorthodox and even apparently illogical means, sometimes resulting in an unexpected resolution. This is therefore opposed to the traditional method of reasoning and thinking, in logical steps, which is 'vertical thinking'. The terms were devised as recently as the 1960s by the British specialist on thinking processes, Dr Edward De Bono. The terms themselves imply that usual thinking works 'up and down', like the steps of a ladder, but that 'lateral thinking' explores routes to the side of the normal track of reasoning. In some ways, the split is the same as that of the pair **vertical/horizontal**, or even more, **synchronic/diachronic** and the next entry below.

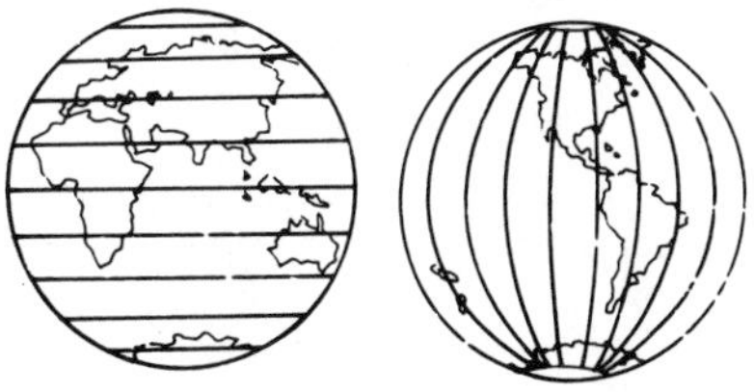

latitude longitude

latitude/longitude
In their geographical sense, which is where the contrast is best observed, 'latitude' is the angular distance of a place expressed in degrees north or south of the equator, which itself has a 'latitude' of 0°. 'Longitude' is the converse of this, in other words the angular distance of a place in degrees east or west of a so-called 'prime meridian', this usually being Greenwich, which therefore has a 'longitude' of 0°. The two terms are sometimes confused (and 'longitude' wrongly said as 'longtitude'), doubtless because if a place has a 'latitude' at, say, 20° south (of the equator), one may well travel a distance south from the equator along a 'longitude' to reach it. Geographers express the location of a place with the 'latitude' first, then the 'longitude', usually giving both degrees and minutes, and using N (S) or E (W) accordingly for the compass

bearing. For example, Palm Beach, in the United States, is 26° 46′N, and 80° 0′W. It is rather a pity that the location 0° 0′N, 0° 0′W is not actually on land but off West Africa in the Gulf of Guinea.

latter see **former**

laugh/cry
'I didn't know whether to laugh or cry', we may say, on hearing or experiencing something that could be either comic or tragic (such as one's nextdoor neighbour stuck on his roof, or one's own embarrassing display of ignorance when asked an easy question). Not surprisingly, the two contrasting actions are linked in several sayings, such as 'Laugh and the world laughs with you, cry (or weep) and you cry alone', and 'Laugh before breakfast, you'll cry before supper'. To 'laugh' is of course to express one's happiness, pleasure or amusement, and to 'cry' to show one's sadness, unhappiness or grief. But basically the two actions are very similar ('tears of joy', 'hysterical laughter' and so on), and this is a good example of a pair of opposites in which extremes virtually meet. (Look up 'laugh' in the *Oxford English Dictionary* and you will find a description which for much of its extent could be that of 'cry': 'spasmodic utterance of inarticulate sounds, facial distortion, shaking of the sides', etc.)

lay see **clerical**

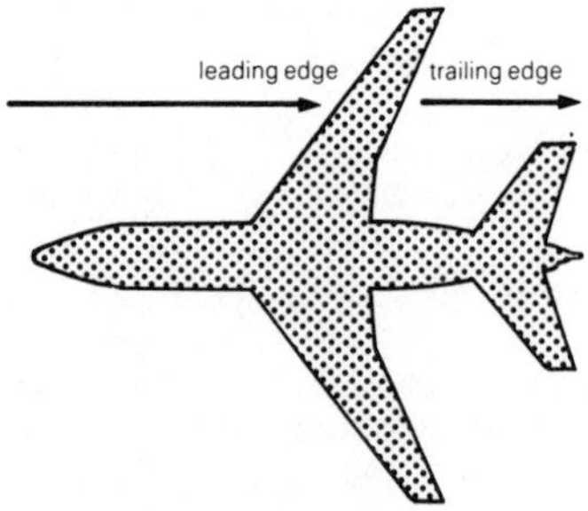

leading edge/trailing edge
These are the terms used for the front and rear edge of an aircraft's wing or tailplane, or of the blade of a propeller as it moves through the air. (Of a ship, the terms can also apply to its screw as it progresses through the water.) The forward edge thus 'leads' the way, while the rear edge 'trails' behind it or follows.

learn see **teach**

leave it see **take it**

lee/weather
In nautical terms, the 'lee' side of a ship is the side that is sheltered from the wind, so that the 'weather' side is the side exposed to it. The distinction is thus very similar to that of the pair **leeward/windward** (see next entry). 'Wind' and 'weather' are associated both in their meaning and in their origin, because it is likely they both stem from the same basic Indo-European root.

leeward/windward
Still mostly in nautical terms, 'leeward' means 'away from the wind', 'to the sheltered side', so that 'windward' means 'into the wind', 'to the exposed side'. The names are familiar as those of different groups of islands that are either relatively protected from a prevailing wind or exposed to it, with probably the best known being the 'Leeward' and 'Windward' Islands in the West Indies.

left/right
Two diametrically opposed words, with several important usages and connotations. For most people, their 'left' hand is weaker than their 'right', and it is thus the latter that they use for such everyday acts and tasks as cutting, pointing, writing, throwing, stirring, cleaning and so on. (For raising food to the mouth when eating, the 'right' hand is also used with a fork or spoon alone, but the 'left' hand when the 'right' holds a knife.) In politics, officially and generally, 'left' has traditionally come to mean 'radical', 'socialist', 'democratic', 'revolutionary', 'Communist' or 'worker-oriented', while 'right' has

come to mean 'traditional', 'conservative', 'reactionary' or 'establishment-oriented'. The origin of the particular sides in this sense lies in the seating arrangement of the French National Assembly of 1789, in which the nobles took the seats to the 'right' hand of the President, as a mark of honour, while members of the Third Estate (the 'commoners' or townsmen) sat to his left. Both words are frequently coupled with 'wing' or 'hand' to denote political standpoint ('left-wing views') and direction or location ('right-hand bend') respectively. (See the next entry for more on this.) On the whole, 'left' and 'right' apply to the physical viewpoint of the observer, but if I talk about your 'left' eye, I mean the one that is 'left' to you, even though it is to the 'right', as I look at it, of the other one. Sometimes, too, an object that is on the 'left' will be on the 'right' when viewed from another standpoint, such as the 'left' window of a house, which will be on the 'right' when seen from outside. The 'left' bank of a river, however, is the one on this side when the observer is facing downstream, and the 'right' the one when facing upstream. (See **rive droite/rive gauche** in this respect.) See also **sinister/dexter**.

left-hand drive/right-hand drive
Britain is famous (or notorious) for its 'right-hand drive' cars, because road transport drives on the left, not on the right, as in many other countries, including everywhere in Europe and the United States and Canada. Throughout the world, there are also other countries where vehicles drive on the left, mainly in former British colonies. Among them are Australia, New Zealand, India and Indonesia. In Japan, too, vehicles drive on the left, making the transfer of Japanese motor manufacture technology to Britain a relatively easy procedure. (In 1986 the Japanese firm of Nissan opened a large new factory in north-east England.) British motorists taking their cars to the Continent sometimes have difficulty adjusting to the 'right-hand drive' rule, because it can seem as if they are driving on the 'wrong' side of the road.

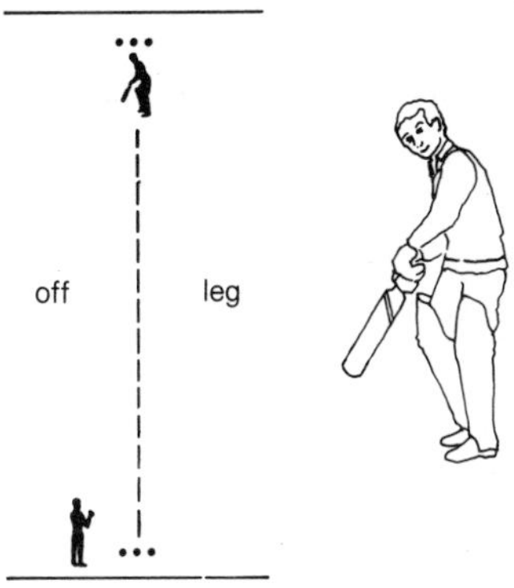

leg/off
Cricket is renowned for its esoteric vocabulary ('square leg', 'silly mid-off'), and 'leg' and 'off' are two of the basic opposites that lie behind some of them (including the two just quoted). Basically, the words correspond to the pair **left/right** from the point of view of a right-handed batsman when he is facing the bowler. If an imaginary line is drawn from his middle stump to the middle stump of the wicket at the bowler's end, everything to the left of this will be on the 'leg' side, and anything to the right of it will be 'off'. (Care is needed here, since what is on the 'off side' in cricket is nothing to do with being 'off side' in football, where the expression refers to a player who is illegally in front of the ball!) The terms themselves fairly obviously refer to the batsmen's legs, which are to the left of the middle stump as he stands at the wicket, and to the right side regarded as 'off' in the same sense as the word in the pair **near/off** (which see). Rather more logically (or confusingly, depending on one's view), an alternative term for 'leg' is 'on'. For more about this, see **on/off**.

legato see **staccato**

lend/borrow
If I 'lend' you my pen, you are 'borrowing' it, so the distinction is really that of 'act done by me at the same time as you' versus 'act done by you at the same time as me',

with these differentiated. (For similar pairs, compare **buy/sell**, **give/take**, among others.) Children sometimes say 'lend' when they mean 'borrow' ('Can I lend your bike?'), perhaps half echoing the use of the word as a noun meaning 'loan' (so that 'Can I have a lend of your bike?' would be acceptable, if colloquial). 'Lend' and 'loan' are related, but 'borrow', believe it or not, is related to 'borough' and 'bury'. The linking concept is of the object being a sort of 'security', something that is held safe.

length/width
The contrasting words denote the distance or measurement of something longways on the one hand, and across it on the other, with the basic adjectives of 'long' and 'wide' behind the nouns. In one popular sporting use, the words are used of the measurements of a swimming pool, with a swimmer's ability or stamina judged by his or her covering of so many 'lengths' or even 'widths' ('Jane swam three lengths yesterday, but John still can't even manage a width'.) The final '-th' is characteristic of many English measurements, including also 'depth' and 'breadth', so that one quite frequently even hears the erroneous 'heighth' (sounded as the ending of 'eighth'), instead of 'height'.

lento see **allegro**

lesbian see **homosexual**[2]

lesser see **greater**

leucocytes/erythrocytes
These are the medical terms meaning respectively 'white blood corpuscles' and 'red blood corpuscles'. The 'leucocytes' are white or colourless, have nuclei, do not contain haemoglobin, and are mainly concerned with the defence mechanisms of the body. The 'erythrocytes', which have their characteristic red pigment, contain haemoglobin and carry oxygen to the tissues. The Greek-derived names mean simply 'white cell' and 'red cell'. See also more generally **red/white**.

lexis/taxis
The words as they stand are pure Greek, meaning respectively 'word' and 'arrangement'. The terms are used in so-called computational stylistics (i.e. the method of analysing an author's writing by means of a computer) to denote his actual vocabulary on the one hand (his 'lexis') and the arrangement of his words on the other (his 'taxis'). The combination of the two will reveal such things as the frequency of particular words, the lengths of words (by letters or syllables) and the author's use of particular grammatical features (e.g. subordinate clauses or proper nouns). The results can be quite interesting when the author is someone like James Joyce, and quite useful when it comes to reconstructing doubtful passages in an important text (for example, the Dead Sea Scrolls).

ley see **arable**

liabilities see **assets**

libel/slander
Both are damaging to a person's reputation. Basically, 'libel' is something harmful that is written about a person, while 'slander' is something spoken. However, with increasingly sophisticated methods of communication, the terms need to be qualified. 'Libel' can now include pictorial matter (e.g. a cartoon), and 'slander' can in some circumstances include recorded words. (Words broadcast by radio, however, are 'libel'.) In modern legal terms, too, 'libel' may be punished criminally, while 'slander' is purely a civil offence. 'Libel' has its origin in Latin *libellus*, 'little book', while 'slander' comes from Late Latin *scandalum*, 'cause of offence', so is related to modern 'scandal'.

librettist/composer
The 'librettist' writes the words and the 'composer' writes the music, à la Gilbert and Sullivan. The 'librettist' is named after the libretto that he writes, this being literally (in Italian) the 'little book' with the words of an opera or oratorio. It does not follow that all operas had a separate

'librettist', and Wagner, for example, was his own 'librettist'. Even so, there have been some famous 'words and music' combinations, with the 'librettist' called the 'lyricist' in more recent and popular works, e.g. Rodgers and Hart, Rodgers and Hammerstein, Lerner and Loewe (of *My Fair Lady*), and Tim Rice and Andrew Lloyd-Webber (*Jesus Christ Superstar*). Probably *the* 'librettist' of all time, at any rate in classical music, was the eighteenth-century Metastasio (real name Pietro Trapassi), whose fifty or more libretti were used by many famous composers, including Mozart, Handel, Haydn and Gluck. See also **Gilbert/Sullivan**, **words/music**, **classical/popular**.

life/death
Two extremes, about which one can be duly philosophical, in any sense of the word. Here we would do best to concentrate on the linguistic and semantic contrast. A 'matter of life and death' is a matter of extreme urgency. The implication is that if steps are not taken, 'life' may become 'death'. Inevitably, there are several proverbs and quotations to point to a few basic truths about the two. Many of the best known quotations are from the fine poet George Herbert, and include: 'Life without a friend, is death without a witness', 'In life you loved me not, in death you bewail me', and 'Between the business of life and the day of death, a space ought to be interposed'. In the more prosaic world, a 'life' mask is one made (usually in plaster of Paris) from the face of a person while he is alive, while a 'death' mask is a case of the face taken soon after 'death'. Is there 'life' after 'death'? Christians believe so. Compare **death/resurrection**.

Lifeguards see **Blues**[2]

liger/tigon
Who says there ain't no such animal? A 'liger' is the offspring of a lion and a tigress', while a 'tigon' is the reverse, so to speak, the offspring of a tiger and a lioness. The respective beasts were produced as the result of cross-breeding in various zoos from the 1930s, which was when the cross-bred names themselves first appeared. The 'tigon' is also sometimes known as a 'tiglon'.

light[1]/dark
Some things that are 'light' have a 'dark' counterpart. Among them are shades of colours ('light' blue and 'dark' blue) and, although in a much more specialized sense, consonants that have a 'light' or 'dark' pronunciation in phonetics. For example, the English letter 'l' is usually 'dark' or somewhat resonant when it comes at the end of a word (say, 'hall'), but this letter in French is usually pronounced as a 'light' consonant (for example, *ville*). However, there are many more opposites to be found for the pair **light/heavy**, for which see the next entry. Compare also **darkness/light** for a slightly more literary consideration.

light[2]/heavy
Although spelt exactly the same as the 'light' above, this 'light', with its opposite of 'heavy', is not of the same origin. (The 'light' meaning 'bright' relates to Latin *lux*, 'light', and this 'light', meaning 'of little weight', relates to Latin *levis*, 'light'.) Most of the contrasts here relate directly to weight, such as the different boxing weights, which are fairly complex, and even include a 'light-heavyweight' (who weighs not more than 12 stone 7 pounds if professional, or between 75 and 81 kilogrammes if amateur, with more complexities in the different weight systems used). Some of the more common contrasts include the following: a 'light' sleeper is easily awakened, but a 'heavy' sleeper is difficult to rouse; 'light' industry usually produces goods that go straight to the consumer, but 'heavy' industry produces goods that are mainly used to produce other goods, and that are certainly heavy, such as coal, steel and machinery; 'light' cavalry (for example) carries little armour or weapons, as distinct from 'heavy' cavalry which is well loaded with armour and arms; 'light' traffic means few vehicles travelling on the road, but 'heavy' traffic, as in the rush

hour, involves many vehicles. Do you find all this 'light' reading, or diverting and easy to read, or 'heavy' reading, so that it is complicated and difficult to take in? 'A light-heeled mother makes a heavy-heeled daughter', runs the old proverb, meaning that if the mother is active and does all the work, the daughter will sit idly and become lazy. See also **lightface/boldface**, below.

light[3]/shade
Here the contrast is mostly an artistic one. If something is in the 'light', it is clearly visible, but if it is in the 'shade' it is difficult to see. The 'lights and shades' of a painting, therefore, are its clearer and more obscure parts. Sometimes the contrast is a figurative one, as in Pope's 'lights and shades' of life (whose 'well-accorded strife' gives life its 'strength and colour'). In fairly recent times the contrast has also transferred to other 'artistic' areas, such as the 'light' and 'shade' of a stage performance (especially the way a particular part is varied as the actor performs, and the way in which he modulates and 'throws' his voice).

light[4]/upright
Try this small puzzle:

My first is a member that's able to hold,
My next is the name of an emperor of old,
My last is a plucking, a sharp twanging sound,
My whole is a sausage, a peppery hound.

Any luck? The answer is HOT DOG, and the puzzle itself is an acrostic, with each line of verse the clue to a word whose first and last letters are needed for this overall answer. So the arrangement is:

(My first . . .) H A N D (a 'member')
(My next . . .) O T T O (the famous German emperor)
(My last . . .) T A N G (a 'sharp twanging sound')

And HOT DOG (My whole . . .) not only appears reading down the first and last letters, but is clued descriptively ('sausage') and cryptically ('peppery hound'). The point of all this is to illustrate the two terms of the entry. In an acrostic, the 'lights' are the words that appear reading across (HAND, OTTO, TANG), and the 'uprights' are the words that appear reading down (HOT DOG). The difference is that of **vertical/horizontal**. The term 'lights' apparently originated because the words across resemble a 'window' bounded by the two 'uprights'. The word is also sometimes used for the answers that appear in a crossword, with the blank spaces also seen as 'lights' which need to be filled in. (See **across/down** for more on this.)

light see (1) **darkness** (2) **sound**

lightface/boldface
In printing, 'lightface' is the relatively thin and light type used for setting normal text, as in this sentence. By contrast, 'boldface' is a thicker, darker type used for headings and for special emphasis. In this dictionary, as in many others, it is used for the entry headings. 'Light' here means light in weight, and 'bold' means 'prominent'.

lightning see **thunder**

Lilliput/Brobdingnag
The former name here is much better known than the latter, no doubt since it is easier to say and spell, and probably because its significance is in itself more 'homely'. 'Lilliput' was the imaginary country of tiny inhabitants in Swift's *Gulliver's Travels*, while 'Brobdingnag', in the same book, was the country of tall people or giants. It was in 'Lilliput' that the Big-Endians opposed the Little-Endians (see **Big-Endians/Little-Endians**). The words have to some extent passed into the English language, so that 'Lilliputian' can mean 'very small', and (although much less commonly), 'Brobdingnagian' can mean 'gigantic'. Swift seems to have based the name 'Lilliput' on two foreign words, such as Danish *lille*, 'small' and Italian *putto*, 'child'. 'Brobdingnag' (sometimes

incorrectly spelt 'Brobdignag') has a more obscure origin.

linear/painterly
The terms relate to art, and particular to painting. 'Linear' applies to a painting that derives its effect chiefly from its lines, that is from the edge of objects as clearly delineated, rather than from colour and light. 'Painterly', on the other hand, applies to a picture that derives its effect more from blocks of colour than from lines. Although 'linear' was in use in this sense in the late nineteenth century, 'painterly' seems to have emerged (as a translation of German *malerisch*) somewhat later. The terms can of course be applied retrospectively to the 'old masters', so that Botticelli can be said to be a 'linear' painter, while Rembrandt is 'painterly'.

lingam see **yoni**

Lion

Unicorn

Lion/Unicorn

> The lion and the unicorn
> Were fighting for the crown.

But who were they? The two beasts originated in heraldry, with the 'Lion' traditionally representing England and the 'Unicorn' Scotland. The former royal coat of arms of Scotland had two 'Unicorns' as its supporters (on either side of the shield). When James VI of Scotland became also James I of England, in 1603, he 'imported' one of the two 'Unicorns' and used it to replace the Red Dragon (representing Wales) that was one of the supporters on the English coat of arms, where the other supporter was already the 'Lion'. The two arch rivals thus became joint supporters on the shield of the new combined kingdom of England and Scotland, and they remain today on the royal coat of arms of Great Britain.

liquid see **solid**

literal/figurative
'Literal' language is language that describes what actually happens. For example, 'The river winds its way through the hills'. 'Figurative' language is language that, by contrast, uses a figure of speech, especially a simile or a metaphor. For example, 'The river snakes through the hills' (here, a metaphor). 'Figurative' language is thus more imaginative, even poetic, while 'literal' language is plain and straightforward. See also **simile/metaphor**.

literate[1]/illiterate
As popularly used, 'literate' means 'able to read and write', while 'illiterate' means 'unable to read and write', otherwise 'badly educated'. More recently, a contrast has emerged between 'literate' and 'numerate'. See the next entry.

literate[2]/numerate
The two terms are frequently applied in an educational context, so that a child who is 'literate' is one who can read and write satisfactorily (i.e. can handle letters), while one who is also 'numerate' can handle numbers, and be competent in arithmetic or mathematics generally. In other words, the contrast is simply in the kind of written symbols that are used for communication, letters and figures. Ideally, a child should be both 'literate' and 'numerate', an aim formerly expressed by the basic 'three Rs' ('Reading, 'Riting and 'Rithmetic'). 'Numerate' formerly existed as a word meaning 'numbered', with this usage becoming obsolete. In the present sense, the word first became prominent only from the 1960s. It seems to have been devised for use in a government report on secondary education published in 1959, where the word appeared in quotation marks followed by the comment 'if we may coin a word to represent the mirror image of literacy'.

litotes see **hyperbole**

little/large
How does this pair of opposites differ from those of **big/little** and **large/small**? Apart from the alliteration, which helps to bind the two, there really is no great distinction between 'big' and 'large' when they come to be contrasted with 'little'. A few proverbs have the pair, such as 'A little kitchen makes a large house' (i.e. economise on space to gain extra room), and the words have also been adopted as stage names for a pair of tall and short comedians, but otherwise the particular coupling is not all that frequent. However, we should not perhaps overlook the attractive dedication in the prayer book sent by the seventeenth-century poet Richard Crashaw to 'Mrs M. R.': 'Lo here a little volume but a large book'.

little see **big**

little end see **big end**

Little-endians see **Big-endians**

little slam see **grand slam**

live[1]/dead
This pair of opposites is not quite the same as the ones in **alive/dead** (which see). It can come close to it, however, as when contrasting the 'live' weight of an animal (when it is alive) and its 'dead' weight (when it is not). The words mainly apply to things, however, that are respectively 'active' and 'passive'. Examples are 'live' coals, which are glowing and burning, and 'dead' coals which are cold and extinguished. A 'live' wire is one that has an electric current running through it, while a 'dead' wire has no current. More technically, a 'live' load is a variable one, such as that of traffic passing over a bridge. A 'dead' load, however, is the unchanging weight of a structure, as the sum of its parts. In sport, the ball is 'live' when it is in play, but 'dead' when it is not (and usually when it has gone over the line marking the playing area). Colloquially, glasses or bottles in use by drinkers in a pub or elsewhere can be 'live' or 'dead': 'live' glasses are still in use and may be refilled, and a 'dead' bottle is an empty one that is useless. See also the next two entries below. (See also **life/death**.)

live[2]/recorded
The terms here apply mostly to radio or television broadcasts. A programme that goes out 'live' is one that is broadcast as it happens, while a 'recorded' one has been prerecorded (obviously enough). The majority of broadcasts are 'recorded', if only for convenience and in order to achieve the desired standard and length, with 'retakes' possible and with the result edited down.

live birth/still birth
A 'live' birth is the hoped-for one (normally), when the baby is born alive. A 'still' birth occurs when the child is born dead. The concept is of a baby that either shows signs of life, and moves, or that does not, and so is still. The opposite of 'stillborn', to describe such a child, is thus 'liveborn'. There was a dialect word 'deadborn' but this is now virtually obsolete. Perhaps 'still' (instead of 'dead') arose as a sort of euphemism, although other languages do not seem to require it. ('Stillborn' in French is *mort-né*, in German *totgeboren*, and in Russian *mertvorozhdënny*, for example, all of which mean 'deadborn'.) Compare **live/dead** (above).

living/fallen
The contrast here is usually between people who are still alive and those who have been killed in war or battle, with 'fallen' a euphemism for 'killed', implying 'felled by a bullet' rather than 'fallen asleep'. This sense of 'fallen' is quite recent, apparently dating from not much earlier than the eighteenth century. One of its first occurrences is in a poem by Mrs Felicia Hemans (who gave us the famous 'stately homes of England' and 'The boy stood on the burning deck'), in the line from *Abencerrage* written in 1819:

> There bleed the fallen, there contend the brave.

The word became widely current in and immediately after the First World War.

local anaesthetic/general anaesthetic
A 'local anaesthetic', usually administered for a fairly minor operation, is one that numbs or deadens only the part to be operated on, such as a tooth or a finger. A 'general anaesthetic', on the other hand, is one that renders the patient totally unconscious, and is normally used for more serious or prolonged surgery. The respective terms 'local' and 'general' originate from medical parlance in an older sense, with a 'local' disease affecting only a particular part of the body, and a 'general' one affecting all of it. The usage came to apply to treatments for such diseases, and eventually to the two types of anaesthetic.

local call/national call
The terms relate to telephone calls. A 'local call' is one made within one's own neighbourhood, and within fixed limits (which can nevertheless be quite extensive), and is one that is generally cheaper than a 'national call'. The latter, until the early 1980s normally known as a 'long-distance call' or a 'trunk call', is one made over a substantial distance, and is thus more expensive. In Britain, the distance dividing a 'local call' from a 'national call' has for some years been notionally fixed at 35 miles (56km), although in practice the actual range can vary, depending on the location of the caller and the person called.

lodging see **board**

long/short
The basic contrasts here apply in a number of everyday or familiar contexts. A 'long' drink is an alcoholic drink that is relatively weak in alcohol and large in amount, typically beer. A 'short' drink is a much smaller one with a relatively powerful alcoholic content, as typically spirits (especially whisky or gin). A 'long' wave is a radiowave with a wavelength greater than 1000 metres, while a 'short' wave is less than this, and almost always between 10 and 100 metres. As commonly used, a 'short' wave is the main one for amateur radio transmissions, although it is also used professionally (and confusingly) for long-range broadcasts. 'Long' trousers ('longs') are or were mostly those worn by men, while 'short' trousers ('shorts') are associated with small boys. The transition from 'shorts' to 'longs' was formerly regarded as something of a rite of puberty, 'boy into man'. 'Short' hair has long been associated with men and boys, and 'long' with women and girls. In the Bible, St Paul told the Corinthians that this was the natural order of things ('Doth not even nature itself teach you, that, if a man hath long hair, it is a shame unto him? But if a woman hath long hair, it is a glory to her', I Corinthians 11:14, 15). Today things are often different. 'Longhand' is normal writing, with words their full length, but 'shorthand' is an abbreviated form of writing, as traditionally used by secretaries. A 'long' position of a fielder in cricket is one far from the wicket, such as 'long leg'. A 'short' position, however, is one close in, where it is often actually called 'silly' (such as 'silly mid-on'). In the financial world, to be 'long' in a commodity, such as wheat, is to possess more than one actually requires of it, so that one is hoping for a rise in prices. If one is 'short' in wheat, one does not have enough to meet demand. Finally (although not exhaustively), 'the long and the short of it' is the expression to indicate the final outcome or essential meaning of something. And the long and the short of it is that this must be the final sentence of the entry. (But compare **tall/short.**)

longitude see **latitude**

long jump see **high jump**

long-range/point-blank
A 'long-range' shot is one fired from some distance away, and a 'point-blank' shot is one fired at minimum range, very close to the target. 'Point-blank' is rather a curious term, and probably originates in an archery shot that was fired at the 'blank' or white centre of the target. Such a shot

was made horizontally and fairly close to, without any allowance for a drop in the flight of the arrow. (Today, however, the centre of an archery target is gold or yellow.)

long-sighted see **short-sighted**

lord/lady
A nobleman and noblewoman, respectively, or in medieval terms, the master or mistress of a manor. There are fairly complex rules about which aristocratic ranks can be called by one title or the other, which are too complex to detail here. In the Christian religion, however, it is worth noting that 'Our Lord' is a title of Christ, and 'Our Lady' a title of the Virgin Mary. 'Lords and ladies' is a colloquial name for the plant also known as the cuckoopint (*Arum maculatum*). The reference is to the contrasting colours of the flower-spikes, which are a mixture of dark ('lords') and light ('ladies'). The words themselves are interesting, since they are two of the very few Old English (Anglo-Saxon) terms that have survived to apply to persons of high rank, whereas most similar titles are of Norman-French origin (such as 'duke', 'duchess', 'baron' and 'marshal'). Their literal meanings are suitably rural, since 'lord' meant 'loaf ward' (i.e. the 'bread protector' of the crops), and 'lady' meant 'loaf kneader' (i.e. the 'bread maker' of the household). See also **king/queen**, **Sir/Madam**, as well as the next entry.

Lords/Commons
The 'House of Lords' and 'House of Commons' are respectively the upper and lower chambers of the British parliament, with the former composed of the peers of the realm ('lords' as well as 'ladies'), and elected for life, and the latter the more familiar assembly of Members of Parliament ('MPs'), elected for the parliamentary session only, and representing the current Government and Opposition. The title 'Commons' alludes to the fact that the members are not peers. See also **lord/lady**, **Government/Opposition**, **spiritual/temporal**, and compare the names of similar bicameral assemblies, such as **House of Representatives/Senate**, **Bundesrat/Bundestag**, **Lagting/Odelsting**.

lose see **win**[1]

loss see (1) **gain** (2) **profit**

loud/soft
Apart from the familiar senses, relating to sounds or noises of high or low volume, 'loud' and 'soft' have a few special applications. On a piano, for example, there is a so called 'loud' and 'soft' pedal. The words are misleading, because the 'loud' pedal (for the right foot) does not increase the volume but merely sustains the notes played when it is held down. The 'soft' pedal does 'dampen' or decrease the sound, however. (See **piano/forte**.) 'Loud' clothes are garish ones, but sober-coloured clothing is not 'soft' but 'quiet'.

love/hate
Two basic and potentially powerful emotions, that of great liking or affection on the one hand and great dislike or loathing on the other. The 'polarity' of the pair has long been recognized at a popular level, and the words, in their most basic usage, have featured in tattooed form on the four fingers of the left and right hand. (This is wittier than it might at first appear: 'love' on the one hand, and 'hate' on the other!) Needless to say, the contrast between the two can be found in many sayings and quotations, one of the oldest deriving from the Greek of Aristotle to mean: 'Love as in time to come you should hate, and hate as you should in time to come, love'. In much more recent times, and in English, the expression 'love to hate' has become popular, even when used comically or trivially (as typically by a TV compère in an introduction, for instance: 'Here he is, folks, the one you love to hate . . .'). This itself refers to the alternating 'loving' and 'hating' that can exist in any close relationship (is there anything worse than to be 'hated' by the one you 'love'?),

and also alludes to the psychologist's 'love-hate complex', originally used to describe ambivalent feelings of one and the other emotion towards someone. (In Freudian psychology, this was bound up with the contrasting pair **pleasure/pain**.) The whole phenomenon was summed up in Catullus's *Odi et amo*, ('I hate and I love') (For another of his contrasts, see **hail/farewell**.)

low see **high**

lower see (1) **higher** (2) **raise**

Lowlands see **Highlands**

Loyalists see **Republicans**

LP/EP
Common abbreviations for two types of gramophone record (disc). 'LP' means 'long-playing', and usually refers to a record that is 12 inches (30cm) or 10 inches (25cm) in diameter and that rotates at 33⅓ revolutions a minute. An 'EP' is an 'extended play' record, usually 7 inches (18cm) in diameter and played at a speed of either 45 or 33⅓ revolutions a minute. When they first appeared in the 1950s, 'LPs' were contrasted with the so-called '78s' (from the speed of revolutions per minute), whose running time was, even when 12 inches in diameter, usually less than five minutes. The new 'LPs' thus had a running time, thanks to their micro-grooves, of around 20 minutes. The 'EPs', in their turn, are also known as '45s' and are contrasted with the popular short-playing 'singles', which have, or originally used to have, a running speed of only 45 rpm. But things change fast, so see **record/cassette**.

Ltd/plc
The two abbreviations are commonly found after the name of a firm or company, such as 'Joe Bloggs Ltd', or 'The Ocean Exporting Company plc'. Somewhat confusingly, the first word appears in the full form of the second abbreviation, since 'Ltd' means 'Limited' and 'plc' (or 'PLC') means 'public limited company'. So what's the difference? Companies that are 'Ltd', which are greatly in the majority, are those that are technically 'private', while those that are 'plc', as the title indicates, are technically 'public'. The chief distinction between the two is that only 'plc' companies can offer their shares for sale to the public, whereas 'Ltd' companies (by definition, all those that are not 'plc') cannot. 'Plc' companies are thus normally much larger than most 'Ltd' ones. The 'limited' in each case means that the shareholder's responsibility for any debts that his company may incur is legally restricted or 'limited' to the nominal value of his shares. (In the case of a 'Ltd' company, the shareholder will be a member of the company.) The division into the two types of company was brought about by the Companies Act of 1983. Before this date, most 'plc' companies were 'Ltd' ones.

lunar see **solar**

lunch/dinner
The distinction between the two meals works on a number of levels. As a main midday meal, 'lunch' is the name used by most professional or business people (so-called upper or middle class), while 'dinner' is used for the meal by working or artisan people ('lower class'). However, 'dinner' is also the word for the meal when it is eaten by young 'upper-class' children and by the pets of such people, such as dogs and cats. In another way, where these same 'professional' people have 'lunch' as their midday meal, they may well have 'dinner' as the evening meal, especially when the latter is their main meal of the day (so that the 'lunch' will be a light one). 'Working-class' people, on the other hand, having 'dinner' as their main meal (at or near midday), will have a late afternoon or evening meal that is either 'tea' or 'supper'. So the difference is one of social class, eating habits, age, and timing, among others. 'Lunch' is an odd word. It is short for 'luncheon' and may be related to 'lump'. However, other authorities say that 'luncheon' is an alteration of 'nuncheon', an old word of similar

meaning (although basically meaning 'noon drink'). Browning mentions both in the well-known lines from *The Pied Piper of Hamelin*:

So munch on, crunch on, take your
  nuncheon,
Breakfast, supper, dinner, luncheon.

Mm

machismo/marianismo
'Machismo' is the cult of virility and the he-man. 'Marianismo' is the cult of femininity, especially as practised by some feminists who hold that women are semi-divine, and are spiritually and morally superior to men. The contrast between the two particularly applies to the **man/woman** duality experienced in Latin America, where the terms originated quite recently. 'Machismo' derives from Mexican Spanish, ultimately from Spanish *macho*, 'male', while 'marianismo' refers to the Virgin Mary, who in Roman Catholic eyes was the perfect mother, and divine progenitor of Christ through the perfect birth (the 'Immaculate Conception').

mackerel sky/mare's tail sky
A 'mackerel sky', so named from its small, white, fleecy clouds resembling the markings on the back of a mackerel, is one that usually denotes the end of a period of unsettled weather, so is therefore a good sign. A 'mare's tail sky' (or simply 'mare's tails'), so named from the appearance of its long, thin, wispy clouds suggesting the tail of a horse, is normally one that indicates approaching bad weather, so is an unwelcome sign. Technically (i.e. meteorologically), the clouds in a 'mackerel sky' are altocumulus or cirrocumulus, while the 'mare's tails' are cirrus. See also **cumulus/stratus**.

macrocosm see **microcosm**

macron see **breve**

Madam see **Sir**

madame see **monsieur**

made-to-measure see **off-the-peg**

Mahayana/Theravada
The names are those of the two basic types of Buddhism. 'Mahayana' (literally 'great vehicle') is the more outgoing and 'loving' of the two, teaching belief in a single God and preaching the need for social awareness. 'Theravada' ('doctrine of the elders') is the more rigorous and 'purer' type of Buddhism, stressing the importance of the intellect and involving strict self-discipline. Its particular characteristic is its doctrine of nirvana, otherwise the ultimate state of bliss achieved by the select few. 'Theravada' is also known as 'Hinayana', which more accurately contrasts with 'Mahayana' because it means 'little vehicle'. However, Hinayan Buddhists themselves usually prefer the title as here (and westerners adopting Buddhism usually prefer 'Mahayana').

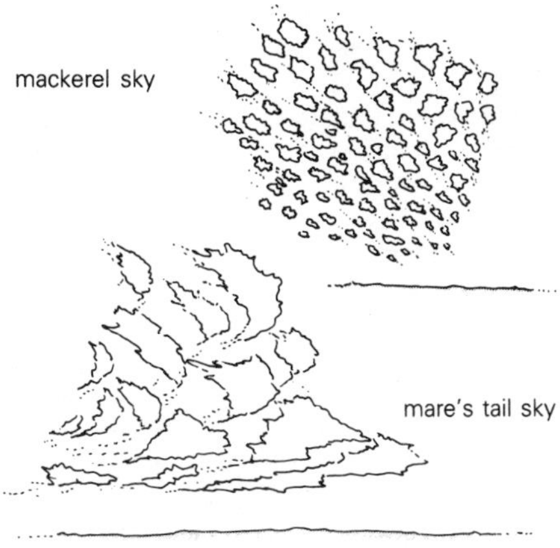

mains see **battery**

maintained school/independent school
The difference is basically the same as that of the pair **state/private**, as relating to

types of school. A 'maintained school' is thus a state one that is 'maintained' or funded by a local education authority, while an 'independent school' is one that raises its funds from the fees charged to the students' parents, so that it is 'independent' of state finance. Most (but not all) public schools are 'independent schools'. For more on the subject see **public/private**.

major/minor
As well as their general senses of 'more important', 'greater' and 'less important', 'lesser', the two words have several reasonably specialized uses. In music, a 'major' key is one based on a 'major' scale, which is one that has semitones between the third and fourth and the seventh and eighth steps. Thus, the 'major' scale of C on the piano ascends or descends only on the white notes, giving the pattern: tone, tone, semitone, tone, tone, tone, semitone, with the semitones occurring between E and F and between B and C. A 'minor' scale, used for a 'minor' key, has semitones between the second and third, fifth and sixth, and seventh and eighth steps if a so-called 'harmonic' scale, or between the second and third and seventh and eighth ascending (second and third and fifth and sixth descending) if a so-called 'melodic' scale. (See **harmony/melody**.) 'Major' keys give the music a positive or joyful sense, while 'minor' keys make the music sound introspective and even mournful. In the Roman Catholic and Orthodox Churches, a 'major' order is one of the holy orders of bishops, priests or deacons, while a 'minor' order has a clerical rank lower than this. In the game of bridge, a 'major' suit is one of hearts or spades, having a higher scoring value, while a 'minor' suit is one of clubs or diamonds, having a lower value. In the Old Testament, a 'major' prophet is Ezekiel, Isaiah or Jeremiah (or the book named after him), so that a 'minor' prophet is any book (or its author) from Hosea to Malachi. In logic, a 'major' premiss is a statement of what is affirmed or denied (as a 'predicate') with regard to the subject of a syllogism (which states that if all As are as B, and C is an A, then C must be B). So if Fido is a dog, and we assume the 'major' premiss that all dogs are descended from wolves, then Fido is descended from a wolf. A 'minor' premiss, on the other hand, is the statement that contains the subject of the conclusion drawn, so that if we assume the 'major' premiss that all dogs are descended from wolves, and accept the 'minor' premiss that Fido is a dog, then Fido must be descended from a wolf. In law, a 'major' is someone who has attained his majority (in Britain, the age of 18, when he has full legal rights and responsibilities), while a 'minor' is someone under this age. See also the next entry below.

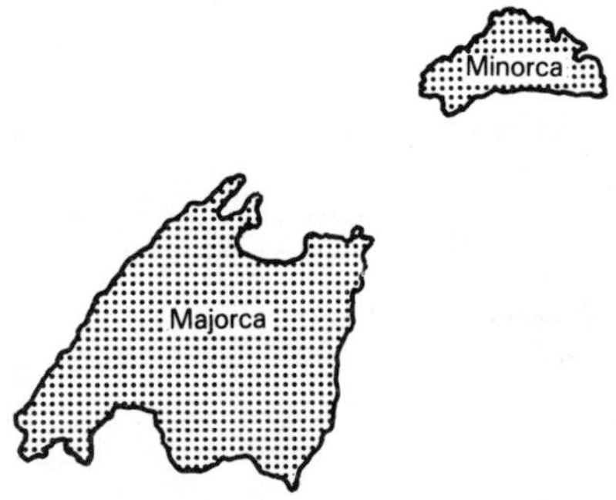

Majorca/Minorca
'Majorca' (called 'Mallorca' in Spanish) is the largest of the three Balearic Islands, off the east coast of Spain, while 'Minorca' (Spanish 'Menorca') is the second largest. (The third largest is Ibiza.) The names of the two mean respectively 'greater' and 'lesser' (or 'major' and 'minor'), and so correspond to similar names for large and small islands elsewhere, such as Scotland's Great Cumbrae and Little Cumbrae, or indeed any places or objects such as towns and rivers that are named respectively 'Great' and 'Little', in whatever language.

majuscule/minuscule
A 'majuscule' letter, in handwriting, is a capital one, while a 'minuscule' letter is a small one. Some scripts use only 'majuscule' letters, in particular the so-called 'uncial' style of writing, with largish

rounded letters, found in Latin and Greek manuscripts from the fourth to the eighth centuries. The terms themselves derive from Latin, and mean respectively 'rather large' and 'rather small'. 'Minuscule' has also acquired a general sense of 'very small', as in 'They only gave us minuscule portions at the hotel'. See also **capital letter/small letter**.

make/break
'Make or break'. The rhyming expression is quite widely used to denote something that will specifically either succeed or fail, especially when it is something crucial: 'It was make or break whether we would win the election or not'. However, 'make' and 'break' have two technical opposites when referring to electricity or electronics, since to 'make' a circuit is to close it, allowing the current to flow, and to 'break' it is to open or interrupt it, preventing the current from flowing.

male/female
The biggest division – and bond – between the sexes, that has intrigued man (and woman) for centuries, ever since the Garden of Eden and Adam and Eve ('Male and female created he them', Genesis 1:27). The biological differences between the sexes are familiar (one hopes) to all. What is interesting is the actual usage of the words as applied to men and women over the years. In the nineteenth century, 'woman' came to have undesirable sexual overtones (as it still has in stock expressions like 'Wine, Women and Song'), so began to have 'female' substituted for it. But this word also acquired a demeaning connotation (the *Oxford English Dictionary*, published in the late nineteenth century, says it is 'now commonly avoided by good writers, exc. with contemptuous implication') and was in turn replaced by 'lady'. 'Male', on the other hand, has never taken on a derogatory connotation. Not surprisingly, many feminists have strong feelings on the subject, as no doubt they have on the technical uses of 'male' and 'female' as applied to screws, plugs and the like. A 'male' plug has a projecting element that fits into its 'female' counterpart, so that a 'female' plug is one with a hollow part that can receive such an element. There is no etymological connection between the words 'male' and 'female', despite their similarity. 'Male' derives (through French) from Latin *masculus*, 'masculine', while 'female' comes ultimately from Latin *femina*, 'woman'. The spelling of English 'female' was thus influenced by that of 'male'. See also **masculine/feminine** and the next entry below.

malevolent see **benevolent**

malignant see **benign**

malison see **benison**

man/woman
Most people are aware of the feminist objection to the use of 'man' to mean not simply 'male person' but 'person' (of either sex) or, more widely still, 'human race' (as in 'the descent of man'). Hence such devices as the use of 'person' to conceal the actual sex (for example 'chairperson', 'spokesperson' and so on), or the respelling of 'women' in a way such as 'wimmin', in order to blur the 'men' element of the word. Both are unplanned developments in the language, as can happen, and in actual fact the main sense of 'man' in Old English was 'human being', with the adult man denoted by the word 'wer' and the adult female by 'wif' (compare Latin *vir*, 'man' and modern English 'wife'). Later, 'man' also came to be used of the adult male, while 'wif' added 'man' (in the 'human being' sense) to produce today's 'woman', with the vowel 'i' changed to 'o'. And although 'wimmin' is a modern creation, it is actually quite close to one of the many earlier spellings of the word down to the fourteenth century or even later. (These include, for the plural, 'wifmen', 'wimmen' and 'wymmen', admittedly all with 'men'.) Because of the two senses of 'man', compounds ending '-man' (such as 'chairman') are much more common than ones with '-woman'. The simple fact, too, that most such designations apply to posts

or roles adopted by males will also mean fewer '-women' compounds. Something like true equality exists for the following, however, where the 'woman' is just as fully recognized as the 'man': policeman/policewoman, serviceman/servicewoman, airman/airwoman, horseman/horsewoman, salesman/saleswoman, businessman/businesswoman, sportsman/sportswoman, yachtsman/yachtswoman, countryman/countrywoman, madman/madwoman. For the following, a '-man' equivalent is rare or freakish: 'needlewoman', 'washerwoman', 'charwoman' (all depressingly domestic, as feminists will notice immediately). See also Appendix II (p. 291).

management see **workers**

Mandarin/Cantonese
Both are languages of China. 'Mandarin' has been the official language since 1917, and is spoken by about two-thirds of the population, as well as being taught in schools throughout the country. 'Cantonese' is spoken in the port of Canton, Kwangtung and Kwangsi provinces, Hong Kong, and outside China, and takes its name from the first of these. In recent years, 'Mandarin' has come to be known as 'Northern Chinese', since 'Cantonese' is spoken chiefly in the south. The languages are technically dialects, and are written in the same ideograms (symbols) while being spoken differently. This means that when a 'Cantonese' audience watches a film in 'Mandarin', they need subtitles (which are printed vertically, on either side of the screen). All 'Mandarins' watching the film would find the subtitles superfluous, however! 'Mandarin' gets its name from the mandarins, the court and official of the Chinese Empire, who spoke it. See also **Pinyin/Wade-Giles** with regard to the spelling of Chinese place-names.

Man of Kent/Kentishman
A 'Man of Kent' is one born east of the river Medway in this county, while a 'Kentishman' is born west of the Medway. The 'Men of Kent' are said to have welcomed William the Conqueror in 1066 with green branches, and as a result had their ancient rights and territory confirmed by him. However, there appears to be little rivalry between the two, at least today, and a joint 'Association of Men of Kent & Kentish Men' still exists 'to foster a sense of pride in the County of Kent' among its 5000 members. (It was founded in 1897.)

manque/passe
In roulette, 'manque' is the name of the section of the cloth with the low scores, from 0 to 18, while 'passe' is for the higher numbers, from 19 to 36. The French words mean literally 'fail' and 'pass', so that 'manque' implies that the ball fails to reach a number over 18. See also **odd/even**, **red/black**, and even **pass/fail**.

mantissa see **characteristic**

manual/automatic
The broad distinction is between something that needs to be operated by hand, and something that is 'self-programmed' and works without the need for constant human control or adjustment. A car, for example, can have 'manual' gears, changed by hand, or 'automatic' ones, changing as the speed and engine power require. Many cameras, too, now have 'automatic' focussing and aperture control, as distinct from 'manual'.

many/few
Quotations spring to mind immediately. 'Many are called, but few are chosen' (Matthew 22:14); 'Ye are many – they are few' (Shelley, *The Mask of Anarchy*); 'So much owed by so many to so few' (Churchill, speech in House of Commons, 20 August 1940); 'All communities divide themselves into the few and the many' (Alexander Hamilton, American statesman, 1787). And these quotations are only a 'few' of the 'many' contrasting the two words. (Nor should we overlook the proverb, 'Few words and many deeds'.) In each case, the 'few' is singled out for its good or bad qualities, since the word can imply either 'the elect' on the

one hand, or 'the powerful bosses' on the other. Most of us therefore finish up somewhere in the 'many', who are neither the elect nor the repressors.

marchioness see **marquis**

mare see **stallion**

mare clausum see **mare liberum**

mare liberum/mare clausum
The Latin expressions mean literally 'free sea' and 'closed sea', respectively, and belong to maritime law. 'Mare liberum' denotes a sea that is open to the shipping of all nations, while 'mare clausum' is a sea that falls under the jurisdiction of one nation only, so is closed to all others. The Yellow Sea was formerly famous as a 'mare clausum'. The terms themselves were actually titles of books. *Mare clausum* was the title of a Latin work written in 1635 by the English jurist John Selden in answer to the *Mare liberum* of the Dutch jurist Hugo Grotius, written in 1609. The titles used the expressions that arose in the seventeenth century to refer to the struggle for supremacy at sea between England and the Netherlands. (See **auction/Dutch auction** for more on this aspect.)

mare's tail sky see **mackerel sky**

margarine see **butter**

marianismo see **machismo**

marquis/marchioness
A 'marquis' is a nobleman who ranks above a count (outside Britain) or above an earl but below a duke (in Britain), while a 'marchioness' is either the wife or widow of a 'marquis' or a woman who holds the equivalent rank in her own right. The feminine equivalent of 'marquis' is not thus 'marquess', which is simply an alternative form for 'marquis', as preferred by most noblemen of this rank in Britain. (However, many Scottish 'marquesses' prefer the form 'marquis', which is the French spelling, and is thus commemorative to them of the 'Auld Alliance' between France and Scotland.) The spelling of 'marchioness' is actually closer to the origin Medieval Latin word *marchio*, genitive *marchionis*, 'marquis' (literally 'captain of the marches', i.e. of the boundaries).

married/single
This is the usual pair of opposites to denote a person who either has a spouse or has not. The opposite of 'married' is not therefore normally 'unmarried', which somehow suggests a deliberately selected state (whereas 'single' tends to imply a temporary state before possible marriage). Inevitably, there are a number of quotations that combine the two. One of the most original is perhaps that of Richard Crashaw, the seventeenth-century poet, who in his poem *On Marriage* wrote:

> I would be married, but I'd have no wife,
> I would be married to a single life.

Mars/Venus
'Mars' was of course the 'he-man' god of war in classical mythology, while 'Venus' was the beautiful goddess of love. Their astronomical symbols (since they are planets) have been adopted for use in biology to denote male or female organisms, plants, cells or the like, with '♂' standing for 'Mars' and '♀' for 'Venus'. The symbols themselves are said by some to represent the attributes of the god and goddess, with the 'Mars' symbol showing a simplified thunderbolt, and the 'Venus' one a mirror (in which the goddess admired her beauty). However, it is hard to deny an apparent sexual reference in both, whether in modern 'explicit' terms or not. (Biologists denote a hermaphrodite by '⚥'.) For a sensitive (and sensuous) artistic rendering of the mythological pair, see Botticelli's painting *Mars and Venus* in the National Gallery, London.

Martha/Mary
These are the names of the two sisters of Lazarus in the Bible, with 'Martha' coming to represent, in the Christian life,

a person who is active and assiduous, and 'Mary' one who is more contemplative and intellectual. The precise reference is to Luke 10:38–42, where the two sisters are entertaining Jesus. 'Mary' is keen on obtaining spiritual advice from him, whereas 'Martha' bustles about getting him a proper meal. When 'Martha' complains to Jesus that her sister has left her to do all the work, she is quietly rebuked by him, and reminded that 'Mary' has chosen an aspect of daily life which she herself had overlooked, even though she was 'careful and troubled about many things'. The two names have been used in their symbolic sense in various modern works of fiction, such as Elizabeth Goudge's *Towers in the Mist* (1938): 'She belonged to that noble army of Marthas who cook the dinners that the Marys gobble up to keep them going between their visions and their dreams'. Significantly, the name 'Martha' actually meant 'mistress of the house' in the original Aramaic.

Mary see **Martha**

masculine/feminine
Although basically meaning 'male' and 'female', these two words are on the whole linked mostly with the 'technical' side of one sex or the other, either in a narrow sense, as when used for grammatical gender, or in a more general sense to indicate something characteristically male or female, respectively. In the latter usage, they are thus closely linked with the corresponding nouns 'masculinity' (the quality of being male) and 'femininity' (the quality of being female). However, this does not mean that 'masculine' need always apply to males, or 'feminine' to females, so that a woman can have a deep 'masculine' voice, for example, or a man can make a 'feminine' gesture of the hand. When it comes to grammatical gender, the words frequently (but by no means exclusively!) denote animate beings that are normally male or female, as the case may be. The difficulty begins with inanimate objects, as any student of French soon discovers (the word for 'window', for example, is 'feminine', but 'floor' is 'masculine'). In some languages, there is a third gender to be reckoned with. This is 'neuter', whose name really means 'neither masculine nor feminine'. In verse, a 'masculine' rhyme is a single monosyllabic one at the end of a line (such as 'born' and 'morn'), while a 'feminine' rhyme is one of two syllables or more (such as 'daughter' and 'bought her'). Compare **male/female**.

masochist see **sadist**

mass noun see **count noun**

Master[1]/Miss
The words were long used as the standard polite titles or forms of address for a boy and a girl, respectively (e.g. 'Master John Brown' and 'Miss Kate Smith'). Today, although still occasionally found, they are increasingly rare. However, 'Miss' still lives in various contexts, from 'Miss World' as the supreme beauty contest winner (on criteria that are perhaps suspect) to the more down-to-earth 'Miss Patricia Goldring' whose engagement in announced in the up-market press. Neither of these are in contrast to 'Master', however, which is usually employed during boyhood, whereas 'Miss' can be used up to and into adulthood, and indeed until marriage or even for the rest of life, if no marriage occurs. However, 'Master' also exists as an adult title for certain Scots noblemen or their relatives, in particular for the heir to a peerage. Thus the son of Lady Sempill is known as the 'Master' of Sempill, and the son of Lord Belhaven and Stenton (a double designation) is known as the 'Master' of Belhaven. In R. L. Stevenson's novel *The Master of Ballantrae*, the main character is the elder son of Lord Durrisdeer and Ballantrae (whose family name is Durie).

master[2]/mistress
These are the corresponding terms for a male and a female 'boss' of some kind, with both words still frequently found in official titles, such as 'Master of the Rolls' as the presiding judge of the Court of

Appeal, and 'Mistress of the Robes' as a lady with special duties in the royal household. Despite these 'lofty' senses, 'mistress' has gained a much more lowly status as the word for a woman with whom a man has a sexual relationship outside marriage. The sense here altered over the centuries from 'woman who is courted by a man' to 'woman who is seduced by a man'. Both words are still used, however, as the designations of a male and female schoolteacher, especially in independent (private) schools. This is simply a special usage of the 'boss' concept. Etymologically, 'mistress' is simply the feminine form of 'master', i.e. it evolved as a form of what could have become 'masteress'. For more about the school 'mistress', see **Sir/Miss**.

master[3]/servant
Here is the 'boss' again (see entry above) and the one he bosses, otherwise the one who commands and the one who obeys. The contrast between the two has long been a popular one in literature and folklore, from Goldoni's play (from the Italian) *A Servant of Two Masters* to the many proverbs such as 'Servants make the worst masters' and 'One must be a servant before one can be a master'. The two are also paired when contrasting something with extreme characteristics, for example, 'Fire is a good servant but a bad master' (i.e. it can aid in many ways but can also kill). Despite the medieval ring of 'master and servant', the words are also used today in quite technical senses to denote a mechanism that controls a device and the device that is so controlled. (For more on this see **slave/master**.)

master see **slave**

match play/stroke play
The terms here relate to golf, or more precisely to methods of scoring in golf. 'Match play' is scoring according to the number of holes won (and lost), while 'stroke play', as its name indicates, is scoring according to the total number of strokes made. Originally, amateur championships were at 'match play' and open championships and most professional events at 'stroke play', although some amateur events have now switched to 'stroke play'. (The latter in fact requires a greater degree of consistency in a player, since one lapse into a high figure at a hole can cost him his victory, whereas in 'match play' he loses only that one hole.)

material/spiritual
'Great men are they who see that spiritual is stronger than any material force, that thoughts rule the world' (Emerson, *Letters and Social Aims*, 1876). This is the great dichotomy here, the duality of mind ('spiritual') and matter ('material'), or even invisible and visible, or intangible and tangible. The terms basically have a philosophical reference, therefore. And is a person's inner will stronger than his physical strength? There are certainly some instances where the 'spiritual' can triumph over the 'material', as such religions as Christianity hold, for example. But here we are becoming metaphysical, and the reader would do best either to ponder the contrast further unaided, or more prosaically to see such entries as **visible/invisible**, **death/resurrection**, **spiritual/temporal**, **mind/matter**, **body/soul**.

materialism/idealism
In philosophy (as in the entry above), 'materialism' is the doctrine that matter is the only reality, and that mind, the emotions, the soul and the like are simply functions of it. On the other hand, 'idealism' holds that thought or the mind is the only reality, and that external objects consist merely of ideas. For more in the same contemplative way, see the entries listed at the end of the entry above.

matins/evensong
These are the alternative names of the two Church of England services known rather more formally as 'morning prayer' and 'evening prayer' in the Prayer Book. 'Matins' is also the first of the seven so-called 'canonical hours' (prayer services) observed daily in the Roman Catholic Church. Its name (also spelt 'mattins')

obviously links up with French *matin*, 'morning' and relates to the time of day when it is held. 'Evensong', on the other hand, really corresponds to what the Roman Catholic Church calls 'vespers', with this also a 'canonical hour'. (The name clearly refers to an 'evening song' and is an old one, dating back to at least the eleventh century.) Both words were employed by romantic poets to denote birdsong at dawn or in the evening, so that today they each have a rather sentimental ring to them, as well as a religious one.

matriarch see **patriarch**

matt see **glossy**

matter see **mind**

maxi/mini
The two words, originating as shortenings of 'maximum' and 'miniature' (with 'mini' also influenced by 'minimum'), became popular from the 1960s to indicate objects that were respectively long or small versions of the standard, especially vehicles and clothes. For vehicles, it was 'mini' that predominated, and the word was adopted as the proprietary name ('Mini') for the small car of 1959 made by British Motors. For clothing, the items to be designated one or the other *par excellence* were the 'maxi'-coat, which reached almost to the ground, and the 'mini'-skirt, which went up several startling inches above the knee. (There was also a 'maxi'-skirt, but understandably it caused less of a sensation, since it was essentially nothing new.) 'Mini' in particular became widely used to designate a whole range of other things and occurrences, among them (but by no means exhaustively) being 'mini' bikes, bottles, budgets, cameras, computers, elections, guns, holidays, marathons (!), pigs, pills, recessions, shifts (the garment), skis, submarines, tankers, vans and even wars. But apart from the 'Mini' car, the 'minicab' also took to the streets as a new type of small handy taxi, as did the 'minibus', as a scaled-down bus seating only a few passengers. (This last word, however, already existed in the nineteenth century to refer to a small kind of horse-drawn omnibus.) Both 'maxi' and 'mini' were joined by a third party, the 'midi' (from 'mid-' or 'middle'), so that a 'midi'-skirt, for example, was one that was longer than a 'mini' but shorter than a 'maxi'. (After the 'Mini' car, British Leyland produced the Austin 'Maxi' in 1969.) For more 'maxis' and 'minis', see the next entries below.

maximalist/minimalist
A 'maximalist' is a person who favours direct 'all-out' action to achieve his aims, while a 'minimalist' advocates minimal action, for whatever reason. Spelt with a capital letter, 'Maximalist' and 'Minimalist' were sometimes used in English in the 1920s to translate the Russian 'Bolshevik' and 'Menshevik', although somewhat confusingly 'Maximalist' was also used earlier to translate the Russian equivalent word (*maksimalist*) used for a member of the near anarchic faction of the Socialist-Revolutionary party in the 1900s. See also **Bolsheviks/Mensheviks**.

maximin/minimax
In mathematics, a 'maximin' is the highest or largest of a set of minimum values, while a 'minimax' is the lowest or smallest of a set of maximum values. The terms are obviously based on combinations of the first elements of 'maximum' and 'minimum'.

maximize/minimize
To 'maximize' something is to make the most of it, to increase it as much as possible, as when a factory 'maximizes' its output. To 'minimize', therefore, is the opposite, to reduce something or 'play it down' as much as possible, as when one 'minimizes' a risk by taking particular precautions.

maximum/minimum
This pair of opposites is the basis of the four pairs above, since 'maximum' means the greatest possible of something, and 'minimum' the least possible. As can be expected, the terms have wide use in

precise sciences such as mathematics and astronomy. At a more homely level, one may have a 'maximum-minimum' thermometer in one's garden or greenhouse. This records the highest and lowest temperatures over a given period. From the 1960s, the 'maximum' security prison became well known as an establishment specially designed to prevent prisoners from escaping, i.e. having 'maximized' security (see the entry above). The words themselves are pure Latin meaning 'greatest' and 'least'.

May Week/Eights Week
The names are those of the respective highspots of the rowing year at Cambridge and Oxford, in the summer, when the end of the year is celebrated with inter-college boatraces and lavish dances ('college balls'). At Cambridge, 'May Week' is now a double misnomer, since it is actually a fortnight in June. The boatraces themselves are usually known simply as the 'Mays' and the 'Eights', and the latter, at Oxford, are traditionally watched by many while indulging in extravagant tea parties on decorated boathouses along the course. ('Eights', of course, refers to the teams of eight oarsmen or women in each boat.) See also **Oxford/Cambridge**.

me see **you**

mean time see **true time**

medical/surgical
As applied to the treating or healing of a disease or illness, 'medical' is used of medicine or drugs that the patient must take, while 'surgical' relates to the actual operation on the body, or part of it, in order to effect a cure. The ordinary family doctor or 'G.P.' uses 'medical' methods of treatment, while any 'surgical' aid will have to be carried out by a surgeon in hospital (usually). See the relevant **physician/surgeon**.

medusa see **polyp**

melody see **harmony**

men/de
The Greeks had a word for it, or in this case two words, traditionally used to express a contrasting statement and meaning respectively 'on the one hand' and 'on the other'. Here they are in a quotation from Socrates: *Alla gar ēde hōra apiēnai, emoi men apothanoumenō, hymin de biōsomēnois* ('But already it is time to depart, for me on the one hand to die, for you on the other to go on living'). There is also a 'de' (but no 'men') in the shorter quote on p. ix.

mensheviks see **bolsheviks**

merit system/spoils system
The contrasting terms relate to appointments and promotions in the civil service in the United States. In a 'merit system', these are based on ability or general competence. In a 'spoils system', on the other hand, public offices and their resulting financial awards are regarded as 'spoils' or prizes to be awarded to the members of the victorious party in a political election. The two terms thus imply correctness on the one hand, and corruption on the other.

metachronism see **prochronism**

metaphor see **simile**

metric/imperial
The two terms are those of conflicting systems of weights and measures, with 'metric' being the basic decimal system and 'imperial' relating to several different standards long established in Britain (where both 'metric' and 'imperial' now jointly reign in supreme confusion). Thus 'metric' will relate to the metre, gram, kilometre and 'metric' tonne, while 'imperial' includes the inch, mile, ounce, pound, gallon and ton. The dual existence of both systems thus means that in many instances both appropriate weights or measures will have to be given, even in such a simple domestic procedure as making a dish in the kitchen ('Take 2lbs/900g apples, 4oz/100g chopped raisins', etc.), with each page of the cookbook

sternly worded 'Use only one set of measurements! Do not mix metric and imperial!' Similar chaos still reigns in Britain when it comes to expressing a temperature – see **Fahrenheit/Celsius**. 'Imperial' weights and measures date from the Weights and Measures Act of 1824 which established a gallon as '10 imperial pounds weight of distilled water' in an effort to sort out the muddle. The so-called avoirdupois system of weights, with its pound of 16 ounces and ton of 112 pounds, is an 'imperial' one. See also **kilometre/mile**.

mho see **ohm**

microcosm/macrocosm
'Micro-' means 'small', and 'macro-' means 'big' (see p. 286), so a 'microcosm' is a miniature version of something, and a 'macrocosm' a large complex structure, such as the universe, especially when it is seen as complete in itself. The former word is the more common, if only since most of us 'see small' rather than 'think big'. Because the second half of each word relates to 'cosmic' (Greek *kosmos* means 'world'), a 'microcosm' is therefore often used of a 'mini-world', such as the English public school was often said to be. (Many have disagreed with this, however: 'We were told that "School is the world in miniature" and as far as my experience goes it isn't', E. M. Forster, 'Letter from the College', in *The Fleur-de-Lys* [magazine of King's College School, Cambridge], December 1961.) In the ancient world, 'microcosm' was a philosophical term designating man as being a 'little world' in which the 'macrocosm', or universe, was reflected. The concept has been taken up subsequently by several philosophers and thinkers, from Paracelsus in Renaissance times to Rudolf Lotze and his *Mikrokosmus* of 1864.

midday/midnight
The two opposing times of 12.00 noon and 12.00 at night, with neither really being in the middle of the day or middle of the night, as their names imply, unless one reckons 'day' as 6.00 a.m. to 6.00 p.m. and 'night' as 6.00 p.m. to 6.00 a.m. In literary or fictional use, 'midday' suggests a bright and burning sun, as in the French 'Midi', or South of France, while 'midnight' conjures up mystery, romance and general murkiness. *The* great magical 'midnight' of the year is of course that of 31 December, when the New Year is seen in. And what happened to Cinderella when she hurried home at 'midnight'?

Middle Ages/Dark Ages
In European history, the 'Middle Ages' are, broadly, the thousand years from the fifth century A.D. to the fifteenth, or more narrowly, from about A.D. 1000 to about A.D. 1500. On the other hand, the so called 'Dark Ages' (named thus since they were considered to be unenlightened or 'barbaric') extended from the late fifth century A.D. to about A.D. 1000. The former period may or may not, therefore, include the latter.

Middle East/Far East
Roughly, the 'Middle East' includes those countries that are located to the east of the Mediterranean, especially Israel and the many neighbouring Arab states, such as those of North Africa and, to the east, Iran. The 'Far East' comprises the countries of eastern Asia or the 'Orient', especially China, Japan and North and South Korea. There used to be a 'Near East', which was really the same as present 'Middle East', although the name could also apply to the former Balkan States and Ottoman Empire. 'Far East', too, has sometimes been used loosely as a name for all countries east of Afghanistan, including India. However, although 'Near East' is a more obvious opposite to 'Far East' than 'Middle East', the last name does reflect fairly accurately the location of the region that borders the Mediterranean (whose own name means 'Middle Land').

midnight see **midday**

MI5/MI6
'MI5' is the popular name (formerly official) for the counter-intelligence agency of the British Government, while 'MI6'

(with name of similar status) is the intelligence and espionage agency. The abbreviation actually stood for 'Military Intelligence', with '5' and '6' the numbers of the particular departments. Today, the official titles are instead 'Security Service' and 'Secret Intelligence Service' (SIS), with the former approximating to the United States FBI and the latter to the CIA.

migrant/resident
In zoological terms, a 'migrant' is an animal that moves from one habitat to another, as migrating birds do annually, while a 'resident' is one that does not migrate, but 'stays put'. In Britain, swallows are 'migrant', while thrushes, for example, are 'resident'. (As a rough guide, animals and birds seen only in the summer months are likely to be 'migrant', while ones seen throughout the winter as well are probably 'resident'.) See also the related **emigrant/immigrant**.

milady see **milord**

mile see **kilometre**

military see **civilian**

milk chocolate/plain chocolate
'Milk chocolate', as its name indicates, is chocolate that has been made with milk, so that it is lighter in colour than 'plain chocolate' and has generally a creamier and sweeter taste. 'Plain chocolate' is therefore made without milk, as a consequence of which it is darker in colour and has a slightly bitter taste. Some people regard 'plain chocolate' as more 'refined' (socially, if not in taste) than 'milk chocolate', just as black coffee is sometimes thought of as 'superior' to white. (See also **tea/coffee**, **black/white**.)

milord/milady
The two words were formerly used as continental titles for, respectively, an English gentleman and an English gentlewoman, that is, not necessarily a 'lord' and a 'lady' in the strict sense as a member of the nobility. The terms, which fairly obviously derive from 'my lord' and 'my lady', also suggest 'grand' Englishmen and women travelling abroad, or even somewhat mocking designations for a 'stuck-up' person ('What does milord want now?', 'Is this enough for milady?'). 'Milord' became a French word in its own right (*un milord très riche*) and even came to be used as the name of a type of horse-drawn vehicle (known in English, grandly enough, as a 'victoria').

mind/matter
In Cartesian philosophy, 'mind' and 'matter' were viewed as the two basic modes of existence, with 'mind' the term for the human spirit and intellect, and 'matter' the human body and the material world. In its popular conception, the conflict or contrast is usually seen as a battle between the two, especially of 'mind over matter', where a physical barrier or opposition can perhaps be overcome by the force of the mind, i.e. of willpower. See also **heart/mind**.

mind see **heart**

mini see **maxi**

minimalist see **maximalist**

minimax see **maximin**

minimize see **maximize**

minimum see **maximum**

minor see **major**

Minorca see **Majorca**

minuend see **subtrahend**

minus see **plus**

minuscule see **majuscule**

misandry see **misogyny**

MI6 see **MI5**

misogyny/misandry
The opposing terms can be used to mean 'hatred of women' and 'hatred of men', respectively, with the roots in Greek *misein*, 'to hate' (in both words), *gynē*, 'woman' and *anēr*, genitive *andros*, 'man'. The former word is generally better known than the latter, since there appear to be more women-hating men than men-hating women (except for certain militant feminists). 'Misogyny' should not be confused with 'misogamy', which means 'hatred of marriage', and 'misandry' should not be confused with 'misanthropy', which means 'hatred of mankind' (i.e. of one's fellow men and women).

miss see **hit**

Miss see (1) **Master**[1] (2) **Sir**[2]

mistress see **master**[2]

mixed/straight
These terms belong to the realm of alcoholic drinks. A 'mixed' drink is one containing two or more ingredients, such as a cocktail or a 'punch'. A 'straight' drink is one containing a single ingredient, such as a neat whisky or gin. The 'mixing' does not necessarily involve the addition of alcoholic elements, and a gin and lime can be referred to as a 'mixed' drink, as can a whisky and soda. 'Straight', however, does usually imply that the drink is undiluted.

mixed see **single-sex**

mobile/stabile
We are here dealing with art forms. A 'mobile' is a type of delicate and usually abstract sculpture that is suspended in such a way that its parts revolve or move in the currents of air. A 'stabile' is exactly the same, except that its parts do not move, but are stationary. The pioneer of the 'mobile' is generally regarded as the American sculptor Alexander Calder, and 'stabiles', too, were largely developed by him.

modern see (1) **ancient** (2) **old face**

mods/rockers
The 'mods' and the 'rockers' became famous (or infamous) in the 1960s in Britain as rival groups of teenage gangs. There was a distinction, however. The 'mods' dressed stylishly (in a 'mod' or modern or even modish manner), had short hair, and rode motor scooters. The 'rockers', on the other hand, wore leather jackets (often studded), had long hair, and rode motorcycles. To some extent, 'mods' survive even today, especially where teenage groups congregate at seaside resorts on bank holidays in Britain looking for an 'opposition', and press reports noted a clash between 'mods' and 'rockers' at Southend even as recently as 1982. However, 'rockers', named for the rock 'n' roll or (later) rock music that they favoured, have now mostly passed into history, and 'mods' and 'rockers' have generally been superseded by Hell's Angels and skinheads, respectively, the latter substituting a closely shaven head for the long hair of the 'rockers'.

monarchy/republic
The countries of the world are mostly divided up into those that have royal heads of state, and those that do not. The former are thus the 'monarchies', and the latter mostly the 'republics'. Today, 'monarchies', in whatever country, are easily outnumbered by the many 'republics'. They include the following (as at 1987): Bahrain (emirate), Belgium (kingdom), Bhutan (kingdom), Brunei (sultanate), Denmark (kingdom), Japan (empire), Jordan (kingdom), Kuweit (emirate), Lesotho (kingdom), Liechtenstein (principality), Luxembourg (grand duchy), Morocco (kingdom), Nepal (kingdom), Netherlands (kingdom), Norway (kingdom), Oman (sultanate), Saudi Arabia (kingdom), Spain (kingdom), Swaziland (kingdom), Sweden (kingdom), Thailand (kingdom), Tonga (kingdom), United Arab Emirates, United Kingdom. Most countries in the Commonwealth are also at least nominally 'monarchies', since they recognize the British sovereign as their head.

monastery/nunnery
At their most basic, a 'monastery' is a religious establishment for monks, and a 'nunnery' one for nuns. Formerly, 'monastery', like 'convent', could be used for a religious house of either monks or nuns. Today, however, 'monastery' is used exclusively of monks, and 'convent' almost always of nuns.

monism see **dualism**

monk¹/friar
Although the terms can sometimes be used interchangeably, depending on the context, the broad difference between a 'monk' and a 'friar' is that the former leads his life mostly within the walls of a monastery (see entry above), where he practises poverty, chastity and obedience, while the latter combines monastic life with a preaching (formerly also mendicant or begging) existence outside the monastery, so being in touch with the real world. Most 'friars' are members of the Roman Catholic Church, and belong to a specific order, among the best known being the Black Friars (or Dominicans), Grey Friars (Franciscans), White Friars (Carmelites) and Austin Friars (Augustinians). The word 'monk' is related directly to 'monastery', and 'friar' derives ultimately from Latin *frater*, 'brother'. See also the next entry below.

monk²/nun
A 'nun' is the female equivalent of a 'monk' or a 'friar' (or a combination of both, since there is not the same division for female members of religious orders or communities). She thus lives in a nunnery where she practises poverty, chastity and obedience, but often combines this with nursing or teaching work. The word 'nun' derives from Late Latin *nonna*, a form of address to an elderly woman. See also the two entries above.

mono/stereo
The two terms are short for 'monophonic' and 'stereophonic', and relate to sound systems (as of radios or record players) that have respectively one speaker or two speakers or channels, the latter giving a spatial or 'real' effect, as experienced when listening to an orchestra, for example. 'Mono' means 'one', 'single', of course, but in place of the expected 'bi-' one has Greek 'stereo', meaning literally 'solid' (although 'stereophonic' may well have been influenced by 'stereoscopic', since it refers to sound that has been recorded stereophonically and that is then played back to the listener through headphones ('binaural' means literally 'two ears')). An enhanced form of 'stereo' exists in 'quadraphonic', i.e. 'four-channel' sound, where the listener is located at a point in the middle of a 'square' with a speaker at each corner, two in front of him and two behind. Some cars are fitted with speakers to give 'solid sound' by means of such a system.

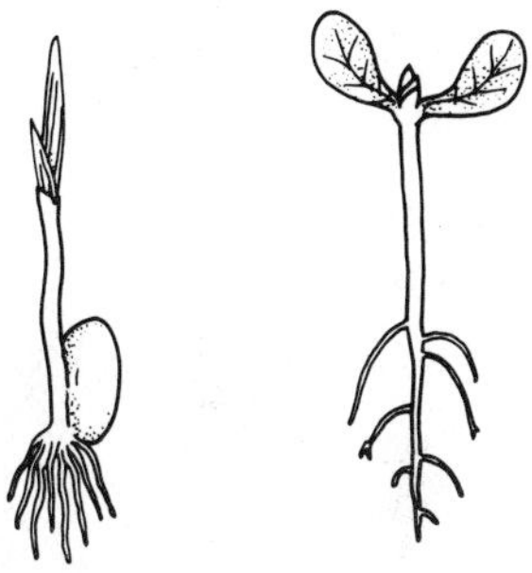

monocotyledon dicotyledon

monocotyledon/dicotyledon
These are the terms for the two principal subdivisions of angiosperms or flowering plants. The 'monocotyledons' or 'monocots' are those flowering plants that have a single embryonic seed leaf, leaves with parallel veins, and flowers arranged in three parts. They include grasses, lilies, palms and orchids. This means that the 'dicotyledons' ('dicots') are virtually all the rest, and in the majority, since they form two seed leaves when the plant begins to grow. They include most flowering trees and shrubs, have varied leaves, often rounded, and flowers mostly

arranged in four or five parts (petals). The words are Greek-based, with 'mono-' and 'di-' meaning 'one' and 'two' and 'cotyledon' (a word in its own right) meaning literally 'cup-shaped', 'hollow'. See also **angiosperm/gymnosperm**.

monolithic/hybrid
In electronics, a 'monolithic' integrated circuit is one that has all its components formed from or produced in or on a single crystal, such as a 'monolithic' silicon chip. By contrast, a 'hybrid' integrated circuit consists of one or more other integrated circuits and other components that are attached to a ceramic base. 'Monolithic', from the Greek, literally means 'single stone', with the implication here that a 'monolithic' integrated circuit is a single powerful unit.

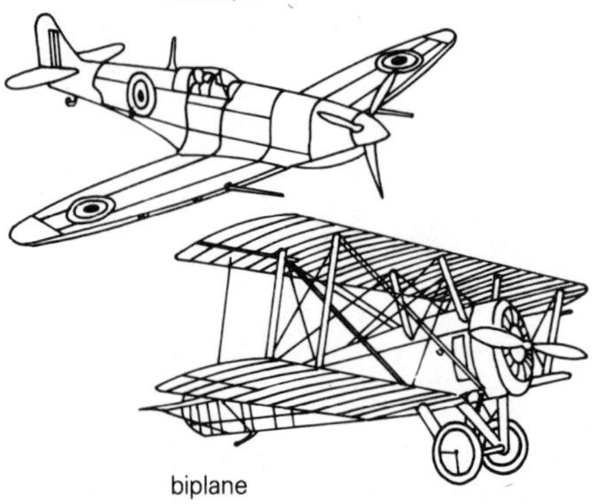

monoplane/biplane
A 'monoplane' is an aeroplane with two wings, as most of them have. A 'biplane', more common in the earlier days of flying, is an aircraft with double pairs of wings. There were even 'triplanes' with three pairs of wings, and rare and wonderful 'quadriplanes' (although the word is hard to find in dictionaries). 'Biplanes' were common in the First World War since they were easier to brace than the 'monoplane' or triplane. One of the best known 'biplanes', at least in Britain, is the Tiger Moth.

monopoly/monopsony
Two quite useful terms in economics. A 'monopoly' arises when a firm or company has the sole market for its goods or services, such as the Post Office in Britain before 1981. And whereas a 'monopoly' is thus a 'single seller', a 'monopsony' is a 'single buyer', otherwise a market that is dominated by one sole purchaser. 'Monopsonies' are in the nature of things much rarer than 'monopolies', but one classic example exists in the Central Selling Organization, which despite its name is the diamond buying department of De Beers. Since the 1930s it has bought up almost 80 percent of the value of world diamond production, then selling the diamonds as a 'monopoly'. The words literally mean what they say in Greek, respectively 'single seller' and 'single buyer'.

monopsony see **monopoly**

monosemy/polysemy
These terms relate to the meanings of words, so are relevant here! 'Monosemy' means 'single meaning', and is used of a word that has just one meaning, and so cannot be ambiguous. An example might be 'Sellotape', which can only mean 'brand of adhesive tape'. 'Monosemy' is rarer than one might think, and 'polysemy' or 'multiple meaning' is much more common, since most words have more than one meaning. For example, 'ruler' can mean both 'person who rules' and 'device of wood or plastic for measuring'. 'Monosemy' is mostly found in technical and scientific terms, such as 'monosemy' itself (and also 'polysemy'). The second half of each word derives from Greek *sema*, 'sign' (as in 'semantics', the study of meaning in language).

monsieur/madame
The French equivalent to English 'Sir' and 'Madam' or 'Mr' and 'Mrs'. The words are sometimes used in English in the third person by way of affectation or mockery, as in 'How would monsieur wish to pay for the meal?' and 'Would madame care to try this hat?' This usage imitates the

French. The words themselves break down into the French equivalents for 'My Lord' and 'My Lady' (*mon sire* and *ma dame*).

Montagnards see **Girondins**

Montagues/Capulets
The two feuding families in Shakespeare's *Romeo and Juliet*, with the 'Montagues' the family to which Romeo belonged, and the 'Capulets' the family of Juliet. (Romeo and Juliet themselves were of course 'a pair of star-cross'd lovers'.) The names themselves are the Frenchified versions of Italian Montecchi and Cappelletti, both native to Verona:

> Two households, both alike in dignity,
> In fair Verona, where we lay our scene,
> From ancient grudge break to new mutiny,
> Where civil blood makes civil hands unclean.

moon see **sun**

morning[1]/afternoon
As commonly regarded, the first part of the day and the second, before and after the midday meal. It would be neater, of course, if 'morning' were called 'forenoon', to match 'afternoon'. This alternative is no longer in popular use, however, although can still be found in some legal contexts and is still current in the navy, where the day is divided into 'watches' rather than precise hours.

morning[2]/evening
The first and the last part of the day, popularly equated with sunrise and sunset, or getting up and going to bed. The 'evening', however, can be quite a lengthy period following the afternoon (see the entry above), and is usually regarded as that part of the day that comes after tea (or supper). 'Morning' dress, for men, is a formal kind of daytime dress (not necessarily worn in the 'morning'), consisting of a 'morning' coat (a cutaway frock coat), grey trousers and top hat, while 'evening' dress, as also applied to men, comprises a dinner jacket with tails at the back ('tail coat'), white shirt, white waistcoat and white bow tie. (A popular alternative to this is a dinner jacket or tuxedo with a black bow tie.) For women, 'evening' dress has a floor-length gown as its principal garment. On a loftier plane, the 'morning' star is a poetic name for the planet Venus (not a star at all), when seen in the sky just before sunrise. And the 'evening' star is exactly the same celestial body but observed at a different time: Venus seen shining brightly in the west just after sunset. The two names arose because in olden times people believed that these were two separate bodies. The actual word 'morning' was based on 'evening', and was originally just 'morn' (compare German *Morgen*), while formerly 'even' meant 'close of day' and 'evening' meant 'clos*ing* of day' (as a particular time). See also **a.m./p.m.**, **matins/evensong**.

mortal/immortal
Although 'immortal' is clearly the negative form of 'mortal', the two opposing senses are rather more than just 'positive' and 'negative'. After all, 'mortal' means 'subject to death', but 'immortal' means 'living for ever'! To be 'immortal' has been man's dream and desire from times immemorial, and the word has been used, if only semi-seriously, to apply to various groups of 'great' men, notably the forty members of the French Academy. (The name may have arisen from the fact that a crown of laurel with the words 'A l'immortalité' was engraved on the seal that was originally used for countersigning the Academy's documents.) In Greek mythology, the 'immortal' gods were the ones who lived on Mount Olympus, such as Zeus, Apollo, Athena, Aphrodite, Artemis, Hermes and Demeter. Lesser gods were 'mortal', like men and women. See also the next entry.

mortal sin/venial sin
Theologically speaking, a 'mortal sin' is one that involves a complete loss of divine grace, as it is one that is deliberately committed and serious in nature, i.e. it is one of the 'Seven Deadly Sins' (pride,

covetousness, lust, envy, gluttony, anger and sloth). The sin is so called since it entails spiritual death. By contrast, a 'venial sin' is one that is comparatively slight, and that involves only a partial loss of divine grace. It is usually regarded as a sin that is committed, too, without full reflection on the consequences, or without the full consent of the perpetrator. 'Venial' really means 'pardonable', from Latin *venia*, 'favour', 'indulgence'. Both types of sin are so categorized in the teaching of the Roman Catholic Church.

mortar see **pestle**

mortgagee/mortgagor
A 'mortgagee' is the person or organization (such as a building society) that makes a loan to a person who needs a mortgage in order to purchase his house. The 'mortgagor' is thus the person who takes out a mortgage, and who receives the loan. The difference depends on the endings (see the suffixes '**-er**' and '**-ee**' in Appendix I, p. 289).

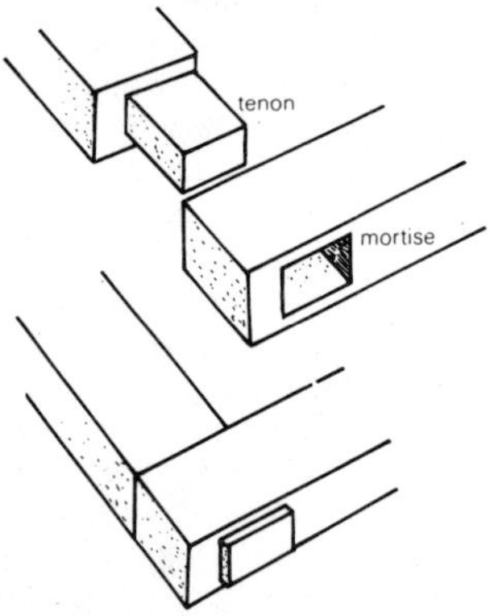

mortise/tenon
A 'mortise' (also sometimes spelt 'mortice') is a slot or recess cut in a piece of wood (less often, stone) in such a way that it can receive a projecting piece, the 'tenon'. The aim of the two devices is to fasten or 'lock' timbers or joists together at right angles. (A similar method is used for a 'rabbet', which is a recess or groove cut into a surface or along the edge of a piece of timber to hold a mating piece, such as a panel.) The word 'mortise' ultimately derives from Arabic *murtazz*, 'fixed in', while 'tenon' is directly related to French *tenir*, 'to hold'.

moth see **butterfly**

mother/father
The 'equal and opposite' pair of parents whose union has produced an offspring, with 'mother' the female and 'father' the male. Both words are used as titles of respect in many contexts, such as the political 'Mother of Parliaments' and 'Father of the House', and a person's native land can be regarded as a 'motherland' or 'fatherland'. (The French traditionally have a 'motherland', *La Patrie*, while the Germans have a 'fatherland', *Das Vaterland*.) Two British festivals, both imported from the United States, are 'Mother's Day' and 'Father's Day', the former now coinciding with (and confused with) Mothering Sunday, the fourth Sunday in Lent, the latter falling on the third Sunday in June. (In the United States, where they originated, 'Mother's Day' is on the second Sunday in May, but 'Father's Day' is the same as now in Britain.) See also **patriarch/matriarch**.

mule/hinny
A 'mule' is the (usually sterile) offspring of a mating between a female horse and a male donkey, while a 'hinny' is a similar hybrid offspring of a male horse and a female donkey. 'Mule' is also used as the term for a sterile offspring of other breeds, such as a 'tigon' (see **liger/tigon**). 'Hinny' is not derived from 'whinny', but simply comes from Latin *hinnus*, just as 'mule' comes from *mulus*.

mullion see **transom**

multiply/divide
The two mathematical processes are related to each other much as 'add' and 'subtract' are, with 'multiply' producing a larger figure (usually) and 'divide' a smaller. 'Multiplication' is thus the method that calculates the product of two or more numbers, and is usually denoted by the sign '×' or by a dot between the figures or amounts ('a.b.') or, especially in

algebra and geometry, by writing the two symbols together ('ab'). Thus 16 × 34 = 544 (said either 'sixteen multiplied by thirty-four . . .' or 'sixteen times thirty-four'). 'Division' is thus the inverse of this, and the method by which the so-called quotient of two numbers is calculated, usually with the smaller number (the 'divisor') 'going into' the larger one (the 'dividend') so many times. The traditional sign for this is '÷', the dot below the line representing the divisor, and the one above the dividend. Thus 544 ÷ 34 = 16 (said 'five hundred and forty-four divided by thirty-four is sixteen' or more colloquially 'thirty-four into five hundred and forty-four goes sixteen times'). 'Long division' (but not 'long multiplication') was a former favourite arithmetical exercise for schoolchildren in which all the calculations are written out systematically, thus, 'dividing' 12 into 64959:

```
     5413
   ______
12 |64959
    60
    --
     49
     48
     --
      15
      12
      --
       39
       36
       --
        3
```

Ans. 64959 ÷ 12 = 5413, remainder 3.

mushroom/toadstool
'Mushrooms are edible, toadstools are not'. That sums up the popular differentiation between the two types of fungi, and broadly speaking it is true, since botanically speaking there is no difference between 'mushrooms' and 'toadstools' as they are both members of the same species of fleshy fungal fruiting structures. However, some people would classify some edible fungi as a 'toadstool' rather than a 'mushroom', which can be misleading. One example is the chanterelle (*Cantherellus cibarius*), which is not only edible but pleasantly tasty. Perhaps it would have been best if English had only one word for both kinds, as happens on other languages: French *champignon*, for example, can mean 'mushroom' or 'toadstool', as can Russian *grib*. 'Mushroom' looks like a word with an interesting origin, but its precise source is unknown. The 'toadstool' is so called since it was fancifully regarded as a 'stool' on which (poisonous) toads sat. The name dates back to at least the fourteenth century.

music see **words**

Mutt/Jeff
'Mutt' and 'Jeff' arose as the names of two characters, the first tall, the second short, in a popular cartoon series by the American cartoonist H. C. Fisher (1884–1954). Subsequently, 'Mutt' came to be the 'dumb' one, who was always kicked around, while 'Jeff' did all the work. Alternatively, although on similar lines, 'Mutt' was the 'hard' man, and 'Jeff' the soft, and the phrase 'Mutt and Jeff' came to be adopted for the alternating 'cruelty and kindness' treatment used to break down prisoners under interrogation. ('Mutt and Jeff' in a more exclusively British context also came to be rhyming slang for 'deaf'. Also in Britain, 'Mutt' and 'Jeff' were nicknames for the War and Victory medals awarded to many servicemen who served in the First World War. If you had the 1914–15 Star as well, however, the three metamorphosed into the names of three different cartoon characters, Pip, Squeak and Wilfred.) 'Mutt' got his name as an abbreviation for 'mutton-head', i.e. a stupid or awkward person, while 'Jeff' appears to have been named after Jefferson Davis, American President of the Confederate States in the 1860s. Compare **hard/soft**, **tall/short**.

myopic/hypermetropic
The scientific (more precisely, ophthalmological) terms mean simply 'short-sighted' and 'long-sighted' respectively, and in the original Greek would have meant 'blink-eyed' and 'over-measuring-eyed'. 'Hypermetropic' can also be 'hyperopic'. The corresponding nouns are 'myopia' and 'hypermetropia' (or 'hyperopia'). See also **short-sighted/long-sighted**.

Nn

nadir see **zenith**

name/number
It is difficult to think of any person who cannot be identified by a 'number' as well as his or her 'name'. Any serviceman or woman is all too aware of this, and today most civilian citizens are. Among the 'numbers' that can identify a person, at least in Britain, are: one's National Health Service 'number', National Insurance 'number', Income Tax Assessment 'number', bank account 'number', telephone 'number', credit card account 'number', passport 'number', gas, electricity or water board account 'number', and many others, including one's vehicle registration 'number' and driving licence 'number'. At least some of these, perhaps all, will be held somewhere by computer, so that we are all 'numbered'. If 'name' means 'unique designation of a person', then in a sense many of our 'numbers' have the status of a 'name'. Some people have even applied to change their traditional 'name' to a 'number', although the courts do not normally look favourably on such a procedure. In any case, what would be the 'pet' or familiar version of, say, 'D/MX 919207'? One is reminded of the possible solution offered by Noël Coward, who wrote a letter to Lawrence of Arabia when the latter had joined the air force, and began it: 'Dear 338171, or may I call you 338 . . .?'.

nanny goat see **billy goat**

narrow see **broad**

narrow gauge see **broad gauge**

nasty see **nice**

national bank/state bank
In the United States, a 'national bank' is a commercial bank that is incorporated under a Federal charter and that is obliged to be a member of the Federal Reserve System. On the other hand, a 'state bank' is incorporated under a State charter and is not obliged to be a member of the Federal Reserve System. (The latter organization is the central banking authority which acts as a fiscal agent for the government and that issues the country's paper currency.) In practice, both types of bank offer the same service and are governed by the same general regulations. There are more 'state banks' than 'national' banks, however, since the latter cannot operate nationwide but may be confined to a single state or even branch. (A 'national bank', too, will often have the word 'National' or 'First National' in its title.)

Nationalist China see **Communist China**

nationalists/unionists
The words in this pair are in effect a political alternative to those of the pair **Republicans/Loyalists**. They refer to the same division or main faction in Northern Ireland, with the 'nationalists' campaigning for Northern Ireland to be politically integrated with the Republic of Ireland, and the 'unionists' standing for the union of Northern Ireland with Britain. On signing the now contentious Anglo-Irish agreement of November 1985, allowing the Republic to contribute to government policy in Northern Ireland for the first time since 1922, the Prime Minister, Mrs Margaret Thatcher, described herself as 'a Unionist and a Loyalist'. Belfast is itself split into the two political groupings: the Shankill Road

district is militantly 'unionist', while the Falls Road is 'nationalist'. See also the relevant **Catholic/Protestant**.

nationalization/privatization
These jargonistic terms are fairly often found in the press and in government publications to refer respectively to the transferring of a private company or business to state control and the restoration to private ownership of a state-controlled enterprise. A virtual synonym for 'privatization' is thus 'denationalization'. The basic verbs that describe such transference of ownership to the state and back are 'nationalize' and 'privatize'. In the 1980s, the Conservative government under Margaret Thatcher in Britain embarked on a plan to 'privatize' many former state-owned organizations and companies.

native/foreign
The terms are properly used to describe someone who was born in a place or country, and someone who was born elsewhere, so is an 'outsider' in some way. Both words can be regarded as offensive, however, with 'native' implying 'uncultured person' and 'foreigner' suggesting 'unwanted intruder who does not speak the language', at least in insular British use. Yet 'native' derives from Latin *nativus*, 'born', so is really the correct word for a person who was born in a place.

NATO/Warsaw Pact
These are the two military blocs of west and east, with 'NATO' regarded as American-oriented, and 'Warsaw Pact' as Soviet-oriented. 'NATO' (North Atlantic Treaty Organization) includes not only the United States and Canada, but Belgium, Denmark, France, Greece, Iceland, Italy, Luxembourg, Netherlands, Norway, Portugal, Spain, Turkey, United Kingdom and West Germany. Most of these joined in 1949, when the Treaty was originally signed, with Greece and Turkey joining in 1952, West Germany in 1955, and Spain in 1982. The total makes fifteen member states. The 'Warsaw Pact' was signed in 1955, and is now an alliance of seven countries: Bulgaria, Czechoslovakia, East Germany, Hungary, Poland, Romania and the USSR. (Albania formerly belonged, but opted out in 1968.) Inevitably, the 'Warsaw Pact', which is virtually synonymous with Comecon, sees 'NATO' as a highly aggressive association and itself as a necessary grouping formed in self-defence, while acting as a union to promote its member-countries' 'friendship, cooperation and mutual aid' (*Soviet Encyclopaedic Dictionary*, 1980). There is a noticeable disparity in size and geographical disposition, with 'NATO', as its name implies, straddling the Atlantic, and containing twice as many countries as the East European 'Warsaw Pact'. When it comes to military might, however, the disparity is less marked, and there is a more equal 'balance of power' and strike/defence potential.

natural virtues/theological virtues
From war to peace (compare the previous entry). The 'natural virtues', in scholastically theological terms, are those of which mankind is capable without the special help of God, in particular justice, temperance, prudence and fortitude. The 'theological virtues' are thus those that are infused in mankind by a special grace of God, specifically the familiar faith, hope and charity. The 'natural virtues' are also known as the 'cardinal virtues'. The 'theological' virtues were those selected by St Paul as the basis required for a Christian life.

nay see **yea**

neap tide see **spring tide**

near[1]/far
'Near' means 'close', whereas 'far' means 'distant', with both words functioning as either adjectives or adverbs ('near escape', 'nowhere near ready'; 'far side', 'far into the sky'). 'So near yet so far' is a common phrase to denote something desirable yet still unattainable, a thing almost obtained, but not quite.

near[2]/off
'Near' means 'left' when used of the legs

of a horse or the wheels of a vehicle, so that in Britain the 'nearside' of a car is the one nearest the edge of the road. The 'off' is thus the 'right' side. Compare the cricketer's **leg/off**.

needlepoint see **pillow lace**

negative see (1) **affirmative** (2) **positive**

neither/nor
The words denote two objects or expressions which were not involved or affected by the verb or allusion in question. For example, 'It is neither hot nor cold' means that it must be lukewarm or of even temperature, and 'He is neither fat nor thin' means that he is of average build. When a person says 'That's neither here nor there', he means it is irrelevant. In older literary texts, 'nor' is sometimes found without a preceding 'neither', especially when repeated more than once, as in the tenth of the Ten Commandments, which states that a man shall not covet his neighbour's wife 'nor his servant, nor his maid, nor his ox, nor his ass, nor any thing that is his'. Compare **either/or**.

neologism see **archaism**

nephew/niece
The words for a person's brother's or sister's son or daughter, respectively, so that the person is the uncle or aunt. 'Nephews' and 'nieces', as relatives, are often used as surrogate sons and daughters by unmarried or widowed uncles and aunts, probably to the benefit of both. There are similar words for the two in many European languages, such as French *neveu* and *nièce*, German *Neffe* and *Nichte* and Italian *nipote* (for both), all ultimately, like the English words themselves, deriving from Latin *nepos*, genitive *nepotis* ('nephew') and *neptis* (originally 'granddaughter'). See also **uncle/aunt** for further comments.

net see **gross**

nether see **upper**[3]

neurosis see **psychosis**

new see **old**

next see **last**

NHS see **private**

nice/nasty
Otherwise 'pleasant' and 'unpleasant'. The homely words, with their 'attraction of opposites', have been frequently associated because of their similar sounds. Many quotations and phrases combine them, such as Swift's 'A nice man is a man of nasty ideas', and Isaac Goldberg's definition of diplomacy as doing and saying 'the nastiest thing in the nicest way'. See also the epigraph to this book (page vi).

niece see **nephew**

night/day
Two of the most fundamental of opposites, each in turn associated with a member of another well-known pair, such as (for 'night') 'moon', 'dark' and 'sleep', which have as respective opposites 'sun', 'light' and 'wake' (associated with 'day'). There are many popular sayings combining the two, from the Bible (Genesis, and the Psalms) to Shakespeare to Browning (whose *Pippa Passes* has the vivid line: 'O'er night's brim, day boils at last'). There are proverbs, too, such as 'The day has eyes, the night has ears' and 'It's never a bad day that has a good night' (both these have double contrasting pairs), and familiar expressions such as 'night and day' (all the time, continually) and (thanks to the Beatles) 'a hard day's night' (now usually taken to mean 'a well-earned night after a hard day's work', although the original sense was sexually oriented). Although English 'day' is related to German '*Tag*' it is surprisingly not linked with Latin '*dies*'. On the other hand, the words for 'night' in many languages are similar and linguistically linked, such as Greek *nyx*, Latin *nox*, French *nuit*, German *Nacht*, Russian *noch'*, Welsh *nos*, and so on. Compare **diurnal/nocturnal**.

no see (1) **aye** (2) **yes**

noble/ignoble
Apart from the obvious opposites, with 'ignoble' the negative form of 'noble', the two words have a special contrast in falconry. 'Noble' is used of a long-winged falcon that captures its quarry by swooping down on it from above. 'Ignoble' is used of a short-winged falcon that captures its quarry by speed and adroitness of flight. The terms date from at least the time of Shakespeare, but are not recorded in any of his works.

nocturnal see **diurnal**

nominal wages/real wages
'Nominal wages' are wages measured in actual money, whereas 'real wages' are measured in their purchasing power. Because of inflation, it is therefore misleading to quote 'nominal wages' when comparing two dates (e.g. to say that a person was earning 'only' £10 a week in 1956 but £100 a week in 1986), and 'real wages' are a more accurate guide to the two when making a comparison since they do not take inflation into account.

non-fiction see **fiction**

non-smoker see **smoker**

non-U see **U**

nor see **neither**

north/south
Apart from the 'up there' and 'down there' geographical concept, and the associated pair **Arctic/Antarctic**, the 'north/south' split can have a deeper significance. In Britain, for example, there is a real social divide between north and south, with neither really understanding the other. Thus northerners are popularly said to be blunt, generous, sociable and shrewd, while many say that southerners are 'smooth', introvert, complex and relatively unsociable, or at least 'private'. The southerner thus thinks of the northerner as crude and lacking subtlety (with his motto of 'Where there's muck, there's brass [i.e. money]'), while the northerner regards the southerner as devious and inscrutable. Apart from this, the 'south' of England has (to oversimplify) the jobs, the wealth, the sophistication (including London) and the warmer weather, while the 'north' of England has the unemployment, the relative poverty, the 'raw edges' (and the many dialects) and the colder, wetter weather. Other countries have their own versions of the north/south split, with national differences. France, for example, has its culture in the 'north', where Paris is, but its rich life and warm weather in the 'south', where the Riviera is. In Italy, again, the 'north' is well known for its prosperity, and the 'south' for its alleged backwardness (although the region of Apulia is said to be the exception here). In England, the expression 'north of Watford' is used to designate the supposed culturally barren part of the country that lies beyond the sophistication of London. 'North' and 'South', too, occur as elements in many geographical names. (Perversely enough, in London itself, the prosperous sector, where most people live and where the important buildings are, is 'north' of the river Thames, while the area 'south' of the river is often regarded as not part of 'London proper' at all, and has less prestige and fewer amenities, even fewer underground railway lines.)

northing see **easting**

not content see **content**

not guilty see **guilty**

nothingness see **being**

noughts/crosses
The two words, or rather symbols 'O' and 'X'), are familiar from the children's paper-and-pencil game also known as 'tic-tac-toe'. In a sense, the symbols themselves are opposites, since although they are both quite symmetrical, the 'nought' is the embodiment, if that's the word, of 'roundness', and the 'cross' of angularity. The symbols are additionally used to

represent respectively a hug and a kiss (see **hug/kiss**). In the nineteenth century, the game of 'noughts' and 'crosses' was sometimes known as 'oughts and crosses', probably since 'a nought' was taken to be 'an ought'.

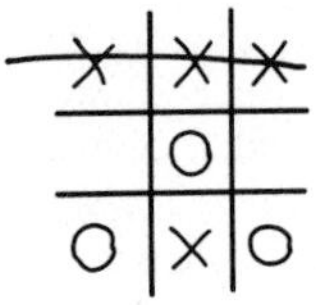

novel/short story
By definition, the 'short story' is (usually) short, and the 'novel' mostly fairly long. Between the two there is also a 'novella', designated as either a long 'short story' or a short 'novel'. (Literary experts sometimes express the different lengths in figures: a 'novel', they say, is 30,000 words long or more, a 'novella' is from 10,000 to 20,000 words in length, and a 'short story' is from 500 to 5000 words long. Moreover, a 'novel' is usually a complete book, while a 'short story' is often published in a newspaper or magazine, as well as being found in a collection published in book form.) In many languages, the word for 'novel' relates to 'romance', such as French *roman*, German *Roman*, Italian *romanzo*, Russian *roman* and so on. (The reference is not so much to 'romance' in the modern sense, despite the popular romantic 'novel', but to a tale originally told in the spoken language of the Romans, rather than in formal Latin.) Similarly, many languages do not emphasize the 'short' aspect of a 'short story', and the French word for it is simply *conte*, like the Italian *racconto*. The English word 'novel' also goes back ultimately to Latin roots, as it represents *novella narratio*, 'new story', meaning a tale that has never been told before.

number see **name**

numerate see **literate**[2]

numerator/denominator
In a mathematical fraction, the 'numerator' is the figure that is above the line, while the 'denominator' is the one below the line and that indicates how many parts the 'numerator' is divided into. For example, in the fraction $3/8$, the 'numerator' is 3 and the 'denominator' is 8. The terms are also respectively known as 'dividend' and 'divisor' (see **multiply/divide**).

nun see **monk**[2]

nunnery see **monastery**

nut/bolt
A 'nut' is a smallish piece of metal, usually square or hexagonal, that has a hole in the centre with an internal screw thread and that is thus screwed on to a corresponding rod, with a matching external thread, to fasten something between them. This latter rod is therefore the 'bolt', and since the two devices are frequently used to assemble a framework or basic structure of some kind, the phrase 'nuts and bolts' has arisen to mean 'essentials', 'practical workings', as in 'Once you've mastered the nuts and bolts of word processing, you'll find the job much easier'. For more about the screw, see **male/female**.

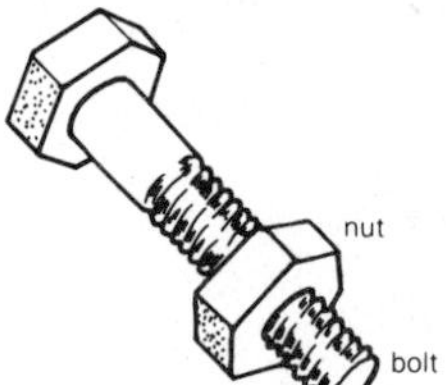

nyctolopia see **hemeralopia**

nymphomania/satyriasis
The medical or psychiatric terms denote, respectively, excessive sexual desire in a female or a male. The terms are classically based, although in Greek mythology it was usually the satyrs who chased the nymphs rather than the other way round. The second half of each word means respectively 'madness' and 'disease'.

Nynorsk see **Bokmål**

Oo

object see **subject**

objective see **subjective**

oblate see **prolate**

obligate see **facultative**

obovate see **ovate**

obreption/subreption
In church law, 'obreption' is the illegal obtaining of a special dispensation or gift by means of giving false information. 'Subreption' is the similar gaining of a gift, but by concealing the facts. The two are thus special examples of fairly common instances of duplicity, otherwise getting what you want by twisting the facts (e.g. claiming you are 18 when you're not) or by carefully omitting facts that would bar you (e.g. neglecting to point out that you are under 18). 'Obreption' derives from Latin *obrepere*, 'to creep up to', 'steal up', so is related to 'reptile'. 'Subreption' has the same basic verb, *repere*, 'to creep', with 'sub-' in the sense of 'secretly', 'underhand', as in 'suborn', which means 'obtain by underhand means'.

obtuse see **acute**[3]

obverse reverse

obverse/reverse
These opposites are best known to numismatists, since they are the respective terms for the 'heads' and 'tails' side of a coin. 'Obverse' means literally 'turned towards', and 'reverse' means 'turned back'. The 'obverse' is thus the side of the coin that normally has the main design or device, often the head of the ruler reigning when the coin was issued. On certain older coins, however, it is difficult to say which is the 'obverse' and which the 'reverse'.

occidental see **oriental**

October Revolution see **February Revolution**

odd/even
The 'odd' numbers are the ones that progress in twos from 1 (i.e. 3, 5, 7, etc.), so that the 'even' numbers are the others (2, 4, 6, etc.). In what sense are the first set of numbers 'odd', however? The answer is that such numbers cannot be divided by two, so whenever any such division is made, they represent the 'extra' left over, or the 'odd man out'. (The modern general sense of 'odd' meaning 'peculiar', 'strange', followed later.) An 'even' number is thus one that can be exactly divided by two, so will have no remainder and will be 'level'. Typically, it is English that has the rather obscure words to denote the two types, and many other languages call 'even' and 'odd' by more obvious words, such as French *pair* and *impair*, German *gerade* and *ungerade*, Italian *pari* and *inpari*, Russian *chëtny* and *nechëtny*, and so on. See also **manque/passe**.

Odelsting see **Lagsting**

Oedipus complex/Electra complex
In psychoanalysis, an 'Oedipus complex' is the sexual attraction of a child (usually a boy) towards the parent of the opposite sex (i.e. his mother) while at the same

time excluding the parent of the same sex (his father). An 'Electra complex' is the opposite: a sexual attraction of a girl towards her father, while excluding her mother. The terms derive from classical mythology. Oedipus was the Greek king who unwittingly killed his father (Laius) and married his mother (Jocasta), while Electra incited her brother (Orestes) to kill their mother (Clytemnestra), who had murdered their father (Agamemnon). Without Greek mythology, what would modern psychologists have done to designate these two particular personality disorders? Several languages besides English use the same expressions.

off/on
The two little words, which can be easily misheard if pronounced unclearly or too rapidly, in effect denote an object or state that is either 'negative' (not operative) or 'positive' (operative). When a water tap is 'off', it is thus shut, and no water flows from it; when it is 'on' it is open, and water flows. If a football match is 'off' for some reason, it will not take place; if it is 'on' it will, especially when there has been some doubt about it. Then, in horseracing, the cry 'They're off' means the horses have started to run, so the actual race is 'on'! In cricket, again, the 'off' side of the field is the right one, while the 'on' ('leg') is left. (See **leg/off** in this respect.) However, care is needed here, since in the devious game of cricket, a statement such as 'Bloggs is on now' will probably mean 'It is Bloggs who will bowl now'! 'Off' can also mean 'right' of the wheels of a vehicle or legs of a horse, but here the opposite is not 'on' but 'near' (see **near/off**). The phrase 'on and off' (or 'off and on') means 'intermittently', 'from time to time' ('It rained on and off all day'). However, 'on and on' means 'continuously', 'without stopping', 'We drove on and on, but couldn't find a garage'. See also **offside/onside** (below).

off see (1) **leg** (2) **near**

offer price see **bid price**

Official IRA see **Provisional IRA**

offside/onside
In a sport such as football or hockey, 'offside' is the illegal position of a player ahead of the ball when it is played, usually in the opponents' half of the field. For being in this position, the team will normally have a penalty declared against it. 'Onside' thus means that the position of the player ahead of the ball is legal, and play can continue without a penalty. The literal implication of 'offside' is that of being away from one's side, and of being on the wrong side (of the ball). See also **off/on**.

off-the-peg/made-to-measure
A suit that is 'off-the-peg' (or 'ready-to-wear', or 'ready-made') is one that has already been tailored for a particular size and fit, and that can be satisfactorily worn by the purchaser (or the person for whom it is bought). A suit that is 'made-to-measure' (or 'tailor-made') is just that – one that is made from measurements taken from the actual person who is to wear it. The latter type of suit will naturally be (or should be) a more exact fit than any 'off-the-peg' one, but will also be more expensive, because of the work involved. Today, 'off-the-hanger' would be a more accurate equivalent for 'off-the-peg', although no commercial firm would dream of using either term.

ohm/mho
An 'ohm' is a unit of electrical resistance, named after the German physicist G. S. Ohm (died 1854). Its reciprocal, a unit of electrical conductance, used to be known as a 'mho', this being 'ohm' spelt backwards. Usually, however, it is now known as a 'siemens', named after the German electrical engineer W. von Siemens (died 1892). This new term was introduced by the British physicist, W. T. Kelvin (Baron Kelvin, died 1907), whose own name was adopted in 1968 for the 'kelvin', as a unit of temperature, after the Kelvin scale that he had invented. The use of reversed names of scientific units to denote their

reciprocal in this way occurs elsewhere. For example, the reciprocal of a 'farad', a unit of electrical capacitance, came to be called a 'daraf', with the original name derived from that of the English physicist Michael Faraday (died 1867).

old/new
'Something old, something new, Something borrowed, something blue', runs the old wedding rhyme, and one does not have to look much further to find many contrasting quotations and expressions with 'old' and 'new'. We live in a changing world, so there is always something 'new' to contrast with or supersede what is 'old', even though the thing itself may now be far from 'new'. (This is notably so in place-names: Newcastle has a name dating from the twelfth century, and the 'New' Forest was recorded as *Nova Foresta* in the 'Domesday Book' a century earlier.) Among the fixed expressions are the following. 'New Style' is the present system of reckoning dates according to the Gregorian calendar, while 'Old Style' formerly used the Julian calendar (see **Gregorian calendar/Julian calendar**). The 'New' Testament, in the Bible, is the second, Christian half, originally written in Greek and recording events from the birth of Christ onwards. The 'Old' Testament is the first, Jewish half, originally written in Hebrew. (In both cases, a better word than 'Testament' would be 'Covenant', since this is what was promised by the prophets: 'Behold, the days come, saith the Lord, that I will make a new covenant with the house of Israel, and the house of Judah', (Jeremiah 21:31.) The 'New' World is a name for the Americas (hence Dvořák's 'New World' Symphony, believed to have been based on Negro spirituals), while the 'Old' World is the rest of the world, i.e. those countries that were known before America was discovered. However, the opposite of a 'new' moon is a 'full' moon, not an 'old' one. See also the next entry below and **young/old**.

old see **young**

old face/modern
The names are those of contrasting printing types. 'Old face' is a style that originated in the eighteenth century and that has little contrast between the thick and thin strokes. 'Modern', on the other hand, originating near the beginning of the nineteenth century, has an exaggerated difference between the thick and the thin strokes. See the example, and compare **serif/sans serif**.

old face modern face

omega see **alpha**

on see **off**

one[1]/other
The words are used to designate alternatives: 'Take one or the other', 'Neither one thing nor the other'. As so regarded, 'one' is usually seen as the basic thing, while the 'other' can often be a sort of 'second best'. (This was basically the theme of Simone de Beauvoir's feminist essay *The Second Sex*, where man is seen as regarding himself as 'the one' while regarding woman as 'the other', according to the existentialist argument.) Certainly 'one' is normally the first thing mentioned and specified, with 'other' the second or following, whether identical or not. If you raise 'one' hand and then the 'other', you thus probably raise your right hand first (if you are right-handed), as it is the dominant one, and if you close 'one' eye and then the 'other', you probably close whichever eye is weaker first, so that your 'good' one can still see. The next entry below continues this theme.

one[2]/two
Without numbering any further (since many things are in pairs), 'one' will usually contrast with whatever is desig-

nated 'two' and be more prominent than it, or have some primary sense. In this way, whatever is regarded as 'one' is unique, and the first of its kind, while whatever is 'two' is compared and usually contrasted with it. World War 'One' was originally known as the 'Great War', until World War 'Two' occurred, and in this latter war, the Germans bombarded Britain with the robot bomb called the 'V-1' (the 'doodlebug') before they came to use the 'V-2' rocket. In counting marching steps or other rhythmic movements ('one, two, one, two'), it is the 'one' that leads and is normally stronger. This priority of 'one' is even present when 'two' designates something larger, i.e. has its numerical value, and 'one' hundred has to exist in order to have a higher 'two' hundred. (The latter may have a higher value, but does not have the priority.) See also **first/second**, **primary/secondary**, and the next entry below.

One Thousand Guineas/Two Thousand Guineas
The 'One Thousand Guineas' is a famous annual horserace for fillies, run annually at Newmarket since 1814. The 'Two Thousand Guineas' is a similar race, also run at Newmarket (since 1809), but for both colts and fillies. The races are usually run within a couple of days of each other in spring, the 'One Thousand Guineas' first. It is thus possible for a good horse (so long as it is a filly) to win both races, and this happened, for example, in 1902 when Sceptre won not only these two Classic races but also the Oaks (also for fillies only) and St Leger. The sums of money refer to the original respective prizes for the winners. See also **colt/filly**, as necessary.

onside see **offside**

OP see **prompt**

opaque see **transparent**

open[1]/closed
The two opposites are probably associated first and foremost with the shop door sign, or the sign on some other kind of public premises. However, there are certain combined expressions that also use the contrasting words. An 'open' book is something that is quite free from mystery, that is 'transparent': 'I can read your mind like an open book'. A 'closed' book, on the other hand, is something that is mysterious or obscure: 'Astrology is a closed book to me'. In the world of education, an 'open' scholarship is one for which any student may compete, while a 'closed' scholarship has certain preconditions (e.g. may be applied for by students from a particular area only). In industry, a 'closed' shop is a factory or industrial enterprise in which all workers must belong to a union, while an 'open' shop is an establishment where workers are taken on and employed whether they belong to a particular union or not. Sometimes the opposite of 'open' is 'close', as in an 'open' season and a 'close' season. In the former, it is legal to hunt game or catch fish; in the latter, such hunting and fishing is banned by law. See also the next entry below.

open[2]/shut
What is the difference between this pair of opposites and the one above? On the whole, it is that 'shut' implies permanently or securely 'closed', and 'closed' only temporarily 'shut'. But as this last sentence illustrates, 'closed' and 'shut' are virtual synonyms. Compare, however, a 'closedown' with a 'shutdown'. The former usually implies an opening up again, like the nightly 'closedown' of television broadcasts; the latter suggests a permanent cessation of activity, but can also mean merely a suspension of work, such as a factory's annual 'shutdown' for the summer holiday. 'Shut', too, is more literal: you 'open' your mouth to speak or eat, and 'shut' it afterwards, and you basically 'open' and 'shut' a door. ('Close' the door suggests doing so carefully or deliberately.) An 'open-and-shut' case is one that is easily settled. The reference is to a legal case that is 'opened', easily dealt with, and then 'closed'.

opera buffa/opera seria
In music, an 'opera buffa' (Italian for 'comic opera') is a satirical or farcical opera, as it were 'played for a laugh'. An 'opera seria' (Italian 'serious opera'), by contrast, is what it says, and is typically an eighteenth-century one based on a mythological tale, such as Gluck's *Orpheus and Eurydice.* An example of an 'opera buffa' is Rossini's *Barber of Seville*, and even Mozart's *Don Giovanni* could be regarded in this category.

opera seria see **opera buffa**

Oppidans/Collegers
These young gentlemen belong to Eton College. The 'Oppidans', who are in the majority, do not live in the College but in boarding houses in the town. (Latin *oppidans* means 'townsman', from *oppidum*, 'town'.) The privileged 'Collegers', or 'King's Scholars', on the other hand, live in the College. They are normally 70 in number and are the students who have won scholarships to the school. Compare **commoners/scholars**.

opposition see **conjunction**

Opposition see **Government**

optimist/pessimist
An 'optimist' is a person who hopes for the best and looks on the bright side. A 'pessimist' expects the worst, and regards the outlook as gloomy. The words derive from Latin *optimus*, 'best' and *pessimus*, 'worst'. It was the American novelist James Branch Cabell who wrote, 'The optimist proclaims that we live in the best of all possible worlds; and the pessimist fears this is true'. 'Optimist' first arose in English in the eighteenth century, borrowed from the French, and 'pessimist' followed a hundred years later as a depressing opposite.

optional see **compulsory**

or see (1) **and** (2) **either**

Oracle see **Ceefax**

oral[1]/aural
These alternatives exist in educational terminology, especially with regard to language learning. 'Oral' thus relates to the ability to speak a language correctly, and 'aural' to that of hearing (and understanding) a language. Since the words are so alike, 'aural' is sometimes given a distorted pronunciation as 'owral' (as in 'our rule'), in order to distinguish it from 'oral'.

oral[2]/written
This is a more common education contrast to the one above, and relates to the respective skills needed to speak and write a language correctly. Most language examinations thus have an 'oral' element and a 'written' one, the former usually involving a conversation or discussion with an examiner, and the latter often including a translation. In Britain, relatively little importance is attached to the ability to speak a language, while competence at a 'written' translation usually wins the majority of the marks. But, by definition, language is speech, not writing (Latin *lingua* is 'tongue', not 'pen')! Compare **translator/interpreter**.

ordinal number see **cardinal number**

ordinary/proper
In the Roman Catholic Church, the 'ordinary' is that part of the Mass that does not vary from day to day, i.e. it is 'fixed', and belongs to the regular order of the service. The 'proper', however, varies according to the particular day or feast, and is 'proper' or appropriate for that occasion. The terms are also used by some Anglicans to the corresponding parts of a communion service, with the fixed prayers being the 'ordinary', and the Collect, Epistle and Gospel (among others) being the 'proper'. (See **epistle/gospel**, if necessary.)

ordinary shares/preference shares
'Ordinary shares' are those that entitle their holder to a dividend after all other demands have been met, with such a dividend being variable. 'Preference shares',

however, entitle their holder to a dividend before anything is paid out to the holders of 'ordinary shares', although such dividends are fixed. The American equivalent terms for such shares are respectively 'common stock' and 'preferred stock'.

organic/inorganic
In chemistry, 'organic' and 'inorganic' are the two main divisions. 'Organic' implies 'coming from life', and includes only compounds of carbon, as it was believed that these compounds could not be synthesized from the elements, but had to come from an organism that had lived. Therefore 'inorganic' involves all the rest of chemistry, and deals with the various combinations of all the other elements apart from carbon. Carbon has a peculiar facility for combining in long chains with itself to make the complicated compounds necessary to maintain life. 'Inorganic' compounds tend to have fewer atoms in them. See also **element/compound**.

organic disease see **functional disease**

oriental/occidental
The two words mean simply 'eastern' and 'western', so have the same basic geographical contrast. The origin of the words is a classical one, respectively Latin *oriens*, 'rising' and *occidens*, 'falling', referring to sunrise and sunset. This provenance has therefore given the terms a poetic or formal use, the formal seen in the names of steamship companies such as 'P & O' ('Peninsular and Oriental'), the poetic in Marlowe's Persian fleet which:

> Sailing about the oriental sea,
> Have fetch'd about the Indian
> continent.

'Oriental' particularly relates to the 'Orient', with its exotic and 'inscrutable' overtones, and has been preserved in a number of witty or frivolous quotations, such as Kipling's Parsee in his *Just So Stories*, whose hat reflected the rays of the sun in 'more-than-oriental splendour' and Johnson's description of Swift washing 'with oriental scrupulosity'. The fact that all these references are to 'oriental', not 'occidental', serve to show that the latter word is much less common, doubtless since the 'Occident', or western world, has much less glamour and colour. However, the 'Epistle Dedicatory' by the English translators of the Authorized Version of the Bible, does refer to 'the setting of that bright *Occidental Star*, Queen *Elizabeth* of most happy memory' to remain as one noble example of its usage. See also **east/west** for more basic considerations.

orthodox/heterodox
'Heterodox' really equates with 'unorthodox', and so relates to anything that is not 'orthodox', especially in matters of belief or doctrine in religion. Hence Bishop William Warburton's famous remark to Lord Sandwich that 'Orthodoxy is my doxy; heterodoxy is another man's doxy'. The words themselves are Greek based, and mean literally 'correct belief' and 'other belief'. (Words with 'hetero-' often have a contrasting word beginning 'homo-', see **homogeneous/heterogeneous**, **homosexual/heterosexual**.) See also the next entry below.

orthodox sleep/paradoxical sleep
The terms are medical ones for the two main categories of sleep. 'Orthodox sleep' is basically that part of a night's sleep which is dreamless, while 'paradoxical sleep' is sleep in which dreams occur. The two types of sleep are also known respectively as 'non-rapid eye movement' (NREM) and 'rapid eye movement' (REM), because eye movements apparently occur only during a sleeper's dream. The latter type of sleep is called 'paradoxical' because the brainwaves of a sleeper in this part of the cycle are similar to those of a person who is fully awake.

orthography/cacography
The terms are rather grand ones for 'correct spelling' and 'wrong spelling', with the derivations in the Greek words for 'right writing' and 'bad writing'. The usage of the terms is mainly confined to language study, with 'orthography' the standardized spelling of a language (where it exists), and 'cacography' any departure

from this standard. The causes of 'cacography' are complex, and can range from illiteracy to the subconscious influence of another, similar spelling (e.g. the surname 'Batchelor', commercially prominent, resulting in the spelling of 'bachelor' in this way).

other see **one**

other-directed see **inner-directed**

out see **in**

outboard see **inboard**

outdoor see **indoor**

outer see **inner**

outerwear see **underwear**

outfield see **infield**

output see **input**

outside see **inside**

outswinger see **inswinger**

outwardly see **inwardly**

ovate/obovate
In botany, a leaf that is 'ovate' is shaped like a hard-boiled egg cut lengthwise, with the broader end at the base, while an 'obovate' leaf is the inverse of this, and has the narrower end at the base. The words are based on Latin *ovum*, 'egg', with the prefix 'ob-' meaning 'inverse', 'upside down'.

over/under
The two opposites here can refer to position ('over the moon', 'under the sea'), condition ('over-heated', 'under-cooked') or quantity ('over 60', 'under a week'). Many words beginning 'over-' have no opposite in 'under' but simply denote an 'extra' or excessive state of the basic word or indicate a position or movement 'over' where there would not be one 'under', e.g. 'overboard' (no 'underboard'), 'overflow' (no 'underflow'), 'overhead' (no 'underhead', although there is an 'underfoot'). Examples of 'over-' words with an 'under-' opposite include: 'overage', 'overarm', 'overcharge', 'overdone' (of cooked food), 'overestimate', 'overlay', 'overpay', 'overshoot' (go beyond a target) and 'overthrow' (throw too far, as in a ball game such as cricket). Sometimes apparent 'over-' and 'under-' words are not opposites but have quite different meanings: 'overtake' means 'pass a person or vehicle by going faster', but 'undertake' means 'contract to do something'. 'Over or under?' is often a question asked by a shop assistant or stall holder of a customer who is purchasing something by weight, especially when a precise measurement is difficult, e.g. 'Two pounds of apples, please', (Assistant, weighing some) 'Over or under?' (i.e. 'It won't be exactly two pounds: do you want less than this or more?').

overheads/prime cost
In running a business, one needs to balance both types of costs. 'Overheads' are expenses such as rent that cannot be accurately calculated or attributed to any particular department, but have to be generally assessed. By contrast, 'prime cost' is the price of production, the portion of the cost of a commodity that normally includes materials and labour and that varies with the amount of production. While 'prime cost' thus varies, 'overheads' are fixed. Compare **fixed/variable**.

oviparous see **viviparous**

ox/bull
The general difference between the two types of male cattle is that the 'ox' is castrated, and used chiefly for draught work and for its meat, while the 'bull' is uncastrated and is used for breeding. However, both words are sometimes used quite loosely for any male bovine animal, whether castrated or not. Compare **cow/bull** and, in quite a different market, **bear/bull**.

Oxbridge/redbrick
The contrast here is between the ancient university foundations of Oxford and Cambridge (blended into a single identity as 'Oxbridge'), and the relatively modern provincial universities founded in the nineteenth century and first half of the twentieth. The particular reference is to the red brickwork of the buildings of the latter universities, as against the mellow grey stone of 'Oxbridge' colleges, with the two types of architecture themselves seen as standing for long-established and firmly founded learning on the one hand, and 'science and industry' and innovation on the other, with the red colour even suggesting a revolutionary spirit, as indeed found formerly in some 'redbrick' universities. A further contrast is also sometimes made between 'redbrick' and 'plateglass', the latter being a term used for the most modern British universities of all, those founded in the 1960s. Here the symbolism of the architectural style lies more in a mood of brightness and optimism, incorporating Harold Macmillan's dictum of the day: 'You've never had it so good'. The contrasts are as much geographical, too, as academic, since most 'redbrick' universities are in the Midlands or north of England (typically, Manchester, Leeds and Birmingham), while the 'plateglass' universities are both in the south (Universities of Surrey and Sussex) and the north (Universities of York and Lancaster). London University, however, would be regarded as 'redbrick', despite its location and the mainly inaccurate designation of its buildings. See also the next entry below.

Oxford/Cambridge
Apart from their geographical locations – 'Oxford' borders on the West Midlands, 'Cambridge' is in East Anglia – what is the chief difference between Britain's two ancient universities and rivals? Broadly, 'Oxford' (which is older than 'Cambridge') has a reputation for arts subjects, and especially for classics and theology, while 'Cambridge' is famed for its sciences and its innovative intellectualism. Put another way, 'Oxford' is more 'staid and sober', while 'Cambridge' is more 'showy' and extrovert. This difference *may* have something to do with the respective geographical locations, because 'Cambridge' is a much more isolated city than 'Oxford', and thus has had to develop its own image more self-consciously. Politically, therefore, 'Oxford' is on the whole more right-wing, while 'Cambridge' veers noticeably to the left. (At 'Oxford', the college of Christ Church is famous for the Conservative politicians and especially prime ministers it has educated, while at 'Cambridge', King's College is still a left-wing citadel.) There are differences in nomenclature too numerous to list here, but for a few see **scout/gyp**, **gyp/bedder**, **quadrangle/court**, **May Week/Eights Week**. See also **Isis/Cam**. When all is said and done, however, it must be admitted that the actual colleges at both universities are equally attractive, with beautiful gardens, and that the basic tutorial and academic systems of both universities are quite similar. Collectors of perverse differences will wish to know that the degree of Doctor of Philosophy is known at 'Oxford' as 'D. Phil.', and at 'Cambridge' as 'Ph. D.' The first of these is short for 'Doctor of Philosophy', the second for Latin *Philosophiae doctor*.

oxidation/reduction
The terms are used in chemistry. 'Oxidation' originally meant that the substance 'oxidized' was made to combine with oxygen, so that iron was 'oxidized' from Fe to FeO. It then meant raising the valency state from say 2 to 3, e.g. by 'oxidizing' FeO to Fe_2O_3. Now, 'oxidation' is understood more generally to mean removing electrons from a compound, or an element in a chemical action. 'Reduction' is the reverse, and involves removing oxygen (for example, to reduce an oxide to the element, or adding one or more electrons to an atom. The word 'reduction' has alchemical and mining origins, because ores are 'reduced' to metals. Common oxidizing agents are ferric oxide (Fe_2O_3), hydrogen peroxide (H_2O_2) and sulphuric acid (H_2SO_4). Reducing agents include iron oxide (FeO), sulphur dioxide (SO_2), and metals that dissolve in acid. See also **proton/electron**.

Pp

pacer see **trotter**

Pacific see **Atlantic**

page/folio
In publishing and printing, 'page' refers to a printed page (that is, numbered) and 'folio' to the page of the manuscript or typescript. Since both manuscript and book will have numbered pages, it is necessary to specify whether 'page' or 'folio' is meant when quoting a number. A 'folio', too, will be numbered on one side only, with the other often blank, while a printed page has two sides, numbered consecutively. The related verbs are 'paginate' and 'foliate', the former implying numbering in sequence, and the latter relating to numbers that may not be in sequence. See also **quarto/folio**; **recto/verso**.

page proof see **galley proof**

pain see **pleasure**

painterly see **linear**

pair-oar/double scull
In rowing, a 'pair-oar' is a racing boat or shell in which the two oarsmen sit one behind the other, each having one oar. 'Double scull' has an identical arrangement of the rowers, but they have two oars each, not one. (Generally, 'rowing' implies that the rower has a single oar, which is manipulated with both hands, while 'sculling' means that the oarsman has two oars, one in each hand.)

PAL/SECAM
The two abbreviations are those of the two main colour television systems of the world, both based on 625 lines. 'PAL' (standing for 'phase alternation line') is the one used in Britain and around fifty other countries, although not the United States, which has its own NTSC (National Television Standard Committee). 'SECAM' (French *Système électronique couleur à mémoire*, 'Colour electronic system with memory', or according to other sources *séquentiel à mémoire*, 'memory sequence') is the system used in France and many East European countries. In terms of practical effect, there is little difference between the two colour systems, and both are modifications of the American NTSC, which came first. The difference lies in the countries that adopted the systems, and their mutual incompatibility.

paleface/redskin
The names are those of the two basic racial groups of North America, with the 'palefaces' being the white European settlers (British, French and others) and the 'redskins' being the native Indians ('Red Indians'). The term 'paleface' is said to have arisen as a nickname for the white men among the 'redskins' themselves, and became familiar from the novels of Fenimore Cooper, Mayne Reid and other 'frontier' writers. 'Redskin', however, is first recorded in the seventeenth century as a name for the Indians, some two hundred years before 'paleface' appeared.

paperback/hardback
The two basic forms of book, respectively with paper and cloth covers, the latter still being in many people's minds the 'real' book, complete with dust jacket. 'Paperbacks' are generally cheaper than 'hardbacks', so sell (or are intended to sell) in greater quantities. They are also less bulky and in many cases less 'permanent', since the cover can tear easily. Conversely, a 'hardback' edition is more expensive and weightier, but more durable. (Typical

prices in 1987 for a novel of either type were 'paperback' at around £4.95 and 'hardback' at £10.95.) Until fairly recently, a 'paperback' edition of a book would appear only after a 'hardback' one, although now many first editions appear in 'paperback'. 'Paperbacks', too, were formerly printed in larger quantities than 'hardbacks', but now this is not necessarily the case. There are alternative terms for the two types, with a 'paperback' also being 'soft-cover', and a 'hardback' being 'cloth' or 'cased'. (A 'limp' book is not the same as a 'paperback', but is a book with a binding not stiffened by boards. Many school books are 'limp'.)

parachronism/prochronism
A 'parachronism' is the dating of something (in literature or elsewhere) at a later time than it really should be, while a 'prochronism' is the dating or timing of something earlier than it actually was. The 'prochronism' is thus really an 'anachronism' (see **anachronism/parachronism** for more on the subject, and also the related **prochronism/metachronism**).

paradoxical sleep see **orthodox sleep**

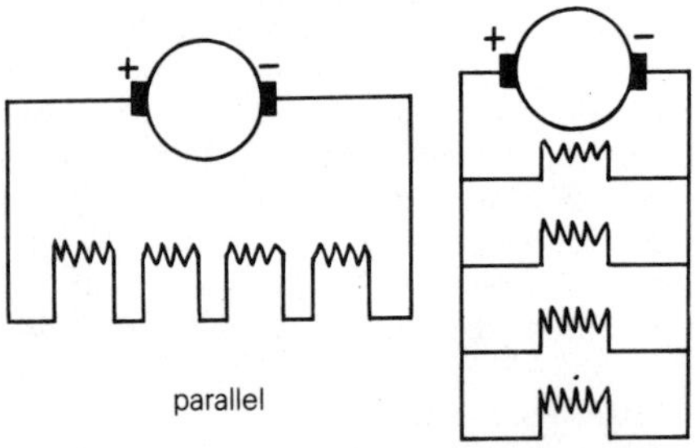

parallel

series

parallel/series
When two or more electrical devices are connected 'in parallel', they have their electrodes or terminals connected to one single current source and their negative points linked to a single 'outlet', so that they share the power (voltage) between them. When they are connected 'in series', however, the current passes through each device in turn. Batteries 'in series' will thus give a higher voltage. See also **series winding/shunt winding**.

paralogism see **sophism**

Parliamentarians see **Royalists**

parole see **langue**

parquet/coulisse
The French words literally mean 'main floor' and 'wings' (as in a theatre), and relate to the French Stock Exchange or Paris Bourse. The 'parquet' is the main part of the Bourse where officially listed securities are traded. The 'coulisse', by contrast, is that part of the Bourse where unofficial securities are traded. The terms originally had specific locational references, since the 'outside' dealers traded in a narrow hallway or passage called *La Coulisse*, while the official dealers traded, as they still do, in a central 'Ring', physically railed off from the rest of the main floor of the exchange. The 'outside dealers' in the 'coulisse' were given recognized status in 1901, however.

particular/universal
In logic, 'particular' is used as a term applying to an affirmation or denial made about only some members of a group, such as 'Some cats are grey'. A 'universal' proposition is one that affirms or denies something about all members of a group, such as 'All people die some day' or 'No one knows everything'.

part-time see **full-time**

pass/fail
The contrasting terms belong chiefly to examination results, with every student hoping to 'pass', not 'fail'. There can be various degrees of a 'pass', however, and even of a 'fail', and many examinations have a particular 'pass' mark or grade, e.g. 60% or a grade 'C' (with 'D', say, being a close 'fail' and 'E' a clear one). 'Pass' and 'fail' grades (in letters or figures) applied to the former GCE and

CSE school-leaving examinations, and there was some comment that when the new combined GCSE examination was introduced, in 1988, a student could not 'fail' but would be simply awarded a particular grade (one of the letters 'A', for the best result, to 'G', for the worst). There are of course various other tests that one can 'pass' or 'fail', such as a driving test, an eye test, or a medical check-up. By an odd quirk of usage, a custom has arisen in certain quiz games and knowledge contests of a person saying 'pass' when he 'fails' to answer a question. But he is actually addressing the questioner or 'quizmaster', telling him to 'pass' to the next question.

pass degree/honours degree
At many universities, a student can be awarded either a 'pass degree' or an 'honours degree' for succeeding in a final examination. In general, students aim to get an 'honours degree', which itself can be graded into 'I' (the best), or 'II' (good average), or 'III' (satisfactory). 'Pass degrees' are awarded by many polytechnics, and also by the Open University, with in some cases an 'honours degree' being awarded after a further year's study. In Scotland, too, the M.A. (Master of Arts) is a 'pass degree'.

passe see **manque**

passive see **active**[2]

past see (1) **future** (2) **present**[2]

patriarch/matriarch
In the most basic sense, a 'patriarch' is the male head of a tribe or clan, while a 'matriarch' is a similar female head. 'Patriarch', too, has come to be used as the title of various religious dignitaries or spiritual heads, from the three ancestors of the Hebrew people in the Bible, Abraham, Isaac or Jacob, to certain bishops in the Roman Catholic and Eastern Orthodox Churches. A 'patriarchy' is thus a social organization in which a male is the head of the family and descent is traced down through the male line, father to son. 'Matriarch' is much less often used as a title of honour, although in a 'matriarchy' the social organization is similar to that of the male line, but with descent being traced down, mother to daughter, from an original female head. Some modern anthropologists and sociologists say that a true 'matriarchy' has never existed, a fact which understandably infuriates feminists, who maintain (at least, some of them) that a primeval 'matriarchy' existed long before the current 'patriarchy'. The terms obviously derive from Latin *pater*, 'father', and *mater*, 'mother', with 'matriarch' based on 'patriarch'.

patrician/plebs
In Ancient Rome, a 'patrician' was a member of the hereditary aristocracy, and in the early republic it was the 'patricians' who held all the high offices. The 'plebs' were by contrast the common people of Ancient Rome (the word functions as a collective plural). 'Patrician' is sometimes used today to apply to a 'grand' or refined person, while 'plebs' has produced the derogatory term 'pleb' for someone who is 'plebeian', or crude and coarse in taste or manners. 'Patrician' derives ultimately from Latin *pater*, 'father', while 'plebs' is a pure Latin word, itself indirectly related to Latin *plenus*, 'full' (with this English word also indirectly related to the Latin).

P-Celtic/Q-Celtic
These terms are not the origin of 'minding one's P's and Q's', although one might suppose so, from the learned languages they respectively designate! 'P-Celtic' is the name for the division of the Celtic languages that includes Welsh, Cornish and Breton. 'Q-Celtic' is the branch that includes Irish Gaelic, Scottish Gaelic and Manx. A glance at the entry **Brythonic/Goedelic** will show that the terms are in effect alternative designations for these names. 'P-Celtic' is so called since the basic Indoeuropean sound *qu* developed in the languages concerned into *p*, while in the 'Q-Celtic' languages it was retained unchanged. For example, Latin *quinque*, 'five', is represented by *cuig* in Irish, but *pump* in Welsh.

peak/trough
The two words are sometimes used to designate a 'high point' and a 'low point' in a particular progression or development, whether visually on a graph or more generally in a person's career or even life. The not very original metaphorical references are to a mountain and a ditch. On the whole, 'peak' is more commonly used than 'trough', probably since people are much more interested in 'peaks' than 'troughs'.

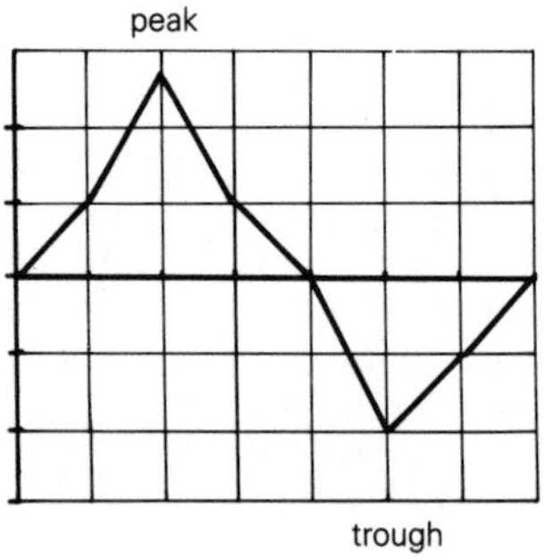

pearl see **clear**

pedal/freewheel
Two contrasting ways of progressing on a bicycle! The rider will need to 'pedal' mostly along the flat, and certainly uphill, but can blissfully 'freewheel' downhill. 'Freewheel' indicates the mechanism by which the rear wheel of a bicycle can rotate freely while the 'pedals' remain stationary. Early bicycles had no 'freewheel', and its appearance around the end of the nineteenth century caused a revolution in cycling.

pejoration see **amelioration**

pen/pencil
The two writing implements are invariably associated and implicitly contrasted: a 'pen' is used for a permanent record, while what is written with a 'pencil' is erasable and correctable. Although similar words, they are of quite different derivations. 'Pen' comes ultimately from Latin *penna*, 'feather', while 'pencil' has evolved from Latin *penicillum*, itself a diminutive of *peniculus*, 'brush'. (English 'penicillin' comes from the same source, since its sporangia, or spore-producing organs, are like little brushes.)

pencil see **pen**

pentameter see **hexameter**

pentathlon/decathlon
These sporting names mean respectively 'five contests' and 'ten contests', and are included as contrasting multiple athletic events in sporting competitions, among them the Olympic Games. The 'pentathlon' can be a series of contests for men or women. For women, it comprises the 100-metre hurdles, shot put, high jump, long jump, and 200-metre sprint. For men, as the 'modern pentathlon' (compared to the classical one), it comprises the 300-metre freestyle swim, 4000-metre cross-country run, 5000-metre horserace (with 30 jumps), épée fencing, and target shooting at 25 metres. The 'decathlon', for men only, comprises the 100-metre, 400-metre and 1500-metre races, 110-metre high hurdles, and the javelin, discus, shot put, pole vault, high jump, and long jump.

penumbra see **umbra**

pepper see **salt**

per capita see **per stirpes**

père/fils
The two French words, 'father' and 'son', are traditionally used for two well-known people who are father and son and who have the same name, for example Alexandre Dumas 'père', who wrote *The Three Musketeers*, and Alexandre Dumas 'fils', who wrote *La Dame aux camélias*. The words are sometimes also used, in self-conscious or affected writing, for English people (or native English speakers), e.g. in the following: 'So it will be seen that there was a Harkaway *père* and a Harkaway *fils*' (E. S. Turner, *Boys will be Boys*, 1948). The

words are normally italicized like this because of their French origin.

perfect/imperfect
'The morality of art consists in the perfect use of an imperfect medium', wrote Oscar Wilde in *The Picture of Dorian Gray*, and the two words have been contrasted in many other general ways quite effectively. In many instances, however, the contrast is a specialized one. For example, in music a 'perfect' cadence is the satisfactory last two chords that close most works of the classical period, while an 'imperfect' cadence, or 'half close', is the one often found halfway through a composition, leaving the listener unsatisfied and expecting more. A 'perfect' interval, too, is a chord made with the keynote and the fourth, fifth and octave of the scale (e.g. C and G, as a fifth), while all other intervals are 'imperfect', and lack the 'pure' quality that the three 'perfect' ones have. In language, again, the 'perfect' tense is the one that denotes a completed action, with the verb as in 'We have eaten', while the 'imperfect' tense denotes in incomplete or continuing state in the past, as in 'We were eating' or 'We ate (every day)'. Finally, a 'perfect' flower, in botany, has both male and female reproductive structures (stamens and pistils), while an 'imperfect' flower has these organs in different flowers, so that the female flowers have to be pollinated (by insects or the wind, for example). See also **imperfective/perfective** and, if botanically curious, **stamen/pistil**.

perforate/imperforate
As philatelists will know, 'perforate' (or 'perforated') is the term used of a stamp or set of stamps that has a line of small holes along its margins so that it can be detached from adjacent stamps. This is the standard method. 'Imperforate' (or less often, 'imperforated') denotes a stamp that lacks any perforations or other means of detachment. This is unusual and often makes the stamp much more valuable than its 'perforate' equivalent. (Early postage stamps were 'imperforate' anyway.) The relevant abbreviations 'perf.' and 'imperf.' soon became familiar to stamp collectors, especially when they acquire a perforation gauge for the former type.

perigee see **apogee**

perihelion/aphelion
The 'perihelion' of a planet or comet is the point when it is nearest to the Sun. Its 'aphelion' is thus the opposite, the point in its orbit when it is furthest from the Sun. 'Perihelion' means 'near the Sun', and 'aphelion' means 'away from the Sun'. Compare **apogee/perigee**.

period/group
In the periodic table of chemical elements, a 'period' is one of the horizontal rows, always starting with an alkali metal and finishing with a rare gas. A 'group' is thus one of the vertical columns in this table, containing elements that all have similar electronic structures, properties, and valencies. The periodic table is of great importance in the study of inorganic chemistry (see **organic/inorganic**), and was devised by the Russian chemist Mendeleev in 1869. ('Period' refers to the 'periodic law', according to which the elements, arranged in order of their atomic numbers, show a periodic variation in most of their properties.)

perishables see **durable goods**

perissodactyl see **artiodactyl**

permanent see **temporary**

permutation see **combination**

personal property/real property
From a legal point of view, 'personal property' is any property that can be moved, such as money and furniture. 'Real property' is therefore immovable, and the term particularly applies to freehold land.

per stirpes/per capita
In law, and as applied to an inheritance, 'per stirpes' relates to the provision by which the children of a descendant divide

between them only that share that would have been their parent's (if still alive). By contrast, 'per capita' means that all share alike. The Latin phrases mean respectively 'by stems' and 'by heads'.

pessimist see **optimist**

pestle/mortar
A 'pestle' is a clublike implement for pounding or grinding a substance in a 'mortar', which is a type of bowl. The two specialized words do not have a figurative or proverbial usage, except on a rather sophisticated literary level, such as the biblical verse in Proverbs 27:22: 'Though thou shouldest bray a fool in a mortar among wheat with a pestle, yet will not his foolishness depart from him'. ('Bray' here means 'pound', 'grind'.) 'Pestle' derives ultimately from the Latin verb *pinsare*, 'to pound', while 'mortar' comes from Latin *mortarium*, 'basin in which mortar is mixed'. Thus the builder's substance ('bricks and mortar') is named after the vessel in which it was prepared, and the 'mortar' that is a type of artillery gun is also the same word, and is so called from its squat shape, like that of the basin.

petit mal see **grand mal**

petit point see **gros point**

phanerogam see **cryptogam**

phloem/xylem
Botanically, 'phloem' is a tissue in the 'higher' plants, such as trees and shrubs, that takes synthesized food substances to all parts of the plant. Greek *phloos* means 'bark'. 'Xylem' is the plant tissue that conducts water and mineral salts from the roots of the plant to all other parts, and that forms the wood of trees and shrubs. Greek *xylon* means 'wood'. The two tissues are thus in effect the ways by which plants 'eat' and 'drink'.

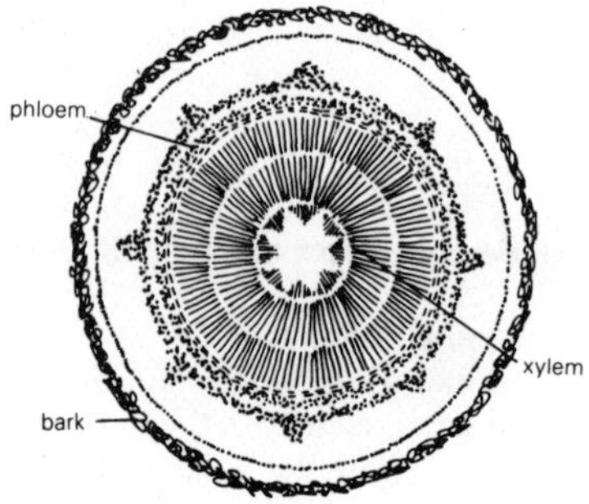

physician/surgeon
These are the two main types of medical men. The 'physician' is a doctor of medicine who thus treats a condition or illness by any means other than surgery, with the 'surgeon' making the latter his speciality. This despite the fact that the family doctor or 'G.P.', who is a 'physician', sees his patients in a 'surgery'. See also **medical/ surgical**.

piano/forte
The two words are Italian for 'soft' and 'loud', and have neatly combined musically to form the full name, 'pianoforte', for one of the most popular and versatile of musical instruments, the 'piano'. The instrument was so named since it could play *piano e forte*, 'loud and soft', that is, it could vary its loudness (unlike its predecessors, such as the harpsichord, which could vary its tone from loud to soft only by having two sets of keys, one for each). In the eighteenth century, the earlier forms of 'pianoforte' were known as a 'fortepiano'. As a distinct musical direction today, 'piano' is normally abbreviated as 'p' (with 'pp' meaning 'very soft' and 'ppp' meaning 'extremely soft'). Similarly, 'f' means 'loud', and 'ff' means 'very loud'. (The abbreviation 'pp' is usually referred to as 'pianissimo' and conversely 'ff' as 'fortissimo'.)

pica/elite
'Pica' (pronounced like 'hiker') is a size of typewriter type providing ten characters to the inch. 'Elite' provides twelve characters to the inch. The two are the standard sizes of typewriter type, with probably 'elite' more common. 'Pica' was also a size of printer's type of approximately twelve points (a 'point' being a unit measuring

0.351mm, or almost 1/72 inch), and there was formerly also a printer's type called 'elite'. 'Pica' has an interesting origin. The word is Latin for 'magpie', and was adopted (in Latin) to be used as a term for a list of ecclesiastical regulations, the link probably being that such a list was varied, and suggested a magpie's love of collecting miscellaneous objects. 'Elite' is the same word as the standard one meaning 'select', 'exclusive'.

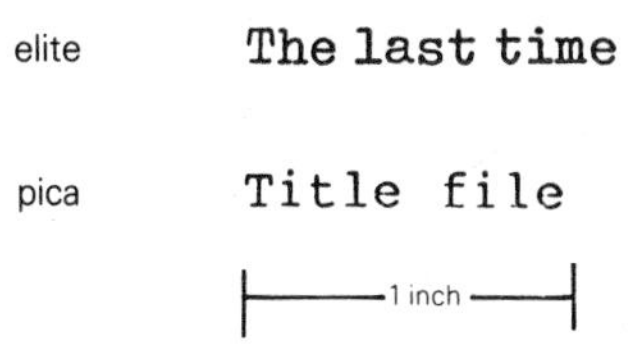

pidgin see **creole**

piece-dye/yarn-dye
To 'piece-dye' a fabric is to dye it after it has been woven or knitted, when it is already a 'piece' of material. To 'yarn-dye' is thus to dye a fabric before it has been woven or knitted, when it is still in that 'yarn' stage.

piecework/timework
'Piecework' is work that is paid for at a set rate per unit, for example, work done by a typist at a rate of £5 for every 2000 words or five pages typed. 'Timework' is work paid for at a set rate for a period of time taken to do it, usually so much per hour. Thus the same typist might be offered payment of £5 per hour for the work.

pillow lace/needlepoint
'Pillow lace' is lace made by winding thread round bobbins on a padded cushion or board, this being the 'pillow'. 'Needlepoint', or 'point lace', is lace made worked with a needle (especially in a so called 'buttonhole stitch') over a paper pattern. Both methods are quite old, and date back to at least the sixteenth century.

pinniped see **fissiped**

Pinyin/Wade-Giles
These are the names of the two best-known contrasting methods of transcribing Chinese in English letters. The older and still probably the more familiar of the two is the 'Wade-Giles' system, first published by Sir Thomas Wade in 1859 and serving as the basis for the Chinese–English Dictionary of H. A. Giles published in 1912. In 1958, however, the Chinese government approved the system called *pinyin zimu* ('phonetic alphabet') for the romanization of the language, since it was more accurate and simpler, and was preferred by teachers of Chinese. (In 'Wade-Giles', for example, the sound approximating to the 'j' of 'jump' was rendered as 'ch', whereas 'Pinyin' uses 'zh'. 'Wade-Giles', too, has a complex use of apostrophes, so that the 'Pinyin' equivalents of 'chih' and 'ch'ih' are respectively 'zhi' and 'chi'.) For the man in the street in the western world, the main difference between the two will be noticed in China's geographical names, so that Peking (more a 'Wade-Giles' equivalent than a true 'Wade-Giles' spelling) is now Beijing, and Tientsin (in 'correct' 'Wade-Giles', T'ien-chin) is now Tianjin. Most modern atlases, such as *The Times Atlas of the World*, published in 1985, now use the 'Pinyin' spellings.

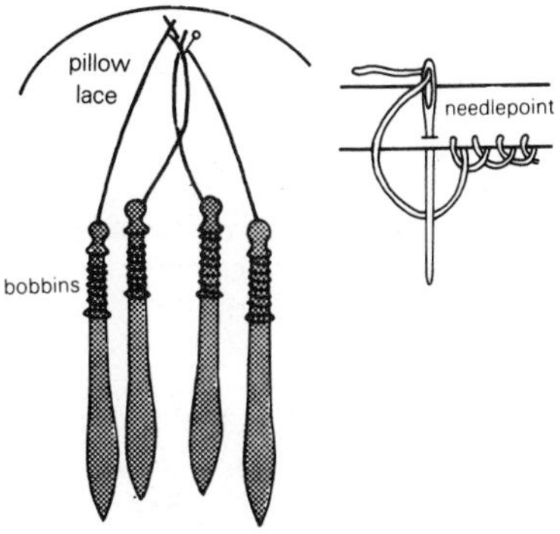

pipe organ/reed organ
There are musical organs and organs. The 'pipe organ' is the familiar one found in churches, with pipes and pedals. The 'reed organ' is one in which the sound is produced by air passing through reeds, such as the harmonium, accordion or harmonica ('mouth organ'). See also **positive organ/ portative organ**.

pistil see **stamen**

piston engine/jet engine
The two types of engines are familiar from aircraft, where 'jets' have 'jet engines' (actually, gas turbines) and other and older aircraft have 'piston engines', or the ordinary internal combustion engine, as used in cars. (In aircraft, the propeller was driven by the 'piston engine'.) In terms of ton/miles per gallon of fuel, a 'jet engine' is much more efficient, and moreover uses a cheaper and safer fuel (kerosene, not gasoline). Nor is this the sole advantage. Aircraft with 'jet engines' can maintain sustained speeds that are much faster than those of 'piston engines', and the word 'jet' is still regarded as synonymous with 'trendy', 'fast-paced' as a result, especially in the phrase 'jet set' to apply to the wealthy people who fly to fashionable resorts all over the world by 'jet' aircraft.

pitch[1]/roll
When a ship 'pitches', its bow rises and falls. When it 'rolls', its deck tilts alternately to port and starboard. There is thus a longitudinal and a latitudinal contrast of movement here. (When a ship 'heaves', additionally, it rises and falls in the water, and this can similarly contrast with either its 'pitch' or its 'roll'.) When a ship does all three simultaneously, as it can in a rough sea and a strong wind, it 'tosses', and the result is extremely unpleasant for all except the most experienced of sailors or passengers.

pitch[2]/strike
The words are used in a semi-technical or specialized sense for setting up and disbanding a camp (or military encampment). One thus 'pitches' a camp or a tent at the beginning, and 'strikes' camp (but not a tent) at the end, when moving on or returning. This may seem an unusual use of 'strike', which often implies an advancing ('striking' at the enemy), but really means basically 'taking a course of action', so is the same verb as the 'strike' that means 'cease work in protest'.

place see **win[2]**

placebo/drug
A 'placebo' is a 'drug' that is not really a drug at all, since it is given purely for its psychological effect, to 'keep the patient happy' or to serve as a 'control' in an experiment. (The word is Latin for 'I shall please', and derives from the opening of a prayer for the dead, ominously enough.) The only real opposite to a 'placebo' is thus the genuine article, the 'drug' that does actually contain the medicinal substances.

plain see (1) **purl** (2) **rich[1]**

plain chocolate see **milk chocolate**

plain clothes see **uniform**

plaintext/code
If a message is in 'plaintext', it is in its original standard form, in normal language. When in 'code', its text will be disguised or reorganized in apparently arbitrary letters, figures or symbols, so that it cannot be readily understood. The term 'plaintext' is often used of a message before it has been 'coded'. Then, when it has been decoded, it will be in 'plaintext' again. An alternative term for 'plaintext' is 'clear', especially when the message may not be put into 'code' anyway.

plaintiff/defendant
In a court of law, the 'plaintiff' is the person who brings a civil action against someone else, i.e. he is legally 'complaining' about him. The person so accused is therefore the 'defendant', because he has to 'defend' himself against the charge. Compare **prosecution/ defence**.

plan/elevation
In a scale drawing of a building, a 'plan' is a representation of a horizontal section at a given level (for example, ground floor, first floor, etc.). The opposite to this is an 'elevation', which is a drawing to scale vertically, either of the front or back of a building, or of one of its sides. Both types of drawing are commonly seen in the work of architects. To the layman, a 'plan' is really a sort of map of a building, while an 'elevation' is a more realistic 'picture' of one of its sides.

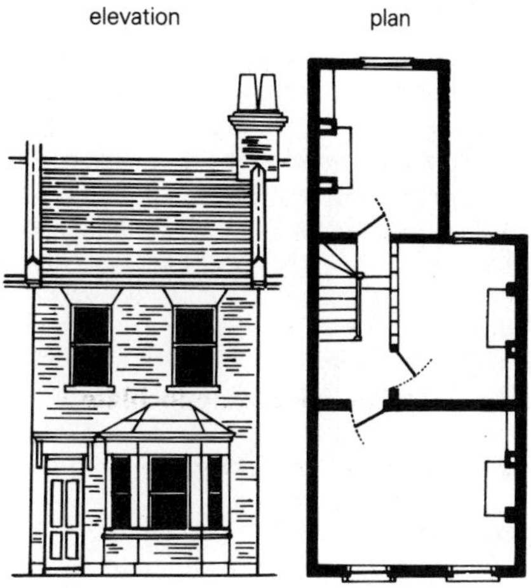

planet see **star**

platyrrhine see **catarrhine**

play see **work**

play by ear see **sight-read**

PLC see **Ltd**

pleasure/pain

> The pain that is all but a pleasure will change
> For the pleasure that's all but pain.

So Gilbert and Sullivan, in *Patience*. The two keenly felt opposites, like the pair **laugh/cry**, can sometimes overlap, so that extreme 'pleasure' can seem painful (have you ever 'laughed till it hurt'?), and extreme 'pain' can even perversely give 'pleasure' (see **sadist/masochist**). Indeed, some intense physical acts really combine the two, in a fusion of opposites, among them long-distance runs and (at a more modest level) scratching a bite. The dichotomy has long intrigued mankind, and it was Swinburne who wrote of 'grievous pleasure and pain', as if unable to envisage the one without the other. See also **love/hate**.

plebs see **patrician**

plenum see **vacuum**

plug/socket
One is not much use without the other, the 'plug' being the electrical device with three (or less often, two) pins that fits into a 'socket' (a 'power point') in order to receive an electric current and pass it via a cable to some electrical appliance. Sometimes the appliance itself may also have a 'socket' into which a 'plug' on the other end of the cable or lead needs to be fitted. This system works with some radios, for example. Rather perversely, we often call the 'socket' in the wall the 'plug', especially when considering it individually, e.g. 'Why do you have the plug in such an awkward place?' In this usage, or misusage, the device is also called a 'wall plug', which at least helps to make it clear what is meant. See also **male/female**.

plummet see **soar**

plural see **singular**

plus/minus
The two basic mathematical opposites, with their respective signs ('+' for 'plus', '−' for minus), are also used in a general sense, especially 'plus'. 'Our garden is quite private, which is a big plus'; 'The constant noise from the motorway is a distinct minus'. In these two sentences the words have the respective meanings 'advantage' and 'disadvantage'. The terms are also familiar in the academic assessment of a student's work, especially with

a Greek letter, with 'alpha plus' the best, and (usually) 'delta minus' (or even 'double minus') the worst. (The narrator in Margaret Drabble's novel *Summer Bird-Cage* at one point rates Scott Fitzgerald's novel *Tender is the Night* as 'beta minus'.) The mathematical symbol '±' means 'plus or minus', and refers to an approximate quantity, or to a figure that need not be precisely accurate, e.g. the boiling point of gold is 2807±2°C, i.e. somewhere between 2805 and 2809°C. In arithmetic the signs '+' and '−' indicate 'add' or 'subtract', as every schoolboy still knows. He may not know, though, that in astronomy the same signs denote respectively 'north' or 'south' (of latitudes or declinations). See, as necessary, **add/subtract**, **right ascension/declination**, **latitude/longitude**.

p.m. see **a.m.**

pneumatic/hydraulic
Anything 'pneumatic' is to do with air or gas (Greek *pneuma*, 'breath', 'wind'), and anything 'hydraulic' is to do with water (Greek *hydor*, 'water'). These two elemental forces thus lie behind the names of various machines or devices that are operated by either air or water, such as a 'pneumatic' drill operated by compressed air, or a 'hydraulic' ram that raises fluids also by means of pressure. The scientific studies of the forces, as they apply to engineering, are called respectively 'pneumatics' and 'hydraulics', with the latter also known as 'fluid mechanics'.

poacher see **gamekeeper**

pocket see **banker**

poetry[1]/prose
'Poetry' is literature in metrical form, with or without rhyme (and even with or without metre), otherwise 'verse' (but see the next entry below!). 'Prose' is literature in non-metrical form, although when arranged in linear form (i.e. in displayed lines of differing length) can become 'poetry'. Thus this sentence is 'prose': 'In spring the leaves appear on the trees and the flowers emerge from the earth'. But this arrangement is (more or less) 'poetry':

> In spring the leaves
> Appear on the trees
> And the flowers emerge
> From the earth.

It was Molière who made this profound judgment on the difference: 'Tout ce qui n'est point prose est vers; et tout ce qui n'est point vers est prose' ('All that is not prose is verse; and all that is not verse is prose') (*Le Bourgeois Gentilhomme*).

poetry[2]/verse
Although 'poetry' is often *in* 'verse', it is not always properly 'verse' itself, but something loftier and more 'deep-felt'. On the whole, therefore, 'poetry' is superior, and often carefully composed, while 'verse' is in the main less weighty and runs fairly easily, even naively. Shakespeare's sonnets are thus 'poetry', but Edward Lear's limericks are 'verse'. Significantly, we talk of 'light verse', not 'light poetry'. 'Poetry' does not have to be serious, however, and many poets have written humorous or witty poems, from Byron to Betjeman.

poikilothermic see **homoiothermic**

point see **square leg**

point-blank see **long-range**

poison/antidote
The 'antidote', of course, is designed to counteract or neutralize the 'poison'. But why is it not called an 'antipoison', or why is a poison not called a 'dote'? The '-dote' of 'antidote' ultimately derives from the root of the Greek verb *didonai*, 'to give', so an 'antidote' is really an 'antidose', or something given to have a cancelling effect. The word came into English from Old French or possibly direct from Medieval Latin.

polemics see **irenics**

polliwog/shellback
In dialect British usage, a 'polliwog' is a tadpole, so called because it 'wiggles its poll' or head. In colloquial North Amer-

ican usage, however, a 'polliwog' is also a nickname for a sailor who has not crossed the equator, since he is a mere 'tadpole'. By contrast, a 'shellback' is a sailor who has, otherwise he is an 'old salt'. 'Shellback' is otherwise a general colloquial term for a marine turtle.

polyandry/polygyny
These two opposing terms mean respectively 'the state of having more than one husband' and 'the state of having more than one wife'. However, the latter state is usually described by the term 'polygamy', so that 'polyandry' and 'polygyny' are more precisely used of animals, with 'polyandry' describing a female mating with more than one male in a breeding season, and 'polygyny' relating to a male doing the opposite. Plural marriages of the human kind have existed in a number of cultures, from that of pagan Ireland to modern tribal Africa, as well as India and China. The latter half of the words represents respectively Greek *aner*, genitive *andros*, 'man', *gyne*, 'woman' and *gamos*, 'marriage'.

polygyny see **polyandry**

polyp/medusa
Of these two types of marine creatures, the 'polyp' is stationary and does not reproduce sexually, while the 'medusa' is mobile and reproduces sexually. Examples of a 'polyp' are the sea anemone and coral, while a common type of 'medusa' is the jellyfish. 'Polyp' literally means 'many-footed', while the 'medusa' is so named after the Greek goddess Medusa whose hair was changed into serpents: the jellyfish has tentacles that look like snaky locks.

polysemy see **monosemy**

poor see **rich**[2]

pop see **classical**[1]

pope/antipope
The 'pope' is the head of the Roman Catholic Church and 'Bishop of Rome'. Who, then, were the various 'antipopes' of history? As their name suggests, they were rival 'popes', elected in opposition to those 'popes' who had been canonically (i.e. legally) elected. (In some cases they were not actually elected, but still claimed the title of 'pope'.) There were 'antipopes' from the third century A.D. (St Hippolytus is generally agreed to have been the first), but their prominence was attained in the fourteenth-century division in the Western Church known as the 'Great Schism', when there were rival 'popes' (and therefore 'antipopes') in Rome and Avignon. The last 'antipope' was Felix V, who was born in France in 1383. He submitted to the lawful 'pope', Nicholas V, in 1449, however, and became a cardinal.

popular paper see **quality paper**

port/starboard
Most people are aware that on ships and aircraft, 'port' means 'left' and 'starboard' means 'right'. However, 'port' is a relatively recent word, and replaced the earlier 'larboard' in the seventeenth century, since 'larboard' and 'starboard' can sound alike when used in spoken commands at sea. The origin of 'port' is still uncertain, but it could derive from the other 'port' that is a harbour, because this side of the ship was turned to the land when loading was taking place. (This origin seems to be supported by 'larboard', which literally means 'lade board', i.e. the side of the ship where the cargo was loaded on board.) 'Starboard' means literally 'steer board', as it was originally over this side of the ship that she was steered by means of a paddle.

portative organ see **positive organ**

positive/negative
The words have both specialized and general use as opposites. Among the special applications one has the mathematical one of 'positive' for a number greater than zero, and 'negative' for one less than zero (so that 'positive' equates to 'plus', and 'negative' to 'minus') and

the physical sense of 'positive' for an electric charge that has a polarity opposite to the charge of an electron, and so the same charge as that of a proton, while 'negative' denotes a charge that has a polarity the same as the charge of an electron. Probably more familiar will be the medical test, which if 'positive' indicates the presence of a suspected disease or organism, and if 'negative' denotes the absence of any disease. (This is therefore one of the few instances where 'positive' indicates something bad, and 'negative' something good.) Even more familiar will be the photographic 'positive', which is a print or slide showing the photographed object in its natural colours and shades, while a 'negative' has these reversed or opposed (black for white, yellow for blue, green for red, and so on). More generally, 'positive' denotes certainty, affirmation or a 'forward-looking' attitude, while 'negative' indicates a lack of these qualities, or implies a denial. Compare **affirmative/negative**, **plus/minus**, **proton/electron**.

positive organ/portative organ
In the Middle Ages, a 'positive organ' was a type of non-portable church organ with one manual and no pedals. A 'portative organ', as its name implies, was portable and had its air supplied by bellows worked by the player's arm. The 'positive organ' was so called as it occupied a fixed position in the church. See also **pipe organ/reed organ**.

positron see **electron**

possible/probable
'Possible' is generally used of something that may or may not happen, but that would cause little surprise if it did not. 'Probable', on the other hand, is more likely, and the thing that may or may not happen will cause considerable surprise if it does not. In sport, trial matches are sometimes organized between two sides, the 'probables' against the 'possibles', with the former being the stronger side and expected to win (and to be selected for the main competing team). The two words are sometimes combined to denote an extremely likely situation, or unlikely, when preceded with a negative word, as in Gilbert and Sullivan's *The Gondoliers*:

> Of that there is no manner of doubt –
> No probable, possible shadow of
> doubt –
> No possible doubt whatever.

posterior see **anterior**

postlude see **prelude**

poulard see **capon**

practice see **theory**

precentor/succentor
The terms are ecclesiastical titles. The 'precentor', in a cathedral, is the cleric who directs the choral services or who actually leads the singing in some parts of the services. The 'succentor' is his deputy, especially in cathedrals that have retained their statutes since before the Reformation. The Latin names mean literally 'leader singer' and 'deputy singer'. For more about cathedral singers, see **decani/cantoris**.

predecessor/successor
A person's 'predecessor' came before him, either as an ancestor or as a former holder of his office or position. His 'successor' is therefore the person who comes after him, whether a descendant or someone who will supersede him in his job or role. A 'predecessor' thus precedes, while a 'successor' succeeds!

preference shares see **ordinary shares**

prefix/suffix
A 'prefix' is a meaningful element attached to the front of a word or stem, so that the 'prefix' of 'prefix' is 'pre-', meaning 'before'. The suffix is the opposite, and comes at the end. The 'suffix' of 'motherhood' is '-hood', meaning 'condition of being (a mother)'. 'Prefix' can also be used of a name or title that precedes a person's main name, as for example the 'prefix' of 'Lord' in 'Lord Peter Pauly', or simply of

'Mr' or 'Mrs' in 'Mr John Brown', 'Mrs Mary Green'. 'Suffix' is not used to denote the opposite, as this does not occur in the same way. See also **enclitic/proclitic**.

preformation/epigenesis
In biology, 'preformation' was the theory (now discredited) that every egg contained a fully formed version of the adult creature in miniature, and that this simply grew in size when developing. 'Epigenesis' is by contrast the now widely accepted theory that an adult creature develops by the gradual differentiation of a single undifferentiated egg cell in such a way as to produce the creature's various parts. 'Epigenesis' literally means 'being born after'. The two terms first became prominent in English in the early nineteenth century.

prelude/postlude
A 'prelude' is a piece of music that precedes another, usually more important or longer than it, such as a fugue or suite or the act of an opera. An organ 'voluntary' is in effect a 'prelude' to the main organ music of a church service. A 'postlude', although a rare term, is a piece of music used to conclude or round off a work or performance, and in a church service is the 'voluntary' that is played as a final piece, while the choir processes out or the congregation leaves. The second half of the terms derives from Latin *ludere*, 'to play'. 'Prelude' can also be used generally of any preliminary or introductory event or action, such as the dispute between workers and management that is the 'prelude' to a strike. 'Postlude' is hardly used at all in a general way, although it can be a synonym for a spoken or written epilogue, otherwise an 'afterword'. See also **prologue/epilogue**.

premarital/extra-marital
Both words relate to something (usually sexual relations) that occur outside marriage. 'Premarital' refers to anything that happens before marriage; 'extra-marital' to something that occurs during a marriage but outside the ties and duties to a person's spouse, and so implies infidelity and (to put it crudely) 'a bit on the side'. It's simply a matter of prefixes, with 'pre-' meaning 'before' and 'extra-' meaning 'outside'.

premium see **discount**

prescriptive/descriptive
The two words are sometimes used of different types of dictionary. A 'prescriptive' dictionary tells the reader what he *should* say (spell, pronounce, etc.). A 'descriptive' dictionary gives the senses and usages of words and phrases as they actually are, without distinguishing 'good' from 'bad' English. In effect, almost all dictionaries are 'prescriptive', and contain guidance as to correct usage or at least indications that a particular word or phrase is 'less acceptable' (as *Chambers Twentieth Century Dictionary* says of the spelling 'alright' by comparison with 'all right').

present[1]/absent
The words may smack of school registers, but are correct to denote generally that something or someone either is or is not actually in a particular place. 'Present' frequently has overtones of satisfaction or happiness, while 'absent' can imply sadness or loss. (Compare 'the present company' and 'absent friends'.) As the proverb runs, 'Absence sharpens love, presence strengthens it'.

present[2]/past
The contrast between what is happening now and what has happened before has long intrigued us. How does the 'present' differ from the 'past', and how will it compare with the future? Perhaps it was T. S. Eliot who best encapsulated the eternal problem in the lines from *Burnt Norton*:

> Time present and time past
> Are both perhaps present in time
> future,
> And time future contained in time past.

More simply, the proverb reminds us that 'Things present are judged by things past', as indeed they have to be, since we have no other criterion. In grammar, the term 'present' is used of a verb that expresses what is happening now, and 'past' for what has happened earlier. Foreign learners of English find the 'present' fairly complex, as there are so many ways of expressing it, and we can say 'I play', 'I am playing', 'I have been playing', 'I do play' and so on to denote different types of action or time. (It is almost as bad in the 'past', with 'I played', 'I was playing', 'I have played', 'I used to play' and the like.)

presentationism/representationalism
These impressive terms, not surprisingly, are philosophical contrasts. 'Presentationism' is the theory that objects are identical with the way we perceive them, while 'representationalism' (or 'representationism') is the doctrine that objects are not identical with our perceptions of them but are either true copies of them or else representations that have been modified in our minds. The next time you see that tree or pass that house, think about it!

press-button telephone see **dial telephone**

primary[1]/historic
In Latin and Greek grammar, 'primary' is used of a tense that refers to present or future time, while 'historic' refers to a past tense. In Latin, therefore, it is the Present, Future Simple and Future Perfect tenses that are 'primary', and the Imperfect and Pluperfect that are 'historic'. The Perfect, however, can be either. When it means 'I have said' (*dixi*) it is 'primary', but when it means 'I said' it is 'historic'. This is because 'I have said' really relates to the state I am in now, at present. (When you say 'We have moved', you are thinking about your present new address, not the old one.) See also the next entry below.

primary[2]/secondary
The two words are frequently used to express contrasting or complementary things or concepts, with 'primary' indicating the greater or first. Among others, we thus have a 'primary' school for younger pupils, and a 'secondary' one for older students, 'primary' colours (red, green, blue) that can be combined to make other colours, and 'secondary' colours that are so made from them, a 'primary' electric cell that cannot be recharged, and a 'secondary' cell that can (like an accumulator), 'primary' processes in psychoanalysis, which are our unconscious thought processes (seen best in dreams), and 'secondary' processes, as our logical and conscious thoughts, and many others. Sometimes 'primary' does not have a contrasting 'secondary', as with the American 'primaries', or elections in which local candidates are selected for political office, with the ensuing major elections simply known as the 'final' ones.

prime cost see **overheads**

prime number/composite number
A 'prime number' is one (apart from 1) that cannot be divided by any other number, but only by itself and 1, such as 2, 3, 7 and 11. The converse of this is a 'composite number', that can be divided by other numbers, such as 4, 6, 9, 10, 12. All 'prime numbers' apart from 2 are thus odd numbers, but 'composite numbers' can be odd or even.

primo/secondo
The two Italian words (meaning 'first' and 'second') are most common in music written for piano duet, where 'primo' indicates the upper or right-hand part, and 'secondo' denotes the lower or left-hand part. Although the 'primo' will necessarily often have the 'tune', a well-balanced duet will give both players an equally important contribution, so that the left-hand player need not feel 'secondary' in any subordinate sense.

primogeniture/ultimogeniture
In law, 'primogeniture' is the right by which an eldest son succeeds to the estate of his ancestor, to the exclusion of everybody else. The opposite of this, much less commonly, is 'ultimogeniture', whereby it is the youngest son that succeeds. The terms literally mean 'first birth' and 'last

birth', denoting the eldest and youngest sons respectively. Compare **patriarch/matriarch**.

prince/princess
Both the male and the female title are common in many royal families for a descendant of the sovereign, respectively, with 'princess' also used for the wife of a 'prince'. In general use, 'prince' can apply to any person of high standing in his class or profession, such as a 'merchant prince', while 'princess' is mostly reserved for a very beautiful and graceful woman or girl, although it can likewise be used of talent, as a 'princess of the stage' who is a gifted actress. Reflecting the 'physical' side of the title, a 'prince' can similarly be a handsome young man, as the pantomime hero 'Prince Charming' is (see, by coincidence, the next entry below).

princess see **prince**

principal boy/dame
The 'principal boy' is the chief character in the English pantomime, although traditionally acted by a woman. Similarly, the 'dame' is a leading comic female character in the pantomime, although traditionally played by a man. Apart from these double gender opposites, there is a further contrast in the two characters, as the 'principal boy' is a handsome young man, while the 'dame' is an unprepossessing elderly woman, representing either the mother of the 'principal boy' or one of a pair of so-called 'ugly sisters'. Well-known 'principal boys' are the characters of Aladdin, Dick Whittington, Robinson Crusoe, Idle Jack (in 'Jack and the Beanstalk') and Prince Charming (in 'Cinderella'). Familiar 'dames' are Aladdin's mother Widow Twankey, Idle Jack's mother Dame Trot (or sometimes Dame Durden), and Cinderella's 'ugly sisters', who go by a variety of absurd paired names (e.g. Hugga and Holda or Popsy and Mopsy). Recently, however, the 'principal boy' has come to be played increasingly by a male actor, often a television personality or pop star, although the 'dame' is still mostly played by a man, if only a recognizable comic 'in drag'. The title of 'principal boy' is rightly subconsciously associated with 'prince', and indeed in 'Cinderella' he actually *is* a 'prince'. (It is worth remembering, too, that in 'Beauty and the Beast' – a contrasting pair if ever there was one – the Beast turns into a 'prince' in the happy ending.) See also the entry above.

print/transparency
A photographic 'print' is a positive image in black and white or colour produced on paper from a negative film, that is, it is the standard 'snap'. A 'transparency' or 'slide', by contrast, although also a positive photograph, is reproduced on a transparent base as a film that can be projected on to a screen. Outwardly, it resembles a negative, although as stated it is actually positive. (The German word for a 'transparency' is *Diapositiv*, serving as a reminder of its positive quality.) See also **positive/negative**, **colour/black and white**, **transparent/opaque**.

private/NHS
These two colloquial abbreviations are used to denote the contrasting types of medical and surgical treatment available in Britain. Most people are 'NHS', or receive their treatment through the state-provided National Health Service, where treatment is free, but a fixed charge is made for medicines and certain appliances and services. 'Private' means that the patient pays to receive his treatment, either from a 'private' doctor, in a 'private' hospital, or in some other specialist but fee-paying centre such as a clinic or nursing home. The treatment either way can be equally good, although 'private' implies that lengthy waiting can be avoided, either to see a doctor or to occupy a hospital bed. A growing number of people are taking out insurance to enable them to 'go private', however, partly for convenience, partly because 'NHS' treatment and standards have in some instances been below par or have involved lengthy delays. See also **public/private** and, if necessary, **medical/surgical**.

private see (1) **public** (2) **state**

privatization see **nationalization**

pro¹/anti
In any argument or dispute or discussion, there will be a 'pro' side, in favour, and an 'anti' side, against, and in any debatable or controversial matter one can be either 'pro' or 'anti', e.g. 'pro' corporal punishment or 'anti' it, 'pro' nuclear disarmament or 'anti' it. The words are simply Latin for 'for' and 'against'. Compare the pair of opposites in the next entry, which have rather a different usage.

pro²/con
The two words are probably used the most frequently in the expression 'pros and cons', meaning the points for and against something, the advantages and disadvantages. When travelling abroad, you might therefore need to consider the 'pros and cons' of plane as against train, or weigh up the 'pros and cons' of buying a television set instead of renting one. Some of the entries in this book consider the 'pros and cons' of the two contrasts, e.g. **gas/ electricity**.

proactive/retroactive
In psychology, 'proactive' inhibition is the tendency for a person's early memories to interfere with recent ones, when the latter need to be recalled for factual reasons. 'Retroactive' inhibition is thus the opposite, and means that the keen attention given to something new that is learned may impede the recall of material learned earlier. All students are aware of both phenomena.

probable see **possible**

processed peas/garden peas
Most people know that 'garden peas' are the 'real' ones. But how real are they? Are they really fresh from the garden? They always were originally. Today, however, the term, like that of 'processed peas' is simply commercial jargon for a type of canned peas. 'Processed peas' are dried peas that have been soaked to bring them back as much as possible to their original size before they go through the same canning procedure as 'garden peas', which themselves are peas that have been canned when they are fresh. So the only true 'garden peas' are those you pick in your garden.

prochronism/metachronism
These two terms are sometimes used as alternatives to the pair of **anachronism/ parachronism**, otherwise dating an event too early, or too late. For another relevant entry on this, see **parachronism/prochronism**. 'Pro-' means 'before', and 'meta-' means 'after'.

prochronism see **parachronism**

proclitic see **enclitic**

produce see **get**

producer/director
In the making of a film or television programme, the 'producer' is the person who is responsible for the administrative side of things, especially the finance, but also the casting and filming schedules. The 'director', on the other hand, is responsible for the artistic side of things and for ensuring that the actual process of filming goes ahead in the way it should. In short, the 'director' tells the cast and cameramen what to do to make the film, while the 'producer' gives him the facilities and backing to do this. In the theatre, the British usage was formerly to call the person responsible for the actual staging of the play the 'producer', but now the American custom of calling him the 'director' has been adopted. Most of the financial side, on the other hand, is handled in Britain by the manager (but the 'producer' in America, as for films).

producer see **consumer**

profane see **sacred**

professional see **amateur**

profit/loss

In accounting, whether commercially or privately, the 'profit' is the excess of income or earnings over expenditure, while the 'loss' is the opposite, the undesirable excess of expenditure over income. A business or company normally issues an annual or more frequent 'statement of accounts', showing if it has made a 'profit' or a 'loss' over the period, and usually comparing the figures to those of the previous year or period.

programme music/absolute music

'Programme music' is classical music that is composed with the aim of conjuring up a particular scene or 'picture'. The term originated with Liszt in the nineteenth century, although 'programme music' itself existed long before this. Examples include Couperin's eighteenth-century harpsichord pieces with titles such as 'The Frightened Linnet' and 'Mountebanks with their Bears and Monkeys', as well as later compositions such as much of Beethoven's 'Pastoral' Symphony. 'Absolute music' is therefore 'pure' music, where the composer has no special pictorial or literary scene in mind. Examples include Bach's preludes and fugues and Mozart's sonatas. Even so, some 'absolute music' may evoke *some* scenes or emotions in the listener's mind, so the terms are really rather subjective.

progressive/regressive

Generally, 'progressive' means 'moving forwards' and 'regressive' means 'moving backwards'. There are one or two specialized usages, however, such as 'progressive' tax, which is heavier in proportion for the rich (perhaps rightly), and 'regressive' tax, which is heavier in relation to their incomes for the poor.

progressivism/essentialism

In education, 'progressivism' is the doctrine that emphasizes the importance of the child as an individual, of informality in the learning environment, and of the encouragement of self-expression, in other words, what is known as 'progressive education'. 'Essentialism', by contrast, concentrates on traditional methods, with an emphasis on the acquiring of an 'essential' basic but comprehensive knowledge of the culture of a particular country. 'Progressivism' is still regarded as suspect or even 'cranky' by some, while many people cannot envisage education in terms other than that of 'essentialism'.

prolate/oblate

'Prolate', of a spheroid object, means that it has a polar diameter greater than that at the equator, while 'oblate' means that it is flattened at the poles, so that its equatorial diameter is greater. Our Earth is an 'oblate' sphere, since its diameter at the poles is 7900 miles (12,713 km), but at the equator is 7926½ miles (12,756 km).

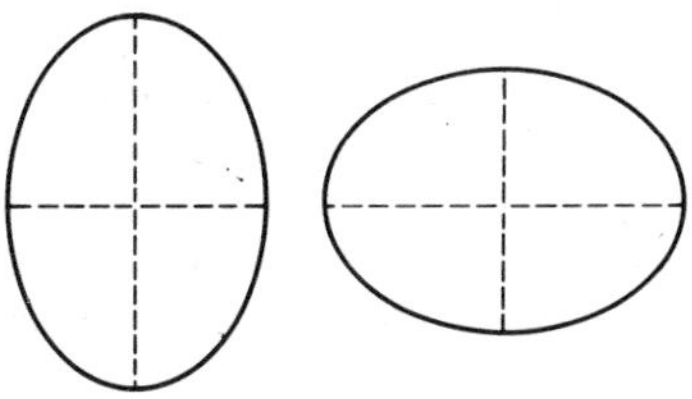

prologue/epilogue

In its most literary form, a 'prologue' is a passage that introduces a play, where it traditionally occurred in seventeenth- and eighteenth-century drama as a 'chorus' (actually spoken by one person). Perhaps the best-known example of a 'prologue' in English literature is the one that opens Chaucer's *Canterbury Tales*, beginning with the fine poetic lines evoking an English spring:

> Whanne that Aprille with his shoures sote [i.e. sweet]
> The droghte of Marche hath perced to the rote [root].

Conversely, therefore, an 'epilogue' closes a play, or ends a fable (giving its moral). A dramatic one usually asks the audience to approve the play they have just seen, and aims to dismiss them in an agreeable frame of mind. There is a short 'epilogue' at the end of Shakespeare's *All's Well That*

Ends Well, where the King of France speaks six rhyming lines, of which the final two are:

> Ours be your patience then, and yours our parts;
> Your gentle hands lend us, and take our hearts.
>
> [*Exeunt*.

promisee/promisor
In contract law, a 'promisee' is a person to whom a promise is made, and a 'promisor' is the person who makes that promise. The two endings '-ee' and '-or' (or '-er') are also found in other instances, such as **mortgagee/mortgagor**, and 'employee' and 'employer'. See also Appendix I, p. 289.

promisor see **promisee**

prompt/OP
These two terms are theatrical jargon for the two sides of the stage, left and right. 'Prompt' refers to the prompter, who in Britain traditionally sits off the left side of the stage, but in the United States off the right (i.e. from the point of view of an actor facing the audience). 'OP' means 'opposite prompt', and therefore denotes the opposite side, right in Britain, left in the USA. However, 'left' and 'right' are regularly used also in stage directions, such as 'exit left' or 'enter right'. See also **upstage/downstage**.

prone/supine
When used narrowly, 'prone' means 'lying face downwards', 'prostrate', while 'supine' means 'lying on the back, face upwards'. However, 'prone' can also be used, as 'prostrate' can, to mean merely 'lying flat', whether face down or on one's back. The Latin origins show the true positions, however, since 'prone' comes from *pronus*, 'bent forward', and 'supine' from *supinus*, 'face upwards'. (The Latin grammatical 'supine' that is a type of verbal noun also derives from this, although why the noun should be 'face upwards' is difficult to see. Perhaps in some way it was regarded to be *sub* or 'under' the grammatical influence of an accompanying word.) In physiology, to 'pronate' is to turn the palm of the hand downwards, and to 'supinate' is to turn it upwards.

proper see **ordinary**

proprietary/ethical
In medicine, 'proprietary' is the term used of a drug that is made and sold under a trade name, and especially one that is available to the general public as a 'patent medicine'. An 'ethical' drug, however, is one that is available to the public only by means of a doctor's prescription, whether under a trade name or not. (It is 'ethical' since it conforms to professional standards.) Moreover, 'proprietary' medicines are widely advertised to the public, but 'ethical' preparations are advertised only to the medical profession.

prose/unseen
Until quite recently, the two terms were used in academic language teaching to denote respectively a passage translated from English into the foreign language, such as a 'French prose' or even a 'Latin prose', and one translated into English from an unprepared foreign text, such as a 'Latin unseen' or a 'French unseen'. 'Prose' implies a composition in prose as the standard written language (not verse), while 'unseen' indicates a text that is not from a prepared literary work or 'set book'. The terms particularly applied to examinations.

prose see **poetry**

prosecution/defence
In a criminal court of law, the 'prosecution' is a collective term for the lawyers who are putting the case against a person on trial. The 'defence' thus comprises the defendant (see **plaintiff/defendant** for civil cases) and his legal advisers, who may seek to prove either that the defendant did not commit the crime, or that there were special circumstances that prompted him to.

protagonist see **antagonist**

protasis see **apododis**

Protestant see **Catholic**

proton/electron
Both a 'proton' and an 'electron' are elementary physical particles, as parts of an atom. The 'proton' carries a positive charge, and is in the nucleus of the atom, together with neutrons (except in hydrogen, where it *is* the nucleus). It is 1830 times as heavy as an 'electron'. The 'electron' thus has a negative charge, and moves in an orbit around the nucleus, where it is the part of the atom that engages in chemical reactions. 'Proton' means 'first' in Greek, presumably implying that 'positive' comes before 'negative'. However, the *Supplement* to the *Oxford English Dictionary* suggests that the word may have been prompted by the name of William Prout, the English chemist and physicist who first propounded in the early nineteenth century that hydrogen was a constituent of all the elements. 'Proton' is first recorded later than 'electron', which is itself based on 'electric'. See also **electron/positron**, **element/compound**, **positive/negative**.

Provisional IRA/Official IRA
The 'Provisional IRA', or 'Provos', has been the name since 1969 of the faction of the Irish Republican Army (the organization of militant nationalists) and Sinn Féin (the republic political party linked to it) that traditionally pursues a policy of terrorism in order to achieve unity in Ireland. The 'Official IRA', on the other hand, places more emphasis on political rather than guerrilla activity. (It is not Marxist, like the 'Provisional IRA', but merely 'good Catholic'.) The IRA itself arose in the late nineteenth century, and Sinn Féin (Irish for 'we ourselves') in the early twentieth.

proximal see **distal**

psychosis/neurosis
A 'psychosis' is a type of severe mental disorder in which a person's contact with reality becomes distorted or even lost altogether. An example of such a condition is schizophrenia. A 'neurosis' is a relatively mild nervous disorder, without any disease of the nervous system, in which a person's normal life is made difficult because of obsessions, phobias, anxiety and the like. A 'psychoneurosis' is not a blend of the two, but a special type of 'neurosis' in which a person's 'inner conflict' affects his or her normal behaviour.

Ptolemaic system/Copernican system
The two systems contain the respective names of their propounders. Ptolemy was the second-century A.D. Greek astronomer who held that the Earth lay at the centre of the universe, and that the Sun, Moon and known planets revolved round it. Copernicus (the latinized name of Mikołaj Kopernik) was the sixteenth-century Polish astronomer who in 1543 published his thesis that overthrew Ptolemy's views, and which stated that the Earth and planets rotated round the Sun. His 'heretical' work was placed on the 'Index Librorum Prohibitorum' ('list of banned books') by the Roman Catholic Church until 1835. See also **geocentric/heliocentric**.

public/private
Almost every individual's life revolves round what is 'public', or accessible to everybody (at least in theory), and what is 'private', or particular to himself. There is thus a 'public highway', that all may travel on, and 'private property', to which only the owner or specially named persons have access. However, there are some special instances of 'public' and 'private', and also some anomalies. A 'public company', for example, is a company whose shares can be purchased by the 'public' and traded on the open market, while a 'private' company does not issue shares for 'public' subscription. (See also **Ltd/plc**.) Similarly, 'public enterprise' is a term for a nationalized organization of some kind, while a 'private enterprise' is one that is not run by the state but is in 'private' ownership. (See also **nationalization/privatization**, **state/private**.)

However, a 'public school' is not normally (at least in England) a state one, and is so called because it is owned by a publicly accountable trust.

pull see **push**

pulp magazine see **glossy magazine**

pure/applied
'Pure' mathematics or 'pure' science is so called since it is studied for its theoretical aspects rather than its practical application. It follows that an 'applied' science or other discipline is one studied so that it can be put to practical use. Compare **theory/practice**.

purl/plain
In knitting, a 'purl' stitch is a basic one that is the opposite of a 'plain' stitch. A 'purl' stitch is when 'knots' are formed on the front of the row being knitted, while a 'plain' stitch produces a knot on the back. (In the 'plain' stitch, the right needle is put through a loop on the left needle from the front to the back; in the 'purl' it is inserted from the back to the front.) 'Purl' comes from an old dialect word meaning 'twist'.

plain

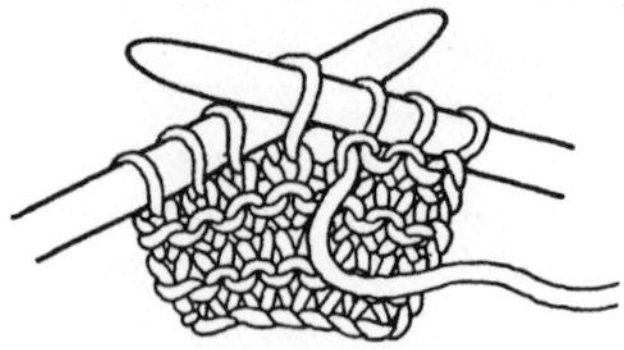

purl

push/pull
The two opposing ways of moving or transporting something (or someone), familiar from their use in written directions on doors. (Visitors to Russia need to learn that the equivalents for 'PUSH' and 'PULL' are 'OT SEBYA', literally 'from oneself' and 'K SEBE', that is, 'towards oneself'.) A 'push-pull' device is an arrangement of electronic components, such as valves or transistors, giving an alternating input and so sending an electric current through a load alternately, with such a current called a 'push-pull' circuit. A 'pushme-pullyou' is a policy or attitude that vacillates or lacks coherence. The name derives from a weird creature like a llama with a head at both ends that appears in Hugh Lofting's *Doctor Dolittle* books (where he spelt them as 'pushmi-pullyus'). These archetypes became popular from the film *Doctor Dolittle* released in 1967. Finally, from the mid-1980s (and hardly yet recorded in the dictionary), a 'push-pull' came to be a colloquial term for a free local advertising newspaper, so called because the person who delivers the paper usually 'pushes' it halfway through the letter-box, leaving the occupant of the house to 'pull' it right through.

put see **call**

putt see **drive**

Qq

Q-Celtic see **P-Celtic**

quadrangle/court
The words are those used for the college courtyards at, respectively, Oxford and Cambridge, with 'quadrangle' often shortened to 'quad'. The design and layout of the courtyards is basically similar at both universities, in the main consisting of a grass lawn with footpaths running round it and sometimes across it. 'Quadrangle', as a word of Latin (and mathematical) origin, is apt for a university that has a reputation for classics, and 'court', similarly, is a suitable and functionally brief term for a university famed for its science and 'progressiveness'. See also **Oxford/ Cambridge**.

quadrivium/trivium
The terms designate the twofold division of the seven liberal arts in medieval times. The 'quadrivium', which were more advanced, comprised the mathematical sciences, i.e. arithmetic, geometry, astronomy and music. The 'trivium' consisted of grammar, logic and rhetoric. The former thus approximates to our modern 'sciences', while the latter is closer to the 'arts'. 'Quadrivium' literally means 'meeting of four ways' (otherwise 'crossroads'), while 'trivium' means 'meeting of three ways'. It was the latter Latin word that gave modern English 'trivial', the allusion being to something that is discussed in public at the crossroads.

qualitative/quantitative
In scientific or technical usage, 'qualitative' relates to distinctions or measurements based on quality, while 'quantitative' involves considerations of size and amount. In chemistry, for example, 'qualitative' analysis implies the analysis or breaking down of a compound into its elements in order to establish what those elements are, while 'quantitative' analysis aims to find out the amount of each element or constituent.

quality paper/popular paper
The expressions are used for the two basic divisions of English newspapers into 'serious' or 'upmarket' (for the 'discerning reader') and 'undemanding' or 'downmarket' (for the reader who seeks entertainment and titillation rather than sober opinion and detailed facts). The 'popular papers' (also known by some as 'the gutter press', for their interest in sensational news stories and scandals) have a much larger circulation than the 'quality papers' (which are also known as 'the heavies', for their weighty views and even larger size). The 'popular papers', too, are still mainly tabloids, while the 'quality papers' are broadsheets (see **broadsheet/tabloid**). In the late 1980s, the division between the 'qualities' and the 'populars', was as follows, with the order that of the newspapers' foundation ('D' means 'daily paper', 'S' means 'Sunday paper', where this is not obvious from the title): 'Qualities': *The Times* (D), *The Observer* (S), *The Guardian* (D), *Sunday Times*, *Daily Telegraph*, *Financial Times* (D), *Sunday Telegraph*, *The Independent* (D); 'Populars': *News of the World* (S), *The People* (S), *Daily Mail*, *Daily Express*, *Daily Mirror*, *Sunday Express*, *Sunday Mirror*, *The Sun* (D), *Morning Star*, *The Star* (D), *Mail on Sunday*, *Today* (D), *Sunday Sport*, *News on Sunday*.

quarto/folio
At their most basic, 'quarto' denotes a book size obtained by folding a sheet of paper into four, and 'folio' a size obtained by folding a sheet into two. The words themselves derive from New Latin *in quarto*, 'in quarter' and *in folio*, 'in leaf'. As

applied to the works of Shakespeare, his earliest plays are described as either 'quartos' or 'folios' according to the folding of the printed sheets, with the 'folios' being large tall volumes and the 'quartos' being relatively small, square books. (If a sheet of paper is folded into eight, the resulting size is called 'octavo', abbreviated '8vo', and if into 16, it is known as 'sixteenmo', or more correctly 'sextodecimo', abbreviated as '16mo'.)

quantitative see **qualitative**

queen see **king**

question/answer
From ecclesiastical catechism to school examination and everyday conversation, there have long been 'questions' in our lives that sought an 'answer'. ('Sought' is right here, as 'question' derives from Latin *quaerere*, 'to seek'. 'Answer' is a good Old English word related to 'swear'.) However, some 'questions' have no 'answer', such as Pontius Pilate's 'What is truth?' and nonsensical ones such as 'What is the difference between a duck?' The phrase 'Like question, like answer' implies that a strange or unusual 'question' must be expected to have an equally unusual 'answer'. See the next entry below.

question mark/exclamation mark
The 'question mark' or 'interrogation mark' (or simply 'query') is the sign ('?') that denotes a question, while the 'exclamation mark', or 'note of admiration' as it was formerly called, is the sign ('!') that indicates an emphatic answer or denotes a statement specially worthy of notice for some reason. The former thus requires information; the latter vigorously supplies it. The two signs have been adopted for some specialist uses outside those of normal punctuation, and have likewise acquired colloquial or jargonistic names, such as 'shriek' or 'bang' for an 'exclamation mark'. Of all the quotations using the signs, probably the best known, and certainly the briefest, is that of the letter sent by the French author Victor Hugo to his publishers, Hurst and Blackett, in 1862 to ask how his novel *Les Misérables* was selling, and the publishers' reply. Hugo wrote '?'. His publishers replied '!'.

quick/slow
As distinct from **fast/slow** (which see), the pair 'quick' and 'slow' are used more of a regular action, such as a 'quick' pace or a 'slow' one. In dancing, too, the teacher traditionally calls 'slow, slow, quick, quick, slow', and of progress at school one says that one child is 'quick' to learn, but that another is 'slow'. In a broader sense, therefore, a person can be 'slow' to scold and 'quick' to forgive (or the other way round, alas).

quote/unquote
The two words came to be used in a dictation to denote the start and finish of a quoted passage, i.e. one to be written in quotation marks. Later, the pair were used in everyday speech to quote a real or imaginary word or phrase in the middle of a sentence, for example, 'We stayed at a quote Queen Elizabeth slept here unquote hotel'.

QWERTY/DSK
For many years, the keyboard layout of a standard English language typewriter has had a top line of letters beginning 'QWERTY'. This non-alphabetic arrangement was devised in the 1870s by the American inventor Christopher L. Sholes with the aim of separating keys that jammed when struck at speed. In effect, he was thus slowing typists down. By the mid-1980s, however, with the prominence of electric and electronic typewriters and word processors, it clearly became desirable to find a new arrangement of letters that would be more conducive to speedy typing. The new layout was devised by an American psychologist, August Dvorak, whose 'DSK' ('Dvorak Simplified Keyboard') placed all five vowels on the centre row, together with the five most common consonants, so that they lay right under the fingers of the typist. 'DSK' has not yet even begun to supersede 'QWERTY', but it seems likely to. For

comparison, here are the two keyboard layouts (slightly simplified):
'QWERTY':

1 2 3 4 5 6 7 8 9 0 - =
Q W E R T Y U I O P ½
A S D F G H J K L ; :
Z X C V B N M , . ?

'DSK':

1 2 3 4 5 6 7 8 9 0 =
" , . P Y F G C R L ?
A O E U I D H T N S ·
Q J K X B M W V Z

Perhaps this will come to be known as the 'PYF' keyboard, rather than the 'DSK'? Note that the latter finally abolishes all fractions and substitutes the decimal point. See also **electronic/electric**.

Rr

rabbit/hare
Both animals are quite closely related, but a 'rabbit' is smaller than a 'hare' and has shorter ears. Moreover, baby 'rabbits' are born without any fur, while young 'hares' have fur on their bodies when they are born. As a third distinction, 'rabbits' live under the earth in burrows, while 'hares' inhabit nests of grass on the surface of the earth, where their homes are known as 'forms'. More of a contrast comes in the custom still observed by some young children of saying the word 'hares' last thing at night on the last day of the month, and 'rabbits' as the first word in the morning of the first day of the month. The origin of this is not clear. For another contrast, compare **hare/tortoise**.

rabi see **kharif**

radial/cross-ply
The terms describe the two main contrasting types of motor tyres. 'Radial' tyres, which are designed for faster speeds and are longer lasting than 'cross-ply', have internal cords that are laid at right-angles to the centre line of the tread. They are thus like 'radii' from it as they go round the tyre. 'Cross-ply' tyres, on the other hand, have cords that are bonded crosswise so as to strengthen the tread. The outer casing is thus more flexible in a 'radial' tyre, and more rigid in a 'cross-ply' one. 'Radial' tyres are now mostly superseding 'cross-ply'.

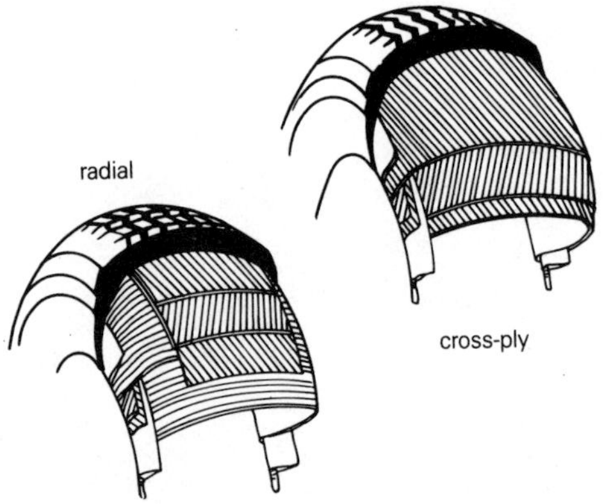

radial symmetry/bilateral symmetry
'Radial symmetry' is a term used of an organism (or part of an organism) that, when cut vertically through its axis in two or more planes, will give halves that are mirror images of each other. By contrast, 'bilateral symmetry' means that the mirror images will occur only if the organism is cut in one plane. 'Radial symmetry' is thus so called since it applies to creatures where

parts of the body 'radiate' from a central axis, such as starfish and jellyfish. 'Bilateral symmetry' relates specifically to creatures where the cut would have to be made down the middle ('head to tail') to give the two sides. Most animals are like this, even where internal organs are asymmetrical, as in man.

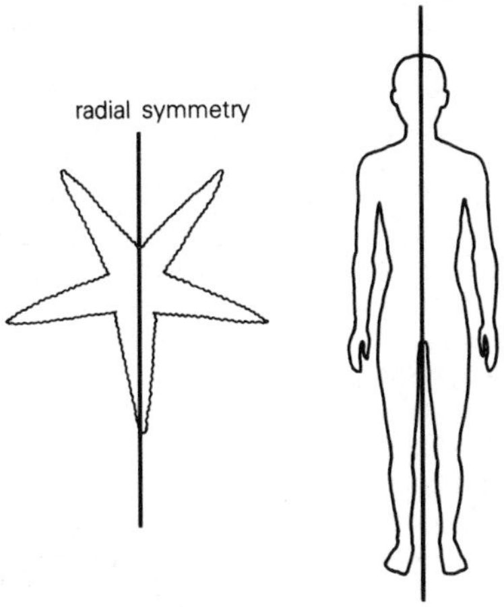

radio/TV

Undoubtedly, 'TV' is the more popular medium, with much of 'radio' used simply as 'background' when the listener is doing something else, such as working or driving. Clearly, too, the visual impact of 'TV' is much more 'real' and vivid than a medium which relies on one sense only, that of hearing. On the other hand, 'radio' can produce mental pictures that are much more vivid than any 'TV', since they are produced within our own imagination and are much more part of us. (In this sense, they can be regarded as relatively 'active', while 'TV' images are received by viewers in a more or less 'passive' frame of mind.) The contrast between the two media is marked when it comes to the recounting of a major disaster. 'TV' pictures can make us feel like indecent voyeurs, while 'radio' listeners can interpret and even tone down the news to suit their own degree of acceptability, as when reading such news in a newspaper. Discussing this aspect of the media in *The Times* (19 October 1985), Philip Howard wrote that television was 'a medium of irrationality and emotion compared with radio and the written word', and this points to another contrast between the two. 'TV' is much more 'unpredictable' than the controlled medium of 'radio'.

radius/ulna

The names are those of the two bones of the forearm. The 'radius' is the outer and shorter of the two; the 'ulna' the inner and longer. The words come straight from Latin, with 'radius' meaning 'staff', 'spoke', and seen as the main bone of the two, while 'ulna' literally means 'elbow', since the bone extends from the elbow to the wrist.

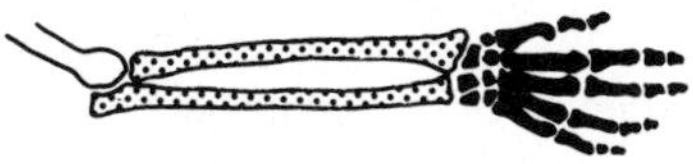

rail/road

For the main differences between travel by 'rail' or by 'road', see the contrasting pair **bus/train**. The two alliterative words are popular with advertisers when promoting transport or travel by one or the other (e.g. 'It's quicker by rail' or 'It's cheaper by road'), although British Rail itself combines the two words in what it calls its 'rail-road links', meaning sections of a route where the passenger *has* to travel by 'road' to get to a particular town or point since there is no 'rail' station there. (Some quite large towns in Britain now have no railway stations, and if you want to travel, say, to Buckingham by 'rail' from London, the best you can do is go to Bletchley, and then complete the final twelve miles of the journey by 'road'.) In the United States, 'railroad' is the term for the British 'railway' (although originally British 'railways' were also known as 'railroads').

raise/lower
The two opposites are familiar from a number of everyday phrases, where to 'raise' an object is usually to initiate an action or make a communication of some kind, and to 'lower' it is to cease an action or complete a communication. For example, a person will 'raise' his hand to convey a message of some kind ('Stop', 'I wish to vote', 'Here I am', 'Please, teacher . . .'), will 'raise' a flag on a ship to send a signal, will 'raise' a sail on a boat to proceed on a course or to alter it, and will 'raise' the gas in order to cook a meal. A person will 'raise' her eyes to look up at someone or something, and 'lower' them in order not to look, or because the act of looking has finished. The general connotation of 'raise' and 'lower' is that provided by the pair **high/low**, or **up/down**.

rajah/rani
A 'rani' (or 'ranee') is a Hindu queen or princess, and especially the wife of a 'rajah'. Similarly, a 'maharani' is the wife of a 'maharajah', who himself is a Hindu prince ranking higher than a 'rajah'. 'Rajah' derives ultimately from a Sanskrit word meaning 'king' (to which English 'royal' is related), and 'rani' is the feminine form of this. The 'maha-' of the two more elevated titles means 'great'. (Hence also the title 'mahatma', which means 'great souled'.) English 'much' is indirectly related to 'maha-'.

ram/ewe
A 'ram' is a male sheep, technically an uncastrated male one (a castrated sheep is called a 'wether'). A 'ewe' is an adult female sheep. The 'ram' gave its name to the battering 'ram', because the sheep is known for its ability to butt hard with its head. However, 'ewe' is a more general word for a sheep linguistically, since it is related to Latin *ovis* and hence English 'ovine', meaning 'sheeplike'. 'Rams' are known as much for their strong sexual drive as their butting, hence the reference in Shakespeare's *Othello*, when Iago wakes Brabantio to warn him (referring to the Moor, Othello, and Brabantio's daughter, Desdemona) that:

> Even now, now, very now, an old black ram
> Is tupping your white ewe.

Rangers see **Celtic**

rani see **rajah**

rank/file
The phrase 'rank and file', meaning 'the great majority', 'most people', is so common that we tend to overlook the fact that 'rank' and 'file' are individual military terms of contrast. As applied to soldiers drawn up on parade, for example, a 'rank' is a line of soldiers standing abreast, next to one another, while a 'file' is a line of soldiers behind one another, in marching formation. Moreover, 'rank and file' is itself a military term contrasting with 'officers', since it means the ordinary soldiers. 'Rank' and 'file' also serve as contrasting terms in the game of chess, with 'rank' denoting one of the eight horizontal rows of squares, and 'file' one of the eight vertical rows. Chess, after all, represents the strategy and tactics of a military battle, with the pawns the infantrymen and the knights on horseback as 'cavalry'. (See **cavalry/infantry** for a development of this theme.)

rare see **well-done**

rave see **slam**

raw/cooked
Most foods are divided into those that are eaten 'raw' (i.e. uncooked) and those that need to be 'cooked'. Some vegetables, especially salad plants, are almost always eaten 'raw', such as cress and lettuce. Much fruit is also eaten 'raw' especially strawberries and citrus fruits, such as oranges and grapefruit. But even these *can* be 'cooked', and some fruits have two distinct categories or kinds, one for eating 'raw' and one for eating only 'cooked'. For an example, see **cooking apple/eating apple**. Meat is virtually always eaten 'cooked', although some steaks, when very

rare, are almost nearer a 'raw' steak than a 'cooked' one. (A 'smoked' food, such as fish, is one that has been cured by exposure to smoke.)

read/write
'Reading' and 'writing' are normally regarded as complementary activities, since in 'reading' we are being communicated to, by someone who has 'written', and in 'writing' we are ourselves communicating, so that someone else will 'read' our words. The two combined indicate that we are literate, and traditionally, when 'reading' and 'writing' are combined with 'arithmetic' we have the 'three Rs' ('reading, 'riting, 'rithmetic'), and a person who is competent at all three is both literate and numerate, or basically educated. (See **literate/numerate**.) 'Read' and 'write' are also contrasting terms in operating computers, for when a computer 'reads' information it takes it from its memory, where it will have been stored or 'written' by the operator. For a somewhat similar contrast in music, see **sight-read/play by ear**. Compare also the next entry below.

reader/writer
The terms denote even more clearly the people who perform the contrasting acts expressed by 'read' and 'write', as outlined in the entry above. 'Readers' are thus people who take in what 'writers' have to say to them, and 'writers' write so that they can communicate to their 'readers', of whom you, dear 'reader', are one. However, some see the distinction as an increasingly blurred one, as does the following 'writer' and poet:

> There used to be writers and readers
> So readers would profit from writers
> And writers would profit from readers
> But the latter learnt more from the
> former
> Than the former could learn from the
> latter
> So the readers then became writers
> And the writers no longer had readers.

(D. J. Enright, 'Short Thoughts', from *Instant Chronicles*, 1985)

reality see **appearance**

real property see **personal property**

real wages see **nominal wages**

rear see **front**

rearguard see **vanguard**

receiver see **transmitter**

record/cassette
The contrast here needs to be considered from two angles. For sound only, a 'record' (or 'disc') will usually give better reproduction, since it has a greater surface (played by stylus) for electronic information to be retrieved than a 'cassette' tape. On the other hand, 'cassettes' are generally handier than 'records' and can be played on portable instruments. But 'records' have had the marked edge in quality since the appearance of the compact disc (in 1983), as the latter plays longer, lasts longer, and has eliminated almost all 'surface noise'. (The difference between a compact disc and a conventional one is actually that between 'digital' and 'analogue': see **analogue/digital**.) Then, when it comes to both sound and vision, there are video 'cassettes' and video 'records' (or 'discs', as they are more usually called) to consider. Discs are less bulky than tapes, and produce a better quality of sound, as the LP 'record' did when compared to the original 'cassette'. However, at present it is not possible to re-record on a video disc, as one can on a video 'cassette'. Compare **audio/video** for a similar dichotomy.

recorded see **live**[2]

recto/verso
In printing and publishing, 'recto' is the term used for the right-hand pages of a book, i.e. the ones with the odd numbers. 'Verso' is therefore used for the left-hand pages, bearing the even numbers. The words come from the respective Latin phrases *in recto folio*, 'on the right-hand page', and *verso folio*, 'the page having been

turned'. See, as required, **odd/even**, **left/right**, **quarto/folio**.

rector see **vicar**

red[1]/black
The most obvious contrast here is in the expressions 'in the red', meaning 'overdrawn' (of a bank account), 'in debit', and 'in the black', meaning 'having funds', 'in credit'. The terms refer to the different coloured inks used for recording the relevant 'debit' and 'credit' figures. 'Red' and 'black', too, are the two contrasting colours of a gaming board, the 'rouge' and the 'noir', with even bets placed on either. (The French writer Françoise Sagan recorded in her autobiography *With Fondest Regards* how she always, when gambling, preferred 'black' to 'red', odd numbers to even, and low numbers to high.) French 'rouge' and 'noir' are a reminder that the colours are also those represented in Stendhal's famous novel *Le Rouge et le Noir*, where the 'rouge' stands for the army (and the blood shed in battle) and the 'noir' is the church (the colour of a priest's cassock). (However, other literary experts say that the 'rouge' of the title represents republicanism, and that the 'noir' stands for the forces of clerical reaction, so the precise interpretation remains somewhat uncertain.) Finally, as a less contrived contrast, one should note the 'redcurrant' and the 'blackcurrant', respectively *Ribes rubrum* and *Ribres nigrum*. The former of these is the more acid, and the latter the sweeter. Both can be used for making jelly, however. For more on the gaming board 'red', see **manque/passe**.

red[2]/blue
'Red' and 'blue' occur as contrasting colours in certain contexts, with probably the most common being 'red' to indicate 'hot' and 'blue' to indicate 'cold', especially on water taps. In politics, 'red' is the colour of the Labour Party, and 'blue' that of the Conservatives. The former has the socialist connection that the Communist 'red flag' has, i.e. blood shed in a worthy cause, and the latter is the colour of constancy, itself perhaps referring to the 'blue' of the sky or the sea, or even to some constant dye. In sport, the two opposite corners in a boxing ring are 'red' and 'blue', and in chemistry, a 'red' litmus paper (indicator strip) denotes the presence of an acid, while a 'blue' paper indicates an alkali.

red[3]/green
The most common contrast here is the international one of 'red' for 'stop' and 'green' for 'go', especially on traffic lights or the flags of railway guards. Customs posts, too, have a 'red' channel and a 'green' channel, for arriving passengers who have something or nothing to declare, respectively. In some cases, too, one finds 'red' and 'green' denoting 'hot' and 'cold', much as 'red' and blue can do (see previous entry). Finally (for this entry), London's 'red' buses serve the urban and central areas of the city, while 'green' buses and coaches (the 'Green Line') serve country districts. The suggestion is that the 'red' lifeblood flows in the capital, while the rural areas are predominantly 'green' in colour, with their fields and trees.

red[4]/white
As basic colours, 'red' implies 'revolutionary', and 'white' counter-revolutionary especially with regard to Russia and her early Soviet period. (Although 'White' Russia is nothing to do with this, but is simply a name, current in pre-revolutionary times, for one of her peoples.) A 'red' blood cell (or corpuscle) is one that transports oxygen and carbon dioxide to and from the tissues of the body, while a 'white' cell does not transport oxygen but deals with the defence mechanisms of the body and tissue repair. (The technical terms for the two types of cell are 'erythrocyte' and 'leucocyte', see **leucocytes/erythrocytes**.) The 'Red' Ensign is the flag of the British Merchant Navy, and has the Union Jack in one corner on a 'red' background. The 'White' Ensign, however, is the ensign of the Royal Navy (also, the Royal Yacht Squadron), having a 'red' cross on a 'white' background and, like the 'Red' Ensign, the Union Jack in

one corner. 'Red' meat is any meat that is dark in colour, such as beef and lamb, while 'white' meat is light-coloured, such as veal or turkey breast. 'Red hot' means 'very hot' (600°–800°C), while 'white hot' means 'incandescent' (over 1000°C). Compare also **paleface/redskin**.

redbrick see **Oxbridge**

red card see **yellow card**

redskin see **paleface**

red squirrel/grey squirrel
The 'red squirrel' (*Sciurus vulgaris*) is the one that is increasingly rare in Great Britain, since it has been driven out by the introduced 'grey squirrel' (*Sciurus carolinensis*). The colours obviously refer to the animals' respective furs. The legend persists that 'grey squirrels' are harmful (which they are, since they extensively damage deciduous trees), but that 'red squirrels' cause no harm. This is not really true, and indeed the 'red squirrel' was destroyed in large numbers in Scotland precisely because of its damage to forest trees. It also feeds on fruits and shoots, not simply innocently stored nuts. But the 'grey squirrel' is the real pest, and the 'red squirrel' is actually now a protected species.

reduce see **enlarge**

reducing agent see **oxydizing agent**

reed organ see **pipe organ**

reef knot/granny
A 'reef knot' (sometimes called a 'square knot') is a symmetrical knot made from two half-knots tied in opposite directions. A 'granny' (or 'granny knot') is asymmetrical, and has two half-knots tied the same way. The 'reef knot' is thus secure, and should not slip or jam. The 'granny' is insecure, and can do either. The 'reef knot' is so called since it was (and still is) used for securing sails when they are rolled up or 'reefed'. The 'granny' is so called because it is the type of knot 'tied by women or landsmen, and derided by seamen because it cannot be untied when it is jammed' (Admiral William Henry Smyth, *The Sailor's Word-book*, 1865).

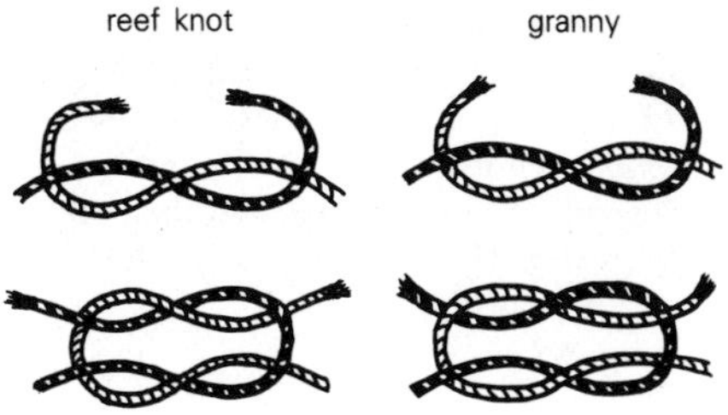

reel-to-reel/cassette
The terms describe the two basic methods of running a tape on a tape recorder. 'Reel-to-reel' means that the tape runs from one separate reel to another, and needs to be threaded on to the empty spool before playback or recording can begin. In a 'cassette', the tape is enclosed in a case, and although arranged on two spools, does not need to be threaded since it is already attached to both. The latter method is popularly used for sound and videotapes, whether blank or pre-recorded.

re-entrant see **salient**

referee/umpire
The main difference between the two officials is that of the various sports in which they arbitrate. 'Referees' officiate in football, boxing, ice hockey, tennis and rugby football, among others, while 'umpires' operate in cricket, hockey, tennis, lacrosse and baseball. Tennis features for both here, since the 'umpire' who arbitrates in a match (and who is sometimes verbally abused by contentious players) is appointed by a 'referee' who himself is in charge of the actual tournament.

refined see **coarse**

reflector/refractor
A 'reflector', or 'reflecting telescope', is one that uses a concave mirror to reflect

the image of the observed object. A 'refractor', or 'refracting telescope', forms the image through lenses, thereby 'refracting' the light rays instead of 'reflecting' them. A 'reflector' is often larger than a 'refractor' because it can be lighter as the light does not have to pass through the glass. 'Reflectors' have a better definition, however, because they are wider. (Newton invented the 'reflector' because he believed it was impossible to avoid chromatic aberration in a 'refractor'.)

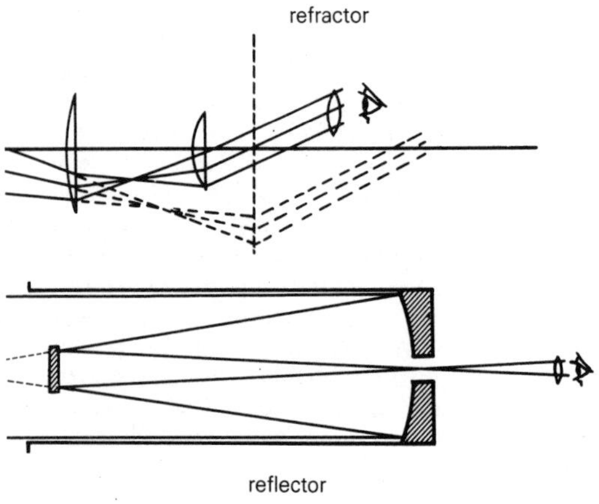

refractor see **reflector**

regina see **rex**

regressive see **progressive**

regular/secular
A 'regular' priest is one who belongs to a religious order, and so who lives in a community such as a monastery (see **monastery/nunnery**). By contrast, a 'secular' priest is the familiar one who lives 'in the world' as a parish priest. The terms apply mainly to Roman Catholic clergy (see **Catholic/Protestant**).

relativism see **absolutism**

rendered see **brick**

repel see **attract**

representationalism see **presentationism**

republic see **monarchy**

Republican see **Democrat**

Republicans/Loyalists
The names relate to the two 'camps' in Northern Ireland, with the 'Republicans' seeking to achieve a united Ireland (as a republic), and the 'Loyalists' loyal to Great Britain. The pair thus corresponds to the pair **nationalists/unionists**, and as a religious division, to the pair **Catholic/Protestant**. The emphasis of the terms 'Republicans' and 'Loyalists', however, is more historical and geographical than political or religious, and at the same time more 'militant'. In the latter respect, compare **Provisional IRA/Official IRA** (Where the 'R' stands for 'Republican').

resident see **migrant**

resurrection see **death**

retail/wholesale
The terms relate to the selling of goods. 'Retail' goods are those sold individually or in fairly small quantities to consumers and customers, especially in shops and stores. 'Wholesale' goods are sold in large quantities to retailers (who resell them as 'retail' goods, therefore). However, the size of the quantities are smaller than those in which the wholesaler purchases the goods from the manufacturers. The economics of the process means that 'wholesale' goods are cheaper than 'retail' ones. If they were not, the retailers would make no profit. Sometimes customers are fortunate enough to be able to purchase goods at 'wholesale' prices, although this is the exception rather than the rule. 'Retail' derives ultimately from French: compare French *tailler*, 'to cut' (and English 'tailor'), indicating that only a portion of goods is supplied or sold. 'Wholesale', on the other hand, implies that goods are sold in a 'whole' or complete amount, not a part or portion.

retard see **advance**[1]

retire see **advance**[2]

retroactive see **proactive**

retrograde see **direct**[2]

return see **single**[2]

reverse see (1) **forward**[2] (2) **obverse**

revolution see **rotation**

rex/regina
The words are Latin for 'king' and 'queen' respectively, and form part of the title of a king or queen, although today found more commonly only in legal documents, inscriptions on coins, and the like. For example, Queen Elizabeth II is officially Elizabeth 'Regina', and when the crown or state is involved in the legal case, the title will appear in a typical formula as 'Regina v. Miller' (*The Times*, 6 May 1986). When the sovereign is a king, 'Regina' will change to 'Rex'.

rheme see **theme**[1]

rhyme see **blank verse**

rich[1]/plain
A 'rich' food is one that is highly seasoned, fatty, oily or sweet, such as Christmas pudding, marzipan or pancakes. A 'plain' food is one that lacks an excess of fat, oil, sugar or seasoning, with the term particularly applying to cakes and biscuits that have small quantities of such ingredients. 'Plain' flour, too, does not contain a raising agent. It is usually considered healthier to live on a 'plain' diet than a 'rich' one. 'Plain' living is admired by some, too, as it involves a modest way of life, with little indulgence. 'Rich' living thus attaches much importance to material goods and wealth, which some regard as 'symbols of success'. 'Plain' can also mean 'ordinary' as applied to a 'man in the street' (as in the title of books such as *The Plain Man's Guide to Wine*), and even smacks of the naive or innocent. The opposite of this is not 'rich', however, but a word such as 'sophisticated' or 'knowledgeable'.

rich[2]/poor

> The rich man in his castle,
> The poor man at his gate,
> God made them, high or lowly,
> And order'd their estate.

Thus the popular image for many years, although this particular verse of the children's hymn 'All things bright and beautiful' is usually omitted today. (It was composed in solid Victorian times, in 1848.) In modern times, however, 'rich' and 'poor' is still used of nations and countries, as in such statements as the following: 'By 1972 the gap between the rich and poor nations had become an issue in international politics' (*The Times Atlas of World History*, 1978). For related comparisons, see **haves/have-nots**. The division of the nations of the world in this way in effect equates with the industrialized countries on the one hand, and the developing (formerly, 'underdeveloped') countries of the Third World on the other.

Richard Roe/John Doe
The fictional names traditionally used in a legal case to represent, respectively, the defendant and the plaintiff (see **plaintiff/defendant**). 'John Doe' later became a name in American usage for someone whose real name was not known, or for a typical 'man in the street', like the British 'Joe Bloggs'. The original use of both names in legal cases dates from the eighteenth century, however.

ridge/trough
The terms are used in meteorology as an equivalent to the pair **peak/trough** (which see). A 'ridge' is thus an elongated area of high pressure developing from an anticyclone, while a 'trough' is a similar area of low pressure formed from a depression (or cyclone). The image is thus that of 'hills' and 'valleys'.

right/wrong
'Two wrongs don't make a right', we say

to a child who attempts to cover up one misdeed by performing another. 'Wrong never comes right', runs another proverb. Much of our lives and our moral attitudes is governed by what we believe to be 'right' and what we regard as 'wrong'. For children, too, 'right' and 'wrong' assume a more 'black and white' image as 'correct' and 'incorrect', even as a tick for a 'right' answer and a cross for a 'wrong' one. (The tick serves to mark the answer, to pick it out, while the cross symbolically obliterates it.) However, the second saying quoted above is surely untrue, and it is possible to 'right' a 'wrong', or correct what is faulty or in error.

right see **left**

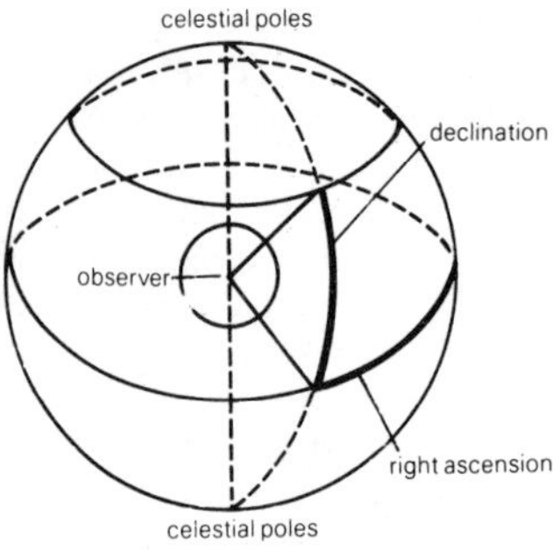

right ascension/declination
These are astronomical opposites. The 'right ascension' is the angle that is measured eastwards along the celestial equator between the vernal equinox and the point at which the meridian (line drawn from the celestial pole) intersects the celestial equator through a particular heavenly body. It thus corresponds roughly to longitude on Earth. The 'declination' is the angular distance of a celestial body north or south of the celestial equator as measured along a great circle passing through the celestial poles. It therefore approximates to latitude on the Earth. The two coordinates can thus be used to pinpoint the exact location of an object in the sky. Unlike latitude and longitude, however, which are both measured in degrees, 'right ascension' is measured in hours, minutes and seconds, and only 'declination' in degrees (as well as minutes and seconds as divisions of a degree). Astronomers have calculated the position of many celestial bodies years ahead, so that on 28 February 1992, for example, they know that the position of the planet Neptune will be: 'right ascension' 15h 37m 14s, 'declination' −3° 59′ 57″. For some of the technicalities here, see as necessary **vernal/autumnal**, **equinox/solstice**, **latitude/longitude**.

righthand drive see **lefthand drive**

right side up see **upside down**

ringing tone/engaged tone
When making a telephone call, the chances are that the person one wishes to speak to will either not be talking on the phone or that he or she will be. In the first instance, the caller will hear the 'ringing tone', which (at least in Britain) is a repeated 'burr-burr'. If the person one is ringing, however, is already using the phone, the caller will hear a repeated, fairly high-pitched tone, heard at more frequent intervals and somehow more 'urgently' than a 'ringing tone'. There are other, less frequent tones, such as the 'purring' dial tone, and the continuous 'number unobtainable' tone but these two are the most common and represent the contrast: either the number called is free, or it is engaged. (For a not dissimilar concept, compare **vacant/engaged**.)

rise/fall
Otherwise 'go up' and 'go down', or 'ascend' and 'descend'. 'Rise' often implies an improvement, an ascent to greater things or to importance, while 'fall' can mean a descent to a lower state or even to ruin. As the proverb runs, 'One may sooner fall than rise', however, and there is a kind of superstitious fear that 'what goes up must come down'. We are all half aware of the many 'Rise and Fall' titles, such as William L. Shirer's *Rise and Fall of the Third Reich* (itself echoing Gibbon's *Decline and Fall of the Roman Empire*). In

recent years the punning expression 'rise and rise' has evolved as a variant on this, with reference to someone or something that prospers and continues to prosper, such as a commercial undertaking or a personal reputation.

rising trot see **sitting trot**

rive droite/rive gauche
The French names mean 'right bank' and 'left bank', and properly apply to those parts of Paris that lie respectively north ('right bank') and south ('left bank') of the Seine. The 'rive gauche', in particular, acquired a reputation in the nineteenth century for its 'progressive' intellectual views, since it is there that the university (the Sorbonne) is located, as well as the 'Quartier Latin' or 'Latin Quarter', where artists and students live. ('Latin' refers to the fact that Latin was spoken here in medieval times.) 'Rive droite' is thus more a negative than a positive description to denote the 'right bank', and really implies that the region lacks what the 'rive gauche' possesses. It is pure chance that 'left' here happens to coincide with the 'progressive' sense of 'left-wing', 'socialist'. Certain other cities could be said to have a similar disposition of districts north and south of their river, and even in Moscow, for instance, the university and student hostels lie south of the Moskva.

rive gauche see **rive droite**

road see **rail**

roaring/whistling
This unlikely pair of contrasts relates to two of the main kinds of breathing defect occurring in horses. The terms are used by veterinary surgeons, with 'roaring' denoting a laborious intake of breath accompanied by a harsh rasping sound, and 'whistling' applying to the early stages of the condition, in which a high-pitched shrill sound is heard when the animal breathes in. Both effects are symptoms of an inflammation of the respiratory tract or of a chronic malformation of the air passages, and both conditions cause the animal considerable distress and discomfort. Horses in one state or the other are known respectively as 'roarers' and 'whistlers'.

roast coffee see **instant coffee**

robbers see **cops**

rockers see **mods**

roger/wilco
'Roger' is a jargonistic term used by signallers (typically, RAF pilots) to denote that a message has been received and understood. As such, it is frequently followed by the expression 'out', meaning that the communication has been completed. 'Wilco', by contrast, means that the message just received will be acted on. In other words, 'roger' implies a 'passive' comprehension and acceptance, while 'wilco' indicates that an 'active' move or manoeuvre will follow. 'Roger' is the former signalling codeword for the letter 'R', here denoting 'received'. 'Wilco' is an abbreviated form of 'I will comply'.

roll see **pitch**[1]

rolled see **folded**

roller skates/ice skates
The basic difference between the two types of sporting footgear is that 'roller skates' have wheels, and are used for progressing over land, while 'ice skates' have blades, and are used to move over ice. 'Ice skates' were in use long before 'roller skates', and were originally called simply 'skates' until the arrival of 'roller skates' (in the nineteenth century) required the prefix 'ice' to denote the difference. 'Ice skating' has always been a more athletic and graceful sport than 'roller skating' (Pepys described it as 'a very pretty art' in 1662).

roman see **italic**

Romance/Germanic
These are the names of two of the main language families represented in Europe and, by colonization, elsewhere in the

world. The 'Romance' languages are those that derived from Latin as spoken by the Romans, and are today found, among others, as French, Spanish, Italian, Portuguese and Romanian. The 'Germanic' languages (formerly often called 'Teutonic') are those that developed from a now extinct language spoken over an area centred on modern Germany, and they today include English, German, Dutch, the Scandinavian languages (Danish, Norwegian, Swedish), Flemish and Afrikaans. However, although certainly of 'Germanic' origin, as spoken by the Anglo-Saxons and Jutes who settled in Britain from the fifth century, English is today really a blend of 'Germanic' and 'Romance' elements, because French was introduced to England by the Normans in the eleventh century, and Latin later gained prominence as a 'language of learning'. This means that as far as its vocabulary is concerned, English is now approximately half 'Romance' and half 'Germanic' in content. As basic language families themselves, 'Romance' is usually regarded as representative of arts and 'culture' or learning, while the 'Germanic' languages are seen as more basic and 'earthy' or practical. The contrast can be seen in the respective 'Romance' and 'Germanic' words for one and the same thing in modern English, such as 'Romance' 'mutton' (meat prepared for table) and 'Germanic' 'sheep' (the animal that produces the meat), or 'Romance' 'chair' (for sitting on when dining) and 'Germanic' 'stool' (for sitting on when working).

Roman numerals see **Arabic numerals**

Romans see **Greeks**

romantic see **classical**[2]

root/branch
Botanically, the 'root' of a shrub or tree is its basic 'attachment' in the ground from which it gains its moisture or absorbs its water, while its 'branch', in the air, is its main stem or bough from which it gains its 'food' (by manufacturing it via the process of photosynthesis through its leaves) and by means of which it 'breathes' (again, via the leaves). The two organs are thus contrasted functionally and in their location ('roots' are low down, and 'branches' high up), hence the modern expression 'root and branch' to denote an entity or completeness of something, especially when it is destroyed or defeated, as 'We must ban this evil practice root and branch'. (The reference is to the eradication or destruction of a dangerous or deadly tree.)

rotary/cylinder
The terms relate to different types of mowing machine. A 'rotary' mower is one that has a flat circular set of cutters, rotating horizontally. A 'cylinder' mower, the older, more traditional type, has a 'cylinder' or blades that rotates vertically to cut the grass. 'Cylinder' mowers can be hand pushed or powered (by electric or petrol motors). 'Rotary' mowers are usually driven by electric or petrol motor, and can hover, but some can be hand-pushed on wheels. In the 1980s, a kind of 'war of the mowers' developed among manufacturers of either type, each claiming that their system had the advantage over the other. At first, some 'rotary' mowers were relatively unsophisticated, and not provided with the grass-collecting boxes that most 'cylinder' mowers had. Later, each type became more efficient, and there is now little to choose between them. However, many people prefer a 'cylinder' mower since they know it will give the neat 'stripy' effect that can look so attractive when the lawn has been mown.

rotation/revolution
The two terms are used for different types of movement of heavenly bodies in astronomy. 'Rotation' describes the turning or 'spinning' of a body around its own axis, as the planets do. 'Revolution' applies to the orbital motion of one body round another, as also the planets do when they revolve round the Sun. Planets thus 'revolve' as they 'rotate', and it is the 'revolution' of the Earth round the Sun, for example, that produces the changes in

the seasons, while it is the 'rotation' of the Earth that gives the sequence of day and night. For a related topic, see the pair **equinox/solstice**.

rotor/stator
A 'rotor' is a rotating part in a machine, especially an electrical one such as a motor or generator. A 'stator' is a fixed part, that does not revolve. Any revolving drum or fan is thus a 'rotor', while the bearing to which it is fixed is a 'stator'. The two terms are said to have been coined by the Scottish-born electrical engineer and plastics pioneer Sir James Swinburne (1858–1958), with 'rotor' based on 'rotator' and 'stator' partly based on 'rotor' and partly based on Latin *stator*, 'one who stands'.

rough/smooth
In their general senses, 'rough' denotes something that is uneven, uncouth or in some way coarse, while 'smooth' indicates a levelness, 'polish' and general refinement not present in anything 'rough'. Thus 'rough' can often have an overtone of 'incomplete', while 'smooth' suggests 'perfectly finished'. A fabric or garment that has a 'smooth' finish on the outside may have some 'rough' joins or stitching underneath. There are one or two interesting uses of the contrasting words. In tennis, for example, two players will usually spin a racket when starting, in order to determine who plays which end and who is to serve first. One actually does the spinning, while the other calls 'rough' or 'smooth' to refer to the threading of the small strings at the top and bottom of the face of the racket. The spinner stops and examines the racket to see which side is uppermost. This is therefore the equivalent of tossing a coin, as is customary in other sports. Then in ancient Greek, 'rough' breathing means that a sound like the letter 'h' precedes certain vowels at the beginning of a word (this technically known as 'aspiration'), while 'smooth' breathing means that no 'h' will be sounded. The two types of breathing are indicated by special symbols over the initial vowel, one facing one way, the other facing the other. For example, ἕτερος (transcribed *heteros*, 'other') has a 'rough' breathing, but ἐτεος (*eteos*, 'true') has a 'smooth' breathing. The expression 'to take the rough with the smooth' in English means 'to accept the bad things with the good', 'to put up with the disadvantages while enjoying the advantages'.

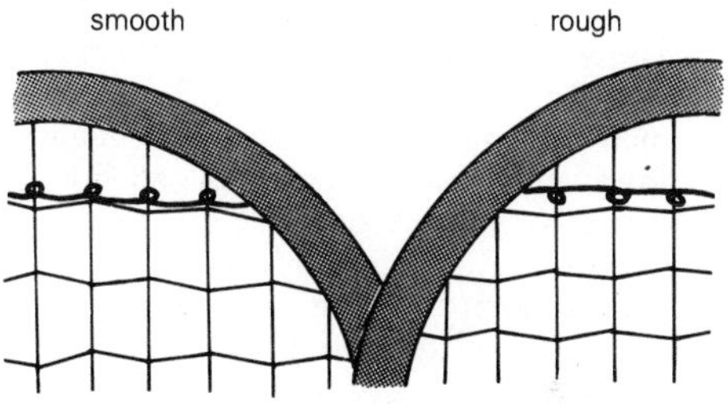

round/square
'Round' implies a circle or sphere, with all points on the curve equidistant from the centre, while 'square' is a figure having four equal lines with corners of right angles. The two shapes or contours are familiar in many household objects, so that 'round' describes such things as plates, glasses, door-knobs, lampshades and flower-pots, while 'square' will apply to most tables, chairs, books, television screens and radiators. Many 'round' objects are thus containers, while 'square' objects are not. Hence the expression 'like a square peg in a round hole', used of someone who is a misfit, especially a person who is in the wrong job. The contrasting shapes can also be found in street formations, where a 'round' area is often called a 'circus'. Thus Piccadilly Circus in London is (more or less) 'round', while Leicester Square is 'square' and has a street running along each side. See also the next entry below.

roundabouts see **swings**

round brackets/square brackets
These are the two contrasting types of brackets or parentheses. 'Round brackets' are the standard sort, appearing as '()'. 'Square brackets', appearing as '[]', thus

have special uses, for example when supplying words to make a quotation understandable, or when enclosing something that is already in 'round brackets'. Thus in the following, the words in 'square brackets' supply what is necessary for the reader to understand the rest of the phrase: 'He blew out the candles [on the birthday cake]', and in the following sentence the 'square brackets' are used inside the 'round' ones: 'A frame tent of considerable size (around 20 feet [six metres] square) is ideal for family camping'. Printers sometimes call 'round brackets' 'parentheses'.

Roundhead/Cavalier
In English history, the 'Roundheads' were the supporters of parliament in the Civil War of the mid-seventeenth century, so were opposed to the king, Charles I. The 'Cavaliers' were therefore royalists, or supporters of the king. (For a few more details, see **Royalists/Parliamentarians**, below.) The 'Roundheads' were so nicknamed because they cut their hair short, while the 'Cavaliers' were the royal horsemen. The latter nickname was a disapproving one at first, and was given to the Royalists for their militant, 'swashbuckling' attitude.

rowing/sculling
A contrast is sometimes implied between 'rowing' in an eight (or other group), using a single oar, and 'sculling' as an individual rower, using two oars. However, there are exceptions to this basic differentiation, since an oarsman using two oars in a boat on his own is obviously 'rowing'. Moreover, a rower who is 'sculling' sits on a sliding seat. See also **pair-oars/double sculls**.

Royalists/Parliamentarians
These were the official designations of the two opposing sides in the English Civil War of the mid-seventeenth century, when supporters of Charles I (the 'Royalists') clashed with supporters of the House of Commons (the 'Parliamentarians') regarding their respective prerogatives. After several battles, the 'Parliamentarians' won, and Charles was executed in 1649. See also above **Roundheads/Cavaliers**.

rugby league see **rugby union**

rugby union/rugby league
The broad difference between the two forms of rugby football is that 'rugby union' has teams of 15 players on each side, and is restricted to amateurs, while 'rugby league' has teams of 13 players each and can be played professionally. 'Rugby union' is the more widespread form of the game, at least in Britain, and until recently 'rugby league' was played mostly in the north of England (Yorkshire, Lancashire, Cumbria). There are also certain differences in the rules and scoring systems. The two forms of the game arose as the result of a split in 1893, when the Rugby League broke away from the Rugby Union with the aim of developing a more 'open' game that would be more interesting to watch.

rule/exception
'The exception proves the rule', we say, meaning that a 'rule' would not actually be one unless it had an 'exception'. A 'rule' thus states that something is so (or is not so), and the 'exception' states a case of deviation from this 'rule'. Foreign language learners are all too familiar with grammatical or spelling 'rules' that have one or more 'exceptions'.

ruled/plain
The two contrasting terms are common in commercial use for writing paper ('notepaper') that either has lines or does not. When sold in pads, 'plain' sheets of writing paper are often provided with a 'guide rule', a sheet with heavily ruled lines that is designed not to be written on but to be placed under the paper so that the lines appear through it and serve as a type of 'ruling'.

running rigging/standing rigging
On a sailing vessel, the 'running rigging' is a term for all the movable ropes and wires that are used for adjusting the sails.

The 'standing rigging', on the other hand, includes the stays, shrouds (sets of ropes or cables) and other devices that remain mainly fixed, although that are adjustable, and that are used to support the masts. 'Running' here thus implies 'moving over blocks and pulleys'.

rural/urban
'Rural' means 'belonging to the country', while 'urban' relates to the town. Britain formerly had local government bodies known as 'rural' district councils and 'urban' district councils, respectively. Compare the basic **town/country**. The words are Latin-based, from *rus*, genitive *ruris*, 'country', and *urbs*, 'town'.

Ss

saccule/utricle
Here we have crept into the inner ear, where in the so-called 'membraneous labyrinth', or sensory structures, the 'saccule' is the smaller of the two parts, while the 'utricle' is the larger. The words really mean both the same thing literally, since both Latin *saccus* and *uter* mean 'bag'. 'Saccule' is obviously also related to English 'sack', but 'utricle', surprisingly, is not related to 'uterus', which has the same meaning in Latin ('womb') that it has in English.

sacred/profane
'Sacred' implies respect for a god, 'holy', while 'profane' implies that disrespect is shown, 'unholy', 'abusive'. Both the opposites are portrayed in Titian's famous painting 'Sacred and Profane Love', which has one clothed female figure and one nude. (The figures have been variously interpreted as representing either earthly love and heavenly love, or the virtues of grace and truth. The former seems more likely, so that the work in a sense illustrates the contrasts 'terrestrial' and 'celestial': see **celestial/terrestrial**.) 'Profane' literally means 'outside the temple' (Latin *pro fano*), and therefore 'not consecrated'.

sadist/masochist
A 'sadist' is one who takes pleasure in hurting others; a 'masochist' is one who derives pleasure from being hurt. The two are therefore allied to the pair **active/passive**, and are also both individually an inextricable blend of the pair **pleasure/pain**. It would be interesting to know what the psychosexual perversions would be called if it were not for Messrs Sade and Masoch, or more precisely the Marquis de Sade and Leopold von Sacher-Masoch. The former (actually a count) was an eighteenth-century French soldier and writer who specialized in describing the infliction of pain on a loved one. (Do you really want to hurt me?) The latter was a nineteenth-century Australian novelist who described the converse in his fiction, which included *The Legacy of Cain* and a number of erotic short stories about Polish Jews. A 'sadomasochist' is a person who displays (or conceals) both attributes. See also **love/hate**.

safety/touchback
In American football, 'safety' is the tactic employed when a player puts down a ball behind his own goal line when it has been sent over the line by someone on his own side. This is as opposed to 'touchback', when a player similarly puts the ball down behind his own goal line, but one sent over it by an opponent. A 'safety' counts as two points for the defending team, while a 'touchback' gives two points to the attackers. (It must not be confused with a 'touch*down*', which is a straight score over the line, worth six points.)

sag see **hog**

sagittal/coronal
The terms are anatomical. The 'sagittal' plane through a body is the one that divides it into two from front to back, typically passing through centrally placed features as the nose and the navel. The 'coronal' plane divides the body at right angles to this, i.e. laterally, so passes through the hips (and the arms, if extended horizontally). 'Sagittal' derives from Latin *sagitta*, 'arrow', because this weapon was usually thrown straight at a person from the front. 'Coronal' comes from *corona*, 'crown', since the plane cuts across the head or skull from one side to the other. Compare similar contrasting

planes or positions, such as **anterior/posterior**, **dorsal/ventral**, **superior/inferior**, **cephalic/caudal**.

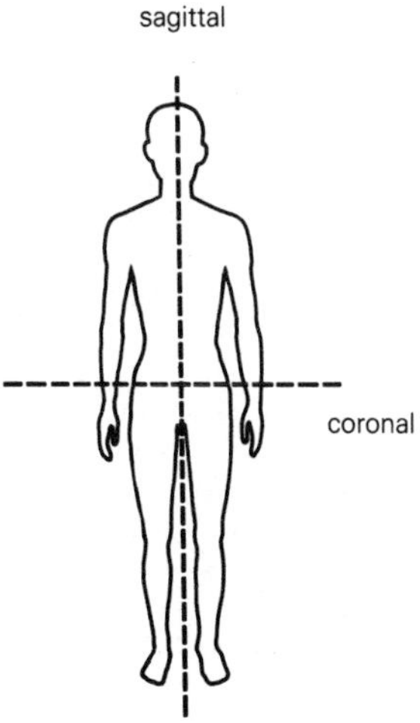

saint/sinner
The two alliterative terms are frequently coupled as opposites, in such words as 'He's more a sinner than a saint', and there are fairly familiar proverbs containing the two, such as the perceptive 'The greater the sinner, the greater the saint', and 'Young saints, old sinners'. When paired like this, the terms usually have a fairly trivial sense, not a deep religious one, although saints and sins properly belong to religion.

salary see **wage**

salient/re-entrant
These opposites belong to mathematics (geometry) or geography, in the main, and basically mean 'pointing outwards' (of an angle, for example) and 'pointing inwards'. The terms occur in historical descriptions of military fortifications, too, which can thus speak of a 'salient' as a defensive work that projects from a larger structure, and of a 're-entrant' as an angular arrangement from which shots can be fired. 'Salient' literally means 'leaping', and was first used in heraldic descriptions to apply to a lion that was portrayed as if about to leap. 'Re-entrant' seems an odd word: why not just 'entrant'? The answer is that a 're-entrant' angle is regarded as one that is normally 'salient', or pointing outwards, but that has 'gone back in again'. That is, an angle is normally made by a projection formed from within a figure; when it does the opposite, it 're-enters' that figure.

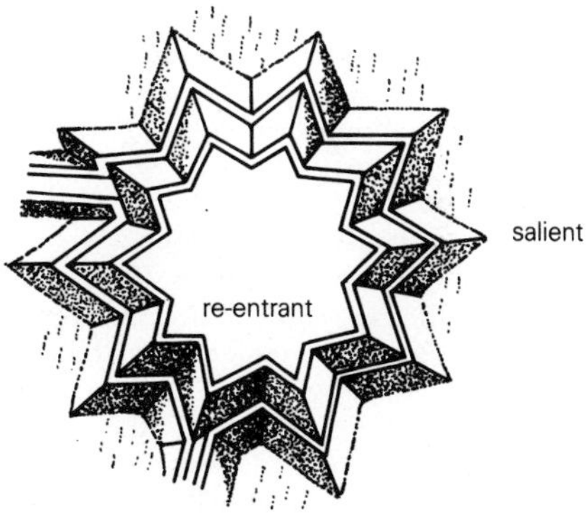

salt/pepper
Two basic condiments, one to give tang, the other to give 'pep'! 'Pepper' is finer in consistency than 'salt', so is traditionally dispensed from a pot with several small holes, whereas 'salt' is poured from a jar ('saltcellar') with a single hole. (Outwardly, a 'pepper' pot and a 'salt' cellar are often virtually indistinguishable, until one looks at the top, although if transparent, the white 'salt' can be clearly distinguished from the brown 'pepper'.) 'Pepper-and-salt' is used as a term to describe a flecked colour, such as a combination of black and white or brown and white (or simply dark and light). Hence one can wear a 'pepper-and-salt' coat, and the army major can sport a 'pepper-and-salt' moustache (a blend of brown hair and grey). The colour distinction therefore falls in the class of **brown/white** or **black/white**.

salt see **fresh**[1]

same/different
Two identical objects are the 'same'; two nearly but not quite identical objects are therefore slightly 'different'. We are always comparing things, and find it difficult to make up our minds at times: things that are the 'same' are welcome since they are recognizable and familiar, while things that are 'different' are also welcome since they are new or novel, and provide a change. Perhaps the best compromise is something that is 'the same, only different', i.e. recognizable but subtly altered. This phrase seems to have been imported to Britain by Americans in the Second World War. Americans, of course, speak the 'same' language as the British, only 'different'.

samizdat/tamizdat
Not the names of two **Tweedledum/ Tweedledee** twins, but two contrasting Russian terms that have to some degree made their way into other western languages. 'Samizdat' is the system by which secret or banned literature gets printed and distributed in the USSR on a 'do-it-yourself' basis. (The word literally means 'self-publishing'.) 'Tamizdat', the lesser known of the two, is the reverse process: the publication of literature in the West which is then smuggled into Russia. An example of 'tamizdat' is Pasternak's novel *Doctor Zhivago*, which was published in Milan (in Russian), with copies later finding their way back to the Soviet Union, where it had been originally written. The word literally means 'publishing there' (Russian *tam*, 'there').

Sandinistas/Contras
These are the names of, respectively, the pro-government and anti-government forces in Nicaragua, the latter being a guerrilla organization. The 'Sandinistas' are named after the Nicaraguan nationalist leader Augusto César Sandino (1893–1934), and arose in his lifetime as a revolutionary force. The name is now used, however, to apply to the similar force that was founded in his name in 1963, and that overthrew the former President Anastasio Somoza in 1979. (He was assassinated the following year.) Officially, the 'Sandinistas' are the National Liberation Front, otherwise a junta. As such, they are supported by the USSR and Cuba. The 'Contras', who are based in Honduras, are 'anti' or against them, as their name implies, and are supported by the United States. (President Reagan has described them as 'freedom fighters'.) The 'Sandinistas' won 63 percent of the votes in elections held in 1984.

sane/insane
Obviously, 'sane' means 'of sound mind' and 'insane' means 'of unsound mind', 'mad'. The pair are here simply to illustrate the fact that the negative of an adjective can be more common than the positive, that is, that 'insane' is more commonly used than 'sane', simply because it is more remarkable. In most cases, of course, the sense is not literally 'mad' but more 'crazy', 'absurd' as in an 'insane' idea or an 'insane' remark.

sans serif see **serif**

satem/centum
The terms are linguistic ones, used to describe different groups of Indo-European languages. The 'satem' group, which includes Iranian and Slavonic languages (among others), was the one in which the sound *k* changed to *s*. The word 'satem' is itself an example of this, as it is the Avestan for 'hundred'. The 'centum' group, which includes the Hellenic, Italic and Germanic languages (i.e. Greek, Latin and English, therefore), did not have this change. 'Centum', Latin for 'hundred', thus represents the original *k* sound. The distinction between the two groups was made by nineteenth-century philologists. (The fact that modern English 'century' is pronounced with an *s* sound is nothing to do with this law, but developed through the 'vulgar' Latin language and, more obviously, French. Originally in Latin, *centum* was pronounced 'kentum'.)

Saturday/Sunday
The two halves of a typical British

weekend, with 'Saturday' traditionally devoted to Mammon, and 'Sunday' to God. The distinction between the two has become increasingly blurred in recent years, but 'Saturday' is still really regarded as a sort of 'working holiday' day, when many weekday operations are still carried out (shops are open, letters are delivered, and so on), while 'Sunday' remains basically a 'rest' day, with quite a different routine. Put another way, 'Saturday' is the 'uphill' or effortful half of the weekend, while 'Sunday' runs downhill, and is relatively effortless. 'Saturday' night is thus (or could be) the high spot (remember 'Saturday Night Fever'?). 'Sunday' morning is the one after that night before (remember *Saturday Night and Sunday Morning*, Sillitoe's novel or the fine film of it?).

satyr see **faun**

satyriasis see **nymphomania**

savoury see **sweet**[2]

scholar see **commoner**

sciences see **arts**

scientific socialism/utopian socialism
'Scientific socialism' is Marxist socialism, embodying such doctrines as those of dialectical and historical materialism, a class struggle, and a 'dictatorship of the proletariat' ('Workers of the world, unite!') in power until a classless society has been achieved. 'Utopian socialism' is socialism as advocated by Robert Owen and others, and involves capitalists peacefully surrendering the means of production through persuasion, moral conviction, and so on. The latter seems unlikely to work (not for nothing does 'Utopia' literally mean 'no place') but the former involves enormous complexities, and is itself to a large degree 'utopian' or idealistic.

scout[1]**/guide**
The designations of the young males and young females who are members of the youth movement founded by Robert Baden-Powell in the early years of the twentieth century, with the 'Boy Scouts' first camping in 1907 and the 'Girl Guides' following three years later. The words themselves had long been in use for military agents: a 'scout' reconnoitres and a 'guide' shows the way, giving information about the enemy's position and so on. (The modern army still has 'scout' cars, and there was a French *Corps des Guides* in the Napoleonic Wars even before the Queen's Own Corps of 'Guides' was raised as a regiment in the Indian Army for frontier service in the wars against the Sikhs in 1846. So the name is historic.) For more homely equivalents, see their junior counterparts, **cub/brownie**. Until fairly recently there were also 'rovers' as a term for older 'scouts', and there still are corresponding 'rangers' or 'ranger guides' for senior 'guides'. (Older 'scouts' are now called 'venture scouts'.)

scout[2]**/gyp**
A 'scout' is a college servant at Oxford, while a 'gyp' is his equivalent at Cambridge (and also Durham). For a different division of college labour, see **gyp/bedder**. The exact sense of 'scout' here is not certain, for the servant hardly 'scouts out' in the accepted manner, nor does the word appear to have originated as a term of abuse, as 'scout' once was (perhaps still is, in Scotland). On the other hand, perhaps it did, as 'gyp' is short for 'gypsy', which can be used to mean 'rogue', and in American use still, 'gyp' means 'fraud', 'cheat'.

sculling see **rowing**

Scylla/Charybdis
The phrase 'between Scylla and Charybdis' means 'between two equally dangerous alternatives', otherwise 'between the devil and the deep blue sea'. In Greek mythology, 'Scylla' was a sea nymph turned into a sea monster who was believed to drown sailors navigating the Straits of Messina (between mainland Italy and Sicily). She was identified with a rock on the Italian side. 'Charybdis' was a ship-devouring monster who was ident-

ified with a whirlpool on the Sicilian side of the strait, opposite 'Scylla'. So although geographical opposites, either monster could send hapless sailors to a watery grave. (On his return journey home after the Trojan War, Odysseus lost six seamen to 'Scylla' when steering clear of 'Charybdis'. Later, his ship was driven back to 'Charybdis' and was destroyed, with Odysseus surviving by clinging to a fig tree over the pool.)

sea see **land**

SECAM see **PAL**

second see **first**[2]

secondary see **primary**[2]

secondo see **primo**

secular see **regular**

sell see **buy**

seller's market see **buyer's market**

Senate see **House of Representatives**

senior/junior
The words are straight Latin for 'older', 'elder' and 'younger', which is one of their most common senses still in English. A 'junior' post is usually held by a younger person, and a 'senior' by an older. Schools, especially, have 'senior' and 'junior' departments, classes and pupils. Not every 'senior' designation has a 'junior' equivalent, however. This is because 'senior' itself has come to acquire authority and importance (and experience), whereas 'junior' suggests the opposite (a lack of these qualities). Thus 'senior', but not 'junior', is found in a number of military ranks, such as 'senior' aircraftman in the RAF, 'senior' chief petty officer in the US Navy, and 'senior' master sergeant in the USAF. British hospitals, too, have 'senior' house officers and 'senior' registrars. And there is no opposite number to the 'senior' citizen who is an old age pensioner or retired person. However, many universities and colleges have a corresponding 'Senior' Common Room (SCR) for the teaching staff and a 'Junior' Common Room (JCR) for the students. 'Senior' is itself related to all those foreign words for 'Mr' or 'Sir' or 'Lord', such as 'seigneur', 'signor', 'señor' and 'sir' itself, as well as 'senator'. 'Junior' has its best known equivalent in the actual word 'young', as well as the more obvious 'juvenile'.

senza see **con**

Sephardi see **Ashkenazi**

septentrional see **austral**

sequential access see **direct access**

seraphim see **cherubim**

Serbian/Croatian
'Serbian' and 'Croatian' are usually regarded as one and the same language, the Serbo-Croat of Yugoslavia. However, Serbs or 'Serbians', who currently make up about 36 per cent of the population, are Eastern Orthodox Christians, and so write the language in the Cyrillic script (like Russian), while the Croats or 'Croatians', who represent some 20 per cent of the population, are Roman Catholics, and thus write the language in Roman script (like English). This means that many street signs are in both scripts, much as in Ireland they are in Irish (Gaelic) and English. True, there are minor differences in the language, as spoken by each race, but normally 'Serbians' will understand 'Croatians' perfectly, and vice versa. (Serbo-Croat is the main, but not the only language spoken in Yugoslavia. There is also Slovenian and Macedonian.)

serenade/aubade
Two rather attractive, indeed literally musical words, to describe respectively a piece of music played in the evening, at dusk, or in the early morning, at dawn. The object is usually to woo a woman, while at the same time extolling the beauties of the dusky evening or the dawning day. The terms can also be used

of a poem similarly declaimed or read at these times and to these ends. A 'serenade', by its very nature, is a more common creation than an 'aubade' – one must be truly inspired to make music or read poems at dawn – and its purely musical sense can be a much wider one, to denote any lyrical composition in several movements, especially an instrumental one. Both words are from the French, however: 'serenade' (related, as one would hope, to 'serene') comes ultimately from Latin *serenus*, 'clear', while 'aubade' goes back eventually to Latin *albus*, 'white'. In their origin, therefore, the extremes almost meet.

series winding

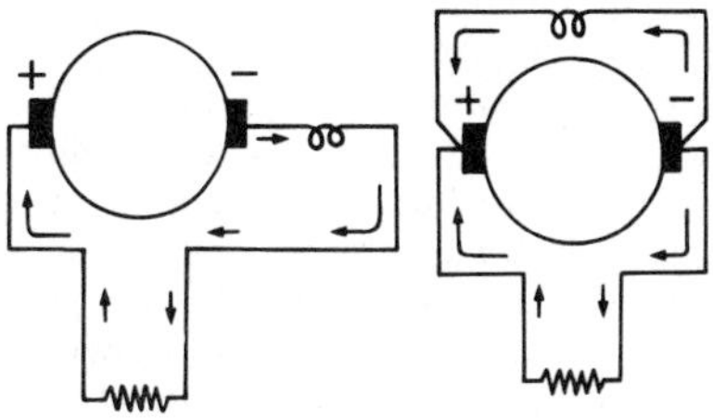

shunt winding

series see **parallel**

series winding/shunt winding
'Series winding' relates to an electric motor or generator in which the field and armature circuits are wound in series (see **parallel/series**). With 'shunt winding' the circuits are connected in parallel (ditto). 'Shunt winding', as its name implies, thus establishes a current path that is auxiliary to the main circuit, and can be used for taking off surplus current if the main current for a particular appliance is too great.

serif/sans serif
A 'serif', as all printers know, is the name of the little line that appears at the end of a main stroke in a printed letter, where it is at an angle to that stroke. For example, the 'feet' of a capital 'A' are 'serifs', as are the small lines at the end of the three main strokes of a capital 'E'. This is the standard form of type. 'Sans serif', as its name implies, is therefore a typeface where these small lines are absent, and where the characters have no 'serifs'. 'Sans serif' is commonly used for bold advertisements and newspaper headlines, the latter mainly in the 'popular' press. (For good examples of 'serif' type, see *The Times*, and especially its 'masthead' or title, printed in capitals, where every letter has from two to four 'serifs'.) 'Sans' is French for 'without', but 'serif' is not a French word. It is probably Dutch *schreef*, 'stroke', 'line', so related to English 'scribe'. 'Sans' is pronounced to rhyme with 'Hans'.

serif sans serif

servant see **master**[3]

service ceiling/absolute ceiling
Both terms relate to the altitude at which an aircraft flies. When an aircraft reaches its 'service ceiling', in standard conditions of flying, it cannot rise any higher except at a particular designated small rate of climb, for example 100 feet a minute. When it reaches its 'absolute ceiling', it cannot rise any higher at all, and must fly only horizontally (or down). Such 'ceilings' are measured above sea level. 'Service' here means 'economical', 'effective'.

several see **joint**

shade see **light**[3]

shadow cabinet/cabinet
In Parliament, the 'shadow cabinet' consists of those ministers of the Opposition who would form an actual 'cabinet' if they were in power, while the 'cabinet' is the executive body of ministers of the government of the day. Each member of the 'shadow cabinet' can be designated as

'shadow' before his would-be title, such as 'shadow' Chancellor and 'shadow' Home Secretary. (This does not apply to the proposed Prime Minister, however, who is not the 'shadow' Prime Minister but the 'Leader of the Opposition'.) 'Shadow' here means 'copy', 'counterpart', and the special political usage seems to have originated during the premiership of A. J. Balfour in the opening years of the present century. See also **Government/Opposition**.

shall/will
The two auxiliary verbs have caused lengthy debates. Should one say 'I shall expect you tomorrow' or 'I will expect you tomorrow'? The standard rule was that one used 'shall' for the first person pronoun ('I', 'we'), and 'will' for the others ('you', 'he', 'she', 'it', 'they'), unless a special emphasis was needed, as in 'You *shall* come with us', 'I *will* be there'. The issue became somewhat blurred since both the Scots (and Irish) and Americans (and Canadians) reversed this principle, saying for example 'Will I open the door for you?' or 'They shan't see us here'. This led to uncertainty of usage among native English speakers. But perhaps we should attempt some guidance here, if only for the benefit of non-native English-speakers. (Like the legendary Frenchman who fell from a boat into the river, and being unable to swim, cried, 'I will drown, and no one shall save me!') As a general rule, 'will' can always be safely used to express the future in all three persons, so that it is quite acceptable to say 'I will expect you tomorrow', and 'You *will* come with us', even for emphasis. In actual practice, the form of 'will' (or 'shall') is reduced to simply ''ll' in many cases, thus avoiding any need for choice. The Frenchman could thus have well said, 'I'll drown, and no one'll save me!' He would have been more certain of rescue that way. ('I'll save you; you'll be all right!')

shallow see **deep**

sharp[1]/blunt
'Sharp' is used of something that is pointed or that can cut easily; 'blunt' is the opposite, and means that an object will not pierce or cut. (Although an attacker can harm his victim equally with a weapon that does either, by cutting or slashing him with a 'sharp' knife, or hitting him hard with a 'blunt' weapon.) 'Blunt' often implies that something that was formerly 'sharp' no longer is so, such as a 'blunt' knife or a 'blunt' pencil. But there are certain instances where 'blunt' will not be the opposite of 'sharp'. A 'sharp' cry, for instance would have a 'gentle' cry as its opposite, or perhaps a 'low' cry, while a 'sharp' bend would have a 'gradual' bend as its contrary. Similarly, a 'blunt' comment has a 'tactful' one as an opposite.

sharp[2]/flat
These are the musical opposites. A 'sharp' (#) is a sign indicating that a note must be raised by a semitone, for example C to C#. A 'flat' (♭) is the opposite, lowering a note by a semitone, such as B to B♭. If a person is singing 'sharp', it means that his voice tends to be pitched higher than it should be, whereas someone who sings 'flat' is out of tune by singing too low. Many European languages have a word for the symbols that are derived from classical roots, and the word for 'sharp' (French *dièse*, Italian *diesis*, etc.) comes from Greek *diesis*, 'quarter-tone', while the equivalent of 'flat' (French *bémol*, Italian *bemolle*, etc.) derives from medieval Latin *B mollis*, 'softened B'. This last was the term devised for an extra note that was needed a semitone lower than B, and it later came to be used of any 'flattened' note. The note itself was written as a rounded 'b', and this is the origin of the modern 'flat' symbol. In German, a 'flat' is simply *das B* even now (although a 'sharp' is *Kreuz*, 'cross'). Pianists will be aware that what may be a 'sharp' note in one piece will be a 'flat' in another, depending on the key. Thus C# (the black note between C and D) can also be D♭. These are really two distinct notes, but on the piano, because of the limited number of actual notes (keys), double up as one.

she see **he**

sheep/goats
If we sort out or separate the 'sheep' from the 'goats' (figuratively), we are selecting the better or superior people. So what's wrong with 'goats'? The expression has a biblical origin: 'And before him shall be gathered all nations: and he shall separate them one from another, as a shepherd divideth his sheep from the goats' (Matthew 25:32). Here, the animals represent the righteous and the wicked. So, again, what's wrong with 'goats'? The truth is that although both animals were (and are) kept for their meat and milk and coats (wool and hair, respectively), the 'sheep' has the edge, and what it can offer man is a better and purer and also more abundant quality and quantity of these commodities. In biblical times, too, 'sheep' were more easily herded, and kept together, while 'goats' tended to wander off and go astray. They mostly still do, unless tethered.

shellback see **polliwog**

Shi'ite/Sunnite
In the world of Islam, the 'Shi'ites' are those Muslims who do not recognize the first three caliphs who succeeded Muhammad (the founder of Islam) and who follow Ali, Muhammad's cousin and son-in-law, claiming that he was endowed by divine will. Ali was the first in a line of imams, and 'Shi'ites' believe that the last recognized imam will return as a 'messiah'. Hence they are sectarian or partisan, which is what Arabic *shi'ah* means. The 'Sunnites', therefore are the orthodox Muslims, who recognize the caliphs who succeeded Muhammad. Unlike the 'Shi'ites', they hold that all believers are equal before God, whereas the 'Shi'ites' have a type of clergy. (The Ayatollah Khomeini is their head.) The 'Shi'ites' thus reject the tenet of the 'Sunnites' that the people themselves have the right to select their ruler, and strive to established guided clerics in their place. (For the effect the religious differences have had in the Middle East, and in particular in the Gulf War, see **Iran/Iraq**.) Arabic *sunna* means 'path', because the 'Sunnites' hold that they are following the true path, and that the 'Shi'ites' have deviated from it. In the Muslim community as a whole, there are only about 15 per cent 'Shi'ites' as against 85 per cent 'Sunnites'. In Iran, however, the 'Shi'ites' are in the majority, while in Iraq the 'Sunnites' are in a minority.

short see **long**

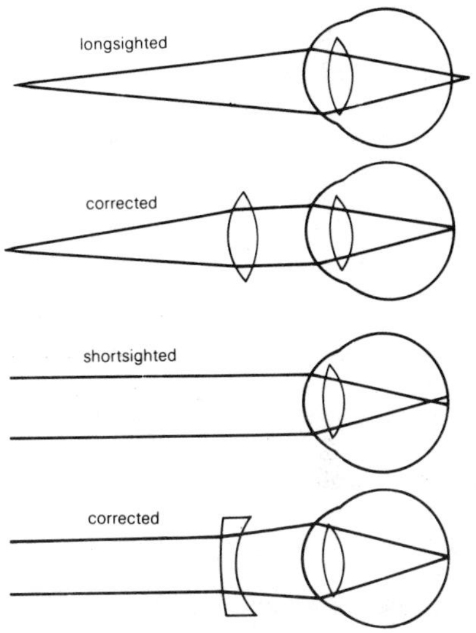

short-sighted/long-sighted
For some reason, it is sometimes supposed that a 'short-sighted' person is someone who cannot see things close to. In fact the reverse is true, and he can see nearby objects well, but not ones at any distance. It follows that a 'long-sighted' person is one with good vision for remote objects, but possibly (although not necessarily) finds it hard to see nearby objects. No doubt the confusion arises among normal-sighted people, who sometimes see a 'short-sighted' person taking off his glasses

to have a better look at an object near him. (The general necessity to wear glasses is due to the phenonemon known as 'presbyopia', when the lens of the eye loses its elasticity and the eye finds it hard to focus.) To be 'short-sighted' is a much more common defect than to be 'long-sighted'. See also **myopic/hypermetropic**.

short story see **novel**

shower meteor/sporadic meteor
As far as astronomers are concerned, meteors come in two types. A 'shower meteor' is one that travels in a stream or 'shower' together with many others. Sometimes such showers can last for days. 'Shower meteors' are generally regarded as the debris of a comet. On the other hand, 'sporadic meteors', as their name suggests, come individually. They can be observed travelling over a section of the night sky for a period up to about 30 seconds. 'Shower meteors' have a fixed time of appearance, so that the Perseids can be seen in the first half of August, for example, and the Taurids in November. (They are named after the constellation from which they appear to radiate.)

shunt winding see **series winding**

shut see **open**[2]

sickle see **hammer**[1]

siderite see **aerolite**

cross-saddle

side-saddle

side-saddle/cross-saddle
Most people when they ride a horse sit 'cross-saddle', that is, with the legs astride the horse. 'Side-saddle', with both legs on the near side of the horse (see **near/off**), is the posture adopted only by women (who can of course equally well ride 'cross-saddle'). The 'side-saddle' attitude was originally designed for women wearing long skirts when riding, and is today used mainly on ceremonial occasions, such as (formerly) by the Queen when present at the Trooping of the Colour. A 'side-saddle' rider has only one stirrup, not two, and a special balance strap to hold. The saddle of a 'side-saddle' rider will also have two crutches or pommels near the front: one, called the 'near' or 'second' pommel near the head of the saddle, over which the rider places her right leg, and the other, called the 'leaping head' or 'hunting horn' (incorrectly, 'second pommel'), placed close to the near side and lower down than the 'near' pommel, under and against which the rider places her left leg. Otherwise the 'side-saddle' itself is built basically on the same lines as the 'cross-saddle', but is slightly heavier.

side-wheeler

stern-wheeler

side-wheeler/stern-wheeler
Two contrasting types of paddle steamer. The 'side-wheeler' has two large paddle-

wheels, one on each side. The 'stern-wheeler', unsurprisingly, has a single large paddle-wheel at the stern. The wheels on a 'side-wheeler' were relatively narrow, while the one at the rear of the 'stern-wheeler' was more like a revolving drum. I say 'was' and 'were' here, because although paddle steamers still exist, they have largely been superseded by conventional steamers with propellers ('screws').

sight/sound
'Sight' and 'sound' are not only the contrasting 'thing seen' and 'thing heard', as perceived by the two senses of seeing and hearing, but the complementary attractions or attributes of many objects, such as the 'sights' and 'sounds' of a city or of a more contrived enactment such as a concert performance. We nearly always expect and even demand to have something to see when we listen, and to hear when we look. Hence the attraction of an opera or a ballet, or any staged or filmed performance, or television in general. The inability to see 'sights' or hear 'sounds' (i.e. blindness or deafness) is one of the greatest disabilities and deprivations we can experience. The two are frequently coupled in literature, such as in Rupert Brooke's 'The Soldier' ('If I should die . . .') where he longs for the 'sights and sounds' of England, and it was Swinburne who wrote (in 'Ave atque Vale'):

> There lies not any troublous thing
> before,
> Nor sight nor sound to war against thee
> more.

Interestingly, 'sight' can mean both 'ability to see' ('good sight') and 'thing seen' ('not a pretty sight'), whereas 'sound' can mean only 'thing heard'.

sight-read/play by ear
A pianist will often be better at doing one than the other. If he 'sight-reads' well, he is good at playing, often unprepared, from sheet music, 'reading' the notes. If he is better at 'playing by ear', he can reproduce music or a tune that he has heard, but may not be able to 'sight-read' at all. The best pianists, or other musicians, can do both equally well. For a singer, the corresponding terms are 'sight-sing' and 'sing by ear'. Most of us are the latter.

sign/symptom
For a doctor, a 'sign' is an objective indication of a disease or disorder, such as an enlarged gland or an irregular heart-beat, which he himself can detect in his patient. Conversely, a 'symptom' is what the patient experiences, and is something that the doctor may need to be told about. Indeed, it may not be the indication of a disease or disorder at all, as 'symptoms' can be subjective or even 'all in the mind'. An example of a 'symptom' might thus be difficulty in breathing or dizziness. (For the latter, see also **body/soul**.)

silver see **gold**

similar see **congruent**

simile/metaphor
Both a 'simile' and a 'metaphor' are figures of speech used to compare one thing to another. In a 'simile', the comparison is straightforward, and is indicated by a word such as 'like' or 'as', for example 'legs like tree-trunks' or 'warm as toast'. In a 'metaphor' (which literally means 'transference'), there is no 'like' or 'as' but instead one thing is described *in terms of* another, for example 'The ship ploughed the waves' or 'The tennis champion motored to victory'. Much poetry contains 'metaphors', because they are subtle and evocative, such as Milton's 'Under the opening eyelids of the morn' and Shelley's 'See the mountains kiss high heaven'. A 'simile' is thus explicit, 'spelt out', while a 'metaphor' has a comparison that is implicit (see **implicit/explicit**).

simple[1]/complex
Apart from the general contrasting senses of 'easy' and 'complicated', the two terms have certain precise uses. For example, in grammar, a 'simple' sentence is one with a single main clause, as in 'We arrived at the house', while a 'complex' sentence is one with a main clause and at least one subordinate clause, as in 'We arrived at

the house where our friends lived'. (This is not the same as a *compound* sentence: see next entry.) There are more opposites for 'simple' and 'compound' than 'simple' and 'complex', however, as the following entry shows.

simple[2]/compound
Unlike the pair **simple/complex** (above), these opposites have several precise applications. Among the best known are the following. A 'simple' fracture is one in which the bone does not penetrate the skin, whereas in a 'compound' fracture it does. In the world of finance and investment, 'simple' interest is interest paid on the principal (the basic sum loaned) alone, while 'compound' interest is interest paid on the principal plus any 'simple' interest it has earned. A 'simple' microscope has a single lens, like a magnifying glass, but a 'compound' microscope has two or more lenses, one with a short focal length and the other with a long, that further magnifies the image. In grammar, a 'simple sentence' is one with a single main clause (see entry above), while a 'compound' sentence has at least two main clauses, joined with a conjunction such as 'and' or 'but', for example 'We arrived at the house and stopped the car'.

simple vow/solemn vow
In the Roman Catholic church, a 'simple vow' is one taken by a person entering a religious order that permits him or her to retain property and that recognizes any marriage that may be entered into under canon law (church law). A 'solemn vow' makes no such concessions, and is also irrevocable. It prevents the person from owning any property and bans any marriage from being entered into. Both types of vow are made in public.

simplex/duplex
These terms are used in some technical senses to imply 'one-way' or 'two-way'. For example, a 'simplex' telecommunications link allows communication in one direction only, while a 'duplex' link allows it in both directions at the same time. The words mean literally 'one-fold' and 'two-fold'. In North America, a 'duplex' apartment is one on two floors, but a one-floor flat is not normally known as a 'simplex', because most apartments are on a single floor anyway.

single[1]/double
A fairly large number of domestic objects and arrangements are either 'single' or 'double', apart from the obvious 'single' bed for one person and 'double' for two. 'Single' cream, for instance, can be poured, and is lighter and thinner than 'double' cream, which is meant for whipping. It also contains nearly three times as much butterfat as 'single' cream. Then, in clothing, a 'single'-breasted coat or jacket fastens at the centre with a 'single' row of buttons, while a 'double'-breasted coat has an overlapping piece and two rows of buttons (but only one row of buttonholes). A 'single'-decker is a bus (or a cake) with one deck or layer, while a 'double'-decker has two. Incidentally, a 'singlet' (the vest, as worn by athletes) is so called since it has only one thickness of material, as distinct from the old 'doublet' (the man's jacket of Elizabethan times), which had two. And talking of athletes, we must not forget the tennis 'singles', with two players, as against the 'doubles', with four.

single[2]/return
The usual sense here is for a 'one-way' ticket or a 'there and back' one. ('One-way ticket' is actually the American equivalent of the British 'single'.) 'Single' here refers to the one journey that the passenger will make. Oddly, the British concept does not refer to the actual direction or to 'going' (as distinct from coming back) that other languages have. In French a 'single' ticket is an *aller* (a 'going'), and even the American 'one-way' implies a journey that will be made in one direction, not two. (British English does not talk of a 'single' street, for example, but a 'one-way' street.)

single see **married**

single-sex/mixed
Terms sometimes but not consistently

used to denote, respectively, a school for one sex only (usually boys, unless otherwise stated) or for both, i.e. coeducational. Much educational discussion, informed and uninformed, has been devoted to the relative merits and disadvantages of one system or the other. The general opinion seems to be that 'single-sex' schools produce better academic results, especially for girls, but that 'mixed' schools prepare their students best for life in general. As schools are suppose to achieve both these aims, this makes for something of a dilemma.

singular/plural
One of the most familiar grammatical divisions, into 'one' ('the house') and 'more than one' ('the houses'). Some pedants sometimes get worked up about such phrases as 'the government are' instead of 'the government is', claiming that you can't have a 'plural' verb with a 'singular' subject. But since 'government' implies 'members of the government', there is little need for them to worry. Some languages have, or used to have, a 'dual' in addition to a 'singular' and a 'plural', this being used for two objects. Classical Greek had it, as did Russian, and modern Arabic still has it. In languages where it used to exist, it has now blended with the 'plural'. In non-grammatical derivatives, the contrast hardly exists, so that 'singularity' is not the opposite of 'plurality'.

sinister/dexter
As purely heraldic terms, 'sinister' means 'left' and 'dexter' means 'right'. Hence the infamous 'bend sinister' that denoted a bastard. (It is a band that runs diagonally from the upper right to the lower left of a shield. The 'bend' represented a sword belt.) It was not this usage that led to the modern meaning of 'sinister' as 'evil', 'ominous', however, because this goes back to Roman times, when augurs regarded the left-hand side to be the unlucky one. (*Sinister* is a pure Latin word, as is *dexter*.) 'Dexterous', however, means 'skilful', 'clever', because the right hand is most people's 'best' one. Compare the next entry for a much more specialized use.

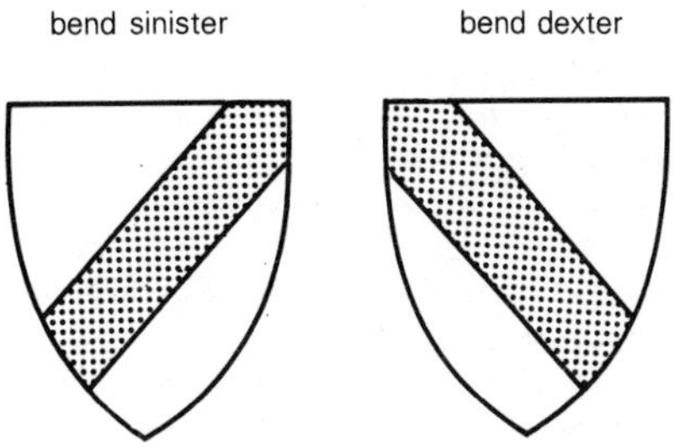

sinistrorse/dextrorse
Two botanical words used of climbing plants. Ones that are 'sinistrorse' climb in a spiral that turns from right to left, while 'dextrorse' plants spiral to the right. (That is, to the left and right from the plant's point of view, not from that of someone looking at it. Ambiguity is possible here, just as it can be for the pair **left/right** itself.) The honeysuckle is 'sinistrorse', but the hop 'dextrorse'. (Sweet peas are neither, but climb by means of tendrils.) The '-orse' of the terms is related to Latin *versus*, 'turned'.

sinner see **saint**

Sir[1]/Madam
Forms of polite address to a man (gentleman) and woman (lady), respectively. Both are used as formal letter-starters, without the name: 'Dear Sir', 'Dear Madam'. However, when it comes to 'Sir' as a title for a knight, put before his first name ('Sir James Smith'), his wife will not be called 'Madam' but 'Lady'. (As such, she will either have 'Lady' before her surname, as 'Lady Smith', or with her Christian name preceding this, as 'Jane, Lady Smith', but not 'Lady Jane Smith', unless she is to be distinguished from another 'Lady Smith', and even then her Christian name should be put in brackets when in written form, as 'Lady (Jane) Smith'. Wives of knights were also formerly called 'Dame'.) Both terms are of French origin, with 'Madam' literally

'my lady' (*ma dame*). See also **monsieur/madame**, **senior/junior**, and the two entries below.

Sir²/Miss
Traditional forms of address by a school pupil to a male or female teacher respectively. Some schoolchildren even use the words virtually as names: 'Sir said we were not to do that', 'I gave my book in to Miss'. 'Sir' goes for a married or unmarried male teacher, as does 'Miss' for his female counterpart. This despite the fact that many female school teachers are married. (Formerly, and typically, they were not, so 'Miss' was correct.) See also the previous entry, and **Master/Miss**.

sire/dam
The words are chiefly used in animal breeding and rearing, especially horses and dogs, where they refer respectively to a young animal's male and female parent. The terms are obviously closely linked to the pair **Sir/Madam** above, and came into English similarly through French. 'Sire' was also formerly a form of address to a monarch, as familiar in the Christmas carol 'Good King Wenceslas', where the page says to the king: 'Sire, the night is darker now'. See also **monsieur/madame**.

sister see **brother**

sit see **stand**

sitting trot/rising trot
In horse riding, a 'sitting trot' is a trot made by the horse while the rider sits still in the saddle. In a 'rising trot', the rider thus rises in the saddle in time with the trot (on every second beat). The latter method is much less tiring for the rider, and also looks more harmonious. It was formerly also known as the 'post trot', as this was the method of trotting favoured by postillions (post boys) when accompanying mail or stage coaches. A further name for the 'rising trot' was also 'English trot' because of this, while the 'sitting trot' was also known as the 'cavalry trot' or 'French trot'.

skilled/unskilled
The distinction here is the standard one to refer to a worker or employee, or an applicant for a job, with 'skilled' meaning that the person has been trained in particular craft or trade, and 'unskilled' meaning that he hasn't. In official statistics, where people are graded socially (by class) from A down to E, a 'skilled' working class person is graded as C2, while an 'unskilled' person is DE (i.e. a combination of the two lowest grades). (C1 belong to the middle class, together with A and B.) In a way, it is rather odd that the lack of knowledge of a particular skill should put one low down the social scale, as there are a number of upper and middle class people who also do not posses any skill, whatever other knowledge they may have.

skim milk/whole milk
'Skim milk' (or 'skimmed milk') is milk from which the cream has been removed, i.e. it has been 'skimmed off'. 'Whole milk' is therefore normal, natural milk, with nothing removed. 'Skim milk' is preferred by slimmers since it has a lower fat content.

skin/hide
To the man and woman in the street, the two words may well seem synonyms, for an animal's 'skin' is also its 'hide', and vice versa. To a tanner, however, 'skin' is the term for the actual leather made from an animal's 'hide', while this latter term is used to refer to the animal's 'skin' while it is still raw or at the most only tanned, and not fully treated as leather. After all, we talk about leather goods as 'pigskin', 'sheepskin', 'calfskin' or whatever when referring to the unfortunate animal who provided the particular 'hide' for the article.

Skinfaxi see **Hrimfaxi**

sky wave/ground wave
In radio communications, a 'sky wave' is a radio wave reflected back to the earth by a communications satellite, so avoiding difficulties created by the curved surface

of the earth. Such a wave can also be reflected from the ionosphere (the upper region of the earth's atmosphere). This means that a 'ground wave' is a conventional one, beamed from a transmitter on the ground to a receiving aerial, also on the ground. A 'ground wave' is also sometimes known as a 'surface wave' (and is often confined to line of sight, moreover).

slam/rave
Semi-jargon words used by journalists and reporters to mean either 'harsh criticism' on the one hand, or 'extravagant praise' on the other. 'Slam' is more common as a verb ('The art critic slammed the exhibition'), while 'rave' often occurs in the phrase 'rave review' ('Minister's first play gets rave review').

slander see **libel**

slave/master
The mechanical or technical equivalents of (with the boss first) **master/servant.** A 'slave' is a name for a device that is controlled by, or copies the action of, another device, the 'master'. For example, in a hydraulic braking system, the 'slave' cylinder is a small cylinder containing a piston that actually works the brake shoes or pads, while the 'master' cylinder is the main one containing the working fluid (also with a piston). In a computer, the typewriter unit is a 'slave', as it is controlled by the computer itself, the 'master'.

slow/fast
Unlike the pair (in reversed places) **quick/slow**, 'slow' and 'fast' are the general terms to indicate time or speed, especially of mechanical things ('slow running' of an engine, or 'fast flying' of an aircraft). When a clock is 'slow', or tells a time earlier than it really is, it is because its mechanism is running 'slow' for some reason. When a clock is 'fast', the opposite happens. In photography, a so-called 'fast' film is one that is highly sensitive to light, while a 'slow' film is less sensitive. Hence the 'speed' of a film, which is really its sensitivity (as it is actually called in some languages, such as German *Empfindlichkeit* and Russian *chuvstvitel'nost'*). In cinematography, a 'slow' motion film is actually achieved by filming at a 'fast' running speed. On a motorway, the outer, right-hand lane is sometimes inaccurately called the 'fast' lane, implying that the others are 'slow'. In fact it is not intended for continuous high-speed driving but simply for overtaking (see the Highway Code, section 156!).

slow see **quick**

slow handclap see **applause**

slug/snail
'Slugs and snails and puppy-dogs' tails', says the nursery rhyme, are 'what little boys are made of'. (Surely they are not *all* that repellent?) The main difference between the two types of gardener's enemy is that 'slugs' do not have shells, whereas 'snails' do. Oddly, the need to differentiate does not seem to have arisen until the eighteenth century. Before this time 'snail' was the general word for both creatures, with or without a shell. This distinction apart, they are basically the same terrestrial gastropod mollusc.

slump see **boom**

small see (1) **great** (2) **large**

small letter see **capital letter**

smoker/non-smoker
With the increasing publicity given to the dangers of smoking, it is not surprising that the numbers of 'smokers' have decreased in recent years, while 'non-smokers' have increased. More manifestly, the number of 'non-smokers' (train compartments or carriages in which no smoking is allowed) has also increased, to the extent that all trains on the London Underground are now 'non-smokers'. 'Non-smoker' is thus one of the few negative terms that is really quite positive. We really need an equivalent to 'teetotaller' or 'abstainer' to avoid the negative-seeming 'non-'.

smooth see **rough**

snail see **slug**

snakes/ladders
Those familiar with the children's board game will know that the 'ladders' take the lucky player up to a higher number when his piece lands at the foot of it, while a throw of the dice that sends him to the head of a 'snake' will mean a drop to a lower number, at the end of its tail. Rather like the pair of **swings/roundabouts**, the terms are sometimes used figuratively, even in the singular, to mean a rise and a fall, or an advantage and a disadvantage. In its issue of 30 April 1985, *The Times* described Lord Home as the only person in a television programme with 'the honesty and clearsightedness to see television as both snake and ladder'.

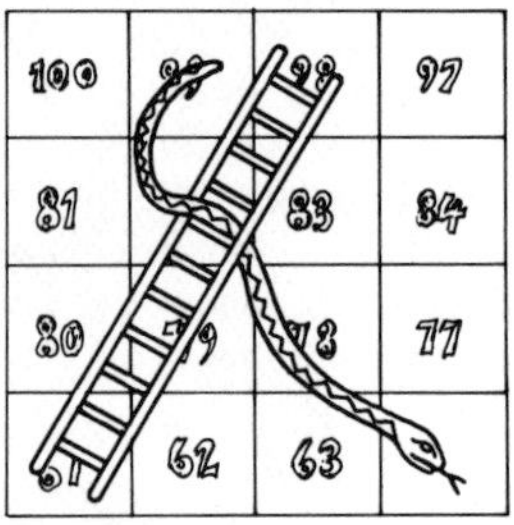

snob/inverted snob
Which is the more objectionable? A 'snob' tries to associate with 'top people', and looks down condescendingly on others. An 'inverted snob' (surely there must be a neater term?) is someone who rejects his own upper or middle class values and affects an identity with those of a lower class. The first is a prig, the second a hypocrite.

soar/plummet
The two words are used by journalists to describe things that have rapidly risen or dramatically fallen, such as prices, shares and the temperature. The verbs therefore occur fairly commonly in headlines, such as 'Gold soars', 'Shares plummet'. ('Soar' literally means 'expose to the breeze', deriving ultimately from Latin *ex-*, 'out' and *aura*, 'breeze'. 'Plummet' is related to Latin *plumbum*, 'lead', i.e. the heavy metal.)

sober see **drunk**

social/solitary
These terms relate to bees and other insects. 'Social' bees live with others in colonies while 'solitary' bees, also known as 'nonsocial' bees, do not. ('Social' bees live in nests or hives; 'solitary' bees usually dig a burrow in the ground. Ants are well-known 'social' insects.) For more about bees see **bee/wasp**, **drones/workers**.

socket see **plug**

soft see (1) **hard** (2) **loud**

softwood see **hardwood**

solar/lunar
The correct scientific adjectives to be used respectively for the pair **sun/moon**, as in a 'solar' eclipse or a 'lunar' crater. They derive directly from Latin *solaris* and *lunaris*, themselves coming from *sol* and *luna*. The latter pair form the basis for many modern words for 'sun' and 'moon' in non-English languages, such as French *soleil* and *lune*, Italian *sole* and *luna*, and even Russian *solntse* and *luna*.

sole see **upper**[4]

solemn vow see **simple vow**

soli/tutti
The Italian words are musical terms to indicate, respectively, a passage of music to be performed by soloists, for example in an opera or oratorio, and a passage to be performed by all the singers, or all the members of the orchestra. The literal meanings are 'alone' and 'all' (i.e. are the plural forms of Italian *solo* and *tutto*). The latter word is the more common, and is found in music reviews, for instance, as a standard English word ('After a hauntingly beautiful solo on the cor anglais and a perfectly timed pause, the piece

concluded with a magnificent tutti, with not a note out of place').

solid/liquid
Otherwise the general principle behind the **food/drink** pair or even (in reverse order) the **urinate/defecate** couple. As occurring in more specialized terms, 'solid' and 'liquid' frequently have no matching opposite, so that there is no 'liquid' geometry to counter 'solid' geometry, nor any 'solid' crystal display to set off the 'liquid' crystal display (LCD) seen in calculators. The nearest one can get here is perhaps 'solid' fuel and 'liquid' fuel, the former perhaps being coal, and the latter petrol or paraffin. Yet another doublet in the same basic category is that of **land/sea**.

solitary see **social**

solstice see **equinox**

son/daughter
Male and female offspring, of course, with the former also familiar in the names of family businesses, such as 'James Cooper & Son'. Occasionally, and pleasantly, one also finds the opposite, such as the London butcher and fishmonger Wainwright & 'Daughter'. The two relationships are so basic, that one finds similar words in many other languages besides English, such as German *Sohn/Tochter*, Swedish *son/dotter*, Russian *syn/doch'*, and, where it all started, Greek *hyios/thygatēr* (the first word having *h* where we now have *s*). There are a number of sayings and proverbs that bring out a more domestic contrast, too, such as 'My son is my son till he has got him a wife, but my daughter's my daughter all the days of her life', and 'Marry your son when you will, your daughter when you can'.

sophism/paralogism
In logic, a 'sophism' is an argument that is deliberately specious or invalid, but a 'paralogism' is one that is unintentionally false. A great perpetrator of 'sophisms' in classical times was the philosopher Eubulides of Miletus. He came up with the following, for example: 'What you haven't lost, you have. You haven't lost any horns. Therefore you have horns.' (Another of his paradoxes was the mind-teasing 'Does a man who says he is now lying, speak truly?') We are probably all guilty of 'paralogisms' at some time or other, such as when we reason: 'If Jim is a trustworthy person, then he can be entrusted with this new post; but he is not a trustworthy person, so he can't be entrusted with the post'. (We have committed the fallacy or 'paralogism' of mistakenly reaching our conclusion from the original statement, or what is technically known as denying the antecedent.) 'Sophism' gets its name from Greek *sophisma*, 'clever trick', ultimately from *sophos*, 'wise' (hence 'sophisticated', as many 'sophisms' are). 'Paralogism' means literally 'reason aside'.

soul see **body**[2]

sound/light
'OK for lights? OK for sound?' was long the standard filmmaker's check before 'shooting', and the two complementary requirements are certainly essential for any visual and aural recording: without 'light', you will see nothing; without 'sound', you will hear nothing. As with the pair **sight/sound**, both are key elements in many types of performance and 'show', from stage productions and films to the more specialized '*son et lumière*', the historical re-enactment that is named precisely after the two components. However, there is natural 'sound' and 'light' as well in daily life, and nature herself can put on her own '*son et lumière*' with a dramatic display of **thunder/lightning**. In this pair, 'lightning' is obviously related to 'light', and although I have not seen it in any etymological dictionary, I do not think it too fanciful to see an ultimate (primeval) link-up between 'thunder' and 'sound'. (The words are still close in some languages, such as French *tonner* and *sonner*, and the Latin *tonare* and *sonare* from which they derived. Compare, too, Greek *bronte*, 'thunder' and *bromos*, 'sound', especially a roaring or clashing one.)

sound see **sight**

sour see **sweet**[3]

source language/target language
Two rather awkward terms used when translating from one language into another. The 'source language' is the one from which the translation is made, while the 'target language' is the language into which the translation is made. The 'target' implies that one is 'aiming' at the other language, with the hope of scoring more hits than misses.

south see **north**

sovkhoz see **kolkhoz**

spade/spoon
Both words are types of oar used in rowing. A 'spade' is an oar with a blade that is relatively broad and short, like the garden implement, while a 'spoon', like the domestic utensil, has a blade that is curved at the edges and tip. The advantage of this latter type is that it gets a good hold on the water by its 'scooping' action.

spare see **strike**

sparkling see **still**

spay see **castrate**

spear side/distaff side
Two rather poetic terms used to denote, respectively, the male and female sides or branches of a family. By today's liberated standards, the basic 'spear' and 'distaff' are hopelessly stereotyped for each sex, but they go back to Old English, and so to an age when man's work was with the 'spear' (for killing) and woman's with the 'distaff' or spindle (for spinning).

specialist/generalist
A 'specialist' is a person who makes a close and detailed study of a particular subject or discipline, or who is an expert in it. A 'generalist', by contrast, has knowledge and interests that extend to several fields or activities. A familiar example of a 'generalist' is the family doctor, actually called a 'general practitioner' ('G.P.') because he treats all illnesses and does not specialize.

species see **genus**

spin drier see **tumble drier**

spinster see **bachelor**

spirits see **wines**

spiritual/temporal
'Spiritual' relates to things that are of the spirit or soul, and that are therefore to do with religion and the church. 'Temporal' relates to things that are in a sense 'temporary', in other words to human life, which has a finite span. As opposed to 'spiritual', 'temporal' thus means 'lay', 'secular'. The terms are best known in the titles 'Lords Spiritual' and 'Lords Temporal' in the House of Lords. The former are the bishops of the Church of England; the latter are all the other peers. The terms date back to at least as early as the fourteenth century. Compare **clerical/lay**, **body/soul**, **church/state**, **temporary/permanent**, **material/spiritual**.

spiritual see **material**

split ticket see **straight ticket**

spoils system see **merit system**

spoken/written
The contrasting terms here relate mostly to two types of examination, especially in a foreign language, that is, they equate with the pair **oral/written** (which see, above). But more widely, they also relate directly to **read/write** and to everyday communication, which can be by voice ('spoken') or by pen or pencil ('written'). The latter has generally more authority than the former, if only because it is a permanent record, 'in black and white'. In many legal instances, however, a 'spoken' word is as binding as a 'written' one, especially when it is a promise or under-

taking of some kind (for example, an instruction to someone to sell or buy, e.g. by telephone to a stockbroker regarding shares).

spoon see **spade**

sporadic meteor see **shower meteor**

spring[1]/autumn
The two seasons that have the same opposition to each other as have those of the pair **summer/winter**, with 'spring' seeing the 'birth' of plant life, and 'autumn' its culmination or fulfilment, as particularly in the harvest. (In fact in Old English, 'harvest' was the actual word for what is now 'autumn', as it can still be seen to be in German *Herbst*. Compare 'the seedtime and the harvest' of the harvest hymn, itself translated from the German, 'We plough the fields and scatter/The good seed on the land'. 'Autumn' has its origin in Latin *autumnus*, itself sometimes said to be related to *augere*, 'to increase', with reference to the fruition of crops.) Inevitably, there are sayings and folk wisdom linking the two, including the corny 'That which doth blossom in the spring will bring forth fruit in the autumn'. Poets, too, for whom both 'spring' and 'autumn' have been a permanent inspiration, frequently link the seasons, as in Shakespeare's 'Three beauteous springs to yellow autumn turn'd' in one of his 'Sonnets'. See also **vernal/autumnal**.

spring[2]/neap
A 'spring' tide has the greater range, and occurs (in Europe) just after a full or new moon. A 'neap' tide thus has the smaller range, and takes place at the first and third quarters of the Moon. 'Spring' does not relate to the season, but has the sense 'rise', as in a 'spring' of water. 'Neap', which relates only to tides, is a word of uncertain origin, deriving from Old English. Other languages sometimes use opposite terms based on 'syzygy' (for 'spring' tide) and 'quadrature' (for 'neap'). These rare words have an astronomical sense in English, the first referring to position of the Sun, Moon and Earth in a straight line, the second describing the situation when the Sun and the Moon are at an angle of 90° to the earth. It is these precise positions that alter the gravitational influence of the Sun and Moon, which is what causes the tides in the first place. ('Syzygy' is a Greek word meaning 'yoked together', referring to the double attraction of the Sun and Moon.)

spring wheat/winter wheat
'Spring wheat' is wheat that is sown in spring and harvested later the same year. 'Winter wheat' is sown in the autumn (rather than the actual winter), and is harvested the following year, usually in the summer.

springwood/summerwood
'Springwood' is the wood produced by a plant in the spring as the softer portion of an annual ring of wood. 'Summerwood' is formed later in the season as the harder portion of the annual ring. 'Springwood' is also more porous than 'summerwood'. See also **phloem/xylem**, since the latter is involved here.

square see (1) **feather** (2) **round**

square brackets see **round brackets**

square leg/point
Two opposite positions of fielders on the cricket field. 'Square leg' is a fielder to the left of the batsman (the 'leg' side if he is right-handed), and at right-angles to his wicket. Hence the name. 'Point' is at right-angles to the batsman on the other side of the wicket, where he will be facing the 'point' of the batsman's bat (if he is right-handed). Hence the name. In general, 'point' is closer to the wicket than 'square leg', who can be up to halfway to the boundary. 'Point' is well positioned for a catch at short range, especially one inadvertently sent his way by the batsman. 'Square leg' will usually have to deal with more powerful hits, although catches can come in his direction, too.

stabile see **mobile**

staccato/legato
In music, 'staccato' playing gives short, sharp, 'detached' notes, while 'legato' playing produces smooth, connected notes. The two Italian words (usually abbreviated 'stacc.' and 'leg.' in music scores) mean literally 'detached' and 'tied'. They can also be indicated by symbols, with 'staccato' notes having a dot under or over them, and 'legato' notes joined by a curved line (a 'slur'). 'Staccato' can also be used of an abrupt or sharp voice or sound (a 'staccato' bark), but 'legato' is rarely used in this more general way.

stag party/hen party
A 'stag party' is a party of men only, while a 'hen party' has only women. Why 'stag'? Or, to make the contrast more obvious, why not 'cock'? The reference is to the male animal, the deer, of which the female is the doe. No doubt the 'crude animal spirits' element is implied, too, as it is with similar male animal names such as 'buck', 'bull', 'ram' and 'cock' itself. Not for nothing is a 'stag party' traditionally held on the eve of a bridegroom's wedding as a sort of male parody of the (presumed) night that follows it. So the 'hen party' preserves the usage of bird names for females, as with 'chick' and 'bird' itself.

stalactite/stalagmite
The names of the two formations, found in limestone caves, are confusingly similar. The 'stalactite' is the one that hangs down from the ceiling of the cave, and the 'stalagmite' the one that projects upwards from the floor. (If in doubt which is which, remember that the 'stalactite' has 'c' for 'ceiling', and the 'stalagmite' has 'g' for 'ground'.) The two terms both derive ultimately from Greek *stalassein*, 'to drip', and the single letter that marks one from the other is also the only differentiation in many other languages besides English, because the words are 'internationally scientific'.

stalagmite see **stalactite**

stale see **fresh**[2]

stallion/mare
A 'stallion' is a male horse, especially one used for breeding, and a 'mare' is a female, also regarded as one of breeding age. The name 'stallion' is related to 'stall' and 'stand' (and, though less directly, 'stud'), and came into English from Old French, but 'mare' is pure Old English (originally *mere*), so is not related to French *mère*, 'mother'.

stamen/pistil
The 'stamen' is the male reproductive organ of a flower, consisting of a stalk ending in a so called anther, where the pollen is produced. The 'pistil' is the female reproductive part of a flower, consisting of one or more so called carpels, which are designed to receive the pollen from the 'stamen'. The transference of pollen from one to the other ('pollination') is usually carried out by birds or insects, or by the wind, but some flowers are self-pollinating, as most flowers have both a 'stamen' and a 'pistil'. 'Stamen', though coming from Latin, is related to 'stand', while 'pistil' has the same origin as 'pestle'.

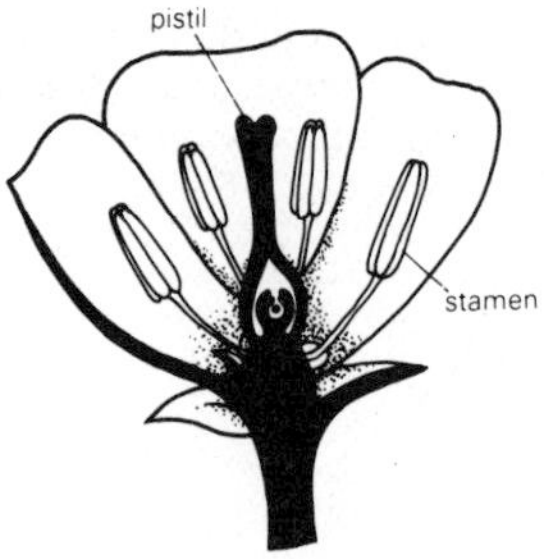

stand/sit
The two verbs represent the two most common motionless positions adopted by human beings during the day (while for animals, the alternatives are usually standing or lying). 'Standing' is more tiring, especially for any noticeable length of time, while 'sitting' is more comfortable,

since there is no need to balance in the same way, and the body is relaxed. Many public performances and enactments, from concerts to sporting events, have provision for the audience to either 'stand' or 'sit', with those who 'stand' often paying less. A political candidate 'stands' for an election in the hope of winning a 'seat'! Soldiers can sometimes 'sit' to attention, instead of 'standing' to attention. (They do this when seated in a lecture room, for example, when a senior officer comes in.) Ultimately, both 'stand' and 'sit' are related words, with the 'st' of both indicating something that is 'still' (which word is itself related). Compare also some of the words with 'st' above and below.

standard gauge/narrow gauge
In Britain, most railway lines are 'standard gauge' (1.435 metres, or 56½ inches), while several light railways are 'narrow gauge' (one metre or less). (A few railways use model locomotives, such as the Romney, Hythe and Dymchurch Light Railway, 'The World's Smallest Public Railway', whose 'narrow gauge' is only 381 millimetres.) 'Standard gauge' lines can be easily converted to main lines, if the traffic warrants it. That is their big advantage. 'Narrow gauge' railways have the edge, however, in that they allow greater flexibility in their curves. Outside the UK, many countries have a broad gauge system, i.e. one with a gauge wider than the 'standard gauge'. Indian Railways has all three types, with the broad gauge measuring 1676 millimetres and the 'narrow gauge' 762 millimetres.

standing rigging see **running rigging**

star/planet
A child's guide to the night sky would probably tell him that a 'star' twinkles, but a 'planet' does not. This is as good a working distinction as any, although one can obviously be more scientific. 'Stars', for example, shine by their own light, while 'planets' shine by means of reflecting the light of the Sun (which is itself a 'star'). 'Stars', too, are infinitely more numerous than 'planets', which including our own Earth are (so far) only nine in number. Confusingly, the Morning 'Star' and 'Evening' Star are not only one and the same celestial body but are not a 'star' at all. They are popular names of the 'planet' Venus. Such confusion is confounded by the fact that in astrology (see **astrology/astronomy**) people talk of 'stars' that are really 'planets' (e.g. 'Your love is like a red, red rose as velvet Venus perfumes the air with the rich scent of amour', Russell Grant, 'What your stars foretell', in *TV Times*, 5–11 July 1986). In 1984 astronomers got quite excited when they discovered what appeared to be both a 'star' and a 'planet' as a single body. They called it Van Biesbroeck 8B, as a companion to the genuine 'star' Van Biesbroeck 8. However, probably the best term for the new object is really a 'brown dwarf', previously only speculated to exist. 'Star' ultimately has the 'st' element, as did Latin *stella* and Greek *aster*, that relate it distantly to 'stand'. 'Planet' comes from Greek *planetes*, literally 'wanderer'. (To the ancients, they appeared to 'wander' through the constellations of 'stars', which are fixed.)

starboard see **port**

start/finish
The 'start' of something is the initial moment or spot where it begins, and the 'finish' is the similar, corresponding time or place where it ends. As such, the terms denote a fairly precise point. As sporting terms for the place where a race begins and where it ends, they have even entered other languages, such as French and Russian. The original sense of 'start' in Old English was 'jump' (compare modern 'startle'), while 'finish' has a more classical origin in Latin *finis*, 'end'. The words are commonly linked in the expression 'from start to finish', meaning 'right the way through', 'omitting nothing', especially with reference to a narrative or account of events ('Right, I want to hear everything about your trip, from start to finish'). See also **beginning/end**.

start see **stop**[2]

starting price/antepost
In horse racing, the 'starting price' (often abbreviated to 'S.P.') is the latest odds offered by bookmakers at the start of a race, just before the 'off' (see **on/off**). 'Antepost' refers to an earlier bet, one placed before the numbers of the runners are put up on the board. Such a bet can thus be made several days before the race. It is the 'starting price', however, that is quoted in the press (in the racing columns). The distinction is thus between a late bet and an early one. The 'post' of 'antepost' refers to the 'posting' of the numbers, not to the starting post!

state/private
The two terms are normally used of organizations and businesses that are either controlled by the government or are run as a commercial concern by one or more persons independently. In Britain there are thus 'state' industries (often called 'British' something, such as British Rail or British Coal), and the 'private' companies, and there are 'state' schools and 'private' schools. (Confusingly, the latter include 'public' schools: see **public/private**.) For more about the 'state' industries, see **nationalization/privatization**, also **Ltd/plc**.

state see **church**[2]

state bank see **national bank**

static see **dynamic**

stator see **rotor**

steady state theory see **big bang theory**

steam iron see **dry iron**

steeplechase/flat race
These are the two main types of horse races. A 'steeplechase' is run over a variety of jumps (hedges, fences, streams, etc., or collectively 'over the sticks'), while a 'flat race', as its name implies, has no obstacles, merely a grass course ('the turf'). The 'steeplechase' is closer in form to the actual course ridden by huntsmen when riding (or chasing) across country, since they will have to negotiate a number of hedges and ditches as they cross the fields. It got its name from the prototype race of this kind, which was a race across country to a church steeple, which served as a convenient visible 'finishing post'. Whether a particular steeple was involved is uncertain, but there were regular 'steeplechases' of this sort in the eighteenth century. As a professional sporting term, it has now passed from English to other languages in a variety of pronunciations and spellings, such as French *steeple-chase* (pronounced approximately 'stip-le-tchaize') and Russian *stipl-chez* or *stipl-cheyz* (pronounced something like the English but with a final 'z').

stem/stern
The 'front end' and 'back end' of a ship, or, more nautically, her bow or prow and her rear end. The words are common in the phrase 'from stem to stern', meaning 'from one end to the other'. The 'stem' is so called as it is the part of the ship that 'stems' the waves, i.e. makes headway against them (not the other, opposite sense of 'stem', which is 'stop', 'check'). 'Stern' is related to 'steer', as this is the part of the boat where the rudder is. See also **fore/aft**.

stenotropic/eurytropic
The terms relate to ecology and the natural environment. If an animal or plant, or its species, is 'stenotropic', it can tolerate only a limited amount of change in the environment. If, however, it is 'eurytropic', it can put up with a large number of environmental changes. Fish are notoriously 'stenotropic', because they are vulnerable to even mild pollution or other disturbance of their watery environment. On the other hand, dandelions, docks and other weeds are relatively 'eurytropic', because they are highly resistant to herbicides and other deterrents devised by man. More correctly, the words should be 'stenotopic' and 'eurytopic', and they appear to have been influenced by 'tropic'. Literally, they respectively mean 'narrow place' and 'broad place'.

stereo see **mono**

stern see **stem**

sternum/tergum
In an arthropod such as a crab or shrimp, the 'sternum' is the horny plate that covers its ventral (under) surface, while the 'tergum' is the corresponding covering for its dorsal surface (its back) (see **dorsal/ventral**). However, and more familiarly, the 'sternum' is also the technical name for the breastbone in animals (and man), although we have no 'tergum' to correspond to it. (One could make a sort of opposite pairing of 'breastbone' and 'backbone', however, although the correspondence is not very precise.) 'Sternum' is nothing to do with English 'stern', but comes from Greek *sternon*, 'chest', 'breastbone', while 'tergum' is the Latin for 'back'.

stern-wheeler see **side-wheeler**

stet see **dele**

stick[1]/carrot
The allusion is to a donkey, who needs alternately a 'stick' to punish him and a 'carrot' to encourage him, or alternatively a 'stick' to drive him on from behind, and a 'carrot' to lead him on from the front. So the implication is respectively a punishment on the one hand, or an incentive on the other. It is not clear when the phrase arose, although 'sticks' and 'carrots' have been proverbially associated with donkeys for some time. The metaphor is mostly seen in journalism, although often the other way round ('Carrot and stick in South Africa', heading in *The Times*, 9 July 1986).

stick[2]/twist
In the card game pontoon (vingt-et-un), to 'stick' is to be unwilling to play a turn, or to refuse a card from the dealer. The opposite is to 'twist', which is to request another card from the dealer. A player 'sticks' since he stays or 'sticks' where he is, or with the card value he already has. When he 'twists', he gets the card with its face turned up ('twisted'). (He would otherwise get a card face down, by laying an additional stake. When he 'twists', he pays nothing, but everyone can see his card.)

stiff/tender
These are not opposites in the general sense, but they are in a nautical one. When a sailing boat is 'stiff', it is fairly resistant to heeling and rolling, and will stay reasonably upright as it sails. If it is 'tender' it is easily heeled over by the wind. The terms seem to have originated in a metaphor referring to a muscle: if a muscle is 'stiff' it is not moved much, but when 'tender' it is sensitive and responsive.

still/sparkling
Two basic types of wine or drink in general, such as a 'still' orange drink that is not effervescent and a 'sparkling' drink that is. (Of non-alcoholic drinks, however, the more common word in the latter case is 'fizzy'.) A wine is made 'sparkling' either by having carbon dioxide added or by undergoing a secondary fermentation. The archetypal 'sparkling' wine is of course champagne (not for nothing colloquially known as 'bubbly' or 'fizz').

still birth see **live birth**

stitch/unpick
A rather curious pair of opposites, since one would expect either 'unstitch' as the standard contrary, or 'pick' as the positive form. To 'stitch' something is therefore to

sew it, with stitches, and to 'unpick' it is to remove those stitches. (There *is* a verb 'unstitch', but it is not regularly used for the process.) In fact the use of 'un-' here is a very rare one, and it has no negative force. (If you 'pick' a lock, for example, you 'undo' it in the same way that you 'undo' the stitches when you 'unpick' them.) About the only other word still surviving with a 'redundant' 'un-' like this is the verb 'unloose', although people sometimes say 'unpeel' when they mean 'peel off' ('He unpeeled his overalls'). No doubt the 'un-' survived in these cases as we are actually reversing a previous positive process, 'stitching' and putting on respectively.

stinging nettle/dock leaf
The 'dock' has long been regarded as a popular plant for effectively counteracting the sting of a 'nettle'. Conveniently, too, there are usually 'dock leaves' available not far from the 'stinging nettles'. So here one virtually has a situation of **poison/antidote**. The association of the two goes back several hundred years, especially in the folk saying 'In dock, out nettle', which occurs in Chaucer. (The full form of this 'charm', according to the *Oxford English Dictionary*, is 'Nettle in, dock out, Dock in, nettle out, Nettle in, dock out, Dock rub nettle out', this to be recited during the rubbing process.) The precise efficacy of the 'dock leaf' against the 'stinging nettle' is uncertain, although there must be something in it, as there often is in many folk remedies.

stop¹/go
Two of the most common opposites that exist, since we spend most of our lives doing one and the other, as does much of the natural and mechanical world around us. Traffic on the whole 'goes', although is all too frequently obliged to 'stop' at a point other than a vehicle's destination, possibly at road works where one of the workmen is controlling the traffic with 'stop-go' boards. In economics, a 'stop-go' policy is one resulting in alternate activity and inactivity. The government can cut taxes, for example, to make the economy 'go'. When signs of inflation appear, they can then raise taxes, and make the economy 'stop'. Britain underwent a 'stop-go' phase in the 1950s and 1960s. (After that, 'stop-go' became more 'stop-stop', as inflation increased.) For more about the traffic situation, see **red/green**. See also the next entry.

stop²/start
To 'stop' an action is to cease doing it; to 'start' one is to begin it. The two verbs are therefore diametrically opposed. 'Stopping and starting' is a fairly common phrase used of something that moves or progresses irregularly, whether mechanical or intangible, like a country's economy (where it has more or less the same sense as the 'stop-go' of the entry above). See also **start/finish**, **beginning/end**.

straight¹/bent
Apart from their standard meanings, 'straight' is a slang word for a person who is honest and reliable, while 'bent' means that he is dishonest or corrupt. ('Bent' is often used of an official who one would normally expect to be law-abiding but who is not, such as a 'bent' prison warder or a 'bent' policeman.) The two terms can also be used to denote, respectively, a heterosexual and a homosexual. (Compare **gay/straight**.)

straight²/crooked
Again, as for the entry above, the words can have a general sense, or share the same slang senses of 'law-abiding' on the one hand, or 'corrupt', 'dishonest' on the other. However, 'crooked' cannot mean 'homosexual', as 'bent' can.

straight³/curved
Here the opposite senses are standard English, and not slang, referring to something long, such as road or a surface of some kind, that either keeps to a level and undeviating course or gradually turns away from it (to one side or upwards or downwards). The two adjectives are sometimes specially associated with the human body: a man's body is mostly (or should be) 'straight', but a woman's is 'curved'.

See some classical statues, or the real thing.

straight see (1) **gay** (2) **mixed**

straight fight/three-cornered fight
In politics, a 'straight fight' is one between two candidates of opposing parties, traditionally those of the pair **Conservative/Labour**. A 'three-cornered fight' is between three candidates. In Britain, the 'three-cornered fight' has become more common from the early 1980s with the rise of the Social Democrat-Liberal Alliance. The metaphor is from boxing, with its 'corners' (but only two contestants, of course).

straight glass/jar
Most regular pubgoers have their preference for drinking beer either from a 'straight glass', without a handle, or a 'jar', with one. A stranger to a pub may well be asked which he prefers if he orders a pint (although sometimes the wording varies, and the alternatives may be suggested as 'straight or handle'). On the whole, English northerners prefer their beer in a 'straight glass', while southerners tend to settle for a 'jar' with a handle. This is presumably illustrative of the northerner's directness (he wants no frills) and the southerner's alleged greater sophistication (he attaches some importance to presentation). Characteristically, the 'straight glass' is quite unornamented and basic, while the 'jar' often has a fluted bottom. The 'straight' of the 'straight glass' also suggests that the drinker likes his beer 'straight', without any fancy receptacle. 'Jar' on its own can also be colloquial for 'drink of beer', 'pint' ('Fancy a jar?'). See also the related **jug/bottle**.

straight ticket/split ticket
In American politics, a 'straight ticket' is a ballot cast for all the candidates of one party. (The elector votes for all at once, often by means of a voting machine.) A 'split ticket' is a ballot cast for the candidates of more than one party. The 'ticket' is the list of candidates for election.

strain see **stress**

stratus see **cumulus**

strength/weakness
These are the nouns that have evolved to correspond to the adjectives **strong/weak**. They are often contrasted in assessing something, such as a plan or a person's character, his 'strengths and weaknesses'. One finds the two contrasted in literature. For example, it was Charles Lamb who said 'Credulity is the man's weakness, but the child's strength', and Emily Dickinson wrote:

> Not to discover weakness is
> The Artifice of strength.

In sexual stereotyping, 'strength' is a male characteristic and 'weakness' a female.

stress/strain
We are probably all familiar with the 'stress and strain' (or 'stresses and strains') of modern life, its hazards, problems and difficulties. But 'stress' and 'strain' have a more precise specialized contrast. In physics, the 'stress' on a body is the force that deforms it, or more exactly the intensity of such a force. The 'strain' is the converse: the deformation of such a body when it is under 'stress'. As such, the 'strain' can be expressed as the amount of change in dimension of the body (for example in length or volume) divided by its original dimension. Such 'stresses' and 'strains' are important in engineering and various types of construction.

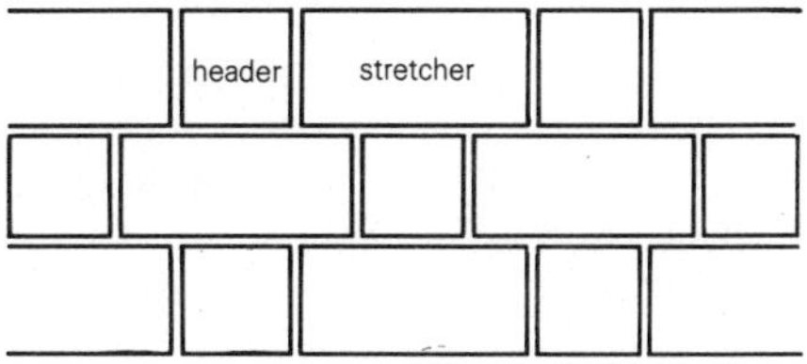

stretcher/header
Bricklayers will know that a 'stretcher' is a brick laid longside on in a wall, while a

'header' is one laid at right angles to it, so that its 'head' faces outwards. Many walls have alternating 'stretchers' and 'headers'.

strike/spare
In tenpin bowling, a 'strike' is made when all the pins are knocked down with the first bowl of a frame. The next best thing is a 'spare', when two bowls are needed to knock down all the pins. The 'spare' is so called since a player has only two deliveries in a single frame, and has used his 'spare' ball (after the first delivery) to complete the knockdown.

strike see **pitch**[2]

stripping see **stuffing**

stroke play see **match play**

strong/weak
Apart from the obvious contrasts, the adjectives have certain special uses, some narrower than others. Drinks, and especially tea, can be 'strong' or 'weak', depending on the consistency of the base, and the taste of the drinker (although 'strong drink' itself also means generally 'alcoholic drink'). A 'strong' stomach is one that is not easily upset or nauseated, while a 'weak' stomach is a delicate one, disturbed by 'strong' food. A 'strong'-minded person is 'bloody, bold and resolute', but a 'weak'-minded person lacks decisiveness or 'character'. (The term is also sometimes used as a synonym for 'feeble-minded', or mentally deranged.) The same type of contrast goes for a 'strong'-willed person and a 'weak'-willed. In grammar, a 'strong' verb is one that changes a vowel in its past tenses and forms, such as 'sing', 'sang', 'sung', while a 'weak' verb simply adds a small ending ('sew', 'sewed', 'sewn') and does not change its vowel. (German is a language of 'strong' verbs more than English is: compare its *lassen, liess, gelassen* with its English equivalent, the unchanging 'let'.) Traditional sexual stereotyping has the 'strong' man but the 'weak' woman (see **strength/weakness**), but rejecters of the latter will find support in the Apocrypha ('The first wrote, Wine is the strongest. The second wrote, The king is strongest. The third wrote, Women are strongest.', I Esdras 3:10).

strophe/antistrophe
'Strophe' (literally 'turning' in Greek) has three main senses in literature. It is the first of two movements made by a chorus in an ode in Ancient Greek drama, the first part of the actual ode itself as sung during this movement, and, more generally, the first of two metrical arrangements used alternately in a poem. It follows that the second such movement, part, and arrangement, respectively, will be the 'antistrophe', or 'counterturning', as it were. In poetry, 'strophe' is now little more than 'stanza' or simply 'verse', and in the technical sense, 'strophe' and 'antistrophe' are mostly used to refer to classical literature.

stuffing/stripping
The words look coarse, but they are actually technical terms used in marine transport (which explains their forthright if not exactly 'salty' nature). 'Stuffing' is the packing of containers, and 'stripping' the unpacking. So that's all there is to it.

subject/object
In grammar, the 'subject' of a sentence is the word or phrase about which something is said, or that (more colloquially) 'does the action', like 'John' in 'John drove the car'. The 'object' is therefore the word or phrase that is on the 'receiving' end of the verb, or that 'has the action done to it', like 'car' in this same sentence. In English and many other European languages, the 'subject' usually comes at the beginning of a sentence, and the 'object' at the end. However, in a general sense, there is little difference between 'subject' and 'object' when the meaning is 'person or thing that is studied or examined', so that one can say either 'Fieldmice have long been a popular subject for photographers' or 'Fieldmice have long been a popular object for photographers'. Purists might claim, however, that 'object' has a sense of 'focus of attention' ('objective', in fact), that

'subject' lacks. See also the next entry below, as a related topic.

subjective/objective
A 'subjective' judgment is one made in the mind of the thinking 'subject', so does not take into account all the facts of the 'object' of the judgment. By contrast, an 'objective' judgment is based on known facts, and is unbiased, without any personal prejudice or failing on the part of the person who makes it. The 'subject', therefore, is the person involved with whatever is said to be 'subjective', while the 'object' is the thing actually regarded as 'objective'. Sometimes a thing can be both 'subjective' and 'objective'. For example, the way I write in this book is largely 'subjective', but what I write about is (I hope) mostly 'objective', unless I make it clear that it is not.

subjunctive see **indicative**

sublime/ridiculous
It was Napoleon who said (although others have cited Talleyrand) 'Du sublime au ridicule il n'y a qu'un pas', and that is the origin of the English equivalent. (Napoleon is said to have made the comment to the French diplomat, Dominique de Pradt, after his retreat from Moscow in 1812.) We now regard the 'sublime' and the 'ridiculous' as supreme opposites, one the height of experience or achievement, the other a ludicrous debasement following it. However, it is possible to interpret the relationship between the two rather differently, as Thomas Paine did in his 'Age of Reason': 'The sublime and the ridiculous are often so nearly related, that it is difficult to class them separately. One step above the sublime makes the ridiculous, and one step above the ridiculous makes the sublime again'. However, he wrote that in 1795, *before* Napoleon's comparison as we are now familiar with it, so the contrast was not then so explicit.

submarine/surface vessel
It is a pity that English does not have a handier term to express the opposite of a 'submarine', but there is no 'supermarine', except in the name of the former 'Supermarine' Aviation Works, who manufactured the famous 'Supermarine' Spitfire fighter. Other languages have a more exact correspondence, such as German *Unterseeboot* and *Überwasserfahrzeug* ('over-water-travel-thing') and, even closer, Russian *podvodnaya lodka* and *nadvodny korabl'*. Still, the 'sur-' of English 'surface' is a sort of opposite to the 'sub-' of 'submarine', so all is not quite lost.

subreption see **obreption**

substratum/superstratum
Literally 'underlayer' and 'overlayer'. The terms are used in linguistics and apply respectively to a 'native' language that is replaced by that of a conquering or occupying people in a country, and, conversely, this 'colonizing' language itself, as replacing the indigenous one. This is most often found in former colonies, such as the English imported to Australia and New Zealand, or the French still found in several African countries. In the United States, English has again become the 'superstratum', with the Indian languages each a 'substratum', while in Britain, the Norman French brought over with the Conquest can be regarded as a 'superstratum', since it had a marked effect on the existing Anglo-Saxon.

subtract see **add**

subtrahend/minuend
In arithmetic, the 'subtrahend' is the number that must be subtracted from another number (the 7 in $10 - 7 = 3$), so that the minuend is the number from which the 'subtrahend' is subtracted (in this example, 10). The learned words are from Latin and mean 'that which is to be subtracted' and 'that which is to be diminished'. See also, as required, **add/subtract**.

succentor see **precentor**

successor see **predecessor**

succubus see **incubus**

suck/blow
To 'suck' something is to draw it into the mouth, and to 'blow' is to breathe out or expel something from the mouth with a puff of air. The mouthorgan or harmonica is a musical instrument played by both 'sucking' and 'blowing' to achieve all its available notes, and the piano-accordeon and concertina also work on a 'suck-blow' basis, although here the suction and blowing are gained by means of the bellows. (Most wind instruments, however, are operated by 'blowing' only.) Somewhat confusingly, in sex slang, to 'suck off' is the same as to carry out a 'blow job', i.e. to practise fellatio (see **fellatio/cunnilingus**). To raise this topic to a more academic level, it is worth pointing out that 'blow' is actually related, if indirectly, to Greek *phallos*, English 'phallus', 'penis'.

suffix see **prefix**

suggestio falsi see **suppressio veri**

Sullivan see **Gilbert**

summer/winter
Long familiar and frequently quoted opposites, as in the biblical 'While the earth remaineth, seedtime and harvest, and cold and heat, and summer and winter, and day and night shall not cease' (Genesis 8:22, a fine verse for contrasts) and Shakespeare's famous opening to *Richard III*:

> Now is the winter of our discontent
> Made glorious summer by this sun of York.

There are plenty of proverbs, too, to bring out the contrast: 'No summer but has its winter' and, more optimistically, 'Good winter, good summer' and 'After rainy winter, plentiful summer'. People wear lightweight clothes (even called 'summerweight') in 'summer', but heavier clothing in 'winter', and in some favoured cities, the monarch had both a 'Summer' Palace and a 'Winter' Palace. (Peter the Great did in St Petersburg, now Leningrad. They are still there, even if museums.) Strictly speaking, 'summer' begins at the June solstice and ends at the September equinox in the northern hemisphere, and does the opposite in the southern. (See **equinox/solstice**.) 'Summer' is almost always associated with 'sun', and 'winter' frequently with 'wind', from the similarity of the words as well as their appositeness. However, the words are not linked etymologically, and 'summer' goes back ultimately to a Sanskrit word meaning 'season', 'year', while 'winter' can be traced back to a basic connection with 'wet'. (For the 'summer' sense here, compare the poetic equivalent in expressing people's ages, usually those of young women, such as a 'maiden of sixteen summers'.) The famous Old English song beginning 'Sumer is icumin in', incidentally, was altered by Ezra Pound to the following pleasantry in his 'Ancient Music':

> Winter is icumen in,
> Lhude sing Goddamm,
> Raineth drop and staineth slop,
> And how the wind doth ramm!

It is worth noting that in Britain 'winter' is itself a season of contrasts, and is either cold and dry or mild and wet. See also **spring/autumn**, **vernal/autumnal**.

summerwood see **springwood**

sun/moon
The temptation to quote contrasting passages is great here, but must be resisted or we will burst at the seams. Suffice it to say that there are many associated contrasts with each respective celestial body, so that 'sun' suggests summer, light, heat and day, at the least, and 'moon' conjures up winter, darkness, cold and night. It is a curious astronomical coincidence, however, that although the 'sun' is around 400 times greater in diameter than the 'moon', the two are almost exactly the same size in the sky when we look at them. In a solar eclipse, for example, when the 'moon' comes between the earth and the 'sun', it exactly covers it. But back in the

world of opposites: what greater contrast exists than that between Sunday (named after the 'sun') and Monday (named after the 'moon')! See also **solar/lunar**, **gold/silver**, and even **Saturday/Sunday**.

Sunday see **Saturday**

Sunnite see **Shi'ite**

sunrise/sunset
The primal cause of the pair **dawn/dusk**, or more generally **morning/evening**, to say nothing of the implied **start/finish** (day, work). A less common quotation gently combining the two is the following, from the nineteenth-century American educationalist Horace Mann: 'Lost, yesterday, somewhere between Sunrise and Sunset, two golden hours, each set with sixty diamond minutes. No reward is offered, for they are gone forever' ('Lost, Two Golden Hours'). Although 'sunrise' and 'sunset' are themselves opposites, the pair together have a sort of contrasting duo in 'moonrise' and 'moonset'. However the latter, although occurring regularly, do so at an interval of 25 hours, and do not begin and end the night in the same way that 'sunrise' and 'sunset' begin and end the day. See also **east/west**.

sunset see **sunrise**

superior/inferior
The words derive respectively from Latin *superus* and *inferus*, 'upper' and 'lower', and are used in a number of specialized senses as well as the popular meanings 'better', even 'supercilious', and 'lowly', 'debased'. In anatomy, for instance, a 'superior' part of the body is above another, as a 'superior' artery, while an 'inferior' part is below a corresponding one (the 'inferior' maxillary bone in the lower jaw). A 'superior' planet, in astronomy, is one that has an orbit further from the Sun than that of the Earth, so that an 'inferior' planet's orbit is nearer the Sun. (In this sense, we are still geocentric.) In printing, a 'superior' figure is one printed, usually in smaller type, above the line, as in 'pitch^2', while an 'inferior' figure comes below the line, as in chemical formulae such as 'H_2SO_4'. Lake 'Superior', in the Great Lakes of Canada and the USA, is so called because it lies geographically above (north of) the others, although there is no Lake 'Inferior'. (In France, the former *départements* of Seine Inférieure and Loire Inférieure were renamed respectively as Seine Maritime and Loire Atlantique in the 1950s, because of the 'degrading' connotation of 'Inférieure'!)

superstratum see **substratum**

supine see **prone**

supply/demand
The opposites are mostly associated with economics. At its most basic, this means that if there is a 'demand' for a product or commodity, there needs to be someone to 'supply' it. Not that it is by any means always quite so simple. More precisely, the 'supply' of a commodity is the amount that producers are willing and able to offer, at a particular price, while the 'demand' for that commodity is the amount that consumers are willing and able to purchase, at the same price.

suppressio veri/suggestio falsi
The rather rarefied Latin legal terms translate literally as 'suppression of the truth' and 'suggestion of the false' respectively. 'Suppressio veri' involves the suppression, in a one-sided statement, of some material fact on the other side (which ought to be made known), while 'suggestio falsi' is a misrepresentation by which something incorrect is implied to be true, in other words, it is an indirect lie. The two terms frequently occur in conjunction with each other, and have even turned up in literature, as in Kipling's *Stalky and Co* (1899): 'It seems [. . .] that they had held back material facts; that they were guilty both of *suppressio veri* and *suggestio falsi*'.

supra/infra
Two learned opposites used in academic works to mean 'above' and 'below', i.e. before a certain point in the text, or after

it. They often occur with 'v.' ('see'). All three are straight Latin, meaning respectively the English words given here (with 'v.' the abbreviation for *vide*). Since they are Latin words, they are usually printed in italics. Compare **superior/inferior** (*supra*).

surface mail see **airmail**

surface structure see **deep structure**

surface vessel see **submarine**

surgeon see **physician**

surgical see **medical**

surname see **Christian name**

swash see **backwash**

sweet[1]/dry
The terms are used of contrasting wines. A 'sweet' wine has a fairly high sugar content, while a 'dry' wine has a low content. On the whole, a 'dry' wine is considered a 'superior' one (at least socially) to a 'sweet'. This particularly applies to the social world of sherry drinking, where the drier the sherry, the better it is considered to be (and certainly, the more expensive it is).

sweet[2]/savoury
Here the contrasts relate to food dishes, especially pies and puddings. A 'sweet' pie will thus contain sugar and probably fruit, but a 'savoury' pie could contain meat. In British use, a 'savoury' dish or course is typically one served as an hors d'oeuvre or 'starter' before a meal, or as a final dessert or 'finisher' at the end of it. For example, pâté would be a 'savoury' dish to begin a meal, and scotch woodcock (anchovies and scrambled eggs on toast) is a 'savoury' course to conclude a dinner. 'Savoury' literally means little more than 'tasty', and only began to acquire its present meaning, through the sense 'stimulating the palate', in the seventeenth century.

sweet[3]/sour
Anything 'sweet' tastes of sugar, and is agreeable; anything with a 'sour' taste, such as lemon juice or vinegar, is disagreeable unless carefully regulated to 'point up' something sweet (like lemon juice on pancakes). 'Sweet' foods and drinks are normally bland; 'sour' ones are acidic and 'sharp'. In transferred use, someone with a 'sweet' nature is friendly and good-tempered, but a person with a 'sour' expression is probably humourless and even morose. However, we are fond of combining a 'sour' ingredient with a 'sweet' in our meals, as reflected in the proverb 'Sweet meat will have sour sauce'. (This despite the saying that 'What is sweet in the mouth is oft sour in the stomach'.) The expression 'take the sweet with the sour' means 'accept equally what is good and bad', 'be resigned to the changing fortunes of life'. And back in the dining room or restaurant again, why not sample a 'sweet-and-sour' dish, that is, one cooked in a sauce made from both 'sweet' ingredients (such as sugar) and 'sour' (such as vinegar)? Compare **bitter/sweet**.

sweet see **bitter**

sweet chestnut see **horse chestnut**

swing bridge/drawbridge
These are the two main types of 'opening' bridges. A 'swing bridge' opens horizontally, by having a central section that rotates round a vertical axis. A 'drawbridge' opens vertically, by having one or more sections that are raised by turning on a horizontal axis. There is a large 'swing bridge' over the St Lawrence River in Canada, and a notable one in Britain over the Manchester Ship Canal at Barton-upon-Irwell, Greater Manchester. London's Tower Bridge, technically a 'bascule bridge', is really a type of 'drawbridge', because its two halves or 'bascules' are drawn up. (In fact, a bridge like this is really *two* 'drawbridges', one each side.)

swings/roundabouts
The two fairground attractions are contrasted in the common expression 'swings and roundabouts', meaning that what is lost in a particular deal or enterprise will be offset by a gain elsewhere. (The full phrase is usually 'gain on the swings and lose on the roundabouts'.) The origin lies in the irregular income or profit made by showground owners: what they lose on the 'swings', they hope to regain on the 'roundabouts'. (This seems to suggest that 'roundabouts' are a more popular fairground attraction than 'swings', perhaps as they are more accessible.) There is another contrast here that should not be overlooked: 'swings' move in a vertical plane, up and down, while 'roundabouts' usually revolve horizontally. In fact, the direction of movement is similar to that of the two types of bridge in the previous entry.

swing wing/fixed wing
An aircraft that is 'swing-wing' is one having wings which can be 'swept back' during flight, so that any shock waves are minimized, but which are returned to the conventional position during take-off and landing in order to provide the necessary lift. An aircraft which is 'fixed-wing' is thus the standard one, with wings that cannot be swept back. The F-111 aircraft, in service with the US Air Force, has a 'swing wing' that can be pivoted from an angle of 72° back to only 25°. ('Swing wing' is also known as 'variable geometry'.)

symphile/synoekete
The Greek zoological terms mean literally 'mutual lovers' and 'mutual dwellers' (more precisely, 'co-residents'). 'Symphiles' are insects who live in the nests of other so-called 'social' (as distinct from 'solitary') insects, such as ants, and who are fed and reared by their hosts. 'Synoeketes' are similar insects, living in the nests of ants, for example, but without receiving any attention from them. Some types of beetle have become such long-established 'symphiles' that they have ceased to have wings and in some cases cannot even move. The 'n' of 'syn-' becomes 'm' in the first word because of the usual form 'sym-' before 'ph' (as in 'symphony'). See also **social/solitary**.

symptom see **sign**

synchronic/diachronic
'Synchronic' means 'happening at the same time', while 'diachronic' means 'happening throughout time'. The contrasting terms are thus as it were the temporal equivalents of 'horizontal' and 'vertical', or, alternatively, of 'geography' and 'history'. They are chiefly applied in linguistics, which when 'synchronic' studies the forms of one or more languages at a particular stage in their development. By contrast, 'diachronic' linguistics studies the changes undergone by languages over a long period of history. (It is this, long-established study that traces languages back to a common primeval or 'protolanguage', such as Indo-European.) 'Synchronic' linguistics developed in the first half of the twentieth century as a reaction to the mainly 'diachronic' studies of the nineteenth century. Today, however, the value of both systems is appreciated. See also **vertical/horizontal**, **history/geography**.

syncline/anticline
Terms that are geological opposites. A 'syncline' is a 'trough' (like an inverted arch) of stratified rock in which the sides dip or run downwards from either side to the centre. In an 'anticline', the formation is the other way up, like an arch, with the layers running downwards on either side from the top. The words are based on 'cline' (from Greek *klinein*, 'to lean'), with the contrasting prefixes 'syn-' ('with') and 'anti-' ('against').

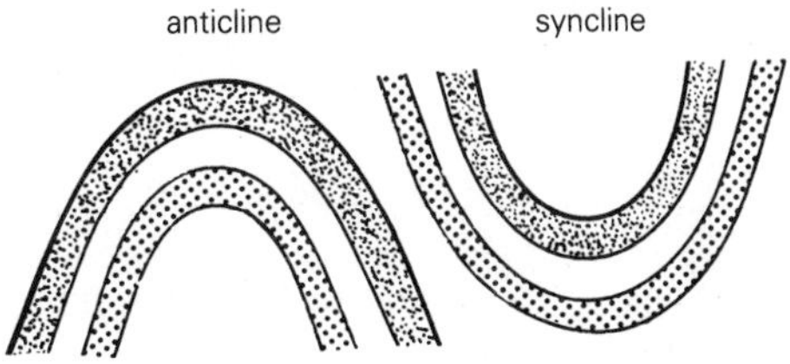

synergist see **antagonist**[2]

synoekete see **symphile**

synonym/antonym
Words that are 'synonyms' have the same, or nearly the same, meanings, such as 'cold' and 'chilly'. (Often there is some small but detectable difference in the precise senses, although the basic general meaning is usually the same for both.) 'Antonyms' are what this dictionary is all about, as they are words of opposite, or near-opposite, meaning. Thus 'antonym' is the 'antonym' of 'synonym'! The literal senses of the terms are 'naming with' and 'naming opposite'. The words really caught on only in the nineteenth century in English, although obviously the phenomena themselves had existed for centuries before, in many languages. Earlier English terms for the two were 'term' and 'counterterm', which although more readily comprehended are not perhaps quite right for what is actually involved.

synthesis see **analysis**

systolic see **diastolic**

Tt

table/chair
Two common but complementary items of furniture, although of course one can have a 'table' without a 'chair' and a 'chair' without a 'table'. 'Tables' are for things; 'chairs' for people. (A 'chair' is even created in the image of man, because it has a 'back', two 'arms', 'legs' and a 'seat'.) A 'table' usually implies work, or activity, while a 'chair' has a connotation of rest, or inactivity, even when the two are not together. Many 'tables' are associated with standing, and they themselves stand; a 'chair' always implies sitting, although they themselves also stand. 'Tables' are usually relatively high, while 'chairs' are mostly fairly low. (When not in use, many 'chairs' can have their seats placed under a 'table'.) In many Christian churches, the worshippers sit on 'chairs' (or pews), while the priest or minister stands at the 'Lord's table' (the altar), with the one facing the other. Similar arrangements apply elsewhere, such as in the House of Commons, where 'the table' is the one that stands in front of the Speaker's 'chair'.

table d'hôte see **à la carte**

tabloid see **broadsheet**

tachycardia/bradycardia
In medicine, 'tachycardia' is the term for an abnormally rapid beating of the heart, especially over 100 beats a minute. 'Bradycardia' is the opposite, and indicates an abnormally low heartbeat. The common '-cardia' is the Greek for 'heart', while 'tachy-' means 'rapid' (as in the 'tachograph' that records the speed of a lorry) and 'brady-' means 'slow' (found only in technical or scientific words, like the one here).

tai chi chuan/kung fu
Two contrasting types of Chinese martial art. 'Tai chi chuan' is the 'internal' type, where what is important is the technique of the exponent. In 'kung fu' the system is 'external', and what is important is the effect on the opponent. 'Tai chi chuan' has slow, graceful movements, while 'kung fu' has fast, sharp movements. 'Tai chi chuan' is more suitable for the elderly and those of gentle nature; 'kung fu' is for the young and aggressive. 'Tai chi chuan' means literally 'extreme limit fist' (it has been described as 'yoga in motion', and is said to balance the opposing forces of the pair **yin/yang**). 'Kung fu' means simply 'boxing principles'. The Chinese name for the martial arts, sometimes found in English literature on the sport, is 'wu shu' (meaning literally 'military technique').

tail see (1) **head**[1] (2) **top**[2]

take see **give**

take it/leave it
'Take it or leave it!', the common exasperated rejoinder to someone who hesitates or disputes. The phrase is not just a twentieth-century one, and goes back at least to the time of Shakespeare. (In 1576, William Lambarde, in his *A Perambulation of Kent*, said that he would 'leaue the Reader to his free choice, to take or leaue the one, or the other'.) In more recent times, a 'take-it-or-leave-it' manner or the like is one that implies either acceptance or rejection. The opposing phrases have even acquired a specialized use, so that in polo a player will say 'Take it' to a member of his team when he wants him to hit the ball, and 'Leave it' when he does not want him to hit the ball because he intends to hit it himself. Finally, Shakespeare himself:

Lear. Will you, with those infirmities she owes, [. . .]
Take her, or leave her?
Duke of Burgundy. Pardon me, royal sir;
Election makes not up on such conditions.
Lear. Then leave her, sir.
(*King Lear*, 1605)

tame/wild
The adjectives are used for animals that have been domesticated and those that have not, so that most household pets and farm animals are 'tame' and those living lives untouched by man are 'wild'. When it comes to plants and flowers, however, one can have 'wild' flowers, growing naturally in the countryside, but not 'tame' ones. (One must talk of 'garden' flowers.) The opposites are occasionally found in proverbs, such as 'The most deadly of wild beasts is a backbiter, of tame ones a flatterer'. In a more general sense, 'tame' is used of a mild or submissive person, with a 'tame' personality, while a 'wild' person is aggressive and unruly, with a 'wild' nature.

tamizdat see **samizdat**

tant mieux see **tant pis**

tant pis/tant mieux
Somewhat trendy French phrases uttered on occasions to mean respectively 'too bad' (when regretting something) and 'so much the better' (when approving something). In his *Sentimental Journey*, Laurence Sterne commented: '*Tant pis* and *tant mieux* being two of the great hinges in French conversation, a stranger would do well to set himself right in the use of them'. That was in the eighteenth century, when the phrases themselves first gained currency in English.

tape see **disc**

target language see **source language**

tax avoidance/tax evasion
There's a subtle difference here! 'Tax avoidance' is the reduction or minimizing of one's tax liability by lawful methods. 'Tax evasion', however, is doing this by illegal methods.

tax evasion see **tax avoidance**

taxis see **lexis**

tea/coffee
The two most popular hot drinks in Britain, both similar in colour, and both drunk weak or strong, with milk or without, with sugar or without. On the whole, 'tea' is a popular or 'lower-class' drink, while 'coffee' is more 'refined' and 'classy'. 'Tea', too, is definitely the more popular drink in Britain: according to a report by the Tea Council in mid-1986, half a Briton's daily drink is 'tea', but only 21 per cent 'coffee'. 'Tea' is mainly drunk from a largish 'tea'-cup, while 'coffee' imbibers like to take their drink from a small cup. In relation to this, 'coffee' is sipped in polite company, but (in run-of-the-mill company) 'tea' is on the whole 'slurped' or drunk in large mouthfuls. (On the Continent, however, where 'coffee' is the more popular drink, 'tea' has a higher social status.) In origin, 'tea' is made from dried leaves, and first came from China. 'Coffee' is made from berries, and originated from the Yemen. Both drinks contain caffein, although the caffein found in 'tea' is chemically different from that found in 'coffee'. ('Caffein' and 'coffee' are related.) The names of both beverages have exotic origins: 'tea' (and its colloquial name, 'char') comes from a Chinese word, while 'coffee' is ultimately Arabic (*kahwi*). ('Look here, Steward, if this is coffee, I want tea; but if this is tea, then I wish for coffee'. Caption of cartoon showing disgruntled sea passenger, *Punch*, vol. 123, p. 44, 1902.)

teach/learn
To 'teach' something is to pass on knowledge of it to others; to 'learn' is to have this information passed on to one. That much everyone knows. Those who 'learn' foreign languages, however, also know that in some languages the opposing concepts are named by a single verb, or

by only slightly differing grammatical constructions. For example, in French, both 'to teach' and 'to learn' are *apprendre* (as in Italian they are *apprendere*), and in German the words for 'to teach' (*lehren*) and 'to learn' (*lernen*) are mutually related. Even in Russian the verb 'to learn' (*uchit'sya*) is merely the reflexive form of the verb 'to teach' (*uchit'*). What's more, colloquial or ignorant English has 'learn' instead of 'teach' ('That'll learn you!'). So what is happening? The truth of the matter is that although 'teach' and 'learn' are opposites, the action involved is a single one, so that to 'teach' a person is to enable him or her to 'learn'. The transference of knowledge is a one-way process, not a reciprocal one. So formerly in English 'learn' was the sole verb, and was the standard for the process. Even as late as the nineteenth century 'learn' was used to mean 'teach' in a literate text, for example 'We made up our minds to learn him a lesson' (Rolf Boldrewood, *Robbery Under Arms*, 1889) and as the second verb in 'Learn to know the House; learn the House to know you' (Disraeli, *Coningsby*, 1844). And although 'teach' existed all this time in English in its present sense, it has now taken over as the standard verb for the imparting of the knowledge, while 'learn' has remained in use for the acquiring of it. The division of meaning is found as early as Chaucer, whose 'Clerk of Oxenford' did both: 'And gladly wolde he lerne, and gladly teche'.

teletext/viewdata
'Teletext' is the system, familiar from the 1970s, by which a television set can display a printed text such as news, sports results or weather reports. In Britain, the two best-known systems of 'teletext' are those of the pair **Ceefax/Oracle**. The text is transmitted over existing TV channels, with the receiving set suitably adapted. By contrast, 'viewdata', although also a similar type of display, is transmitted from a computer over a telephone line. The best-known example of a 'viewdata' system in Britain is the Prestel one operated by British Telecom. (The name 'Prestel' is apparently a blend of 'press' and 'telephone', with perhaps a suggestion of 'presto' for rapid information.)

temporal see **spiritual**

temporary/permanent
Something that is 'temporary' is of limited duration, while a 'permanent' thing lasts indefinitely. In *Dombey and Son* (1848), Dickens makes a character say: 'Being only a permanency I couldn't be expected to show it like a temporary'. Here 'temporary' means a casual worker, and is the forerunner of today's 'temp', the 'temporary' typist (who may sometimes turn out to be 'permanent', especially as the verb 'to temp' has almost come to mean 'to work as a typist', and indeed advertisements actually for 'permanent temps' have been seen in recent years). However, a 'perm' is not a 'permanent' employee but a 'permanent' wave, that is, a long-lasting (but not literally 'permanent') wave set in the hair by the means of special heat treatment and the application of special chemical preparations.

tender see **stiff**

tenon see **mortise**

tercel see **falcon**

tergum see **sternum**

terminus ad quem/terminus a quo
Two grandly classical expressions denoting respectively a goal or aim on the one hand, and a starting point or point of origin on the other. The terms have been particularly favoured by theologians over the centuries. For example, the English scholar James Rendel Harris wrote in *The Guiding Hand of God* (1905) that he regarded death 'more and more as a starting-point', as 'a *terminus a quo* and not a *terminus ad quem*'. The Latin phrases themselves originated in the Scholastic Latin of the thirteenth century, and are found in the writings (in Latin) of such great theologians as Thomas Aquinas, Roger Bacon and Duns Scotus. They literally mean 'the end to which' and 'the end from which'.

terminus a quo see **terminus ad quem**

terrestial see **celestial**

text/graphics
In terms of informational displays and the like on television and computer screens, 'text' is 'printed' matter, in letters and figures, while 'graphics' in stylized pictures and diagrams, used to accompany or illustrate a 'text' much as pictures, sketches and diagrams illustrate a book.

Thanatos see **Eros**

that see **this**

thaw see **freeze**

theist see **deist**

them see **us**

theme¹/rheme
In modern (post-Second World War) linguistics, 'theme' is the term adopted to denote the part of a sentence that indicates what is being talked about, while 'rheme' is the part of the sentence that says something new about the 'theme'. The dichotomy is thus similar to that of 'topic' and 'comment' (in the sense linguists talk about them), or to the distinction between 'old' information and 'new'. (It is *not* the same, however, as 'subject' and 'object'.) For example, in the sentence 'I haven't seen that picture before', 'I' is the 'theme' and all the rest is the 'rheme'. But I could also say 'That picture I haven't seen before', where 'that picture' is the 'theme' and the rest is the 'rheme' (giving new information about 'that picture', which is the topic). Yet grammatically 'that picture' is the 'object' of the sentence. However, if I say '*That* picture is one I haven't seen before', then '*that* picture' (stressed) is the 'rheme', since it is the new information. The words literally mean 'thing laid down' and 'word'. ('Rheme' is related to 'rhetoric'.)

theme²/variation
The terms are familiar in musical compositions, where a 'theme' or subject is played first, as a straightforward melody or 'tune', and is then repeated in a series of embellished or even distorted versions, often increasing in complexity, or at any rate varying in tempo, instrumentation, character and so on. In more general use, we can talk of 'variations on a theme' to mean loosely 'much the same thing' ('All the vicar's sermons are just variations on a theme'). In some older musical titles, 'Theme with Variations' is replaced by 'Air with Variations'. One of the best known musical 'theme' and 'variations' is Elgar's 'Enigma Variations', written as musical 'portraits' of his friends. See also **harmony/melody**.

theological virtues see **natural virtues**

theory/practice
'In theory we should be there by six o'clock.' 'Yes, but in practice we won't, because there's always a traffic hold-up on this section of the motorway.' 'Theory' is thus what we plan to do, and 'practice' what we actually manage to do, and all too frequently the 'practice' falls short in some way of the 'theory'. The contrast of 'in theory . . ., in practice . . .' has been current in English since about the seventeenth century, and exists equally in other languages (French '*en théorie . . ., en pratique . . .*', Russian '*v teorii . . ., na praktike . . .*', and so on), showing the international source of the words in classical Greek.

Theravada see **Mahayana**

there see **here**

thermoplastic/thermosetting
If a synthetic plastic or resin is 'thermoplastic', it will become soft when heated and will then reharden on cooling (in a new shape, as desired) with only a very slight change in its original properties. If it is 'thermosetting', however, it hardens permanently after a single heating and pressing. As such, it cannot be remoulded.

thermosetting see **thermoplastic**

thesis¹/antithesis
In logic, the first stage of an argument is the 'thesis'. This is then countered by a second stage, which is the 'antithesis'. Finally, the argument is resolved at a higher level in the 'synthesis'. The development strictly belongs to the dialectic of Hegel, the (mainly) nineteenth-century German philosopher. One development of the Hegelian dialectic was that of Marxist thought and its dialectical materialism.

thesis²/arsis
The Greek words literally mean 'setting down' and 'raising up', and are used to describe the 'upbeat' and 'downbeat' in classical Greek verse. The long syllable of a dactyl was the 'thesis', so that the 'arsis' was the two short beats. See **anapaest/dactyl**.

thick¹/clear
The opposites here are used of soup. A 'thick' soup is one to which flour, potato, etc. has been added, such as Scotch broth. A 'clear' soup is a more or less transparent one with a virtual absence of solid content, such as a consommé, which is made from a meat broth. (A broth can thus be 'thick' or 'clear'.)

thick²/thin
As well as the general meanings ('broad', 'dense'; 'narrow', 'not dense'), the two opposites have a number of specialized and phrasal senses. As noted in the previous entry, 'thick' can denote a soup with a dense consistency. The opposite of this, especially on menus, is usually 'clear', although one can also talk of a 'thin' soup. The same distinction applies to other liquids, such as a 'thick' paint and a 'thin' one, although a 'thick' syrup is not necessarily an opaque one but a very viscous or 'sticky' one, so that a 'thin' syrup would be more liquid and 'runny'. A 'thick' person is, colloquially, a stupid or 'dense' one, but the opposite is not 'thin' but simply 'clever' or 'bright'. The phrase 'through thick and thin' means 'through good times and bad', 'in all fortunes'. The expression goes back at least to the days of Chaucer in the fourteenth century, and apparently refers to a 'thick' wood (even a 'thicket') or a 'thin' one, where the literal senses apply ('dense', 'sparse'). Spenser's *Faerie Queene* has it in this meaning:

> His tyreling
> Jade [i.e. horse] he fiersly forth did push
> Through thicke and thin, both over banck and bush.

And of course the words are found in proverbs, such as 'Thick sown, thin come up' (meaning that an abundant sowing does not guarantee a good harvest, or some similar metaphorical application).

thin see (1) **fat** (2) **thick²**

thirteen see **twelve**

this/that
'We talked about this and that', we say, meaning that we had a nice chat on all kinds of subjects, some of them probably rather trivial. Yet 'this' and 'that' are essential words to differentiate, especially when talking of two similar or even identical things. ('This road leads south; that road goes north'.) Of the two, 'this' usually indicates the nearer or more immediate thing, so that 'that' is considered as a secondary object or action, as in W. S. Gilbert's:

> You hold yourself like this,
> You hold yourself like that,
> By hook or crook, you try to look, both angular and flat.
>
> (*Patience*, 1881)

So 'this' is one thing, but 'that' is another. And that's that.

thorn/edh
Not the names of two comics, the joker and his stooge, but terms for the Germanic letters that respectively indicated the sound of 'th' in modern English 'thin', and 'th' in 'then'. They occur today still in modern Icelandic, as 'þ' and 'ð', and they also occurred in Old English, although they were both by then pronounced the same (as in 'thin'). 'Edh' (also spelt 'eth') is similarly used in some modern phonetic

alphabets to convey the 'th' sound of 'then'. The words themselves are simply random ones, selected since they contain the two types of 'th' (unvoiced and voiced).

three-cornered fight see **straight fight**

three-piece see **two-piece**

thrombus see **embolus**

thrust/drag
Two opposing forces in aerodynamics, especially as applied to aircraft. 'Thrust' is the forward-moving force obtained either from the propeller or a jet stream; 'drag' is the opposing, retarding force, caused by the resistance of the air to the surface of the aircraft. 'Thrust' and 'drag' must be equal, or the plane will fly faster and faster (as stated in Newton's Law). The same forces also work on the same principles in hydrodynamics, with 'thrust' coming from the propeller or other motive force of the boat, and 'drag' coming from the resistance of the water to it. In both cases, the degree of 'drag' will depend on the configuration of the craft, its speed, and the viscosity of the medium through which it is moving. 'Drag' can be reduced by streamlining.

thunder/lightning
Nature's own 'son et lumière' (see **sound/light**), with the 'lightning' usually preceding the 'thunder', if only fractionally. Many people enjoy 'Donner und blitzen!' as a sort of joke German imprecation, corresponding (roughly) to the pair, although no English person curses 'Thunder and lightning!' except in humour. However, in the eighteenth and nineteenth century, 'thunder-and-lightning' was used to describe garish clothing, often with brightly contrasting colours (what today we would call 'flashy' or 'loud'), and in Thackeray's *Yellowplush Papers* (1839) he writes: 'I recollect my costume very well: a thunder-and-lightning coat, a white waistcoat, [. . .] a pair of knee-breeches'. The proverb 'There is lightning lightly before thunder' means 'There is usually a warning when a disaster is about to occur' ('lightly' means 'commonly' here), although many would disagree with this. Scientifically, the 'thunder' and 'lightning' are simultaneous, only light travels faster than sound.

tibia/fibula
These are two of the main bones in the leg, with confusingly similar names. They are located between the knee and the ankle, where the 'tibia', or shinbone, is the inner and thicker of the two, and the 'fibula' is the outer and thinner. The respective Latin names mean literally 'pipe' and 'fastener', although the Romans themselves used *tibia* for the shinbone. See also **radius/ulna**.

tied house see **free house**

tight see **easy**

tigon see **liger**

time deposit see **demand deposit**

time exposure/instantaneous exposure
In the early days for photography, a 'time exposure' was the standard method of taking a picture, using a film with a very slow speed. The photographer opened the shutter at the beginning of the 'shot', then closed it again after an interval. Today, an 'instantaneous exposure' is the norm, where the shutter 'clicks' open and shut almost instantaneously, at a speed of fractions of a second. 'Time exposures' will now be used, therefore, only for special effect.

time loan see **call loan**

timework see **piecework**

to see **from**

toad see **frog**

toadstool see **mushroom**

toe see (1) **finger** (2) **head**[2] (3) **heel** (4) **top**[2]

together/apart
To some, the words may conjure up gymnastic exercises ('Apart, together! Apart, together!'), while others think of a more basic and lengthy undertaking, living 'together' or 'apart'. 'Together' usually implies what is right and 'homely', while 'apart' suggests deviation and alienation. 'Together' smacks of unity and happiness ('the more we are together . . .'), but 'apart' conjures up a lone effort or kind of detachment, possibly an unhappy one. Of a complex or assembled object, containing many elements, 'together' suggests a completeness and wholeness ('put together'), whereas 'apart' implies that it has been made useless or even broken ('take apart'). 'Together' is related to 'gather', while 'apart' derives from Old French *a part*, 'by the side'.

tongs see **hammer**[2]

top[1]**/bottom**
The upper point or half of something and the lower, as the 'top' of a hill or a cabinet and the 'bottom' of one. 'Top' usually has a connotation of superiority (think of 'top' drawer, 'top' dog, 'top' hole, 'top' notch, 'topping' and the like, as colloquial terms for someone or something that is excellent or the best), so that 'bottom' can imply the reverse, although colloquial terms containing it are not common (and 'bottom' drawer is not the opposite of 'top' drawer, but is simply a drawer where a woman keeps her clothes, linen and so on before her marriage). English uses 'bottom' as a fairly common colloquial word for the buttocks, otherwise the 'behind', which gives the word something of a 'degrading' association. (Other languages do not see the human seat as a 'bottom' but only as a 'behind', which it more logically is; compare German *Hintere*, French *derrière*, Italian *deretano*, Russian *zad*.) The phrase 'from top to bottom' means 'right through', 'thoroughly' ('I cleaned the house from top to bottom'), and in an allusion to this, an advertising slogan for toilet paper was 'Tops for bottoms' (quoted in Walter Redfern, *Puns*, 1984). See also below.

top[2]**/toe**
The entire length of a person standing is 'from top to toe', and the phrase can denote whatever the person is wearing or is covered in ('wearing white from top to toe') or mean simply 'through and through' ('an Englishman from top to toe'). 'From top to bottom' (see entry above) can also mean this, but the alliterative phrase is shorter and more common. Compare the next entry, too.

top[3]**/tail**
A phrase similar to the one in the entry above, and just as alliterative, although the length this time is taken to the 'tail' not to the 'toe'. 'Topping' and 'tailing' are words sometimes used for the process of cutting off the upper and lower part of something, or of attending to them. Some vegetables and fruits have 'tops' and 'tails' that need to be cut off before they are cooked, such as carrots (the 'tops' are either the leaves or the hard upper end) and gooseberries. (An alternative term for this is 'top and lop', an expression from woodland management.) See also the two previous entries above.

top coat see **undercoat**

top loader see **front loader**

topspin/backspin
In tennis, 'topspin' is a hit made in such a way that the ball spins forwards as it travels, enabling it to go further, higher, or faster. If a ball is hit with a 'backspin', it will rotate backwards, and travel less far, high, or fast than it would otherwise have done. A ball hit with a 'topspin' will bounce sharply on impact; one with 'backspin' will slow suddenly after making contact.

tortoise see **hare**[2]

Tory see **Whig**

touchback see **safety**

town[1]/country
In many countries, the overall contrast for many purposes, from the domestic to the economic, is 'town', where 'civilization' is, and 'country', where things are more 'primitive'. Yet to counterbalance this, the 'country' is natural, and so has a charm and beauty that the manmade 'town' usually lacks. (Some people like a compromise, and choose to live nearly in the 'country' on the edge of a 'town'.) Again, 'country' has an association of wealth and 'blue blood' that 'town' does not have. This is because it is in the 'country' that many wealthy or aristocratic people have their residences, and where they pursue their 'upper-class' sports of 'huntin', shootin' and fishin''. As a further type of contrast, 'town' often implies the modern and progressive, while 'country' suggests the out-of-date, or at best the historic. But many 'town' dwellers hanker after the 'country', and like to visit it and read about it. ('Country' has a nostalgic ring to it that 'town' never has; it conjures up one's childhood, the summer, holidays, and even one's own ancestral 'roots'.) It is interesting to see what word has settled for 'country' in other languages. In French, *campagne* is directly related to *champ*, 'field'; in German it is *Land*, which has all the English meanings of 'land' as well as 'national territory'; in Russian it is *derevnya*, which also means 'village'. And in English itself, 'country' acquired its 'rural' sense only in the seventeenth century, so that the 'national' one came first. See also **rural/urban**.

town[2]/gown
The rhyming words are used to denote, respectively, the native residents of a university town or city and the students or undergraduates, since between these groups there is an implied keen contrast, even rivalry. Those who are 'town' are the 'real' inhabitants, and it is their own city. Those who are 'gown' are visitors, 'upstarts', and regard themselves as academically and socially superior (which they often are). The terms particularly apply at Oxford and Cambridge, where the division undoubtedly arose in medieval times, since the universities were granted privileges which adversely affected the commercial livings of the city merchants. (Today, though, the presence of the university certainly boosts local trade.) The actual use of 'gown', too, implies a sartorial difference, because the garment is a symbol of academic interests, whereas those who are 'town' have no distinguishing dress. And although there are still clashes or expressions of hostility sometimes between 'town' and 'gown', at least there are no longer the murderous riots of the Middle Ages, when many lost their lives in armed confrontation.

town[3]/village
Much of what has been said above regarding 'town' and 'country' applies to the general contrast between 'town' and 'village', as the latter is in the country and is therefore thought of as primitive/attractive/historic/nostalgic or whatever. But there is another contrast – that of size. A 'town' is a relatively large collection of houses and buildings, while a 'village' is small. When does the latter become the former, or how small can a 'town' be without actually being a 'village'? There is an uneasy connection, too, between 'village' and French *ville*, 'town'. Nor are we helped much by the *Oxford English Dictionary* which notes: 'The distinction between a small town [. . .] and a village is somewhat indefinite; there are also decayed towns [. . .] which are surpassed in population by many villages'. I would suggest the following guidelines, therefore. A 'town' is usually larger than a 'village', with a greater population, and with local government offices (DHSS, Jobcentre, magistrate's court, and the like). It is also often more systematically laid out, and will frequently have a market place where a weekly market is held. Finally, it is usually located on a main road leading directly to another 'town'. (Note that I do not mention a church, because a small 'town' may have only one church, just as a 'village' does.) And English 'village' and French *ville*? They are both ultimately

from Latin *villa*, 'country house', with French *village* ('group of country houses') borrowed direct as our 'village', while French *ville* continued for the more important and larger populated region that is our 'town' (which we in turn kept from the Old English word, *dūn*, meaning 'enclosure' – just as small in area originally as the Roman *villa*). In the United States, most 'towns' are actually known as 'cities' (except in New England).

traducianism see **creationism**

tragedy see **comedy**

trailing edge see **leading edge**

train see **bus**

transitive/intransitive
In grammar, a 'transitive' verb is one that has an object (see **subject/object**), as in 'Sue opened the door'. An 'intransitive' verb is thus one without an object, as in 'We rose early that morning' (you can't 'rise' something). Some verbs can be either 'transitive' or 'intransitive' as in 'We called Pete' ('Pete' is the object) and 'We called' (no object). The term itself is intended to denote (classically) that the action is passed over ('trans-') to the object.

translator/interpreter
The usual distinction here is that a 'translator' works on written translations from one language to another, while an 'interpreter' works orally, translating what one person says to another as he says it. The latter is generally regarded as the harder process, since the translation has to be done on the spot, without recourse to dictionaries, whereas the 'translator' has time to think and to look up words in a dictionary. Not all languages observe the distinction. French does (*traducteur*, *interprète*), as does German (*Übersetzer*, *Dolmetscher*), but Russian doesn't (*perevodchik* for both).

transmitter/receiver
In radio telegraphy, the 'transmitter' is the instrument that sends the signals, and the 'receiver', obviously enough, the instrument that receives them. Thus radio communication is made. An instrument that is a combined 'transmitter' and 'receiver', and that specifically uses the same devices for both these functions, is called a 'transceiver', as a blend of both words.

transom/mullion
A 'transom' is a horizontal crosspiece in a window, and a 'mullion' a vertical one. 'Transom' itself is a word with the 'trans-' element that means 'across', but 'mullion' is of less certain origin. Since most windows have only one 'mullion', it may derive from French *moyen*, 'middle', as a central vertical bar.

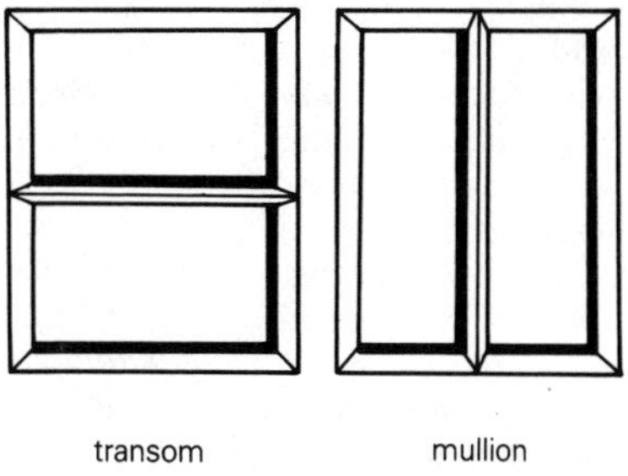

transparency see **print**

transparent/opaque
If a thing is 'transparent', you can see through it, and if it is 'opaque', you can't. That is the basic difference. The words can also be used to mean metaphorically 'easy to understand' and 'hard to understand', so that you can talk of a 'transparent' remark, or an 'opaque' comment. In linguistics, a 'transparent' word or element has an obvious or clear meaning, whereas an 'opaque' one is obscure or meaningless. The terms particularly apply to name studies: 'Newcastle' is a 'transparent' name, since you can easily see what it means; 'Bristol' is an 'opaque' name, apparently with no meaning, and you need to know that it derives from a

blend of the former words for 'bridge' and 'stow' (meaning 'place'). Many apparently 'transparent' names are red herrings, so that 'Bridgwater', in Somerset, does not mean 'bridge over the water' but 'Walter's bridge'. 'Transparent' itself means literally 'appearing through', although 'opaque' really is an 'opaque' word, because it comes from Latin *opacus*, whose own origin is uncertain. (Perhaps it is somehow connected with Greek *ops*, 'eye'?)

transubstantiation/consubstantiation
Two rather forbidding theological terms. 'Transubstantiation' is the (mainly) Roman Catholic doctrine that the consecrated bread and wine in the eucharist changes into the 'substance' of the body and blood of Christ. 'Consubstantiation', on the other hand, is the doctrine held by many High Church Anglicans, stating that in a more complex way the consecrated bread and wine contains both the 'substance' of the body and blood of Christ as well as the 'substance' of the bread and wine itself, so that the two (or four) coexist. It was Martin Luther who originally evolved the doctrine of 'consubstantiation'. The respective prefixes indicate the differences between the two doctrines ('through' and 'with'). See also **body/blood**, **bread/wine**, **Catholic/Protestant**.

treat see **trick**

treble/bass
The 'high notes' and the 'low notes', to put it at its most basic, otherwise the musical registers that belong characteristically to certain instruments (such as the flute on the one hand and tuba on the other) and certain voices (such as those of many women and most boys on the one hand, and those of many men on the other). Many instruments, of course, can extend their ranges well into the 'treble' or 'bass', with probably the most familiar example being the piano, which has sheet music conventionally printed in the 'treble' and 'bass' clefs. (The symbols for each clef centre on a note that is respectively five notes above middle C or five notes below, viz. G and F.) More generally, 'treble' and 'bass' refer to the high-frequency gain or low-frequency gain of an audio amplifier, such as a radio or tape recorder, which normally have 'treble' and 'bass' controls. The origin of the actual terms is of mixed difficulty. 'Bass' is obviously from Italian *basso*, 'deep', which word itself lies behind the names of two 'bass' musical instruments, the double bass and the bassoon. 'Treble' is harder, as it is not immediately apparent what there is 'three' of, since that is what the word means. Perhaps originally the 'treble' (Latin *triplus*) part was one added above the 'high' (*altus*) and 'low' (*bassus*). One would really expect the contrasting ranges or pitches to be called something like 'alt' (from Italian *alto*) and 'bass', rather than 'treble' and 'bass'.

trick/treat
Most Americans, and now many Britons, are familiar with the annual 'trick or treat' dodge enacted house-to-house at Hallowe'en by children. The whole thing is really a sort of con: the luckless householder must give the children a 'treat' (sweets or money) if he doesn't want them to play a 'trick' on him. So it's really a sort of double-dealing contrast: give something good, or you'll get something bad. The origin of the dubious tradition is obscure, and the *Supplement* to the *OED* does not trace the formula back (in American usage) earlier than 1947.

trimaran see **catamaran**

trivium see **quadrivium**

trochee see **iamb**

Trojans/Greeks
The famous Trojan War was fought between the 'Trojans' and the 'Greeks'. But surely Troy, where the 'Trojans' came from, was an ancient Greek city? Yes, it was, but only as a result of the War, when the 'Greeks' won and sacked the city. The 'Trojans' were probably descended from Thracian immigrants, while the 'Greeks' settled on the Balkan Peninsula originally as emigrants from Achaea and Ionia, respectively from the west and the north. In fact, it would be more accurate to say that it was the Achaeans who fought the 'Trojans', rather than the 'Greeks'. As told in Homer's *Iliad* and *Odyssey*, the cause of the War was the abduction of Helen from her Greek husband Menelaus by Paris, son of the Trojan king, with the 'Greeks' aiming to wreak their revenge on the 'Trojans' for this. But this is classical legend, and the historical cause of the War, which archaeology confirms as indeed having taken place, is still uncertain. We do know that for some reason the Achaeans devastated a wonderful and opulent city . . .

trotter/pacer
In the sport of harness racing, more popular in the United States than in Britain, the horses (harnessed to two-wheeled vehicles called 'sulkies', in which the driver rides) are divided into 'trotters' and 'pacers'. 'Trotters' lift their forelegs and opposite side hind legs at the same time, but 'pacers' move their forelegs and hind legs on the same side together. Put another way, 'trotters' move their legs in diagonal pairs, and 'pacers' in lateral pairs. The latter have a slightly faster gait, although both types of horse have a common, standardbred ancestry.

trough see (1) **peak** (2) **ridge**

truant/absentee
According to some authorities (e.g. Carol Dyhouse in *Girls Growing Up in Late Victorian and Edwardian England*, published in 1981), 'truant' was the word used by British school boards in the nineteenth century for a boy absent from school, while a girl similarly away was called an 'absentee'. The reason for the different terminology was said to be that when a girl was away from school, she was helping look after younger brothers and sisters at home, whereas a 'truant' boy was simply 'missing from school'. (The feminist implication here is that the girls were given a discriminatory label.) However, an 'absentee' can also be absent lawfully, with permission, and is not necessarily 'skiving' or 'playing hooky'.

true/false
Opposites to verbally conjure with! What *is* 'true', and what 'false'? Without getting too philosophical, we generally accept that something 'true' is 'real', and is what we think and believe it is, whereas something 'false' is not what it should be, and is even deliberately deceptive. A person's 'true' name is the one he was born with, or given at birth; a person's 'false' name is a different one that he has adopted, probably for a criminal purpose. (Yet which is the 'true' name and which the 'false' when one considers a writer's pen-name? H. H. Munro, who wrote as 'Saki', adopted a name that was his 'true' or genuine one for writing purposes. He did not aim to deceive by adopting it.) The words have been set off against one another frequently in literature, but perhaps never so nicely as in Tennyson's famous double oxymoron (figure of speech combining contradictory terms): 'Faith unfaithful kept him falsely true'. (Tennyson's works are full of contrasts, incidentally, as witness the following from *The Idylls of the King*:

> For men at most differ as Heaven and Earth,
> But women, worst and best, as Heaven and Hell.

Those two lines contain five contrasting pairs, and possibly six if one takes 'most' as the opposite of 'worst', which is already contrasted with 'best'.)

true time/mean time
'True time' is the 'real', solar time, as shown on a sundial, so that when the sun is at its highest point, the 'true time' is

midday or noon. Such a point will vary slightly each day. On the other hand, 'mean time' is measured in terms of a 'mean sun', which is an imaginary one that moves at a constant speed round the celestial equator, thus giving a standard for the 24-hour day. Hence Greenwich 'Mean Time' (GMT). Compare **GMT/BST**.

tsar/tsarina
These are the terms we conventionally use in English for the former ruler of Russia and his wife (or his female counterpart). For some reason we have distorted the actual Russian for the feminine title, which is properly *tsaritsa*. The altered spelling perhaps came to English through German, where *-in* is a standard feminine ending (e.g. *Freund*, 'boy friend', *Freundin*, 'girl friend'), and certainly the standard German word for 'tsarina' is *Zarin* (while 'tsar' is *Zar*).

tsarina see **tsar**

tu/vous
The French equivalent of the former English 'thou' and 'you', chosen for contrasting purposes here as French is the best-known foreign language for most native English speakers. Basically, 'tu' is always singular, while 'vous' can be either singular or plural. 'Tu' is also used mainly when talking to a member of one's family, a close friend, a child, or an animal. Some people feel happier talking to God as 'tu', too. So 'tu' is basically friendly and intimate, even familiar. This means that 'vous' is polite and formal, used for speaking to strangers and people socially or otherwise more elevated than oneself. For this reason, some people feel that they should address God as 'vous', as he is (in the proper sense of the phrase) 'high and mighty'. But 'tu' can also be used as a term of verbal abuse, derision or dismissal, implying that the person spoken to is inferior or ill-educated. All these differences of class, age, social standing and emotional attitude formerly existed for English 'thou' and 'you' (and 'thee' and 'you', the object forms), with 'ye' also used as a plural form of respect, or even a singular one, like 'thou'. Similar shades of usage and differentiation exist in other languages besides French today, such as German *du* and *Sie*, Italian *tu* and *Lei*, Spanish *tú* and *Usted* (although many of these are singular forms only now) and Russian *ty* and *vy*.

tub see **drum**

tumble drier/spin drier
A 'tumble drier' dries newly washed clothes by 'tumbling' them in a rotating heated drum, often at a fairly slow speed. A 'spin drier' dries clothes by 'spinning' them, often at considerable speed, in a rotating drum without the use of heat, so that they are left damp. (The water is driven from the drum by centrifugal force. See **centrifugal/centripetal**.) Almost all domestic washing machines have 'spin driers', although separate driers will usually be 'tumble driers'. See also **front loader/top loader**.

tungsten lamp/fluorescent lamp
A 'tungsten lamp' is the conventional electric light bulb, while a 'fluorescent lamp' is the 'strip lighting' frequently found in workplaces and large premises. In a 'tungsten lamp', the light comes from the heated filament, but in the 'fluorescent lamp' it comes from electrons hitting the fluorescent powder that coats the inside of the 'tube'. They do this when an electric current is passed through it. (Tungsten is the metal out of which the filament is made. It has a high melting point, obviously a necessary quality.) When respectively in use, the 'tungsten lamp' gives a warmer light (and a lot of heat, which can be a drawback), but is more expensive to run than a 'fluorescent lamp' and does not last so long. A 'fluorescent lamp' thus is more economical and is brighter (for the same amount of electricity as a 'tungsten lamp' it will give about four times as much light), but its light is cold, and the lamp itself is apt to flicker and 'hum', which can be disturbing for working conditions. It is also slower to light than a 'tungsten lamp' when switched on.

tunnel see **bridge**

tutti see **soli**

TV see **radio**

Tweedledee see **Tweedledum**

Tweedledum/Tweedledee
The two plump twins are familiar to all readers of Lewis Carroll's *Through the Looking-Glass*, where they monopolize a whole chapter. At first sight, or first reading, they appear to be identical. But read more closely: whatever 'Tweedledum' says, 'Tweedledee' contradicts, coming in with 'Contrariwise', at least to begin with. And look more closely at John Tenniel's drawings, too. Tenniel went to considerable pains to portray the 'inner sense' of what Carroll wrote, and in his picture of Alice and the two fat men, he shows that they are exact mirror images of each other, what scientists call 'enantiomorphs' (chemical compounds or crystals whose molecules have this precise 'mirror-image' relationship with each other). The twins stand side by side with one arm round each other, in such a way that the right arm of 'Tweedledum' (marked 'DUM' on his collar) hangs by his right side, while the left arm of 'Tweedledee' ('DEE') hangs by his left. Moreover, when they shook hands with Alice, 'they held out the hands that were free', so that 'Tweedledee' held out his left hand. In their talk, there are frequent contrasts, so that when 'Tweedledum' says he has toothache, 'Tweedledee' says he has a headache, and when 'Tweedledee' says that he hits every thing he can see, when he fights, 'Tweedledum' says he hits every thing in reach whether he can see it or not. Carroll did not invent the twins – they already existed in a nursery rhyme or folk rhyme, having a battle. Their origin is uncertain, although their names were used in the eighteenth century by the hymn-writer and shorthand pioneer John Byrom to represent the composers Handel and Bononcini, who were bitter rivals. Perhaps Byrom actually invented the names, since they can be taken as a sort of imitation of violin-playing.

tweeter see **woofer**

twelve/thirteen
There is more to 'unlucky thirteen' than meets the eye . . . Centuries ago, the Babylonians regarded 'twelve' as the perfect number. It was ideal for reckoning, because it can be divided by 2 and 3 and 4 and 6 without a remainder. The Babylonian astronomers favoured it, too. Observing the apparent motion of the sun in the sky, they measured time: to each day and each night they assigned 12 hours, and each hour they divided into 60 minutes, i.e. five groups of 12 minutes each. Even the year had 12 months. And we still have these main divisions today. But 'thirteen', one more than 'twelve', was in marked contrast to it. It could not be divided by any number except itself. (see **prime number/composite number**.) It was thus regarded as a 'fateful' number. Hence the present 'unlucky' quality still held by 'thirteen'. (Superstitious people usually quote the biblical story of the Last Supper, where there were 'thirteen' people present – Christ and his 'twelve' disciples. One of these was Judas, who would betray him, thus giving support to the 'fateful' influence of 'thirteen'.)

twist see **stick**[2]

two see **one**[2]

two-piece/three-piece
A 'two-piece' suit, fairly clearly, consists of two garments, an upper (jacket) and a lower (trousers), and other 'two-piece' garments will have similar matching halves. A 'three-piece' suit, additionally, will have a waistcoat. In another domestic area, a 'two-piece' suit*e* (one extra letter) will comprise a settee and an armchair, while the more common 'three-piece' suite will have a settee and two armchairs. (Both 'suit' and 'suite' are related, though not to 'set' but to 'sue', because the components follow in matching sequence.)

two-stroke engine see **four-stroke engine**

Two Thousand Guineas see **One Thousand Guineas**

Uu

U/non-
'U' stands for 'upper class', and the opposing terms were devised by Professor Alan Ross, a linguist, for an article he wrote in 1954 on the English language. He entitled the article 'Linguistic class-indicators in present-day English', and in it he sought to prove his theory that upper-class people used a different type of English to the 'lower' classes, and that their differing vocabulary and pronunciation was really what marked them as 'upper-class'. For example, he said that upper-class ('U') people said 'rich', but 'non-U' people said 'wealthy', that 'U' people spoke of a 'napkin', while 'non-U' people called it a 'serviette'. He extended his theory to the way people actually lived, so that 'U' people had their main meal of the day in the evening (as 'dinner'), while the 'non-U' ate at midday. And although many of his distinctions have now become obsolete, the general theory still holds good to a large extent, even in Britain's supposed 'classless' society (as some now see it). So today one might cite the following examples of 'U' and 'non-U' usage: 'U' 'woman' ('She's such a dear woman')/'non-U' 'lady' ('Mind out of the lady's way!'); 'U' 'goodbye'/'non-U' 'bye', or 'ba-bye!', or 'bye now', or 'cheers'; 'U' 'ice'/'non-U' 'ice-cream' (stressed on the first syllable). Various books have pursued the phenomenon, including *What Are U?*, edited by Professor Ross and published in 1969, and *U and Non-U Revisited*, edited by Richard Buckle and published in 1978.

ulna see **radius**

ultimogeniture see **primogeniture**

ultramontane see **cisalpine**

ultra-violet see **infra-red**

umbra/penumbra
An 'umbra' is a region of shadow caused by the total obscuring of a light source by an opaque body. The classic scientific example of this occurs during an eclipse of the Sun, when the shadow of the Moon is cast over the Earth. A 'penumbra' is a partial shadow cast in the same way, but with the opaque object not completely obscuring the light source. Astronomers also use 'umbra' for the darker, inner region of a sunspot, and 'penumbra' for the lighter, outer region. 'Umbra' is simply Latin for 'shadow'; the 'pen-' of 'penumbra' means 'almost' (Latin *paene*), in the same way as for a 'peninsula', which is 'almost an island'.

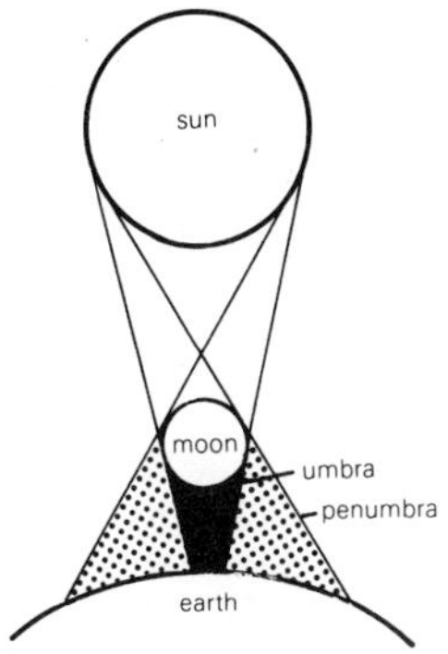

umpire see **referee**

uncircumcised see **circumcised**

uncle/aunt
The names for a parent's brother or sister, or for the latters' respective wife or husband. Children also use the names for a male or female adult friend of their parents (as 'Uncle George' or 'Auntie

Doris'). The 'uncle' in the latter case is usually a friend of the child, too, although if the child's mother is a single or unmarried parent, the 'uncle' may simply be the mother's partner or 'boy friend', and not be interested in the child. 'Uncles' are traditionally jovial and generous, distributing gifts of money on birthdays and at Christmas ('Here you are, my boy, get yourself something with this!'), whereas 'aunts' have a traditional reputation for prim morals and for being spinsters. (Hence the nickname 'Auntie' for the BBC, as a supposedly strict guardian of the nation's morals.) Learners of English as a foreign language should note that in Scotland and the north of England, 'aunt' is pronounced 'ant', a fact not stated in many dictionaries. The adjective meaning 'like an uncle' is 'avuncular' (an 'avuncular' smile), but there is no corresponding adjective for 'like an aunt', which is perhaps a pity. 'Uncle' is also a slang term for a pawnbroker. Compare **nephew/niece**.

under see **over**

undercoat/top coat
An 'undercoat' is a coat or layer of paint, or some other substance, applied as a base before the final 'top coat' is applied. (In the United States, it is also the term for what in Britain is called the 'underseal', that is, a waterproof coating applied to the underside of a car or the like.) However, if 'undercoat' is used in its rare sense of 'coat worn under another', then the outer coat will usually be called an 'overcoat', although 'topcoat' certainly exists as a term for a rather special overcoat worn over a suit, when it will usually be fairly lightweight.

underwear/outerwear
This pair of contrasts is here to show what the opposite of 'underwear' is, that is, the term used for top or outer clothing generally. (One would not thus say 'overwear'.) As an opposite for 'underclothes', a synonymous term for 'underwear', one can say 'outer clothing' or 'outer garments'.

unearned income see **earned income**

Unicorn see **Lion**

uniform/plain clothes
Many people have to wear 'uniform' at some stage in their lives, at school, in the armed services, at work or elsewhere. But what do they wear when they are 'off duty', or have left the community that required them to wear 'uniform'? Probably the most common term is 'plain clothes', although this is not really used for schoolchildren on holiday, for instance, and indeed can specifically denote a policeman such as detective who is purposely carrying out his work out of 'uniform' so that he will not be recognized, or so that he can gain easy access to certain public places. Service personnel usually talk of 'civvies' (i.e. 'civilian' clothes, as distinct from a military 'uniform'), although some members of the forces still also use the rather old-fashioned 'mufti'. (The origin of this clearly non-English word is uncertain. It may derive from the Muslim legal expert called a 'mufti', who was sometimes represented on the stage in what looked something like a dressing-gown and slippers, which are obviously anything but formal 'uniform'!) At the end of the Second World War, when many conscripted servicemen returned to civilian life, they were issued with a 'demob suit' as a 'demobilized' person (i.e. one discharged from military service).

unilateral/bilateral
'One-sided' or 'two-sided', in their literal senses, with the terms frequently associated with political agreements or policies. 'Unilateral' disarmament is favoured by those who feel that a single nation's disarmament (i.e. renunciation of nuclear weapons) should suffice to serve as a nuclear deterrent to others, while also serving as an example. In some countries, a 'unilateral' policy of some kind has lasted long, a notorious example being the 'Unilateral' Declaration of Independence (UDI) of Rhodesia (now Zimbabwe) in 1965. (Britain wished any such independence to include provision for ultimate

majority rule by Africans, but Rhodesia was not prepared to have this, so announced 'UDI'. Britain immediately declared it illegal. 'UDI' lasted until 1979, when the country changed its name and a limited majority rule was introduced.) In sociology, 'unilateral' relates to a person's ancestry as traced back through one sex only, e.g. his male line of descent, so that 'bilateral' refers to a line of descent through both sexes. 'Unilateral' and 'bilateral' can have literal senses, too, as when botanists talk of a 'unilateral' plant, that is, one with flowers or other parts on only one side of its stem.

unionists see **nationalists**

universal see **particular**

unpick see **stitch**

unquote see **quote**

unseen see **prose**

unskilled see **skilled**

up/down
These basic opposites begin a short run of related entries. Apart from their literal senses, 'up' and 'down' have certain special uses in British English. Most people, when travelling to London, will say they are going 'up' to London, even when geographically they are travelling south (or 'down') to it. This usage is reflected in railway terminology, as the 'up' platform of a station will be for the 'up' train to London (if that is where the line leads, of course). Conversely, when leaving London, people say that they are travelling 'down' from it, and on the railway, a 'down' train will stop at the various 'down' platforms on its way from London to some other destination. In a similar way, a student going to a university, especially Oxford or Cambridge, is said to go 'up' to it and to come 'down' from it at the end of the term or at the end of his career there. (While actually at the university, he is thus 'up'. 'When were you up?', as a question to a graduate, means 'When were you at university?') Both these usages reflect the overall concept that what is 'up' is important, and what is 'down' is less important. However, in the phrase 'to round up', the sense is purely numerical, and the verb means 'to give an approximate total to the next highest whole number' (or to the next ten, hundred, etc. when reckoning in tens or hundreds). Similarly, to 'round down' is to reduce the total to the whole number (ten, hundred, etc.) immediately below the actual precise amount.

upbeat/downbeat
In their literal sense, the terms refer to the movement of a conductor's baton, with an 'upbeat' coming as the last beat in the bar, and the 'downbeat' given on the first, accented beat of a bar. In colloquial use, 'upbeat' means 'cheerful', 'optimistic', while 'downbeat' means 'gloomy', 'depressed', 'pessimistic'. The latter usage derives from the former: when a conductor indicates an 'upbeat', he has his baton high, at the top of its stroke, and he awaits the new bar that must follow it. He may even look up with a smile or animated expression at this point. On a 'downbeat', his baton moves sharply down, and the conductor may look down as he gives this indication, and have a serious or concerned expression. Watch a conductor in action to see how the emotional figurative senses developed.

upper[1]/downer
In drug parlance, an 'upper' is a drug that gives a 'high', or acts as a stimulant, so making the person who takes it feel 'up'. The opposite is a 'downer', a depressant drug, that brings the drug-taker down from his 'high'. See also **high/low**.

upper[2]/lower
As literally used, anything that is 'upper' is more elevated, and something that is 'lower' is further down, so that one can have an 'upper' floor, at the top of a house, and a 'lower' shelf of two in a cupboard, for example. For a printer, an 'upper' case letter is a capital one, while a 'lower' case letter is a small one. In their 'social' appli-

cations, of 'superior' and 'inferior', 'upper' is used in such phrases as 'upper' class (and its jokey equivalent, 'upper' crust) and 'lower' deck, meaning the petty officers and men in the navy or on a ship, as distinct from the officers. (The latter, however, are not called the 'upper' deck, but are referred to collectively as the 'quarterdeck', which in many ships is still actually on the 'upper' deck at the stern of the vessel.) Somewhat symbolically, in some firms and business houses, an official letter dictated by a senior member, and typed by his secretary, will have a notation combining his initials in capital letters ('upper' case), and hers in small letters ('lower' case), for example in the form 'MGP/cs', which must certainly infuriate feminists. Finally, although not exhaustively, 'Upper' and 'Lower' are used for various bicameral ('two-chamber') legislative bodies, typically as the 'Upper' House (like the British House of Lords) and the 'Lower' House (the House of Commons). 'Upper' has its usual 'more important' sense here, of course, whether the chamber is physically located above the 'Lower' one or not. See also **majuscule/minuscule**, **capital letter/small letter**.

upper[3]/nether
In some cases, 'nether' serves as the opposite of 'upper', especially in formal terminology, such as 'nether' lip instead of 'lower' lip. However, one of the best-known examples of the word, in the 'nether' regions, as the regions below the surface of the earth, does not have 'upper' regions as its opposite, but simply some phrase such as 'on the surface', 'above ground'. In literature, too, the 'netherworld' is a synonym for the mythological 'underworld', or regions of the dead or damned (like Hell). But it likewise has no true corresponding opposite using 'upper'. Perhaps most commonly 'Nether' survives in place-names, where there will often be a corresponding 'Upper', as in 'Nether' Heyford and 'Upper' Heyford, villages in Northamptonshire, and, slightly differently, the Wiltshire villages of Netheravon and Upavon.

upper[4]/sole
Here the contrasting pair relates to footwear, and particularly shoes. The 'upper' is all that part of the shoe that is above the 'sole', which is itself the underside, on which the wearer walks (like the sole of the foot). This 'upper', incidentally, is the one in the phrase 'to be down on one's uppers', meaning 'penniless', 'broke'. The picture is of someone who has walked so far looking for work, or while out of work, that he has worn through the 'soles' of his shoes or boots and is now 'walking on his uppers' (as the phrase originally was in American usage).

upright/cylinder
Two contrasting types of vacuum cleaner. The 'upright' cleaner, which is the more common of the two, is the one that stands vertically and that has its dustbag either inside or attached externally. The 'cylinder' or 'canister' cleaner, is basically a chunky horizontal box on two wheels (or hovering) with an internal dustbag and a hose. The latter feature makes it more versatile, as the sucking head on the end of the hose can be easily directed under beds, chairs and so on, and can be easily raised for cleaning stairs and curtains. It also has a stronger suction than the 'upright'. However, its hose can be seen as a disadvantage, since the person doing the cleaning will constantly have to manoeuvre it with one hand, while moving the cleaner itself with the other. Here the 'upright' has the edge, as it can be used with one hand. Pricewise there is currently little difference between the two. See also **rotary/cylinder**.

upright see (1) **grand piano** (2) **light[4]**

upside down/right side up
When something is 'upside down' it has been overturned, and is usually in the wrong position ('A plate lay upside down on the carpet'). This means that things should normally be 'right side up'. However, a so-called 'upside-down' cake actually is 'right side up'. It is whimsically so called because it is made with a fruit layer underneath, but is then inverted

before being served up. The actual phrase 'upside down' looks as if it indicates that the 'up' side is 'down'. Originally, however, the expression was 'up so down', with the 'so' perhaps an alteration of 'to'.

upstage/downstage
On a theatre stage, 'upstage' is at the back of the stage, further away from the audience, while 'downstage' is at the front, nearer to the audience. Formerly, the back of the stage was higher than the front, which meant that an actor 'upstage' would have been more prominent than one 'downstage'. Hence the use of the verb 'to upstage', meaning to make an actor turn his back on the audience to speak to an 'upstage' actor facing them. See also **prompt/OP**.

upstairs/downstairs
The opposites have more than a locational sense ('on an upper floor', 'on a lower floor'), but have come to mean, mostly in a historical sense, 'masters' on the one hand and 'servants' on the other, otherwise 'employer' and 'domestics'. The specific reference is to an Edwardian household, where the ground floor of the house was occupied by the resident family, while the servants had their quarters in the basement, where also the kitchen would be. The phrase is sometimes used in the form 'upstairs-downstairs', especially when indicating a social contrast, e.g. 'They treat their au pair like a real upstairs-downstairs girl', i.e. they treat her as belonging to a socially inferior class. The term gained wide popularity with the TV series about the life of an Edwardian family and its servants, entitled *Upstairs, Downstairs*, first broadcast in 1971 and since repeated.

upstream/downstream
The literal senses are 'against the current of a river' and 'with the current of a river'. German has an equivalent pair, *stromauf* and *stromab*, but some other languages express the contrasting concepts in a more roundabout way, such as French *en amont* and *en aval*, Italian *a monte* and *a valle* (both in a sense meaning 'up hill' and 'down dale') and Russian *vverkh po techeniyu* and *vniz po techeniyu* (literally 'upwards according to the current' and 'downwards according to the current'). 'Upstream' and 'downstream' can also be used in certain chemical or other processes where a product flows one way or the other, as in an oil refinery. There appear to be no figurative senses of the words, which is perhaps rather surprising.

uptown/downtown
The terms are still more American than British, and refer respectively to the higher or upper part of a town, where the main residential area is and where wealthy people live, and the lower part of a town, where the main business district is. The distinction is thus frequently a geographical one, with the residential area on the higher ground, and 'downtown' implies 'business district', and should not be confused with the British usage of 'down town' in 'I'm going down town this afternoon', meaning 'I'm going to the town centre this afternoon'. However, 'upstate' and 'downstate' do not have these same meanings, and really mean 'to or in the northern part of the state', and 'to or in the southern part of the state', although 'upstate' can also imply a direction or district away from a state's metropolitan areas, and 'downstate' the reverse.

upwind/downwind
To travel or fly 'upwind' is to go into (against) the wind, and to travel 'downwind' is to go with the wind. On the whole, aircraft aim to take off and land 'upwind', or into the wind, to get the necessary lift (which they need not only to rise when taking off but to control a landing). When in flight, an aircraft will obviously fly faster when it is going 'downwind', with a tail wind behind it. The terms really correspond to a boat's **upstream/downstream** conditions.

urban see **rural**

urinant/haurient
The first word of this pair has purely an etymological link with the first word of

the pair below. The terms are heraldic: 'urinant' means 'with head downwards', and 'haurient' therefore 'with head upwards'. They are used chiefly of aquatic creatures on shields, such as fishes and dolphins. They derive respectively from Latin *urinari*, 'to dive' and *haurire*, 'to draw' (i.e. the fish looks as if it is drawing water out of the sea, or as if it had raised its head to draw in air.) The common etymological link between 'urinant' and 'urinate' is Greek *ouron*, 'water'.

haurient

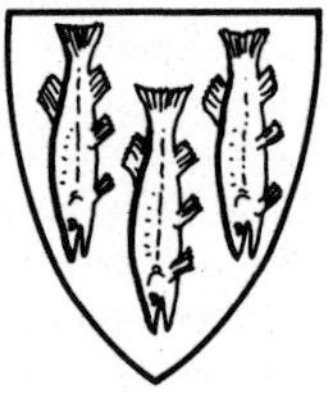
urinant

urinate/defecate
It would be wrong to overlook these two opposites, as they are quite interesting. There are several contrasts. First, to 'urinate' is to pass a liquid, while to 'defecate' is to expel a solid. Then, to 'urinate' is to perform a repeated yet fairly trivial and brief action, several times a day, while to 'defecate' is to carry out a more important, longer-lasting action, perhaps only once or twice a day. For males, again, to 'urinate' is to stand and face one way, while to 'defecate' is to sit and face the other. Yet although 'urinating' is a relatively minor act, compared to 'defecating', it can also be a more urgent one, and this can perhaps explain the colloquial terms 'number one' and 'number two', respectively. Two other common colloquial words for the acts or the products, especially among children, are 'wee-wee' and 'biggies'. The latter is self-explanatory, for the reasons already alluded to. As for the former, some dictionaries are quite po-faced when suggesting an etymology, saying something like 'of unknown origin', or at best 'babytalk', implying a sort of onomatopoeic link. But surely it is not so fanciful to suggest that 'wee' here means what it says, 'small', 'little', especially in view of its opposite number? As for the formal words, it is noteworthy that only 'defecate' has an 'out' or 'removal' prefix (as in 'delouse'), reflected in the 'ex-' of 'excretion'. It is therefore a sort of negative verb. By contrast, 'urinate' has no similar prefix, suggesting that the process is almost productive. (We do after all talk of 'making water' in this sense.) Perhaps this results from the positive uses of urine over the ages, whether for alchemical purposes or for diagnosing, as today, the state of the body. In view of the daily necessity of 'urinating' and 'defecating', it is strange that English has not evolved an adjective meaning 'needing to urinate' or 'needing to defecate', as it has (in common with other languages) for 'needing to drink' ('thirsty') and 'needing to eat' ('hungry'), all the more as the processes of drinking and eating are the converse of the subsequent actions.

us/them
'It's us against them', we say, implying that we, on the side of the 'little man', are up against a big impersonal employer or state body. We almost all of us belong to an 'us', whether socially, politically, religiously or in some other way, and we all feel at times that we are up against 'them', 'the big boys'. Sometimes, too, we win.

utopian socialism see **scientific socialism**

utricle see **saccule**

Vv

vacant/engaged
Familiar legends on the doors of public lavatories, to show whether they are free or occupied. English uses formal words for the purpose, whereas many other languages use simply the ordinary words for 'free' and 'occupied', such as French *libre* and *occupé*, German *frei* and *besetzt*, Italian *libro* and *occupato* and Russian *svobodno* and *zanyato*. The words can occasionally occur as opposites in other situations, such as a 'vacant' table (an unbooked one) and an 'engaged' table (a booked or reserved one), but even here the usage is not common, and we would be much more likely to talk of a 'free' table and a 'reserved' one. The nearest common sense of 'engaged' to mean 'in use' is that of an 'engaged' telephone line: see **ringing tone/engaged tone**.

vacuum/plenum
As used scientifically, a 'vacuum' is a region or area that contains no matter, while a 'plenum' is a space that is quite full. A 'vacuum' cleaner is so called because it produces a partial vacuum by suction. In this respect it differs from the earliest models which produced the same effect by blowing. (The French call it an *aspirateur*, since it 'breathes in' the dust, while the Germans call it a *Staubsauger* and the Russians a *pylesos*, both literally meaning a 'dust-sucker'.) See also **suck/blow**.

vair see **ermine**

vale see **ave**

valid/invalid
If a document such as a ticket or pass is 'valid' it is in force or 'good', and if it is 'invalid' (stressed on the second syllable) it cannot be lawfully used since it has expired or is faulty in some way. An 'invalid' (stressed on the first syllable), otherwise a sick or inform person, is so called because he is weak (Latin *invalidus*, literally 'not strong'). The word in this sense was borrowed by English from the French, where *invalide* came to be the term for a disabled soldier from the sixteenth century. The *Hôtel des Invalides* in Paris was a home for disabled soliders until quite recently.

valley see **hill**

vanguard/rearguard
The terms arose in English in the fifteenth century as words for the foremost and rearmost divisions of an army, respectively, and were themselves borrowed from French, as many military terms have been. The 'van-' of 'vanguard' represents French *avant*, 'before', while 'rear-' came from Old French *rere* (modern *arrière*), 'behind' (Standard English 'rear' as a separate word probably developed as a short form of 'rearguard', just as 'van' did from 'vanguard'. This is not the same 'van' as the vehicle, however, although this is also a shortening, of 'caravan'.) The modern French equivalents of the words have taken on special senses in English: see **avant-garde/arrière-garde**.

variable see **fixed**

variation see **theme**[2]

vegetable see (1) **animal** (2) **fruit**

vein/artery
In the body, the 'veins' carry blood to the heart, which pumps it back through the 'arteries', having sent it through the lungs to be recycled with oxygen on the way. Many of the major 'veins' and 'arteries'

in the body run virtually parallel to one another. 'Veins' are usually thought of as carrying blue blood, and 'arteries' as red. To an extent this is true since blood in the 'veins' has been depleted of oxygen, whereas in the 'arteries' it is oxygen-enriched. (The only 'artery' that carries deoxygenated blood is the pulmonary 'artery', which takes blood from the heart to the lungs.) Apart from this, 'arteries' are thick and elastic to withstand the pressure of the heart pumping, while 'veins' have valves to stop the blood flowing back down the body. Figuratively, 'artery' means 'highway', as an 'arterial' road, which is a main road. 'Artery' is etymologically related to 'aorta', which is itself the name of the main 'artery' that takes the blood from the heart and feeds it into smaller 'arteries' for distribution round the body. For what goes on in the heart, see **atrium/ventricle**.

venial sin see **mortal sin**

ventral see **dorsal**

ventricle see **atrium**

Venus see **Mars**

verkrampte/verligte
The two terms relate to South African politics. A 'verkrampte' (literally 'restricted' in Afrikaans) is (or was until recently) an Afrikaner Nationalist who is completely opposed to any liberalization in government policies, especially in racial matters. He is thus ultra-conservative, and in favour of apartheid. A 'verligte' ('enlightened') is a white member of any political party who favours a more liberal attitude, again, especially as regards racial policies. However, today most 'verkramptes' are not in the Nationalist Party but in the Conservative Party, founded in 1982, which is politically to the right of it. This means that the main-stream of the Nationalist Party has now been mostly taken over by the 'verligtes'.

verligte see **verkrampte**

vernal/autumnal
The adjectives corresponding to the nouns of the pair **spring/autumn**. 'Vernal' is less common than 'autumnal', presumably because it is quite different from its noun. However, it certainly flourishes in formal use (as for the 'vernal' equinox: see **equinox/solstice**) and in poetry ('purple all the ground with vernal flowers', Milton). 'Vernal' derives from the Latin word for 'spring', *ver*.

verse see **poetry**[2]

verso see **recto**

vertical/horizontal
'Vertical' (at right angles to the horizon in direction) is so called since it leads to the 'vertex', or highest point. 'Horizontal', more obviously, is named after the horizon, as it runs laterally across in the same direction. In economics, 'vertical' integration is the process whereby a firm buys up other companies that are involved in the same business but at different stages of production, as when an oil company owns everything from the basic oil well to the final filling station. Such production is seen as progressing 'vertically', or upwards to the end product. In 'horizontal' integration, all the firms acquired would be engaged in the same stage of production, or would be manufacturing identical products. In a television set, the electron beam in the cathode-ray tube (that produces the picture on the screen) moves in two time bases, a 'vertical' (so called 'frame time base') and a 'horizontal' ('line time base'). The latter gives the particular number of lines used to denote the transmission system used, for example '625 lines' (i.e. the beam scans 625 'horizontal' lines across the screen in a set time, in this case 0.04 seconds). Sometimes musicians talk of 'vertical' music, where the important feature is the harmonies or chords, as distinct from 'horizontal' music, where the main thing is the melody (see **harmony/melody**). In some non-English crossword puzzles, the clues are given 'vertically' and 'horizontally' (in the

native language) instead of 'down' and 'across' (see **across/down**).

vertical thinking see **lateral thinking**

veteran car/vintage car
Two similar names for old cars, especially carefully preserved ones. Strictly speaking a 'veteran car' is one made before 1904, while a 'vintage car' is one made between 1905 (or according to others, 1917) and 1930. Some people also designate cars made between 1905 and 1910 as 'Edwardian cars'. To see examples of fine 'veteran cars', station yourself on the London to Brighton road (the A23) for the annual 'Brighton Run' held on the first Sunday in November. (Or, perhaps better, go to see them at Hyde Park, where they start, for many fall by the wayside.)

VHS see **Beta(max)**

vicar/rector
A 'vicar' is the clergyman in charge of a parish who, in former times, did not receive any tithes from it, i.e. did not receive any of the tax charges for the upkeep of the church. A 'rector', on the other hand, although similarly in charge of a parish, *did* receive tithes. Hence the title of the 'vicar', who originally was a deputy to the 'rector', i.e. he acted 'vicariously' on his behalf. (He would have been appointed by the monasteries who 'appropriated' the tithes.)

vice see **virtue**

vice-chancellor see **chancellor**

video see **audio**

viewdata see **teletext**

village see **town**[3]

villain see **hero**

vintage car see **veteran car**

virtue/vice
In the loosest sense, a 'virtue' is a good or favourable quality of a person or thing ('The great virtue of her home is that it's easy to clean'), while a 'vice' is a bad quality, even a merely 'naughty' one ('I'm afraid blue cheese is one of my vices'). But, as we all know, 'patience is a virtue', so there must be more precise and solemn definitions for the words. There are. For the 'virtues', see **natural virtues/theological virtues**. For 'vice', see the *Oxford English Dictionary* ('Depravity or corruption of morals; evil, immoral, or wicked habits or conduct; indulgence in degrading pleasures or practices'). (Blue cheese seems a very trivial 'vice'!) The words, both because of their radical contrast and their alliteration, have been constantly contrasted since the earliest times, well before Chaucer, and there are countless instances in literature where they are opposed. Here we shall perhaps do best to confine ourselves to a single proverb, worth pondering on: 'Vice is often clothed in virtue's habit'. See also **mortal sin/venial sin**.

VISA see **Access**

visible/invisible
Apart from the literal common opposites ('what can be seen', 'what cannot be seen'), the two terms are fairly familiar from reports on the economy in the media, when one reads of 'invisible' exports, for example, or 'visible' trade. 'Visible' imports and exports (and trade) are those that are actual, tangible goods, rather than services, for example cars, corn and cigars. (Such goods are sometimes crudely described as 'those you can drop on your foot'.) By contrast, 'invisible' imports and the like are services that do not result in a tangible end product, so they include such things as insurance, banking, shipping, and foreign travel, all of which are things 'that you can't drop on your foot'. However, 'invisible' trade can be financially quantified, just as 'visible' trade can, and it is important in a country's economy.

viviparous/oviparous
Most mammals are 'viviparous', that is, they give birth to live offspring that develop in the womb. ('Viviparous' means 'bringing forth alive'.) However, a few mammals are 'oviparous' ('bring forth as eggs'), notably the duckbilled platypus, and certainly fishes, reptiles and birds are overwhelmingly in this category, because they produce eggs that hatch outside the body. A few creatures again, however, are 'ovoviviparous', and produce eggs that hatch inside the body of the mother. Among this rare breed are certain lizards and snakes, such as the viper.

vixen see **fox**

vous see **tu**

vowel/consonant
Many languages have an alphabet consisting of several different 'consonants' and a rather smaller number of 'vowels'. Strictly speaking, however, a 'consonant' (and a 'vowel') is a sound rather than a single letter, so that English has the 'consonants' represented by the letters 'ch' and 'sh', for instance. In short, a 'consonant' is a sound produced when the stream of air above the vocal cords, as a person speaks, is obstructed or impeded in some way, for example by the tongue or the teeth. (It does not matter whether the voice is actually sounded or not, so that both 'p', without the voice, and 'b', with it, are 'consonants', and the impeding is done by the lips.) A 'vowel' is thus the opposite, and is a stream of air that comes 'straight', without any obstruction, even though the shape of the mouth (as a 'resonance chamber') may alter. The famous five English 'vowels' are 'a', 'e', 'i', 'o' and 'u', with 'y' sometimes a 'vowel' (as in 'symbol') and sometimes a semi-vowel (as in 'yawn' or 'yacht'). 'Consonant' means literally 'sounding at the same time', and is so called because it cannot be sounded unless it is 'sounded with' a 'vowel' (which is not really quite true, as it is possible to utter an unvoiced 'consonant' such as 'p' without any accompanying 'vowel'). 'Vowel' is ultimately related to Latin *vox*, 'voice', and therefore to 'voice' itself.

Ww

Wade-Giles see **Pinyin**

wage/salary
The difference between the two payments for work done is really that of the pair (here reversed) **white-collar worker/ blue-collar** worker, that is, a 'wage' is for the 'worker' proper, and a 'salary' for a professional employee. Moreover, 'wages' are usually paid by the week, whereas a 'salary' is mostly paid monthly. Again, many workers still receive their 'wages' in actual cash (in a 'pay packet' or 'wage packet'), while most employees who receive a 'salary' are either paid by cheque or have the amount credited direct to their bank account.

wale see **course**

Walloon see **Fleming**

wane see **wax**

warm see **cool**

warm-blooded/cold-blooded
'Warm-blooded' animals and birds are those who maintain a constant warm body temperature, usually slightly higher than their surroundings. 'Cold-blooded' creatures, such as fishes and reptiles, have a body temperature that varies with the surrounding environment (that may not literally be always 'cold'). The scientific terms for the two adjectives are those of the cumbersome pair **homoiothermic/ poikilothermic**. In a general way, a 'warm-blooded' person is ardent or passionate (in *Castle Dangerous*, Walter Scott wrote of the 'young and warm-blooded valour of England'), while 'cold-blooded' means 'lacking feeling or sympathy', 'callous' (as in a 'cold-blooded' murder).

warm front see **cold front**

warp/woof
In weaving, the 'warp' is the arrangement of the yarns lengthways in the loom. They thus form the threads through which the 'woof' (or 'weft', as it is also called) passes, this being the term for the crosswise threads. The expression 'warp and woof', favoured mostly by journalists, means 'essence' (i.e. 'fabric'), so that we can regard the media as 'weaving' its way into the 'warp and woof' of our daily lives. 'Warp' comes from an Old English verb meaning 'throw' (compare modern German *werfen*); 'woof' is related to 'weave' and so to 'weft'.

Warsaw Pact see **NATO**

wasp see **bee**

water see **fire**

wax/wane
The verbs are particularly associated with the phases of the moon, which 'waxes' from a new moon to a full moon, then 'wanes' until it is invisible. So the basic senses are 'increase' and 'decrease'. Apart from this usage, the words are decidedly literary, although at one time 'wax' was the standard verb in English for 'grow' ('But Jeshurun waxed fat, and kicked', Deuteronomy 32:15). The alliteration of the verbs, together with their opposite senses, has resulted in many quotations combining them, such as Bishop Jewel's translation of Latin *Mali proficiunt: Boni deficiunt*: 'The wicked wax: the godly wane'.

weak see **strong**

weakness see **strength**

weather see **lee**

well-done/rare
Two opposing methods of cooking meat, usually steak or roast beef. 'Well-done' is self-explanatory; 'rare' means that the meat is not cooked right through, so that the inside is still almost raw, and red in colour, or in other words so that it is underdone. This 'rare' is not the same word as the common 'rare' that means 'unusual' (a 'rare' species of plant), but arose as a form of 'rear', apparently from a verb meaning 'stir' (compare German *rühren* in this sense). But as 'rare' meat is an acquired taste, preferred by the discriminating diner, no doubt many feel that 'rare' is an appropriate word, since it can mean 'excellent' (a 'rare' treat).

west see **east**

wet/dry
There are many special senses in which 'wet' is the opposite of 'dry'. Here are a few. A 'wet' cell is a battery cell in which the electrolyte (the substance that conveys the electric current) is a liquid. In a 'dry' cell it is a paste. For an angler, a 'wet' fly is an artificial fly that moves below the surface of the water, whereas a 'dry' fly floats on the surface. (These flies are designed for different types of fish.) A 'wet-and-dry thermometer', also called a 'psychrometer', is a thermometer with a 'wet'-bulb thermometer and a 'dry'-bulb one, the former having a bulb covered by a damp muslin bag, and the latter having an unmoistened bulb. The two together are used for measuring the humidity of the atmosphere. In politics, a 'wet' is a 'liberal-minded' member of the Conservative Party who is opposed to the monetarist 'hard-line' policies of Mrs Thatcher. By contrast, a 'dry' (the term is much less frequent) favours such policies. ('It used to be customary to analyse ministerial changes in terms of the balance between wets and dries', *The Times*, 22 May 1986.) A 'dry' country or community (such as a ship's crew) is one where alcohol is not sold or permitted, but in a 'wet' one it is. Incidentally, 'dry' cleaning is so called because garments that could not be laundered were rubbed when 'dry' with french chalk and then brushed clean with the chalk to remove the grease. Today, organic solvents (which are actually 'wet', but which will not mix with water) are used to dissolve the grease. See also **sweet/dry**.

Whig/Tory
In the seventeenth century, the 'Whigs' were the political party in England who opposed the succession to the throne of James, Duke of York, as he was a Roman Catholic. They were mostly aristocrats and rich middle-class people at first, but later crystallized as supporters of a limited monarchy and increased parliamentary power. In the nineteenth century they formed the basis for what evolved as the Liberal Party. The 'Tories' were the great royalists of the eighteenth century (at first particularly supporting the Stuarts), and they sought to preserve the existing parliamentary structure and so opposed any reform. They were the forerunners of the Conservative Party of today. (See **Conservative/Labour** for a contemporary picture, rather than this historical one.) The names are unusual. 'Whig' is short for 'Whiggamore', the nickname of one of the Scottish rebels who joined in an attack on Edinburgh in the seventeenth century, with their own name probably from Scottish *whig*, 'to drive', and *more* 'mare'. The 'Tories', somewhat unexpectedly, have a name of Irish origin, and the derivation is in Irish *tóraidhe*, 'pursuer'. This is because the original 'Tories', before the English ones, were Irish royalist outlaws in the seventeenth century. So the two respectable political titles evolved from disrespectable raiders and robbers, respectively!

whiskey see **whisky**

whisky/whiskey
Although basically one and the same 'Scotch', the slightly differentiated spellings are used for Scottish 'whisky' (the original, and still regarded by many as the only genuine type) and for Irish or

American 'whiskey'. The word itself, however spelt, comes from Scottish *uisge beatha* (or Irish *uisce beathadh*), 'water of life'. (Compare French *eau de vie*, 'brandy', 'spirits', and 'aquavit' (Scandinavian spirits), from Latin *aqua vitae*, 'water of life'.)

whisky see **brandy**

whistling see **roaring**

white/yolk
The 'white' of an egg is the viscous material containing albumen that surrounds the 'yolk', which is the round yellow mass in the centre. When uncooked, the 'white' is almost transparent, but gets its name from the colour it becomes when solidifying under heat. 'Yolk' is actually related to the word 'yellow' and the word for 'yolk' in some languages is quite close to the colour name, (e.g. French *jaune d'oeuf*, German *Eigelb*, Russian *zheltok*, and so on).

white see (1) **black** (2) **brown** (3) **coloured** (4) **red**[4]

white-collar worker/blue-collar worker
A 'white-collar worker' is an employee in a non-manual post, typically a clerical one in an office, and usually receiving a salary rather than a wage (see **wage/salary**). He is so called because he (traditionally) wears a white collar, unlike the coloured collar worn by employees in protective clothing or overalls. Therefore a 'blue-collar worker' is a manual worker, paid in a weekly wage, whose work makes it desirable for him to wear special clothing, although not always blue. The terms themselves arose in the United States, apparently in the 1930s, although a white collar was regarded as a typical garment of an office clerk some years before this.

white hole see **black hole**

white tie see **black tie**

whoa see **gee-up**

wholefood/junk food
The two terms are not commonly contrasted, as such, although they *are* opposites. 'Wholefood' is a food that has been processed or refined as little as possible, and so is near enough in its natural state. Examples would be wholemeal flour, natural yoghurt, brown rice, and so on. At the other end of the dietetic scale is so called 'junk food'. This is food that has been extensively processed and that has a high carbohydrate content but low nutritional value. Examples of 'junk food' might be hot dogs, candy floss, and chips (without the fish). A further distinction between the two sorts is that 'wholefoods' are usually eaten at home, as part of a balanced meal, while 'junk foods' are eaten away from the home (often, simply in the street near the shop or stall where they were bought). Many children love 'junk foods', but 'wholefoods' are the preferred choice of discriminating adults, especially those regulating their meals or watching their diet. Again, 'junk foods' are bought all over the place, at various sale points (often holiday resorts, or 'down-market' districts), while 'wholefoods' are usually bought at rather superior 'health food shops' and the better class of chemist's shop or drugstore. Both types of food can be quite expensive (think of muesli or potato crisps). The term 'junk food' originated in the United States in the late 1970s, while 'wholefood' arose somewhat earlier. It is no coincidence that the words 'whole' and 'health' are etymologically related. See also **skim milk/whole milk**, **brown/white**.

whole milk see **skim milk**

wholesale see **retail**

widow/widower
The common terms for a woman whose husband has died, and a man whose wife has died, respectively. An unusual feature of the pair is that the term for the male developed later than the term for the female (originally 'widow' served for both). Feminists claim that this is because the wife's loss of her husband's financial

support was regarded as more important than a husband's bereavement or loss of female companionship. 'Widow' has its recognizable counterpart in other languages, such as French *veuve*, Italian *vedova*, German *Witwe* and Russian *vdova*, all of them ultimately related to Latin *viduus*, 'bereft', and so to French *vide*, 'empty' and English 'void'.

widower see **widow**

width see **length**

wife see **husband**

wilco see **roger**

wild see **tame**

will see **shall**

Wilton/Axminster
A 'Wilton' carpet has its design woven directly into it, in loops of cut or uncut pile, whereas in an 'Axminster' carpet, the pile tufts are inserted into its backing while it is being woven. 'Axminster' carpets were originally manufactured at Axminster, in Devon. Now they are manufactured at Wilton, in Wiltshire! This paradox came about because the Axminster concern merged with that of the Wilton Royal Carpet Factory in the early nineteenth century. However, both types of carpet are also manufactured elsewhere in the country.

win[1]/lose
'Win some, lose some', we say philosophically or phlegmatically, resigning ourselves to a 'lose' in some situation when we had been expecting a 'win'. Life is all about 'winning' and 'losing', and as for the sporting sense, why, it's only a game, isn't it (we say, when we have 'lost')? Then there is the old dodge of the trickster: 'Heads I win, tails you lose'. Optimistically, we always want to 'win'; realistically, we know we will sometimes 'lose'; pessimistically, we come to believe that we *always* 'lose'. It is hardly surprising that the contrasting pair features regularly in literature of all kinds. Among proverbs, there are 'Win at first and lose at last', and the rather more encouraging 'Either win the horse or lose the saddle'. So go all out to 'win', you've nothing to 'lose'! (According to Karl Marx: 'The workers have nothing to lose but their chains. They have a world to win.')

win[2]/place
In horseracing or gambling, a 'win' is a horse that comes in first, or a bet that he will. A 'place' is a horse that finishes second or third, or a bet that *that* is where he will finish. An 'each way' bet is one for either a 'win' or a 'place'. (In America, 'show' is used instead of 'place' for a horse that comes in third.)

winder see **flier**

windward see **leeward**

wine see **bread**

wines/spirits
Two basic types of alcoholic drink, with 'spirits' stronger than 'wines', and usually needing to be diluted as a mixed drink (see **straight/mixed**). On the whole, 'spirits' are about four times as strong alcoholically as ordinary table 'wines', or twice as strong as so-called fortified 'wines', such as sherry. Typical 'spirits' are gin, whisky, rum and vodka. There are hardly any typical 'wines', but see **red/white**, **still/sparkling**. 'Spirits' are so called because they are regarded as the 'essence' of the grain from which they are (mostly) distilled. 'Wine', usually made from grapes, is a similar word in many languages. Here are a few: French *vin*, Italian *vino*, Spanish *vino*, Russian *vino*, German *Wein*, Latin *vinum*, Greek *oinos*. It's not only love that makes the world go round, apparently . . .

winter see **summer**

winter wheat see **spring wheat**

wire wheel see **disc wheel**

witch see **wizard**

with/without
English is unusual in repeating the positive word in its negative equivalent here, so that 'with' appears in both, even if in the opposite it is 'out'. Compare French *avec* and *sans*, German *mit* and *ohne*, Russian *s* and *bez*, Latin *cum* and *sine*, and so on. Almost every day of our lives we are faced with the choice of doing or having one thing 'with' or 'without' another, if only in what we eat or drink ('with' sugar or 'without'?). However, in many senses 'without' is not really an opposite form for 'with', and it cannot always be substituted to indicate the contrary. For example, you can do something 'without' any trouble, but not 'with' trouble, and you can say that 'without' doubt you will arrive on time, not 'with' doubt. This is because the nouns themselves denote something undesirable (you never wish for trouble or doubt). But the same also applies when positive verbs are involved, so that you can walk by the shop 'without' seeing it, not 'with' seeing it. 'Without' needs careful handling!

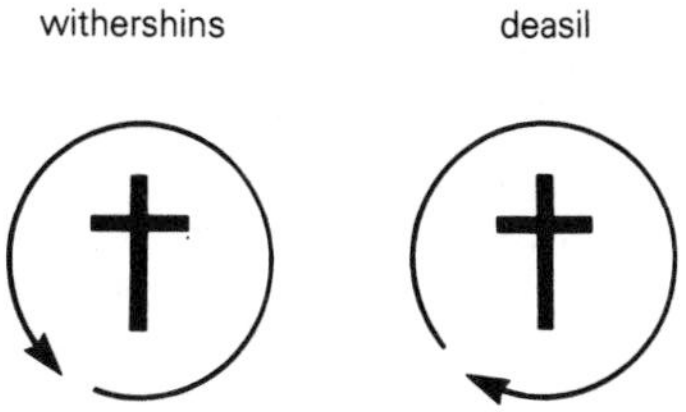

withershins/deasil
These attractive-sounding opposites mean respectively 'anticlockwise' and 'clockwise', with the implication that 'withershins' is the 'wrong' direction (turning against the direction of the sun), while 'deasil' is the 'right' way to turn. The terms themselves relate chiefly to folklore and superstition, with witches inevitably flying 'withershins', but a procession round a church in a wedding ceremony, for instance, being 'deasil'. The words are Celtic in origin, so the related beliefs and practices are themselves Celtic, and especially Scottish. 'Withershins', also spelt 'widdershins', literally means 'going back' (compare modern German *wider*, 'against', 'contrary to'), with the second half of the word later associated with 'sun'. 'Deasil' (pronounced 'dezzle' or 'dessle' or even 'deshle') is related to Latin *dexter*, 'right-hand', and so to English 'dexter' as well. See also **clockwise/anticlockwise**, **sinister/dexter**, and even **left/right**.

without see **with**

wizard/witch
Although the two words are commonly associated, with a 'wizard' regarded as a sort of male 'witch', and a 'witch' being a kind of female 'wizard', they do not have a common origin. 'Wizard' is directly related to 'wise', with the '-ard' ending that often has a 'bad' sense (as in 'bastard' or 'coward'). 'Witch', on the other hand, evolved as the feminine form (in Old Englich *wiċċe*) of the male *wiċċa*, meaning 'sorcerer', 'magician' (i.e. someone who 'bewitches'). This means that for some time 'witch' could be a person of either sex, and there may even be some remote places where this sense is still current in local use. (The *OED* quotes a text dated 1914 where it is stated that near Criccieth, in Wales, 'there lives a long-haired, haggard old man whom the people about speak of as a "witch"'.) In popular modern usage, a 'wizard' is someone who is gifted in some way (a 'wizard' at tennis), and perhaps the subconscious association with 'whizz' helps here (a 'whizz-kid' is surely a 'wizard' at something). 'Witch', on the other hand, usually means 'ugly old woman', 'hag', although it could formerly mean 'fascinating woman', 'temptress' ('For my part I find every woman a witch', Bulwer-Lytton, *The Last Days of Pompeii*, 1834). Feminists have used the letters of 'witch' to serve as the initials of various groups of 'action women', such as '*W*omen *I*ncensed at *T*elephone *C*ompany *H*arassment', '*W*omen *I*ntent on *T*oppling *C*onsumer *H*olidays' and '*W*omen's *I*ndependent *T*axpayers, *C*onsumers and *H*omemakers'.

woman see **man**

woodwind/brass
The two main sections of wind instruments in an orchestra, with 'woodwind' including the flutes, even though today they are frequently made of metal. (The other stock members of the 'woodwind' family are the oboes, clarinets and bassoons, where the name is more appropriate. The German for 'bassoon' is *Fagott*, showing a clear 'woody' link, as it is basically the same word as English 'faggot', in the sense 'bundle of sticks'.) The 'brass' comprises those instruments that are equally found in a 'brass' band, that is, the trumpets, trombones, horns and tuba. Some of these instruments are still literally made of 'brass', although other metals are also used, so the term should not be taken absolutely literally. One important distinction is in the method of playing: the 'woodwind' (except the flutes) have reeds, but the 'brass' are played by applying the lips to a mouthpiece. The tones of both combine well in a wind band. Of the 'brass' instruments in an orchestra, the horns are reckoned to be closest in sound quality and musical tone to the 'woodwind', hence the positioning of the horns next to the 'woodwind' in the usual seating arrangement of an orchestra today.

woof see **warp**

woofer/tweeter
The agreeably non-technical names are used for quite technical objects. In a hi-fi system, a 'woofer' is a loudspeaker that reproduces low audio frequencies, while a 'tweeter' reproduces the high-pitch sounds. In size, a 'woofer' is usually larger than a 'tweeter'. The sounds produced by each do not bear much resemblance to a dog bark or birdsong, but one can appreciate the analogy. The actual terms date from at least the 1930s.

words/music
The two complementary features that comprise many types of standard musical entertainment and performance, from grand opera at one end to the musical at the other, taking in hymn singing and pop songs on the way. The basic contrast here is thus between the human voice and the musical instrument, with the former providing almost (but not quite) as much variety as the latter. In some instances, the 'words' that go with the 'music' have a special designation. In opera, for example, the 'words' are the 'libretto' (Italian, 'little book'), while for a musical they are the 'lyrics'. 'Words' are 'written', but 'music' is usually 'composed'. For related themes, see **librettist/composer**, **opera seria/opera buffa**, **Gilbert/Sullivan**. And for one middle-of-the-road example of the things themselves, see the musical *Words and Music* (or better, and easier, the film version of it, released in 1948).

work/play
An interesting pair of contrasts. On the face of it, an obvious one, since 'work' usually involves a fairly serious 'earning a living' or 'job', while 'play' is light-hearted and relaxing, and serves as a welcome break from routine or even boring 'work'. But consider: a professional footballer or musician 'plays' for his 'work', and we must all have experienced an activity when 'play' of some kind was as demanding, physically or mentally, as 'work'. If I write a letter to a friend, is that 'work' or 'play'? We tend to pigeonhole all our daily activities into one category or the other, and there must surely be many things we do which are neither 'work' nor 'play'. So when the famous proverb says that 'All work and no play makes Jack a dull boy', it is really saying that we must combine the serious with the frivolous, the purposeful with the pointless, if we are to get the most out of life and be a 'complete' person.

workers/management
In business and industry, a common way of describing the employ*ees* on the one hand and the employ*ers* on the other is to talk of 'workers' and 'management'. (Although it is actually the employers who pay the wages.) The duality somewhat suggests an **us/them** division. Perhaps 'employees' and 'employers' is a less

emotive pair. In Germany, the equivalents are the much more satisfactory *Arbeitnehmer* ('work taker') and *Arbeitgeber* ('work giver').

workers see **drones**

worse see **better**

wove/laid
'Wove' paper is made in such a way that no fine lines run across it, as they do in 'laid' paper. 'Wove' paper is so called since originally it was made on a mould of finely woven wire. 'Laid' paper was made by having a raised wire 'laid' along each of the crossbars of the mould to which the other wires were fastened, so giving it its characteristic 'ribbed' appearance (the fine lines that are seen). Many people choose 'laid' paper for their private letters, because they regard it as more 'classy', especially if it has a deckle. The watermark it contains, too, give it an appearance of exclusivity.

wow/flutter
A pair of technical terms of the same order as those of **woofer/tweeter**, and similarly relating to the electrical reproduction of sound. The meanings are different, however. 'Wow' is the word to indicate a distortion heard as a slow rise and fall in the pitch of the sound, and is caused by an irregular speed in the sound-reproducing system itself, such as a faultily revolving turntable (in a record player) or tapedrum (in a tape recorder). 'Flutter' has the same basic cause, but is a much faster rise and fall in pitch. The terms themselves are vaguely imitative, with 'wow' implying a wailing sound, and 'flutter' an oscillating or 'trembling' sound or motion. 'Wow' is also sometimes known as 'wobble'. The terms originated in the 1930s.

write see **read**

writer see **reader**

written see (1) **oral**[4] (2) **spoken**

wrong see **right**

Xx

x/y
The two letters have long been in use for contrasting unknown terms or quantities (with 'z' often providing the third unknown factor). In mathematics more generally, an 'x'-axis of a graph is the horizontal one, and the 'y'-axis the vertical one. In genetics, an 'X'-chromosome is a sex chromosome (strand of gene-carrying material) that is usually paired with another 'X'-chromosome in one sex, and with a 'Y'-chromosome in the other sex. As far as human beings are concerned, two inherited 'X'-chromosomes means that the sex is female, and an inherited paired 'X'-chromosome and 'Y'-chromosome means that the sex is male. The 'Y'-chromosome is moreover shorter than the 'X'-chromosome. Since 'X' has the common meaning 'unknown' (as mentioned above), 'Y' is sometimes used as a contrast to it when talking about two people whose names are not stated or known, for example, 'Mr X then spoke to Miss Y', in a court case, say.

xylem see **phloem**

Yy

y see **x**

Yahoos see **Houyhnhnms**

yang see **yin**

yarn-dye see **piece-dye**

yea/nay
'Let your yea be yea; and your nay, nay', the Bible advises us (or, more precisely, whoever was the author of the Epistle of James). Here the two words correspond to, but are not the same as, 'yes' and 'no', i.e. 'an affirmative' and 'a negative'. Originally, 'yea' was an affirmative answer to a positive question, while 'yes' was an affirmative answer to a negative question (see **yes/no** below). 'Nay' was a negative answer to any question, as 'no' is today. Curiously, the two words virtually mean one and the same thing when they are used in a sentence or statement to introduce a more precise or more emphatic word or phrase than one just said. For instance, this quotation by Wesley (which actually has 'yea') could equally well have 'nay': 'Some of them use improper, yea, indecent expressions in prayer' ('Some of them use improper, nay, indecent expressions in prayer'). Either word will serve to introduce 'indecent', which is a stronger word than 'improper'. Today, both words are almost obsolete, although 'nay' can still perhaps be used in formal speech or writing in its 'emphatic' sense. See also **aye/no**.

yellow card/red card
In football, a 'yellow card' is a yellow-coloured card held up by the referee to show that a player is having his name taken for committing an offence. A 'red card', similar, only red, is one shown to indicate that the offending player is being sent off the field. In English football, both cards were abandoned in 1981, but were reintroduced in the 1987 season.

yes/no
'Yes' and 'no' must be two of the commonest words in the English language. ('Oh no they're not!' 'Oh yes they are!', as the familiar pantomime dialogue runs.) As mentioned in the entry **yea/nay**, 'yes' was originally used to give an affirmative response to a negative question, much as French *si* and German *doch* still are today. A good example comes in Shakespeare's *Two Gentlemen of Verona*:

> *Valentine*. What means your ladyship?
> Do you not like it?
> *Silvia*. Yes, yes: the lines are very
> quaintly writ.

However, this was in 1591, and 'yes' did not have this special usage as a regular feature much after about 1600. (It does comes four times in the Authorized Version of the Bible published in 1611, however. In the 1881 Revised Version, the revisers altered all these to 'yea', apparently in ignorance of the fact that 'yes' was precisely the correct response to a negative question, by contrast with 'yea', which followed an affirmative one.) This is not to say, however, that 'yes' could not be used as a response to a positive question. It could, although it was rather more emphatic than 'yea'. All of which brings us back to the present, with our sometimes hesitant or deliberately careful 'yes and no', meaning that the answer could be 'yes' when seen in one light, but 'no' when regarded in another. ('Do you enjoy reading this book?' 'Well, yes and no – it's interesting but the author keeps changing the subject.') In 1925 the musical 'No, No, Nanette' was first performed. And yes, it was a success. Two years later, by a different writer, the musical 'Yes, Yes, Yvette' was staged. But no, it was not a success.

yin/yang
'Yin' and 'yang', in Chinese philosophy, are diametrically opposed principles. 'Yin' is expressed in terms of the negative: the moon, the female, dampness, water, cold, and the passive. 'Yang' is expressed in terms of the positive: the sun, the male, dryness, fire, heat, and the active. (We westerners traditionally think in terms of the 'yang' quality first.) In a perfect world, 'yin' and 'yang' combine to produce the entire universe. Many people, including westerners, believe that 'yin' and 'yang' can be achieved through a correctly balanced diet, and this is really what macrobiotics is all about. (In a macrobiotic diet, the balance should be five parts of 'yin' to one of 'yang'. One of the best known such diets is the ten-day brown rice one, since grain has already a natural 'balance'. For more, see the related **wholefood/junk food**.) In Chinese, *yin* actually means most of the 'yin' principles, e.g. 'shade', 'feminine', 'moon', etc., while **yang** has the 'yang' senses, such as 'sun', 'positive', 'male genitals'. The so called 'yin-yang symbol' is one representing the blending of the two cosmic forces, and consists of a circle with an 'S'-shaped line dividing it into a dark segment and a light one, the 'S' shape itself indicating that the 'yin' contains a 'seed' of the 'yang', and vice versa.

yolk see **white**

yoni/lingam
In Hinduism, 'yoni' is a (stylized) representation of the female genitals, found in Hindu temples, where it is regarded as the divine symbol of sexual pleasure and of generation. 'Lingam' is the converse, a representation of the male genitals, shown as a stylized phallus. 'Yoni' literally means 'vulva', and 'lingam' (or 'linga') has the literal sense 'characteristic'. Both are Sanskrit words.

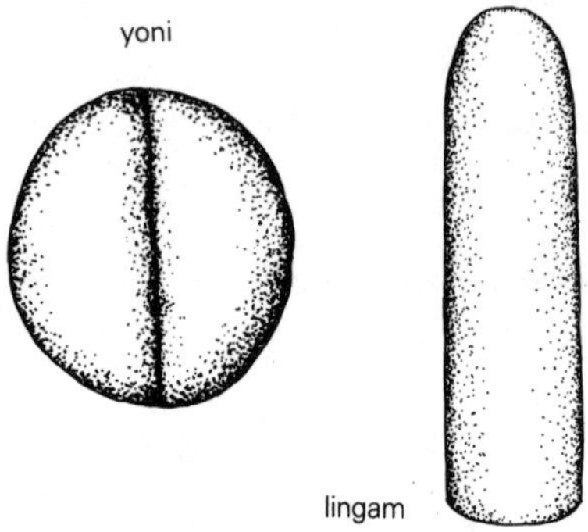

York/Lancaster
The contrast, or rather the opposition, is a historic one for these two cities, referring to the Wars of the Roses, when in the latter half of the fifteenth century there was a struggle for the throne between the house of York (whose symbol was a white rose) and the house of Lancaster (whose symbol was a red rose). (However, there are some hard-faced historians who say that the roses were a later romantic addition to the affair. Even so, they gave their names to the conflicts.) The struggles ended with the battle of Bosworth Field in 1485, when the Yorkist king Richard III was killed (see Shakespeare's play of this name for more) and the Lancastrian Henry Tudor became king as Henry VII, at the same time uniting the houses of 'York' and 'Lancaster' by marrying Elizabeth of York, eldest daughter of the Yorkist king Edward IV (who had died two years earlier). To this day, there is a sense of rivalry between the two cities, or more precisely between the counties of Yorkshire and Lancashire, if only on the cricket field. (Yorkshire have been County Champions eight times in the annual matches since 1948, but Lancashire only once, and neither county at all since 1968.) See also **Canterbury/York**.

you/me
The contrast is constant and implicit: 'you' are 'you', and I am 'me', and (grammatically, at any rate), 'you' are the second person, while I am the first. Some linguists have noticed a curious fact, which may or may not be simply a coincidence. In saying the word 'you', our lips move outwards towards the person we are speaking to, but in saying 'me' the lips are drawn in to the speaker. The same principle applies in other languages, so that French *vous* and *tu*, as well as Italian *voi* and German *du*, are all 'outwards' words, while even in English 'I', 'we' and 'us', as well as 'me', are all 'inwards' words. 'You' and 'me' have been coupled in ways too numerous to mention, but mostly in or out of a loving relationship, from John Betjeman's tennis goddess, Miss J. Hunter-Dunn ('We in the tournament – you against me!'), to Michael Drayton's parting over three centuries earlier ('Nay, I have done: you get no more of me').

young/old
As with 'you' and 'me' (see previous entry), the contrasts here are so basic and vital that there are proverbs, sayings and quotations at every turn to point up the differences. (But let us not forget the similarities, too. There is much in common between the very 'young' and the very 'old', in the best sense. That is why they get on so well together. Not for nothing is a happy 'old' age sometimes called a 'second childhood'.) People have been discussing for centuries when the 'great divide' comes, separating the 'young' from the 'old'. When even is so-called 'middle age'? The truth of the matter seems to be that it is all relative. And we can safely say that anyone younger than us is, by comparison, 'young', even if we are sixty and he or she is fifty. Conversely, everyone older than we are is 'old'. In history, the 'Young' Pretender was Charles Edward Stuart, alias 'Bonnie Prince Charlie', the Scottish claimant to the British throne in the mid-eighteenth century. He was the son of the 'Old' Pretender, James Francis Edward Stuart, who made two unsuccessful attempts to claim the throne. 'Young' and 'Old' are fairly common to distinguish between two people of the same name, whether they are related or not ('Old' Mr Bloggs and 'Young' Mr Bloggs). 'Youngster' and 'oldster' are sorts of opposites, for a 'young' person (or animal) and an older one, although the second word is not so common as the first. English is slightly unusual in having no single one word to correspond to 'youth' – we have to say 'old age'. (Other languages are tidier, such as French *jeunesse* and *vieillesse*, German *Jugend* and *Alter*, Russian *molodost'* and *starost'*.) Language-wise, 'young' is a much more 'universal' word than 'old', and all these words are related to it: French *jeune*, Italian *giovane*, Spanish *joven*, German *jung*, Russian *yuny*, Welsh *ieuanc*, Irish *óg*, Latin *juvenis*. Compare **senior/junior**.

Zz

Z see **A**[2]

zenith/nadir

Taking the words scientifically, in astronomy, the 'zenith' is the point on the celestial sphere (the 'dome' of the night sky) that is directly above an observer, while the 'nadir' is the point directly below him exactly opposite the 'zenith'. The words are Arabic, as are many astronomical names. 'Zenith' ultimately derives from *samt*, 'path', i.e. the path overhead, while 'nadir', simply enough, comes from *nazīr*, 'opposite'. The words can be used loosely to mean 'peak', 'high point' (at the 'zenith' of her career) and 'depths', 'low point' (the 'nadir' of despair). The difference in spelling between 'zenith' and the Arabic original appears to have arisen from the fact that at some stage, when the Arabic characters had been transliterated to Roman (as *samt*), the 'm' was misread as 'ni'.

zero/infinity

'Zero' (written '0') is the lowest number you can have, i.e. nothing, 'one below one'; 'infinity' (written '∞') is the highest number you can have, so high that you can never reach it. Mathematically, $0 = 1/\infty$. (Also mathematically, $\infty + a = \infty$, if 'a' is finite, and $\infty + \infty$ is nonsense.) 'From zero to infinity' is a phrase that can mean 'comprehensively'. As might be expected, 'zero' is a word of Arabic origin, from *sifr*, 'empty', which also gave English 'cipher'. 'Infinity' is of Latin origin, indicating a value that is 'not finite', or 'endless'.

zygodactyl/heterodactyl

The terms belong to ornithology, and relate to the feet of birds, or more exactly their toes. A 'zygodactyl' is a bird whose first and fourth toes point backwards, while its second and third toes face forwards. A 'heterodactyl' is the opposite: its first and second toes point backwards, but its third and fourth face forwards. Such things can make a difference to the bird's ability to climb, for example, so that parrots can climb in their cages (or anywhere else, for preference) since they are 'zygodactyls', as also are woodpeckers. On the other hand, tropical birds of the Trogonidae family, such as the quetzal, are 'heterodactyls'. They do not climb, but they do need to perch. Hence their particular toe arrangement. 'Zygodactyl' literally means 'with toes yoked' (referring to the second and third, which in some birds, such as the hornbill and kingfisher, are actually united), while 'heterodactyl' means 'with toes opposite', which is no great surprise.

Appendix I
Contrasting prefixes and suffixes

A cursory glance through the headings in the Dictionary will soon show that many contrasting pairs, especially those of a scientific or technical nature, have different prefixes or suffixes to denote their opposing senses. In the main, these are of classical origin, and are often the Greek or Latin root words meaning 'above' or 'below', 'in front' or 'behind', 'up' or 'down' and the like, so frequently seem more imposing than they are. The learned couple 'brachycephalic' and 'dolichocephalic' thus turn out to mean nothing more alarming than 'short-headed' and 'long-headed', and 'anadromous' and 'catadromous' mean simply 'running up' and 'running down'. Such terms were devised by scientists to denote opposing physical phenomena, and have the advantage of being understood internationally, since Latin and Greek are classical languages recognized by most civilized societies.

In this Appendix, some of the more common distinguishing prefixes and suffixes are given, together with their meanings and examples of their usage. The prefixes, which are generally greater in number, are in Section A, while the suffixes are in Section B. In some cases, prefixes or suffixes of identical meaning are virtually interchangeable, and 'cacogenics' is the same as 'dysgenics', while a 'postfix' is an alternative name for a 'suffix'.

A little familiarity with contrasting prefixes or suffixes can be a dangerous thing, however, since although the words themselves are exact etymological opposites, they may not be so in their current sense. For example, a 'benefactor' is not the exact opposite of a 'malefactor', because the good that he does affects others directly, while the 'malefactor' is simply a miscreant or 'misbehaver'. Similarly 'matrimony' is not the opposite of 'patrimony', although the contrasting pair 'mother' and 'father' lie behind the words. On another, more technical level, a 'microphone' is not normally regarded as the opposite of a 'megaphone', despite the fact that the words themselves derived from Greek meaning respectively 'little sound' and 'big sound'. (Readers of an inventive turn of mind can amuse themselves devising as yet unrecorded scientific instruments by using such contrasting prefixes, although it is hard to envisage what use could be found, for example, for a 'benescope' or a 'malescope', unless the former is a type of rose-coloured spectacles and the latter a 'glass darkly'.)

Certain structural or spelling alterations must be expected with some prefixes, so that 'dis-', for example, can also occur as 'di-' or 'des-' or 'de-', while 'in-' changes its second letter depending on the letter that follows, so is found as 'il-', 'im-', 'ir-' etc. when the next letter is the same.

Such deviations and peculiarities are mentioned in the individual entries, where appropriate. For the words themselves containing such prefixes and suffixes, only a literal definition is given, not a scientific discourse, and readers who want to know what creature could exactly be called 'brachycephalic' or 'anadromous' should refer to a specialized work or to a 'big' dictionary such as the *OED*. Contrasting words that have their own entries in *this* Dictionary, however, are printed in italics, and more information about the precise senses will normally be found there.

Finally, it should be pointed out that many prefixed words have a contrasting sense to an *un*prefixed word. In other words, it is merely the presence of the prefix that indicates the contrast. Usually this is to give a negative or 'bad' sense, or to denote an absence or reversal of something. The obvious example is the negative prefix 'un-', which is added to a basic word to give its opposite meaning: 'tie' and 'untie', 'happy' and 'unhappy', 'certain' and 'uncertain'. 'In-' is used in the same way: 'hospitable' and 'inhospitable', 'logical' and 'illogical'. Yet another such negating prefix is 'dis-': 'order' and 'disorder', 'please' and 'displease', 'mount' and 'dismount'.

In some cases, the opposing, negating or 'cancelling' sense of the prefix is all too apparent, so that one has 'violent' and 'non-violent', 'march' and 'countermarch', 'indicate' and 'contraindicate' (in medical jargon), and so on.

The little Greek prefix 'a-' has the same negating effect as English 'un-' or Latin 'in-': 'chromatic' and 'achromatic', 'moral' and 'amoral', 'sexual' and 'asexual'. Before vowels, it usually occurs as 'an-': 'aerobic' and 'anaerobic', 'echoic' and 'anechoic'. (It should not be confused here with 'ana-', meaning 'up', 'back', even though this can also have a contrasting sense, as in the 'anadromous' and 'catadromous' already mentioned.)

Sometimes one finds different negating prefixes used to express different shades of meaning. Thus 'amoral' (with Greek 'a-') means 'not moral', i.e. outside the domain of morality, but 'immoral' (with Latin 'im-') means 'wrong', 'wicked'.

Other negating or opposing prefixes in similar uses are 'mis-' ('understand' and 'misunderstand'), 're-' ('invest' and 'reinvest'), and 'de-', as distinct from 'dis-' ('activate' and 'de-activate'). Sometimes the prefix indicates a new action rather than an opposing one, and the contrast lies in the comparison between what is new and what is old. 'New-' itself can be used in this way, so that a 'newcomer' is seen in a different light from those who came earlier, but more often a classical prefix such as Greek 'neo-' is found, and a 'neo-classical' style of architecture is implicitly contrasted with a 'classical', while in art 'neo-Impressionism' is compared with 'Impressionism'. A prefix can also indicate a lack of genuineness or importance. Thus 'pseudoclassicism' is contrasted with genuine 'classicism', and a 'paramilitary' force is by implication compared with a standard 'military' one. (Care is needed with this prefix: a 'paramedic' is a person who helps a doctor, but a 'paradoctor' is a doctor who drops in on his patients by parachute!)

A: Prefixes

acro-, 'top'/**basi-**, 'bottom', or **acro-**/**bathy-**, 'depth'
'Acro-' is from Greek *akron*, 'tip', 'point', 'summit', while 'bathy-' is from *bathos*, 'depth'. 'Basi-' is really as much English 'base' as Greek *basis*, literally 'step', 'pedestal'. Examples are 'acropetal' and 'basipetal' ('seeking the top' and 'seeking the bottom'), and 'acrophobia' and 'bathyphobia', otherwise 'fear of heights' and 'fear of depths'.

ad-, 'to'/**ab-**, 'from'
The prefixes are Latin *ad* and *ab* in the sense given. In botany, 'adaxial' means 'towards the axis', so that 'abaxial' is 'away from the axis'. See also *absorb/adsorb* in Dictionary and compare 'adjure' ('charge on oath', literally 'bring on oath') and 'abjure' ('renounce on oath', literally 'take away on oath').

ana-, 'up'/**cata-** (**kata-**), 'down'
These are Greek prefixes in the senses stated. See *anabatic/katabatic* in Dictionary, and compare 'anadromous' and 'catadromous', as already just mentioned above, as well as biological 'anabolism' (chemical 'upbuilding' of substances in living matter) and 'katabolism' (or 'catabolism') (disruptive process of chemical change, otherwise a destructive metabolism).

andro-, 'male'/**gyno-** (**gynaeco-**), 'female'
The roots here are Greek *aner*, genitive *andros*, 'man', and *gyne*, genitive *gynaikos*, 'woman'. 'Andrology' is the branch of medicine that deals exclusively with men's diseases, as opposed to the more common 'gynaecology' which concerns itself with diseases and disorders in women. Compare in Section B the suffixes '-androus' and '-gynous'. In botany, 'gyno-' (or '-gynous') denotes the pistil in a plant (see *stamen/pistil* in Dictionary), so that an 'androphore' is a prolongation of the receptacle containing the stamens, and a 'gynophore' one that carries the carpel (or pistil).

ante- 'before'/**post-**, 'after'
Two fairly familiar Latin prefixes, as also found in such contrasting pairs as *anterior/posterior* and the first words of the abbreviations *a.m./p.m.* The prefixes mostly occur in words denoting opposites in time rather than position, as in 'antedate' (date before the true date) and 'postdate' (date after the true date) and 'antenatal' ('before birth') and 'postnatal' ('after birth'). In some words beginning 'anti-' the source is actually 'ante-', as in 'anticipate', although here there is no contrasting 'postcipate'. Compare, so as to distinguish, the prefixes 'pro-' and 'anti-' (below).

apo-, 'away', 'off'/**peri-**, 'round', 'near'
The Greek prefixes, with the meanings given, are common in contrasting terms in astronomy. See for example *apogee/perigee* in Dictionary, as well as (reversed) *perihelion/aphelion*. (English 'off' is actually related to 'apo-'.)

aristo-, 'best'/**kakisto-** (**cacisto-**), 'worst'
Greek prefixes found in a few erudite contrasts, e.g. 'aristocracy' (literally 'rule by the best') and 'kakistocracy' ('rule by the worst'). Socialists and Communists would claim, in modern terms, that an 'aristocracy' is a 'kakistocracy'.

auto-, 'self'/**hetero-**, 'other'
Greek *autos* is 'self', and *heteros* is 'other'. The two are not commonly contrasted, but occur in 'autonomous' ('self-governing') and 'heteronomous' ('subject to outside laws'). See also the more common pairs 'homo-' and
'hetero-' and 'ortho-' and 'hetero-' (below) and compare the related Latin pair 'ego-' and 'altero-'.

bene-, 'good', 'well'/**male-**, 'bad', 'ill'
For examples of the Latin opposites, see *benevolent/malevolent* and *benison/malison*, as

well as *benign/malignant*. A 'benediction' is a blessing, and a 'malediction' a curse, respectively a literal 'speaking well' and 'speaking ill'. (See also *bless/curse* in Dictionary.)

brachy-, 'short'/**dolicho**-, 'long'
Greek *brachys* and *dolichos* mean respectively 'short' and 'long', and are found mainly in zoological and geological terminology, to refer to creatures that have or had short or long heads, toes, wings or whatever. See the introduction to this Appendix (above) for one such pair. Compare also the Latin equivalents in the next entry below.

brevi-, 'short'/**longi**-, 'long'
The contrasting Latin prefixes occasionally occur in place of their more common Greek equivalents (see previous entry), for example in 'brevipennate' ('short-winged') and 'longipennate' ('long-winged').

calli-, 'beautiful'/**caco**-, 'bad'
The two Greek prefixes are not often in direct opposition, but they can be seen in such a pair as 'calligraphy' ('beautiful writing', or the art of it) and 'cacography' ('bad writing', 'illegible writing'). Compare the pair 'ortho-' and 'caco-', below, and the more common 'eu-' and 'dys-'.

calo(**ri**)-, 'hot'/**frigo**(**ri**)-, 'cold'
The Latin prefixes have as their roots *calor*, 'heat', and *frigor*, 'cold'. 'Calorific' thus means 'causing heat', and 'frigorific', by contrast, 'causing cold'.

Cis-, 'this side'/**Trans**-, 'across' (i.e. 'that side')
The Latin prefixes have mainly a historical or geographical use, as in 'Cisalpine' ('this side of the Alps', i.e. the Roman side) and 'Transalpine' ('across the Alps'), or 'Cispadane' ('this side of the Po') and 'Transpadane' ('across the Po'). Even more academically, 'Cisleithian' means 'this side of the Leitha' (a river that formerly divided Austria and Hungary), therefore 'Austrian', so that 'Transleithian' equates to 'Hungarian'. Applying to London, 'cispontine' means 'north of the Thames' (literally 'this side of the bridges'), and 'transpontine' therefore 'south of the Thames'. But 'cismontane' ('this side of the mountains') usually has 'ultramontane' ('beyond the mountains') as its opposite. Compare in Dictionary *cisalpine/ultramontane*.

con-, 'with', 'together'/**dis**-, 'not', 'apart'
'Con-', also found as 'com-' as well as 'col-' and 'cor-', ultimately derives from Latin *cum*, 'with', while 'dis-' (also occurring as 'di-', 'des-' and 'de-'), from the identical Latin prefix, has a general negating, separating or indeed 'dissociating' sense. Common examples (see Dictionary) are *concord/discord*, *consonant/dissonant*, *constructive/destructive*. Similarly, 'consent' is 'agreement', but 'dissent' is 'disagreement', and 'concrete' is 'formed into a single mass' (literally 'grown together'), while 'discrete' is 'separated', 'consisting of distinct parts' (literally 'grown apart').

ego-, 'I'/**altero**-, 'someone else'
The best known pair here (in reversed order) is *altruistic/egotistic*. The prefixes are respectively Latin *ego*, 'I' and *alter*, 'other' (i.e. the second of two). Compare the pair 'auto-' and 'hetero-' (above).

endo-, 'in'/**exo**-, 'out'
The prefixes are Greek, with *endon* meaning 'within' and *exo* meaning 'outside' (and equating to Latin *ex*, 'out'). 'Endo-' can also occur as 'ento-', and 'exo-' as 'ecto-'. The prefixes are frequently but not exclusively found in botanical terms, e.g. 'endocarp' ('inner layer of the pericarp', for example as a plum stone) and 'exocarp' ('outermost layer of the pericarp', for example the plum skin). Compare in Dictionary the pair *endogamy/exogamy*, and see also the next entry below.

eso-, 'inside'/**exo**-, 'outside'
These prefixes are the less common equivalents of those in the entry above, so similarly derive from Greek (*eso* is 'within', like

endon). Probably one of the best known pairs is *esoteric/exoteric* (see Dictionary).

eu-, 'good'/**dys-**, 'bad'
The Greek prefixes have the sense given, with 'dys-' having the same 'reverse' usage as Latin 'dis-', although not related to it. Words with the prefixes are found in a range of artistic and scientific fields, such as *euphemism/dysphemism* in Dictionary. Thus 'eulogistic' means 'praising', but 'dyslogistic' means 'censorious', while 'euphoria', denoting a heightened sense of well-being, has an opposite 'dysphoria' in medical terms, meaning 'lack of sense of wellbeing', 'morbid restlessness'. For some terms, 'caco-' is used to mean the same as 'dys-' (see the prefix 'calli-' above), so that one can have 'cacogenics' or 'dysgenics' as the opposite of 'eugenics', this latter word relating to 'race improvement', and the former words to 'race degeneration'. A word 'cacotopia' has thus been devised as the opposite of 'Utopia', to denote a place where everything is bad, with an alternative name for this place also 'dystopia'. See also the pair 'ortho-' and 'caco-' below.

giga-, 'giant'/**nano-**, 'dwarf'
The senses here are the literal ones for the Greek origins, respectively *gigas* and *nanos*. Mathematically, 'giga-' means 'ten to the ninth power' (i.e. 10^9), while 'nano-' means 'one thousand millionth' (i.e. 10^{-9}). Obviously, there are factors (multiples and submultiples) higher and lower than these, but at least the prefixes themselves denote basic opposites (see *giant/dwarf* in Dictionary). Compare the prefixes 'mega-' and 'micro-' below.

holo-, 'whole'/**mero-**, 'part'
The Greek prefixes are rather rarefied, deriving respectively from *holos*, 'whole', 'entire' and *meros*, 'part'. Thus in biology, 'holoblastic' means 'dividing completely into separate cells' (of an egg), while 'meroblastic' means 'dividing only partially into cells' (because the yolk impedes the division).

homo-, 'same'/**hetero-**, 'different'
Probably two of the best-known contrasting pairs with the prefixes are *homosexual/heterosexual* and *homogeneous/heterogeneous* (see Dictionary). The terms are Greek (so therefore not Latin *homo*, 'man', for 'homosexual'), and are respectively *homos*, 'same' and *heteros*, 'other' (see also the prefix 'auto-' above). Note that 'hom(o)eo-', 'like', although related to 'homo-', actually means 'like', so will have an opposite 'allo-', 'different', as in the pair (reversed in Dictionary) *allopathic/homoeopathic.*

hyper-, 'over'/**hypo-**, 'under'
Two confusingly similar opposite prefixes, from the Greek words with these respective senses. The medical condition of 'hypothermia' (subnormal body temperature caused by exposure to cold) has more than once appeared in the media as 'hyperthermia', which would imply dangerous overheating of the body. The prefixes are found in music as well as medicine, e.g. 'hyperdorian' mode in ancient Greek music (above the so called Dorian mode), and 'hypodorian' mode (below it).

in-, 'in'/**ex-**, 'out'
Two opposite Latin prefixes, with 'in-' often occurring as 'il-', 'im-', 'ir-', etc. before these consonants, and 'ex-' often appearing as simply 'e-'. Examples are frequent, e.g. *ingress/egress*, *inhale/exhale* and the more common *include/exclude* (see Dictionary for these), as well as other technical opposites where the sense has altered somewhat, e.g. 'inhibit' ('keep back', literally 'have in') and 'exhibit' ('show', literally 'have out') and the pair 'inspire' ('stimulate mentally', but literally 'breathe in') and 'expire' ('die', but literally 'breathe out'). See also in Dictionary (in reverse order of prefixes) *emigrant/immigrant*, and compare the pair of prefixes 'intra-' and 'extra-' (below).

infra-, 'below'/**ultra-**, 'beyond'
Latin prefixes sometimes used in opposite terms, e.g. the familiar scientific *infra-red/ultra-violet* (see Dictionary) as well as 'infrasonic' (of frequencies below the usual audible limit) and 'ultrasonic' (of

frequencies above the higher audible limit). (Compare with this the better known 'supersonic' and 'subsonic' quoted below under 'super-' paired with 'sub-'.) See also below 'supra-' and 'infra-'.

intra-, 'within'/**extra**-, 'outside'
Latin prefixes directly related to the pair 'in-' and 'ex-' (see above), with 'intra-' having an alternative form 'intro-' (but not 'inter-', which means 'between'). For examples in Dictionary, see *intrinsic/extrinsic* and *introvert/extravert*, and compare such obvious opposites as 'intraterritorial' ('within a territory') and 'extraterritorial' ('outside a territory'), as well as the academic 'intramural' (literally 'within the walls', of tuition within a university or college) and 'extramural' (tuition outside a college, e.g. by correspondence).

maxi-, 'most'/**mini**-, 'least'
The prefixes, fashionable in the 'Swinging Sixties' ('maxi-coat', 'mini-skirt'), are actually short forms of 'maximum' and 'minimum', referring to length here. See in Dictionary *maximum/minimum*, *maximize/minimize* and *maxi/mini* themselves.

mega-, 'big'/**micro**-, 'little'
The Greek prefixes, respectively from *megas*, 'big' and *mikros*, 'little', are found in a wide field of scientific and specialized applications, e.g. 'megacephalous' ('big-headed') and 'microcephalous' ('small-headed'), 'megalith' ('big stone' in a historic structure, like those at Stonehenge) and 'microlith' ('little stone', otherwise a very small Stone Age implement), and 'megascope' (instrument for projecting an enlarged image) and the more familiar 'microscope' (for examining small objects). In mathematical factors, 'mega-' means 'to the millionth power', or 10^6 (as in 'megaton'), while 'micro-' means 'a millionth part', or 10^{-6} (as in 'microbar'). See also comments in introduction above on 'megaphone' and 'microphone', and compare the next entry below.

micro-, 'little'/**macro**-, 'great'
These Greek prefixes, with 'macro-' deriving from *makros*, strictly speaking 'long', sometimes occur as alternatives to the pair in the entry above. See in Dictionary, for example, *microcosm/macrocosm*, and compare such pairs as 'microfossil' (a fossil too small to be seen with the naked eye) and 'macrofossil' (one discernible to the naked eye). Since in modern science and technology small is increasingly beautiful, many 'micro-' objects have no corresponding 'macro-', however. A 'microprocessor', in computing, can be accommodated on a single chip, so who needs a 'macroprocessor'?

mono-, 'one', 'single'/**di**-, 'two', 'double'
The Greek prefixes are commonly used to contrast and compare two objects or states where the first has only one feature or property and the other has two, as in *monocotyledon/dicotyledon*. But Latin 'bi-' is also used to oppose Greek 'mono-' as for instance in 'monolingual' ('speaking one language') and 'bilingual' ('speaking two languages'). Consider, too, a 'monocle', which is a single lens placed in one eye, and 'binoculars', which one looks through with both eyes. Similarly a 'monocycle' has only one wheel, while a 'bicycle' has two. But note that although a 'monologue' is spoken by one person, a 'dialogue' can be spoken by two *or more*, since the prefix here is not 'di-' but 'dia-', meaning 'across'. (However, a 'duologue' *is* spoken between two persons, since it has the Latin prefix *duo*-, 'two'.) For another contrast to 'mono-', see the next entry below.

mono-, 'one', 'single'/**poly**-, 'many'
This is the same 'mono-' as in the entry above, but now contrasted with 'poly-', from Greek *polys*, 'much'. See *monosemy/polysemy* in Dictionary for one example, and also compare 'monochromatic' ('in one colour') and 'polychromatic' ('in many colours', like Joseph's coat). For the Latin equivalent, see below 'uni-' and 'multi-'.

neo-, 'new'/**palaeo**-, 'old'
Greek *neos*, 'new' and *palaios*, 'old' give these contrasting prefixes, which are

chiefly associated with geological terms, such as 'neolithic' (relating to the later, i.e. newest or last period of the Stone Age) and 'palaeolithic' (relating to the earlier, i.e. oldest or first period of the Stone Age), or the similarly named 'Neozoic' and 'Palaeozoic' eras, literally translating as 'new life' and 'old life'.

ob-, 'towards', 'in the way of'/**sub-**, 'under', 'below', hence 'away'
The Latin prefixes serve as opposites for a few pairs, of which probably the best known is (with order reversed) *subject/object.* See this in Dictionary, as well as *obreption/subreption* for a more subtle distinction. To 'obtrude' is literally to 'thrust towards', and there is a 'subtrude' meaning 'push in stealthily'. Here, however, the 'sub-' has a 'secret' sense, as it has in 'suborn' ('induce to commit an illegal act'), so it is not a proper opposite.

ortho-, 'straight', 'correct'/**caco-**, 'bad'
Greek *orthos* means 'straight', 'right', so that 'orthodox' literally means 'true opinion'. (For 'caco-' see 'calli-', above.) For an example of opposing terms with the prefixes, see *orthography/cacography* in Dictionary. There is also a 'cacodoxy' to serve as an opposite of 'orthodoxy', although a more usual equivalent is 'heterodoxy' (see *orthodox/heterodox* in Dictionary). 'Para-', meaning 'beside' (Greek *para*) can also occasionally serve as a sort of opposite of 'ortho-', so that a 'paradox' is an opinion that is contrary to the usual one, i.e. to the 'orthodox'. In this respect, see *orthodox sleep/paradoxical sleep* in Dictionary.

patri-, 'father'/**matri-**, 'mother'
These contrasting elements, from the Greek, are not true prefixes, but are sometimes regarded as such in contrasting gender pairs such as 'patricide' and 'matricide' (killing one's father/mother). See also in Dictionary *patriarch/matriarch.* As mentioned in the Introduction (p. 281), 'patrimony' and 'matrimony', although technical exact gender opposites, have now changed their meanings to be respectively 'inheritance from one's father' and 'wedlock'. The difference is equally marked in 'patron' and 'matron', where the former word now has no specific gender sense, and the latter has acquired a medical aura.

phil-, 'love'/**mis-**, 'hate'
The Greek prefixes (from *phileein*, 'to love' and *miseein*, 'to hate') are typically seen in the contrasting pairs 'philanthropist' ('one who loves his or her fellow men', i.e. one who likes other people) and 'misanthropist' (for someone who dislikes people), although the former word now has the specific implication of being a generous donor and patron. More obviously gender-related are the contrasting 'philogynist' (who loves women) and 'misogynist' (who hates them). Note that the 'mis-' prefix here is not the same as the one in 'misinterpret' or 'misbehave', which is a purely English prefix meaning 'wrong', in fact 'amiss'.

poly-, 'many'/**oligo-**, 'few'
The Greek origins here are *polys*, 'much' (see 'mono-' above) and *oligos*, 'little', 'few'. There are not many words with the prefixes, although one better known pair is 'polyarchy' ('government by many') and 'oligarchy' ('government by few', implying a small and exclusive ruling class). At a more rarefied level, 'polycythaemia' is a medical condition in which there are too many red cells in the blood, while in 'oligocythaemia' there are too few (the second half of the word consists of Greek *kytos*, 'vessel' and *haima*, 'blood').

pre-, 'before'/**post-**, 'after'
The Latin prefixes are familiar in a number of pairs, such as the obvious 'prewar' and 'postwar' and 'prenatal' ('before birth') and 'postnatal' (after it). See also *prelude/postlude* in Dictionary. There is also a 'postfix' to serve as the opposite of a 'prefix', in other words to act as a 'suffix'. This is itself a reminder that 'sub-', meaning 'below' (in position or importance) can also serve as an opposite to 'pre-'. See in Dictionary, for example, *precentor/succentor*, *predecessor/successor*, and of course *prefix/suffix.*

('Sub-', like 'in-', can vary its third letter to match the following one.)

primo-, 'first'/**ultimo-**, 'last'
Two Latin prefixes (from *primo* and *ultimo*, 'first' and 'last' in an adverbial sense) are used less often than one might suppose, but see *primogeniture/ultimogeniture* in Dictionary.

pro-, 'for'/**anti-**, 'against'
The Latin prefixes are chiefly used to express current opposing or controversial attitudes, as in 'pro-Apartheid' and 'anti-Apartheid', or 'pro-nuclear' or 'anti-nuclear'. Often, too, 'anti-' is added to a basic word without the use of 'pro-' to denote a positive attitude, e.g. 'anti-establishment' for a person opposed to the 'establishment', and, in the literary world, an 'anti-hero' who is a principal character of a novel lacking the traditional qualities of a 'hero'. Similarly an 'anticlimax' is the opposite of a 'climax'. However, such pairs do not involve attitudes, as 'pro-' and 'anti-' normally do, so are strictly speaking not in the same category. See also *pro/anti* themselves in Dictionary, as well as the next entry below.

pro-, 'forward'/**retro-**, 'backward'
Here the opposites are mostly those of direction, so that 'progression' is 'moving forward' and 'retrogression' is 'moving backward'. (Strictly speaking, Latin *retro* means 'behind', but the English sense is usually 'backward', as it can be for 're-': see *progressive/regressive* in Dictionary.) In the same way 'project' literally means 'throw forward', and 'retroject' – 'throw backwards'. See also in Dictionary *proactive/retroactive*, and compare the entry above.

super-, 'above'/**infra-**, 'below'
Both prefixes are Latin, and 'super-' can often occur in the alternative form 'supra-'. (Latin *super* and English 'over' are actually related, if distantly.) Thus 'supersonic' relates to sound that is above the audible limit, while 'infrasonic' is below the usual audible limit. Similarly, in medicine 'supracostal' relates to something on or above the ribs, while 'infracostal' means 'beneath the ribs'. See also in Dictionary (in reverse order) *infralapsarian/supralapsarian*, and *supra/infra* themselves. Compare, too, the prefixes 'infra-' and 'ultra-', above, as well as the next entry below.

super-, 'above'/**sub-**, 'below'
There are many terms with the opposite Latin prefixes, such as 'superhuman' ('more than human') and 'subhuman' ('less than human'), and 'supersonic' ('faster than the speed of sound') and 'subsonic' ('below the speed of sound'). A 'superacute' condition is a medical one that is more than acute, while a 'subacute' condition is only moderately acute (more exactly, between acute and chronic: see *acute/chronic* in Dictionary). There is even a 'superterranean' to mean 'living on the earth's surface', as the opposite of 'subterranean'. See also in Dictionary (in reversed order) *substratum/superstratum*, as well as the entry above.

syn-, 'with', 'together'/**anti-**, 'against'
The Greek prefixes can be seen in such pairs as *syncline/anticline* and *synonym/antonym* (both in Dictionary). Compare, too, 'sympathy', which is literally 'feeling with', as opposed to 'antipathy', which is 'feeling against'. Sometimes 'dia-' ('through') acts as a kind of opposite to 'syn-', see *synchronic/diachronic* in Dictionary.

tachy-, 'fast'/**brady-**, 'slow'
The prefixes here derive respectively from Greek *tachys*, 'swift' and *bradys*, 'slow' (to which English 'broad', however, is not related). Terms with them are mainly medical, relating to body processes such as the heart beat and digestion that can proceed fast or slowly. See *tachycardia/bradycardia* in Dictionary.

uni-, 'one', 'single'/**bi-**, 'two', 'double'
These prefixes are the Latin equivalents of Greek 'mono-' and 'di-' (see above). Words containing them are mostly more general in meaning than the Greek equivalents, however, and include *unilateral/bilateral* (see Dictionary), as well as such pairs

as 'unisexual' and 'bisexual' (with however 'unisex', as a fashion term, really meaning 'bisexual'!), and 'univalve' (of a mollusc having a shell with only one valve or half) and 'bivalve' (having two). At times the Greek prefixes are merely used as alternatives for the Latin, so that there is little if any difference between 'unilingual' and 'monolingual', or 'bipetalous' ('having two petals') and 'dipetalous'. However, there can be a subtle difference, and although a 'monocycle' is simply a cycle with one wheel, a 'unicycle' is a special 'monocycle' used by acrobats. See also the next entry below, and the pair of prefixes 'mono-' and 'poly-' above.

uni-, 'one', 'single'/**multi-**, 'many'
This is the equivalent Latin pair to Greek 'mono-' and 'poly-' (see above), and the prefixes have a fairly wide range of applications, from the general ('unidirectional' and 'multidirectional', 'unilateral' and 'multilateral') to the highly specialized ('univoltine' and 'multivoltine' are used of silkworms that have respectively one or many broods a year, literally 'one winding' or 'many windings'). Some words with 'multi-' are rather contrived, like the 'multiversity' that is a large 'university' with many campuses. See also the entry above.

B: Suffixes

-androus, 'male'/**-gynous**, 'female'
Terms with the Greek suffixes (compare the prefixes 'andro-' and 'gyno-' above) are mostly either sociological or zoological (or botanical), so that 'monandrous' can mean either 'having one husband at a time' or (of a plant) 'having one stamen', and 'monogynous' will thus mean either 'having one wife at a time' or 'having one style' (containing the stigma). Compare in Dictionary *polyandry/polygyny*. By switching both prefix and suffix one can arrive at a sort of bisexual balance, so that 'gynandrous' means the same as 'androgynous'. However, the first of these is specifically botanical, relating to plants such as orchids that have their stamen and pistil in a single column (see *stamen/pistil* in Dictionary, if necessary), while 'androgynous', as well as any special scientific sense (e.g. to refer to a hermaphrodite) can mean little more than 'seductively feminine in appearance' (of a male, such as certain pop singers in the Effete Eighties). This latter sense, incidentally, is not recorded in most dictionaries.

-er, 'one who does'/**-ee**, 'one to whom it is done'
The contrasting suffixes are familiar mainly in legal terms, such as 'mortgagor' and 'mortgagee', where the first is the person who gets a mortgage (to buy a house, for example) and the second is the person or organization that gives him the mortgage (see *mortgagee/mortgagor* in Dictionary). Other similar legal opposites are 'lessor' and 'lessee' (the first grants the lease to the second) and 'assigner' and 'assignee' (the former assigns a right or property to the latter). One can also have an 'employee' regarded as a person working for an 'employer', and even a 'tutee' receiving tuition from a 'tutor'. In many cases, however, the '-ee' person does not suggest a contrasting '-er' (or '-or'), so that a 'trainee' is simply a person under training, and a 'licensee' someone to whom a licence has been granted. Note that not all words ending in '-ee' will have this sense: an 'escapee' is simply someone who has escaped, and an 'absentee' a person who is absent. This is because an intransitive verb is involved here, not a transitive one. (Even an 'escaper' and an 'absenter' are the same as an 'absentee' and an 'escapee'.)

-er, 'male'/**-eress** (**-ress**), 'female'
For a sample of contrasting male and female designations with these suffixes (where '-er' can also be '-or') see Appendix II, below. For interest, compare also the next entry below.

-er, 'male'/**-ster**, 'female'
Historically, the suffix '-er' frequently designated a male, before the sixteenth century, while the '-ster' suffix designating the female who performed the same work or task. For example, a 'weaver' was a man who wove, while the woman was a 'webster', and while a man who baked bread was a 'baker', a woman who did so was a 'baxter'. (Hence, incidentally, the origin of the surnames Webster and Baxter.) A modern spin-off, if I may say so, from this system is the word 'spinster', who was a female 'spinner'. (See *bachelor/spinster* in Dictionary.) After around 1600, such female designations, where they survived, came to be used for males, however, and in turn developed a new feminine suffix to designate the female equivalent. Thus 'songster' was now a male singer, not just a female, and 'songstress' was (possibly still is) a female one. Hence the origin of 'sempstress', for a woman who sews. A man who did so was a 'seamster' (or 'sempster'), although this term originally applied to the woman.

-iens, 'doing something'/**-iendum**, 'having something done to it'
These learned Latin suffixes have an occasional academic use to indicate an object or provision that performs an action, and one that has an action performed to it, as a sort of active and passive. The only example in the Dictionary (as in most other dictionaries) is *definiens/definiendum*, which see. Grammatically, the '-iens' ending is that of the Latin present participle (here, of the verb *definire*), while the '-iendum' suffix is the neuter of the gerundive of the verb.

-phile, 'lover'/**-phobe**, 'hater'
These Greek suffixes are more or less equivalents of the prefixes 'phil-' and 'mis-' above, although '-phobe' literally means not 'hater' but 'fearer' (from *phobos*, 'fear'). They are mostly used in connection with particular nationalities or peoples, whom one either likes and admires or hates and fears. A 'Francophile' is thus keen on the French and things French, but a 'Francophobe' dislikes them or distrusts them (often irrationally, as with other countries). Two other familar pairs that have evolved over the years are 'Anglophile' and 'Anglophobe', and 'Russophile' and 'Russophobe'. There is also a 'xenophile' who likes things foreign, as distinct from a 'xenophobe' who hates foreigners. One can devise similar pairs for many countries, although the name of the country should be Greek or at least classical, such as a 'Hispanophile' who likes things Spanish, or a 'Sinophobe' who dislikes and mistrusts the Chinese. The conditions of loving or fearing in this way can be designated by '-philia' and '-phobia', and can apply to areas outside the human, such as 'canophilia' (or 'cynophilia'), 'a love of dogs', and 'ailourophobia', 'morbid fear of cats'. One needs to know one's Greek here, though, and be a reasonable 'Hellenophile'.

-ster, 'male'/**-stress**, 'female'
For examples of words with these gender-differentiating suffixes, see Appendix II below, as well as the third '-er' suffix above (paired with '-ster').

-tor, 'male'/**-trix**, 'female'
For examples of designations with these classical gender-differentiating suffixes, see Appendix II below.

Appendix II
Gender differentiation

Most languages, and certainly English, have a way of distinguishing between the male and the female, whether animal or bird or human. In the latter case, there is also frequently a need to distinguish not merely by sex but by rank or occupation, often by way of an altered suffix.

Many animals and birds have quite distinct words to denote the male and the female, such as cock/hen, bull/cow, dog/bitch, ram/ewe, colt/filly, stag/doe, with the male word sometimes used for the particular bird or animal in general, of whichever sex. Thus, 'dog' can mean both 'canine quadruped' and 'male canine quadruped', and in the latter case having 'bitch' to denote the female. Conversely, there may be some other word to denote the animal in general, such as 'sheep' for ram/ewe and 'foal' for colt/filly. In a few instances, it is the female word that can denote either gender as well, such as 'duck', meaning both 'aquatic quacking bird' or the female of the family, so that 'drake' is reserved for the male. The same thing applies to 'goose', which can be either gender or just the female, with the male being 'gander'.

In some cases the respective male and female words can be seen to be related, such as fox/vixen, and in a few animal names, such as tiger/tigress, lion/lioness, the female has merely a suffix to indicate her gender.

Male and female humans can also be designated by quite different words, such as boy/girl, man/woman, lord/lady, monk/nun, bachelor/spinster. (Many of these are in the Dictionary: see as necessary.) On the other hand, many ranks and occupations have simply a distinguishing suffix to denote the female.

The most common such suffix is '-ess', which arrived into English via French from ultimately classical origins (Latin or Greek). In many instances, this suffix is added direct to the male word, such as peer/peeress, heir/heiress, mayor/mayoress, count/countess, host/hostess, steward/stewardess. In other cases the ending of the masculine word is slightly modified before taking the suffix, and perhaps loses a vowel. Examples are waiter/waitress, actor/actress, songster/songstress, master/mistress. A greater difference occurs in marquis (or marquess)/marchioness, although other pairs are simpler, like duke/duchess. 'King' and 'queen' are not related, however, any more than 'man' and 'woman' are, despite their similarity of spelling.

Where there is a perceptible and even necessary distinction between the standing or role of the male and female, this differentiation by suffix is still largely preserved today, although the feminist movement has made strenuous efforts to alter a linguistic situation that it regards as discriminatory and demeaning. Thus, 'flight attendant' is now found in many cases in place of 'stewardess', or 'lady mayor' is used instead of 'mayoress'. In some cases, too, the addition of the suffix can actually indicate quite a different occupation to that of the male. A 'conductress' would not conduct an orchestra, although a 'conductor' could! Similarly, a 'governess' is not the female equivalent (where she still exists) of a 'governor'.

These and other general linguistic and social trends have meant that many words formerly adding '-ess' for the female no longer do so, and the examples listed as 'current' in the *Oxford English Dictionary* would now be regarded as mannered, patronizing, or even downright old-fashioned. They include 'authoress', 'patroness', 'Jewess' and 'tailoress'. The same criterion would also apply today to 'poetess' and 'priestess', although the latter word would be correct for a historical reference, for example, in classical times. Somewhat surprisingly, 'manageress' is still fairly common for a woman 'manager', despite general awareness of sexual equality in employment, and the passing of the Sex Discrimination Act (in Britain) in 1975.

Other suffixes denoting the female as against the male are much less common. One learned one is '-trix', to correspond to the male '-tor'. These came straight from Latin, where for example a *venator* was a male hunter and a *venatrix* a female (or, as formerly in English, a 'huntress'). Any such remaining words are almost exclusively legal terms, such as executor/executrix, primogenitor/primogenitrix, testator/testatrix, procurator/procuratrix. The suffix did spill over at one stage into aeronautics, especially when women took to the air, and a female 'aviator' was an 'aviatrix'. But this word is a curiosity today, and male and female flyers are merely 'pilots'.

Another feminine suffix that has largely disappeared today is the French '-ette', as in usher/usherette, and, more whimsically, undergraduate/undergraduette. Probably the best known example of the suffix, although having no male equivalent, was in 'suffragette', this at a time when women of the world were beginning to unite and break loose from their chains (and were claiming the right to vote in Britain). Even where the suffix is still in use, however, it can be misleading: a 'drum majorette' is not a female 'drum major'! (In fact, in this example the '-ette' has almost as much a 'diminutive' sense as a feminine one, as in 'kitchenette' and 'maisonette'.)

Other French suffixes still survive, however, in such pairs as masseur/masseuse, comedian/comedienne, where the words themselves are French. A similar example is Italian 'ballerina' for a female ballet dancer. 'Heroine', as the feminine equivalent to 'hero', although coming into English from French, ultimately goes back to Greek *heroine*. (And many heroic women today are 'heroes', not 'heroines', which now smacks of schoolgirl escapades and romantic or adventurous sacrifices: such accounts were still published quite recently as children's books, for example 'Tales of Young Heroines' in the *True Adventures Series* by the prolific E. G. Jerrome, issued by Blackie in the 1950s.)

A much more practical method for differentiating between the sexes at a professional level is simply to use '-woman' instead of '-man'. This pairing is still quite common in sports and the services, for example horseman/horsewoman, airman/airwoman (and in the RAF, as an official rank, aircraftman/aircraftwoman). This is not exactly a suffix, of course, but a separate word, although 'horsewoman', for example, was written as one word, not two, as early as the sixteenth century. This manner of distinguishing is especially common to denote a nationality: Englishman/Englishwoman, Frenchman/Frenchwoman, and so on. However, where the male nationality does not normally end in '-man' one must simply add 'woman' to the adjective to denote the female: Russian/Russian woman, German/German woman (the '-man' not being 'man' here, of course), Swede/Swedish woman, Pole/Polish woman, and the like. But if there is no need to denote the female sex so specifically, or if it is clear from the context (e.g. after a female name or pronoun), then one can simply say 'Russian', 'German' and so on ('He married a Swede').

Finally, the traditional semi-romantic pairing of 'man' and 'maid' is still in some current use for certain occupations. A female 'barman', for example, is often called a 'barmaid', and 'dairyman' and 'dairymaid' are also more or less equivalents. Similarly, a male 'mermaid' is called a 'merman'. However, one needs to be careful with the occupations, because a 'milkman' is not a male 'milkmaid': he delivers the milk, but she milks cows. And while a 'housemaid' is a domestic servant, a 'houseman' is anything but – he is a newly qualified hospital doctor. (He is so called since he is a 'house' physician or surgeon, that is, he is resident, and the hospital is the 'house' where he lives. See also **physician/surgeon**.) Some 'maids' by occupation have no corresponding 'man' to represent their male equivalent, either. A 'meter maid' is thus a female 'traffic warden' (there is no 'meterman'), and a 'bridesmaid', a girl or young unmarried woman who attends a bride at her wedding, has her male half in a 'page'. In a few cases, moreover, there is no male equivalent at all to do the job, at least in the normal course of events, and there is no 'nurseman' to look after young children in the way in which a 'nursemaid' does. (Particular care is needed here, because an alternative name for a 'nursemaid' is a 'nurserymaid', and there *is* a 'nurseryman'. But he cultivates plants for sale!)

Gender differentiation, at least occupationally, is thus not always a straightforward matter.

By Way of a Bibliography

It would be impossible to list individually all the printed sources I consulted for information or confirmation when working on the Dictionary. As the reader will have seen, many subjects and specialities are involved in the various entries, from theology to botany, from philosophy to philology, and in some cases I needed to consult a particular book or article only once, simply to check the facts. Moreover, to list all titles consulted would not only give undue emphasis to certain works, whose contribution was very tiny by comparison with many others, but would look all too much like an exercise in academic self-aggrandizement. It is true, I *did* put in my thumb and pull out some plums, but the last thing I want to do is to say 'What a good boy am I!'

All that perhaps should be said about such sources is that they ranged from the scholarly to the ephemeral, and from the specialized to the trivial. They included not only standard reference works but fictional literature and 'the media', the latter mainly in the form of magazines and newspapers, whether as professionally written articles or advertisements aimed at the consumer.

However, there is one type of reference work that I clearly must (and certainly wish to) acknowledge, and that is the English dictionary. Many dictionary compilers and editors obviously feel that it will be helpful to their readers to indicate the antonym or opposite of a particular word or phrase, when appropriate, or at least to end an entry with a little 'compare' or 'see also' indication. Some dictionaries are better than others in doing this. The great *OED* will sometimes provide a discreet 'cf.' with the opposing or contrasting word printed in light capitals, while *Collins English Dictionary*, which on the whole avoids academic abbreviations like the plague, distinguishes such antonyms clearly by a separate sentence 'Compare . . .', with the required contrast printed conspicuously in bold (but lowercase) black. It would be invidious to single out any one dictionary for this particular feature, or its treatment of it, but *all* the dictionaries listed below deal with the matter in some way or other, either sporadically or systematically, and I consulted them all during my own compilation. So they will be the sole works to be fully listed here in what is otherwise a rather unconventional bibliography.

Burchfield, R. W. (ed.), *A Supplement to the Oxford English Dictionary*, OUP, Volume I (A–G), 1972, Volume II (H–N), 1976, Volume III (O–Scz), 1982, Volume IV (Se–Z), 1986.

Gove, Philip B. (ed.), *Webster's Third New International Dictionary of the English Language*, G. & C. Merriam, Springfield, Mass., 1971.

Hanks, Patrick (ed.), *Collins Dictionary of the English Language*, Collins, London and Glasgow, 1979, 2nd ed., 1986.

Hanks, Patrick (ed.), *Encyclopedic World Dictionary*, Hamlyn, London, 1971.

Hoad, T. F. (ed.), *The Concise Oxford Dictionary of English Etymology*, Clarendon Press, Oxford, 1986.

Kirkpatrick, E. M. (ed.), *Chambers Twentieth Century Dictionary*, W. & R. Chambers, Edinburgh, 1983.

Longman Dictionary of the English Language, Longman, Harlow, 1984.

Murray, James and others (eds), *The Oxford English Dictionary*, OUP, 1888–1933.

Onions, C. T. (ed.), with the assistance of G. W. S. Friedrichsen and R. W. Burchfield, *The Oxford Dictionary of English Etymology*, Clarendon Press, Oxford, 1966.

Partridge, Eric, *Origins: A Short Etymological Dictionary of Modern English*, Routledge & Kegan Paul, London, 1966.

Wyld, Henry Cecil (ed.), *The Universal Dictionary of the English Language*, George Routledge, London, 1934.